AGING AND THE ELDERLY

Gerontology

EDITED BY

STUART F. SPICKER
KATHLEEN M. WOODWARD
DAVID D. VAN TASSEL

INTRODUCTION BY

ERIK H. ERIKSON
JOAN M. ERIKSON

AFTERWORD BY

ROBERT N. BUTLER M.D.

AGING AND THE ELDERLY

humanistic perspectives in gerontology

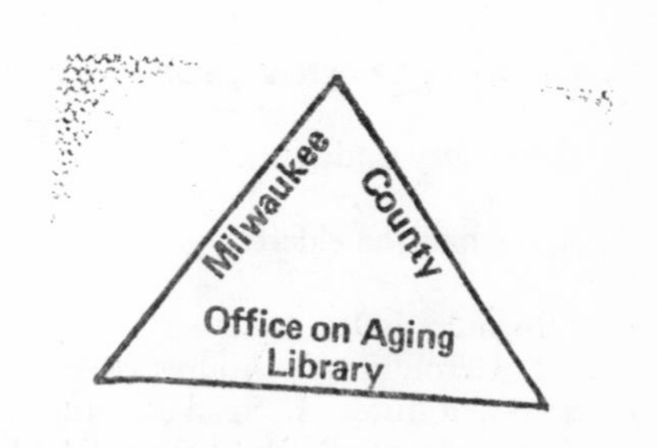

HUMANITIES PRESS, INC.
Atlantic Highlands, New Jersey

Publication of this work was made possible by a
grant from The National Endowment for the Humanities

First printing

Printed in the United States of America

Library of Congress Cataloging in Publication Data

Main entry under title:

Aging and the elderly.

Includes index.
1. Gerontology—Addresses, essays, lectures. 2. Old age in literature—Addresses, essays, lectures. I. Spicker, Stuart F., 1937—I. Woodward, Kathleen M. III. Van Tassel, David Dirck, 1928—[DNLM: 1. Aging. 2. Geriatrics. 3. Social conditions. WT100 A265]
HQ1061.A457 301.43'5 77-25815
ISBN 0-391-00559-6 (cloth)
ISBN 0-391-00560-X (paper)

Table of Contents

PREFACE

This collection of essays by humanists on aspects of human aging represents the first fruit of a project conceived in 1972, a year after the Second White House Conference on Aging, and supported two years later by the National Endowment for the Humanities under the title "Human Values and Aging: New Challenges to Research in the Humanities." When the project first began, there were few humanists working in this field, and little existed in the way of published research, either in monographic or article form. Why? Perhaps it was because humanists assumed that it was not an appropriate subject for their inquiry or that there was no significant material available. Perhaps, on the other hand, as many social scientists assumed, old age was an experience and social problem faced only by the twentieth century.

Whether or not the assumption of social and medical science was correct, twentieth-century civilization had certainly discovered old age as a social, economic, and health problem of growing proportions, and has gone about surveying the situation in horizontal cuts with miles of questionnaires and computer print outs, laying bare in cold statistics the lives, the pains, the hopes of a contemporary generation of elderly. Yet a whole dimension of the growing field of gerontology was being neglected—the humanistic. The fundamental assumption upon which I based the project was that there does indeed exist an important body of material and that humanists should be studying this vast and untapped source of human experience recorded in history, literature, folklore, artifact and art, created by past generations and cultures. These are materials which should be located, brought to light, and refined by scholars in the humanities. Such an effort would not only give new perspectives to the field of gerontology and widen the horizons of each of the disciplines of the humanities, but above all would enhance the appreciation and understanding of the later stages of life.

The project was designed to go through three phases over a period of three years. The authors of the essays in this volume were among thirty Research Associates carefully selected, following a national competition, by an Advisory Committee composed of members of the humanities, social science and medical faculties of Case Western Reserve University. Once selected, they were invited as Research Associates or Observers, to attend a conference held in November 1975, on the campus of Case Western Reserve University. The first conference consisted of papers read by senior scholars in the social sciences, medicine, and the humanities who had been involved in some way in the study of aging, such as Leon Edel, Erik Erikson, Leslie Fiedler, Joseph Fletcher, Juanita Kreps, Peter

Laslett, and others. During the intensive discussions of the papers by the Research Associates and invited Observers, a certain ambivalence surfaced. It was clear that old people had many problems in modern society. It was also clear that the growing proportion of the elderly in Western populations posed a social problem. Some of the participants sought immediately to find ways in which the humanities might help solve these problems. Others began to see aging and old age as an experience of the human condition, which the disciplines of the humanities had neglected to illuminate.

During the following year the Research Associates completed projects of their own and produced papers discussed at a second conference held in New York City in October 1976, in conjunction with the annual meeting of the Gerontological Society. At that time a certain electricity was produced by the convergence of forces. The Research Associates discussed each other's papers, many of which appear as essays in this volume, with a new intensity and confidence in their value. Amongst the gerontologists, there was an awareness of a new group meeting on their fringes. There had long been a need for a greater voice from the humanities in all areas of gerontology. This need had been demonstrated by the frequent use of fiction, poetry, and philosophy in courses and programs in gerontological education. Joseph Freeman, M.D., an internist in gerontology and a founder of the Gerontological Society, had been most prominent in calling for formal recognition of this need. Finally, in response to the increasing interest of humanists, and the motion which was presented by Dr. Freeman, the Council of the Gerontological Society recognized the existence and potential contributions of the humanities and arts to gerontology by passing the motion which established its Ad Hoc Committee on Humanism and the Humanities in Gerontology.

This volume, however, is very largely the product of the work of Stuart F. Spicker, a Research Associate, and Kathleen M. Woodward, an invited Observer. They are mainly responsible for the conception and imaginative organization of the volume, as well as the selection of the two additional essays to give it a balance it would not otherwise have had. Kathleen Woodward undertook the arduous and creative task of editing each of the essays to bring them into focus. The authors responded with grace and promptness in supplying the revisions based on the discussions at the second conference and Kathleen Woodward's useful editorial suggestions. For any errors of commission or omission, I take full responsibility, but credit for all that is good in this volume must go to my co-editors and the authors.

David D. Van Tassel
Project Director

EDITORS' FOREWORD

Aging is too vast a subject to be left solely to social and physical scientists. Because aging is a uniquely personal experience, because one measure of the humaneness of a culture is its treatment of the elderly, the humanities have a vital contribution to make, one which has only recently engaged the joint attention of humanists and gerontologists.

The scholars in this collection represent various disciplines—literature, history, art history, philosophy, religion, law, and political science—which devote themselves to the value-laden dimensions of human experience as well as to the more strictly cognitive clarification of the language in which all experience is reflected. As a distinguished scholar of the humanities has written, the essential values of the humanities are "the spiritual values of freedom, dignity, and beauty, and the critical values of openness, toleration, and a measured skepticism of all dogmas."[1] Yet value is inseparable from an ethical commitment. Thus humanists have a unique role to play in deepening our understanding of the aging process (or should we say processes?). While humanists are primarily attracted to the past and its cultural traditions in religion, art, and literature and therefore are not usually oriented toward the solution of contemporary problems, it is worth noting that, in the present volume, they have shown themselves concerned with the significance of attitudes, aspirations, and cultural practices throughout human history underlying the ineluctable fact of age. And it is just this perspective of the past which gives us the possibility of imagining a meaningful, human future. Until we know what we have been, we cannot know what we can become. For this both vision and humility are required.

In a sense we were all unprepared, and it was not until the demographic reality of the growing number of elderly members in Western society confronted all of us that we had to "discover" the elderly. The last to realize that aging was an important twentieth-century phenomenon in the West were the academic humanists; and the last to realize that the humanists have important insights to offer to the study of old age were the professional gerontologists. By the time the reader completes this volume, we hope that it will have established the claim that the humanities have something valuable to contribute to the understanding of senescence and senectitude.

The question, then, is no longer whether literature, philosophy, history, and other humanistic disciplines can present a variety of humanistic perspectives in the investigation of aging, but, more to the point, in what ways shall persons educated in and by the humanities make a joint contribution with those who

constitute the multidisciplines of gerontology and clinical geriatrics. Multidisciplinary engagement is difficult, but humanists have come a long way during the past few years. Still, the humanities can (and usually do) make only a modest claim. The present work does not pose as the reader's salvation, certainly, but as a first step in the effort to view the contemporary problems of the elderly in an aging society from the standpoint of other societies, past and present, other values, other cultural traditions, as well as our own, and thereby to enhance our understanding.

The Editors are deeply indebted to Erik and Joan Erikson for their gracious gift which introduces these essays, and to Robert N. Butler, M.D., Director of the National Institute on Aging, for concluding this volume with his call to those whose creative vision as humanists and artists entitles them to be heard and seen as visionaries into aging and the aged among us.

We are also indebted to Geri Berg and Sally Gadow for allowing us to publish their essay, "Toward More Human Meanings of Aging: Ideals and Images, from Philosophy and Art," and Thomas Halper for his essay "Paternalism and the Elderly," and finally, Barbara Rosenkrantz for her co-authorship of "The Invisible Lunatics: Old Age and Insanity in Mid-Nineteenth-Century Massachusetts."

We are pleased to acknowledge the hard work of Mary Jevnikar, Secretary to the Project, who typed and retyped many of the manuscripts and carried on correspondence with the individual authors, as well as that of Dr. Judith Cetina, Research Assistant to the Project.

The project was supported by the National Endowment for the Humanities under Grant AV-22113-75-111, one product of which is this volume. We acknowledge with gratitude the material support of the Endowment and in particular we wish to thank Richard Hedrich, Ph.D., of the Endowment for his encouragement and assistance in enabling us to bring this volume before the public.

October 1977 The Editors

Note

[1]O.B. Hardison, Jr., *Toward Freedom and Dignity: The Humanities and the Idea of Humanity* (Baltimore: Johns Hopkins Univ. Press, 1972), p. xxiv.

Erik H. and Joan M. Erikson

INTRODUCTION: REFLECTIONS ON AGING

The scholars in this volume who are engaged in the wide search for new meaning in old age have asked us for a message which would help link their work to that of gerontology and geriatrics. If we do respond, it is not because we can claim any formal connections with these fields. Rather, this request has a more general and more personal appeal.

We met with most of the contributors in 1975 at the meeting on "Human Values and Aging" described in the Preface. There were two well-defined groups of participants. The first consisted of persons of advanced academic and clinical standing who brought their long and varying experience to bear on the subject. Another, younger group consisted of "Research Associates" who participated in discussions and scheduled encounters but were expected to make their main contributions at a later date: this date. We, however, belonged to a third, *very* small group which was not officially defined. We were the seniors in the senior group and thus, in a discussion on aging, were not only participant observers but also participants under observation. For one inescapable concern in the proceedings was: where does "real" old age begin? The national statistics had, by then, announced that persons over sixty-five years old constituted more than ten percent of the American population: by surviving in such numbers, the aging were obviously losing some of the exceptional status that once made age so venerable or so deplorable or both. But we were in the seventies; and as the vocabulary used in the discussion began to test thresholds—who is aging or aged, elderly or old, or even penultimately old—we few felt ourselves to be the object of more or less furtive, if sympathetic, glances.

After the opening dinner, one of us (E.H.E.) had the ceremonial privilege of presenting some reflections on the keynote film—Ingmar Bergman's *Wild Strawberries*[1]—which had been shown in the afternoon and which confronted us with old age in the professional class to which we all belonged. The hero, Dr.

Borg, is seventy-six years old. (We will refer to him, here and there, in parenthesis.)

This first meeting was followed by a meeting of the Research Associates a year later. There, *they* had their full say, which in all its eloquence appears in these pages. We were not present at that meeting, nor could we acquaint ourselves with all the papers presented there. And yet we were asked to help open this volume with some reflections. Is it too personal to assume that in this function we represent not only our professional concern with the "elderly," but also this newly discovered human subspecies itself?

Since the meetings on Human Values and Aging make a point of bringing the humanities and other fields concerned with old age closer together, we decided to reorient ourselves in regard to the wide field of humanism by consulting Webster's brevity. The overall definition of the humanities as "the branches of polite learning regarded as primarily conducive to culture" was not immediately suggestive. Another, "faith in the supreme value and self-perfectibility of human personality" was more promising—for does not Bergman's film decisively assume such perfectibility as it shows an old man receiving the highest honor in his field and yet also facing the most creative despair hidden in his inner self—and both most believably so in terms of modern psychology? But closest to our concerns is Walter Lippman's suggestion that humanism "takes as its dominant pattern the progress of the individual from helpless infancy to self-governing maturity." For what faces us today is, first of all, a need to demarcate the stages of life—now that infants are so very much surer to survive the beginning of life, and adults, middle age—while old people can no longer expect to be the rare and revered specimens of special luck or divine distinction. We should note in passing that something paradoxical is happening to those "self-governing" middle years: today, when death seems to be more definitely postponed, there is almost a search for dangerous transitions and critical passages *within* life, threatening the survival of the individuality of the person now that physical survival seems so much more certain.

The humanities are directing their attention to middle life too.[2] But here we are concerned with the changing values of aging; and in order to add another decade of perception to ours we turn to an octogenarian (and analytical psychologist):

> But we also find that as we age we are more alive than seems likely, convenient, or even bearable. Too often our problem is the fervour of life within us. My dear fellow octogenarians, how are we to carry so much life, and what are we to do with it?
>
> Let no one say it is "unlived life" with any of the simpler psychological certitudes. No one lives all the life of which he was capable. The unlived life in each of us must be the future of humanity.[3]

What exceptionally perceptive and expressive representatives of old age have been able to verbalize over the ages must now be understood and formulated as

part of the more common fate of common people.

Much of the quality of old age is, of course, determined by the prevailing world view which gives the stages of life specific connotations. We can best introduce this subject with a remark addressed by one of our grandsons to his grandmother when he was four years old. "Grandma," he had asked, "Are you going to die?" She had answered, "Yes, of course, but probably not right now. When people get very old they all die." After a pause, he said, "Grandma, you are old and I am new." This is a clear and simple statement not to be burdened with more meaning; and yet, does it not fit the conception of old age in a country which has put such a premium on newness (from the New Man to new products to new ideas, and from the New World to the New Deal and the New Spirit) that to be young means to have the choice of always becoming new again, and to be old the loss of that choice? At any rate, the study of the connotations of the life stages and of life as a whole within the dominant world view is all the more urgent since such study is so rare. The humanists' classical example is, of course, Shakespeare, who lists seven ages or "parts played by man": the infant and the schoolboy (no play age, no adolescence), the lover and the soldier, the justice—and then the old man with his "big manly voice turning again toward childish treble" and, finally, the man facing second childishness and mere oblivion, "sans teeth, sans eyes, sans everything." Here man grows up to an adult stature of short duration, only, at it were, to grow *down* again—and fall apart. One must take this playful "scheme," of course, for what it is in its literary setting. In contrast, consider the elaborate Hindu scheme which lists no childhood as such, just a stage of apprenticeship, and then the "householder's" adulthood, charged with the "maintenance of the world." Aging, however, has two stages: first, the gradual renunciation of one's earthly position—and then self-chosen anonymity and oblivion. The Hindu, then, grows up so that he may grow *beyond*—beyond his one life cycle and into the spiral of rebirths which will eventually fuse with the universal spirit. Unnecessary to say, in these and other world views, womanhood, closer to nature, is only the maternal ground from which man's spiritual fate arises. Even Shakespeare acknowledged only a nurse as the "pewking infant's" initial support; the Hindu life cycle takes the manifold mothering of the extended family for granted as the cultural matrix from which the human (that is, male) life stages will emerge. That such schemes will in no way do for the life cycle in our time makes momentous demand on our reformulations.

As we turn, for a moment, to the concept of the life cycle which we have been using in our work (ever since we formulated it for the Midcentury White House Conference on Children and Youth), it must be clear that such (then, very rare) total schemes and their subdivisions emerge from theoretical concerns intrinsic to a historical and conceptual "moment." Each, therefore, has an inner coherence which is discernible and becomes arguable only in comparative studies, which take into account the relativity of standpoints on which different views of life rest.

In our case, the need for an attempt to sketch at least one trend within the whole life cycle followed Freud's discovery of distinct stages in the previously

unrecognized, if not repressed, infantile portion of man's *psychosexual* development. From this—and from Piaget's *cognitive* stages of development—the need arose to trace the corresponding *psychosocial* stages—and this not only in childhood and youth but also up into adulthood and old age. For each such stage we postulated a conflict and a crisis which has to come to a relative solution in order to permit further development. It all starts with an early crisis in infancy of what we called *"Basic Trust"* and *"Basic Mistrust"* from the dialectics of which the basic human strength Hope emerges; and it continues with a sequence of critical stages (which are listed and explained once more in the account of Dr. Borg's search for his previous selves). But let us account here only for old age and its precursor, mature adulthood. In "our book," the last crisis is a confrontation of what we call *"Integrity"* and *"Despair"*; and if the relative resolution of each crisis helps to mature a basic human strength, in old age it is *"Wisdom."* All these are ancient words, much too high sounding, it would seem, for the experience of the unpretentious, not to speak of the powerless among us. But being concerned with the psychosocial, that is, the interdependence and interplay between the individual life cycle, on the one hand, and the structure and history of the collectivity on the other, the oldest and most universal word roots serve best to present the basic human scheme reborn with each child. In spite of their "classical" tone, however, these words are conceived as connoting an active *adaptation* rather than a passive *adjustment* to the inner and outer conditions of one's development. The adaptive potential of integrity and wisdom has, throughout history, formed the very basis for the private and public service of the old in some advisory, priestly, or judicial context—whether personified by the Roman senator in his rarified atmosphere or by the Chinese grandmother in ancient family life. (And those who remember Bergman's Dr. Borg will be impressed with the surprising state of activity aroused in this quiet man by his daughter-in-law's confrontation. Thus, we witness the way in which an old age crisis in one life becomes interlocked with a crisis in the younger generation.) We have named the adult life crisis that of *"Generativity"* (that is, the commitment to progeny, production, and creativity) and *"Stagnation,"* a basic conflict necessary for the development of the basic adult strength of *"Care."* (This crisis, as Dr. Borg's fate illustrates, can recur and reactivate in the older generation what already had seemed forfeited to death.) At the same time, all this illustrates that old age *"Despair,"* in some balance with the forces of *"Integrity,"* is by no means a pathological or expendable state of mind, to be "cured" or avoided at all cost: it is an essential component for the last stage. For man develops through conflict.

And this is our central point. What remains true for the last stage in life is in the *epigenetic nature* of the life cycle from the beginning. While each new development must wait for the inner and outer conditions which make its full unfolding possible and necessary, each previous development is always relived and can (and must) be renewed in each subsequent one. (Thus, we can recognize in Dr. Borg's old age crisis a reactivation of the "Intimacy" crisis of early adulthood as well as the "Identity" crisis of adolescence—and so on, back to the childhood stages.) At the same time, the fate of old age clearly reflects the

way in which ingrown habituations and social mores can inactivate an individual's potentials, even as they isolate and incarcerate him—actually and symbolically—from the beginning to the end of life.

It is true that our approach to life histories originated with case histories reconstructed in clinical work. Here we should note how often we learn about human resources from the liberation of segregated and inactivated classes of people. It is from clinical work that we have learned to understand the human struggle with specific manifestations of anxiety on each stage of life and, above all, with the persistent danger, multiplied in the aged, of partial regressions to earlier and earliest conflicts. But it is from clinical work, also, that we have learned to appreciate the power of the human ego—in the sense of an integrative inner center—to sustain step for step that basic orientation each of us needs and all of us must try to guarantee to one another: a sense of, well, being *central* in the space-time of the world rather than shunned to a periphery, *active* rather than inactivated, and *planful* rather than disoriented. But clinical work has confronted us not only with inner conflict but also with the self-deluding and colluding deals which our inner life can make with social conditions—and vice versa. It is one of the most insidious aspects of human nature that we are inclined to bolster our central sense of worth by excluding from our "kind" and from our "world" some classes of people, by classifying them into restrictive categories including age groups; by excluding them from our scheme of activity; and, finally, by inactivating and segregating them in some more or less pernicious way. On the other hand, religious and ideological counterschemes have, at decisive historical moments, undertaken to reinclude "the possessed" and "the poor" in ever more universal schemes of Agape and Caritas, or the enslaved or exploited in revolutionary schemes of liberation. But every historical period has its own shifts in world view, including new healing endeavors; and in ours the holistic trend in the healing professions demands a unified approach to all stages of life.

Men and women can begin to face the issue of neglected potentialities as early as in their forties and fifties, realizing that social commitments have been closing in on their choices and chances. Many fear and resent the bureaucratic closure of their full participation in daily economic life at a set date, and this not the least because of the satisfying social patterns that they have developed at work: and, no doubt, the economy will have to find ways to utilize the potentials of an increasing number of the aging. Given some leeway and choice, however, the most promising meaning of old age is, for many, the opening up of alternative paths. The really inviting open door is the prospect that, after retirement or when the children are on their own, there will be time "to play with" and that with some foresight and preparation it can be a deeply meaningful time. After all, laying an early groundwork for the height of vocational life is always accepted as realistic. Could it not be argued that the later stages of life could also be more fully lived as a time of further personal

development if they had been prepared for early enough in the whole life plan?

Perhaps the most challenging gift that the increase in available time after retirement offers is the opportunity to delve into those life-enriching areas of learning and doing that were of necessity bypassed in the pressures and demands of the commitment to the middle stages of life. And there is impetus abroad now to make such study available and to "sell" it with sometimes glamorous or Madison Avenue type names. In our county (Marin, California), an "Emeritus College" lures older students into a curriculum with a wide range of studies. The Gray Panthers encourage their members at long last to learn to become political activists. In Texas, TRIMS (Texas Research Institute of Mental Sciences) helps older people to manage to get the benefits that make it possible for them to live proud and useful lives, while again from California, SAGE (Senior Actualization and Growth Exploration) reaches out across the country offering the concept that through activities stimulating the potentialities of the aging a new image of the elderly will emerge in the public view and in their own perception of themselves.

The organizations mentioned are only a small sampling of the many groups which are mushrooming up everywhere to meet the demands of the growing number of elderly citizens. But many of them, commendable and necessary as they are, have one disadvantage: they segregate older people in peer groups devoted to "special" interests. This may appear to be comfortable and efficient, but such exclusiveness could tend again to be impoverishing.

Our clinical and communal work suggests that today's late and massive efforts be complemented and eventually absorbed by lifelong and gradual endeavors to balance the specializations of modern life. Ideally, one could envisage the development of community centers,[4] serving circumscribed city areas and neighborhoods and facilitated by public transportation, where planned activities could be programmed that would promote the continued growth of individuals of all ages by offering opportunities to develop both known and undiscovered potentials. Why should there be "special" classes for either the elderly or for the convalescent, or, for that matter, for children and young people who are not challenged enough by their schools and their environment? Courses in the arts and crafts as well as in variations of body movement, in basic and social science as well as in music, dance and poetry, could bring together, in appropriate groupings, a wide range of ages and thus help prevent the erection of age barriers now considered and deplored as unsurmountable.

As the arts and sciences and the humanities would tend to cross-fertilize one another in such an activities center setting—broadening and stimulating through interrelatedness—so also the generations might learn to profit from the acceptance of the idea that life, at whatever stage you may be, is part of an ongoing cycle in which, in time, you will inevitably play all the parts.

In this sense, we were impressed with a political perspective which Thomas Ganschow reports from behind that great curtain which is beginning to lose its intransigence, namely, Mao's suggestion (in view of the radical changes in the

evaluation of old age in ancient and revolutionary China) that there should be a Three Way Alliance between the old, the middle aged, and the young.

In the context of activities, something should also be said to celebrate the skills of fashioning materials of all kinds—clay, glass, metal, textiles, leather, wood—and this especially for those who have not been privileged to make some of these skills an early part of their lives. Materials offer to the coordinated senses and musculature unique experiences; each demands a disciplined approach appropriate to its texture, strength and potentiality—its very nature. Each will respond and verify uses which are in accord with its essence or it will simply and without argument refuse to be misused. This experience of working with a variety of media in non-verbal communication gives new dimensions to things and words in a technological world dominated by machine-made objects. We underscore such instruction not only because a concrete experience of basic crafts can help to convey the unity of human culture through the ages, but also and especially because a fundamental series of human skill-capacities are reborn with each person, are built into the human life cycle and are, we believe, neglected at great risk for personal and communal development regardless of where technology may lead specialized man.

There are those who preach withdrawal in old age and others who decry this detachment as conducive to apathy and prescribe full-scale activity of mind and body as the necessary road to the fruition of life. Perhaps the answer is to subscribe to both approaches in appropriate ratio. Surely one can use the valuable release from timebound scheduling to learn *how* to do things for which one had no opportunity or time before. But it offers also the supreme opportunity to reconsider those urgent and perplexing *why* questions which were the concern of childhood and were usually brushed aside by one's elders with the dead-end answer "because that is how things are." With a lifetime of experience as "data" and a mind less beset with career problems or economic five- or ten-year plans there is another chance to quietly seek out answers. Our eighty-two year old agrees: "I want to tell people approaching and perhaps fearing age that it is a time of discovery. If they say—'Of what?' I can only answer, 'We must each find out for ourselves, otherwise it won't be discovery.' "[5]

Medical and social progress, we conclude, has not artificially stretched a life span "meant" to be shorter, but it has technically confirmed what was potentially given all along. If this forces us to adjust previous conceptualizations, it only means that we must discern potentialities built into the ground plan of human life. But, as we have learned during the "century of the child" as well as the half-century dedicated to the study of youth, no part of the life cycle can be intensively reassessed without opening itself and all others to a new consciousness: In the long run, the overall status of old age cannot be reevaluated without considering how infancy may be planned so as to create—or, at any rate, not to foreclose—the conditions for a viable old age; and how old

age may be planned so as to bring to fruition what each stage of life may have to contribute to the subsequent ones and to the last. For no doubt there is much in a child's world which presages some of the liberated wonder of aged experience. In this sense, we also found significant much of what Stuart Spicker reports on *mentation* and liked what Sally Gadow and Geri Berg say so perceptively about the changing sense of *time* in old age:

> The slowing down process in aging is one of its most dominant symbols or, in clinical terms, 'symptoms.' . . . It may be that with age we realize time has the dimension of depth as well as duration. . . . We slow ourselves to be more gentle with these experiences, to take care to let their possibilities, their rich density emerge. We continue moving through time, but we also move into time, allowing it to expand in depth for us though its objective duration diminishes.

Among other enlightening data the humanities report (see Kathleen Woodward's essay) how creative and prophetic people saw their lives as a whole: people who often were already a bit "old" as children and retained their playfulness in old age—and people who in having their life stages creatively upset knew, more intimately than most people, periodical feeling of fragmentation and isolation.

Clinical and humanist enlightenment makes it plausible that old age at its height or in its high moments seems to be equipped to reconcile as meaningful counterpoints what the years of adult over-commitment tended to emphasize as mutually exclusive: rationality and intuition, sociability and privacy, action and reflection, hereness and spirituality—all once dubbed opposites with implications of masculinity or femininity, of youthfulness or old age, or of various group affiliations. And by their work, the humanities may help to keep the field of old age concerns out of the eager hands of those moralists who might take it upon themselves to tell the aging and the aged in all detail what they *must* do instead of enabling them to make choices from among truly viable alternatives and thus to find their own way of concluding life during that precious time when one's life time runs out.

Notes

[1]E. H. Erikson, "Reflections on Dr. Borg's Life Cycle," *Daedalus* (Spring 1976), 1-28.

[2]See, for example, *Daedalus* (Spring 1976).

[3]Florida Scott-Maxwell, *The Measure of My Days* (New York: Alfred Knopf, 1972), p. 138.

[4]Joan M. Erikson, *Activity, Recovery, Growth* (New York: W. W. Norton, 1976).

[5]Florida Scott-Maxwell, p. 142.

David E. Stannard

GROWING UP AND GROWING OLD: DILEMMAS OF AGING IN BUREAUCRATIC AMERICA

"You know about birds?" she asked.
"What about them?"
"You know what *old* birds do when their time has come?"
No, he didn't. Was there anything of interest he actually knew?
"Well, when they are old, and their time has come, they just go off alone in the woods and die. That's why you never see any old dead birds, you realize that? There's just millions of birds and they have to die, sometime, but you never see a one of them unless they're hurt."
It amazed the boy to realize the truth of that, and shamed him to think that he hadn't known it.
"It's nature's way," she said, "and people should live according to nature. Some people really do."

Wright Morris,
Fire Sermon (1971)

In the United States today, the aged are the fastest growing of our many groups of minorities. During the past century the aged population of America has increased in size seventeen times—more than triple the rate of the population in general—and current demographic projections estimate another fifty percent increase before the completion of barely one more generational cycle. Such projections, of course, are somewhat problematic, dependent as they are on the stability of presently perceived demographic trends; nonetheless, the common and conservative wisdom of the most perspicacious of our population experts is that in the relatively near future between one out of four to one out of five living Americans will be over sixty-five years of age.

By themselves, these figures are a mere curiosity. For they measure quantity, not quality of life. There are, however, other numbers—batteries of them—

that suggest a dire picture of the life being led and to be led by much of this swelling segment of our people. Income level is the most obvious such measure. And, just as the elderly are the fastest-growing minority group in America today, as Robert N. Butler has recently shown, they are also our fastest growing poverty group.[1] According to the most restrained government estimates, at the same time that in recent years the gross incidence of poverty has been steadily declining for the population at large, it has been climbing for those ages sixty-five and over. The aged have increasingly become dependent on Social Security payments for income (Social Security now represents the largest single source of income for older Americans), but even that limited well of funds—a present maximum of $3,300 per year—is dangerously close to running dry. The structural unsoundness of the system itself is such that it probably will be unable to bear the pressures that will inevitably be placed on it by the future shifting of the nation's age composition.[2]

But the problems of population size and income distribution for the elderly, stark as they may be, only *suggest* the nature of the dilemmas that presently beset us and appear to be in store for the future. This is so because our discussions of the elderly generally fail to consider the fact that age discrimination begins long before the official recognition of old age at sixty-five, and also neglect to seek the roots of such discrimination, roots that spread through and intertwine with the most essential elements of our culture.

Age discrimination, of course, is neither new nor uniquely confined to our society. What is new, however, is the specific *character* of that discrimination among a people who pride themselves as the most affluent and technologically advanced representatives of the human race since the dawn of time. It is a kind of discrimination that is so insidiously a part of our way of life that it will take a virtual reshaping of that way of life if we are to even have hope of undoing the problem. But first we must perceive it. And to do that it will be helpful to take a few steps back from the present in order to view it in a more inclusive context.

I

Almost three-quarters of a century ago a young French sociologist named Robert Hertz wrote a long essay exploring the question of why, in different societies, the death of one individual might sometimes seem to cripple the society, while the death of another might be scarcely noticed.[3] In some societies the death of a king or an important warrior or leader can send the survivors into such a state of shock that entire villages will be burned or deserted, while at the same time in some of those same societies the aged will be left to die of exposure and dead infants will be tossed away with seemingly no more emotion than one might display in disposing of a pot that had cracked in the kiln. As Simone de Beauvoir points out in *The Coming of Age,* it is not at all uncommon for poor and nomadic tribes of people to practice both infanticide and the killing of the aged. "Both are parasites," writes de Beauvoir,

"and sometimes in the case of extreme poverty, this leads to rivalry between them: the children steal the old people's share of food."[4]

Hertz's answer to the question was set in almost crudely functionalist terms, but it was an answer that has inevitably crept into subsequent, more sophisticated treatments of the same problem. The individual in society, Hertz wrote, was possessed of a social as well as a biological existence, a social existence that is in a sense grafted onto the biological being and that thus invests the biological being with social meaning and social value. If an individual who has been invested with a social existence of apparently great value to that society is then suddenly lost to it, the damage to the social fabric will be so disruptive that a good deal of attention to the loss thus occasioned is necessary in order for the society to in effect "heal" itself, that is, come to terms with the individual's absence. As Robert Blauner was to rephrase Hertz's observation half a century later, "Because death is so disruptive in simple societies, much 'work' must be done to restore the social system's functioning."[5] Needless to say, however, little or no such "work" is necessary if the dead or dying individual is regarded, in de Beauvoir's term, as a social "parasite."

But one society's parasite is another society's hope for the future; another society's parasite may be still another society's source of wisdom and stability. Numerous factors, of course, go into such varied valuation or devaluation (a society is nomadic or settled, stable or unstable, agricultural or technological) but the central point is that in most societies the individual possesses less *inherent* than *situational* value to the society at large. And though the criteria for valuation may be seen to vary almost endlessly throughout the length and breadth of human history, such criteria are almost inevitably tied into a system of perceived growth through the life cycle, growth that is most frequently marked by what have come to be termed, since the work of Arnold Van Gennep, as '*rites de passage*.'

Whatever the particular stage of transition one may happen to be concerned with (and whatever particular model of growth, from Shakespeare to Erikson, that one may care to employ) anthropologists have come to recognize that the sequence of events involved in passage from one life-status to another is quite consistent: the passing of the old status, a period of temporary status suspension (the "liminal" period), and finally rebirth into a new status. It is during that transitional "liminal" period, however, when the individual possesses no clear role or status or function, that anthropologists have recently noted some striking behavior among peoples observed; persons who are thus categorized by a society are often seen as ambiguous creatures, and until transition to the new status has been completed they are often regarded as ritually "unclean" and are thus shunned and avoided.[6] One implication of such work is the suggestion that there may exist a certain universal form of deviance. Whatever the society in question—and however seemingly unique may be its system of defining deviant individuals—it appears as though any group that is perceived and characterized as *without* a clear social role will invariably be treated as deviant. If this observation holds true, it can provide

us with a key to understanding the plight of the aged in America today.

We live today in a society that for at least a century and a half has been characterized by a rapid—some have even argued an accelerating—rate of social change on many fronts. Three of the most noteworthy points of change, at least for my purposes here, have concerned the individual's relationship with work, with the family, and with the society at large. On one front we have witnessed an increasing tendency toward specialization and compartmentalization of employment, a tendency noted by many foreign observers of the American scene since as early as the 1830's.[7] On another we have seen the steady shrinking of the family away from close interaction with the larger community and with its becoming, as Charles Abrams and John P. Dean once put it, "an emotional bulwark against the threats and insecurities of a too-big, too-fast, too-complicated world where one must compete, man against man, for his place in the sun."[8] This, too, is a phenomenon that most social historians now trace to its beginnings in the early nineteenth century. And, finally, we have observed the consistent bureaucratization and institutionalization of our social world from the rise of schools, asylums, and penitentiaries, again beginning in the early nineteenth century, to the burgeoning social welfare agencies of the past several decades.

Many of these changes, seen in isolation, one from another, have been of enormous social benefit. But to be seen in proper perspective they cannot, in fact, be treated in isolation. They are interdependent social phenomena, and together they form much of the web that is the social world all of us today inhabit. And to inhabit that world means to grow up in it, to grow old in it, and to die in it, to move chronologically *through* it, shedding one status and donning another as we become older. At one point, however, far too many of us shed one status only to find that there is nothing left to don. Until death. That point occurs when we enter the state of social ambiguity, of social functionlessness, of social irrelevance that is the American liminal period known as old age. It is no accident, I submit, that the most recent study of the history of aging in America identifies the early nineteenth century, when these three major points of change first appeared on the American scene, as the initial stage when the elderly in America began to lose social status.[9]

The interweaving of the various social changes that have marked American life for at least a dozen decades now has worked incessantly to create that vacuum of an open-ended liminal period waiting for all of us at the end of the life cycle. Our work has become steadily less important in the sense that there are few positions which any of us can now occupy that another individual could not fill just as well. Our families have become increasingly introverted and withdrawn from society, with the result that they are less able to socially "diffuse" and thus absorb without trauma either the shock of death or the tedium of demographically unprecedented decades of isolated companionship with one or two others. And so, in the face of these two crucial barriers to a rich engagement with a stable, ego-supportive community, we have found ourselves more and more dependent on large, impersonal, bureaucratic institutions for even minimal amounts of that needed support.

This harsh confrontation with, yet simultaneous dependence upon, large-scale bureaucracies is the inevitable fate of a people who have spent generations whittling away at what the sociologist Peter Berger has recently termed "mediating structures," those smaller, more intimately meaningful social units such as the church, the family, the clan, the community, that serve as buffers between the individual and the bureaucratic "mega-structures" that now dominate the social order.[10] In one sense, as Berger points out, such change can be liberating in that it can serve to free individuals from the oppressive weight of cultural tradition; in another sense, however, it can be devastating. This is something that Emile Durkheim observed with great prescience even before the turn of the twentieth century when he saw the end result of such change as a time when individuals "without mutual relationships, tumble over one another like so many liquid molecules, encountering no central energy to retain, fix and organize them."[11] In still more eloquent language—and many decades earlier than even Durkheim—Alexis de Tocqueville saw a similar image on the horizon of the future:

> I see an innumerable multitude of men, alike and equal, constantly circling around in pursuit of the petty and banal pleasures with which they glut their souls. Each one of them, withdrawn into himself, is almost unaware of the fate of the rest. Mankind, for him, consists in his children and his personal friends. As for the rest of his fellow citizens, they are near enough, but he does not notice them.[12]

Some, however, are less noticed than others. And they are those whom social circumstance has confined to the periphery of active engagement with the world, those who have been systematically denied a clearly defined social role, those who in a world bereft of viable mediating structures are socially redundant and irrelevant, those who are old.

In a society that measures a person's worth by the degree and style with which he or she is able to produce and consume, the individual who finds that his ability to produce or consume has been taken away—*with no future prospect for its return*—is indeed trapped in a dilemma of the most extraordinary complexity. And it is a dilemma made all the worse by the fact that the individual, finding himself old, alone, and irrelevant, was a seemingly willing participant in the creation of the non-status situation he has now inherited. To live willingly, or at least unthinkingly, in a society that degrades and denigrates the social worth of the aged because of their limited ability to engage in the production and consumption activities that are the central criteria for that society's evaluation of social worth, and then to grow old in that society and find oneself stripped of the power to freely produce or consume is to discover that maintaining a tolerable self-image in old age is one of the most difficult chores one will ever encounter. It is to learn that one is blithely placed in a category with, in the words of a major research organization charged with planning for the future, "chronic invalids and the insane," "those with little or no productive potential," and those who in the

future "a community under stress would be better off without."[13] Thus, rather than being socially disruptive, death for the aged is now regarded, in Ivan Illich's words, as "socially approved" since it occurs "when man has become useless not only as a producer but also as a consumer," when "a consumer, trained at great expense, must finally be written off as a total loss."[14]

II

There have, in recent years, evolved two main theoretical approaches suggested as ways of dealing with the plight of the elderly. One is known as activity theory, the other as disengagement theory. The names are self-explanatory. Proponents of activity theory argue that continuing social involvement is natural and beneficial to the aged, while advocates of disengagement theory maintain that aging is an inevitable mutual withdrawal or disengagement, resulting in decreased interaction between the aging person and others in the social system he belongs to. Those who support the activity theory point to numerous studies indicating a correlation between social involvement and mental health, self-esteem, and general competence. Those who support disengagement theory point to other studies indicating a correlation between isolation and free time late in life and the ability of the individual to then review his past life, come to terms with his achievements and disappointments, and in the end die peacefully and, in the unintentionally chilling words of one writer, "without disrupting vital affairs."[15]

The problem with both of these theories is that they ignore the social umbrella under which the subjects of their studies must be herded. The activities most old people are forced to engage in are make-work projects of low social value to the larger society, often projects similar to those children are offered when it is felt they have too much free time at their disposal; on the other hand, the supposedly rich moments of reflection and review available to those disengaged from the social system are today more often than not moments of loneliness and despair while passing the time until death occurs in the quiet and sterility of a nursing home or hospital. In short, whichever way the old person in America turns today, he is isolated and alienated, from work, from society, and all too frequently from family and long-time friends. In this sort of world, if Erikson's famous critical opposition of potential ego qualities for the aged is correct—the opposition of ego integrity versus despair—it is all too obvious where the thrust of modern American society is pushing most of us.

Still, it can be correctly said that I have been dealing in large generalities. Too much specification of individual cases can, however, raise the opposite charge that one is dealing with unrepresentative and perhaps trivial examples. Let me try, then, to illustrate better the plight of the aged and the discouraging prognosis facing us by turning to some material that is contained in the closing chapter of a book I have recently written on the problem of confronting death.[16] Since most of us will die in hospitals (and if we include nursing homes, the percentages become overwhelming), and since most of our deaths

will occur late in life at the hands of a degenerative disease (seventy percent in 1970 as compared with fifteen percent three generations ago), I think it not unfair of me to attempt to depict this setting as an exemplar of the more general fate awaiting us in old age.

To be old in America, with no valued social function to perform, is to be the social equivalent of terminally ill. It is to be in a social state in which one is dependent upon social service or social control agencies and to be subject to what sociologists call "degradation ceremonies" in the grip of such agencies. It is no accident that this situation is almost a textbook definition of social deviance.[17] And in much the same way that prisons and asylums, beginning in the early nineteenth century, emerged as the proper home for one brand of social deviant, the rest home and the hospital in the twentieth century have come to serve the same function for another brand of deviant, the old and the dying. In the past several years we have all been made quite painfully aware of what life in a rest home can be like (and it is worth noting in passing that in New York State alone, between the mid-1930's and the mid-1960's the aged population barely doubled in size while the number of nursing home beds increased more than seven-fold and the size of the average nursing home itself increased by more than sixty-five percent).[18] But hospitals, perhaps since they are not generally seen quite so obviously as profit-making institutions, have not been so prone to headline-making scandals. That should not, however, lull us into thinking that life—and death—in the ward is a pleasant, humanistic experience. More often than not for the aged, it is an existence marked by fear, loneliness, and despair.

When the aged and dying individual becomes too much trouble for his family (if he is fortunate) or his other associates in life to deal with, in America he is generally thrust out of his accustomed social milieu and into an environment probably more sterile and non-social than any he has ever previously known. He is surrounded by doctors and nurses who, with their own feelings necessarily foremost in mind, resort to various formalized strategies to avoid undue "involvement" with him. With the patient's best interests in mind, it should be noted, the hospital staff does often provide the real service of withholding information from the family as to the seriousness of the dying patient's condition because of the commonly observed tendency of families to then desert the patient; but by and large it is simply essential to the efficiency of hospital operation that death—or, in hospital language, "termination"—have as little impact on the staff as possible. Professional composure must be maintained at all costs. Thus, aged and dying patients are often avoided by doctors and nurses, and when contact cannot be avoided, a frequent strategy is to deal with the individual in a manner of forced aloofness and detachment. As a result, the patient must resort to counteracting strategies of his own, such as that of one individual, observed by Elisabeth Kübler-Ross who made a practice of taking her telephone off the hook, "just to hear a voice."[19]

All to often, in Ivan Illich's terse phrase, when the hospitalized individual now looks into the eyes of a physician, "what he meets is the gaze of biological accountant engaged in input/output calculations," a biological accountant for

whom death is simply "that point at which the human organism refuses any further input of treatment."[20] The aged and hopelessly dying individual who has become inconvenient to society then quickly becomes inconvenient and even something of an affront to the hospital staff as well. But modern medicine has an answer to this problem—sedation. Of the more than two hundred deaths one sociologist observed in hospitals in California and the Midwest in the 1960's, all but about a dozen took place while the individual was in a "comatose" state and none were deaths "of the Hollywood version, wherein the person's last sentence is interrupted by his final breath." The ability to thus reduce the emotionally threatening object—the dying patient—to a socially non-functioning state prior to death, and the frequency of such practice, have given rise to the phenomenon of "social death," "that point," in the words of David Sudnow, "at which socially relevant attributes of the patient begin permanently to cease to be operative as conditions for treating him, and when he is, essentially, regarded as actually dead."[21] At this point the dying individual—particularly if he is old and obviously of little social importance—is conveniently depersonalized. And the nurse can go about her business with a good deal more comfort and equanimity: care may be taken to see that the individual's eyes are "properly" closed for the sake of postmortem convenience; nurses may refer to "riding patients out" (keeping their bodies functioning at least until the shift change to avoid "the tedious and time-consuming task of postmorten care"); or "soon-to-terminate" bodies may be stored on stretchers in supply rooms overnight so as not to waste clean sheets and a good room on them.[22] Indeed, it is not at all uncommon for the aged to be flatly denied life-support or life-saving attention available to others . . . simply *because* they are old, as seen in the case reported by David Sudnow of an intern who refused to give mouth-to-mouth resuscitation to an elderly woman because "he could never bring himself to put his mouth to 'an old lady's like that.' "[23]

Such dehumanizing attitudes and procedures are, of course, shocking to us. Yet apart from instituting some additional relevant courses in a few major medical schools, there appears to be very little we will or can do about the problem; and this is so because whatever we do must be keyed to the bureaucratized, productivity-oriented, profit-making, institutionalized value system that is part and parcel of the social world that we inhabit.

To be sure, there are admirable and unselfish movements at work in the land to deal with such problems. Hospice, for example, a struggling movement imported from England in the past few years, is trying vigorously to humanize the process of dying in its pilot facility now being planned in Branford, Connecticut. But it is instructive to learn that Hospice had first purchased land in neighboring Hamden, Connecticut, but had to sell it and give up its original plans because of community resistance based on the fear that the old and dying residents might "molest" that town's little children. Do we need more evidence that the old and the dying are often regarded as deviants?

But even if Hospice is successful, the *idea* that it suggested to others is already outstripping even *its* most ambitious plans. Self-appointed

"bereavement counselors" and private "thanatologists" have begun to set up shop all over the country to make a profit on the pain and loneliness of the old and dying by appealing to the guilt of the surviving family. In California there is one organization that serves as both a training center and employment agency for "professional companions" to sit with the dying patient in his waning hours, thus allowing the family to go about its other business free of the burden of guilt. Begun by a former public relations man whose most important previous claim to fame resided in the large part he played in organizing Ronald Reagan's first successful run for the California Governorship, this organization has various training programs available, including an eight-hour correspondence course ("the reading has been kept light," a promotional flyer assures us) "specifically designed for Nursing Home Administrators." Business, for this organization, appears to be thriving.

III

In the epigraph that I chose for this paper from Wright Morris' novel *Fire Sermon,* it is suggested that "going off alone" to die "is nature's way . . . and people should live according to nature." If that is in fact nature's way, Americans are living it more and more with every passing year. But Morris has another image in another of his books, an image of a different sort. He was "a man who knew his own mind," Morris writes of one of his characters, a man who "had lived in the manner he believed he had chosen, not knowing that he had been one of those chosen not merely to grow old, but to grow ripe."[24] To grow ripe is to mature, to advance to a condition of peak value; it is also, however, to advance to a state when reaping seems in order. And that state is being reached in America today at an increasingly earlier age.

One simple measure of this tendency is the government unemployment statistic. Although not assembled for this purpose, a close evaluation of these figures invariably shows that the time in an American's life when he is least likely to be unemployed is the decade spanning the years of age twenty-five to thirty-four. From that point on the likelihood of being unemployed leaps at an astonishing rate—by sixteen percent for those aged thirty-five to forty-four, by one hundred and twenty-three percent for those aged forty-five to fifty-four, and by two hundred and seventy-three percent for those aged fifty-five to sixty-four.[25] Although the specific percentages are, of course, different, the same trend is observable in government poverty statistics: the older one grows from that same baseline of twenty-five to thirty-four years of age, the greater becomes the likelihood that one will be living in an officially defined state of poverty; indeed, among unrelated individuals residing in urban areas those aged just forty-five to fifty-four are more than twice as likely to be impoverished than those aged twenty-five to thirty-four.[26]

It is clear, in short, that there is nothing sacred about the designation of age sixty-five as the threshold to old age. If old age is that point in the life cycle when redundant and socially irrelevant individuals are to be removed from

active participation in social life, it is clear that old age is occurring at a relatively earlier age now than ever before. Industry is hard at work devising ever newer retirement plans that encourage earlier and earlier removal from the labor force. Retirement communities that once set minimum admission age at sixty or sixty-five have virtually all lowered that barrier now to fifty-five and, in many cases, even forty-five.

All of these figures are, no doubt, discouraging. But they are not hopeless. They are not hopeless in themselves, that is, because they are merely the product of a society that has a certain perception of the proper way of evaluating human worth. But that perception is itself tied to the vastly complex social web we have woven for ourselves during the past several centuries. And to break out of that web will not be easy. It may, in fact, be impossible. For it appears to me, at least, with every passing year, that that web may in fact be the "iron cage" which Max Weber spoke of at the turn of the twentieth century when he wondered "who will live in this cage in the future" and whether it might not in fact be a cage marked by "mechanized petrification, embellished with a sort of convulsive self-importance."[27] If that is so, if we have reached that stage, then the plight of the aged in America can do nothing but grow worse.

If, on the other hand, we have not reached that point, if, that is, we are still capable of recognizing with Simone de Beauvoir that "it is the whole system that is at issue" and that "our claim cannot be otherwise than radical—change life itself,"[28] then, perhaps, we have a chance. But on the evidence to date, one can only regard the prospects for the future as bleak.

Notes

[1] *Why Survive? Being Old in America* (New York: Harper & Row, 1975), pp. 22-36. On the old as a minority group, see M. L. Barron, "Minority Group Characteristics of the Aged in American Society," *Journal of Gerontology*, 8 (1958), 477-81.

[2] For some recent thoughts on this dilemma, see David Hackett Fischer, *Growing Old in America* (New York: Oxford Univ. Press, 1977), pp. 196-203.

[3] "The Collective Representation of Death" [1907], in *Death and the Right Hand*, by Robert Hertz, trans. R. and C. Needham (Glencoe, Ill.: The Free Press, 1960).

[4] *The Coming of Age* (New York: Warner, 1972), p. 127.

[5] "Death and Social Structure," *Psychiatry*, 29 (1966), 387.

[6] See Mary Douglas, *Purity and Danger: An Analysis of Concepts of Pollution and Taboo* (London: Routledge & Kegan Paul, 1966) and Victor Turner, "Betwixt and Between: The Liminal Period in *Rites de Passage*," in *The Forest of Symbols: Aspects of Ndembu Ritual*, by Victor Turner (Ithaca: Cornel Univ. Press, 1967), pp. 93-111.

[7] See, for example, Michel Chevalier's comments on this matter in his *Society, Manners and Politics in the United States: Being a Series of Letters on North America*, trans. T.G. Bradford (Boston: Weeks, Jordan and Company, 1839), p. 282.

[8] Quoted in Ruth N. Anshen, ed., *The Family: Its Function and Destiny* (New York: Harper, 1949), p. 472.

[9] Fischer, *Growing Old in America*, chap. 2. Cf. W. Andrew Achenbaum, "The Obsolescence of Old Age in America," *Journal of Social History*, 8 (1974), 48-62;

Achenbaum posits a somewhat later dating of what he terms the change from "veneration" to "deprecation" of the aged, but the general trend is similar to that portrayed by Fischer and the discrepancy in specific dating may be attributable to a variety of factors, including, simply, the examination of different data.

[10] Among the several occasions on which Peter Berger has developed this theme, see especially his *To Empower People: The Role of Mediating Structures in Public Policy* (Washington: American Enterprise Institute, 1977).

[11] *Suicide* [1897], (New York: The Free Press, 1951), p. 389.

[12] *Democracy in America* [1848 ed.], (New York: Anchor-Doubleday, 1969), pp. 691-92.

[13] Rand Corporation Memorandum RM—5115—TAB (1966), quoted in Butler, *Why Survive?*, pp. 12-13.

[14] *Medical Nemesis: The Expropriation of Health* (New York: Pantheon, 1976), pp. 206-07.

[15] The literature on these two theoretical stances is enormous and cannot even begin to be summarized here. A brief sampling of some of it might begin with the following: Elaine Cumming and William E. Henry, *Growing Old: The Process of Disengagement* (New York: Basic Books, 1961); Robert N. Butler, "The Life Review: An Interpretation of Reminiscence in the Aged," *Psychiatry*, 26 (1963), 65-76; Robert Kastenbaum, ed., *New Thoughts on Old Age* (New York: Springer, 1964); E.B. Palmore, "The Effects of Aging on Activities and Attitudes," *The Gerontologist*, 8 (1968), 259-63; T. Bell, "The Relationship Between Social Involvement and Feeling Old Among Residents in Homes for the Aged," *Journal of Gerontology*, 22 (1967), 17-22; and P. Jaslow, "The Contribution of Work, Work-Related, and Other Factors to the Morale of Older American Women," Diss. Brandeis University 1973.

[16] David E. Stannard, *The Puritan Way of Death: A Study in Religion, Culture, and Social Change* (New York: Oxford Univ. Press, 1977).

[17] See, for example, Kai T. Erikson, "Notes on the Sociology of Deviance," in *The Other Side*, ed. Howard S. Becker (New York: The Free Press, 1964) and Edwin Lemert, "Social Structure, Social Control, and Deviation," in *Anomie and Deviant Behavior*, ed. Marshall B. Clinard (New York: Macmillan, 1964).

[18] Figures computed from various tables in William C. Thomas, Jr., *Nursing Homes and Public Policy* (Ithaca: Cornell Univ. Press, 1969).

[19] *On Death and Dying* (New York: Macmillan, 1969), p. 44. An early statement on the avoidance of death by physicians is August M. Kasper's "The Doctor and Death," in Herman Feifel, ed., *The Meaning of Death* (New York: McGraw Hill, 1959), pp. 259-70. On the various strategies employed by doctors and nurses for maintaining distance and composure, see Barney G. Glaser and Anselm L. Strauss, *Awareness of Dying* (Chicago: Aldine, 1965), pp. 326-56; and Jeanne C. Quint, *The Nurse and the Dying Patient* (New York: Macmillan, 1967), pp. 173-80. On family rejection and desertion of the dying—particularly the elderly—see Rose L. Coser, *Life in the Ward* (East Lansing: Michigan State Univ. Press, 1962), pp. 119-24; and David Sudnow, *Passing On: The Social Organization of Dying* (Englewood Cliffs, N.J.: Prentice-Hall, 1967), p. 97.

[20] Illich, *Medical Nemesis*, pp. 170, 206.

[21] Sudnow, *Passing on*, pp. 88-90, 74.

[22] These and other practices are described in most of the literature on the subject. For the specific practices cited above, see Sudnow, *Passing On*, pp. 74, 83; and Quint, *The Nurse and the Dying Patient*, p. 34.

[23] Sudnow, *Passing On*, p. 101.

[24] Wright Morris, *A Life* (New York: Harper and Row, 1973), p. 152.

[25] See Harold L. Sheppard, ed., *Towards an Industrial Gerontology* (Cambridge, Mass.: Schenkman, 1970), pp. 102-05.

[26] Ibid., p. 100.

[27] Max Weber, *The Protestant Ethic and the Spirit of Capitalism* [1904], trans. Talcott Parsons (New York: Scribner's, 1958), pp. 181-82.

[28] de Beauvoir, *The Coming of Age*, p. 807.

I. THE WESTERN HERITAGE: IMAGES AND IDEALS

Harold M. Stahmer

THE AGED IN TWO ANCIENT ORAL CULTURES: THE ANCIENT HEBREWS AND HOMERIC GREECE

"You shall rise in the presence of grey hairs, give honour to the aged, and fear your God."

Leviticus, XIX, 32[1]

"Grey hair is a crown of glory, and it is won by a virtuous life."

Proverbs, XVI, 31

"Honour your father and your mother, that you may live long in the land which the Lord your God is giving you."

Exodus, XX, 12

"For a young man all is decorous when he is cut down in battle and torn with the sharp bronze, and lies there dead, and though dead still all that shows about him is beautiful; but when an old man is dead and down, and the dogs mutilate the grey head and the grey beard and the parts that are secret, this, for all sad mortality, is the sight most pitiful."

Iliad, XXII, 71-76[2]

"The hearts of the great can be changed. You know the Furies, how they forever side with the elder."

Iliad, XV, 203-04

"It would be a hard thing if we were to put any slight on the eldest and best among us."

Odyssey, XIII, 141-42[3]

This essay will examine the attitudes toward the elderly in these two ancient cultures, focusing particularly on the extent to which they shared a common

respect for the aged and the ways in which this was manifested in each culture. By tradition, students of Western thought have tended to highlight the dissimilarities between the legacies of Athens and Jerusalem.[4]

My approach to these two cultures differs from traditional studies in two ways. First, I have chosen not to include in my investigation the post Homeric period in ancient Greece nor ancient Israel after the establishment of the Monarchy.[5] My second reason for limiting my research to these two cultures was based originally, not so much on their differences, but rather on certain characteristics common to each. These include a shared interest in legend and history, genealogies, oral tradition and culture, as well as an emphasis on the individual's oral and aural powers.[6] Naturally, there are some sharp differences between these traditions, particularly in the areas of religion and mythology. I chose rather to ignore these differences and concentrate on how aging and the elderly were regarded in two cultures that manifest a respect and interest in tradition and history and the possible role and importance of the elders in preserving and transmitting their respective legacies within each culture. In each tradition during the periods under consideration, there existed no recorded, printed documentation that could be read, studied and passed on to subsequent generations.[7] The history, those events worth preserving, had to be told, transmitted orally, in order for the culture to be preserved. Prior to investigating the ways in which this could be achieved, I assumed, perhaps naively, that the responsibility for preserving and transmitting this legacy would be vested in those most knowledgeable about what a particular tribe or culture had experienced and deemed worth remembering. The aged, those most senior in terms of knowledge and experience, seemed the logical candidates for this responsibility, especially those aged who had been recognized for their responsible leadership during most of their active lives.

I. Oral Tradition in Antiquity

Except for those familiar with the writings of Henri Frankfort, with Biblical hermeneutics, with the Kögel-Kittel theory of lexicography, or the writings of Johannes Pedersen, Martin Noth, Thorleif Boman, or Martin Buber, few can appreciate the oral quality that pervaded the lifestyles of the early Hebrews and, which, subsequently, provided the basis for theologies of the Word in Christianity as well as in Judaism.

Similarly, except for those familiar with the scholarship of such authorities on the subject as Milman Parry, Cedric Whitman, and Albert B. Lord, there are relatively few who can appreciate the unique qualities associated with oral cultures in classical antiquity.

Inasmuch as my interest in the aged in these cultures arose out of my curiosity about oral traditions and cultures, it is appropriate to make some comments about oral tradition in these periods before discussing their attitudes toward the elderly.

II. Oral Tradition in the Ancient Near East and Israel

Ancient man stood in awe of language. Language for him was spirit, being, reality—a powerful force in his life. Throughout Assyria, Babylonia, Egypt, the early West, and the ancient Orient, language—the word, and not only the Divine Word—was creative energy, a dynamic force. Words had the power to produce events rather than, as for most moderns, merely to describe them or articulate private thoughts. The same was especially true for ancient Israel. The foundations of Western civilization, in both the ancient Near East and the Hellenic world, have their origins in a mentality that looked upon reality as essentially personal and dominated by ancient man's reliance upon his oral and aural powers. The phenomena of reality confronted men in terms of speech and address as I and Thou. Hence, the characterization of the ancient oral mentality as mythopoeic—where myth as a form of poetry is the means whereby early man's memorable encounters with the phenomena of reality were shaped and preserved.[8] Ancient man was absolutely incapable of the kind of impersonal reflection and distance from reality that characterize the more modern logical, scientific, and mechanical mentality. The ability to understand reality by distinguishing between the perceiver and the thing perceived—by dividing reality into subject and object, or appearance and reality—in a word, to look upon reality as an It, was totally unknown to ancient man. Understanding for the mythopoeic mentality was an activity of involvement and identification which in most cases especially involved men's aural powers. With respect to the Jew of antiquity, Martin Buber said: "We may state it thus, that the Jew of antiquity, was more acoustically oriented (*Ohrenmensch*) than visually (*Augenmensch*), and more temporally oriented (*Zeitmensch*) than spatially (*Raummensch*). Of all his senses he relied most heavily upon his hearing when forming his picture of the universe."[9]

Among the Israelites, Yahweh is distinguished from the nearby nature gods not only as the transcendent One who immanently speaks creation into existence, but as the One who singles out a particular creature to be fashioned after His own image and likeness and permits His creatures to partake in the Word. Their partnership or covenant was established upon their respective abilities to converse and co-operate with one another in the task of creation. The relationship between Creator and creature among the Israelites constitutes a covenant to the extent that without God's Word—without the sustaining power of *davar*—men would wither and die, and human history would become meaningless. Hence the prophet is a *nabi,* literally a "mouthpiece" of God, who warns, persuades, cajoles, and ultimately provides direction for Israel's destiny.

At the beginning of Israel's history *davar* serves as a kind of seal or testimony of an encounter between God and His creatures or between two or more living creatures. Thus, *davar* cannot be translated simply as "word" unless we realize that whenever spoken, *davar* signifies a happening, a situation that is spoken into existence. The exact process whereby the divine *davar* and human speech are blended remains for all practical purposes a mystery. Human speech is permeated with that which, in one sense, is non-human, and yet there is no

definite way of distinguishing between human speech which partakes of the creative word and that which is not permeated with this sacramental quality.

Ancient man literally sang his unity: it was through song that men were reunited by re-experiencing a common event and thereby were given the power to face the unknown. In the time of the great Patriarchs during the first half of the second millennium B.C.E., we have little in the way of accurate dates and written sources. Whatever we know of this period, of the great historical events upon which great traditions have been established, is through song and legend. The renarrating of great events or the singing of great happenings, such as the Song of Deborah, brought to a great emerging people unity, courage, and life.

Voices proclaim, preserve, glorify, but never merely describe events. For these ancient peoples it was through song and verse—through the hearing of heroic tales narrated by the tribe's story-teller—that generations of peoples were bound together and instilled with a common spirit and purpose. In this connection, Buber noted that the best description of Hebrew style is that it is essentially an acoustical art. "Tone," he writes, "is the simplest form of expression, rhythm the foundation upon which her art is established, and lyrics, the most adequate means of embodying her style."[10] In early Jewish culture, the faculty of hearing, a sense for tone and rhythm, was developed long before the Jews had any kind of significant pictorial art.

III. Oral Tradition during the Homeric Period

Beginning with Homer and the resulting Homeric tradition which persisted throughout most of Plato's lifetime, Greek culture was sustained by the oral power of poetry and rhetoric. The spoken word was the chief instrument of Greek culture, whether in the Senate, in the give and take between citizens and magistrates, or in litigation between lawyers. There were no handbills, circulars, newspapers, or journals and magazines; all information depended upon the spoken word. In the field of entertainment, the human voice—whether on the stage, in informal conversation, or in the listening to the tales of the glory of Greece—provided the communities' diversion. Where written literature existed, it was designed to be read aloud even when reading to oneself. It should also be remembered that in earlier times the art of oral narration allowed for considerable flexibility in much the same way that the teacher in the classroom repeats certain points again and again, using illustrations and digressions which make sense only within the context of the classroom. The seemingly disjointed character of many recorded ancient tales, in other words, has meaning only when viewed in their oral context, where the ears and eyes of the group actually shaped the quality and structure of the tale. In his discussion of Homeric oral traditions, Albert Lord writes:

> Each theme . . . each formula—has around it an aura of meaning which has been put there by all the contexts in which it has occurred in the past. It is the meaning that has been given it by the tradition in its

creativeness. To any given poet at any given time, this meaning involves all the occasions on which he has used the theme, especially those contexts in which he uses it most frequently; it involves also all the occasions on which he has heard it used by others, particularly by those singers whom he first heard in his youth, or by great singers later by whom he was impressed. To the audience, the meaning of the theme involves its own experience of it as well. The communication of this supra-meaning is possible because of the community of experience of poet and audience.[11]

The teller, as well as his audience, was under the spell of oral discourse, and this affected the audience's sense of time which often was presented as the reverse of ours: frequently the latest and most recent events were recited first because they were freshest to the ear, and then the bard proceeded to those events that actually preceded the ones already told. Thus, chronological time was reversed; what was normally the last in a series of events became the first for the storyteller in an oral culture.

Education in the Homeric culture began at an early age in the home where the ear was trained by lullabies, by a teacher or slave whose accent was pure, and by a nurse's tales of Aesop, heroes, and witches. H. I. Marrou sums up the dependence of ancient Greece upon the spoken word this way: "In modern times the spoken word has given way to the all-powerful written word, and this remains true even today, despite the great strides made by the radio and the gramophone. But in ancient Greece, and especially in its political life, the spoken word reigned supreme."[12] To have existed in an oral culture required a tremendous auditory sensitivity which is lacking in our own visually-oriented technological society. Thus, Cedric Whitman's statement:

> Homer's mind is the archaic mind, prephilosophic, primarily synthetic rather than analytical whose content is myths, symbols and paradigms. It is not a primitive mind, however, for the archaic, preconceptual way of thinking has a maturity of its own, fully as valid as later modes, and, to judge from Homer, perhaps more valid. In any case, such mentality is a more fruitful source for poetry than the mind trained to logical and philosophical analysis, for its meanings cluster irridescently around unclear images, with the complexity, and explosive power of high-valence atoms. It is the function of poetry to compress meaning, where prose expatiates upon it, and the *Iliad* seems like a brief poem in the light of its meaning.[13]

For modern man, the technique of memorization is largely a private activity consisting of first reading (using the visual senses) and then shutting our eyes and translating the written signs into sounds which we repeat over and over to ourselves until we have mastered the text. A tremendous amount of individual energy is involved in what is essentially a solitary, quite asocial activity. In an oral society such as Homer's, however, oral memorization did not require the

expenditure and drain of personal energy exacted by today's private act of translating from the visual into the auditory. In a unique way, then, pleasure and recreation were combined with the appropriation of the tribal encyclopedia—those stories and legends regarded as worth remembering by each generation. The poet's utterance is likened to a "flowing" or "gushing river," or perhaps to "arrows," where Hesiod speaks of "feathered phrases." This *Mousike* is thoroughly enjoyed, as evidenced by names for the Muses such as "the Enjoyable," "the Passionate," and by references to the utterances as "sweet-dewed" and "honeyed" and to the dances and chants as "desireful."[14] Eros here is hardly noble Reason: it refers to the integrated powers of the most thoroughly human and creative aspects of personality brought to life, aroused by the spoken word. The reciter as well as the audience unconsciously had committed themselves, placed themselves under the spell of speech. Ideally, in the process, something of the identity of each participant was surrendered in the submission to speech, just as each departed enriched and nourished by this re-creation.

Dependence upon speech was matched by the dependence on and proximity of the gods with whom the people continually conversed. Characteristic of the *Iliad*, for example, is the occasional penetration of the human by the divine as a result of human prompting, and the apotheosis or elevation of humans, like Heracles, to the rank of gods. Aeschylus' words appropriately describe the divine-human partnership: "God is well, whenever man himself takes action, joins with him," and as Whitman writes of Homer, "Homer's divinities depend on human prompting for their deeds; their knowledge is independent and transcendent, but their action as a rule is immanent in human action, or character. Hence all divine participation has something of the effect of apotheosis, and this is true no less of Homer's system of the continuing images than it is of action itself."[15]

In the fields of history, drama, and philosophy, the oral foundation is at once apparent. History began with the stories and genealogies of famous families told around the campfire and passed on to the listening ears of the younger generation or sojourners from foreign lands or provinces. History was oral and had to be told; its lifeblood depended upon its need to be retold, memorized, and in turn transmitted to others. For centuries Greek history was identical with the oral legacy of Homer, epic poetry, and dealt with the events of the Trojan War, the valor of the men of Athens, and the acts of the gods.

IV. The Aged Among the Ancient Hebrews

We know from Biblical texts that, officially, Hebraic culture required that the aged be revered and respected. In *Deuteronomy* (21, 21), for example, we read that a son who disobeys his father should be taken by the father before the elders of the city, and at the town gate, all the men of the town "shall stone him to death." In the Book of *Numbers* (11, 16-18), the political power of the elders is clearly recognized as the Lord tells Moses, "Assemble seventy elders from Israel, men known to you as elders and officers in the community . . . and they

will share with you the burden of taking care for the people; then you will not have to bear it alone."

In *Ecclesiastes* (11, 7-10 and 12, 1-8), we find two somewhat contrasting views of old age. These passages are devoted to advice to young men and begin with the admonition, "Delight in your boyhood, young man, make the most of the days of your youth;" but conclude with the words, " . . . boyhood and the prime of life are mere emptiness" (11, 7-10). In the second passage, the young man is told to, "Remember your Creator in the days of your youth, before the time of trouble comes. . . ." The "time of trouble" refers to old age, to the declining years, when one sees "no purpose in them" (12, 1). The misfortunes of old age are then described in metaphors: "The guardians of the house [the arms] tremble; the strong men [the legs] stoop, the women grinding [the teeth] cease work because they are few, and those who look through the windows [the eyes] look no longer, . . . when the noise of the mill [the mouth] is low, . . . when the blossom whitens on the almond tree [white hair], and the locust's paunch [the stomach] is swollen and caper-buds [the sexual organs] have no more zest." In his concluding remarks, the writer states, "Remember him . . . before the dust returns to the earth as it began and the spirit returns to God who gave it. Emptiness, emptiness, says the Speaker, all is empty" (12, 1-8).

But apart from this rather gloomy picture of old age, the elderly in the Bible are shown as deserving respect not merely on religious grounds, but also because of the political power, authority, or wealth they possess. The religious sanction "Honor thy father and thy mother" implies that those to be honored have walked in the ways of righteousness and obeyed God's laws throughout their lives. Those who have not led righteous lives are punished regardless of age, authority, or seniority. For example, from a much later source, the book of *Daniel and Susanna* in the Apocrypha, two elderly judges are sentenced to death after Daniel discovers that they had falsely accused the attractive wife of a friend of sleeping with a young man, when in fact, they had sought out her favors and been rejected.

Among the ancient Jews, the great longevity of one's ancestors was an indication that they were among God's chosen; longevity was a reward for their steadfastness. This is implied in *Deuteronomy* (11, 21) in Moses' charge to his people that if they obey God's commandments, "Then you will live long, you and your children, in the land which the Lord swore to your forefathers to give them, for as long as the heavens are above the earth." And in *Proverbs* (10, 27), "The fear of the Lord brings length of days; the years of the wicked are few."

Historically, priestly functions and responsibilities were performed by old men. Here are but a few samples as recorded in the Hebrew Scriptures. In *Genesis* (7, 6) we learn that Noah "was six hundred years old when the waters of the flood came upon the earth. And so, to escape the waters of the flood, Noah went into the ark. . . ." After the waters had subsided, "Noah built an altar to the Lord . . . and offered whole-offerings on the altar" (8, 20-21). Although not nearly as old as Noah, Abraham was ninety-nine when he beseeched the Lord to have mercy on Sodom and Gomorrah (*Genesis* 18). The powers of the aged were not, however, limited to calling on divinity. According to Leo Simmons, "The

Hebrew believed that aged parents and especially fathers, could by their blessing or curse determine the fate of their children"[16] In *Genesis* (27, 1-4), for example, Issac prepares to bless Esau: "When Isaac grew old and his eyes became so dim that he could not see, he called his elder son Esau and said to him, 'My son . . . listen now . . . make me a savory dish of the kind I like, and bring it to me to eat so that I may give you my blessing before I die.' " The blessing, which through clever deception fell upon the younger son Jacob, was regarded as a tragic misfortune for Esau. Similarly, King David's dying charge to his son, Solomon, may be regarded as a priestly blessing: "I am going the way of all the earth. Be strong and show yourself a man. Fulfill your duty to the Lord your God . . . " (*I Kings* 2, 1-3). In this same meeting, David tells Solomon not to let an old opponent who cursed him go unpunished: " . . . you are a wise man and will know how to deal with him; bring down his grey hairs in blood to the grave" (*I Kings* 2, 11-12).

On the other hand, depending on sources and textual interpretation, there is ample evidence to support the notion that the Hebrews, particularly those living in the first millenium (B.C.E.), were ambivalent in their feelings and attitudes toward the elderly. As oral tradition and transmission waned and people began to rely on recorded texts rather than on the oral record passed on by the patriarch, as tribal communities consisting of between 200 and 500 joined and became cities and kingdoms, and as power and wealth were amassed by those late in years, there developed feelings of jealously and ambivalence toward them by those imbued with a religious tradition that venerated those whose long lives were a reward from Yahweh, but who were at the same time faced with the political, economic, and social realities of day to day life in a more complex society. For example, the reference in *Proverbs* to the "grey hairs" which I quoted at the beginning of this paper is not in and of itself a complimentary term. In the context of the passage, it appears that you must even love, honor, and obey those with "grey hairs" if for no other reason than that they are old *because* they have been blessed by God. Thus, "grey hairs" is a crown of glory, but *only* as a reward for a life of righteousness.

Against the background of inherited mythologies and traditions stemming from the ancient Near East, it would appear that the Jews emerge as one of the few peoples whose cultural traditions demanded appreciation and veneration for those "full of days." One receives this impression, certainly, from Simone de Beauvoir's treatment of the Jews in *The Coming of Age.*[17] However, in *Hebrew Man*, the Old Testament scholar Ludwig Köhler concludes that the status accorded the aged in Hebraic culture is not so easily defined. Köhler argues that references to genealogy and duration of life (for example, that Adam lived 912 years) are in fact "designed to fit a quite definite eschatological theory" and serve what is basically a "chronological purpose."[18] Such figures, according to Köhler, must "be regarded as unhistorical and mythological. They are an echo of Babylonian history, in which the primeval kings attained much greater ages."[19]

If one begins with the story in *Genesis* of Man being created "in the image of God" and then asks what the qualities are of one whom "the *Lord* is in," then, a

slightly different picture emerges. As was suggested earlier, those "full of days" are blessed *because* they walked in the ways of the Lord all their days, particularly in their earlier days when the Lord was truly *in* them. For those of old age, longevity is a reward and the young and vigorous are told to be tolerant of those with "grey hairs" *because* of their early services to the Lord. The picture presented by Köhler is that the ideal ancient Hebrew in whom the Lord resided must have been healthy, powerful, and vital, as was true of Yahweh Himself. According to Köhler, the starting point for appreciating the *imago dei* concept is an aesthetic one: "Man is beautiful, by the will of God. Whoever is beautiful bears in himself the sign of God's good pleasure. We may well wonder about the heavy cloud which thus weighed upon all those that were deformed."[20]

There was much emphasis, then, on youth. In fact, around the year 1000 B.C.E., the ideal figure of the Hebrew could be said to possess six basic qualities. David, as he is described in *I Samuel* (16, 18-24), illustrates perfectly this ideal: he was cunning in playing (the harp), a man of substance (property), accustomed to warfare (able to overcome his opponents), prudent in speech (able to plead for himself, his family, and those under his protection), and a comely person (a man "who looks something"), "*and the LORD is with him.*" And by the year 200 B.C.E. the emphasis is still on an ideal of youth, on "young men of good looks and bodily without fault, at home in all branches of knowledge, well-informed, intelligent, and fit for service in the royal court" (*Daniel* 1, 4). At this point the only changes are a new emphasis on the capacity to learn, less emphasis on prowess in the field, and greater stress upon knowledge rather than practical ability.

On the basis of this brief excursion into the subject of the attitudes of the ancient Hebrews towards the elderly, we can conclude that the typical stress upon "Honor thy father and mother" as unequivocally symbolizing a special respect due to the aged is an oversimplification. It would seem that, in the final analysis, the ideals of the ancient Hebrews—their emphasis on youth, beauty, and vitality—are much closer to those of the Greeks than had been expected. In fact, were it not for the perpetuation of a kind of religious exemption or protection clause in Hebraic religion toward those who were rewarded by longevity for having walked in the ways of the Lord all their lives, this special attitude might very well have eroded and almost totally vanished centuries, if not millenia, ago.

V. The Aged in the Homeric Tradition

Let us turn now to the ancient Greeks, to Homer and his legacy, and examine for a moment the extent to which attitudes towards the elderly changed appreciably from those held by the ancient Hebrews. To begin with, ancient Greek mythology is filled with tales of conflict between young and old. Prominent among them is the story of Uranus and his children who, cast out by their father, first hide in Gaea's bosom, and then, upon being freed by Gaea, castrate their father. Uranus is despised by his children as a tyrannical despot, but the

pattern is doomed to repeat itself. His own son, Cronus, comes to hate his own children and, legend has it, ate them. And even Zeus, the king among the pantheon of Gods, as a child attacked his father, Cronus, and his brothers, the Titans, and, after taking on not only the Titans, but also the Giants (the half brothers of Cronus), conquered them all.[21]

As we found in Hebraic culture, when the elderly of ancient Greece are blessed with longevity and a happy life, it is due to the beneficence, or the religious exemption or protection clause, of the Gods. In *Old Age Among the Greeks,* Bessie Ellen Richardson states that:

> In Homer's day, although youth and deathlessness were worshipped as at no other period, there was no idea of curing disease or prolonging life by magic. Most of the magic which has survived to us from antiquity in the form of spells and conjurations as well as recipes endowed with mysterious efficacy for the cure of disease by irrational means are not pure Greek but largely Oriental. The Greeks believed that it was the gods alone to whom exemption from old age and death was given, *or in early times they seem to have placed some credence in the fact that the gods could bestow this gift upon whom they might elect.*[22]

Richardson makes it abuntantly clear that the Greeks did not seriously wish to regain their youthfulness as much as they wished to "escape the enfeeblements of which they had an extraordinary dread." She adds that "the condition of the old seems to have been fairly tolerable in Greece" and that the Greeks "were interested in obtaining a long life if they might retain good health and activity. Long life without these blessings possessed no charm."[23]

Historically, the Greek people of Gades erected an altar to Geras, the personification of old age, but we do not know whether they did this out of veneration or out of fear. The latter is probably the case inasmuch as vases portray Heracles clubbing Geras who is decpicted in " . . . the form of a feeble and emanciated dwarf." There is another depiction of Geras helplessly imploring Heracles to spare him. In this picture, Geras is portrayed "as nude and weaponless" with "an emaciated body, thin hair, and wrinkles on the forehead, but is rather agile."[24] All known depictions of Geras portray him as either a gruesome dreaded monster, or as weak, ugly, and enfeebled. But, in each instance, Geras is portrayed as a malevolent force.

The gruesomeness of old age is evident throughout Greek literature. Nestor is a classic example. In the *Iliad,* he can no longer wrestle or box "since now the hardship of old age" is upon him: "My limbs are no longer steady, dear friend; not my feet, neither do my arms, as once they did, swing light from my shoulders. I wish I were young again and strength still unshaken within me. . . ."[25] Nestor says this in response to Achilles having given him the two-handled jar as fifth prize in the Funeral events. After reminiscing on the achievements of his youth and full manhood, he concludes:

> "This was I, once. Now it is for young men to encounter such actions, and for me to give way to the persuasion of gloomy old age. . . . I accept

> this from you gratefully, . . . my heart is happy that you have remembered me and my kindness, that I am not forgotten for my honour that should be my honor among the Achaians."[26]

Nestor is venerated not simply by virtue of being old and therefore deserving of respect accorded all old people; rather, he is honoured *because* of his past achievements and for his "wisdom." Age *was* a positive factor in Homer's time, as it was throughout classical antiquity, if accompanied by the recognition on the part of youth that their elders tended to be wiser, more experienced, and learned than they were (youth was considered to be characterized by brashness and impetuousness). But here we are talking about the aged who still possess most of their mental faculties.

In the *Iliad* this is brought out in a response by Antilochos to Menelaos: "Enough now. For I, my lord Menelaos, am younger by far than you, and you are greater and go before me. You know how greedy transgressions flower in a young man, seeing that his mind is the more active but his judgment is lightweight."[27]

Related to this, Achilles, out of respect for Hector, postpones the battle during Hector's funeral. Upon Odysseus' return, Zeus proclaims to the Earthshaker, "What a thing to have said, Earthshaker of the wide strength. The gods do not hold you in dishonor. It would be a hard thing if we were to put any slight on the eldest and best among us."[28]

It is interesting to note that *gera, geron,* from which we get our word "gerontology," referred in antiquity to those of great age who for one reason or another were to be honored. The word referred "to the privileges of age, the rights of seniority, representative position."[29] It was not then a blanket or umbrella of honour that applied to all simply because they were old. Thus it is not the gerontes Nestor, Laertes, or Priam who win the day for the Greeks; rather, it is men in their prime like Ulysses and Hector. On the other hand, when wisdom and sound judgment are needed by the people in their councils, it is the oldest members who speak first in the assembly. When, for example, Telemachus calls an assembly of the Achaeans, it is Aegyptius, bowed with age and skilled in numerous arts, who speaks first.[30] (It is interesting that while Richardson determined that 29.43 years was the life expectancy among the Greeks, her study of 128 Greek poets, philosophers, historians, orators, and lawyers whose names we remember from this period, lived anywhere from sixty years of age to 124 years.[31])

In Homer's time, and generally throughout classical antiquity, the Greeks tended to speak about the unfortunate aspects or tendencies of old age as, Richardson writes, a kind of "journey along a dusty, shadeless road":

> The Greeks seem to have been conscious of all the infirmities of age due to physical environment. Old age seems to have been considered a punishment, and in some cases there seems to be the belief that it was actually sent by Zeus as such. The Greeks did not sing with Browning:
>
> Grow old along with me,
> The Best is yet to be,

but rather:

> A lingering old age came upon Phineus, son of Agenor, for revealing the prophecies of Zeus.[32]

Except possibly for the earliest primitive tribal communities, we do not know how long the elders in these communities passed down their histories and religious traditions rather than having this function shared by or delegated to those youths skilled with the musical instruments, such as the lyre, of the period. Certainly, the latter was the case during the Homeric period. The poets, or bards as they were called, were considered inspired by contact with deities. In *Daily Life in the Time of Homer,* Emile Mireaux states: "It is not Homer, who sings of the wrath of Achilles, but the 'goddess.' If it is given to him to relate the wanderings of Odysseus, this is because the words come to them from the Muse. 'The god has breathed in me songs of all kinds,' cries Phemius to Odysseus, as he begs for mercy."[33]

In Homer's times, the bards belonged to an elite group whose members were dedicated to poetry, then considered the speech of the gods. They were not, however, drawn from among the aged in their communities. They began to train for their profession at an early age, knowing that a good bard had a repertory of at least a hundred thousand lives and that one has to undergo severe training to develop a mastery of the art. Accompanying himself on the cithara (a three or four stringed instrument that enabled him to give the words he sang their proper measure) and couching his language in conventional poetic diction whose form was adopted to meet the requirements of epic prosody, he was able to ease the strain on the memories and attention of his listeners and make communication easier.[34]

VI. Conclusions

Originally, I set out to examine two instances of oral culture and to compare attitudes toward the aged in each tradition, assuming that in oral as distinguished from print cultures, those most advanced in age might be revered as the repositories and transmitters of the remembered legends and history in their respective cultures. There were indeed patriarchs, heroes, and great leaders, but not all were remembered because of their special wisdom. Most, in fact, seem to have been remembered and venerated because of valiant deeds performed during their youthful years or at the peak of their manhood. And, in most cases, longevity was viewed as a reward for earlier accomplishments or for having walked all the days of one's life in the path of righteousness. In Homer's time and among the ancient Hebrews, old age was viewed with mixed feelings. Although for some it was a noble reward bestowed on one by a divinity, for most, however, it was viewed with fear and apprehension because one's powers declined and the physical symptoms associated with old age began to take their toll. It should also be remembered that many of the elderly in positions of power

and authority were feared as often as they were revered. While alive, many were respected outwardly but mocked and jeered in private. As in all societies there were the privileged and the less fortunate.

While the aged played an important role in both Hebraic and Homeric cultures in determining policy and transmitting the traditions of their pasts, they were not venerated because of age *per se.* They, like mortals of any age, had to earn respect and the right to be remembered, or even to grow old, and to be revered by successive generations. Nor were those who handed down the traditions and lessons of the past necessarily drawn from the aged in each society. Yet, although neither tradition venerated age *per se,* each had a tremendous respect for "the past," for the traditions and events that shaped their present and their futures. And, especially revered were those legendary leaders whose actions, glories, and accomplishments determined the quality and richness of the traditions and history within each culture.

Notes

[1]*The New English Bible: Old Testament* (Oxford and Cambridge Univ. Presses, 1970). All subsequent references will be to this edition.

[2]*The Iliad of Homer,* trans. Richmond Lattimore (Chicago: Univ. of Chicago Press, 1973).

[3]*The Odyssey of Homer,* trans. Richmond Lattimore (New York: Harper and Row, 1967).

[4]Perhaps the most classic statement depicting this cleavage in outlooks was made by Tertullian in the second century A.D.: "What indeed has Athens to do with Jerusalem? What concord is there between the Academy and the Church? What between heretics and Christians? Our instruction comes from the porch of Solomon (*Acts* 3:5) who had himself taught that the Lord should be sought in simplicity of heart (*Wisd.* 1:1). Away with all attempts to produce a mottled Christianity of Stoic, Platonic and dialectic composition!" Etienne Gilson, quoted in *Reason and Revelation in the Middle Ages* (New York: Charles Scribner's and Sons, 1954), pp. 9-10.

[5]Dr. Maria S. Haynes has provided us with a fairly comprehensive treatment of attitudes toward the aged in both ancient Greece as well as ancient Rome. See "The Supposedly Golden Age for the Aged in Ancient Greece: a study of the literary concepts of old age," *Gerontologist,* 2 (1962), 93-98; "The Supposedly Golden Age for the Aged in Ancient Rome," *Gerontologist,* 3 (1963), 26-35. The most exhaustive study of the Greek experience and aging is Dr. Bessie Allen Richardson's *Old Age Among the Ancient Greeks* (New York: Greenwood Press, 1969). Unfortunately, nothing comparable to Dr. Richardson's work exists for Biblical Judaism.

[6]When one speaks of oral traditions and cultures, the reference is not necessarily to a preliterate stage in social development. There are today, as the studies of Albert Lord have shown, oral cultures living side by side with established print dominated cultures. See Albert B. Lord, *The Singer of Tales* (Cambridge: Harvard Univ. Press, 1964).

[7]The dating of the periods under consideration is extremely difficult. No one knows, for example, exactly when Homer lived. For our purposes, I shall consider the Homeric influence to extend from the middle of the ninth century B.C.E. until it was challenged by Plato (428-347 B.C.). Unfortunately, it is equally difficult to determine precisely when the oral tradition began among the ancient Hebrews. It may have begun as early

as the year 2000 B.C.E. and continued until the founding of the Monarchy a thousand years later. As Martin Noth suggests, in *A History of Pentateuchal Traditions* (Englewood Cliffs: Prentice Hall, 1972), the preliterary period may have begun as a series of formulated Hebraic confessions which were customarily recited as particular cultic celebrations and emanated from the original twelve tribes which made up ancient Israel.

[8]Henri Frankfort, *Before Philosophy* (Harmondsworth: Penguin Books, 1951), pp. 12-36.

[9]*Die Jüdische Bewegung* (Berlin: Judische Verlag, 1916), I, 245.

[10]Ibid.

[11]*The Singer of Tales*, p. 148.

[12]*A History of Education in Antiquity* (New York: Mentor, 1964), p. 84.

[13]Cedric H. Whitman, *Homer and the Homeric Tradition* (Cambridge: Harvard Univ. Press, 1963), p. 13.

[14]Eric Havelock, *Preface to Plato* (Cambridge: Belknap Press, 1963), pp. 153-55.

[15]Whitman, pp. 149-50, 238ff.

[16]*The Role of the Aged in Primitive Societies* (New Haven: Yale Univ. Press, 1947), p. 172.

[17]*The Coming of Age* (New York: Warner, 1970), p. 139ff.

[18]*Hebrew Man* (London: SCM Press, 1956), p. 41.

[19]Ibid, p. 42.

[20]Ibid. p. 34.

[21]de Beauvoir, *Coming of Age*, pp. 144-45.

[22]*Old Age Among the Greeks* (New York: Greenwood Press, 1933), p. 71.

[23]Ibid., p. 73.

[24]Ibid., p. 74.

[25]Lattimore, *Iliad*, p. 467.

[26]Ibid.

[27]Ibid., p. 466.

[28]Lattimore, *Odyssey*, p. 202.

[29]de Beauvoir, p. 147.

[30]Richardson, *Old Age Among the Greeks*, p. 49.

[31]Ibid., p. 215. Köhler (p. 62) provides us with the following comparison among the Hebrews: "Father: Hebrew at nineteen, today at twenty-six. Grandfather: Hebrew at thirty-eight, today at fifty-two. Great-grandfather: Hebrew at fifty-seven, today at seventy-eight."

[32]Ibid., p. 14.

[33]*Daily Life in the Time of Homer* (New York: Macmillan, 1967), p. 98.

[34]Ibid., pp. 98-104.

Evelyn Eaton Whitehead

RELIGIOUS IMAGES OF AGING: AN EXAMINATION OF THEMES IN CONTEMPORARY CHRISTIAN THOUGHT

In the conference which signaled the start of this interdisciplinary discussion of aging, economist Juanita Kreps spoke to the question of the value of human aging.[1] Within the evaluative framework of contemporary American economics which stresses the relationship of expenditure to production, she noted, the aged person can be viewed only as a liability. Physician Robert Kohn, whose research has contributed to our understanding of the biology of aging, sounded a similar note.[2] In terms of the dominant values of medicine, he observed, the process of human aging can be viewed solely as negative. Certainly the negative evaluation of aging is not limited to such sophisticated sources. Many involved in the experience of growing older—and of being old—can document the multiple depreciations of aging. Loss of income, loss of role, loss of status, loss of affection, loss of competency, loss of power—these are but a few of the negative elements which characterize for many their experience of growing older.

Is this the whole story? Is loss the unqualified experience of aging? Is depreciation the only realistic evaluation possible of this universal human phenomenon?

We know this is not the case. Human life as well as literature attest to other characteristics of aging—maturity of the personality, a broadening of sensibilities, the ripening of genius, the testing of the spirit. Neither the positive nor the negative characterization of human aging alone are complete. Maturity and loss are common companions in adult experience.

The humanities—those disciplines devoted to the human traditions of thought, art, religion, literature—are rich repositories within which the variegated patterns of human maturity and loss are stored. The humanist's challenge today is to mine these resources of human culture. The goal of this effort will be to explore alternate evaluations of human aging which are not based simply on the diminishment of productive output or of biological

functioning. Can the humanities, with their unique access to the cumulative resources of the spirit, provide the human community with a perspective within which the full ambiguity of the process of human aging can be seen as the basis for a more balanced evaluation of aging and the aged? If the answer is yes, the contribution of the humanities to both public policy discussion and to the critical internal dialogue of personal integration will be of real significance.

One of the veins of the cultural deposit to which humanists are heir is the religious heritage of western Christianity. This vein, to be sure, has produced its share of alloy. That ambiguous lot it shares with art, literature, science and other of humankind's attempts to transcend the limits of the obvious in the effort toward more enduring meaning. The ongoing Christian tradition is a complex system of image and belief, doctrine and symbol. The Bible is of central, even definitive, importance in Christianity, and through the centuries its texts have been subject to a wide range of diverse interpretations. Literal meaning, allegorical significance, congruence with philosophy, verification by history—each of these has been espoused as the basis of the orthodox interpretation of the texts. The heritage of western Christianity includes the checkered history of its efforts to be in the world but not of it, and its often less than successful attempts to stand as a sign of justice and mercy. Christian history documents recurring scandals of internal dissension and institutional arrogance; but it stands, as an ongoing witness of the transforming power of religious belief in people's lives.

Recently aging has become an issue of explicit religious and pastoral concern. Since 1960 we find in contemporary theological writing, as in the literature of the biological and human sciences, a rapid increase in the number and quality of publications considering human aging in its several dimensions. Early on, articles dealing with the practical problems of the aged-in-need began to appear in several ministry journals.[3] Gradually essays emerged dealing more directly with theological and religious themes.

Several contributions to this religious discussion of human aging from the mid-seventies are of particular note. In 1974 Henri Nouwen, an influential religious psychologist, and his colleague Walter Gaffney published *Aging: The Fulfillment of Life.*[4] That same year an issue of *Soundings,* the journal of the Society for Religion in Higher Education, addressed the theme of "Leisure, Retirement and Aging." The next year, under the impetus and editorship of Seward Hiltner, dean of American pastoral theologians, a group of prominent university-based theologians published *Toward a Theology of Aging.*[5] And in its 1976 issue devoted to "Adulthood," as prestigous a journal as *Daedalus* included substantive pieces concerned with human maturity and aging from the perspective of several religious-cultural traditions. William Bouwsma's important article on "Christian Adulthood" appears in this compilation.

If the test of the hardiness of any cultural tradition is its capacity to draw from the resources of its own symbol system those images which can provide meaning for the new, as yet unacculturated, experiences of the next generation, then one way to examine the usefulness of the Christian religious

tradition as a basis for the positive evaluation of human aging is to explore how such contemporary religious writers are themselves drawing upon the resources of the Christian tradition in their considerations of aging. Clearly, the Christian tradition is not the only source to which these religious writers turn in their effort to illumine the human experience of growing older. The philosophic orientations of both phenomenology and linguistic analysis are in evidence; use is made of the psychological categories of Freud, Jung, Erikson. But it is upon the various uses made of the Christian heritage itself that I wish to focus. My concern here is neither to mount an apologetic for religious belief nor to discuss the merits of Christianity in relation to other systems for the interpretation of reality. Rather it is to ask: Which images do these thinkers retrieve from the repository of Christian history and tradition? How do they bring them to bear upon contemporary issues of human aging? And ultimately, of what relevance are these images to the humanist's self-appointed task? Therefore I will focus in this essay only upon a portion of the diverse and ambiguous heritage of Christianity. Following the lead of the French phenomenologist and gerontologist Michel Philibert, I shall use the term "images" in a very general sense. As he writes, "People hold opinions, beliefs, or mental attitudes toward aging which are more or less coherent and which carry images and memories together with the beginnings or outlines of knowledge. We shall call these *multi-form constructions* 'images.' They constitute orientations or perspectives . . . ."[6] In particular, I will consider, in turn, the use made of central images and religious themes in treating three challenges central to the personal experience of aging:

I. establishing a basis for self-worth less dependent upon economic productivity or social role.

II. interpreting the significance of one's own life, and

III. coming to terms with the changes and losses of aging.

1. Establishing a Basis for Self-Worth Less Dependent Upon Economic Productivity or Social Role

The realization that a person is more than what he does is a critical insight of human maturity. With this awareness can come—even if only fleetingly—a sense of liberation from many of the sources to which one ordinarily turns to bolster self-esteem. Reputation, accomplishment, beauty, influence, wealth—these evanescent advantages seem never fully achieved, finally and securely. In so far as a person's appreciation of himself and his worth is limited to these factors, he senses his vulnerability. In so far as one is able to find within oneself and one's own experience of life other sources of positive self-evaluation, sources less dependent upon the exigencies of chance or external control, one is more likely to experience the self as autonomous.

There are many vocabularies appropriate to a discussion of this struggle of the individual to come to a mature sense of personal worth. Psychology has much to say, as do poetry, drama, biography. Religion, too, has considered the

question of the basis of personal value.

The major religious traditions of humankind have rebelled against the identification of the person with his or her usefulness to society. In Buddhism and Taoism as well as in Christianity, uselessness has appeared as a central religious category. As we see in the early chapters of the influential *Vimalakirti Sutra,* the ultimate uselessness of all worldly things is a basic tenet of Buddhism. In Taoism the most memorable celebration of uselessness occurs in Book Four of *Chuang Tzu,* in the story of the massive, ancient tree which at first sight appears attractive to the woodsman. Upon closer examination, however, it is seen to be gnarled and therefore useless to his purposes. Indeed, it is this uselessness, we are told, that guarantees the tree its transcendent longevity. These examples reflect the conviction deep in each of these traditions that a person does not *earn* his or her way into a relationship with that which is ultimate.

The Christian image of God's unfailing love, both unmerited and unmeritable, can be interpreted as a symbol suggesting that the real basis of one's worth is beyond "good works"—beyond one's productivity, vigor, or wealth. This conviction of God's unconditional love for humankind is rooted in the Old Testament accounts of Yahweh's relationship with the people of Israel. *Genesis* relates the story of Yahweh's gratuitous covenant with Abraham, which constituted him father of the chosen people. The subsequent books of the Old Testament recount God's continuing faithfulness to this people, in spite of their frequent disobedience and obstinancy. The Lord's love of the Israelites is unconditional, neither limited by their worthiness nor dependent upon their response. In the New Testament, Jesus reminds his followers that the Father's care for the birds of the air and the flowers of the field is unrelated to their productivity (*Luke* 12). This belief finds expression in Paul's conviction that we are not saved (in more humanistic terms, that we do not achieve self-realization) by our own individual effort (*Romans* 4). Such self-realization is experienced ultimately as a surprising gift, a gracious occurrence in our life beyond our own best efforts at self-instigated growth.

Nouwen and Gaffney turn to this Biblical tradition of unconditional love in an evocative discussion of the "painful suffering of many old people which makes their aging into a way to the darkness." Noting that the painful lot of many among the aged is more a reflection on the evils of our society than upon limitations inherent among the elderly, they go on: "Yet for those who suffer, the rejection by their society can lead to the recognition of an acceptance we ourselves have not been able to give. Out of the recognition that life is determined neither by what one did, had, or achieved, nor by one's friends or relatives, nor even by one's own self-understanding, the way might be found to Him whose heart is greater than ours and who says through His own son, the broken servant of Yahweh: 'You are accepted.' "[7]

William Bouwsma suggests another image in the tradition of western Christianity as a resource to the critical issue of self-esteem in mature age. "The biblical idea of time," Bouwsma asserts, "is the foundation for the conception of the worth of the individual personality."[8] In Christian

mythology, he argues, creation is a true beginning. The temporal dimensions of process and change are real (not illusory) and good (not imperfect manifestations of unchanging ideal forms). The biblical God has underscored the positive significance of time, process, and change through His continuing presence and intervention within the unique and unrepeatable events of human history. Thus, the pattern of the life experience of each individual is unique. The individual's past, as a history of his or her personal encounter with life—and with God—is holy as well. "The past demonstrates God's care and will for men and therefore cannot be ignored or repudiated," writes Bouwsma; "The significance of the past also points to the indelible importance of all human experience. It gives meaning to the particular temporal experiences that have shaped each individual during the whole course of his life."[9]

For Bouwsma, then, the Christian meaning system can provide an interpretation of time, history, and individuality that permits a positive evaluation of one's life based not simply upon what has been done or what can be done. Beyond the record of these "doings," the history of one's life is also an account of God's continuing care and of His saving action in the world. Appreciation of life, therefore, need not be limited to criteria of productivity or social usefulness. One's life is of value—a person is of value—beyond such partial considerations.

These two Christian images—God's unconditional love and the religious significance of personal life history—suggest that there are bases of self-worth independent of economic productivity and social role. Noting this claim, or hope, implicit in this religious language, the humanist may find here a potential resource. The underlying insight—that personal worth does not depend simply on one's usefulness to others—transcends the limits of the various vocabularies in which it is expressed. Its salience for the humanist need not be diminished, indeed, it can be enhanced by a consideration of the particular nuances of meaning that these Christian categories add to the basic human insight.

II. Interpreting the Significance of One's Own Life

As a person grows older the question of the significance of his own life must be faced. Of what use has it been to oneself? To others? Will the values which one has attempted to realize end with death? Are they of meaning in any larger context? Will anything come of one's efforts, often felt to have been less than successful, to find value, to extend value, to preserve value in the world beyond the self?

Erik Erikson designates this central crisis of late adulthood as the challenge of integrity, "the acceptance of one's one and only life cycle and of the people who have become significant to it as something that had to be and that, by necessity, permitted no substitutions."[10] Successfully resolved, this struggle for integrity results in an "accrued assurance" of the meaning of an in-

dividual's life, as well as of the larger flow of generations. Recently Erikson has described this struggle in powerful detail in his analysis of Dr. Borg, the central character in Ingmar Bergman's classic film *Wild Strawberries.* "I found this screenplay an incomparable representation of the wholeness of the human life cycle," Erikson states, "which I now feel I should spell out for this new generation of adults who (after all we have learned about childhood and youth) feel impelled to comprehend, not without some reluctance and distaste, what adulthood and old age are really all about."[11] The film records the day's journey of an elderly Swedish physician from his retirement home in the countryside to the University in Lund, where he is to be honored for fifty years of service in his profession. "But this journey by car on marked roads through familiar territory," Erikson maintains, "also becomes a symbolic pilgrimage back into his childhood and deep into his unknown self."[12] Over the course of the day's events we witness Dr. Borg's struggle to reach a sense of personal meaning that can overcome the threats of despair and disgust. The vital strength of the human spirit which is evoked and tested in this struggle is, according to Erikson, wisdom. "*Wisdom,* in whatever systematic or implicit, eloquent or quiet way it may be expressed, *is the detached and yet active concern with life itself in the face of death itself, . . . it maintains and conveys the integrity of experience, in spite of the decline of bodily and mental functions.*"[13] Such wisdom is the final fruition of hope, which is "the first and most basic human strength."[14] And like hope, wisdom "must rely on the power of unconscious processes as well as on some confirmation by fate—and by faith."[15]

Don Browning, a theologian whose work has been influenced significantly by Erikson,[16] turns to the religious images of salvation and hope in his appraisal of the potential of Christian symbols to illumine this crisis of integrity and the accompanying emergence of wisdom. Characteristic of the earliest narratives and stories of Jesus, notes Browning, is an insistence on the relationship between the present and the future. Jesus calls his followers to participate by their present actions in God's saving action of ushering in the Kingdom. As Browning puts it, "participation of early Christians, both individually and corporately, in God's saving and redeeming work gave them a sense that their own finite efforts were caught up in the activity of God and therefore had an objective significance to them that would transcend their own suffering and eventual death."[17] Through subsequent centuries this understanding of one's own life and actions as participating in God's saving plan for humankind has provided for many believing Christians a sense of ultimate personal significance, and Browning suggests that it might be possible to retrieve this religious image of individual significance as a means of confronting the contemporary crisis of meaning in old age. One's own limited and often apparently fruitless efforts gain potency when understood as part of God's plan for the world.

Within such a context the task of coming to accept the particularity and peculiarity of one's own life can be undertaken with an added measure of hope. One can be confident that the good work which God has begun in the

self (and, through one's efforts, in the world) will be brought to completion (even beyond one's efforts). The active and responsible involvement in the world which appropriately characterizes early and middle adulthood can be transmuted—as one's ability to control and contribute gradually diminish—into a more disengaged concern. Browning suggests that this desire for some sense of the lasting significance of one's life can find its ground in the Christian concept of personal salvation. Quoting psychologist and theologian James Lapsley, he argues that salvation "must refer primarily to the preservation in the life of God of the values realized in the world, especially in the lives of men."[18]

"What does this understanding of hope and salvation in these crucial New Testament sources suggest for the problem of aging?" asks Browning. These images function, he responds, as "symbolic representation(s) of an objective activity on the part of God that transforms the world and preserves the values of those who participate in His work." In addition, they provide "ideological reinforcement to our efforts to make generativity and care victorious over stagnation and self-absorption."[19]

Here again the humanist may look to the deeper human hope for personal significance implicit in this religious language of hope and salvation. It is possible that an image of personal significance, drawn from religious sources or from elsewhere among the traditions of western humanism, could speak powerfully in the contemporary discussion of human aging.

III. Coming to Terms with the Changes and Losses of Aging

For Americans today, growing older is most often accompanied by changes in income, residence, patterns of social interaction and the personal use of time. For many, there is also the experience of loss—of one's spouse, of cherished friends and companions, of status and established social roles, of physical vigor and health. Not all these changes need be, or are, experienced as negative. And many of the debilitating effects of the losses of aging can be mitigated by personal planning and effective social policy. But the alterations of change and loss are endemic to the human experience of growing older. One's ability to in some way come to terms with these inevitable losses of old age is a critical test of human maturity.

The religious authors we are considering make use of several images in their attempts to suggest a religious perspective appropriate to the experience of change and loss in mature age. In the context of our earlier discussion of self-worth, we noted Bouwsma's reference to a Christian understanding of time. Here we will consider his explication of a Christian understanding of adulthood. The essential note of the Christian biblical understanding of human maturity, for Bouwsma, is its emphasis on the dynamic processes of continuing change and growth. This focus on continual development distinguishes the biblical view from a more classical notion of adult maturity as a state which—once achieved—is to be sustained without deviation. In the

Christian conception of human life, according to Bouwsma, the goal of human development is total conformity to the manhood of Christ. But since this is a transcendent goal, the practical emphasis in Christian adulthood is on the process rather than its end. Since it is impossible to achieve perfect maturity in this life, the duty of the Christian is simply to develop constantly toward it. The essential element in the Christian idea of adulthood is, accordingly, the capacity for growth, which is assumed to be a potentiality of any age of life."[20] For the Christian, then, the changes of late adulthood, like those of adolescence and middle age, can be interpreted as continuing opportunities to grow into the full stature of Christ.

Bouwsma does not take up explicitly the issues of old age; his focus is adulthood, not aging. But his discussion of human maturity offers a religious symbol that can be relevant to the individual involved in the significant personal changes of aging—the Christian as pilgrim. "The Christian is not to evade the challenges, the struggles, the difficulties and dangers of life, but to accept, make his way through, and grow in them," remarks Bouwsma. He continues: "This understanding of life finds expression in the figure of the Christian as wayfarer (*viator*) or pilgrim; Christian conversion is thus not, as in the mystery religions, an immediate entrance into a safe harbor but rather, though its direction has been established, the beginning of a voyage into the unknown. . . . From this standpoint, just as the essential condition of Christian adulthood is the capacity for growth, . . . its opposite—what might be called the Christian conception of immaturity—is the refusal to grow, the inability to cope with an open and indeterminate future (that is, the future itself), in effect the rejection of life as a process."[21] The acceptance of life as a process, the appreciation of the open-endedness of both personal and social development, the identification of oneself as a pilgrim-on-the-way—these realizations suggest that one's experience of *change* in aging can be interpreted as an invitation from God to continue the process of growth toward full human maturity.

Among religious writers today there are also attempts to provide a religious perspective upon the *losses* experienced in aging. Of particular interest is the appeal to the images of an ascetical spirituality of "emptying" and "letting go," a tradition found in Christianity as well as in Eastern religious thought. In Christianity, this spirituality of emptying, or *kenosis,* finds its most forceful expression in the Pauline description of Jesus as one who "emptied himself, taking the form of a servant" (*Philippians* 2:7).[22] Eastern religious thought provides even more powerful elaborations of this theme. The development of the notion of *sunyata* in Madhyamika Buddhism,[23] as well as the paradoxical role of emptiness (*hsü*) in Taoism,[24] attest to the central importance of this symbol.

In each of these religious traditions, the ascetical challenge is similar—to let go one's own determinations regarding the self as the prerequisite discipline for undertaking the spiritual quest; to empty oneself of the distracting ambitions and false criteria of value that stand as obstacles to one's realization of the transcendent. In such a perspective, the losses of aging need not be experienced solely as negative. Physical, social, and financial loss can be in-

terpreted as part of a spiritually significant process of "emptying" and "letting go." The individual is invited to recognize the religious possibilities hidden within even those aspects of human aging which are obviously deleterious.

In this context my colleague James Whitehead writes, "the social event of retirement performs a religiously ironic function: it empties out of a person's life perhaps the most sturdy crutch of self-worth, one's social role and usefulness. In this moment of stripping away, of death to a former style of life, the Church's ministry must not be that of substituting ersatz identities, but of celebrating this emptying process which leads to God."[25] Stripped of these partial sources of identity, the religious person can grow to recognize, even celebrate, a deeper truth—that no one ever "earns" his way, that life's meaning is more a gift than a reward.

Sidney Callahan and Drew Christianson, writing in the interdisciplinary journal *Soundings,* suggest the Christian mystical tradition as another point of reference in uncovering a significance to the losses of old age that goes beyond an exclusively negative appraisal of their impact. "Mystics in every tradition," they note, "have pointed to the need for living fully *now,* making 'a sacrament of the present moment' with a concentration on the immediate experience. In obtaining this fullness in the present, a discipline is imposed, as in old age: one must be removed from power, be divested of external social roles, and turn away from the world's claims. So too the remembrance of death and finitude has always been considered an essential means to living fully now. The 'letting go' required of death creates an appreciation of each present hour."[26]

The losses of age can be viewed, in other words, as vivid reminders of the finitude and contingency of all human life. This insight into human contingency is understood as central in religious traditions of both East and West. In facing and accepting the real diminishments of one's own aging, the older person is led to see things as they really are. Thus the quest for spiritual awareness is continued, even brought to maturity, in the challenge of the acceptance of one's old age.

These images of acceptance of aging are potentially powerful vehicles of religious awareness. Care must be taken, however, that they do not deteriorate at the political level into catch-phrases used to sanction individual resignation or communal passivity in the face of society's less-than-adequate response to its aging members. Many of the negative aspects of growing old in America can be changed. Retirement, financial security in mature age, preventive medicine and health care delivery, continuing participation of older Americans in civic life—these issues must be addressed with more creativity than American public policy has shown to date. Religious images, used to delay or divert this public discussion, are misused.

Conclusion

In this paper we have considered six religious images, examining the manner in which they are currently being interpreted in relation to the human experience of aging. These images are:

a. *personal salvation*	The values and achievements of a person's life will be taken up and endure in the continuing life of God.
b. *hope*	Confidence that one's life is a part of God's plan; the efforts toward good that one has begun will not end with one's life; they will be brought to completion beyond the self.
c. *religious sense of time and personal history*	God acts in and through the lives of individuals; there is religious significance in the unique, cumulative experience of the individual's life.
d. *God's unconditional love for the individual*	God's love is not dependent upon one's works; there is thus a basis for self-esteem independent of productivity, social role, physical vigor or beauty; a person is more than what he does.
e. *spiritual discipline of "emptiness" and "letting go"*	The deprivations and losses of advancing age are opportunities to divest oneself of the illusory ambitions and false securities of life which often serve as distractions from the life of the spirit; letting go of these distractions, one is able to live more fully in the present, to see life as it is.
f. *image of the Christian as pilgrim-on-the-way*	It is in the continuing experience of change throughout life that the person develops more fully into the "full measure of Christ," thus the Christian need not fear aging, for the future and its demands for personal change can be interpreted as the invitation of God.

It is likely that for some in American society today the religious quality of these images will enhance their power and efficacy as interpretive devices. Others will find the religious origin of the images irrelevant, or even distracting. Even for this latter company, I suggest, these images may serve as examples of ways in which the imagination of western civilization has attempted to give expression to its awareness of the potentially positive dimensions of aging.

Each of these images resonates with a basic realization or hope of the human spirit. That ones life has significance, that ones worth transcends accomplishments, that apparent "losses" may, in fact, be gains—these intuitions, which often give rise to the religious sense, are not limited to religious

expression. The humanist can trace expressions of these intuitions elsewhere in literature and art, in history and biography. These intuitions, expressed in religious language or in other symbol systems, can lead to an understanding of aging which permits the appreciation of its positive, self-enhancing, developmental aspects. By recalling from our collective cultural memory some of the positive images and models of aging, by attempting to express and to interpret these in contemporary culture, the humanist can expand the range of attitudes toward aging available in American society today.

Michel Philibert reminds us that "our attitude toward aging shapes our experience."[27] Our evaluation of mature age—as "good" or "bad," as a phase of life to be welcomed or to be avoided—will be conditioned by the opinions, beliefs, and images we carry within us regarding the human experience of growing older and being old. If our basic perspective toward aging is developed from largely negative images, it is likely that we shall find in our experience of aging only its negative aspects. If our orientation toward aging can be broadened beyond simply negative categories, it is possible that more positive aspects of the ambiguous human experience of aging may be experienced and savored.

Included among the products of the western imagination collected in our humanistic heritage is a wide range of both positive and negative images of aging. The religious themes we have examined above can be interpreted as positive images of aging. As such these symbols may enable us to contribute to the expansion of the perspective through which the phenomena of human aging can be evaluated and appreciated within contemporary society.

Notes

1 "Human Values, Economic Values and the Elderly," paper delivered at the "Human Values and Aging" project, Case Western Reserve University, Cleveland, Ohio, October 10, 1975.

2 "Biomedical Aspects of Aging," address delivered at the "Human Values and Aging" project, Case Western Reserve University, Cleveland, Ohio, October 11, 1975.

3 The following journals are rich sources of such articles: *Christian Century, Christianity Today, Journal of Pastoral Care, Religion and Mental Health, Review of Religious Research, Pastoral Psychology.*

4 *Aging: The Fulfillment of Life* (New York: Doubleday, 1974).

5 *Toward a Theology of Aging* (New York: Human Sciences Press, 1975).

6 "The Phenomenological Approach to Images of Aging," *Soundings,* 57, No. 1 (Spring 1974), 34.

7 *Aging: The Fulfillment of Life,* p. 131.

8 "Christian Adulthood," *Daedalus,* 105, No. 2 (Spring 1976), 83.

9 Ibid.

10 *Identity, Youth and Crisis* (New York: Norton, 1968), p. 139.

11 "Dr. Borg's Life Cycle," *Daedalus,* 105, No. 2 (Spring 1976), 3.

12 Ibid., p. 1.

13 Ibid., p. 23.

[14] Ibid.

[15] Ibid.

[16] See his *Generative Man: Psychoanalytic Perspectives* (Philadelphia: Westminster, 1973).

[17] "Preface to a Practical Theology of Aging," in *Toward a Theology of Aging,* p. 162.

[18] Ibid., quoted in James Lapsley, *Salvation and Health* (Philadelphia: Westminster, 1972), p. 53.

[19] Browning, *Generative Man,* p. 162.

[20] Bouwsma, "Christian Adulthood," p. 83.

[21] Ibid.

[22] Herbert G. May and Bruce M. Metzger, eds., *The Oxford Annotated Bible* (New York: Oxford Univ. Press, 1962), p. 1422.

[23] See T.R.V. Murti, *The Central Philosophy of Busshim* (London: Allen and Unwin, 1955) and Frederick Streng, *Emptiness: A Study in Religious Meaning* (Nashville, Tenn.: Abingdon Press, 1967).

[24] See especially chapters 3, 4, 5, 15, 16 in *Lao Tse,* trans. D.C. Lau (Baltimore: Penguin Books, 1963).

[25] "The Parish and Sacraments of Adulthood: Access to an Educational Future," *Listening: Journal of Religion and Culture,* 12, No. 2 (Spring 1977), 80.

[26] "Ideal Old Age," *Soundings,* 57, No. 1 (Spring 1974), 11-12.

[27] Philibert, p. 33.

Richard Freedman

SUFFICIENTLY DECAYED: GERONTOPHOBIA IN ENGLISH LITERATURE[1]

> . . . the satirical rogue says here that old men have grey beards, that their faces are wrinkled, their eyes purging thick amber and plum-tree gum, and that they have a plentiful lack of wit. . . .
>
> —*Hamlet,* II, ii

Too often it is assumed by people outside the so-called "humanities" that this loosely grouped field of study is necessarily "humane" in its orientation. In respect to aging, clearly the proper "humane" attitude should be one of gratitude for benefits received, respect for past accomplishment, compassion for current physical and mental decrepitude, and a lofty desire to render their condition as pleasant and productive as the emotional resources of the individual and the economic resources of the community can allow. But literature, generally speaking, tends to be more concerned with the realistic rendition of life as the writer sees it than with the righting of injustices or the immediate betterment of society. The greatest literature, indeed, frequently reveals with unblinking truth the very negative attitudes to the elderly which, if we were honest, most of us would admit we feel.

Even a writer so committed to social action as Simone de Beauvoir reveals in *The Coming of Age* a profound ambivalence about the aging. While on the surface her book is an angry polemic against society's "inhumane" treatment of the elderly, scarcely beneath the surface it is apparent that she shares the feelings of disgust and fear of the aged themselves which perhaps lies at the basis of a culture's seemingly cruel indifference to their plight. She points out that "whatever the context may be, the biological facts remain. For every individual, age brings with it a dreaded decline. It is in complete conflict with the manly or womanly ideal cherished by the young and the fully-grown. The immediate, natural attitude is to reject it, in so far as it is summed up by the words decrepitude, ugliness and ill-health. Old age in others also causes an instant repulsion."[2]

Hamlet, in his ambulatory book report to Polonius which is quoted in my epigraph, adds to de Beauvoir's list some pithier and more concrete indictments of the aged as physically repulsive specimens of humanity. Even if Shakespeare is making fun of Hamlet's youthful callowness when the Prince lectures his by no means elderly mother that at her age "the heyday in the blood" should be "tame,"[3] Hamlet is surely justified in hating Polonius, whose old age has brought not wisdom, but merely an intensification of what was probably a lifelong penchant for gossip, double-dealing and amoral Machiavellianism.

The intention here is not to buttress or even countenance Western society's hostile treatment of the aged, but perhaps to confront that treatment—as The Enemy—in some of its more eloquent and enduring literary manifestations. The hope is to demonstrate that great literature neither takes sides nor necessarily promotes what we think of as social good; that its true greatness, perhaps, lies precisely in its ability to face unflinchingly the lowest, least "humane" instincts of human beings, and that to see literature—or any of the "humanities"—as necessarily benign and affirmative is to make a great mistake about its provenance, basic assumptions, and ultimate value.

From much current thinking about the problems of aging, particularly in relation to possible governmental approaches to them, one gets the sense of nearly total confusion among the words human, humane, humanist and humanities; but added to this semantic problem, one also gets the sense that the humanities are expected to provide some sort of magic balm for the pains of old age, which society in general and the federal government in particular could nod sagely at and then continue to ignore. This state of affairs encourages me to believe that a confrontation of the literary response to aging at its most bracingly negative might be of some use in countering such glibly optimistic views of the role of the humanities, and might point the way to further research into the large body of literary opprobrium to which the aged have been subjected.

For example, one specific value of such an overview might be in dispelling the popular myth that only in very recent times has a degenerate American society ignored and disprized the proverbial wisdom of the aged; the breakup of the "atomic family"—or, indeed, of any family at all—being held responsible for this depressing phenomenon. Yet a knowledge of literature serves to puncture this glibly self-accusatory myth by showing that as far back as 1854, Thoreau, early in *Walden,* was asserting that: "What old people say you cannot do you try and find that you can. Old deeds for old people, and new deeds for new." Thoreau then nastily provides us with an example of what "the wisdom of the aged" usually boils down to: "One farmer says to me, 'You cannot live on vegetable food solely, for it furnishes nothing to make bones with,' and so he religiously devotes a part of his day to supplying his system with the raw material of bones; talking all the while he walks behind his oxen, which, with vegetable-made bones, jerk him and his lumbering plough along in spite of every obstacle."[4] So much for "the wisdom of the aged" as perceived by at least one observant citizen of idyllic, preatomic, Currier-and-Ives nineteenth-century America. And one might go back even a bit further in

Western culture, to Homer's *Iliad,* where that wise old bore Nestor endlessly counsels the troops, to their grudging respect and ill-concealed yawns.

The hope, then, is that the following examples, culled from English literature and representing only the proverbial tip of an iceberg of literary gerontophobia, may demonstrate some of the negative attitudes to aging and the aged held by some of the finest—and most humane—minds the world has known. If only the material plight of the aged is to be at least partially mitigated in our time, this noble endeavor will best be accomplished, not by pretending that old age is any happier a condition than in fact it is, but by honestly facing the worst that has been thought and written about it and rising superior to our own negative feelings which this literature so forcefully expresses.

The most potent weapon of destruction in the literary arsenal is, of course, satire, and one might as well begin, then, with the eighteenth century, the high-water mark of English satire, to find the most vicious excoriations of the condition of old age. This was, after all, an epoch in which good bourgeois mamas and papas, not knowing what to do with their children on a rainy Sunday, would take them to Bedlam to enjoy the antics of the mad. Conveniently at the very outset of the century, in 1700, came the grand climax of anti-sentimental Restoration comedy with Congreve's *The Way of the World,* in which the foolish Lady Wishfort is mercilessly lampooned for having libidinous feelings at the advanced age of . . . fifty-five! At one point in the play Mrs. Fainall says: "Female frailty! We must all come to it, if we live to be old and feel the craving of a false appetite when the true is decayed." On which theme Mirabell, the hero, gleefully embroiders: "An old woman's appetite is depraved like that of a girl. 'Tis the green sickness [a female adolescent form of anemia] of a second childhood; and like the faint offer of a latter spring, serves but to usher in the fall, and withers in an affected bloom."[5] Later in the play, Lady Wishfort, eagerly awaiting her false suitor, Sir Rowland, confides to her servant Foible that her makeup is not all it might be:

> LADY WISHFORT: This wretch has fretted me that I am absolutely decayed. Look, Foible.
> FOIBLE: Your ladyship has frowned a little too rashly, indeed, madam. There are some cracks discernible in the white varnish.
> LADY WISHFORT: Let me see the glass [mirror]. Cracks, say'st thou? Why I am arrantly flayed; I look like an old peeled wall. Thou must repair me, Foible, before Sir Rowland comes, or I shall never keep up to my picture.[6]

Congreve was thirty when he wrote *The Way of the World,* and his cruelty to the erotic aspirations of Lady Wishfort might be ascribed in terms of glib psychologizing to a male's hopes and fears of being seduced by a woman old enough to be his mother.

But surely literary tradition contributes at least as much to Congreve's view of

the world as does his personal psyche. The figure of the grotesquely libidinous old man or woman dates back at least as far as Roman comedy, and it is no accident that in his dedicatory preface to *The Way of the World,* Congreve refers to Terence, one of the masters of that genre, as "the most correct writer in the world."[7] E. F. Watling, in his introduction to some plays by Plautus, Terence's great predecessor, summarizes Plautus' old men as "gullible, irascible, or lecherous,"[8] and as for old women, Scapha, a character in Plautus' play *The Ghost,* inveighs against "Those raddled old creatures who plaster themselves with perfume, toothless hags trying to hide their ugliness with make-up—what with scent and sweat together they smell like as if a cook's been mixing up too many different kinds of stew. You can't tell what they smell of, all you know is they smell horrible."[9] It could almost be a description, nearly two millenia earlier, of Lady Wishfort in *The Way of the World.*

In Plautus, Terence, and Congreve we find the specific butt of satire against the aged to be the disparity between their physical ugliness and decrepitude and their erotic urges: the satirists' complaint seems to be as much esthetic as moral. But returning to the eighteenth century, somewhat later than Congreve, we find in the greatest of all satirists, Jonathan Swift, a far broader range of attack. In Book III of *Gulliver's Travels,* Gulliver hears about a race of immortals known as the Struldbruggs. In typical gullible fashion, he cries out: "as in a Rapture": "Happy Nation, where every Child hath at least a Chance for being Immortal! Happy people who enjoy so many living Examples of antient Virtue, and have Masters ready to instruct them in the Wisdom of all former Ages!" The "wisdom of the aged" again, we see, but the reality turns out to be somewhat different:

> they had not only all the Follies and Infirmities of other old Men, but many more which arose from the dreadful Prospect of never dying. They were not only opinionative, peevish, covetous, morose, vain, talkative; but uncapable of Friendship, and dead to all natural Affection. . . . Envy and impotent Desires, are their prevailing Passions. . . .
>
> If a *Struldbrugg* happen to marry one of his own Kind, the Marriage is dissolved of Course by the Courtesy of the Kingdom, as soon as the younger of the two comes to be Fourscore. For the Law thinks it a reasonable Indulgence that those who are condemned without any Fault of their own to a perpetual Continuance in the World, should not have their Misery doubled by the load of a Wife.

Again we have a revulsion here against geriatric sexuality. But Swift goes on to observe that the Struldbruggs "are despised and hated by all Sorts of People," and rightly so, for:

> They were the most mortifying Sight I ever beheld; and the Women more horrible than the Men. Besides the usual Deformities in extreme old Age, they acquired an additional Ghastliness in Proportion to their

> Number of Years, which is not to be described; and among half a Dozen I soon distinguished which was the oldest, although there were not above a Century or two between them.
>
> The reader will easily believe, that from what I had heard and seen, my keen Appetite for perpetuity of life was much abated.[10]

The added ingredient here is that as a professional clergyman and Christian moralist, Swift's initial impetus is to satirize the heretical desire for literal immortality of the body, rather than spiritual immortality of the soul. But the horrifying vision of the Struldbruggs goes far beyond this conventional doctrinal purpose into an almost gratuitous assault on the old merely for being old, quite apart from the problem of physical immortality, which becomes for Swift merely a *reductio ad absurdum* of age itself. The catalogue of moral and social failings ("opinionative, peevish," etc.) can be added to Hamlet's list of physical shortcomings as applying to the old in general, rather than merely to an imagined race of men growing older unto immortal infinity.

There is, in addition, satire on marriage of the Darby-and-Joan sort, which, Swift the observant bachelor is saying, in effect is what all marriages become given enough time, and the characteristic greater repugnance aroused by old women than by old men ("the Women more horrible than the Men"), which seems to me, ignoring the modish *bêtise* of "male-chauvinism," to be a commonly shared opinion. Gulliver is cured of his sinful desire for physical immortality and his foolish belief that wisdom increases with age; we are given a morbidly accurate description of what we shall look and act like when we are old. There is no escape from Swift's black vision in such contemptible euphemisms as "senior citizens," just as there is no escape from Swift's general assault on human beings for the crime of being human. The only escape from Swift for the sentimental and fuzzy-minded is the one that in fact has been largely adopted, which is to bestow upon one's children a book one lacks the guts to read oneself.

The cold ferocity of Swift's attack on age in *Gulliver's Travels* would leave a worse taste in our mouths than it does if Swift, like most of us, envisioned as his targets only Other People. But why was Gulliver "mortified" by the spectacle of the Struldbruggs if he did not sense in them some connection with his own human destiny? Perhaps a clue lies in the extraordinary "Verses on the Death of Dr. Swift," in which Swift has the moral imagination to envision himself as a Struldbrugg, seeing that "The Time is not remote, when I/Must in the Course of Nature dye." He foresees his deathbed, at which friends and relations will gather to say:

> See, how the Dean begins to break:
> Poor Gentleman, he droops apace,
> You plainly find it in his face:
> That old Vertigo in his Head,
> Will never leave him, till he's dead:
> Besides, his Memory decays,

He cannot call his Friends to Mind;
Forgets the Place where last he din'd:
Plyes you with Stories o'er and o'er,
He told them fifty Times before.
How does he fancy we can sit,
To hear his out-of-fashion'd Wit?
But he takes up with younger Fokes,
Who for his Wine will bear his Jokes. . . .

Swift, then, envisions an old age in which he will share the fate of those he scourged in *Gulliver's Travels.* He, too, will be garrulous, repetitive, a social burden borne for the worst motives and with the worst possible will by his younger contemporaries, who, cataloguing the almost innumerable defects of his senescence, "then hug themselves, and reason thus;/ It is not yet so bad with us."[11]

If more of us had an iota of Swift's moral courage, we would hear less self-serving cant about "the sunset years" (decrepitude as a technicolor travelogue), and would realize that the best we can hope for is either, with the ancient Greeks, a sudden death at the height of our powers or, with the modern socialist countries, some financial mitigation of an otherwise totally intolerable condition. One feels that only his strong Christian faith, bolstered by a deep-rooted cussedness that refused to let the world so easily off the hook, prevented Swift from ending his life on his own terms rather than face any further indignities of old age than those he foresaw in his poem, written fourteen years before his actual death.

A half-century after *Gulliver's Travels,* in 1778, Frances Burney produced her sole masterpiece, *Evelina,* at the age of twenty-six. Although it was wildly popular at the time, and was to be a profound influence on Jane Austen, who was three years old when it appeared, read today, with our hindsight of what Austen would do in this line, *Evelina* seems in many ways a crude and shocking performance, largely because of Burney's inadequate control of her materials. No better example of this exists than the scene toward the end of the novel, in which the young, naive Evelina, with whose "Entrance Into The World" the novel is exclusively concerned, finds herself staying at a fashionable country house, where the bored young bloods decide to bet a hundred pounds on "a race between two old women, one chose by each side, and both of them to be proved more than eighty, though, in other respects strong and healthy as possible."[12] Utterly lacking the breadth and humanity of Swift, this cruel and grotesque race is described in mindless, lip-smacking detail which deserves to be quoted, despite its length, in full:

> Before dinner, came Mr. Coverley, and before five o'clock, Mr. Lovel and some other company. The place marked out for the race, was a gravel-walk in Mrs. Beaumont's garden, and the length of the ground twenty yards. When we were summoned to the *course,* the two poor old women made their appearance. Though they seemed very healthy for

their time of life, they yet looked so weak, so infirm, so feeble, that I could feel no sensation but that of pity at the sight. However, this was not the general sense of the company, for they no sooner came forward, than they were greeted with a laugh from every beholder, Lord Orville [the hero] excepted, who looked very grave during the whole transaction. Doubtless he must be greatly discontented at the dissipated conduct and extravagance, of a man with whom he is, soon, to be so nearly connected.

For some time, the scene was truly ridiculous; the agitation of the parties concerned, and the bets that were laid upon the old women, were absurd beyond measure. *Who are you for?* and *whose side are you of?* was echoed from mouth to mouth by the whole company. Lord Merton and Mr. Coverley were both so excessively gay and noisy, that I soon found they had been too free in drinking to their success. They handed, with loud shouts, the old women to the race-ground, and encouraged them, by liberal promises, to exert themselves.

When the signal was given for them to set off, the poor creatures, feeble and frightened, ran against each other and, neither of them able to support the shock, they both fell on the ground [pure Monty Python, this!].

Lord Merton and Mr. Coverley flew to their assistance. Seats were brought for them, and they each drank a glass of wine. They complained of being much bruised, for, heavy and helpless, they had not been able to save themselves, but fell, with their whole weight upon the gravel. However, as they seemed equal sufferers, both parties were too eager to have the affair deferred.

Again, therefore, they set off, and hobbled along, nearly even with each other, for some time, yet frequently, and to the inexpressible diversion of the company, they stumbled and tottered; and the confused hallowing of *'Now Coverley!' 'Now Merton!'* rung from side to side during the whole affair.

Not long after, a foot of one of the poor women slipt and, with great force, she came again to the ground. Involuntarily, I sprung forward to assist her, but Lord Merton, to whom she did not belong, stopped me, calling out 'No foul play! no foul play.'

Mr. Coverley, then, repeating the same words, went himself to help her, and insisted that the other should stop. A debate ensued; but the poor creature was too much hurt to move, and declared her utter inability to make another attempt. Mr. Coverley was quite brutal; he swore at her with unmanly rage, and seemed scarce able to refrain even from striking her.

Lord Merton then, in great rapture, said it was a *hollow thing;* but Mr. Coverley contended that the fall was accidental, and time should be allowed for the woman to recover. However, all the company being against him, he was pronounced the loser.

> We then went to the drawing-room, to tea. After which, the evening being delightful, we all walked in the garden.[13]

Here, surely, for all Evelina's reiteration of the adjective "poor" and her protestations of feeling "pity at the sight," and for all her lover, Lord Orville's, disdainful self-distancing from the scene, is the brutal eighteenth century of Hogarth's *Gin Lane* and *Beer Alley,* rendered all the more offensive by its taking place in an aristocratic, rather than a slum milieu, and by the cold, anticlimactic indifference of Evelina's concluding paragraph. Considering that the rest of the novel is concerned with making the finest differentiations between truly elegant and merely genteel manners, this racing scene stands out in a way one doubts Burney could have intended. Lack of esthetic control can be blamed for most of the passage's shock-value: one doubts that Burney is fully conscious of the impression the scene itself and the moral inadequacy of her response to it is making on the reader—a mistake Jane Austen would never make—but its technical naiveté makes it all the more convincing as a bald statement of some eighteenth-century attitudes to the aged—especially, we note again, to aged women.

By Austen's time (1775-1817) the most brutal savagery of eighteenth-century satire had long given way to a softer apprehension of life. In *Sense and Sensibility,* Marianne Dashwood is gently mocked for assuming, in her extreme youth and inexperience, that Colonel Brandon, at thirty-five, is too old to be a lover and husband. She is made, in fact, to end up marrying him, but the tone of this conclusion is an ambiguous one: Austen conveys the sense that at least partially this marriage is a punishment for her earlier folly in throwing herself at the dashing young Willoughby. Similarly, at the moral climax of *Emma,* the heroine is upbraided by the admirable Mr. Knightley for having responded impatiently to one of Mrs. Bates' tedious monologues and nearly loses him as a result of having mocked the old lady in such blatant terms as even she could understand. Everybody in the novel—including the unfortunate Mrs. Bates—knows what a fearful bore she is, but Mr. Knightley's point is that elderly, impoverished bores must be suffered in silence and with the best will one can muster. Clearly Austen is on Mr. Knightley's side in this. Yet just as clearly there is a good deal of Austen in Emma, as the author describes Mrs. Bates thus: "Mrs. Bates, the widow of a former vicar of Highbury, was a very old lady, almost past everything but tea and quadrille. She lived with her single daughter in a very small way, and was considered with all the regard and respect which a harmless old lady, under such untoward circumstances, can excite. . . . She was a great talker upon little matters. . . ."[14] A little later, Emma's rather simpleminded protégée, Harriet, notes of another character that "Mr. Weston is almost an old man. Mr. Weston must be between forty and fifty," to which Emma replies: "Which makes his good manners the more valuable. The older a person grows, Harriet, the more important it is that their manners should not be bad—the more glaring and disgusting any loudness, or coarseness, or awkwardness becomes. What is passable in youth, is detestable in later age."[15]

Unlike Congreve or Swift, however, Austen feels guilty about her impatience

with the old at the same time as giving full, hilarious, vent to it. In a letter she comments on a "Poor Mrs. Stent! it has been her lot to be always in the way; but we must be merciful, for perhaps in time we may come to be Mrs. Stents ourselves, unequal to anything & unwelcome to everybody."[16] Of another old lady, she remarks: "at her age, perhaps, one may be as friendless oneself, and in similar circumstances quite as captious."[17] Like Swift, then, Austen can project to herself her own old age, and is fearful above all of committing those social *gaffes* arising from senile egotism, a fate one feels she would have been exempt from in any case, even had she not died at the age of forty-three.

Jane Austen's life straddled the eighteenth and nineteenth centuries, but the roots of her art are deeper in eighteenth-century satiric moral realism (her favorite prose writer was Samuel Johnson) than in the Romanticism which was burgeoning all about her as she wrote. Not until her last completed novel, *Persuasion,* in fact, are there any discernible Romantic preoccupations, and even there, they are muted. As Romantic attitudes to the aging are treated elsewhere in this volume, I shall skip over them into certain tendencies visible in the later nineteenth century, pausing only to remark that a generalized spirit of "humanitarianism" was one of Romanticism's major cultural gifts to us, so that we are more repelled by such scenes as the geriatric race in *Evelina* than Burney's avid contemporary readers would have been: one must search hard in the nineteenth century to find anything approaching the eighteenth century's savagery—or moral realism, depending on how one looks at it—toward aging and the aged.

A handy way of gauging this softening tendency in the nineteenth century would be to compare Swift's Struldbruggs to Tennyson's "Tithonus," where the theme of the folly of desiring immortality is given very different voice. Here, Eos, the goddess of the dawn, has pled successfully with the gods to grant her husband Tithonus eternal life, forgetting to stipulate that what really was wanted was eternal *youth.* Like the Struldbruggs, Tithonus just grows older and older:

> The woods decay, the woods decay and fall,
> The vapours weep their burthen to the ground,
> Man comes and tills the field and lies beneath,
> And after many a summer dies the swan.
> Me only cruel immortality
> Consumes. . . .[18]

In Tennyson's languidly elegiac stanzas there is no hint of precisely what that eternal aging entails physically. This is only to be expected from the nineteenth century, in which Tennyson's heartier contemporary Browning was able to burble enthusiastically: "Grow old along with me!/ The best is yet to be,"[19] and to contemplate death as merely "one fight more,/ The best and the last!"[20] Perhaps only the eighteenth century—and, at its best, our own—can confront unblinkingly the horrors of old age. With exquisite irony, Aldous Huxley used Tennyson's line "And after many a summer dies the swan" for the title of his

1939 satirical novel about an obscene Hollywood mogul determined to live forever by ingesting the triturated entrails of decaying carp. To be sure, Dickens has his vicious portrait of Mrs. Skewton in *Dombey and Son,* but she is easily balanced by the many sentimentally-conceived old people in his novels—the charming Aged Parent in *Great Expectations,* or the pathetic Dr. Manette in *A Tale of Two Cities,* for example.

One place in which consistent gerontophobia does occur in the nineteenth century, surprisingly perhaps, is in the light operas of Gilbert and Sullivan. Beginning with their first opera, *Thespis, or The Gods Grown Old,* in which Diana is described as "an elderly Goddess," and continuing practically unabated through their entire careers right up to the Lady Sophy of *Utopia, Limited,* yet "another man-hungry ugly old woman,"[21] cruel fun is poked at the aged. In their first successful collaboration, *Trial by Jury,* the Judge proudly recounts to the Jury the cynical way in which he climbed to the top of his profession, including his falling in love "with a rich attorney's/ Elderly, ugly daughter." Said attorney, in his relief at getting rid of this encumbrance, assures the young swain:

> 'You'll soon get used to her looks,' said he,
> 'And a very nice girl you'll find her!
> She may very well pass for forty-three
> In the dusk, with a light behind her!'[22]

Most famous, perhaps, of Gilbert and Sullivan's aged butts for satire is Katisha, the appalling virago of *The Mikado,* of whom her reluctant suitor, Ko-Ko, has these flattering things to sing:

> I've got to take under my wing,
> Tra la,
> A most unattractive old thing,
> Tra la,
> With a caricature of a face.[23]

Reconciled to marrying Katisha, he has this grotesque duet with her:

> KO-KO: There is beauty in extreme old age—
> Do you fancy you are elderly enough?
> Information I'm requesting
> On a subject interesting:
> Is a maiden all the better when she's tough?
> KATISHA: Throughout this wide dominion
> It's the general opinion
> That she'll last a good deal longer when she's tough.
> KO-KO: Are you old enough to marry, do you think?
> Won't you wait till you are eighty in the shade?
> There's a fascination frantic

In a ruin that's romantic
Do you think you are sufficiently decayed?[24]

And Katisha joyfully concurs that she is "sufficiently decayed."

Cruelty of all sorts abounds in *The Mikado,* much of it under the guise of satirizing the time-honored Japanese custom of beheadings and other pleasant social rituals, and by implication satirizing perhaps the real target: the *fin-de-siècle* esthetes' faddish adoration of a race capable of such enormities. In *Patience,* the opera exclusively concerned with satirizing estheticism from a doggedly Philistine point of view, the hyper-esthetic rip-off artist Bunthorne melodramatically confides in the audience that: "I do *not* long for all one sees/ That's Japanese,"[25] only pretending to do so because "uttering platitudes/ In stained-glass attitudes" is a proven method of attracting groupies, *circa* 1881.

But satire of this sort exists on a purely conscious intellectual level, which hardly explains the almost demonic intensity of Gilbert's cruelty to the aged throughout his works. Sullivan seems to have been largely exempt from his collaborator's fixation, but cheerfully went along with it—rather less so, though, as he grew older himself. In this very emotional disparity, in fact, lies much of the success of their collaboration, in which the sweetness and genuine gaiety of Sullivan's music mollifies the sting of Gilbert's appallingly savage lyrics. One would hardly know merely from the melodic charm and life-enhancing exuberance of the Sullivan scores what psychologically dark corridors the Gilbertian libretti inhabit. A serious, but idiomatic, psychological-esthetic analysis of the Gilbert and Sullivan *oeuvre* would be a fecund area for research in the field of gerontophobic literature.

Rather than satire, however, a relentless realism, on the surface a more "humane" mode, dominates gerontophobic writing of the late nineteenth and early twentieth centuries. Perhaps the best example of this shift is a powerful passage in Arnold Bennett's unjustly neglected masterpiece of 1908, *The Old Wives' Tale.* Here we see the inexorable toll time takes of two sisters, culminating in the discovery made by one of them, Sophia, of her long-estranged husband Gerald, as he lies dead. Sophia herself is old, but

> In her mind she had not pictured Gerald as a very old man. She knew that he was old; she had said to herself that he must be very old, well over seventy. But she had not pictured him. This face on the bed was painfully, pitiably old. A withered face, with the shiny skin all drawn into wrinkles! The stretched skin under the jaw was like the skin of a plucked fowl. The cheek-bones stood up, and below them were deep hollows, almost like egg-cups. A short, scraggy white beard covered the lower part of the face. The hair was scanty, irregular, and quite white; a little white hair grew in the ears. The shut mouth obviously hid toothless gums, for the lips were sucked in. The eyelids were as if pasted down over the eyes, fitting them like kid. All the skin was extremely pallid; it seemed brittle. The body, whose outlines were clear under the sheet, was very small, thin, shrunk, pitiable as the face. And on the face

> was a general expression of final fatigue, of tragic and acute exhaustion; such as made Sophia pleased that the fatigue and exhaustion had been assuaged in rest, while all the time she kept thinking to herself horribly: 'Oh! how tired he must have been!'[26]

Here the effect is produced neither by conscious satiric wit nor by ill-concealed sadistic impulses, as in most of the examples quoted earlier. Bennett is genuinely compassionate, but as a master of the new realism he had imbibed from such French sources as Maupassant and Zola, his mere accretion of detail, right down to the "little white hair . . . in the ears" of the aged corpse, the sense of disgust is as powerful as anything in Swift. For Bennett as much as for Swift, aging is unmitigated woe, leading inexorably to what for Bennett, the agnostic, is the total catastrophe of death.

One of the esthetic triumphs of *The Old Wives' Tale* is the way in which the aging process of the two sisters, whom we first encounter in girlhood, is rendered. The novel is quite long (640 pages) to be sure, but Bennett does not rely solely on sheer length to convey the passage of time. Instead, he measures the sisters' lives against two opposed coordinates: On the one hand is Mr. Critchlow, the local druggist, who seems old to the two girls at the beginning of the novel (taking advantage of the fact that youth always overestimates the age of its elders) and is indeed incredibly ancient by the end. On the other hand is the succession of short-lived pet dogs the sisters cherish. By plotting his heroines' normal-length lives against the extreme longevity of Mr. Critchlow and the very brief (by human standards) lives of their many dogs, a true sense of the passage of time is magnificently achieved, all culminating in the disillusioned despair of the passage quoted above.

In dealing with these various modes of literary gerontophobia it will be noticed that I have not sought any "explanations" for the authors' attitudes either in their personal psychologies or in the social circumstances under which they wrote. This is partly because I am keenly aware of the limitations of such socio-biographical approaches as suggesting more than they can prove. More important, I think the enduring power of their art itself suggests that it is founded less on personal psychological idiosyncrasy than on an uncanny ability to perceive and express fairly universal attitudes—at least in the West of the past few centuries—toward the aging which few have the desire or the courage to locate in themselves. Literature helps us to identify even those areas in our own psyches which we would least like to contemplate, and in doing so, perhaps serves the complex functions of ridding ourselves of complacently euphemistic cant, of gratuitous, paralyzing guilt (if others have felt as we do, perhaps we are not as monstrous as we thought), and of thus enabling us to address the genuine problems of the aging with free intelligences and clear consciences.

Notes

[1]I use "gerontophobia" in preference to the "ageism" proposed by Robert N. Butler (*Why Survive*? [New York: Harper & Row, 1975], pp. 11-12n), for two reasons: (1) to avoid the faddishness recently associated with the "ism" suffix that gave us "sexism" by loose analogy to "racism"; and (2) because the "ism" suffix is ambiguous and can mean entirely opposite things: "racism" is hatred of races other than one's own, while "Americanism" is super-loyalty to one's country. And how about "humanism" itself? To the objection that "phobia" means fear, not hatred, I would reply that fear and hatred are more closely allied than, say, racism and humanism.

[2]*The Coming of Age,* trans. Patrick O'Brian (New York: Warner Paperback Library, 1973), p. 60.

[3]*Hamlet,* III., iv., ed. Cyrus Hoy (New York: Norton, 1963), p. 60.

[4]*Walden,* ed. Owen Thomas (New York: Norton, 1966), pp. 5-6.

[5]*The Way of the World,* II, in *Restoration and Eighteenth-Century Comedy,* ed. Scott McMillin (New York: Norton, 1973), p. 173.

[6]Ibid., p. 181.

[7]Ibid., p. 154.

[8]*Plautus: The Rope and Other Plays* (Harmondsworth: Penguin, 1964), p. 3.

[9]Ibid., p. 38.

[10]*Gulliver's Travels,* ed. Robert A. Greenberg (New York: Norton, 1961), pp. 177-83.

[11]"Verses on the Death of Dr. Swift," II., in *Poems of Jonathan Swift,* ed. Joseph Horrell (Cambridge: Harvard Univ. Press, 1958), p. 722.

[12]*Evelina,* III., iv., ed. Edward A. Bloom (London: Oxford Univ. Press, 1970), p. 295.

[13]Ibid., III., vii., pp. 311-12.

[14]*Emma* (Harmondsworth: Penguin, 1966), pp. 51-52.

[15]Ibid., p. 62.

[16]Letter to Cassandra Austen, 21 April 1805, in *Jane Austen's Letters,* ed. R. W. Chapman (London: Oxford Univ. Press, 1965), p. 154.

[17]Letter to Cassandra Austen, 27 December 1808, Ibid., p. 243.

[18]*Tennyson: Representative Poems,* ed. Samuel C. Chew (New York: Odyssey Press, 1941), pp. 60-62.

[19]*Pippa Passes and Shorter Poems,* ed. Joseph E. Baker (New York: Odyssey Press, 1947), pp. 480-87.

[20]Ibid., p. 519.

[21]J. S. Atherton, "Gilbert versus Sullivan," *Times Literary Supplement,* 11 March 1977, p. 276.

[22]*The Complete Plays of Gilbert and Sullivan* (New York: The Modern Library, n.d.), p. 47.

[23]Ibid., p. 392.

[24]Ibid., p. 397.

[25]Ibid., p. 199.

[26]*The Old Wives' Tale* (New York: The Modern Library, n.d.), p. 598-99.

Susan S. Tamke

HUMAN VALUES AND AGING: THE PERSPECTIVE OF THE VICTORIAN NURSERY

The values held more-or-less in common by any given society are often expressed most clearly and directly in the process of child-rearing. Children will become successful members of society only if they accept the prevalent attitudes, beliefs, and values of the adult society and so, much of the effort of the child-training process is directed at making the child conform to society's expectations. These expectations are expressed in prescriptions of acceptable behavior and proscriptions of unacceptable behavior; the child is encouraged to behave in certain ways and threatened with punishment if he behaves in other ways. The socialization process further defines roles which are appropriate to individuals depending upon a variety of economic, social, sex, or age factors. Behavior, in turn, is dependent upon role. For instance, while it might be appropriate for an adolescent girl to dress in sexually alluring clothes, the same behavior might be considered entirely inappropriate for an older woman. What any given society defines as proper roles and conduct is determined primarily by that society's structural needs, not by the individual's needs. If the process of socialization is successful, children will internalize the social values of the parents—they will want to do what they have to do; their consciousness of reality will be constructed in such a way that their behavior is most likely to conform to social norms.[1]

Assuming, then, that the didactic literature of the nursery—a literature of moral instruction—can tell us much about the dominant social values as well as role and behavior expectations of a culture, I have surveyed a large number of children's stories, songs, and games from nineteenth-century England.[2] The purpose of the survey was to see how nineteenth-century society valued the aged. Whenever an older person appears in this nursery literature, I have attempted to analyze the role played, the behavior exhibited, and the judgment made or implied by the author about this behavior.

I

In this literature we find three predominant models of the elderly. The first model is of the wise and moral old people who are essentially passive; when they function actively they do so largely through or for other people, primarily children. They teach wisdom and good behavior to children or, if they are wealthy, they can function as gift-givers. Their good behavior is rewarded by admiration, by promises of salvation of their souls in the next world, or, if they are poor, as many are, by charity. These old people are staple characters in evangelical, moralistic tracts. The second model is of foolish or malevolent old people whose conduct is inappropriate to their role as envisaged by Victorian society. They disregard, often flaunt, social conventions by remaining active and self-directed. These characters are found most often in nursery rhymes where their behavior produces laughter, but occasionally they appear in more purposefully didactic literature where their conduct is punished harshly by ridicule, by threat of social ostracism, or even by threat of damnation. The third model is of old people who exhibit no behavior and, therefore, are neither good nor bad but simply old. These old people rarely figure in the didactic literature, but rather appear most often in game rhymes and the older traditional songs and stories. They are rarely treated kindly: because they are old they are laughed at, their physical impairments are the subject of jests, and they are denied the rewards which are given to the young. They are punished simply because they are old.

The models of socially approved or "good" old age in children's didactic literature are passive, passionless people, most often shown only in their relationship to the very young. They are affable creatures: the pictures accompanying the texts portray them as white haired, slightly plump, and smiling. They frequently function as a child's plaything:

> Grandfather sits in his old arm-chair,
> And the ruddy rays from the fireside there
>   Fall soft on his locks of snow;
> And the smile on his old face seems
> To tell of bright happy dreams
>   Of the long ago.
>
> In fancy again he can see
> The days of his youthful glee
>   And merry tricks and sport;
> How oft—Hullo! who's there?
> For he feels a tug at his hair
>   Of no very gentle sort.
>
> He starts with a quick surprise,
> And the merry light in his eyes

Shows that he sees the fun;
Ah, 'tis only Ethel and May,
And for *them* youth's sport and play
Have but just begun![3]

These good old people show no emotions other than a general desire to be beneficent; they delight in the younger generation's play and growth. This lack of emotion puts them outside of the vital part of society—youth; they are extraneous except in their desire to serve youth. These old people have no present; they are expected to, encouraged to, think about their past, which is the only part of their lives that is valued, or about their future, which is defined as life after death.

The passivity of these old people is greatest when the elderly are poor and thus become the objects of casual charity. In Lisa Lockyer's *A Child's Influence; or, Kathleen and Her Great Uncle,* there are a number of elderly characters, all of whom are poor villagers, lonely, pious and consequently content, even grateful, for their lot in life; they rationalize their deprivation as God's beneficent providence. Here is the conversation between Kathleen's friend Basil and old Susan:

"Truly, Susan; but methinks you have little to make you happy; blind, half deaf, very poor, rheumatic, and mostly alone."

"Alone! no, never, the blessed Babe is always with me. Poor! was not He poor. And as to my pains He suffered more for me. And if I am blind and deaf it does but shut out the world to make me think more of Him. And I have my blessing, Master Basil. There's my good son, who never leaves me but for God's house or to go fishing; then I have a roof over my head, and a comfortable bed, and every one is kind to me. . . ."[4]

The function of these old people is to teach the young by their pious example. What they teach is an attitude of gratitude for the status quo and a quiet acceptance and anticipation of death. They sit passively in their cottages, grateful for the ray of sunshine that the child Kathleen's presence brings: " 'Our young lady' was the name she went by in the village; blind Jonas would listen for her footsteps, and lame Willy Green liked his chair to be placed by the cottage door that he might see her pass."[5] They sit and wait in isolation—in the dark of blindness, in the silence of deafness—patiently waiting for death. Their suffering gives them a certain nobility, but they are essentially passive creatures acted upon by God's providence, by the charitable or uncharitable younger people around them, by the aging process that they never question. Sometimes they die before the story's end and when they do, they are eulogized for their patient acceptance.

The passivity of old people is seen especially in the case of old women; in fact, women who are widowed or otherwise left alone are often defined as

"old" not because of their age but because of their helplessness. They can rarely act for themselves and are dependent upon the actions of others. There are many Victorian children's stories about widows who work their fingers to the bone, who sacrifice everything for their children (especially for their sons), and then are rescued by their sons who, because they learned piety and hard work from their mothers, become financial successes. The helpless old mother or grandmother is a stock figure in the enormously popular self-help success genre. The stories value highly productivity and success which are achieved within the existing social and economic structure. Old people in these stories are given a peripheral, passive role; their function is to teach the young, but once this is accomplished they must sit back and wait for those they taught to save them from the miseries of loneliness and possible starvation. Since they are not highly productive they are acted upon by those people—the young—who are productive; they are expected to be acquiescent, non-interfering, even grateful for what benefits they do receive.

Some of the old people in these books do take a slightly active role: they teach young people piety, wisdom, and proper behavior. Mothers and grandmothers, of course, are expected to be models of moral behavior. But old people in the community who have no family connection are also expected to function as models and teachers of wisdom. In one story old Reuben, the gardener at the great house, befriends the young boys of the village: "when school was over, and his work was done, many a walk they took together in the woods. As he was a pious as well as a wise man, they seldom left him without a few words of advice."[6] In another story an old sailor called Norton is used by a middle-class family to take the young boys to the beach where he watches them and offers his homely wisdom.[7] The best-known example of an elderly person who imparts wisdom to the young is found in Robert Southey's poem about a wise and moral old man who teaches his son how to achieve a good old age. This poem, "The Old Man's Comforts and How He Gained Them," was memorized by generations of English children as a school-prize poem:

"You are old, Father William," the young man cried;
"The locks which are left you are gray;
You are bald, Father William,—a hearty old man:
Now tell me the reason, I pray."

"In the days of my youth," Father William replied,
"I remembered that youth would fly fast,
And abused not my health and my vigor at first,
That I never might need them at last."

"You are old, Father William," the young man cried,
"And pleasures with youth pass away;
And yet you lament not the days that are gone:
Now tell me the reason, I pray."

"In the days of my youth," Father William replied,
"I remembered that youth could not last;
I thought of the future, whatever I did,
That I never might grieve for the past."

"You are old, Father William," the young man cried,
"And life must be hastening away;
You are cheerful, and love to converse upon death:
Now tell me the reason, I pray."

"I am cheerful, young man," Father William replied;
"Let the cause thy attention engage;
In the days of my youth, I remembered my God,
And He hath not forgotten my age."[8]

Although the role of teacher is active, the end is a selfless one—the education of the younger generation.

One other active role is allowed and encouraged in good old people: economic self-support. When poverty-stricken old people are introduced as characters in a children's story the reader is assured of their good character by two criteria: their quiescent piety and their efforts to provide for themselves so that they will not be a burden to their family or the community. They labor at small tasks—knitting, gardening, making trinkets—in hopes that their charitable neighbors will buy their wares. Sometimes their labors are heroic, achieved despite pain and debility. Alice Gray, another young heroine who, like Kathleen, spends her time visiting the poor, sick, and lonely, visits Matthew, a retired fisherman:

"How's the rheumatism today, Matthew?" she inquired.

"Badly, Miss, very badly o' nights," he replied: "I scarce rested an hour last night; but, thank God for all His blessings, I felt comfortable and happy thro' the night-watch. I seem to think of all the comforts He has given me, most in the night season, and to praise Him most then!"

Poor old Matthew! I am afraid there are not many in his situation who would have found as much to be thankful for as he did. Bedridden for two years, and often suffering dreadful pain—utterly dependent on his nephew . . . he yet contrived to be always occupied, and to earn almost enough to keep himself, by making and mending nets, and constructing toy boats for children. . . .[9]

The role of good old people in these stories and poems, then, is essentially a passive one; the only active roles they are allowed are not self-directed, but other-directed. They teach the younger generation for the latter's moral betterment and they attempt to provide themselves with sustenance so that

they will not burden the community. They are never viewed as a "self," but as an "other." The only emotions they show are directed toward the young or toward heaven. They do not act, but are acted upon; they are objects rather than subjects. They are outside the human community except as they relate to the young.

This view of old people as objects is seen clearly in the admonitions to respect and honor the aged. The value of the aged is that as recipients of charity, they permit the young to be good; we receive the distinct impression that the purpose of charity is the moral benefit of the giver rather than the well-being of the recipient. For instance, in Mrs. Sherwood's *Fairchild Family,* when an old woman teaches the children that they should care for the aged she quotes from the Apocrypha:

> My son, help thy father in his age, and grieve him not as long as he liveth: and if his understanding fail, have patience with him and despise him not when thou art in thy full strength; for the relieving of thy father shall not be forgotten: and instead of sins, it shall be added to build thee up. In the days of thy affliction it shall be remembered. Thy sins also shall melt away as the ice, in the fair warm weather.[10]

The argument is that kindness to the aged is an investment in one's own salvation. In a poem entitled "Filial Love," the grandfather is treated with kindness and consideration but, again, he is presented not as a person but rather as an objectified recipient of the child's actions:

> Dear grandfather, thy feeble form
> A guiding hand requires;
> For thou hast weather'd many a storm,
> And quenched thy youthful fires.
>
> Come, let me be thy staff and guide,
> I know the shadiest spot,—
> The smoothest paths; for I have tri'd
> All those about our cot:
>
> Can lead thee to a shelter'd seat,
> Thy aged limbs to rest;
> When from the sun's o'erpowering heat
> Thy weakness feels opprest.
>
> In winter, when the cold winds blow,
> I'll place thy great arm-chair
> Close to the fire, and round thee throw
> My own warm coat with care.
>
> Thy silver locks I like to see,
> They make me love thee more:

When I stand list'ning at thy knee,
To tales of times before.

And when I kneel my pray'rs to say,
And see thy lips slow move,
I guess, in secret thou dost pray
That God thy child may love.

Feeble and old I know thou art,
Let me thy cares assuage;
In all thy labours bear a part,
And help to lighten age.[11]

We do not feel that the grandfather is a person; he is self-less. Even when he prays, the subject of the prayer is the child.

The children's literature purports to teach that *all* old people are to be honored and cared for. Kathleen says, "mother used to teach me to respect old people, even when they are tiresome."[12] A mother says prayerfully, "I hope my dear children will always be kind, whenever they meet with the aged and blind."[13] But a careful reading of this literature shows that it is only the good, the deserving aged, who receive this honor, kindness, and charity. There is another model of old age: the active old people who have emotions and desires, who take the roles reserved for the young. Far from being honored, these old people are treated with derision and scorn; they are threatened with social ostracism. As we might expect, bad old people rarely appear in the didactic literature (since the purpose of the literature is to teach by example, most of the examples are good ones). But when they do appear they are harshly treated. One lengthy excerpt from *A Visit to the Bazaar,* a children's book which teaches proper roles and behavior according to social class, economic function and status, sex and age, must suffice here as an example. In the book, the children are taken to a bazaar where they can learn their lessons by observing the world. When they approach the milliner's stall,

> little Caroline again saw something to excite her laughter, and to call forth the smile of her father. A lady, long past the prime of life, but dressed in a style of girlish fashion, with short sleeves which showed her shrivelled arms, and still shorter petticoats, was viewing herself with much complacency, as she placed on her head, the grey hairs of which were concealed by the flowing tresses of an auburn wig, a large straw hat, loaded with flowers and feathers, and only fit for a young woman under thirty.
>
> "Surely, mamma," cried Emily, "that old lady can never intend to buy that hat? It is too gay for one of her years."
>
> "She certainly does," said Maria, "and I dare say believes that it will make her look twenty years younger than she is."
>
> "She thinks wrong then, sister," exclaimed Theodore. "For, unless

> she can hide the wrinkles in her face and neck, and the loss of her teeth, and the leanness of her body, she will only the more expose her age, by dressing so ridiculously."
>
> "Your remark is a just one, my boy," said his father. "Old age of itself is respectable, and calls for the attention and veneration of youth, but when it apes the dress and follies of the latter, it only excites the sneer of contempt, and the laugh of ridicule."

The old woman makes a second appearance later in the book:

> "Mamma! mamma!" cried Caroline, "there is the very same old lady looking at that beautiful crape dress, at the DRESS MAKER'S, who was trying on the large straw hat with such a profusion of feathers and flowers."
>
> "Hush! my lovely girl," said her mamma, "if you are not more silent I must take you home."
>
> "It is just the thing, Mrs. Tasteful," screamed out the old lady. "It will suit my figure exactly. Square bosom, and off the shoulders, why with a lace frill I shall look delightful. A saucy fellow had the impudence to tell me, as I was getting out of my carriage, that I had better wear my petticoat a little longer to hide my legs, and put a shawl on to conceal my neck. The fool had no more taste than a Hottentot. Well, my dear woman, you will let me have this dress immediately. I am going out to a ball this evening, and shall want to put it on. Primrose colored crape over white sarsenet. Charming, I declare!"
>
> "Come on my dears," said Mr. Durnford, hastily, "I have no inclination to listen any longer to such disgusting vanity and folly. The age of that lady ought to have enabled her to set good examples to the younger and inexperienced part of her sex, instead of which she is only a disgrace to it. Come on, my dears, I will not stay a moment longer, lest another burst of weakness should offend my ear."[14]

The old woman's behavior is considered inappropriate because she is active and exhibits the emotions and desires of the young: she wishes to attract attention to herself (presumably, a man's attention). The author punishes her by relentlessly emphasizing the physical characteristics of aging: her grey hair, the shrivelled skin on her arms, the wrinkles of her face and neck, the loss of teeth, the scrawniness of her body, the harshness of her voice. She is told, in other words, that she should hide her body. Two pictures accompany the story which caricature the woman's age: her nose and chin are long and pointed, she is scrawny, she looks much like the traditional witch. The very viciousness of her punishment indicates the strength of the emotions behind the social prohibitions against her taking an active role.

Although the foolish old person who tries to usurp the role and behavior of the young rarely appears in didactic nursery literature, it is a stock character

in more fanciful nursery literature. He appears, for example, as the "ancient Beau" who attempts to "rake" and "ramble" and is punished by falling off a horse, falling into a river, and having his gouty toe trod on in a dance.[15] She appears as the ineffective old woman who tries to trade a penny to care for her needs. Her unsuccessful attempts to take an active role are punished by mockery: she is called an "old jade," a "lame dog," a "testy old wench," and "a pig."[16]

A more malevolent "old" character who tries to usurp the active role of the young is the evil step-mother or the witch of the fairy tales. She is narcissistic (magic mirrors and sycophantic courtiers maintain an illusion of youth and beauty) and demands love and admiration. She attempts to control those around her for her own purposes. She is the opposite of the good, self-less old person of Victorian didactic literature and is always punished by the end of the story, usually by death.[17]

The two models of old people presented above—the "good" old people whose behavior is appropriate to their assigned role and the "bad" old people whose conduct is inappropriate—fit neatly into the Victorian worldview of a just world in which good is rewarded and evil punished. Believing as they generally did (at least the majority of the middle classes avowed that they did) that the social order was divinely ordained, conformity to roles could be required because they were sanctioned by God. Since each person was considered responsible for his own behavior, rewards or punishments were an individual or divine matter and not a social concern; since God was omniscient, one could assume that the rewards and punishments were justly deserved. What may have seemed injustice (such as the extreme poverty and deprivation of many pious and passive aged people) could be justified by the facile explanation that the reward would be received in heaven. Humanitarian individuals were urged to give charity to the less fortunate, deserving individuals in their local communities; charity assuaged doubts about the justice of the social system.

This shallow optimism allowed society to ignore the existence of suffering by reliance on wistful dreams of a just world. That aging in nineteenth-century England most often entailed economic misery was made evident to the public by two major surveys of the aged.[18] Despite statistical evidence to the contrary, most popular adult Victorian literature about aging reflects the same values and attitudes and behavioral imperatives that we find in children's literature: that old age was a time for reflection about death and a withdrawal from the world; that the aged should take a passive rather than an active role, except as teachers of the young; and that if the aged showed secular passions or desires more appropriate to the young or otherwise behaved inappropriately, they deserved punishment.[19] Some popular writers even suggested that the physical characteristics of aging were punishment for previous unwise or immoral behavior. Sir Thomas Bernard believed "that age is not necessarily attended with infirmity of body or asperity of mind; and that when they do occur, it is the effect of unregulated appetites and passions, of a

morbid constitution, or of natural sourness of temper."[20] Walter Forward concluded, after a survey of the ages of the Mosaic patriarchs, that

> it is reasonable to suppose that the constitution of man should have so deteriorated by degrees that the ages attained by successive generations should grow less and less. Such deterioration would be brought about by a violation of natural law, and as century after century has sought out fresh devices for self-indulgence and sensual gratification, so has his stock of vitality been reduced and the period of his mundane existence abridged.[21]

This belief in a just and providential world where rewards and punishments were distributed according to an individual's behavior, is contradicted by the third model of old people in nursery culture. This model is that of old people who exhibit no behavior, but who are separated from the community of the young simply because of their age. They are stock characters in the rhymes and game songs, the origins of which could be ancient.

The rewards they receive are different from those the young receive. One widely familiar rhyme says,

> Cheese and bread for gentlemen,
> Corn and hay for horses,
> Tobacco for the old wives,
> And kisses for young lasses.[22]

Their age is the object of jest and disgust. A rhyme from Gloucestershire said of old women,

> What are old women made of?
> What are old women made of?
> Bushes and thorns and old cow's horns,
> And that's what old women are made of.[23]

In a story-poem about an old woman who sells sweets and whose only behavior indicates her honesty, the old woman is described as "An aged crone of many years— How sour a thing to dwell 'mid sweets."[24] These old people are often punished, physically or verbally, simply because they are old.

> There was an old woman, her name it was Peg;
> Her head was of wood and she wore a cork leg.
> The neighbours all pitched her into the water,
> The leg was drowned first, and her head followed after.[25]

Although it is a nonsense rhyme, the fact that old people are so often the subjects of such rhymes, the objects of casual violence, and the butt of jokes, is significant. There is no reason given why Peg's neighbors are so hostile except that she is old. The same is true of Sam:

Sam, Sam, dirty old man,
Washed his face in a frying pan,
Combed his hair with the leg of a chair—
Sam. Sam. dirty old man.[26]

The prevalence of these much-abused old people in nursery culture indicates a fear of, or dislike of, the aged which has little obvious connection to their behavior.

On the other hand, popular superstitions indicate that old people were considered lucky. E.W.B. Nicholson noted, for instance, that in the fishing village of Golspie, "Before starting for the herring-fishing they get some good old man to pray over their boats: this is thought to bring them a good fishing."[27] And a snapbook of dream interpretations says under the heading "Old": "Dreaming of seeing old men, is a sign you will be very fortunate. For a man to dream he is courting an old woman, and that she returns his love, is a very fortunate omen; it prefigures success in wordly concerns."[28]

The obvious ambivalence toward the aged which we find in these less didactic and more primitive artifacts of nursery culture indicates that nineteenth-century attitudes toward the aged were not entirely dictated by contemporary social, economic, and political values. I suspect that, because aging implies approaching death, any society will treat the aged with some degree of fear and withdrawal in an attempt to put aging and death at a distance. We affirm life by denying or distancing death; this attitude is expressed clearly in the old nurse's song:

Laugh, my baby, beauty;
What will time do to ye?
Furrow your cheek,
Wrinkle your neck;
So laugh, my baby, beauty.[29]

At the same time, because death is an ultimate mystery, mystical powers will be attributed to those closest to death. The fear and awe generated by the relationship between the aged and death create an ambivalence of attitudes toward the aged. The realization that aging will inevitably come to all members of society causes feelings of guilt and fear if the aged are not well cared for. Ambivalence and guilt create psychological tensions which demand resolutions within both individuals and societies.

Victorian society generally resolved this tension by withdrawal into a shallow and unquestioning optimism, a leap of faith in a divinely ordained and beneficent social order. To reinforce this belief which contradicted the observable reality of evil, pain, and suffering, society demanded a conformity to social values. As one poem for children expresses it, personal disappointment was to be ignored and criticism stifled in order to maintain this simplistic illusion:

We cannot hope through life to pass
With all things to our will;
The highest, as the lowest class,
Are liable to ill.

Children should early learn to bear
The cares that prove their lot;
They pass away like summer's air,
And are as soon forgot.

Though evils of a trifling kind
May disappoint our views;
None but a weak ungrateful mind
Will harsh expression use.

To hear the words of discontent
From childish lips proceed,
Unmindful of the good that's sent,
Distresses much indeed.[30]

Robert Graves, in his autobiography *Good-bye to All That,* repeats a nursery story which his mother told him that epitomizes this noncritical approach to life. It was, he writes,

> the parable of the king who had a very beautiful garden which he threw open to the public. Two students entered; and one, of whom my mother spoke with a slight sneer in her voice, noticed occasional weeds even in the tulip-beds; but the other (and here she brightened up) found beautiful flowers even on the rubbish heaps.[31]

The tragedy of life, of which aging and death are two important elements, had to be ignored in order to maintain the fantasy of a just, knowable, and beneficent universe, a world in which people were not required to act and to confront problems.

In an attempt to make reality fit their worldview, the Victorians demanded a conformity to roles. The acceptable role of the aged, as we have seen, was to be passive and selfless. The aged thus became objects rather than subjects so that the problem of aging could be denied rather than be confronted.

II

Developmental psychologists tell us that old age is a stage of life which precipitates crises which, like earlier stages, demand resolutions if the individual is to achieve full potential development.[32] The language which the developmental psychologists use when they talk of "resolution" denotes ac-

tivity. Erik Erikson, for instance, writes of a need to "transcend" and of "engagement," "confrontation," and "renewed struggle." Erikson says, "whatever chance man has to transcend the limitations of his self seems to depend on his full (if often tragic) engagement in the one and only life cycle permitted to him." Further, Erikson defines ***wisdom*** as "the detached and yet active concern with life itself in the face of death itself, and that it maintains and conveys the integrity of experience, in spite of the decline of bodily and mental functions."[33]

It may be that our interest in individual development is only a contemporary concern, befitting the values of the society in which we live. Our belief that the individual is self-made, our concern for the realization of individual integrity, and our conviction that the crisis of aging can best be resolved by the active participation of the individual may be passing fancies in the historical panorama of human ideologies and *Weltanschauungen.* Further, I realize that the application of my own values to any past society is ahistorical. Nevertheless, I cannot resist the speculation that if the developmental psychologists of our own time are correct in positing that old age is a crisis which demands active resolution by the individual, aging in Victorian society must have been a frustrating experience for those citizens who were thoroughly socialized. Social organization often requires the repression of human instinctual responses. When this disparity is immediately felt, the individual must resolve the conflict. What a child is taught about the expected roles and behaviors of the aged will in most cases be accepted without question because he has not experienced the process of aging and is not aware of the inherent conflicts between social expectations and the individual's felt needs. The conflict will become apparent only when the individual who has been thoroughly socialized experiences the process of aging and finds that his instinctual responses or experienced needs differ from the expectations of society. If he has no approved models which suit his needs, he will feel an alienation from the community, compounding the loneliness and fear which are inherent in any stage of transition.

In my search of Victorian children's literature I found only two models of active, self-concerned older individuals who received the wholehearted approval of the author—George MacDonald's "grandmother" in "The Princess and the Goblin"[34] and Hans Christian Andersen's "Aunty."[35] I will not deal with the first character at any length because she is a fairy-grandmother who possesses magical abilities and, thus, is not illustrative of actual old people (it should be noted here, however, that fairy tales and fantasies are a way of subverting social conventions[36]). However, two conversations between the princess and the magical grandmother are worth noting because they give us a very unconventional view of aging. In the first, the grandmother asks the princess,

> "You won't be afraid then to go to bed with such an old woman?"
> "No. You are so beautiful, grandmother!"
> "But I am *very* old."

"And I suppose I am very young. You wouldn't mind sleeping with such a *very* young woman, grandmother?"

"You sweet little pertness!" said the old lady, and drew her towards her, and kissed her on the forehead and the cheek and the mouth.[37]

In the second conversation, the grandmother has changed herself into a young woman:

"Why do you call yourself old? You're not old, grandmother."

"I am very old indeed. It is so silly of people—I don't mean you, for you are such a tiny, and couldn't know better—but it *is* so silly of people to fancy that old age means crookedness and witheredness and feebleness and sticks and spectacles and rheumatism and forgetfulness! It is so silly! Old age has nothing whatever to do with all that. The right old age means strength and beauty and mirth and courage and clear eyes and strong painless limbs. I am older than you are able to think. . . ."[38]

While the magical grandmother uses her powers to help young people, she is certainly not passive and conventional. She uses her wisdom and powers to change and manipulate the world—she goes *against* conventions to create individual happiness.

While MacDonald's grandmother is not realistic, Andersen's Aunty is. She is an old woman who lives alone and has few social contacts, but possessing a passion for the theater, she flaunts social conventions by pursuing that passion. The story, by implication, pokes fun at old women who have no passion in their lives. Aunty lives for the theater and, we read, "her dying words were full of meaning; she asked, 'What are they going to play tomorrow?' " In her will she leaves money to allow a "deserving old spinster, living alone in the world," to go to the theater each Saturday, "for on that day they gave the best pieces. Only one condition was imposed on the legatee. As she sat in the theater, every Saturday, she was to think of Aunty, who lay in her grave. That was Aunty's Religious Foundation."[39]

Andersen's view of aging and dying was a thoroughly secular one, entirely opposed to the view presented in most Victorian children's stories. He believed that the whole of life should be a "religious" experience, that full and active participation in life creates a series of experiences which transcend time and place and, thus, deny the terror of death. For him, then, aging is not a stage which sets one apart from society or one's earlier life; it is a continuation of the process of life, a natural outgrowth of what went before, a continued effort at integration of one's self and experience. His parable of "The Toad,"[40] although not specifically about aging, is about life fully experienced and about death which is accepted naturally as the final experience of a fully developed life. In it the toad leaves his home in a well to see the world and to seek the "jewel" which his mother explains "is something so splendid and precious. . . that I cannot describe it; it is something that one wears to please oneself, and

that others fret to death after." He experiences his various adventures with a perceptual intensity that creates an ecstacy that transcends time and death. A moment before he dies the toad thinks,

> ". . . and all the longing and the yearning which I feel! surely this is better than having a jewel in one's head!"
>
> And it had it—the true jewel; the eternal longing and yearning to go upwards, ever upwards! This was the jewel, and it shone within it, shone with gladness, and beamed with desire.

The story is a denial of social conformity—of roles and "proper" behavior. It speaks clearly to me as I contemplate living and aging and, ultimately, death. But it was a lonely voice in the Victorian nursery.

If the culturally defined roles of the aged presented in Victorian nursery culture were internalized, then the options for personal development, for meeting the crisis of aging in a positive and active manner, and for resolving the conflicts inherent in this crisis, were severely limited. The images of quiescent, grateful, passive old people may have become a self-fulfilling prophecy.

III

In the pages above I have assumed, as most students of culture do, that "culture" (both elite and popular) has an effect on the individual personality. When we look at Victorian society as a whole, we can identify common cultural characteristics; we speak of the "spirit of the times," of a "social ethos," and of "national character." We can see the efforts of the group to impose this ethos or spirit upon individuals in the process of educating the young. But what the effect of this socialization process is, how it is achieved, and how deeply it can be impressed upon or internalized in the individual are questions which demand greater research.

We have subjective evidence from individuals that the effect can be profound. Robert Graves, for instance, has described in his autobiography *Good-bye to All That* his long and difficult struggle to shed the worldview of his Victorian-Edwardian childhood. We have much autobiographical evidence that the socio-cultural ideas and values taught in childhood are deeply impressed on the personality.[41] We can see the effect of specific nursery images which have been embedded in the semi-conscious memory when Juliet Soskice describes her "ancient ugly aunts who lay in beds" by reference to a nursery story:

> They used to stretch out their hands to me, and I used to stand on the strip of carpet between them and seem rude and unwilling to make friends. But it was really because I was frightened, for they reminded me of the wolf when he had eaten Red-Riding-Hood's grandmother

> up, and put on her nightcap and got into bed. They were, in fact, very affectionate, and wanted to be kind to me. It was only because they were so old and dried and wrinkled that I was frightened.[42]

The enthusiasm and delight occasioned by Lewis Carroll's *Alice in Wonderland*, which was in large part a parody of the didactic culture of the nursery, indicate how widely spread and deeply ingrained this nursery culture was. The evidence of psychoanalysis shows us that cultural prescriptions and proscriptions are often internalized despite contrary needs of the individual personality. We know, in other words, that a process of socialization does take place.

This is not to say, of course, that the purposeful process of transferring values from one generation to the next is easily accomplished. First, the influences on a child's life cannot always be completely controlled. The nanny's or stableboy's crude songs, the chum's illicit joke, scenes observed in the street, personal interaction—all of the haphazard incidents of life influence the formation of the child's *weltanschauung*. Children are also amazingly resistant to indoctrination. Anyone who has read *The Swiss Family Robinson* as both a child and as an adult has experienced the shock of non-recognition of the adult: "Surely, this isn't the book I remember." The child remembers the tragedy of the donkey who was swallowed by a boa constrictor, the accomplishment of building a comfortable treehouse and furnishing it with all manner of useful devices, and the adventure of racing ostriches. The adult is confounded by the book's labored piety and moralism.

Despite the difficulties inherent in the socialization process, the Victorian child most probably accepted the role and behavior definitions for the aged which we find in nursery literature. This was so not because the literature was effective by itself but because nursery literature, like all popular arts, tends overwhelmingly to reiterate the traditional ideas, beliefs, attitudes and values which predominate in the general society. That is, the images of aging which a child received from nursery literature were reinforced by all of the popular culture around him.

If we are to better understand the process of aging, we must understand the socio-cultural context within which it occurs, the prescriptions and proscriptions which attempt to channel the individual's actions in socially acceptable directions. We must also work to achieve a better understanding of the relationship between the individual personality and culture. Hopefully, this understanding can be used to make the process of aging a fruitful experience for both the individual and society as a whole.

Notes

[1] The assumptions briefly outlined here about the relationship between cultural values and personality follow the lines of Peter L. Berger and Thomas Luckmann, *The Social Construction of Reality: A Treatise in the Sociology of Knowledge* (New York: Anchor Books, 1966); Alex Inkeles and D. J. Levinson, "National Character: The Study of Modal Personality and Sociocultural Systems," in *Handbook of Social*

Psychology, ed. Gardner Lindzey, 2nd ed. (Reading, Mass: Addison-Wesley, 1969), IV, pp. 418-506; and David Riesman, *The Lonely Crowd* (New Haven: Yale Univ. Press, 1967).

[2] The project entailed six weeks of intensive reading in the children's book and periodical collections in the British Museum Library, the Guildhall Library, the University of London Library, and the Victoria and Albert Museum Library. A research grant from the Bowling Green State University Faculty Research Committee made the research trip possible.

I surveyed over 150 books, chapbooks, and serials. Given the vast resources and the limited time available and the idiosyncrasies of each library's acquisition and cataloging systems, my choice of materials was not systematic. I have tried to include as wide a range of materials as possible: their dates span the entire century, the intended age level of the readers is from earliest childhood to late adolescence, and I have included as many different authors and publishers as possible. Because my survey methods were eclectic and subjective rather than systematic, I have not attempted to quantify the results. Although I included some rhymes and songs of a "frivolous" nature in the material surveyed, my chief criterion for selection was that the work be purposefully didactic—that is, that the intention of the author was to give moral instruction as well as entertainment.

I would like to thank Pamela Ecker for research in Victorian children's songs and games.

[3] "Grandfather," *Little Folks: A Magazine for the Young* (London: Cassell Petter & Galpin), No. 65 (n.d.), p. 207.

[4] Lockyer, *A Child's Influence* (London: Griffith & Farran, 1872), p. 30.

[5] Ibid., p. 58.

[6] "Look to Your Copy," *A Gift for the Young: New Short Stories* (London: Religious Tract Society, c. 1850), p. 4.

[7] Mrs. Sherwood, *Juvenile Forget-Me-Not* (London: Darnton and Clark, ca. 1841).

[8] Lewis Carroll's parody of this poem in *Alice in Wonderland* was most effective because knowledge of the original was so widely shared.

[9] *Alice Gray; or, the Ministrations of a Child* (London: Society for the Promotion of Christian Knowledge, n.d.), pp. 46-47.

[10] Mrs. Sherwood, *The History of the Fairchild Family; or, the Child's Manual* (London: J. Hatchard, 1818), p. 252.

[11] Mary Elliott, *Flowers of Instruction: or, Familiar Subjects in Verse* (London: William Darnton, 1820), p. 42.

[12] Lockyer, *A Child's Influence,* p. 69.

[13] [Elizabeth Turner], *The Daisy; or, Cautionary Stories, in Verse* (London: Griffith and Farran, c. 1849), p. 36.

[14] *A Visit to the Bazaar,* 3rd ed. (London: Harris and Son, 1820), pp. 57-59, 72-74.

[15] *The Ancient Beau* (n.p., ca. 1817).

[16] *A True History of a Little Old Woman Who Found a Penny* (London: Tabart and Co., 1806).

[17] I cannot deal at length with the subject of the older woman, beauty, and sexuality here. The subject is complex and important; I am currently working on such a study.

[18] George Murray Humphry, in his study *Old Age* (Cambridge: MacMillan and Bowes, 1889), reported the results of a survey conducted by the British Medical Association of nearly 900 people eighty years or older. The survey showed that of 337 males surveyed, 40 were affluent, 138 were comfortable, and 159 were poor; of 280 females surveyed, 23 were affluent, 112 were comfortable, and 145 were poor. The

survey was limited to those who were already patients of a member of the B.M.A. Charles Booth, in *The Aged Poor in England and Wales* (London: Macmillan and Co., 1894), showed that in 1891 approximately 30% of the aged population was receiving relief of some kind from the Poor Law Unions (this did not include private philanthropy or the charity of non-public institutions), whereas between 2 and 5% of the total population was receiving relief at the same time.

[19] See, for instance, Sir Thomas Bernard, *Spurinna or The Comforts of Old Age* (London: Longman, Hurst, Rees, Orme and Brown, 1816); C. Walter Forward, *The Art of Longevity: A Guide to Long Life* (London: Nichols & Co., 1889); George MacDonald, *A Book of Strife, In the Form of the Diary of an Old Soul* (London: Unwin Brothers, 1880); Alfred G. Mortimer, *It Ringeth Evensong. Some Thoughts for Advancing Years* (London: Skeffington & Son, 1905); J. M. Neale, *Readings for the Aged,* 4 vols. (London: Joseph Masters, 1850-1858); Emile Souvestre, *Pleasures of Old Age* (London: George Routledge and Sons, 1868); and *To the Aged* (London: Religious Tract Society, ca. 1832).

[20] *Spurinna,* pp. 3-4.

[21] *The Art of Longevity,* p. 8.

[22] *Nursery Rhymes for Children* (n.p., n.d.). Iona and Peter Opie (eds.), *The Oxford Dictionary of Nursery Rhymes* (London: Oxford Univ. Press, 1952), p. 185, gives a variation of this rhyme:

> Wine and cakes for gentlemen,
> Hay and corn for horses,
> A cup of ale for good old wives,
> And kisses for young lasses.

[23] G. F. Northall, *English Folk-Rhymes* (London: Kegan Paul, Trench, Trubner & Co., 1892), p. 316.

[24] "The Village School," *Good Words for the Young,* Dec. 1, 1870, pp. 84-85.

[25] Opie, *Dictionary,* p. 346.

[26] Norman Douglas, *London Street Games* (London: Chatto and Windus, 1931), pp. 29-30.

[27] *Golspie: Contributions to its Folklore* (London: D. Nutt, 1897), p. 56.

[28] Robert Collison, *The Story of Street Literature* (London: J. M. Dent & Sons, 1973), p. 139.

[29] J. W. Elliott, *National Nursery Rhymes and Nursery Songs* (London: Novello, Ewer, and Co., ca. 1870), p. 35.

[30] Elliott, *Flowers of Instruction,* pp. 11-12.

[31] *Good-bye to All That,* 2nd ed. (New York: Doubleday and Co., 1957), p. 30.

[32] See, for instance, Erik H. Erikson, "Reflections on Dr. Borg's Life Cycle," *Daedalus,* 105, No. 2 (Spring 1976), 1-28, and Kenneth Kenniston, "Psychological Development and Historical Change," in *Explorations in Psychohistory: The Wellfleet Papers,* ed. Robert Jay Lifton (New York: Harper, 1974), pp. 149-64.

[33] Erikson, "Reflections on Dr. Borg's Life Cycle," p. 23.

[34] Serialized in *Good Words for the Young* (London: Strahan & Co., 1871).

[35] In *Later Tales, Published During 1867 & 1868* (London: Bell & D., 1868).

[36] See, for instance, Ravenna Helson, "Through the Pages of Children's Books," *Psychology Today* (Nov. 1973), 107-17.

[37] Mac Donald, *Good Words for the Young,* 1 Feb. 1871, p. 189.

[38] Ibid., 1 March 1871, p. 285.

[39] Andersen, "Aunty," *Later Tales,* p. 84.

[40] Andersen, "The Toad," *Later Tales,* pp. 8-17.

[41] See, for instance, Peter Fletcher, *The Long Sunday* (London: Faber and Faber, 1958) and Edmund Gosse, *Father and Son: A Study of Two Temperaments* (New York: Oxford Univ. Press, 1907).

[42] Juliet M. Soskice, *Chapters from Childhood: Reminiscences of an Artist's Granddaughter* (London: Selwyn & Blount, 1921), pp. 8-9.

Geri Berg
Sally Gadow

TOWARD MORE HUMAN MEANINGS OF AGING: IDEALS AND IMAGES FROM PHILOSOPHY AND ART

Introduction

Aging has always been a problematic experience. We may believe, at times, that our century is unique in viewing aging as problematic, but the same ambiguity that surrounds aging now was known to our predecessors: "When death approaches . . . old age is no burden." The tacit implication is that old age is indeed a burden, made lighter only by contemplation of some alternative. To the young, aging is no better than death, while to the old, aging may be life itself, as precious and irreplaceable as youth to the young.

This ambiguity permeates all of our thinking about aging. We are not sure whether it is a phase of living that is both healthy and normal, or unhealthy but still normal, or whether it is unhealthy and abnormal. Is it a stage of life or simply the earliest stage of dying? Is being old worth one's whole life to attain? Shall we revere it, prevent it or cure it? Are we to anticipate growing old with hope, dread, or indifference?

We often approach a difficult problem by trying to understand two things about it. We ask: (1) What is it? How shall we define it? (2) What is its value? Usually, we assume that modern science should answer the first, the humanities the second (science being value-free and the humanities value-oriented). But in fact, because aging is a profoundly human experience and not a purely natural phenomenon, like trees losing their leaves, its definition and its value are inseparable. We cannot answer the question of what aging is without at the same time addressing the question of what value and significance it has for us.

Indeed, the sciences themselves reflect this inseparability. In their account of the "facts" about aging, the physiological, psychological, and socioeconomic sciences offer us their definitions. The physical sciences suggest

that aging is thus far an irreversible, physiological deterioration, a disorganization and disintegration characterized by predictable deleterious changes from total body movement to the level of cells and molecules. The behavioral sciences describe aging as a set of processes resulting in failing mentation, confusion, memory loss, and disorientation. Furthermore, the social sciences inform us that aging is characterized by decreased economic productivity; by social isolation due to non-employment, dying peers, and the exclusively nuclear family; and often, by total dependence upon others. These are the so-called "facts" about aging, and value-free as they are supposed to be, they offer us not a neutral view but an altogether negative one. This "definition" presents an interpretation which not only implies what aging *is,* but also what *significance* it has, and that significance is negative. Medical science, in turn, expresses and applies this negative valuation by treating aging as a disease. All that is missing from the clinical model is a clear cause and a cure (and theoretically both can still be discovered).

What this indicates to anyone not already persuaded, is that we cannot define a human experience with facts alone. We invariably interpret and evaluate the facts in some way. Cellular changes, for example, are not described simply as specific chemical and structural transformations, but as "deterioration." It is thus more honest and useful to acknowledge that we are never talking about the facts as distinct from the value of aging, but are always formulating a view of the two together. In other words, we are not, even in science, expressing a final *definition* of aging, but rather, some tentative *meanings* of aging.

If one such meaning is that which science and medicine offer, what reason is there to seek further meanings from the humanities? The reason is this: the humanities are concerned not only with understanding as fully as possible the depth and scope of human experience—this, they share with the sciences. Beyond this, they are concerned with creating or uncovering more human meanings for our experience. Thus the humanities are ultimately engaged in formulating ideals. By "ideal" or "more human meaning" is meant a way of understanding an experience which enhances the value of the experience for the individual, and at the same time preserves the element of freedom in human existence by opening a door to new possibilities. It might be phrased this way: wherever a locked door presents itself in our experience, a closure which means "here is the limiting concept, feeling, insight, beyond which there is no further understanding of this phenomenon," there, the task of the humanities is to provide a key, either one long forgotten in history, or one newly created for just that door.

The negative meaning of aging is such a door. Insofar as it limits our understanding of aging to the notion of decline, without leaving open the possibility of alternatives, that meaning is not as human as we would wish. It is not yet ideal. Perhaps it is one facet of a larger understanding, but in itself, sheer decline or disintegration is not a sufficiently human meaning of aging.

Our intention is to explore some meanings that are more expressive of the fact that aging is a *human* experience—not simply a physiological-

psychosociocultural-economic experience. And in effect, since we are concerned here with finding meanings alternative to the negative interpretation from science, we are concerned with uncovering or generating positive meanings.

By positive, however, is not meant aging-with-a-happy-ending, or aging that is itself a happy ending. For example, one popular candidate for a positive meaning of aging is the view that one's later years can be rendered as nearly "normal" as possible. Aging is a time in which, barring a few extra maladies, nothing changes. One continues to work, to be active, independent, maintaining the same scope and intensity of social and professional involvement. This positive value of aging is more accurately a neutralization of the negative value, achieved by means of omitting, ignoring, or bypassing aging. It amounts to a false positive, because it assumes that the only way of making aging human is to make it as nearly like youth or mid-life as possible.

From these two views—the negative and the false positive—we can learn something about what a genuinely positive meaning of aging would be. These views are limiting because the one hopelessly overvalues, the other undervalues, the realities of aging: that the body moves slowly, that the senses alter, that some structures grow rigid while others become flaccid, that the skin folds back upon itself, that the memory winds around and restructures itself, that some capacities disappear, and that somewhere dying begins. For the negative view, these spell the doom of aging (or the disease called aging). For the stay-young view, they are excluded from aging.

In searching for more human meanings, then, we can begin by neither devaluing nor ignoring the reality of these processes, but only by accepting them as ciphers, symbols, keys to possible meanings. The meanings that we will propose here are one attempt to interpret these ciphers as possible answers to the question that the humanities alone can answer: Where does aging fit in an ideal scheme of things? What is the value of aging in an ideal human existence?

I. Processes of Aging as Symbols of Meaning

Slowing down—opening time. The slowing process in aging is one of its most dominant symbols or, in clinical terms, "symptoms." How can that phenomenon be understood in such a way that it illuminates in more human terms the experience of aging?

It may be that aging is the part of our lives in which our being slows on all levels, in order to experience situations and persons with more attentiveness and care than is possible when a youthful, fast-paced metabolism and an energetic, vigorous body inspire us to cover great distances at high speed, to finish quickly with one experience in order to hasten on to the next. It may be that with age we realize time has the dimension of depth as well as duration. For most of us, these two dimensions seem to be an either/or, and it is only when the aspect of duration is seen not to be endless that we fully recognize the

aspect of depth or density of time. We slow ourselves then to explore experiences, not in their linear pattern of succeeding one another, but in their possibility of opening for us entire worlds in each situation and each person encountered. We slow ourselves to be more gentle with these experiences, to take care to let their possibilities, their rich density emerge. We continue moving through time, but we also move into time, allowing it to expand in depth for us though its objective duration diminishes.

Wrinkling—articulation. One of the processes of aging that we recognize most easily is the alteration of smooth surfaces and straight lines: skin wrinkles and roughens; posture becomes curved; memory is restructured; formerly unbroken stretches of clarity are marked by peaks and between them hollows called "confusion." What positive human meaning could such phenomena suggest?

It is as though, through these changes, body and mind express the greater intricacies, the finer articulations that are possible in the person for whom reality has become many-layered, folded upon itself, woven and richly textured, a reality no longer ordered in the more familiar linear fashion, but now a world filled with leaps, windings, countless crossings, immeasurably more intricate and perhaps also more true than the world of one-dimensional thought and self-evident distinctions.

Becoming rigid and flaccid—defining the self. Another process of aging—important because it alters both appearance and movement—is revealed in the phenomenon in which certain parts of the body become rigid and fixed, while others become soft and flaccid. If we think of the skeleton as defining the body's essential form, and soft tissue as being inessential to structure per se, then we see that the final firming occurs in the structurally essential parts, while the tissue that grows flaccid is the structurally inessential. The skeleton settles into a final, rigid form, firm in places where previously mobile, while muscles, for example, grow soft and irrelevant.

Is the body expressing something which we might understand as symbolic for the experience of the person as a whole in aging? Perhaps the hardening is a final structuring, a settling on what one's character and essence are to be, once and for all; and the softening, a dropping away of what one decides is not to be incorporated into the essential structure, the completed character. This does not mean that aging is not a time of growth. It is a growing clearer and more decided about the essence, the form, that one wants one's existence to have, a growing firmer in those features that will be the defining shape of the person.

Relating to one's death. It seems that amid all of the changes and indicators of aging that we see, somewhere death is foreseen. One more meaning of aging thus may be the individual's recognition, conscious or not, that life is finite. The sum of all of the changes in aging perhaps indicates a tacit, organic knowledge that death is a reality.

A fatal syndrome has been observed in vigorous, previously healthy persons when told they had cancer; overnight, they became apathetic and withdrawn and within a matter of weeks died, without any satisfactory explanation for

PLATE 1

Dorothea Lange "Ex-Slave with a Long Memory, Alabama, 1938" Dorothea Lange Collection, The Oakland Museum, California

The authors and editors acknowledge with gratitude the generosity of the Dorothea Lange Collection, The Oakland Museum, for permitting the reproduction of this work.

PLATE 2

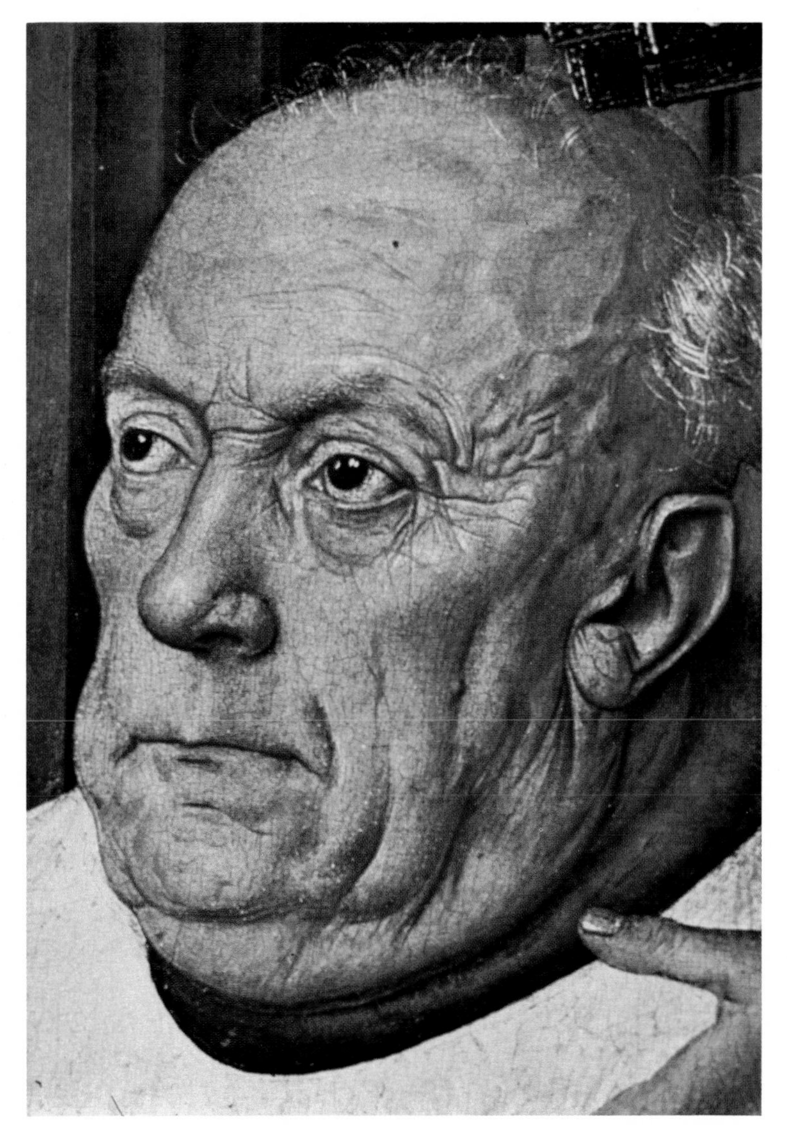

Jan van Eyck "Madonna of Canon George van der Paele" (detail) 1436
Stedelijk Museum voor Schone Kunsten: Groeningemuseum, Bruges, Belgium.

The authors and editors acknowledge with gratitude the generosity of the Stedelijk Museum voor Schone Kunsten, Groeningemuseum, Bruges, Belgium, for permitting the reproduction of this work.

PLATE 3

Rogier van der Weyden "The Descent from the Cross" c.1435, Museo del Prado, Madrid, Spain.

The authors and editors acknowledge with gratitude the generosity of the Museo del Prado, Madrid, Spain, for permitting the reproduction of this work.

PLATE 4

Rogier van der Weyden "Christ on the Cross; Virgin and St. John" 1455-59
Johnson Collection, Philadelphia Museum of Art, Pennsylvania.

The authors and editors acknowledge with gratitude the generosity of the Philadelphia Museum of Art, Pennsylvania, for permitting the reproduction of this work: (J 334/335).

PLATE 5

Paul Cézanne "Mt. Sainte-Victoire" 1885-7
Courtauld Institute Galleries, London, England.

The authors and editors acknowledge with gratitute the generosity of the Courtauld Institute Galleries, London, for permitting the reproduction of this work.

PLATE 6

Paul Cézanne "Mt. Sainte-Victoire" 1906
The Tate Gallery, London, England.

The authors and editors acknowledge with gratitude the generosity of The Tate Gallery, London, England, for permitting the reproduction of this work.

PLATE 7

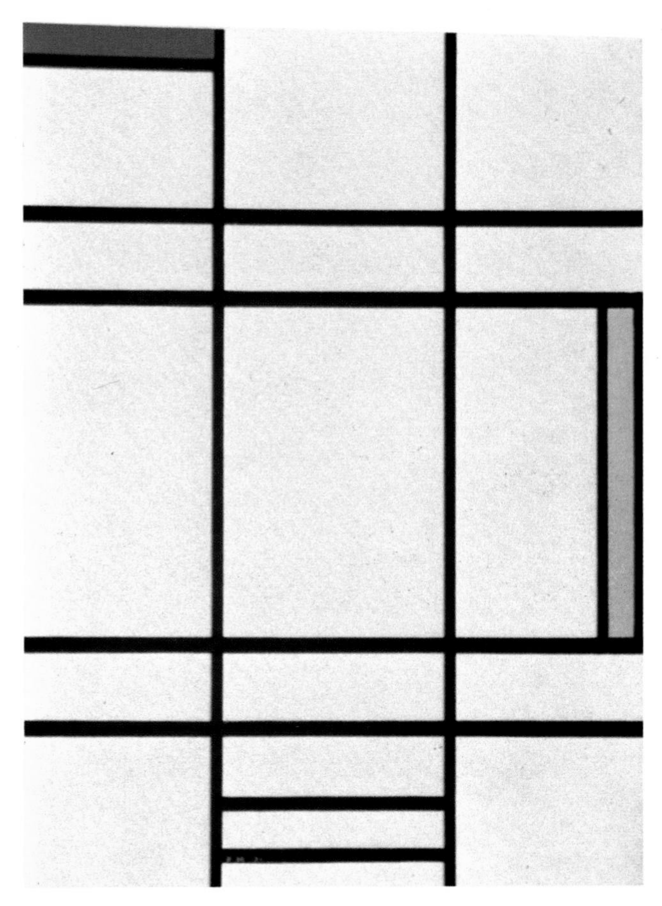

Piet Mondrian "Composition in White and Yellow" 1938
Los Angeles County Museum of Art, California.

The authors and editors acknowledge with gratitude the generosity of the Los Angeles County Museum of Art, California, for permitting the reproduction of this work.

PLATE 8

Piet Mondrian "Farmhouse with Peasant Woman in the Snow: Winterswijk," c. 1898-99, from a private collection, Toronto.

death upon autopsy. It may be that aging is the less dramatic form of this self-willed death. We are not suddenly told that we have cancer, but we are told from the beginning that we are mortal, that we will die. Moreover, we need not hear this from the geriatrician, gerontologist, or the philosopher. We need not hear it at all because we tacitly know it with our body and spirit if not our intellect. The patients described above died when told they had a deadly disease. Perhaps aging is the way in which we begin taking account of death when we know, at least implicitly, that life itself, like a fatal illness, is something from which we will die. If one consciously attends to the body's foresight, aging can be used as an opportunity to personally, freely decide what significance the coming death will have for the life that remains. And it is just that freedom, finally, which is the essence of aging as a human value.

II. Images of Aging

The meanings suggested thus far represent philosophical ideals, alternatives to the unquestioned reality of aging and its assumed negative meaning. But if an ideal is to be more than speculative abstraction, it must derive its strength from the real, as well as finally return there to bear its fruit. For the development of more ideal or human conceptions of aging, one reality in which the proposed ideals are sustained is the artist's view of aging. Some of the strongest examples of aging as a positive human experience can be found in the arts, in statements both about and by the old. Artists, particularly the young, have long been involved in presenting us with outstanding portraits of the old. More recently the camera has been used to aid our eye in noticing and reflecting on the aged among us, as in Dorothea Lange's remarkable portraits of the elderly, for example "Ex-Slave with a Long Memory" (Plate 1) from the 1930's.

Often the old are poignantly contrasted with the very young, as in Domenico Ghirlandaio's portrait "An Old Man and His Grandson" (Paris, Louvre), dating from the late fifteenth century. Too often, we focus on the old man's medical condition (he apparently suffers from rhinophyma) and thus overlook the more human meaning of the love and tenderness portrayed between a child and his grandfather. Rembrandt, too, has juxtaposed the old and the young in several of his paintings, such as in his numerous versions of the "Presentation in the Temple" in which the aged Simeon gently holds the small Christ Child for God's blessing.

Sometimes the elderly are caricatured in both cruel and humorous ways, as in Quentin Massys' "The Ugly Duchess" (London, National Gallery) from the sixteenth century or in "Sketches of Old Men" (Windsor Library) from Leonardo's notebooks of the late fifteenth century. But many outstanding images of the old are to be found in the midst of crowded historical, narrative, or devotional pictures, such as the official portrait of an important man of the Church, the Canon George van der Peale, from a detail of a larger painting, "Madonna of the Canon van der Peale" (Bruges), by the fifteenth-century

Flemish artist Jan van Eyck. A closer view of this painting (Plate 2) reveals a portrait of an old man whose face is wrinkled and flaccid, the infinite details of which speak more about age than privileged position. This portrait, too, has not escaped an impoverished clinical focus through an interesting, if not irrelevant, article by a dermatologist on the "senile degeneration" which he sees here.[1]

III. Personal Statements on Aging

When we turn to the work of artists in the later years of their lives, we find the facts and experiences of aging expressed in a variety of personal statements. Some of their works challenge our conceptions (or misconceptions) of growing old. Is aging, as Rembrandt shows us in his late "Self-Portrait" of 1661 (Amsterdam, Rijksmuseum), a time of quiet introspection and stillness? Or is it still a time of vitality and sexual prowess, as Picasso, age ninety, portrays in "Artist and Prone Woman" (1971) or "Woman and Cavalier" (1968)? Furthermore, must it be an either/or situation? Or are the artists presenting here a purposeful ambiguity? Are the late works of Picasso examples of the false positive view of aging as being as nearly "normal" as possible? Or is Picasso, by offering an exception to our stereotypical notions of sexuality in old age, reminding us that everyone is an exception and that to understand human experience for personal or clinical purposes is to understand its uniqueness as well as its universality?

Let us consider another pair of paintings. Which is the more authentic picture of the old—the firm, austere old ladies, guardians of the poor, whom the eighty-year-old, poverty-stricken Frans Hals portrayed in his "Women Directors of the Haarlem Alms House" (1664, Haarlem, Hals Museum), or the portrait of his wife, "Helene Fourment" (1638/40, Vienna, Kunsthistorisches Museum) which Rubens painted in the last two years of his life? The latter portrait of wrinkled flesh and less than classical beauty, of surprising shyness and modesty, is a private, loving painting and a rare exception to the woman-as-object theme predominant in the history of female nudes in Western Art. Are they not both possible or probable, even in the same person?

IV. Early and Late Works

Turning to a series of early and late works, we can document perhaps better than in any other way the growth—that is, the aging—of the artists selected. We see that for most of them growing old is an enriching, deepening experience; it is distinctly not degenerative or even "business as usual," that is, trying to remain young or "nearly normal." It is a time of slowing down, of rejecting the physical, material world as ideal, of turning in, distilling experiences for their essences, of becoming clearer or in some cases less certain

of knowing it all, and, finally, of determining the personal significance of death.

In the "Descent from the Cross" (ca. 1435, Madrid, Prado), the young fifteenth-century Flemish artist Rogier van der Weyden presents us with a dramatic narrative of an important event in Christian history (Plate 3). Mary Magdalen on the right and St. John on the left form parentheses on either side of this crowded, stage-like scene which has been described by one art historian as "dignity . . . preserved amidst a flow of tears."[2] The bodies of Christ and His Mother parallel each other in form and juxtapose the fainted living with the dead. The entire composition is enlivened by rhythmic curves which flow between and through the figures, binding them together. In contrast, Rogier presents in his later years a distillation of this narrative (Plate 4). In the "Calvary Diptych" (Philadelphia Museum of Art, Johnson Collection), the crowd is gone; only the three essential persons remain. The stillness and icon-like quality of this large painting are reinforced by the broad expanse of grey walls hung with brilliant red cloths against a background of gold. The figures of John and Mary are monumental in their grief; Mary assumes a posture expressive more of worship than collapse. The dramatic, unfolding, rhythmic narrative of the early Rogier is replaced with a still, devotional image confronting us, questioning our assumptions about life and death and affirming those of the artist.

No discussion of art and aging would be complete without considering the great series of self-portraits produced by the artist Rembrandt who, with the exception of one decade, documented almost every year and phase of his life from youth to old age. Rembrandt painted, etched, and drew nearly one hundred self-portraits; they comprise almost ten percent of all of his work. Though he produced an average of two self-portraits a year, there was virtually no market for them. These, then, are the most personal of statements of an artist's life, made essentially for himself. They move from the jauntiness, vitality and even arrogance of youth and early adulthood, to the quiet, introspective and intensely spiritual experiences of old age, concluding with a portrait ("Self-Portrait," ca. 1668, Cologne, Wallraf-Richartz Museum) that seems to unify all of these qualities in a final, definitive expression.

The next comparison—between the early and late work of Michelangelo—is so striking as to almost speak for itself. This difference is dramatically revealed in two "Pietas": one now in Rome, sculpted by the twenty-two year old artist, the other in Milan, which Michelangelo completed in the year he died, nearly ninety. In the early sculpture we sense that it is life, not death, and above all physical beauty, which is being celebrated. Michelangelo's virtuosity in carving marble has rendered the bodies of the Virgin and Christ silky, even sensuous. In contrast, the late "Pieta" rejects the youthful beauty of the early work; the bodies are rough, hacked and hewn from the stone. The boundaries of the bodies of Mother and Son are indistinguishable. The child, now an adult, emerges once again from the body of His Mother; only the faces

are distinct. A work of profound spiritual intensity, the sculpture recalls one of Michelangelo's late sonnets:

> Youth, in its greenness, cannot know, O Lord,
> How taste and love and longing change like weather,
> And how man's thoughts, ah, fear the final step.
> The soul gains more, the more it quits the world;
> My art and death do not go well together:
> What shall I do? From me what do you hope?[3]

We need not, however, turn only to representations of the human figure to disclose attitudes toward the process of aging. We can learn, for example, about the perceptions of the nineteenth-century painter Cézanne by examining his treatment of Mt. Sainte-Victoire, the mountain in southern France near Aix-en-Provence which reappears as an important motif in his painting.

He painted several versions of the mountain, one when he was in his early twenties (Plate 5, "Mt. St. Victoire," 1885-7, London, Courtauld Institute) and another dating from the year he died in his late sixties (Plate 6, "Mt. St. Victoire," 1906, London, Tate Gallery). Cézanne was drawn to the mountain as a symbol of both energy and repose and identified with it "as the ancients with a holy mountain."[4] He always insisted that his art was grounded in nature and that he painted what he saw, but what he *saw* kept changing, and to translate his perceptions into art was a lifetime struggle. In his youth, Cézanne saw the mountain as a monumental contemplative image, solid and eternal. We know of his pausing before each brushstroke, sometimes for hours, to make sure it was just right, painstakingly building the layers of the mountain as if repeating the natural process of weather, rock, and time. The "Mt. Sainte-Victoire" of his old age, however, is at once more free and less certain. The medium of watercolor used in the late painting carries and enhances the less compact, almost tenuous vision of the mountain as symbol of freedom, of lyrical dynamism—but not of eternity.

We see the same kind of change in two portraits by Cézanne. The subject in "Man in a Blue Cap" ("Uncle Dominique," 1865-6, New York, Metropolitan Museum of Art) has been painted in solid, bold form, filling the canvas and brought close to the viewer with a powerful, almost vehement insistence. "The Gardener" (1906, London, Tate Gallery), from the last year of Cézanne's life, presents another vision: the subject moves away from us and is lost in his own thought. The boundaries between body and environment are purposely ambiguous and blurred. The power of the early portrait lies in its brute physical presence, the later in its quiet, reflective inner strength.

Many of us recognize the work of the Dutch artist Mondrian, who died in 1944 in New York City at the age of seventy-two, by his rectilinear grids filled with squares of primary colors (Plate 7) but some will be startled by a glimpse of his early work in Holland, such as the 1898-9 "Farmhouse with Peasant Woman in the Snow" (Plate 8, Toronto). Mondrian's later writing provides a vital link between his art and his philosophy: "Our way leads towards a search

for the equivalence of life's unequal oppositions. Because it is free of all utilitarian limitations . . . art must move not only parallel with human progress but must advance ahead of it. It is the task of art to express a clear vision of reality."[5] Mondrian's vision of reality, his desperate hope for the future, was that all persons would live in universal harmony. He believed that art, architecture, and eventually city planning would provide a model and supportive environment for this way of life. He insisted that "art, although an end in itself, is like religion, a means by which the universal may be revealed."[6] Thus Mondrian's literary vision, like his art, espoused both ascetic and communal ideals; his dedication to both was unrelenting. In his old age, he observed: "What a beautiful task lies in prospect before art: to prepare the future."[7]

In concluding, let us turn briefly to the work of three twentieth-century American painters, all of whom worked throughout their lives in predominately abstract modes. Georgia O'Keefe's painting, although seemingly abstract, is almost always based on objects in nature. Only the focus changes. In mid-life she painted "Black Iris" (1926, New York, Metropolitan Museum of Art), a microcosm of nature, with the flower large, oversized, sensuous, sexual. At seventy-three, her vision and her art turn outward to vast panoramas of sky and cloud trails, serene and limitless.

Mark Rothko, on the other hand, alters basically only the hue and luminescence of his work from mid-life to old age. His paintings bathe the viewer in intense color, moving beyond the canvas boundaries and into the observer's space with warm, soft light. Near the time of Rothko's death by suicide, the palette of his paintings turns dark with somber greys, blacks, and maroons. Yet, ironically, several of these late, dark paintings were designed for a chapel, traditionally a sanctuary for meditation, a place where one might find peace in life or death.[8] Rothko writes that "the progression of a painter's work as it travels in time . . . will be towards clarity, towards the elimination of all obstacles between the painter and the idea and between the idea and the observer."[9] He found the solitary human figure too limiting, a symbol of human incommunicability: "I do not believe that there was ever a question of being abstract or representational. It is really a matter of ending this silence and solitude, of breathing and stretching one's arms again."[10]

Barnett Newman has been quoted after his sudden heart attack at age fifty-two saying, "A heart attack is like instant psychoanalysis."[11] When he resumed painting, he quickly moved beyond his biomorphic canvases of mid-life with their visceral, mystical, life-like forms and created in his old age heroic, monumental paintings which raise color to its highest power. These paintings, completed two or three years before Newman's death, must be experienced in space as well as time. They are not simply vistas; they command the space around them with all the certainty of Cézanne's mountain, affirming the old age of life as clear, strong, and reassuringly solid.

It is this conviction about what growing older means in human terms that Newman shares with other artists across many centuries—aging as an essentially clarifying human experience, at once both simple and direct, as well as infinitely complex and rich.

Conclusion

Through the combined approaches of art and philosophy, images and ideals, it is possible to weave a fabric of meanings which aging appears to manifest, if we remain open to human alternatives other than the definition of aging as deterioration. The metaphor of a fabric suggests itself because none of the meanings presented here, either the philosophical or the aesthetic, is sufficient in itself to unify an entire human experience. But together, interwoven and mutually reinforcing, they form a fabric sufficient to encompass that experience; we are provided with a fabric as variously textured as aging itself, for some of the threads of meaning are strong and palpable, while others are elusive and fragile. Thus it is necessary to weave a dialectic between the fragile abstraction of ideals and the more concrete immediacy of images in order to encompass the complex possibilities of an experience as profound and universal as aging.

That dialectic illuminates for aging the possibility that one of its positive meanings is its advance beyond a simple and unambiguous reality to one rich both in opacity and in finely articulated dimensions. Part of that richness of aging is its non-linear temporality, the fullness of its moments when an experience is slowed to the stillness of a painting and allowed to reveal its internal meaning irrespective of the external sequence in which it exists. Finally, the unity of ideal and image that seems to thread its way throughout the fabric of aging expresses the individual's possibility for determining final forms—both of the self and the world. In this light, the process of aging is a clarifying, a fixing, of the essential character that an individual's self and life-world are to have. That freedom to decide about one's ultimate character and to slow oneself to a temporality more intricate than serial time, is the basis for creating any images of the ideality of aging.

Notes

[1]Erwin Panofsky, *Early Netherlandish Painting* (Cambridge: Harvard Univ. Press, 1966), I, 183, n. 3.

[2] Ibid., p. 258.

[3] Joseph Tusiani, ed., *The Complete Poems of Michelangelo* (New York: The Noonday Press, 1960), p. 151, poem no. 145.

[4] Meyer Schapiro, *Cézanne* (New York: Abrahms, 1965), p. 74.

[5] Hans Jaffe, *Piet Mondrian* (London: Thames and Hudson, 1970), p. 59.

[6] Ibid., p. 54.

[7] Ibid., p. 59.

[8] Rothko Chapel, Houston, Texas.

[9] *Fifteen Americans* (New York: Museum of Modern Art, Exhibition Catalogue, 1952), p. 18.

[10] Mark Rothko, "The Romantics Were Prompted," *Possibilities,* No. 1 (Winter, 1947-48), p. 84.

[11]Thomas B. Hess, *Barnett Newman* (New York: The Museum of Modern Art, 1971), p. 18.

II. DEMENTIA, COMPETENCY AND SENESCENT MEDITATION

Barbara G. Rosenkrantz
Maris A. Vinovskis

THE INVISIBLE LUNATICS: OLD AGE AND INSANITY IN MID-NINETEENTH-CENTURY MASSACHUSETTS[1]

A Congressional Special Committee on Aging opened hearings on Mental Health and the Elderly in September 1975 with a grim reminder of injustices and abuses in the past:

> For years, thousands of individuals have languished in U.S. mental institutions, the victims of involuntary commitment proceedings. Our citizens, especially the elderly, could be placed in such institutions with comparative ease. Generally, all that was involved was the affidavit of a family member and that of a physician. Once housed in an institution, the constitutional rights under the 5th, 8th, 13th and 14th amendments evaporated. Generally, no treatment was forthcoming, and release was out of the question.[2]

Senator Frank E. Moss went on to warn that although recent Supreme Court decisions offered a measure of protection against commitment without due process and long-term hospitalization without therapeutic goals, the vulnerability of the aged left them at special risk as "the present trend to dump mental patients out of State hospitals into boarding-homes" does not assure better care of the aged nor resolution of society's responsibilities.

Dependency is presumably the ambiguous condition that led to institutional arrangements which were once viewed with favor but are condemned today. Most analyses of the origins and nature of dependency associated with the aged mentally ill are customarily placed in an historical context that focuses on the practices and the institutions designated to mitigate that dependency. Usually an implicit assumption is made that dependency has been exacerbated by the increasingly impersonal character of urban life and the growing dissociation of family ties and tenderness. There is a general sense that the contemporary

abuse of the elderly occurs in part because society is more fragmented and less supportive. Contemporary policy analysts often resort to discussions of the past to account for our ambivalence toward the elderly insane. On the one hand, they refer to the past to document persistent institutional custody that violated the rights and needs of aged mental patients. On the other hand, they imply that these invidious practices arose as attitudes towards the elderly deteriorated.

Unfortunately, references to the past are not always accurate or complete. Senator Moss asserts that "mental institutions are historically poor therapeutic environments." This conclusion leads him to raise a series of critical questions which he assumes had been ignored in the past. He asks:

> With respect to the aged, what is the difference between senility and mental illness or are these simply meaningless labels? Where should individuals with these problems be housed? What kinds of services should they be provided? What can be done to insure the release of all patients unnecessarily committed to State mental hospitals? What precautions can be taken to insure that appropriate discharges are made and that therapeutic and recreational services are provided?[3]

This paper will attempt to assess the accuracy of Senator Moss's initial estimate of the therapeutic role of earlier institutions using the very same questions asked by him, for these were indeed the questions asked by the public and the superintendents of institutions for the insane more than a century ago.

Conventional wisdom has its place among the tools of the historian as well as of legislators when it accentuates the distance between reality and aspiration. The place of the aged in our society and the special consequences of the aging process have seldom been the focus of systematic study by historians. Yet attitudes toward the aged are frequently alluded to; this is reflected, for example, in the assumed shift of veneration of the elderly to rejection. This essay will explore the experiences of one particular segment of the aged population at a specific period and place—the elderly insane in mid-nineteenth-century Massachusetts. Though the percentage of the elderly who were judged insane was never very large, their problems do illustrate the difficulties associated with aging in a society which was even then oriented towards the young and vigorous. We will examine the attitudes and responses of both the general public and the physician toward the elderly insane with special emphasis on the problem of discriminating between aberrant and normal behavior.

First, using several different sources of statistical information, we will assess the incidence of insanity identified among the elderly and the likelihood of their being committed to an asylum if found insane. Then we will focus on the reactions of the superintendents of these institutions to the elderly insane using their annual reports to the trustees, the patient casebooks, and contemporary scientific literature. Although this paper should be regarded only as a tentative exploration of old age and insanity, it will hopefully document the risk of insanity associated with age during the first half of the nineteenth century, analyze the function of asylums as indicative of the ambiguous status of insanity

associated with old age, and trace the relationship between medical theory and social expectation in mediating the dependent status of the aged insane.

I. The Incidence of Mental Illness Among the Elderly and the Likelihood of their Institutionalization in Massachusetts in 1854

It is difficult to analyze the extent and nature of insanity among the general population in nineteenth-century America due to the lack of adequate statistical information. Most of the data on the insane was collected by the superintendents of the insane asylums who assembled extensive descriptive statistics on the characteristics of the patients under their care. Though federal and state censuses tried to provide information on insanity among the general population, the number of insane were under-registered.[4]

Fortunately, there was an unusually comprehensive survey of insanity among the general population of Massachusetts in 1854. In an effort to determine the need for constructing a third state hospital for the insane, the Massachusetts legislature in 1854 commissioned a survey of the extent of insanity and of the capacity and efficacy of existing facilities. The survey was conducted by Edward Jarvis, a prominent physician and scholar who already had considerable experience in analyzing the extent of insanity from the federal census returns.[5]

Jarvis argued that previous efforts to survey the number of insane were hopelessly flawed because the federal census marshalls were negligent in collecting the information on insanity and the families interviewed were often reluctant to admit that a member of their household was insane. Rather than relying on incompetent interviewers such as the federal census marshalls or trusting to the self-reporting of insanity by households, Jarvis enlisted the help of local physicians, superintendents of public and private hospitals, keepers of jails and houses of correction, and some clergymen and town selectmen to identify every insane individual in Massachusetts in 1854 by name, nativity, age, means of support, place of residence or confinement, degree of insanity, and prognosis for the future. Altogether, over 1400 individuals co-operated with Jarvis in providing information on the insane by responding to his questionnaire. After Jarvis checked the names of the insane to eliminate duplicate returns, he found that there were 2632 insane persons in Massachusetts in the autumn of 1854.

The Jarvis survey indicates the extent of insanity perceived by selected contemporaries in mid-nineteenth-century Massachusetts. It is an unusually comprehensive effort by relatively knowledgable and concerned individuals to describe the insane population. By re-analyzing the results from the Jarvis survey in conjunction with the characteristics of the Massachusetts population from the state census of 1855, we are able to ascertain the incidence of perceived mental illness among the elderly as well as the likelihood of their commitment to a public or private institution designed specifically for the therapeutic regimen that was widely supported by both physicians and education laymen.[6]

The elderly insane were not perceived by either the public or the physicians as

a major problem or concern in ante-bellum America. For example, there is very little discussion of old age and insanity in the published and unpublished writings of doctors or in the reports of the hospital and asylum superintendents who contributed most of the analyses of insanity in the pre-Civil War period. In terms of the patients in their asylums, the elderly constituted only a very small percentage of the inmates. In the Massachusetts state hospitals at Worcester and Taunton, in the private hospitals at McLean, Pepperell, and Dorchester, and in the municipal hospital at Boston in 1854, only 9.8 percent of the insane were sixty years old and above (see chart number one). In addition, only 3.1 percent of the insane in those institutions were seventy years old and above. At least two other factors associated with these statistics diminished the concern with the characteristics of old age as an influence on insanity. First, as will be shown later in greater detail, patients under seventy years old were not perceived as markedly different from younger persons in the hospital population. Second, those over seventy years old were admitted in substantially worse physical health than other patients, and therefore often were discharged or died soon after admission.

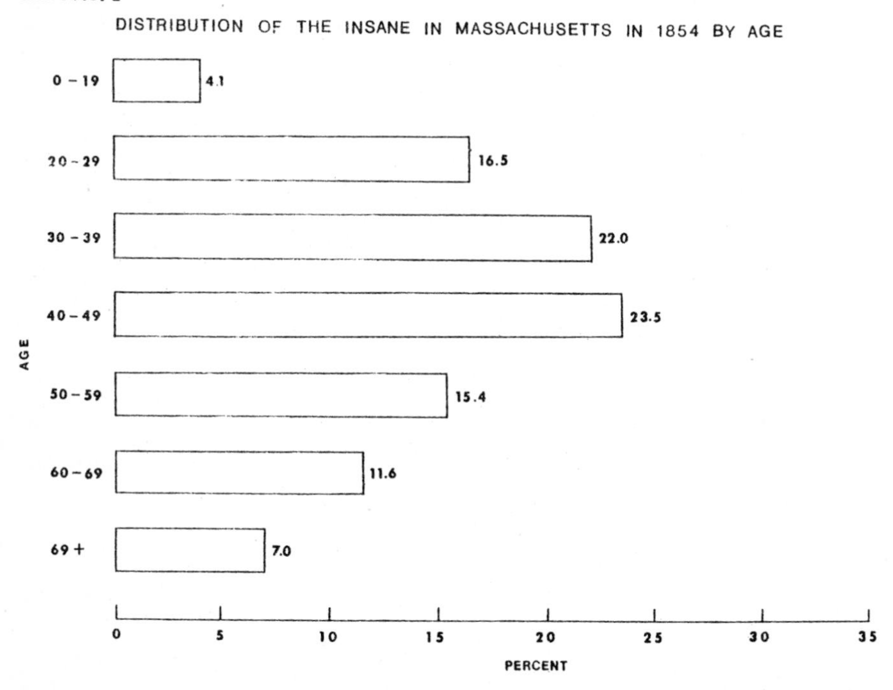

The figures on the percentage of elderly insane in asylums do not provide an accurate picture of the extent of elderly among the insane in the general population in ante-bellum America. Though the elderly insane made up only 9.8 percent of the inmates in Massachusetts asylums in 1854, they comprised 18.6 percent of the insane among the general population in that year (see chart number two). In other words, the extent of the elderly among all of the insane

was nearly twice as large as in the hospitals. Thus, nearly one out of every five insane persons in Massachusetts was over sixty years old.

Chart No. 2

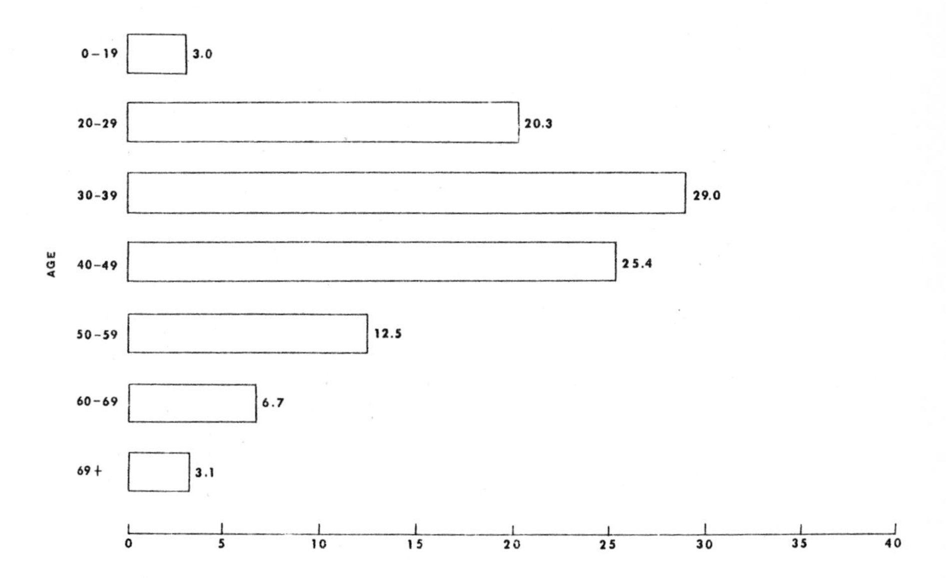

Though the elderly insane did not constitute a large proportion of the elderly population at that time (less than one percent of persons over sixty were insane), they accounted for a sizable proportion of the insane. Most nineteenth-century commentators missed the significance of this fact because they only had access to the age-distribution of insane persons in the asylums. Though Jarvis had laboriously collected data on the ages of the insane, he never published any tables on the age-distribution of the insane population in Massachusetts in 1854. As a result, nineteenth-century analysts failed to recognize the importance of the size of the elderly population among the insane.

Not only did contemporary observers miss the importance of the number of elderly among the insane, they were also unaware of the rates of insanity among the various age-groups of the population. By using information on the age-distribution of insanity from the Jarvis survey and the age-distribution of the population from the state census of 1855, it is possible to calculate the number of insane persons in Massachusetts in 1854 per 100,000 population.

Most nineteenth-century physicians and asylum superintendents focused their attention on the causes and the cure of insanity among young adults in their twenties and thirties. Very little attention was paid to the particular problems and needs of the elderly insane. Yet the results of our calculations of the rates of insanity by age-groups are quite startling—the highest proportions

of insane in Massachusetts were among the elderly (see chart number three). Thus, the extent of insanity among the elderly was two to three times as great as that among individuals in their twenties and thirties—a fact which was not recognized by either nineteenth-century physicians or twentieth-century scholars.

Chart No. 3
NUMBER OF INSANE IN MASSACHUSETTS IN 1854 PER 100,000 POPULATION

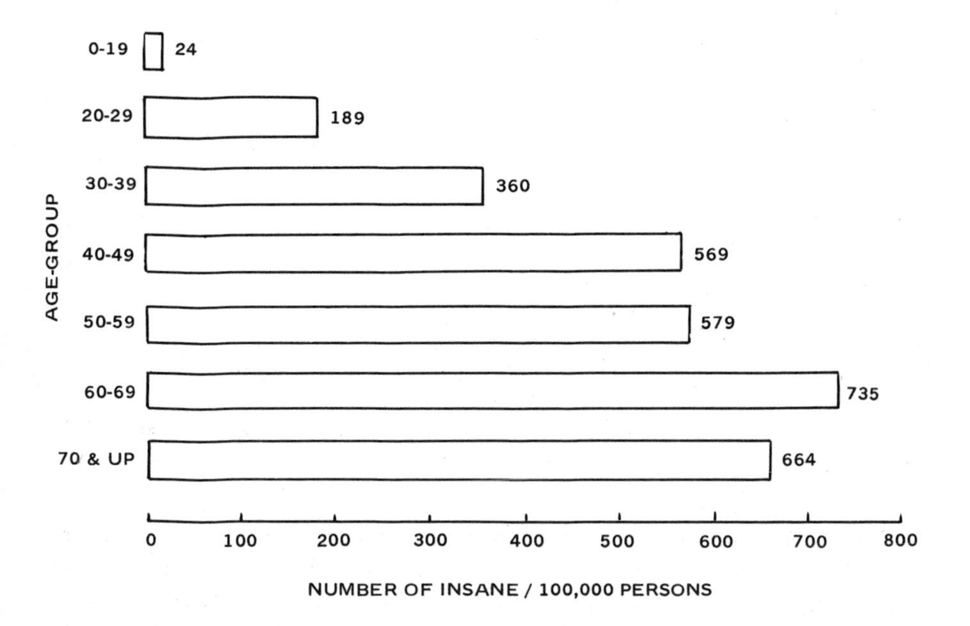

So far we have suggested that nineteenth-century observers underestimated the extent of elderly among the insane as well as the relative proportion of insanity among the aged. Though both of these observations may demonstrate a lack of awareness on the part of nineteenth-century Americans to the elderly, they do not necessarily imply that the elderly insane were forgotten or neglected. Therefore, we now shift our attention to the question of the treatment of the elderly insane in order to see if there was any discrimination against them compared to the treatment of the rest of the insane population in the state.

There was a general agreement among physicians, superintendents, and the public in ante-bellum America that insanity could best be cured in an institutional setting under the careful supervision of a doctor. The decades of the 1830's, 1840's, and even 1850's were a period of great optimism in regard to curing insanity. Most physicians felt that if insane individuals were placed in an asylum within the first year of their attack, chances of recovery were excellent. Cure rates of eighty, ninety, and even one hundred percent for recently admitted patients were commonly cited in the published annual reports of the

superintendents of the asylums. Though these early recovery rates were to be strongly challenged by critics after the Civil War, they were widely circulated and influenced many decision-makers in the earlier period. Consequently, one crude index of the amount of effort expended to treat the insane in the decades prior to the Civil War is the likelihood of their being institutionalized—particularly in one of the recently established asylums such as the Worcester State Hospital or the McLean Asylum.[7]

The Jarvis survey of insanity in Massachusetts in 1854 provides information on the percentage of the insane who were institutionalized (see chart number four). Individuals in their twenties and their thirties were the ones most apt to be institutionalized (67.1 percent and 72.3 percent respectively). The elderly insane were the least likely to be in an institution—only 36.0 percent of those in their sixties were institutionalized and 28.7 percent of those ages seventy and above were in an institution. Thus, in a period of time when the institutionalization of the insane meant better treatment and the possibility of a cure, the elderly were in effect denied equal access to those opportunities.

Chart No. 4
PERCENTAGE OF INSANE IN MASSACHUSETTS@ IN 1854 WHO ARE INSTITUTIONALIZED

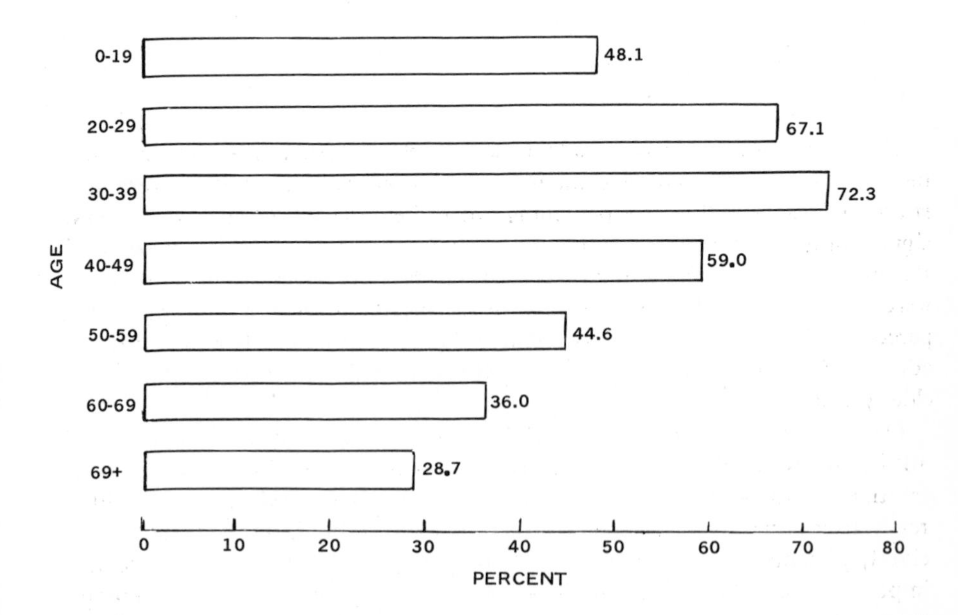

Not only were the elderly less likely to be institutionalized than the rest of the insane population, but those elderly who were institutionalized were more apt to be found in a local jail, state almshouse, or county receptacle where the treatment of the insane was markedly different and judged inferior to that provided in such asylums as Worcester, Taunton, and McLean (see chart

number five). While over eighty percent of the institutionalized insane in their twenties, thirties, forties, and fifties were in the asylums, only about seven percent of the institutionalized elderly insane were in a similar setting.

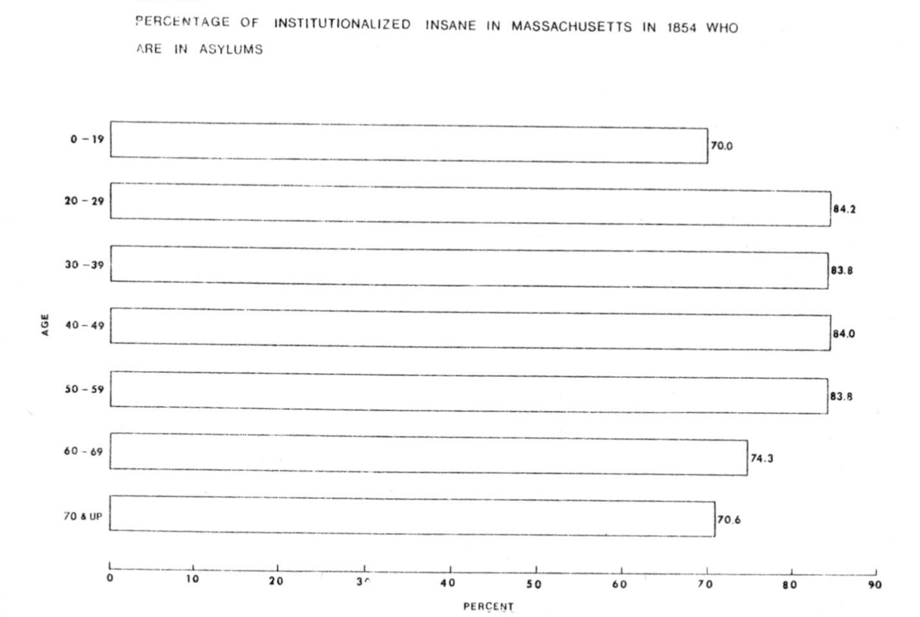

The net result of the processes by which the elderly insane were less likely to be institutionalized and less likely to be in an asylum if they were institutionalized was that the percentage of the elderly insane in asylums was significantly less than those of the other age-groups. While only 26.7 percent of the insane in their sixties and 20.2 percent of the insane ages seventy and above were in asylums in 1854, 56.5 percent of the insane in their twenties and 60.5 percent of those in their thirties were in asylums. In other words, young, insane adults were two to three times more likely to be treated in the asylums than their elderly counterparts.

Our discussion of the institutionalization of the insane in Massachusetts in 1854 strongly suggests that the elderly insane did not receive equal access to treatment in the asylums. But was the relative denial of access to these facilities really discrimination based on age rather than some other factor associated with elderly patients? For example, nineteenth-century medical theory stressed the importance of treating individuals who have recently become insane. Perhaps most of the elderly insane were only denied treatment in the asylums because they had already been insane for such a long time that their physicians and family saw little value in sending them to an asylum for treatment.

In order to test for the possibility that factors other than age were the main determinants of the lack of access of the elderly insane to the asylums, we computerized the personal characteristics of the institutionalized and non-

institutionalized insane from the Jarvis questionnaires. Using multiple classification analysis to predict whether an insane person was in an asylum or not, we included their marital status, age, sex, place of birth, county of residence, duration of present insanity, whether curable or not, and their present and usual condition as the independent variables. The results of our multiple classification analysis show that even after controlling for the effects of the other variables, the elderly were still less likely to be in an asylum than young and middle-aged adults. Thus, nineteenth-century Americans not only ignored the extent of elderly among the insane, but they also denied those elderly insane equal access to treatment.[8]

II. Elderly Patients at McLean and Worcester State Hospital

In the previous section we analyzed the data on insanity in Massachusetts collected by Jarvis for the single year of 1854. We will now focus on the care of the elderly patients over several decades in two of the major Massachusetts asylums—McLean (1818-1860) and Worcester (1833-1861). Using the general registers for patients in each of these hospitals, we assembled information on over 11,000 cases for these years. These data permit us to compare the care that the elderly insane received in a private institution such as McLean and in a state hospital such as Worcester.[9]

The elderly insane were never a very large proportion of the admissions to either Mclean or Worcester during the ante-bellum period (see graph number one). Overall, the proportion of admissions to McLean Asylum who were sixty years old and above during the period 1818-1860 was 8.3 percent and 8.2 percent at Worcester State Hospital for the years 1833-1861.

GRAPH No. 1
PROPORTION OF ADMISSIONS TO ASYLUMS WHO ARE SIXTY YEARS OLD AND ABOVE, 1818-1860

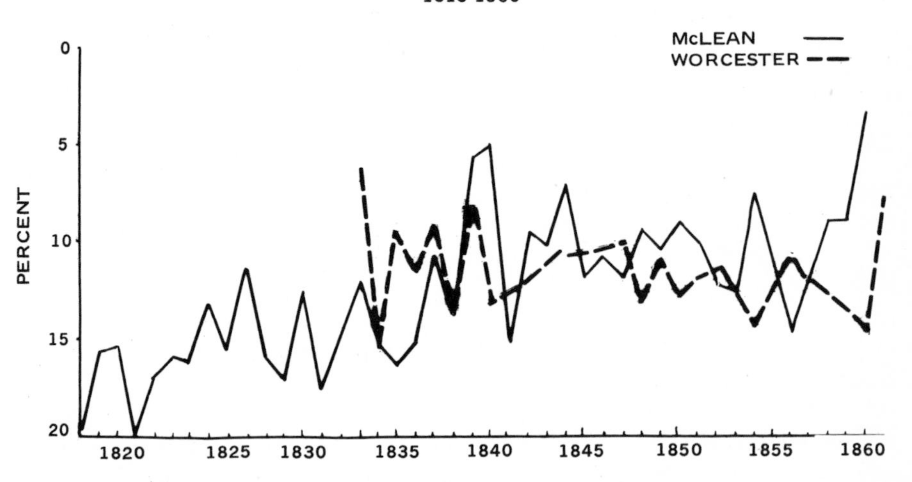

The percentage of elderly patients admitted to McLean and Worcester was generally quite similar for the period 1833-1860, though there are some interesting differences. For example, McLean experienced an unusually high proportion of elderly admissions in the late 1830's which prompted the new superintendent of that asylum to declare that the admission of elderly patients henceforth would be discouraged. What is also interesting is that there was no major increase in the proportion of elderly patients admitted to either McLean or Worcester during the late 1840's and 1850's although the superintendents of those asylums, as we shall discuss later, increasingly began to express doubts in their annual reports about the wisdom of admitting elderly insane to their institutions.

One might properly object that our analysis of the proportion of patients sixty years old and above admitted to these institutions is not a very good indicator of the problems encountered by the superintendents. The proportion of elderly patients in the asylums at any given time could have been considerably higher than suggested by the number of elderly patients admitted since patients who entered in their forties and fifties may have remained there long enough to become part of the elderly population. Therefore, we calculated the proportion of elderly patients sixty years old and above or seventy years old and above in each of the hospitals on December 31st, and compared them with the same figures based on the patients admitted during that past year (see graph numbers two and three).

GRAPH No. 2

PROPORTION OF ELDERLY PATIENTS AT McLEAN ASYLUM, 1818-1860

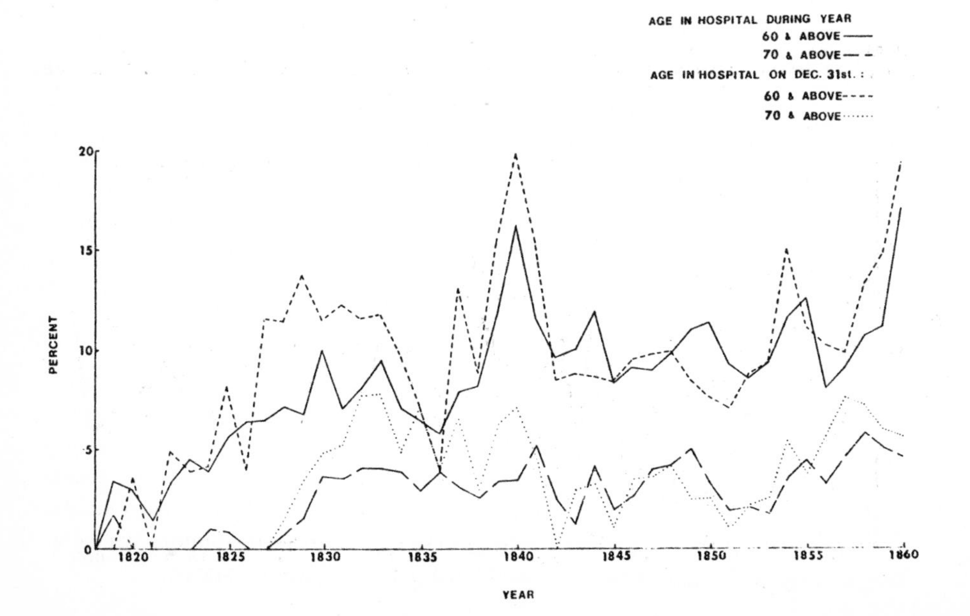

Graph No. 3

PROPORTION OF ELDERLY PATIENTS AT WORCESTER STATE HOSPITAL (1833-1860)

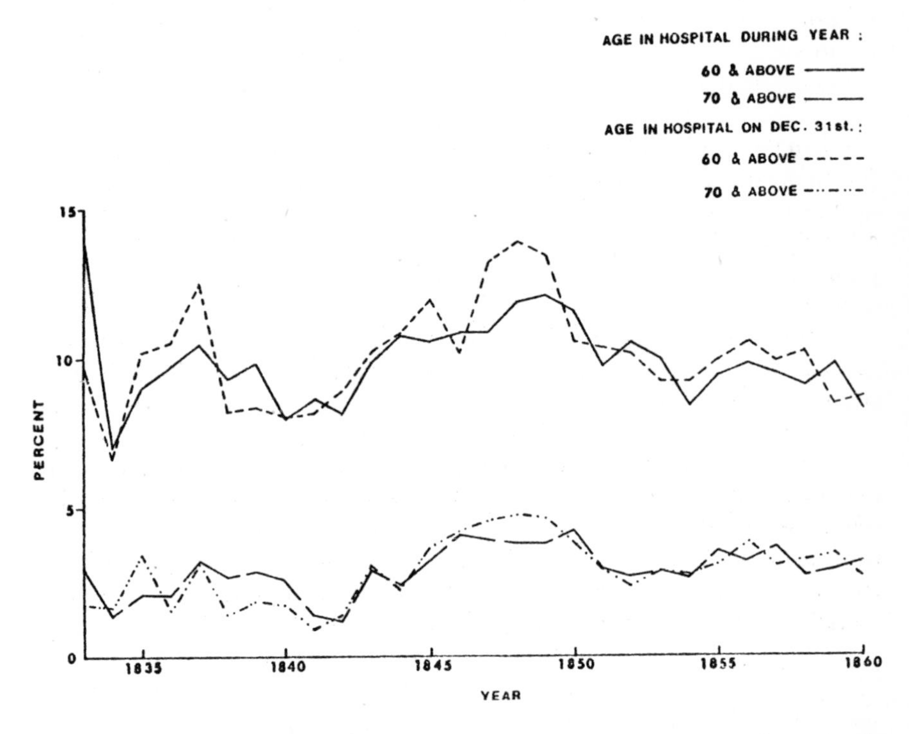

At both McLean and Worcester, the percentage of elderly patients in the hospitals on December 31st was generally larger than the percentage of elderly patients among the admissions during the past year—although the difference usually was never more than a few percentage points. Furthermore, the same pattern we found in our analysis of the age at admission persists; during the 1840's and 1850's there was not a significant rise in the proportion of elderly patients in these asylums. Though there was an increase in the proportion of elderly patients at McLean at the end of the ante-bellum period, there was a decrease in the proportion of elderly patients at Worcester during that same period. Thus, the complaints of the superintendents of those asylums against the admission of elderly patients were not simply the result of a sizable increase in the proportion of elderly patients in their institutions.

The manner in which patients were committed to an asylum varied, but they can be summarized under three broad categories—commitment by the state or the courts, by the local towns, or by family or friends. From the very earliest days, it was assumed under English common law that the state or its courts could commit individuals who were considered insane and dangerous to the community. Thus, in "an act for suppressing rogues, vagabonds, common beggars, and other idle, disorderly and lewd persons," the law stated:

> That when it shall be made to appear to any two Justices *quorum unus*, that any person being within their county is lunatic, and so furiously mad as to render it dangerous to the peace and safety of the good people for such lunatic person to go at large; the said Justices shall have full power, by warrant under their hands and seals, to commit such person to the house of correction, there to be detained till he or she be restored to his right mind, or otherwise delivered by due course of law.[10]

When the Worcester State Hospital was built in 1833, the law was altered to permit the justices to commit "any lunatic, who, in their opinion, is so furiously mad as to render it manifestly dangerous to the peace and safety of the community" to the newly created institution. Furthermore, the legislature stipulated that town paupers could also be sent to the new hospital "for a sum, in no case exceeding the actual expense incurred in their support."[11]

Finally, it was common practice for the friends and the family of insane persons to send them to a private or public asylum during the ante-bellum period. A major limitation on this practice for many families was the considerable expense that was involved in sending someone to an asylum.

We have information on the committment procedures for about 92 percent of the cases at McLean and Worcester. Of these, 45.4 percent of the patients were committed by the state or courts, 7.0 percent by the local towns, and 47.6 percent by their friends and family. Among the elderly insane, the proportion committed by each of these three groups is somewhat different than that for the overall patient population (see chart number six).

CHART No. 6

DISTRIBUTION OF PERSONS AND AGENCIES WHO COMMITTED ELDERLY PATIENTS TO McLEAN (1818-1860) AND WORCESTER (1833-1861)

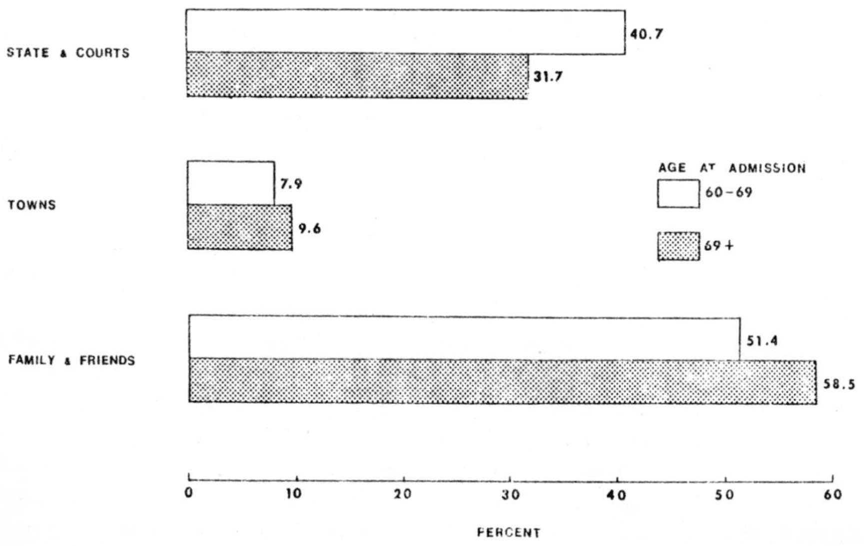

STATE & COURTS
40.7
31.7
TOWNS
7.9
9.6
FAMILY & FRIENDS
51.4
58.5
AGE AT ADMISSION
60-69
69 +
0 10 20 30 40 50 60
PERCENT

While the state and courts were less likely to commit elderly patients to these asylums than younger patients, family and friends were more apt to commit the elderly insane, a practice which frustrated the superintendents who were trying to reduce the number of elderly insane in their asylums in the 1850's and 1860's. These superintendents admonished the families of elderly insane to care for their relatives at home rather than sending them to an asylum.

The pattern of committment at McLean and Worcester was quite different. At McLean, only 2.6 percent of the patients ages 60-69 were committed by the state or courts, .4 percent by the local towns, and 97.0 percent by family and friends (the comparable figures for patients ages seventy and up are 4.6 percent, 0 percent, and 95.4 percent). At Worcester, the state or courts committed 64.0 percent of the patients ages 60-69, the local towns committed 12.5 percent, and family and friends committed only 23.5 percent (the comparable figures for patients ages seventy and up are 48.3 percent, 15.4 percent, and 36.4 percent).

The difference in the pattern of committment between McLean and Worcester is not surprising since the former was a private asylum while the latter was a public one. Though McLean had accepted a slightly larger portion of insane individuals sent by the state, courts, or the local towns in the period before Worcester was built, it was not a very large proportion even at that time. Thus, the development of a state facility for the insane at Worcester in the 1830's provided the state with a better alternative for dealing with the "furious" elderly insane than sending them to one of the county almshouses or jails.

Most physicians in the 1830's, 1840's, and even 1850's were confident that most cases of insanity could be cured if treated within the first year: the longer an insane person went without proper treatment, the less the chances of their recovery. Thus, in *The Report of the Commission on Lunacy,* Jarvis observed that:

> Although three-quarters to nine-tenths may be healed if taken within a year after the first manifestation of the disorder, yet if this measure be delayed another year, and the diseases are from one to two years' standing, the cures would probably be less than half of that proportion, even with the same restorative means. Another and a third year added to the disease diminishes the prospect of cure, and in a still greater ratio than the second; and a fourth still more. The fifth reduces it so low as to seem to be nothing. . . . After this period, insanity is usually deemed to be incurable.[12]

We have information on the duration of the present attack of insanity for the elderly patients prior to their admission to McLean and Worcester (see chart number seven). Of the patients ages 60-69, 68.1 percent were admitted within a year of their attack of insanity; of patients ages seventy and above, 52.2 percent were admitted within a year of their attack of insanity.

Though a majority of the elderly admitted to these asylums received treatment within a year of their attack of insanity, a substantial proportion was only admitted after most physicians had given up hope of recovery since the patients

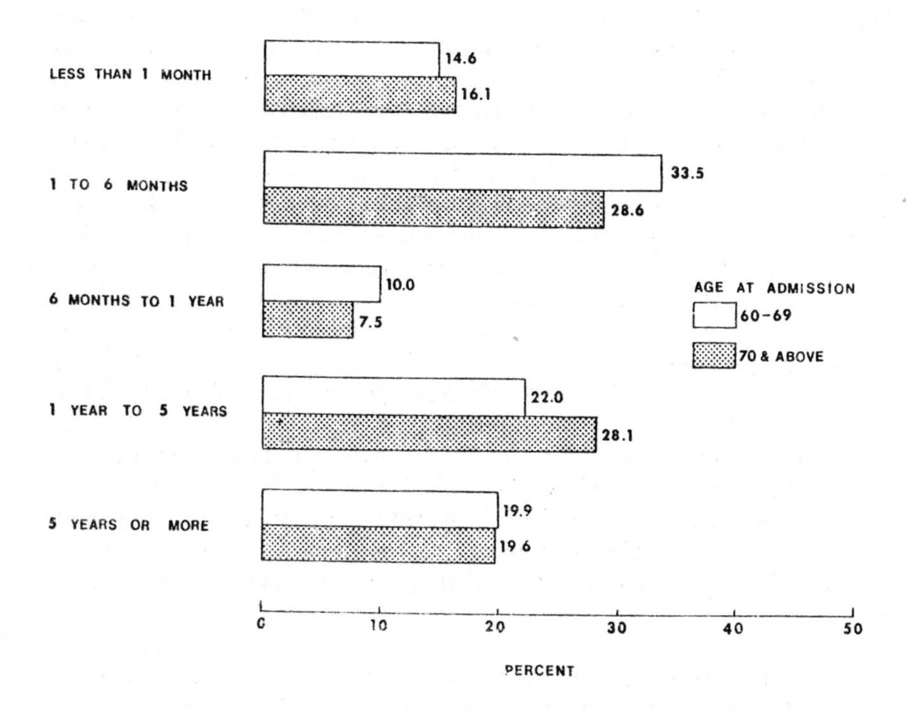

had been insane for many years. Nearly one-fifth of the elderly patients (ages 60-69 and seventy and above) admitted to McLean and Worcester had already been insane for five or more years.

Elderly patients were admitted to McLean sooner after their attack of insanity than those to Worcester. Of the patients ages 60-69, 68.2 percent were admitted within a year of their attack of insanity while only 54.0 percent of that age-group were admitted to Worcester within their first year of insanity (the comparable figures for patients ages seventy and above are 55.9 percent for McLean and 50.7 percent for Worcester).

Compared to other age-groups, the elderly insane were admitted to McLean and Worcester at a somewhat later stage of their insanity. For example, among admitted patients ages 40-49 or 50-59, the proportions entering after five or more years of being insane were 16.6 percent and 16.2 percent respectively—several percentage points lower than for their elderly counterparts.

The data on the duration of the attack of insanity of elderly patients admitted to McLean and Worcester should have been encouraging to the superintendents

since most of the patients found their way to the hospitals within a year of their illness. Furthermore, though elderly patients admitted to these asylums were likely to have had their attack of insanity for a longer period of time than other patients, that difference was not very large—especially when we compare the elderly patients to those admitted in their forties and fifties.

Information is available on who committed the elderly patients to McLean and Worcester, but data are not available on what was the precipitating event that led to their committment. We do not know whether elderly patients were sent to these asylums in order to cure them or to prevent them from injuring or inconveniencing their family or other members of the community. We do have some information on the supposed cause of insanity (data on the supposed

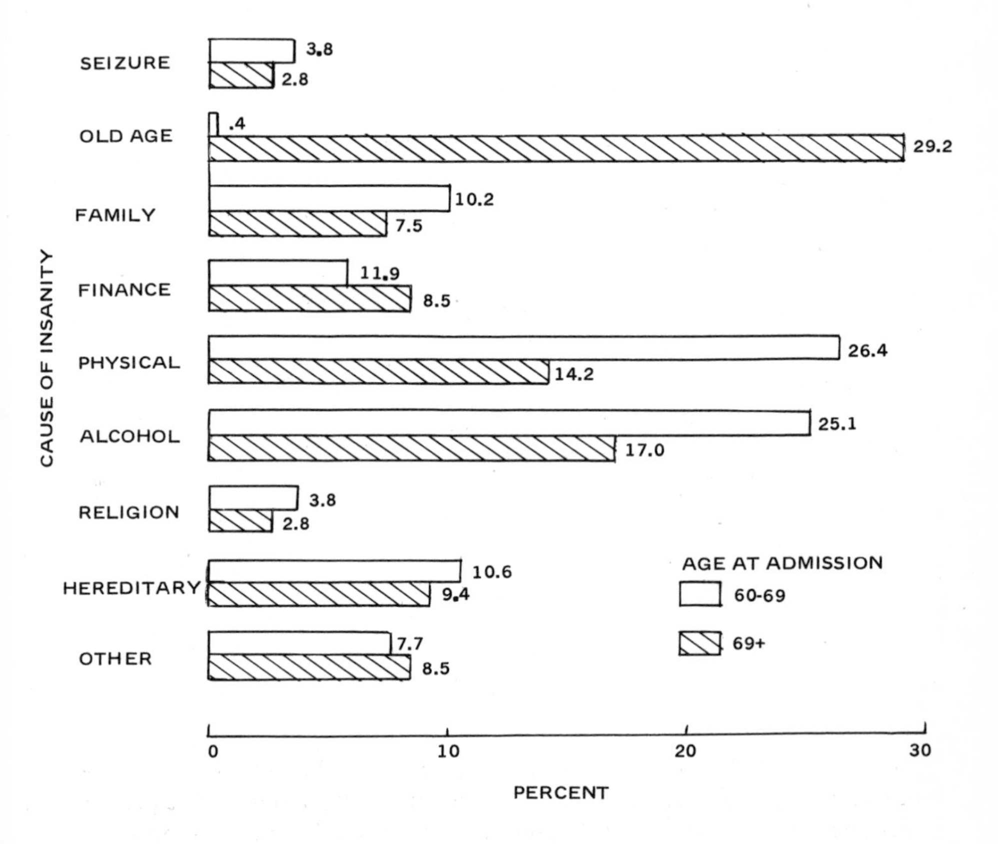

cause of insanity are available for 63.9 percent of the total admissions to McLean and Worcester). This is not necessarily the reason for their being committed since many of the elderly patients had been insane for a considerable

period of time before being sent to either McLean or Worcester. But the supposed cause of insanity does provide information on the diagnosis of insanity among the elderly in ante-bellum Massachusetts.

We separated the supposed cause of insanity of elderly patients in McLean and Worcester by sex since there were some major differences between males and females. Among elderly male patients ages 60-69 admitted to these asylums, alcohol and physical causes were the most common diagnoses of their insanity (see chart number eight). Almost none of these elderly males were insane because of old age. Among the elderly males ages seventy and above, alcohol and physical causes are still important, but they are over-shadowed by old age. Nearly thirty percent of these elderly males were adjudged insane because of old age.

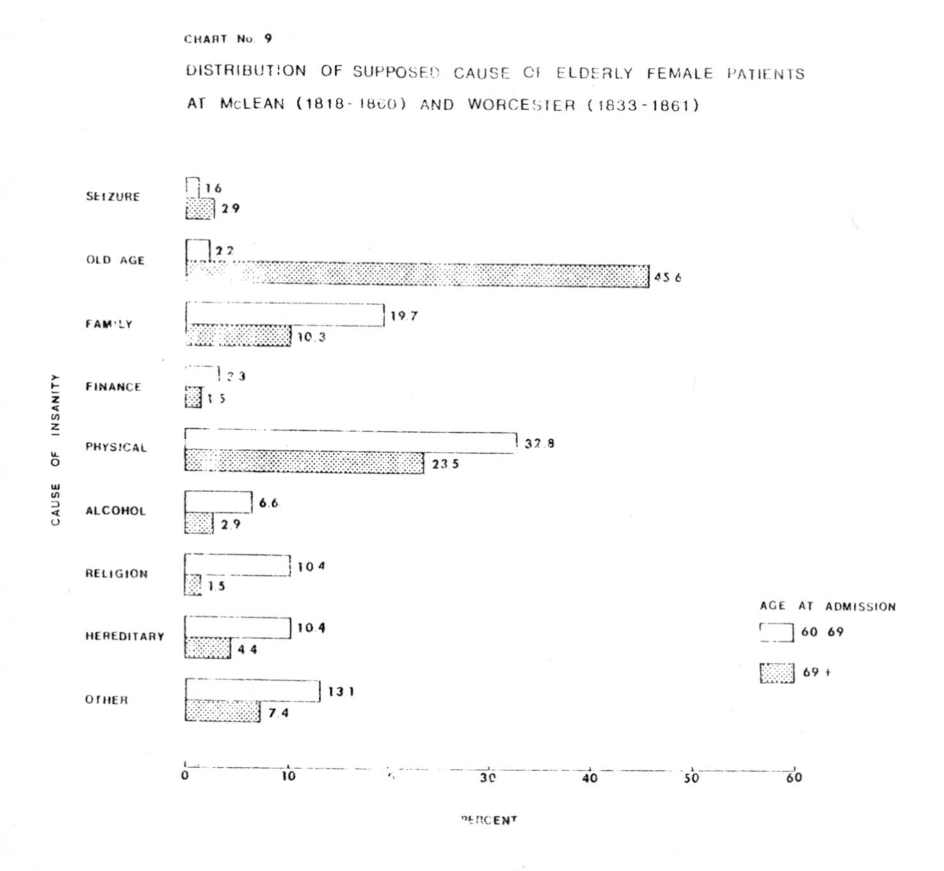

Among the elderly female patients ages 60-69, physical causes of insanity are much more important than among males (see chart number nine). The greater importance of physical causes of insanity among women than men was also true at the younger ages. The next most important category of cause of insanity for these elderly female patients is family problems—again nearly twice as important for females than for males. While nearly one-fourth of the elderly males

ages 60-69 were insane due to the use of alcohol, only 6.6 percent of elderly females were insane because of intemperance. Among elderly females ages seventy and up, physical and family problems were still important causes of insanity, but old age was even more important. Nearly fifty percent of the insanity of these elderly women were diagnosed as being caused by old age—a much higher proportion than for their male counterparts.

It is interesting to observe that it is very rare for anyone ages 60-69 to have old age listed as the cause of their insanity. Yet among elderly patients ages seventy and above, old age was the most frequently cited cause of insanity. It is difficult to ascertain trends in the use of old age as a cause of insanity for elderly patients prior to 1830 since we do not have many cases of elderly patients with such information. However, there is an increase in the use of old age as the diagnosis of insanity of elderly patients ages seventy and above in the following three decades (25.9 percent in the 1830's, 28.4 percent in the 1840's, and 40.6 percent in the 1850's). Thus, the elderly patients, male and female, admitted to McLean and Worcester were increasingly seen as suffering from the ill effects of old age.

We do not have much information on the socio-economic background of the elderly patients admitted to McLean and Worcester. The general patient

CHART No. 10

DISTRIBUTION OF OCCUPATION OF ELDERLY MALE PATIENTS ADMITTED TO McLEAN (1818-1860) AND WORCESTER (1833-1861)

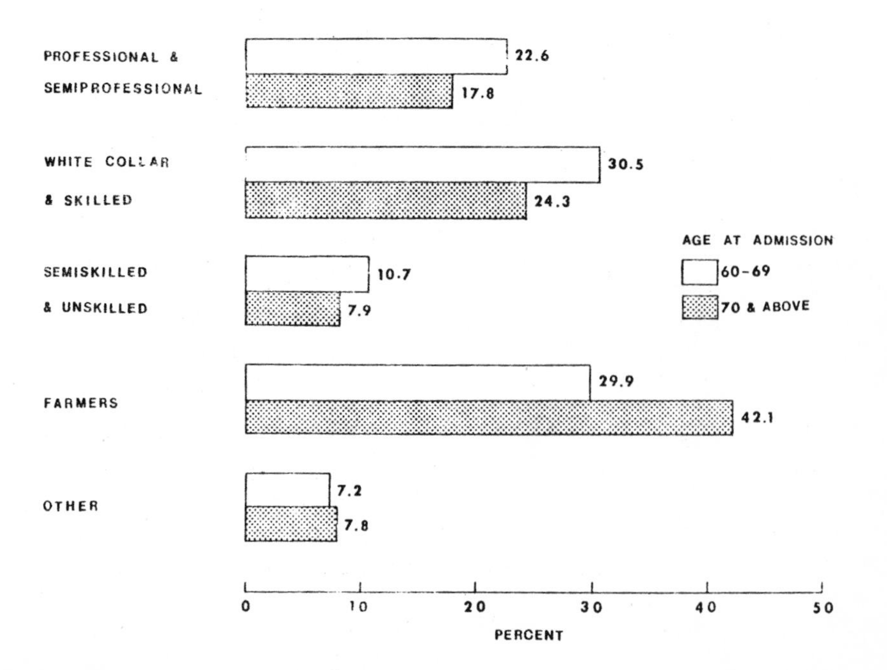

registers did record the occupation of the patients. Though this information is not particularly useful for female patients, since so many of them are listed simply as housewives or housekeepers, the data are more interesting for males because most of them had some specific occupation mentioned (overall, data on occupations were available for 94.8 percent of the males admitted to McLean and Worcester).

The occupations of the elderly male patients were categorized into professionals and semiprofessionals, white collar and skilled, semiskilled and unskilled, farmers, and others (see chart number ten).[13] Most elderly male patients ages 60-69 who were admitted to McLean and Worcester were either white collar and skilled workers or farmers. Among elderly male patients ages seventy and above, about four out of ten were farmers.

The occupations of elderly males at McLean were generally of higher status than that of those admitted to Worcester. For example, among males ages 60-69, 34.9 percent were either professionals or semiprofessionals at McLean while only 13.6 percent of their counterparts at Worcester were professionals or semiprofessionals. On the other hand, while 35.9 percent of the males ages 60-69 were farmers at Worcester, only 21.9 percent were farmers at McLean. The

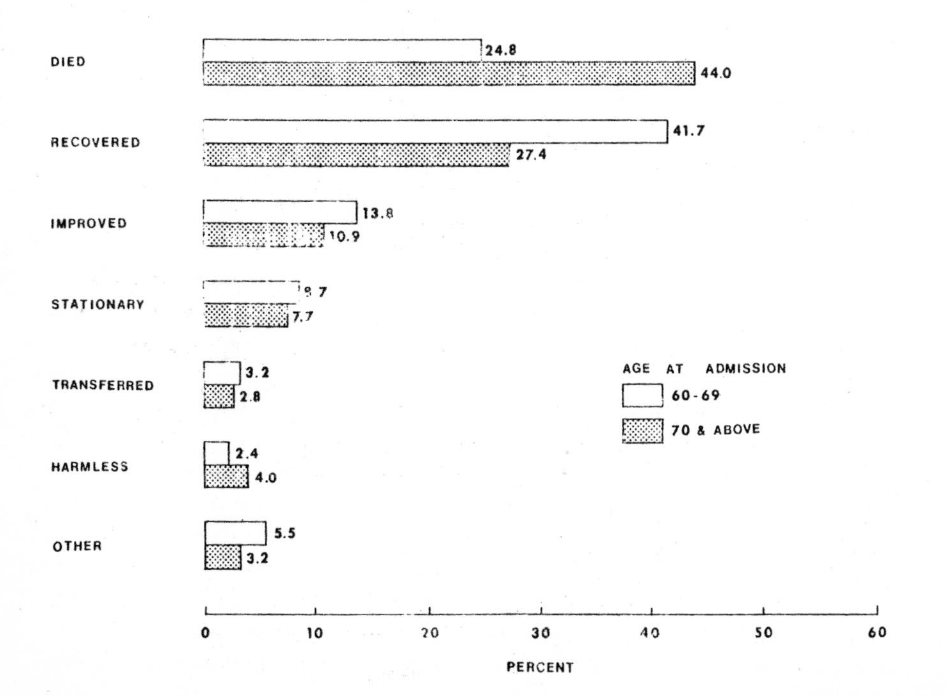

difference in the proportion of farmers at the two hospitals is even greater for male patients ages seventy and above; at McLean, 27.4 percent of them were farmers while at Worcester, 53.8 percent were farmers. These findings are not surprising since most elderly males at McLean were private patients whose family or friends had to be affluent enough to support their treatment while those at Worcester were more likely to have been committed and supported by their local towns or the state because they or their families did not have sufficient resources.

Up to now we have analyzed the characteristics of elderly patients at the time of their admission to McLean and Worcester. Now we will briefly consider the condition of these patients when they were released from the hospital.

Death terminated the stay of 24.8 percent of the patients admitted to these asylums at ages 60-69 and 44.0 percent of those admitted at ages seventy and above (see chart number eleven). Compared to younger patients, the elderly entering McLean and Worcester were more likely to die there (for example, among patients entering McLean and Worcester at ages 50-59, only 18.3 percent died).

The statistics on the mortality of patients might suggest that the superintendents should have hesitated before admitting any elderly patients to their hospitals; yet 55.5 percent of those ages 60-69 and 38.3 percent of those ages seventy and above were discharged as recovered or improved (compared to 60.0 percent of those admitted at ages 50-59). Thus, though elderly patients were less likely to leave the asylums as recovered or improved than their younger counterparts, that difference was not sufficiently striking, at least between those ages 50-59 and those 60-69, that the superintendents at McLean and Worcester should have singled out the elderly patients as particularly problematic for their institutions.

III. The Elderly Insane as Viewed by the McLean and Worcester Superintendents

Our statistical analyses of the perceived extent of insanity among the Massachusetts population in 1854 and of the characteristics of the elderly insane at McLean and Worcester during the ante-bellum period still leave many unanswered questions about the relationship between aging and insanity. Particularly lacking in any statistical investigation is an understanding of how the participants perceived and reacted to what was actually happening. Therefore, in this section of the paper we will discuss the responses of the medical superintendents at the McLean Asylum and the Worcester State Hospital to the troubling issues created by insanity in an aged patient. Some of these questions were addressed directly while others were included within more general considerations of the medical and moral therapy or the problems associated with the increased demand for institutional facilities for the insane. Using case records of individual patients, we will first examine the superintendents' understanding of the relationship between aging and insanity, paying

particular attention to their response to the circumstances that led to hospitalization, the differences between the treatment of elderly and other patients, and the conditions that led to the discharge. These case records have a particular utility for us since they permit a comparison of the behavioral characteristics of those elderly patients whose insanity was caused by "old age" with those elderly whose insanity had other origins. Furthermore, since discharges from the hospitals recorded simply as "cured" or "improved" in the general registers may mask more detailed and accurate comments on the prognosis of the patients contained in their case records, we can look in the case records for evidence of a growing reluctance to admit aged patients that is visible in the annual reports of the superintendents.[14]

Second, we will use these annual reports to suggest how the superintendents publicly responded to the competing expectations of different constituencies. Although McLean Asylum was largely supported by private endowment and patient fees while Worcester State Hospital was financed almost entirely by legislative appropriations, both institutions were governed by a board of trustees. While the superintendents addressed their annual reports to the board of trustees, who maintained a close and generally congenial relationship with them during this period, they also freely acknowledged their accountability to the public at large, to the emerging profession of institutional psychiatry, and to the patients and their families.

And finally, we will briefly describe the substance and tenor of medical literature on insanity of the aged that was available during this period. This includes the rather small number of published articles on senile dementia and other forms of insanity associated with the aged which were published in the *American Journal of Insanity,* established in 1844 as the official journal of the Association of Medical Superintendents of American Institutions for the Insane.

We will first examine some of the problems associated with the elderly insane at the McLean Asylum and the reactions of the superintendents of that small, private institution to those issues. Actually the proportion of aged admitted to McLean in the ante-bellum period was quite small compared to the proportion of aged admitted to our state mental institutions today. Of the approximately 4,000 cases admitted to McLean between 1818 and 1861, only 381 were above the age of sixty (there were 118 female cases and 155 male cases ages 60-69 and 42 female cases and 66 male cases ages seventy and above who were admitted). Though we have no evidence that the first superintendent of McLean, Rufus Wyman, tried to restrict the admission of elderly patients, his successor in 1837, Luther Bell, quickly instituted a policy to limit the admission of elderly patients so that the hospital could maintain its primary therapeutic function.

Those whose insanity was recorded as caused by "old age" formed only a tiny fraction of the elderly patients and they were almost entirely restricted to patients admitted at ages seventy and above. No person was admitted for "old age" before 1834, and of the fifteen women and sixteen men admitted to McLean before 1861 whose insanity was caused by "old age," all but four were seventy years old and above.

Though the superintendents of the hospitals sometimes designated elderly patients as those ages sixty and above, there is little in the case records of those patients between ages 60-69 that differentiates them from those a decade younger, except that there were fewer patients in the older age bracket and that men outnumbered women until the decade of the 1850's (in the younger cohorts women and men are usually about equally represented). Descriptions of behavior within the hospital seldom make references to the age of these patients or to any debility of mental and physical functions that often was used to account for the hospitalization of patients above the age of seventy. In general, neither the reasons for admission nor the regimen of therapy suggest that advanced age played an important role in defining the nature of insanity for most patients in their sixties within the hospital.

By contrast, those who were admitted after age seventy were almost always described as "superannuated." Typically admission followed some specific incident that indicated a benign, helpless elderly person had suddenly transgressed the bounds of propriety and had become troublesome to his family, friends, or community. One woman who had once merely told strange stories about herself "began to sing and dance . . . soon noisy and violent." Another comfortable and respectable widow became subject to "bursts of passion without cause," showed "jealousy and suspicions of persons in her vicinity" and resented being restrained from going into the street. A farmer "became over fond of speculation and has lost considerable sums by buying articles which he did not want or need." Equally typically, these same persons were reported as calm and quiet once they were within the hospital environment, although a number failed to eat and were fed by stomach pump and returned home "unimproved." A disproportionately large number of patients admitted at ages seventy and above died within the hospital, some after only a few short weeks of residence.

The stories of the patients admitted who were seventy years old and above differ in particulars, but the theme is fairly constant. One aged retired professor from Maine, having been partially insane for four years, was admitted at age seventy-eight. He was initially admitted to prevent him from "squandering his property," but since he "was always regarded as an eccentric man, it is supposed that his present condition was brought upon him by want of that regular employment of the mind to which he had been accustomed in former years." After five months at McLean in which his record shows no medication or other specific treatment, he was allowed to return home. Two years later he was back at McLean and was still there two years after being admitted. Though the notation in his record refers to him kindly as "the old Professor," his progressive failure was reported and he was discharged as "unimproved" at the age of eighty-five. In some instances special comforts for this group of patients are afforded: an old man was accompanied by his former servant; a daughter spent two weeks with her father as he dies. But little medication was administered and the theme that appears on the record of one eighty year old farmer might stand for all: "The silver cord is loosed and the golden bowl is broken." There is little indication in the patient records of the value or need of

any specific therapy for these aged patients.

During the first twenty years at McLean, patients who had not responded to therapy were allowed to remain in the hospital. This policy was reversed when Bell became the superintendent. Upon assuming his new office, Bell reviewed the situation of each patient in the hospital in his personal journal and discharged some of the patients who were making little progress. For example, a man who had been first admitted to McLean in 1823 was back in the hospital for the seventh time when Bell arrived. After reviewing his case and observing the patient for a few more months, Bell discharged him at age seventy because he had neither improved nor seemed to be particularly interesting from a medical perspective. Thus, under Bell's leadership, McLean increasingly began to discharge the elderly insane as well as other patients who were not improving from the treatment within the hospital.

In addition to discharging patients who were not being cured, Bell initiated the policy of discouraging the admission of elderly patients. Unlike his predecessor who was silent on this issue, Bell saw the presence of elderly insane at McLean as a threat to the primary therapeutic mission of the hospital. For Bell, the admission of elderly insane was seen only as a last resort.

It is difficult to explain the shift in policy toward the admission of aged patients and the discharge of those who evidenced little improvement at McLean during Bell's administration. The relatively small number of aged inmates, their apparent accomodation to the hospital routine, and their good record of recoveries might well have supported a different policy. Bell's negative attitude toward keeping the elderly insane within McLean preceded a similar reaction among his American medical colleagues by nearly a decade. Perhaps his high aspirations for the McLean Asylum as a leading therapeutic institution as well as the recent addition of an alternative for the treatment of the elderly insane at the new state hospital at Worcester convinced him to define these patients as inappropriate clientele for this private asylum.

With the opening of the Worcester State Hospital in 1833 another institution was available for the care of the elderly insane. All records of patient care between admission and discharge at Worcester as well as McLean were maintained in bound volumes. When a patient was admitted more than once, he or she received a new case number. Although reference was ordinarily made to the earlier admission, the cause and condition of each attack for an individual was not necessarily identical to the previous attack; that is, the cause of insanity might well be altered between one admission and the next. Thus, patients admitted because of insanity caused by "old age" might well have had a previous admission associated with a different cause. In fact, what is particularly interesting is that frequently the same patient is re-admitted to the hospital several years later with almost identical symptoms, but there are now different explanations of that aberrant behavior. These cases provide the opportunity to study the changing assumptions about the elderly as well as the association of aging and insanity at Worcester.

In general, the picture from the case records of patients over seventy years old when they were admitted to Worcester suggests that they were not troublesome

and were kindly tolerated. An illustration of this is the case of a male who was admitted at the age of seventy-four after a bout of influenza. He is described as having been in the same feeble intellectual and physical condition for some time. His illness led him to be "agitated and troubled" so that his family looked to the hospital for relief. He was among the few patients of this age-group whose care included medication (unlike most younger patients who received regular pharmaceutical therapy to stimulate and sedate physical and psychological functions in the late 1840's). This old farmer was dosed with morphine, senna, and paregoric at night, and while he appears to have improved in physical health, his anxieties persisted. He remained in the Worcester Hospital in this uneasy condition from 1847 until the record of January 4, 1852 noted that "he has not been well for a few days and less healthy for a few weeks and today died of old age."

There are several important aspects of this case that illuminate the relationship between the physician superintendent and his "superannuated" patients within the general context of the asylum. Other historians have focussed on the therapeutic mission of these institutions and the extent to which both the public and the professionals were gratified by the successful outcome of institutional care when that therapy was properly utilized. In an earlier section of this paper, however, we indicated situations in which the hospitals fell short of their objectives in respect to the care of the elderly insane and suggested that some of the reasons for these shortcomings were due to the data they collected and the analyses they undertook to assess success. This particular case record of an elderly male patient also indicates how, not through neglect but through care itself, the elderly were absorbed within the institution to the point of being taken for granted. In this institution, in distinct contrast to McLean Asylum under Bell, chronic illnesses rather impervious to cure did not appear to threaten either the physician's general optimism or the daily regimen. In this particular case, the physician simply recorded the patient's complaints, confusions, and delusions and noted that "he asks me why I do not converse with him as I do with others, and then begs me to say nothing lest I should lose my opinion of him . . . refuses to shake hands for fear of giving me some disease. Sleeps well. Appetite good."

Altogether, the thirty-six cases admitted to the Worcester State hospital between 1833 and 1861 for insanity caused by "old age" represented only twenty-six different individuals since in several instances the same patients were admitted more than once for the same cause. Reading these case records suggests that very little differentiated each patient's condition on the first and subsequent admissions. Particularly interesting for the study of the changing assumptions about old age and insanity are the five cases where admission for "old age" is preceded by earlier admissions of different etiology. The most impressive case in this category, in terms of the total frequency of hospitalizations, is a woman whose first commitment took place in 1833 and who was re-admitted on fourteen subsequent occasions. Only the last three admissions (in 1845, 1846, and 1848) were for insanity specifically attributed to "old age." She was first committed by her friends and family at age sixty for

insanity caused by excessive use of snuff and tobacco. Throughout her numerous though brief hospitalizations, intemperance and ill health were cited as the cause of her insanity until the age of seventy-two when admission is attributed to "old age." In each instance but one she was supported as a private boarder, and throughout her visits to the hospital the attending physicians viewed her as an excitable, harmless old lady.

While there is every indication that between 1833 and 1848 the superintendents generally viewed the hospital as an appropriate environment for recovery from the periodical extravagances of fantasy and behavior that characterized this patient, there is no indication that active therapy was sought for her or that she was considered dangerous to herself or to the community. Nor is there any evidence that "old age" when cited as the cause of insanity represents any change in her condition or the distinct delineation of a chronological point in her life cycle. On the contrary, she was always referred to as elderly, but it is not this fact which made hospitalization appropriate.

This case, like many others, suggests that between 1833 and 1849 the Worcester State Hospital was tolerant, perhaps one might even say receptive, to the aged insane. While the hospital was established through legislative authority in order to provide appropriate facilities for the care of patients dependent on public support, both the trustees and the first superintendent, Samuel Woodward, were intent on attracting private boarders as well. Every care was given to the provision of separate facilities for those patients of means who wished to avail themselves of this new institution. Woodward had previously been associated with the Hartford Retreat, an asylum that successfully catered to the requirements of persons from different classes since it was the only large institution for the insane in Connecticut. Because Woodward was concerned lest the Worcester State Hospital become overrun by patients transferred from jails and poorhouses, he may have made special efforts to attract those elderly insane who were not usually committed by the towns or the courts.

Once within Worcester they were treated kindly, but with considerably less specific medical therapy than patients younger in years. Their length of stay varied greatly, but as indicated earlier, while the admission of aged patients increased over time, the annual census of older patients did not rise at Worcester as it did at McLean. This is partly a reflection of the shorter stay of private boarders who frequently found their needs were not easily met when the hospital became more crowded. An eighty year old woman identified as the mother-in-law of the Governor was described as "decrepid from old age. . . .her mind not otherwise affected than the result of old age." She was "discontented" at the hospital, full of complaints and discharged within twenty-eight days. But apparently this patient's haste to leave was not universal; in 1851 an old man was discharged after it was discovered that he had been admitted improperly because he only feigned insanity.

While the case reports of both McLean and Worcester patients indicate decreasing tolerance of aged lunatics over time, it appears that both the timing and the animus of this sentiment had different origins. When we turn to the

annual reports of each institution this difference is evident. McLean's first superintendent, Rufus Wyman, never addresses the problem directly, but as early as 1823 he cautions that the good reputation of the Asylum requires discrimination between incurable patients and those who will benefit from their hospitalization. While noting that "one half of the present boarders have been the subject of insanity for years, and are not expected by their friends to be returned to a sound state of mind," he saw the care of these patients as an obligation of the institution. "It is understood," he continues, "that the principal or sole object of this Asylum is a suitable provision for a great public want—the comfortable accomodation and care of insane persons. It is limited to neither age, sex, nor condition in life."[15]

Despite Bell's desire to minimize the admission to McLean of elderly patients who were not likely to recover, he initially was also quite sympathetic to the plight of the friends and the families. Thus, the *Annual Report* for 1837 noted:

> Regarding the relief and protection of friends and families from the unavoidable distress of having an insane inmate, as an object of this institution, secondary only to that of cure, it has been considered a duty to advise reception indiscriminately of all cases for which application has been made, without inquiring as to any other point than the fact of their derangement, as long as vacancies remain. In conformity to this principle there has been placed under our care, several whose state of health was such as to render speedy death almost certain, as well as many whose cases were hopeless from their long duration or complicated with the imbecility of old age or epilepsy.[16]

Though the report was negative about admitting older patients, the experiences of the fourteen patients over sixty years old who were admitted that year to McLean does not support that position. Eleven of those aged insane were released as "improved" or "recovered" while only two were released as "stationary," and only one had died.

During the next few years McLean continued to struggle with this dilemma, contrasting the legal obligation of the Worcester State Hospital to relieve the burden of families and friends by accepting even hopeless cases with McLean's opportunity and ability to restrict its admissions to those most likely to actually benefit from treatment. Increasingly the superintendents and trustees of McLean sought to restrict the admission of those who had little hope of recovery. Thus, Luther Bell argued in the *Annual Report* of 1840 that "cases of long standing or those where custody only is regarded, should have application made for them prior to its being decided for them to leave home; for it must hereafter be impossible to receive all applications on the instant." He contrasted the Asylum's statistics with those from less favorably endowed institutions and reminded his trustees of "how great a difference should be looked for from differences of regulation as to admissions in an institution for example, receiving only cases of violent excitement and high action, and in one . . . where the exhausted, the aged, the epileptic and the hopeless are brought merely to

relieve friends, or in the desperate hope that some new appliance may renovate the exhausted system."[17]

Whereas Luther Bell expressed grave doubts about the wisdom of admitting elderly patients to McLean by the late 1830's, his counterpart at Worcester, Samuel Woodward, was arguing that the elderly insane were more apt to be cured than younger patients. In his *Fourth* (1836), *Eighth* (1840), and *Ninth* (1841) *Annual Reports,* Woodward noted that insanity in those over the age of forty may be more curable than in those of younger ages. Citing statistics on the recovery of patients between the ages of sixty and seventy-five, he observed that:

> The facts here presented are different from opinions of authors and from the general impression of the public. . . . One Reason that insanity is less curable in the young, is, that it arises in such cases, more frequently from physical causes than in more advanced life, particularly from masturbation. Another reason, probably is, that the brain and the nervous system of the young, being more susceptible are more likely to be affected by organic disease, which renders insanity permanent and incurable.[18]

Throughout the first decade, Woodward's *Annual Reports* stressed three themes that were ultimately relevant to his consideration of the problems associated with the aged lunatic. First, the obligation to provide "safe keeping and amelioration for those who are beyond all hope of cure." Not only was this necessary for the patient's sake, but when these patients were "at large, or improperly and imperfectly in private houses," they were "the cause of grief to their friends, and of uneasiness and alarm to the community. . . ."[19] Second, Woodward constantly feared that the towns and courts would send violent and unruly persons to the hospital, whose behavior would disrupt the institution and whose disease was too far progressed to admit hope of recovery. And finally, Woodward always stressed the pathology of insanity. "We must not for a moment overlook the fact," he wrote in his *Seventh Annual Report* (1839), "that insanity is a physical disease, that the mind, in the most deplorable case, is not obliterated, its integrity is only disturbed. . . .The diseased brain in insanity, the worn out brain of the aged, and the imperfect brain of the idiot, are the only reason why the mind is not as active and intelligent in these individuals as in the rest of mankind. . . ."[20] For Woodward, evidence of a disease of the mind was of greater importance for committing a patient than the possibility of his or her curability and within that context the aged insane could be accepted.

While the *Fifteenth Annual Report* (1847) still expressed optimism about the rate of cure among the aged insane, a decade later this conclusion was reversed as attention was called to the "improper" commitment of "several aged people, suffering simply from mental decay . . . whose friends are ready to admit that these patients are brought here to die. All treatment in such cases must be quite unavailing. Proper attention to hygienic rules is all that can be suggested." Reinforcing this argument is the admonition that depriving the elderly insane "of home with its accustomed pleasures . . . is but a poor exchange for the kind

offices of love and affection."[21]

In the decade before the Civil War, Woodward's successors, George Chandler and Merrick Bemis, not only believed that elderly patients suffered by being hospitalized, but they also argued that this practice was a threat to the family itself. By sending off its oldest and most vulnerable members to the care of others, the family was somehow diminished. Rather than citing any studies by other physicians to support the notion that the elderly insane should be cared for at home by their families, Chandler and Bemis couched their arguments in more general terms. Their reports reflected a dual and contradictory concern for the legitimate needs of the elderly as well as a disavowal of their responsibility as physicians to treat the physical problems of senile dementia which they no longer perceived as amenable to medical cure.

As a result, while the superintendents at Worcester during the 1850's and 1860's were increasingly hostile to committing the elderly to their institution and were becoming more pessimistic about the likelihood of successful therapy, they focused more on the social needs and physical comforts of the aged insane rather than on their access to medical therapy and sustenance. Leaning less on the needs of the hospital itself and stressing instead the requirements of the elderly, their families, and the community as a whole, these superintendents increasingly saw the aged insane as outside their professional jurisdiction. As a consequence of all of these factors, they also may have under-estimated the medical problems of the elderly insane who were within their institutions, as well as those outside, and in a significant way may have altered their conception of the institution's obligation to the public.

Though the superintendents at McLean and Worcester gave quite different reasons for restricting the admission of elderly patients, by the eve of the Civil War they were agreed on the undesirability of treating the elderly insane within their asylums. To account for the sources of their hostility to aged patients is difficult. One possible explanation of the changes in the attitude of these superintendents toward elderly patients may be the impact of European medical literature which provided a scientific rationale for not sending aged patients to an asylum. European writers such as Esquirol, Griesinger, and Voisin described senile dementia as the predominant and ultimately intractable disease afflicting aged patients well before the superintendents of McLean Asylum or Worcester State Hospital had decided that there was little that could be done for the elderly insane within their institutions.

Though Bell was aware of these European writers (he noted their works in a "bibliography of insanity" in his personal journal), neither he nor most of his American colleagues refer to these brief though consistently pessimistic assessments of aged patients. Furthermore, while the *American Journal of Insanity* was publishing numerous articles concerning the management of institutions for the insane, there is no more than an occasional reference to the problems associated with the admission and treatment of the elderly during this period.

The single article in the *American Journal of Insanity* specifically discussing senile dementia was published in 1856 by Dr. John M. Galt, superintendent of

the Eastern Asylum of Virginia. While referring to the works of Burrows, Conolly, Esquirol, and Prichard, Galt notes that there are "but few observations with respect to confining in asylums these sufferers of senile dementia."[22] Galt echoes the sentiments of the superintendents at McLean and Worcester who at that point stressed the inappropriateness of the hospitals for handling the elderly insane:

> We are ourselves very much inclined to think that expediency should be the test here, rather than any definite line of demarcation established between mere natural decay and positive senile dementia. As there is usually but slight hope of a recovery, and the patient is not dangerous, unless under peculiar circumstances, we really consider this to be, in general, one of the instances in which relatives are bound to bear the burden of those to whom life presents but a few years before "the golden bowl is broken," and "the wheel is broken at the cistern."[23]

Though the superintendents at McLean and Worcester could have derived their increasingly negative views of elderly patients from the European writers, this does not appear to have happened since we have very little indication that they utilized this particular aspect of the literature. In fact, the relatively small amount published in American journals on this problem suggests that it was not yet seen as a major issue that deserved extensive discussion and analysis. Instead, it appears that on the eve of the Civil War, there was a general consensus among these superintendents that the elderly insane were not the appropriate clientele for asylums which aspired to remain primarily therapeutic institutions.

If the superintendents at McLean and Worcester did not receive their negative views of elderly patients from the current medical literature, why did they alter their attitudes and behavior toward the aged insane? One might argue that conditions within the hospitals as well as their personal experiences with these patients account for that change. But as we have already noted, neither the changes in the number nor the proportion of elderly patients at McLean and Worcester can account by themselves for the growing hostility toward these patients. Furthermore, our examination of the experiences of these physicians with the aged insane does not provide an adequate explanation for their pessimism about curing these particular patients. The rates of recovery of elderly patients as well as their adjustment within the hospitals could have supported a more positive interpretation of the benefits to be derived from the hospitalization of the elderly insane.

So far we have rejected some possible explanations which we feel cannot fully account for the growing negative expectation of curing the elderly insane within McLean and Worcester. Unfortunately, we cannot conclusively demonstrate what actually induced this change in the superintendents in the period prior to the Civil War. We suspect, however, that these superintendents were reflecting the increasingly negative image of the elderly that was developing in antebellum America. As their perceptions of the elderly in general shifted, they

began to notice selectively those aspects of the elderly insane which suggested that the hospital was an inappropriate setting for these patients. This increasingly negative attitude and behavior of the superintendents toward the aged insane reinforced and contributed to the growing negative image of the elderly among the general population. Thus, we hypothesize that the general shifts in the attitudes toward the elderly in ante-bellum America affected these superintendents and encouraged them to neglect the treatment of the elderly within their asylums.[24]

While the elderly insane had always been less likely to be institutionalized because they were usually less violent and excitable than other patients and because their families, friends, and communities were often unwilling to expend the money necessary to send them to McLean or Worcester, they did not experience any overt discrimination against their admission prior to the 1840's at McLean and the 1850's at Worcester. Yet by the eve of the Civil War, the superintendents at both McLean and Worcester were determined to discourage the admission of these patients by whatever means were at their disposal.

The real irony and tragedy in this situation is that there was a significant increase in the proportion of the elderly insane who were committed to a state mental hospital in the second half of the nineteenth century. But the state mental hospitals at that time were no longer regarded as therapeutic institutions. Instead, these hospitals became mainly custodial institutions where patients were sent with little hope of recovery. Though this shift in the functioning of the state mental hospitals occurred at approximately the same time that the elderly were beginning to be placed in them in much larger numbers, that change was not due to the increasing admission of elderly patients, but more to the changing attitudes of physicians and the public on the possibility of curing anyone who was insane. Thus, the discrimination against the admission of elderly patients to these hospitals only occurred after the institutions were considered to be undesirable by the rest of society.

Notes

[1]Funds for this research were provided by NIH Grant LM-02355, in addition to support received under the "Human Values and Aging" project. We are indebted to Terry Hill, Deborah Hood, and Catherine Whitaker for research assistance and to Mary Vinovskis for programming the data.

[2]U.S. Congress, Senate, Special Committee on Aging, *Joint Hearing before the Subcommittee on Long-Term Care and the Subcommittee on Health of the Elderly,* 94th Congress, 1st sess. (29 September 1975), p. 1.

[3]Ibid., p. 3.

[4]For a discussion of the under-registration of the insane in the early federal censuses, see Gerald N. Grob, "Edward Jarvis and the Federal Census," *Bulletin of the History of Medicine,* 50 (Spring 1976), 4-27.

[5]Massachusetts Legislative Documents, *Report on Insanity and Idiocy in Massachusetts, by the Commission on Lunacy, under Resolve of the Legislature of 1854,* House Document No. 144 (1855). For an extensive introduction to this report, see

the discussion by Gerald Grob in Edward Jarvis, *Insanity and Idiocy in Massachusetts: Report of the Commission on Lunacy,* ed. Gerald N. Grob (Cambridge, Mass.: Harvard Univ. Press, 1971), pp. 1-71.

[6]The original data from the Jarvis survey have been preserved in manuscript form in the "Report of the Physicians of Massachusetts, Superintendents of Hospital . . . and Others Describing the Insane and Idiotic Persons in the State of Massachusetts in 1855. Made to the Commissioners on Lunacy," MS volume in the Countway Library, Harvard Medical School, Boston, Massachusetts. As part of a larger study of insanity in antebellum America, we have computerized and analyzed the individual returns on insanity that were sent to the commissioners.

[7]For extended contemporary discussions of the perceptions of insanity as well as the concerns about institutional arrangements, consult the articles in the *American Journal of Insanity* (1844-). There are numerous secondary analyses of insanity in mid-nineteenth-century America. For example, see Norman Dain, *Concepts of Insanity in the United States, 1789-1865* (New Brunswick, N.J.: Rutgers Univ. Press, 1964) and Gerald N. Grob, *Mental Institutions in America: Social Policy to 1875* (New York: Free Press, 1973).

[8]The complete results of our multiple classification analysis will be presented in our forthcoming reanalysis of the Jarvis data. For an example and discussion of the use of multiple classification analysis in historical studies, see Carl F. Kaestle and Maris A. Vinovskis, "From Fireside to Factory: School Entry and School Leaving in Nineteenth-Century Massachusetts," in *Family Processes in an Historical Perspective,* ed. Tamara K. Hareven (Academic Press, forthcoming).

[9]The manuscript general registers for both McLean Asylum and the Worcester State Hospital were coded and computerized. In addition, we used the casebooks for the individual patients of these institutions in order to add information on such variables as ethnicity and the amount of fee paid.

[10]Massachusetts, *Statutes, 1797,* Chapter 61, p. 457.

[11]Massachusetts, *Statutes, 1834,* Chapter 150, Sections 3 and 5, pp. 185-86.

[12]*Report on Insanity and Idiocy,* p. 69.

[13]There is no satisfactory way of categorizing occupations for mid-nineteenth-century data. Though we followed the suggestions of previous scholars in the field, we readily acknowledge that there are problems associated with any current classification scheme. For discussions of the problems of using nineteenth-century occupational data, see Stuart Blumin, "The Historical Study of Vertical Mobility," *Historical Methods Newsletter, 1 (September 1968),* 1-13; *Clyde Griffen,* "Occupational Mobility in Nineteenth-Century America: Problems and Possibilities," *Journal of Social History,* 5 (Spring 1972), 310-30; Theodore Hershberg, et al., "Occupation and Ethnicity in Five Nineteenth-Century Cities: A Collaborative Inquiry," *Historical Methods Newsletter,* 7 (June 1974), 174-216.

[14]Bound case records for individual patients at Worcester State Hospital from 1833-1861 are deposited at the Francis A. Countway Library at Harvard. Similar records for individual patients at McLean are deposited in the Record Room of the McLean Hospital, Belmont, Massachusetts. We are indebted to the officers of the hospital for permission to consult those records.

[15]*Report of the Massachusetts General Hospital for 1823,* p. 14.

[16]*Report of the Massachusetts General Hospital for 1837,* p. 12.

[17]*Report of the Massachusetts General Hospital for 1840,* p. 35.

[18]Worcester State Lunatic Hospital, *Annual Report,* IV (1836), p. 37. Hereafter cited as WSH, *Annual Report.*

[19]WSH, *Annual Report,* V (1837), p. 5.

[20]WSH, *Annual Report,* VII (1839), pp. 65-66.

[21]WSH, *Annual Report,* XXI (1857), pp. 55-56.

[22]John M. Galt, "Senile Insanity—Hypochondriasis," *American Journal of Insanity,* 12 (1856), 237-44.

[23]Ibid., p. 239.

[24]At the present time, several scholars are trying to date more precisely the growing negative attitudes toward the aged in America. David Hackett Fischer, for example, sees a revolutionary change in age relations occurring between 1780 and 1820; during that period, the authority that had been granted to the elderly was reversed and by 1820 "a new pattern of change emerged—a process of continuous, stable, evolutionary change in which gerontophobia became progressively more intense" (*Growing Old in America* [New York: Oxford Univ. Press, 1977], p. 101). Andrew Achenbaum emphasizes the period 1865 to 1914 as the transitional years during which an increasingly negative image of the elderly emerged. See W. Andrew Achenbaum, "The Obsolescence of Old Age in America, 1865-1914," *Journal of Social History,* 8 (1974), 48-62; Wilbert Andrew Achenbaum, "Old Age in the United States, 1790 to the Present," Diss. Univ. of Michigan 1976. Our own research on the insane asylums suggests that the major change in attitudes toward elderly patients for these superintendents occurred in the 1840's and 1850's. Whether this shift was paralleled by broader changes in the general society remains to be investigated further since our research did not extend much beyond the writings of the superintendents and other physicians.

Lance Tibbles[1]

MEDICAL AND LEGAL ASPECTS OF COMPETENCY AS AFFECTED BY OLD AGE

I. Introduction

As adults grow older, others increasingly treat them as no longer being fully competent to make life decisions that were readily granted them a few years before. Adult children begin to impose their will on their aged parents by asserting their influence on such issues as: should the parent live alone? should the parent sell the large family home? should the parent seek medical treatment? In addition, physicians and adult children often begin to make medical treatment decisions for the aged parents. No longer does the physician discuss the medical problems with the aged person. Instead, he consults with the adult children, and together they decide what action is in the aged parent's "best" interest, joining forces to convince or coerce the parent's compliance. In particular, they often reach an understanding regarding the use of life-sustaining medical technology without even having discussed this issue with the aged parent.

In addition to these activities which occur in the private sector, aged individuals are often the subject of legal proceedings which challenge their competency to write a will or to care for their person or property. If someone alleges that an aged person cannot properly take care of himself or his property, a petition may be filed in court to have him declared incompetent and a guardian appointed to act on his behalf. An aged person's will may be challenged on the ground that he was incompetent at the time the will was made or that he had been unduly influenced by another person. Not all incompetency proceedings and will contests, of course, involve aged persons, but this paper will deal only with those proceedings which do. It will be especially concerned with the effect of these proceedings upon the personal autonomy of the aged person. We must ask what societal values are upheld or undermined by competency proceedings. What criteria should we use to determine when an adult

should no longer be allowed to make the basic decisions affecting his life? Who should determine that the aged person is no longer competent to handle his affairs? Should age alone be sufficient to remove an adult's decision-making power? Age plus physical incapacity? Age plus mental incapacity? Are there alternative procedures that may avoid some of the difficulties of incompetency proceedings?

The following circumstances are often involved in a petition for appointment of a guardian or in a challenge of a will:

(1) An aged person disposes of property to the detriment of family members who, upon the aged person's death, expected the property to be left to them. He may dispose of individual property items, consume assets at a rate that will leave little or nothing for the heirs, or perhaps consume all assets prior to his death, thus requiring others to support him.

(2) An aged person marries or shows affection to a person not approved by family members.

(3) An aged person becomes physically incapacitated.

(4) An aged person becomes mentally incapacitated.

(5) An aged person becomes more susceptible to influence by others.

(6) An aged person refuses a medical procedure that is thought to be necessary to prolong his life.

This paper will look briefly at the medical aspects of aging and their effects upon competency. It will then examine in some detail the legal procedures for determining competency. And finally, alternatives to guardianship proceedings will be explored and suggestions made for future action.

II. Elementary Medical Aspects of Aging and Competency

Debilitating disorders can be generally classified into physical disorders and mental disorders. There are three categories of physical disorders that affect the aged—vascular, musculoskeletal, and sensory loss. The major vascular deficiency is arteriosclerosis, or hardening of the arteries, which involves the narrowing of the vascular channels and results in a reduced blood flow to the vital organs. Osteoarthritis is the most prevalent form of musculoskeletal disorder. Sensory loss includes sight loss, hearing loss, and loss of sensation in the hands. Incapacitating mental disorders are classified as either organic—physically caused, resulting from bodily change in the aging process—or functional—emotionally caused, resulting from socio-economic factors in an aged person's environment.

Senile dementia or psychosis and arteriosclerotic psychoses are the two most common causes of dementia in old age. Dementia is usually the result of slowly progressive cortical disease. Senile dementia is a general term for mental deterioration associated with old age. Dorland's *Medical Dictionary* equates it with "senile psychosis" which it defines as: "mental deterioration in old age associated with organic brain changes and characterized by numerous symp-

toms, including impaired memory of recent events, confabulation, irritability, self-interest, decreased capacity for abstract thought, and sometimes symptoms of paranoia, especially delusions of persecution."[2] It usually begins after the age of seventy, and women are affected more often than men, partially because women are most likely to survive to the age at risk. Brain atrophy is generalized but most marked in the frontal and occipital lobes. By the time an individual suffering from senile dementia is seen by a physician, he may experience episodes in which he is inattentive, confused, and frightened. He may misperceive his surroundings, express ill-formed and poorly sustained delusions of persecution, and wander away from home. Senile dementia is often precipitated by a change in surroundings, for example, an admission to a hospital. Although the onset of the illness may be gradual, once established it usually advances rapidly, bringing about a profound deterioration in memory, intellect, and speech. In contrast to arteriosclerotic psychosis, there soon develops a total dissolution of the personality so that eventually nothing of the patient's former self is recognizable.[3]

"Arteriosclerosis" is a thickening of the walls of the smaller arteries. By the time arteriosclerotic psychoses become apparent, there is usually a history of strokes and paralysis on one side of the body, impairment of speech, and defective vision or blindness in half of the vision field. The illness is punctuated by episodes of clouding presumably due to fresh coagulation of dead cells, which are usually followed by an increase in the severity of the dementia. Although the personality becomes debased, its essence is often preserved and some insight may linger to a late stage. It is unlikely that the damage inflicted by cerebral arteriosclerosis can be both extensive enough to cause dementia and sufficiently selective not to cause other syndromes of brain dysfunction. It is more common in men than in women and occasionally occurs in late middle age.[4]

III. Legal Procedures for Determining Competency

Legal proceedings to challenge the validity of a will or to adjudge a person incompetent and appoint a guardian for him bring into sharp conflict two of our society's basic tenets.[5] The first is "autonomy." Fundamental to our value system is the belief that, to the greatest extent possible, a person should be allowed to live his life as he sees fit. Individual autonomy is the basis of our elected form of government, as well as our free enterprise system, and theories of individual autonomy underlie recent court decisions allowing a pregnant woman to exercise her choice about continuing her pregnancy and allowing a person to refuse life-sustaining medical treatment.[6] Autonomy is also the basis of a patient's right to be informed of the risks and benefits of various medical interventions and to give or withhold consent for them to be used on him.

A second tenet basic to our culture is the protection of vulnerable individuals.

One of the purposes of organized government is to protect individuals from the consequences of their actions that might restrict their future free choice. Because of weakness and frailities, some citizens are more vulnerable to influence by others. Because of their special vulnerability, we have traditionally protected infants, the mentally retarded, and the mentally ill.

Although the principles of "autonomy" and "paternalism" appear to conflict at times, both are well engrained in our society and we try to make them compatible. In fact, one might argue that both are forms of "autonomy." "$Autonomy_1$" might be defined as not overriding competent consent, the nonsubstitution of judgment. "$Autonomy_2$" might be defined as maximizing human potential, the preserving of future opportunities. If a person, whose judgment is severely diminished by dementia, gives away his money, it impinges upon his autonomy because he cannot use his money for his future benefit. When we promote "$autonomy_1$" by not substituting our judgment for his, thus not voiding the gift, we restrict "$autonomy_2$" by preventing him from using his property for his future benefit.

No matter how we conceptualize the issues, society must decide whether it will allow a person to make silly, unreasonable, or foolish choices, or whether it will override an individual's judgment, at least in some cases, and substitute some form of societal judgment. Perhaps the issues would not be so difficult if "competent individuals" always made the same choices. Then we could determine if the individual's choice was the same choice that a competent person would make; if not, society might override that choice. However, not all competent individuals will make the same choice—individuals' values differ and so do their choices based upon those differing values. How, then, does society determine which citizens to protect from their own "ill-considered" judgments?

Under traditional legal classification, a person is considered to be either competent or incompetent. If a person is competent then society cannot appoint a guardian to act for the person; similarly, if a testator (a deceased person who died leaving a will) was competent when he wrote his will, then society cannot void it. Yet, more complicated legal distinctions are made. A person may be held to be incompetent to handle his property, but competent to care for his person and to write a will; a person may be held to be incompetent to handle his property and to care for his person, but competent to write a will; or a person may be held to be incompetent to handle his property, care for his person, and to write a will. But within each of these categories the person can be found only competent or incompetent.[7]

This means that an aged person whose mental capabilities are not as sharp or as quick as they once were, or who because of physical infirmities cannot read fine print or write letters, must be treated as either totally competent or totally incompetent as to the particular matter under consideration. But this dichotomy does not work well when an elderly person is increasingly less able to perform mentally or physically as he has done in the past. If he is treated as "competent," he receives no assistance and continues making his own decisions. If he is treated as "incompetent," the law will remove his right to

handle his affairs and appoint someone to make decisions for him.

One might wish to analogize incompetency in the aged to incompetency in infancy. An infant begins with little or no mental and physical ability to care for himself or property. As the infant advances in age, both his mental and physical capabilities expand. He is increasingly able to care for himself and, perhaps at a slower rate, increasingly able to care for property. The law recognizes this and allots *increasing* legal capacity to the infant as he grows older. For example, he is allowed to ride a bicycle and later allowed to drive an automobile; young adolescents are often permitted to choose which parent to live with when the parents divorce; and adolescents may request or refuse medical treatment. Whereas the infant is given more legal capacity as his mental and physical capabilities grow, the situation is reversed for the aged person. Starting from a position of full, legally recognized mental and physical capability, he may begin to lose mental and physical functions. The process may continue until he can no longer care for either himself or his property. But the law does not recognize *decreasing* areas of legal competence in the aged as it does for increasing areas of legal competence for the infant. As will be indicated later in this paper, however, this analogy overlooks the long future of the infant who has never been competent and the short future of the aged person who has been competent for many years.

The remainder of this section will first analyze briefly the legal proceedings involved in challenging the validity of an elderly person's will and then examine incompetency hearings at some length. In analyzing court decisions, we are restricted to reported cases. Since most states do not report lower court opinions, the reported cases are usually appellate court opinions. Also, most incompetency cases are not appealed because the size of the estate does not justify the cost of an appeal. Thus the opinions available for analysis are the rare incompetency cases that are appealed. After reviewing the case law, we will turn to alternative proposals which may be more conducive to protecting *both* $autonomy_1$ and $autonomy_2$.

A. Procedures to Invalidate a Will Because of Incompetency

It is generally agreed that it is socially undesirable to allow someone to dispose of his property at his death if he is so mentally deficient or unbalanced that he does not appreciate the significance of the disposition.[8] In such a case it is usually considered preferable to invalidate the will and distribute the person's property according to the laws of intestate succession rather than according to the caprice of an unsound mind.

A person's testamentary capacity is determined according to his mental ability to make a will. Thus, even though a person is under guardianship or lacks the ability to make a contract or transact other business, he can have testamentary capacity. Generally, one is judged to have a sound mind for purposes of making a will only when he can understand the nature and extent of his property, the persons who are the natural objects of his bounty, and the

disposition which he is making of the property. He must also be capable of appreciating these elements in relation to each other and of forming an orderly plan as to the disposition of his property.[9]

The usual rule is that insane delusion, eccentricity, prejudice, moral depravity, illiteracy, old age, physical weakness, or severe illness do not necessarily disqualify a person from making a will, although they will sometimes prevent the necessary mental capacity to make a will or will be evidence suggesting a susceptability to undue influence. The essential question in a case is, considering all of the facts and circumstances, whether the will proceeded from and on account of a deranged mind. Wills made in the eighth, ninth and tenth decade of life have been upheld. Advanced years accompanied by mental sluggishness, impairment of memory, childishness, eccentricity, or physical infirmity do not automatically mean a lack of testamentary capacity. Dementia will not invalidate a will unless it has reached the point where the mind is either deficient or deranged under the ordinary tests of capacity.[10]

Legal challenges to the validity of the will are frequently intra-family fights for the ancestor's property. One's sympathies will vary from case to case. It is not always an instance of family members attempting to claim an undeserved bonus. In some cases, for example, promises have been made by the decedent upon which a family member has relied to his detriment by living at home, caring for the decedent, or declining other opportunities. Therefore, the family member may be justified in relying upon the promise that the property will be left to him when his aged parent dies.

English and American law have always preferred that property be left to the decedent's immediate family (children, parents, grandchildren, and brothers and sisters). Property dispositions at or near death which "disinherit" the immediate family and give the property to someone else have invariably been subject to more judicial scrutiny than an identical gift to the immediate family. Thus one of the primary tests employed by the courts to determine whether a testator had capacity to make a will has been whether he knew "the natural objects of his bounty."[11] How does the court determine whether the testator had this knowledge? The cases do not answer this question convincingly, but the fact that the testator gave his property to a non-family member is taken as some evidence that he did not know the natural objects of his bounty. In some cases mental instability, which is not sufficient to show a lack of testamentary capacity, can be used to show either undue influence or a susceptibility to undue influence.[12] A phenomenon that I call the "Trixie Syndrome," which will be discussed at greater length in the section on guardianship, is a case in point. "Trixie" refers to any non-family female who is regarded with fondness by an old man who may spend money on her or even announce marriage plans. Gifts to her of his property to the detriment of the expectant heirs frequently result in a guardianship petition or a challenge to the will. A California case illustrates the point.[13] In 1938, an eighty-five year old man agreed to pay a female housekeeper fifty dollars per month and room and board to care for him the remainder of his life. In his will, he left her his house. His will was invalidated. I think that even if the "natural objects of bounty test" was appropriate in

feudal England, it has long since outlived its usefulness. Requiring a breadwinner to support his spouse and children is unobjectionable. But it is inappropriate to attempt to do this by a uniform rule that a testator must always save his property for his family.

Incompetency to make a will is not necessarily established by the fact that the individual has been adjudged incompetent in a guardianship proceeding prior to writing the will. Although physical disability does not necessarily deprive a person of capacity to make a will, it can cause him to act in ways that may be taken by some courts to exhibit a lack of testamentary capacity. In a 1953 case, an eighty-three year old man became "docile" when he was hospitalized with gall bladder trouble, arteriosclerosis, and senile dementia. In a challenge to a will he made during this period, the trial court said that his changed behavior and the fact that he could not add figures showed mental confusion. However, the appellate court did reverse the lower court's finding of incapacity to write a will.[14] In another case, a sixty-one year old woman did not provide for her husband in her will, which she wrote after having suffered several strokes that left her face twisted and prevented her from speaking above a whisper. Evidence at trial showed that the woman did not speak to people or engage in conversation. The trial court determined that the woman was incompetent. However, the appellate court said that this need not be evidence of mental incapacity:

> Who can say, then, that her reticence was not due to this physical condition, rather than to any serious mental malady? By reason of the condition of her organs of speech and the physical difficulty which she experienced when she tried to talk, it was but natural that she should simply shake her head and smile when spoken to and be more than sparing of her words. . . .[15]

B. Proceedings to Determine Incompetency and to Appoint a Guardian

There is a specific reference to old age or senility in about one-half of the incompetency and guardianship statutes in the United States. Statutes in other states do not specifically refer to the aged or infirm, but have been construed to include such persons within the general category of those who are incompetent to manage their own affairs for any cause. It is frequently stated that the purpose of the guardianship procedure is to protect the individual and to preserve and care for the property of persons who cannot look after the property themselves.[16]

The purposes of guardianship proceedings, especially as applied to the aged, are somewhat contradictory. One purpose is to aid an aged person who is found to be in need of assistance. It is recognized that advancing years will bring some decrease of bodily powers and mental efficiency. But if this decrease is no more than "normal" the courts will not intercede. It is mental incapacity that is important.[17] Weakness, forgetfulness, and normal characteristics of age are

said to be immaterial unless the person cannot intelligently manage his affairs. A second purpose is to protect property. If the estate will suffer material loss because the aged person cannot understand the business he is transacting or the nature and affect of his business affairs, or if he is no longer capable of ordinary discretion, the court will appoint a guardian to prevent property loss.[18] Courts then deprive an aged person of the control of his person or property if they find either that the person needs assistance or that his property needs protecting. This concern for protecting property itself is somewhat strange because our legal system is premised upon rights of individuals. So called property rights are more correctly rights of persons in relation to property. As we have already seen, some courts are concerned not that the property will suffer a loss, but that the expectant heirs will suffer a loss.

Competency and guardianship proceedings vary from state to state. However, the Ohio statute is typical. A hearing is held before a judge who hears the evidence without a jury and determines whether to approve the application for guardianship.[19] If the judge appoints a guardian for an individual, the state removes the ward's constitutional rights to manage his person, his property, or both. The judge determines whether the alleged incompetent, "by reason of advanced age, improvidence, or mental or physical disability or infirmity, chronic alcoholism, mental deficiency, lunacy, or mental illness, is incapable of taking proper care of himself or his property or fails to provide for his family or for other persons for whom he is charged by law to provide. . . ."[20] Although the judge's decision can be appealed, appellate courts rarely reverse the trial judge, who saw and heard the witnesses and observed the alleged incompetent, merely because they do not agree with his evaluation of the evidence. This point is clearly expressed by the following language of an appellate court reviewing the trial court's determination that an eighty-nine year old man with cataracts, arteriosclerosis, and mental deterioration was incompetent:

> Regardless of the view this court might be inclined to take from a reading of the evidence as contained in the transcript, the trial court had the advantage of not only seeing and hearing all of the witnesses, but of observing appellant upon two different occasions and of cross-questioning him; and therefore the trial court was in far better position than we could be in determining the weight to give the evidence which was introduced and to determine the mental condition of the appellant. With the witnesses before it, testifying to the facts disclosed by the record, the court could very properly conclude that appellant's mental faculties were impaired to such an extent as to render him incapable of taking care of his property, and that he was likely to be deceived or imposed upon by artful or designing persons. The testimony of witnesses for the appellant at variance with that of the witnesses who testified in support of the petition for the appointment of a guardian merely raised a conflict in the evidence. Before we can disturb the findings of the lower court upon the ground that they are not supported

> by the evidence, we must be able to conclude as a matter of law that there is no evidence at all to support the conclusions arrived at by the trial court.[21]

In many of the older cases, the allegations are often that the aged individual is "insane," "mentally ill," an "idiot," or a "lunatic." This language was used at least in part because both the statutes and the judges applied these terms to those who were mentally or physically incapacitated by old age.[22] On the other hand, some of the older cases were philosophically more committed to the principle of self-determination than many of the newer cases seem to be. Individuals are increasingly dependent upon others to provide them with necessary requirements of life. People are no longer jacks of all trades, but have a one skill occupation. We rely upon experts to fix our plumbing, dry-clean our clothes, and repair our car. Perhaps advanced uses of technology and of technical experts have created a new desire to substitute experts to make important decisions for individuals.[23]

The use of experts is also important in presenting evidence of incompetency at the trial. Usually there will be testimony by at least one physician concerning a mental deficiency which allegedly caused the defendant to be incompetent. In order to show mental incompetence, a medical expert must establish that (1) some type of mental incapacity exists, and (2) the mental incapacity (a) is the cause of previous "unreasonable" conduct, or (b) may be the cause of future "unreasonable" conduct.[24] However, as we saw earlier, legal incompetency tests are not concerned with the physical condition of the brain. The physician, who speaks as an expert in medical matters relating to mental functioning, is allowed to state his "opinion" as to whether the aged person is competent.

But the medical expert is quickly taken out of his area of expertise and into areas in which he is not an expert. If it is true that there can be legal incompetency regardless of the condition of the brain, then there is no correlation between the brain's condition and the legal criteria for incompetency.[25] Once the testimony turns to evaluating or predicting behavior in terms relating to non-medical standards, the medical expert has no more claim to expertise than any other layman. And if the physician has to use knowledge and experience that come to him from outside his medical expertise then he is no longer testifying as a medical expert. For example, in a 1962 Ohio case: "One of the questions asked of Dr. Artman was whether Mrs. Breece 'had the mental capacity and ability to handle an estate of considerable size.' "[26] Answering this question requires a two step approach: first, a determination of that quantum of mental capacity and ability necessary to handle an estate of considerable size, and secondly, a determination as to whether the aged person possesses that ability. But there is nothing in the good doctor's medical experience or training that tells him what mental capacity is necessary to handle a sizeable estate.

In a California case:

> A medical specialist and expert in nervous and mental diseases testified that appellant [the aged person] was suffering from arteriosclerosis

> accompanied by definite senile deterioration; that this was accompanied by a memory defect, irritability and poor eyesight; that the mental deterioration of appellant was permanent and would grow progressively worse. It was the opinion of this medical expert that appellant was not competent to manage his own affairs and was in danger of being imposed upon by artful and designing persons. This opinion was based, according to the expert's testimony, upon personal observation of the alleged incompetent and upon the physical and mental condition of the latter as the same was noted by the doctor at the time of his examination.[27]

The physician begins by testifying about medical facts, but soon moves into the area of non-medical opinion. In fact, his conclusion that the elderly gentleman was in danger of being imposed upon by artful and designing persons was not even a consequence of medical facts. For instance, how artful and designing must the other person be? Would the aged person have been imposed upon before his arteriosclerosis? Would an ordinary person be imposed upon by artful and designing persons? For a third example, let us turn to an earlier California case:

> One of the physicians called by the petitioner was permitted to testify that he did not believe the appellant [aged person] "capable of going into any business proposition to any depth. I don't believe that he could reason any business proposition."[28]

This statement, although perhaps less objectionable than the previous ones, still requires the physician to state his non-medical opinion about the ability needed to handle business transactions.

In addition to medical testimony concerning the aged person's mental function, the courts usually try to find some physical conduct that can be attributed to deteriorated mental function. Although diagnostic devices can identify pathological anomalies in the brain, the courts are hesitant to label the condition a mental disability if there are no physical symptoms or abnormal actions. Thus, we are dealing primarily with an aged person's actions and conduct which may be evaluated as "abnormal," "unreasonable," or "irrational."[29] Since such terms are not value-neutral, it takes a substantive judgment to label conduct "unreasonable." If "unreasonable" conduct is established, then all that remains is to establish the causal link from a mental disability to conduct. In some cases, courts will infer the existence of a mental disability, finding no other explanation for the "unreasonable" conduct. An extreme case of inferring the existence of a mental disability from physical capacity or conduct is revealed in the following language used by the court to justify its conclusion that the defendant was incompetent: "The testimony disclosed that the gentleman still had a remarkable memory for past events, which in turn indicates that at one time he had had an exceptionally keen, retentive mind."[30]

Without "unreasonable" acts, physical infirmities are usually insufficient to establish incompetency. In an Iowa case, a seventy-eight year old widow had suffered two strokes and her physical disabilities were apparent.[31] The trial court had found her incomptent. But the appellate court could not find any "unreasonable" acts. She trusted her son and grandson but not her daughter. She had not "disinherited" her children in her will. She had hidden a box containing several thousand dollars in her house instead of placing it in the bank. But this had occurred prior to her stroke. Since the disability resulting from a stroke often affects the cognitive functions (perceiving, thinking, remembering), had there been evidence of "unreasonable" acts, the appellate court might have inferred a mental disability and found the lady incompetent.

Contrast this approach with a recent Nebraska case, in which an eighty-year old widow, a Polish immigrant, could not read, speak, or write English.[32] Prior to her husband's death the couple had kept large amounts of cash rather than using a checking account. Her only physical disabilities were high blood pressure and arteriosclerosis. But she could not account for $5,400 that she had recently received. The court found her incompetent to manage her property without assistance.

Poor business judgment or conduct alone are usually insufficient to support a finding of mental incompetency.[33] However, if the alleged poor business conduct involves conveying property, it probably will be more closely analyzed. One of the reasons for this may be that conveyances of property by aged persons often upset the expectant heirs, who then bring incompetency proceedings to protect their expectancy. In an early California case, no one questioned the competency of a seventy-eight year old widow until she sold land worth about $5,000 to her son for $200.[34] It was in reality a gift to her son to induce him to remain in that area and it was understood that she would keep her home on the property. At this point the other children became upset that he had gotten the property, which, had it remained in her estate, they would have shared after her death. A daughter brought a petition for guardianship, which was granted by the trial court. However, this decision was reversed on appeal.

Four years earlier the same appellate court had upheld an order of guardianship when an eighty-four year old man with a poor memory had given away property to a non-family member. The poor memory probably would not have been sufficient for the court to find that the man could not care for his person. But the giving away of property allowed the finding of incompetency to manage his property.[35]

Similarly, many cases involve the "Trixie Syndrome" referred to earlier. Although it may now be true for both sexes, the older cases involve an elderly man who develops a fondness for one or more younger females who are not family members. There need not be a sexual relationship. The man may bestow gifts upon the woman, convey his real property to her, provide for her in his will, or indicate a desire to marry her. His relatives, or sometimes others, may assert that gifts to "Trixie" are invalid, contending that they were made under undue influence or without legal capacity. A gift of money or property to a daughter or a niece will be viewed differently than the same gift of money or property to

"Trixie." In a recent Ohio case, which will be discussed more fully later, an eighty-five year old childless widower was found incompetent on the ground that he had acted unreasonably in giving money to a younger woman, who had taken care of him, "because he felt she needed it."[36] In a Michigan case, which also will be commented upon later, an eighty-year old widower was found to be incompetent. He had purchased a new automobile and had employed young girls to drive the car for him, paying them for these services. He had also purchased a coat for one of the girls.[37] And in a California case, a sixty-five year old widower was found to be incompetent after he showed affection for, and conveyed property to, a practical nurse who cared for his wife in her last illness.[38] I suggest that had the women in these cases been family members, perhaps if they had been men, the results would have been different.

A religious conversion by an aged person is an example of another action that may not meet with societal approval. After his sons had established their own homes and after his wife had died, a seventy-year old man became involved with a religious belief radically different from the family's prior religious beliefs. A dispute arose between the man and his adult son over the ownership of some shares of stock. However, the issue of the father's new religion was stressed by the trial court in granting the son's petition for guardianship. But in granting a later petition for termination of guardianship, the appellate court said: "One should hesitate to declare anyone incompetent to handle his business and personal affairs, because he holds religious views and beliefs different from one's own, or different from that of the majority of the people."[39]

If a person has been declared incompetent, what happens if his mental capacity subsequently returns to normal? Incompetency statutes generally provide that a person who is found to be incompetent can later petition for termination of the guardianship. In the initial competency hearing the person alleging incompetency has the burden of proving that the aged person is incompetent. However, once incompetency has been established, in a subsequent hearing the aged person will have the burden of proving that he is no longer incompetent. Generally this will mean that he will have to show an improvement in mental or physical condition since the determination of incompetency. The Ohio statute, which is typical, states that the court must be presented with "satisfactory proof that the necessity for the guardianship no longer exists or that the letters of appointment were improperly issued."[40] A 1962 Ohio case is an example of the heavy burden that is placed on the person attempting to terminate the guardianship.[41] A ninety-seven year old woman had been declared incompetent when she was hospitalized because of a broken wrist. After she had been released from the hospital and had regained her former physical capabilities, she petitioned to have the guardianship terminated. The Probate Court denied her petition, and the denial was affirmed by the Court of Appeals. Finally, however, the Supreme Court of Ohio did reverse the finding, holding that there was undisputed evidence that the necessity for the guardianship no longer existed. The reluctance to terminate a guardianship is also aptly illustrated by the following judicial analysis from a case in which two brothers in their sixties who, having been adjudicated incompetent because of

advanced age after they each had inherited $34,000, petitioned the court for termination of the guardianships:

> The findings are consistent either with capacity or incapacity at the present time. These findings alone would not support the appointment of a conservator in the first instance. But the petitioners are already under conservatorships as the result of a decree in December, 1936, presumably entered upon adequate evidence. The result of these appeals must therefore depend upon whether a person who seeks to be freed from a conservatorship must show affirmatively that he is then in fact competent to manage his property or must be assumed to be competent until again proved incompetent.
>
> We are satisfied that the burden of proving his present right to be released from protection rests upon each petitioner without the aid of any presumption of present capacity. . . . [The statute establishing the proceeding to terminate guardianship] implies the requirement of proof "that the conservatorship is no longer necessary." . . . The fact of incapacity which presumably justified the imposition upon them of the status of wards is a fact likely to continue to exist. When they ask for a change of that status it is reasonable to require them to prove that their present condition is not such as to demand its longer continuance. . . . The language of our own decisions is consistent with the theory that the burden of proving his capacity rests upon the petitioning ward.[42]

Perhaps the best way to understand what happens to aged persons who are subjected to a competency hearing is to review in some depth the written opinions of two cases. No claim is made that these cases are representative. One hopes that they are not. However, they are cases in which the highest court of two progressive states upheld the trial court's determination that the aged person was incompetent.

In re Johnson's Estate was a petition for termination of guardianship. The probate court, circuit court, and finally the Michigan Supreme Court refused to terminate the guardianship.[43] The Supreme Court said that the Michigan incompetency statute applies to a person whose mind is so affected as to deprive him of sane and normal action. In order to authorize appointment of a guardian of one enfeebled by age, the court must find the elderly person's debility to be such that he cannot intelligently manage his affairs as a result of which his estate might suffer loss or waste. But, the Michigan Supreme Court said, a mere showing that an aged person is unwise, lacks judgment, indulges in folly, or squanders his property is not sufficient for the appointment of a guardian.

This statement of Michigan law was then applied to the facts of the *Johnson* case. An eighty-year old widower owned a considerable amount of property, but expenses for repair and upkeep of the property had put him into debt. Before the hearing in which he was originally declared incompetent, he had, as has

already been mentioned in the previous discussion about the "Trixie Syndrome," purchased a new automobile and employed young women to drive the car for him. He paid them for these services, and had further rewarded one of the girls by buying a coat for her. No sexual relationships were alleged. The aged man was found to be incompetent and his son was appointed his guardian. Two years later it was established at a hearing for termination of the guardianship that during the period of the guardianship the income from his properties was about $90 per month and the guardian, his son, was giving him about $18 per month to live on. It was also found that the aged man did not know the name of the Governor of Michigan or the President of the United States. He was able to do arithmetic problems without pencil and paper but "he failed on equally simple problems." After he had been judged incompetent, he had asked a twenty-four year old woman to marry him and he later married a forty-seven year old woman.

The Michigan Supreme Court said that the facts did not conclusively show either competency or incompetency. However, because the aged man had been determined incompetent two years earlier and because appellate courts seldom overrule the trial court on the determination of facts, the Supreme Court could not conclude that the trial court's decision not to terminate the guardianship was improper. The Supreme Court determined that the aged man:

> [I]s entitled to have his property or income used in every reasonable way that will satisfy his needs and desires, short of the guardian's wasting such estate in expenditures from which the ward could not reasonably be expected to have any enjoyment. It is needless to say that the guardian, even for the ward's benefit or enjoyment, should take no risk in expenditure that might result in petitioner's being made a public charge.[44]

Perhaps this statement is meant to justify the guardian's practice of allowing the aged man to have only twenty per cent of the monthly income from his own property. In addition, the court's language—that the guardian should not allow the aged man to expend money "from which the ward could not reasonably be expected to have any enjoyment"—is curious in light of the conduct which precipitated the first incompetency hearing. How can we say that employing female chauffeurs is an activity from which the aged man could not be expected to have any enjoyment?

The second case that we will examine in depth is a 1962 Ohio case. *In the Matter of Guardianship of Tyrrell* involved an eighty-five year old childless widower. The Ohio Probate Judge described the aged individual in the following language:

> The alleged ward is an elderly gentleman 85 years of age, who was brought to the courtroom in a wheelchair. He was neatly attired in a blue suit, colored shirt and red necktie. His flowing white hair was combed and parted. His face bore no evidence of an adverse or hard

> life. His hands and fingers were smooth and soft. His very appearance told one that he had seen much better days. Throughout the hearing, he sat at the opponent's table and followed the testimony of the witnesses quite carefully.[45]

His sister initiated the proceedings, and prior to the competency hearing she requested that two physicians of her choice be allowed to examine the aged man. The judge granted this request and the physicians talked to him. They later testified that a guardian was needed because the aged man was subject to undue influence. The trial court admitted that much of this testimony was based on what the physicians had previously heard about him rather than upon the interview. Evidence was introduced that he had spent over $9,000 in the prior two years. But there was also evidence that he had purchased a diamond ring for less than the normal selling price and a grave marker costing only a few hundred dollars, and that he had made funeral arrangements for less than $1,000. Perhaps the most crucial evidence in determining the outcome of the case, however, was that during the prior year he had given over $2,000 to a woman who was not a family member.

The Probate Judge found that the aged man was incompetent in that he was subject to undue influence because he had parted with $2,000 for which he had received no service or value. The Judge appointed a guardian for his person and property. The Judge's concluding language is startling:

> The testimony disclosed that the gentleman still had a remarkable memory for past events, which in turn indicates that at one time he had had an exceptionally keen, retentive mind. With respect to the present status of the individual, the Court observed the following: that his smile at times is not normal; his eyes do not focus properly at all times; his gait and reflexes are not normal; and that he is not laying his cane aside, but is dropping it.
>
> These are indications of the lessening of the gentleman's mental capacities. Just what has caused this is not known to the Court. Perhaps there has been arterio sclerosis [sic] or cerebral accident. In any event, there has been a deterioration which would be called mental illness.[46]

The Court of Appeals affirmed the Probate Court's granting of the petition for guardianship and the Ohio Supreme Court declined to hear the case.

The aged individual's brief in the Ohio Supreme Court alleged facts not appearing in the Probate Court opinion.[47] The elderly man had a contract for lifetime care in a rest home for which he paid $2,500 and a hospitalization insurance policy. In addition, the brief alleged that although the Probate Judge noted that the aged man had $10,000 of bank stock, the sister had taken this stock from him. When he began steps to regain the stock, the sister instituted the incompetency proceedings. In any event, the court's language itself raises serious questions as to whether incompetency proceedings are a viable method for resolving the "autonomy" versus "paternalism" dilemma.

IV. *Alternatives to Guardianship Proceedings*

This section will examine conservatorships, powers of attorney, and legal assistants as possible alternatives to the traditional method of determining incompetency and appointing a guardian.

A. *Conservatorships*

Statutory authority exists in a number of states for an individual of sound mind to petition the court for the appointment of a guardian or conservator (the term "conservator" will be used here to identify the individual appointed upon the aged individual's voluntary application). The applicant usually must state that he feels mentally or physically incapable of managing himself or his property.[48] As indicated by the following excerpt, if there is statutory authority courts generally approve such requests even though the petitioner may have some mental disability:

> We are convinced, however, that it was a proper exercise of discretion to allow the ward to have a conservator. This permitted him to obtain competent assistance in the management of his estate without sacrificing either his independence or self-respect. It carried no imputation of unsound mind or surrender of his continued control of his own person, against which he protested throughout the entire proceedings. The appointment of a conservator is authorized "whenever any person shall deem himself unfitted by reason of infirmities or age or physical disability, to manage his estate with prudence and understanding."[49]

In practice, the inducement to voluntarily apply for a conservator often is the fact that someone has brought or threatens to bring a guardianship proceeding.[50]

Some states, including Kansas, California, and Massachusetts, have specific provisions for voluntary petitions; other states, including New Hampshire and Nebraska, have skeletal provisions for voluntary appointments, providing that the appointment of the conservator is to be in the same manner as the appointment of other guardians provided by law.[51] Usually the petitioner can nominate the conservator, although the court is not bound by this choice.

In terms of protecting autonomy there are, however, deficiencies in the conservatorship procedure. The conservator has the same power as a guardian to totally handle the individual's affairs. In addition, the aged person may have as difficult a time removing the conservator as he would in removing a guardian, for the petition for removal of the voluntarily appointed conservator requires the ward to overcome the same type of presumption as in the involuntary appointment of a guardian.[52] Even though the appointing court

might not have acted vigorously to determine that the voluntary petitioner was competent (in fact, incompetency might not have been established at all), the ward may still be unable to terminate a conservatorship because later he might not be able to overcome the presumption of his incompetency. He may be unable to show any improvement in his mental or physical condition that will allow the court to find that he can now capably manage his own affairs. For example, a court was asked to terminate a guardianship of a sixty-seven year old woman who had been granted a voluntary appointment because she was unable to resist her alcoholic son's requests for money. The court found that the son was still an alcoholic, and therefore the conditions had not changed sufficiently for the termination to be in the woman's best interests.[53]

Iowa offers an option that delays the appointment of a conservator until the happening of a later event or condition.[54] The individual can file a petition for the voluntary appointment of a conservator of his property on the condition that the court shall do so only upon the occurrence of a specified event or the existence of a described mental or physical condition of the petitioner. The individual can nominate a person for appointment to serve as conservator, and he can revoke the petition at any time until the conservator is appointed. Thus, an elderly person's option to appoint, while still competent, a conservator effective upon the happening of a later event (such as mental or physical incapacity) is a more effective means of protecting autonomy than are guardianship proceedings. However, once the conservator is appointed, there is the problem of later terminating the conservatorship.

B. Powers of Attorney

A power of attorney is a written document by which an individual appoints another as his agent and confers upon him the authority to perform certain acts on his behalf. Any person having the capacity to appoint an agent may confer upon another the power to act as his attorney in fact. Statutes in some states require that powers of attorney for particular purposes be recorded. In addition, even though not required by statute, powers of attorney usually can be recorded in the same manner as deeds and mortgages of land.[55]

A power of attorney can be terminated by the act or agreement of the parties or by operation of law. The parties can agree that the power will be terminated at the expiration of a specified or reasonable time or upon the accomplishment of the purpose of the power. In addition, the principal can revoke and the agent can renunciate the power at any time, although the reneging party may be liable for damages caused to the other party in so doing. The power of attorney usually will be terminated by operation of law upon the death of either the principal or the agent. Generally the agent's authority is terminated or suspended upon the principal's loss of capacity to become a party to the transaction.[56]

The "Model Special Power of Attorney for Small Property Interests Act" was first published in 1965. It has been enacted in total or in part in Arkansas, Oklahoma, and Wyoming.[57] It provides a simple and inexpensive legal

procedure for assisting persons with relatively small property interests and small incomes who, in anticipation of, or because of physical or mental handicap resulting from injury, old age, senility, blindness, disease, or other similar cause, wish to provide for the care of their property when they are unable to do so. Designed as a less expensive and intrusive alternative to guardianship and conservatorship, the Model Act provides a minimum of procedural safeguards.[58] The power of attorney must be approved by a judge of an appropriate court, filed with the court clerk, and recorded with real property deeds and mortgages. The power will not be invalidated by the principal's subsequent incompetency. It may be restricted to certain matters or grant complete authority to provide for the individual's person and property.

The "Model Special Power of Attorney for Small Property Interests Act" represents a marked improvement over guardianship and conservatorship. Even in the Iowa conservatorship statute with its provision for a delayed appointment of a guardian, a judicial hearing is required both to appoint and to terminate the guardian and the guardian, once appointed, has full control. The moving party under the Model Act is the aged individual himself. He can define the powers which he wants to give his agent, and, perhaps most importantly, he can provide that the powers are not to become effective until the occurrence of some future event. Thus he can anticipate approaching mental or physical disability by executing the document while he is still able. However, there are problems with a power of attorney that is to become effective only upon the happening of some future event. There may be confusion or controversy as to whether the future event has occurred, and therefore the drafting of the power of attorney to take effect in the future requires extreme care in specifying a readily ascertainable condition so that the attorney can begin his duties without controversy.

The Uniform Probate Code, which has been enacted in several states, permits a competent individual to execute a power of attorney which will become effective or remain effective in the event he should later become disabled.[59] If the court subsequently appoints a conservator or guardian, it may either permit the attorney in fact to continue to act or revoke the power of attorney. Under the Uniform Probate Code, the written power of attorney can provide "this power of attorney shall not be affected by disability of the principal," or "this power of attorney shall become effective upon the disability of the principal," or use similar words expressing the intent that the agent is to have the power to act during the principal's disability or incompetence. In this case, the fact that the principal later becomes mentally or physically incapable of caring for himself or his property will not terminate the power of attorney. The Uniform Probate Code does not require that a court approve the power of attorney. This is less of a substitution of judgment than either the conservatorship statutes or the Model Special Power of Attorney for Small Property Interests Act, which require such court approval.

The provisions of the Model Special Power of Attorney for Small Property Interests Act and the Uniform Probate Code are very important because ordinarily a power of attorney is made effective upon execution of the document and terminates when the principal becomes mentally incompetent. These two

provisions are more appropriate for use by an aged person who wishes to have assistance when his mental and physical powers fail, but wants to select his agent, keep some powers to himself, or keep all powers until some future event. Although use of powers of attorney should reduce petitions for guardianship, their use will not entirely eliminate the need for incompetency and guardianship proceedings.

C. Legal Assistant

An additional alternative should be mentioned. One can imagine situations when decision-making authority should remain with the aged person who, however, could use "assistance" to assure that he is aware of or remembers important facts. If an aged person's memory but not his "judgment" is impaired, there may be no need for him to delegate his decision-making authority.

Legislation could provide for a court appointed agent, perhaps called a "legal assistant," to be responsible for reviewing with the aged person all of the major financial transactions which he seeks to undertake.[60] The legal assistant can remind him of prior obligations, legal restrictions, and other complications. However, the legal assistant would not have power to substitute his judgment for that of the elderly individual. The law might also provide that major contractual obligations and property transactions are voidable unless countersigned by the legal assistant who would be required to countersign after advising the aged person.

Of all the alternatives considered here, the Legal Assistant is the least intrusive. Obviously there are problems with this approach. It will be difficult to determine the standard of care to be placed on the legal assistant, as well as the manner of proving that his advice met the established standard. What consequences should follow, for example, if the legal assistant does not remind the aged person that the mortgage is due and the bank forecloses on the property? Suppose the legal assistant says that he reminded the aged person, who has a poor memory, that the mortgage payment was due, and the aged person says that he does not remember the legal assistant so telling him. Should the legal assistant be personally liable for the aged person's loss of property? Moreover, despite a provision that the legal assistant could not substitute his judgment for that of the aged individual, if his countersignature is required, he could refuse to authorize the property transaction. In such a case the aged person might have to bring court action either to compel the assistant to sign or to terminate the arrangement. In either event, he might be inviting a petition to declare him incompetent and appoint a guardian for him.

V. Conclusions and Recommendations

The common law in England and the United States has a preference for lineal descendants to be the natural objects of a person's bounty. Therefore gifts made late in life to other than lineal descendants may be subject to close scrutiny. If

the family members are passed over in preference for a non-family member, especially a woman in whom the aged man shows some fondness, courts often look for an excuse to appoint a guardian or to invalidate the gift. Gifts of property may be struck down by courts for a lack of a donative intent or because the gift was not delivered to the donee. Gifts in wills may be found to be the product of a lack of capacity to make a will or of undue influence. This has been referred to as the "Trixie Syndrome."

The analogy referred to earlier between protecting infants and protecting the aged is of limited usefulness. It is one thing to substitute judgment for an individual who has never been competent but is developing competency which is expected to continue for several years. It is quite another thing to substitute judgment for a person who has been competent but is growing incompetent and has a relatively short life remaining. In this situation, it is less likely that the guardian can preserve property for the aged person to use and enjoy later. If the aged individual is becoming mentally or physically weaker, he will be increasingly less able to enjoy his wealth. Large houses, cars, trips, and gardens bring less pleasure to someone who is no longer mentally or physically capable of using them. For infants, society has more of an interest in "$autonomy_2$"—maximizing potential and preserving opportunities. For the aged, society has more of an interest in "$autonomy_1$"—the non-substitution of judgment.

A long life of frugality followed at sixty-five years of age by the spending of large sums on pleasures foregone in the past may not be a sign of incompetence. It may be a recognition of mortality. Clearly, preserving an aged individual's property, as present policy dictates, may result, not in preserving it for him, but in preserving it for his heirs. Should we have a public policy to override an aged person's autonomy and preserve his property for his heirs? The conclusion of this paper is no.

It has also been shown that many acts used to establish incompetency are not "societally neutral." An act of giving money can be viewed either positively or negatively depending upon the identity of the donee and the circumstances of the donor. Those acts which contradict society's norms and mores are more likely to be interpreted as indicating mental incompetency than acts which agree with society's values.

The use of medical testimony in competency proceedings further complicates matters. A physician testifying as a medical expert must establish the causal connection between the mental or physical condition and the disapproved actions. Medical science does not yet appear capable of doing this. In addition, medical experts are frequently asked to testify to matters that are not within their area of expertise. For example, the terms "likely to be deceived" and "capable of handling complex business matters" are not within the physician's expertise because they are not scientific concepts. Rather, they require judgments in which a layman is as qualified to predict and evaluate behavior as is the medical expert.[61]

Legal proceedings which classify an individual as either "competent" or "incompetent" are inappropriate for aged persons who may be only partially incapable of handling their affairs. We need alternative procedures which will

allow society to preserve an aged person's autonomy while providing the assistance the individual needs to protect himself.[62]

We must protect, in other words, both "autonomy$_1$" and "autonomy$_2$." But we must recognize that for aged individuals "autonomy$_2$"—maximizing human potential and preserving future opportunities—has decreased in importance. Promoting "autonomy$_1$" then assumes primacy. The balance should shift from favoring "autonomy$_2$" for infants, to favoring "autonomy$_1$" for the aged.

Conservatorships are the oldest and most common alternative to incompetency proceedings. They are also the most intrusive and the most depriving of autonomy. The power of attorney appears to be the best procedure to protect both "autonomy$_1$" and "autonomy$_2$" for it does not substitute judgment for an aged individual. Instead it allows him to make his decisions according to his values. But it also provides a method for the aged individual to preserve future opportunities by allowing the agent to act when the aged individual becomes mentally or physically incapable of acting. In this way the individual is assured of having someone of his own choosing, and presumably someone who shares his value judgments, to make decisions for him when he is no longer capable of doing so.

Notes

[1]I wish to express my appreciation for the invaluable assistance provided by John R. Evans, B.A., Kalamazoo College; M.P.A., Maxwell School, Syracuse Univ.; J.D. (expected December 1977) Capital University Law School.

[2]Dorland's *Illustrated Medical Dictionary* (London: W. B. Saunders, 1974), pp. 1283-84.

[3]Martin Roth and D. H. Myers, "The Diagnosis of Dementia," *British Journal of Psychiatry,* Special Publication No. 9 (1975), 87, 94.

[4]Ibid., p. 93.

[5]Milton D. Green in "Undue Influence and Medical Incompetency," *Michigan Law Review,* 38 (1940), 1189 analyzed this problem from the point of view that the conflicting policies are (1) protecting the incompetent or his dependents and (2) upholding the security of transactions.

[6]Roe v. Wade, 410 U.S. 113 (1970) and Doe v. Bolton, 410 U.S. 179 (1970). In re: The Matter of Quinlan, 70 N.J. 10, 355 A. 2d 647 (1976).

[7]Milton D. Green, "Fraud, Undue Influence and Mental Incompetency," *Columbia Law Review,* 43 (1943), 176, 204-05: "Drawing a line always produces hardships in the marginal cases. Especially is this true where the shading from competency into incompetency is so gradual and almost imperceptible. A man may be almost a mental incompetent, but we cannot say his contract or will is almost invalid, or ninety per cent invalid. We are not equipped in our law with a sliding scale of legal results—transaction is either upheld or stricken down—there is no twilight 'legal effect' as there is a twilight zone of near-incompetency."

[8]For a good discussion of the legal history of will contests for alleged incompetency, see Milton D. Green, "The Operative Effect of Mental Incompetency on Agreements and

Wills," *Texas Law Review,* 21 (1943), 554. Green points out in "Proof of Mental Incompetency and Unexpressed Major Premise," *Yale Law Journal,* 53 (1944), 271, that the question of whether the will was "fair" seems to be as important as evidence of legal competence.

[9]Thomas Atkinson, *Handbook of the Law of Wills* (St. Paul: West Pub. Co., 1953), p. 232.

[10]Ibid., p. 250.

[11]In re Estate of Wolf, 174 Cal. 2d 52, 334 P.2d 37 (Dist. Ct. App. 1959); In re Teel's Estate, 25 Cal. 2d 520, 154 P.2d 384 (1944); In re Sexton's Estate, 199 Cal. 759, 251 Pac. 778 (1926).

[12]In re Teel's Estate.

[13]In re Krause's Estate, 71 Cal. 2d 719, 163 P.2d 505 (Dist. Ct. App. 1944).

[14]In re Jamison's Estate, 41 Cal. 2d 1, 256 P.2d 984 (1953).

[15]In re Sexton's Estate.

[16]George J. Alexander, "Surrogate Management of the Property of the Aged," *Syracuse Law Review,* 21 (1969), 87. See also Alexander's recent article: "On Being Imposed Upon By Artful or Designing Persons: The California Experience With the Involuntary Placement of the Aged," *San Diego Law Review,* 14 (1977), 1083, in which he notes that the State of California is the primary user of guardianship proceedings apparently to assure that the state receives payment for its services.

[17]In re Mills, 250 Wis. 401, 27 N.W.2d 375, 377 (1947). See also the philosophical statements in Rhoads v. Rhoads, 29 Ohio App. 449, 163 N.E. 724 (1927) and In re Guardianship of Wilson, 23 Ohio App. 390, 155 N.E. 654 (1926).

[18]In re Cass' Guardianship, 155 Neb. 792, 54 N.W.2d 68, 73 (1952).

[19]Milton D. Green, in "Judicial Tests of Mental Incompetency," *Missouri Law Review,* 6 (1941), 165, states that the actual decision of the judge is dressed in a facade of legal language as a matter of ritual. The actual test used by the courts is an inarticulate behavioristic objective standard.

[20]Ohio Rev. Code §2111.01(D) (Cincinnati, O.: Anderson Pub. Co., 1976).

[21]Guardianship of McConnell's Estate, 26 Cal. App. 2d 102, 78 P.2d 1043, 1045 (1938). To the same effect see In re Towson's Guardianship, 124 Cal. 598, 12 P.2d 1003 (1932) in which a sixty-five year old man abandoned his conservative fiscal habits and conveyed property to a younger woman; Estate of Reed, 198 Cal. 148, 243 Pac. 674 (1926); In re Schulmeyer's Guardianship, 171 Cal. 340, 153 Pac. 233 (1915) which concerns an eighty-two year old man who could not remember business matters.

[22]In re Guardianship of Jacobs, 73 Ohio App. 286, 290, 28 Ohio Ops. 449, 451 (1941):

> It is humane and in keeping with the trend of the times to authorize the designation of one whose mind is in such a state that he requires a guardian, as an "incompetent" instead of a "lunatic" or an "insane person," but, inasmuch as the incompetency which clothes the Probate Court with jurisdiction to name a guardian, against his will, must be mental incompetency, the determination when made is to all intents and purposes synonymous with a finding that the incompetent is insane or a lunatic. This necessarily follows because the terms by which these words are defined in the language of the statute include "every

species of insanity or mental derangement." If one suffers mental disability or infirmity he is mentally deranged. There is a variation of a normal state of mind.

[23] In re Joyce, 19 Ohio Ops. 506, 510, 32 Ohio L. Abs. 553, 558 (Probate Ct. 1940): Liberty is not an unrestricted right to do as one wishes. As society becomes more complex, one's right to action becomes more circumscribed so as to respect the rights of other members of the same society. When society becomes so civilized that it decides to protect the person and property of any of its members, the liberty of its members must be so limited that the state may exercise its authority. And it must follow that when the state provides a statutory method of determining whether one of its citizens deserves the protection of the state, either as to his person or property, or both, that citizen must surrender his liberty to the extent that the state may determine whether his condition is such as to justify the state in exercising its jurisdiction.

[24]For another view of the role of expert evidence in competency proceedings, see Green, "Mental Incompetency," pp. 284-86.

[25]Ronald Leifer notes in "The Competence of the Psychiatrist to Assist in the Determination of Incompetency: A Skeptical Inquiry into Courtroom Functions of Psychiatrists," *Syracuse Law Review,* 14 (1965) 564, 572:

The psychiatrist is trained primarily as a medical physician. His expert status is based on two factors: first, his training in the sciences of anatomy, physiology and chemistry as they are specifically applicable to the detection and alteration of physico-chemical events in the bodily machine; second, his authorization by a civil authority to practice these skills. The legal sanctioning of the physician-psychiatrist is based on his knowledge of the methods of physics and chemistry. However, the methods of communication and not the physico-chemical methods of medicine are utilized in the investigation and description of human affairs. It is interesting to note that no legal test of competency mentions the physical condition (of the brain) as a criterion. . . . If whatever the brain findings may be, the opposite condition of competency is possible, then the brain findings cannot be used in support, since there is no correlation between the state of the brain and the legal criterion of the test. In the face of this unreliable correlation, the enjoinder to exercise caution seems to be a spurious attempt to underwrite the psychiatrist's opinion with medical testimony, for it is not clear what operations would be considered to be the proper exercise of caution. This is another device used by the psychiatrist to give him the appearance of a medical scientist. It is clear that the psychiatrist's primary claim to expert status, his medical training, is irrelevant in the determination of competency.

[26]In re Guardianship of Breece, 173 Ohio St. 542, 184 N.E.2d 386 (1962).

[27]Guardianship of McConnell's Estate, 26 Cal. App. 2d 719, 78 P. 2d 1043, 1044 (1938). To the same effect see, Estate of Reed, 198 Cal. 148, 243, P. 674 (1926).

[28]In re Schulmeyer's Guardianship, 171 Cal. 340, 153 P. 233, 234 (1915).

[29]For a discussion of the importance which the courts place on the finding of a "normal" transaction, see Green, "Mental Incompetency," pp. 298-311.

[30]In the Matter of the Guardianship of Tyrrell, 92 Ohio L. Abs. 253, 256 (Probate Ct. 1962), app. dismissed 174 Ohio St. 552, 190 N.E.2d 687 (1963).

[31]Neidermyer v. Neidermyer, 237 Ia. 685, 22 N.W.2d 346 (1946).

[32]In the Matter of the Guardianship of Malnick, 180 Neb. 748, 145 N.W.2d 339 (1966).

[33]In the Matter of the Guardianship of Valentine, 4 Utah 2d 355, 294 P.2d 696 (1956).

[34]In re Watson, 176 Cal. 342, 168 Pac. 341 (1917).

[35]In re Coburn, 165 Cal. 202, 131 Pac. 352 (1913).

[36]In the Matter of the Guardianship of Tyrrell, p. 254.

[37]In re Johnson's Estate, 286 Mich. 213, 281 N.W. 597 (1938).

[38]In re Towson's Guardianship, 124 Cal. App. 598, 12 P.2d 1003 (1932).

[39]In re Guardianship of Smith, 26 Nisi Prius 533, 538 (Probate Ct. Ohio 1927).

[40]Ohio Rev. Code §2111.47 (Cincinnati, O.: Anderson Pub. Co., 1976).

[41]In re Guardianship of Breece.

[42]Sullivan v. Quinlivan, 32 N.E. 2d 209, 210-211 (Mass. 1941).

[43]286 Mich. 213, 281 N.W. 597 (1938).

[44]Ibid., p. 601.

[45]In the Matter of Guardianship of Tyrrell, p. 254.

[46]Ibid., p. 256.

[47]Brief for Appellant in the Supreme Court of Ohio.

[48]39 Am. Jur. 2d Guardian and Ward §22 (St. Paul, Minn.: West Pub. Co., 1968).

[49]Appeal of Hogan, 194 Atl. 854, 855 (Maine 1937).

[50]See In re Cass' Guardianship, 155 Neb. 792, 54 N.W.2d 68 (1952) where a petition of guardianship was filed against an eighty-one year old woman who had suffered two strokes. She resisted the guardianship and petitioned for the voluntary appointment of a conservator under the Nebraska statute. The trial court found the woman incompetent, appointed a guardian, and denied the petition for conservatorship. The intermediate appellate court reversed and denied the petition for appointment of a guardian and granted the petition for a voluntary appointment of a conservator. The Nebraska Supreme Court agreed, stating that the woman was not incompetent. It seems likely that had the woman not petitioned for the voluntarv appointment of a conservator, the trial court's determination of incompetency would have been upheld.

[51]Kan. S.A. §59-3007 (Supp. 1975); West's Calif. Anno. Probate Code §1754 (Supp. 1976); Mass. G.L.A. c. 201 §16-22 (1958); New Hamp. R.S.A. §464:17 (1968); Neb. Rev. Stat. §§38-901—38-903 (1974).

[52]Mass. G.L.A. c. 201 §18 (1958); New Hamp. R.S.A. §464.21 (1968); Kan. S.A. §59-30 (Supp. 1975).

[53]In re Guardianship of Stark, 118 N.W.2d 537 (Ia. 1962).

[54]Iowa C.A. §§633.591—633.597 (1963).

[55]3 Am. Jur. 2d Agency §§23-33 (St. Paul: West Pub. Co., 1962).

[56]Ibid., §§33-67.

[57]Ark. Stats. §58-501 (1975); 58 Okla. Stat. Anno. §§1051-1062 (1975); Wyo. Stats. §§34-111.1—34-111.10 (Supp. 1975).

[58]Legal Research Center of Univ. of Michigan Law School, *A Handbook of Model State Statutes* (Washington, D.C.: National Council of Senior Citizens, Inc., 1971), pp. 157-64.

[59]Uniform Probate Code §§5-501—5-503 (St. Paul: West Pub. Co., 1972).

[60]Alexander, "Surrogate," p. 166.

[61]See Leifer.

[62]See Alexander, "Surrogate," p. 167.

Stuart F. Spicker

GERONTOGENETIC MENTATION: MEMORY, DEMENTIA AND MEDICINE IN THE PENULTIMATE YEARS[1]

> Or est il mort, passé trente ans,
> Et je remains vielle, chenue.
> Quant je pense, lasse! au bon temps,
> Quelle fus, quelle devenue!
> Quant me regarde toute nue,
> Et je me voy si tres changiee,
> Povre, seiche, megre, menue,
> Ju suis presque toute enragiee.
>
> François Villon[2]

I. Introduction: Ambivalence Toward the Aged

In his brief sketch of Western civilization, a physician, Joseph T. Freeman, writing in *The Gerontologist,* makes the point that the tradition known as humanism "in its aristocratic origin and middle class values long glorified youth and maturity and left old age out of its realm."[3] History, Simone de Beauvoir argues in some detail, "like literature, passes them over in total silence," and the personal experience of the aged "was not appreciated at all . . . in the poets."[4] The Hellenic philosophers, Plato and Aristotle, had already articulated widely divergent theories of aging. For Plato it was consistent to advocate a gerontocracy: since the human mind is not in essence susceptible to deterioration and decay as is the material body, and since governance is dependent on cognitive, not bodily, integrity, a sound mind was the critical requirement which often combined with the extensive experience of the elderly citizen active in the polis. On the other hand, for Aristotle, who rejected Platonic metaphysics at its critical pivots, old age brings with it total

deterioration, and extensive experience is not of particular value. Aristotle is thus totally distrustful of the 'gerontes,' a term derived from *Gera, geron* which, de Beauvoir reminds us, means great age as well as the privilege of age and semantically connects to the notion of honor.[5]

In the present century—on two separate occasions in June, 1941—the American philosopher Ralph Barton Perry addressed the forty-fifth reunions of the classes of 1896 of Harvard and Princeton Universities with his "Plea for an Age Movement." In this speech he remarked that "recently we have fallen to an all-time low . . . "; we witness "the fall of age from its once high eminence." Thus, he concluded, "the time has come to start an 'age movement.' "[6] Perry's position is reminiscent of that of Cicero in *Cato Maior de Senectute* where, speaking of the Roman senators and offering a eulogy to old age, he claims that old men retain their mental powers only as long as they refuse to stop exercising and enhancing them by seeking further knowledge. For Cicero, senile decay (what we tend to equate with dementia) can be avoided by the propaedeutics of preventive action; so-called 'second childhood,' he believes, though not present in all men, occurs in those whose minds are already weak or disposed to diminished powers of mentation.

Aside from eulogies to old age or bitter odes to decrepitude and the organic deterioration of the aging person, what can one find in Western philosophical literature that avoids the *culs-de-sac* of nostalgia, sentimentality, pseudo-compassion, and obvious nods to prevalent biases against aged members of the human commonwealth? Is it for a philosopher, any more than anyone else, to add his or her voice in support of the disenfranchised poor, many of whom are elderly and aged? And if so, is there a contribution for philosophy and philosophers to make beyond clarifying concepts under the rubrics of 'aging' and 'the aged'? Can we not do more than merely reiterate the distinction between objectified chronological age and experienced, subjective, or 'phenomenological' age, the age that we feel? How can we transcend the mesmerizing power of the statistical litany which rehearses in cadence the latest tune: " . . . one tenth of our population is now over sixty-five. If present birth trends continue, an estimated 17% of the population will be 65 and older by the year 2030 compared to 10.5% today" (this reminds us of Perry's observation in 1941: "The vital statistics tell us that the average age of living Americans is rapidly rising.")[7] While forecasting of demographic trends may be more precise in these days of the computer, a critically accurate tally can make it even easier to look the other way, wholly distracted. "22,400,000 or slightly over 11% of the population is over 65," says an entry in *The Congressional Record.*[8] Aside from the self-serving testimony to the medical achievements which began with the discovery of penicillin in 1927, of what import is the rhetoric which underscores the survival of more and more of us? Where did quantity of life, longevity, outrun all interest in quality of life? Have we forgotten our Darwinian heritage?

The fact is that we are much too Darwinian, that is, we have quite unwittingly accommodated ourselves to scientific theory, and have thus neglected to notice that it carries with it a critical value-laden component. Briefly put: the appeal to the Darwinian theory of the long course of human descent—with modification

through variation and natural selection—has too frequently led contemporary intellectuals to accept the thesis that, since the aged members of the species *homo sapiens* have by dint of numerous cultural factors survived, they—as individuals and as a collective biological élite—are the most fit of the species and, therefore, deserve our admiration, respect, and continued care in their penultimate years. But appeal to Darwin and his revolutionary theory of evolution when considering the function of the aged, is, in reality, a futile one: for Darwin's theory begins and ends, we should not forget, with the notion of *reproduction*[9] (as distinct from that of generation).[10] Since only those members of a species *capable* of producing progeny affect the distant future of that species, it follows that only those members of a species capable of reproducing their kind are *valued* when one looks to the center of the theory of natural selection. In fact, one might correctly construe the impact of Darwin's general theory of the mutability of species as serving to further disenfranchise the elderly members of our species, especially the females, since they no longer possess the power to reproduce progeny, though they clearly need not forfeit their sexuality. In other words, from the standpoint of Darwinian theory, postmenopausal females are by definition evolutionarily "irrelevant" and in many instances so too are the males. Teasing out the ethic latent in Darwinism, then, we see that members of the species who are incapable of "transmitting progeny" are no longer considered relevant or of much interest with regard to the long-term ends of the complex processes of selection, survival, and extinction, which are the *idées maîtresses* in the *Origin of Species.*

Whatever the negative influence of Darwinism on the prevailing 'negative image problem' of the elderly (as Robert Butler, M.D., has aptly phrased it), old age is not a disease; it is not even a syndrome, though there are surely "signs" of aging. It is not *une maladie obscure,* to borrow a phrase from a poem of Eustache Deschamps.[11] Nor is aging "just a poor second choice to dying young," as Robert Kastenbaum's analysis of societal attitudes reveals.[12] Yet talk of aging and the aged seems to lead quite readily to talk about death, as if death and dying were only appropriated by the elderly. Even a cursory look at the philosophical literature reveals that insights regarding aging, where they occur, are stillborn at the expense of any significant elaboration. Philosophers eventually become preoccupied with death. Their indexes, as Kastenbaum aptly remarks, read as follows: "Death? See Old Age. Old Age? See Death."[13] So philosophers continuously write of death when they were supposed to attend to aging. Physicians reject death, for death, the enemy, even among the oldest members of the species, is adjudged a physician's failure.[14] This peculiar inference is, in part, explained by the fact that philosophers do not attend the dying, whereas physicians are so charged. They both share in avoiding, wherever possible, reflection on aging and the aged. There is one general exception to this predominant attitude: in the United Kingdom physicians have been organized to care for the very elderly, and there geriatric medicine is indeed a medical specialty, only now beginning to receive its long-deserved recognition in the United States.

Notwithstanding the fact that physicians and philosophers have enjoyed a

dialogue with each other which stretches to the Hellenic period, our contemporary era, generally speaking, does not witness serious formal engagement between philosophers and those persons who care for the elderly. With the rise of geriatric medicine and a slow increment in the number of geriatric physicians who attend, primarily, to the very aged, this dialogue may well take place more frequently. There is, of course, the ever present danger that geriatricians and philosophers will talk past one another. That would be unfortunate. Physicians and other health professionals who care for the infirm aged (the 'frail age' group, as Robert Butler calls them, those persons over 75 or 80)[15] have not, in general, received a philosophical education, and only a very few philosophers are formally trained in medicine and health care delivery, however refined their sentiments and impeccable their sense of justice and equity. Hence, one must be alert to those nonphilosophers who construe philosophy in ways unacceptable to philosophers. For example, in "Geriatric Care in the United Kingdom," Anne R. Somers remarks:

> The overriding philosophy animating all British geriatric care is that old people should be kept at home and as nearly independent as possible; except under extraordinary circumstances where constant medical and nursing services are needed. Irreversible terminal illness is not considered one of these extraordinary circumstances.

She goes on to conclude that "this philosophy differs so markedly from that in the United States."[16]

Surely Anne Somers is correct in her appraisal, but need she refer to it as British or American "philosophy"? All she really intends is to underscore a general attitude and value preference—hardly grounds for anything but a most loosely conceived notion of philosophy. In contrast, T. H. Marshall, in his contribution to the volume, *Needs of the Elderly for Health and Welfare Services,* entitles his discussion "The Philosophy and History of Need"[17] and construes 'philosophy' as the "pursuit of wisdom and knowledge" which includes questions of "distributive justice and equality." His paper, one of the few which relates ethics or moral philosophy to the notion of "need" among the elderly, considers "ethical judgments and their effect upon issues of public policy" as well. But, generally speaking, those persons involved in gerontology and geriatric care have paid little heed to philosophy. Given this abdication, for whatever historical reasons, it is all the more important that philosophers (at least some philosophers) turn their gaze to the aged and examine what has been said of the processes inherent in aging.

Clearly, a visit to a clinic can begin to shed some light on these aging processes in elderly patients. One soon discovers that along with the multiplicity of "organic" problems which afflict the elderly patient, some of the most serious and least understood include the elderly person's *mentation,* the dysfunction of which has generated the concern of psychologists and physicians—so much so, in fact, that the most recent medical literature reveals (as was indicated above) a

new subspecialty called "psychogeriatrics" or "geronto-psychiatry" which is analogous to "pedo-psychiatry."

II. The Aging Organism and Mentation

The term 'mentation,' which according to the *Oxford English Dictionary* originated in the United States around 1850, was originally employed to refer to mental action, especially as attributed to the agency of the brain or other nervous organs. Since it did not make a sharp bifurcation between mind *and* body suggestive of, in my opinion, the worst form of Cartesian dualism and historically degenerate metaphysics, the term conveyed a unified sense of the person or patient. 'Mentation' was taken to refer to embodied and incarnate consciousness, even if brain and central nervous system focused to the general exclusion of the remainder of the patient's body. 'Mentation,' then, was a synonym for the earlier terms 'psyche,' 'soul,' or 'mind,' all of which usually signal a Cartesian model of the amorphous side of the self—that immaterial, impenetrable side having no properties appropriately ascribed to bodies.

Disability with regard to mentation implied "organic" dysfunction (usually something like "organic brain syndrome") and since medicine traditionally defined the boundaries of its realm as necessarily including organic dysfunction, physicians were expected to attend to problems in mentation. This they frequently did even prior to the existence of psychiatry as a medical specialty and psychogeriatrics as its most recent subspecies. This view—that aberrations in mentation are organically based—is, in fact, found as early as the 4th Century B.C. in the writings of Aristotle. Readers of Aristotle may recall the classic *aporia* or impasse created by the dual thesis that (1) reason or intellectual mind, being a kind of imagination, forms a unity with and is inseparable from the body (brain), and that (2) there is at least one activity of soul (intellectual mind) that can exist independently and separately from any connection to a body (brain). Mind, Aristotle sometimes maintained, "seems to be an independent substance . . . and incapable of being destroyed. If it could be destroyed at all," he adds, "it would be under the blunting influence of old age."[18] The next passage in Aristotle's *De Anima* is the historical precursor to the prevalent contemporary view:

> What really happens in respect of mind in old age is, however, exactly parallel to what happens in the case of the sense organs; if the old man could recover the proper kind of eye, he would see just as well as the young man. The incapacity of old age is due to an affection not of the soul but of its vehicle, as occurs in drunkenness or disease. Thus it is that in old age the activity of mind or intellectual apprehension declines only through decay of some other inward part; mind itself is impassible. Thinking, loving, and hating are affections not of mind, but of that which has mind, so far as it has it. That is why, when this

> vehicle decays, memory and love cease; they were activities not of mind, but of the composite which has perished; mind is, no doubt, something more divine and impassible.[19]

The ever-expanding number of elderly persons has led some like Professor Joseph Fletcher to suggest that attention to brain deterioration be given priority by contemporary biomedical researchers. Fletcher asserts that "it is vital, ethically, to overcome the loss of brain cells, which break down commensurately with body cells. Work on neurons and brain physiology is, ethically, a first order requirement."[20] This view is a far cry from Aristotle's concerns as a biologist and philosopher of mind. Since the absolute number of people living beyond 70 has increased significantly since Aristotle's day,[21] Fletcher wishes to direct our attention to the overall quality of those that experience longevity. As an ethicist concerned with the notion of 'person,' an ethical concept, and as an advocate of authentic personhood, Fletcher is led to advocate maximum brain life; the tacit premise is that personhood of necessity requires intact cortical structure. Given this argument, research priorities are dictated by the importance of intact cortical structure for personhood, and biological life prolongation becomes of secondary importance since it is only organic life that is here prolonged, not the life of a person. As Sir George Pickering remarked in response to life prolongation among the infirm aged, "Those with senile brains and senile behavior would form an ever increasing proportion of the earth's population. I find this a terrifying prospect."[22]

Thus, two considerations are implied here: the need for (1) research into the processes and mechanisms which account for cellular aging, and (2) research into the clinical assessment, diagnosis, and management of persons suffering from dysfunctions of mentation in the penultimate years. The first is already supported, in part, by the National Institute on Aging. For example, a notice from the Washington sector reads: "Grant applications are sought for cultured-cell studies of human aging phenomena and an expansion of conceptual and experimental approaches to the relationship between in-vitro expressions of cellular aging and human in-vivo cellular aging." But what of so-called "senile brains" which are, as Sir Pickering remarked, a "terrifying prospect"? Robert Butler reminds us that "perhaps we have forgotten that . . . doctors often find themselves admitting such a person [one suffering from malnutrition] to a hospital with what gets referred to very easily as 'senility' but is simply a function of inadequate food supply to the brain."[23] Voicing a general criticism, not only of physicians, Butler has stressed that "we fail, all too frequently, to recognize a reversible brain syndrome and hastily label it as senility, confusion, forgetfulness, or problems with attention or concentration. We now know that there are approximately 100, if not more, causes of this kind of so-called 'senility.' They range from malnutrition, to excessive medication to unrecognized congestive heart failure, to walking pneumonia, or even to anemia which affects as many as one-fourth of older people." He has also noted that ". . . of the 1.2 million people in American nursing homes, about 1 million are

the elderly. At least half of that group suffers from senile dementia, which means that brain cells have died away."[24]

This idea is, of course, not a particularly cozy one, and one might prefer to take recourse in the more optimistic projection that "the much publicized loss of brain cells in old age . . . is by no means universal."[25] Or one might wish to look enthusiastically ahead to those ever predicted days when technological and scientific advances allow the total "percentage of senile persons in the population . . . [to] decrease."[26] But such hopeful promises on the one hand and fearful anticipations of an "ecological nightmare of endless life"[27] on the other, miss the point. The phenomena to which we should turn are not the cellular, organic, and physiological processes of the brain and central nervous system which are the material conditions and substructure for mentation, the destruction of which entails *modification of mentation* (*quite often but not always resulting in dysfunction or deficit*). Rather, we should inquire into what the psychologist G. Stanley Hall calls "senectitude," "the post-climacteric," or "old age proper."[28] At this point the time has come to throw away the ladder by which we climbed into this paper and to turn to memory and dementia in the setting of psychogeriatric assessment. We will be led to a new non-medical discipline: gerontogenetic mentation.

III. Dementia, Memory, and Geriatric Medicine

A common canard is that "old people live in the past."[29] But such generalizations tend to founder when given a more careful examination. Precisely how do old people mine their past experiences and refine them for personal use in a social context? Would a reevaluation and examination of mentation (memory) in elderly persons, say those over 80, reveal a new appreciation of temporality in these penultimate years?

The gerontological literature reveals—as does the philosophical—an image of aging persons as *reactive* beings, not active constructors of their life world. Psychological investigations of memory tend to approach the experienced past from the vantage point of measurement, as if our power to objectify time and quantify recall is the primordial or primitive condition out of which personal subjective time emerges. But, of course, the truth is just the converse: subjective or personal temporality (memory) is itself a pre-condition for the achievement of objective and measured time; measured time is derived from perceived and lived time. Thus, subjectivity constitutes, in fact, the most fundamental mode of time.

As the contemporary French phenomenologist Maurice Merleau-Ponty explains, "Time is . . . not a real process, not an actual succession that I am content to record. It arises from *my* relation to things."[30] Merleau-Ponty has shown that time is rooted in the *perception* of the actor as well as through his actions in and on the world. Motion is not the condition for subjective, experienced, or so-called 'phenomenal' time. Hence, consciousness, or subjectivity, is indissolubly bound up with time (this has been the motivation for

describing consciousness as a stream or a line).[31] So, paradoxically, time, and therefore memory, are not chronological. To think so would be to erroneously restrict our understanding of human memory.

Aging itself, of course, is predicated on the passage of time and awareness of change. If we expect to understand the experienced and retained past as well as future protentions and expectancies, research into the structure of memorial consciousness in senectitude should—indeed must—abandon the model of time as linear and objectified. Is this not what lies behind our clear intuition that one's chronological age is not the best indicator of one's feeling of age? Aging is a relative process, and individuals of identical chronological age who are called 'aged,' 'elderly,' or 'old' may well represent qualitatively different categories of existence. Therefore, as C. David Hendricks and Jon Hendricks have pointed out, "it is [incorrectly] assumed that individuals of similar chronological age will perceive and interpret time sequence and importance in a like manner."[32] If we use the category of objective time, the time of clock and calendar, then it is true, but trivial, that linear time is "running out" for the aged—a point usually taken with such literal seriousness as to compel philosophers to write of death instead of aging. Subjective time and memorial mentation wear qualitatively distinct faces in different social contexts—home, relative's home, nursing home—such that we are able to attribute a variety of meanings to various phases of our temporal, memorial experience. What assumptions are involved, then, in psychological research into memorial mentation in the aged? Is memory the key indicator of deteriorated intellection and mentation generally? Has memorial consciousness been viewed too simply in terms of a monolinear model? And how has this model affected the assessment we typically make with regard to the aged, whether as friends, relatives, or, as is quite often the case, by physicians and other health professionals charged with the assessment, diagnosis, care, and management of the aged infirm?

These questions seem serious enough to warrant some discussion. For as one physician puts it, "perhaps the most important realization of all is that the commonest presenting pattern of illness in old age is not pain, paralysis, or pyrexia but mental disturbance. This state of confusion and disorientation, which we recognize as the 'toxic-infective' reaction to a very wide range of metabolic, vascular, and infective disorders, is not just evidence of 'senility,' which is still a favourite label in some circles, but is an utterly unjustifiable substitute for an accurate diagnosis."[33] To repeat, "mental disturbance" is no substitute for diagnosis. Yet certainly, the difficulty inherent in accurate assessment of mentation in the elderly is well-known.

First, the range of intellectual performance in people at different times is wide. A Harvard professor with an I.Q. of 170 had a stroke, for example; "after the stroke the professor's I.Q. was 130 but there was virtually no way the physician could recognize the marked decline in brain function."[34] Even the most careful questioning may not always reveal disorientation in regard to time or significant decline in performance involving orientation in space, calculation, or memory. As Dr. Adrian M. Ostfeld has concluded, "There is almost a complete absence of good diagnostic psychological procedures for older

people."[35] Furthermore, medical record-keeping reveals an even more dismal situation. For instance, one five-page form which I have seen entitled "Patient Appraisal and Care Evaluation" has a very small matrix labeled "Orientation: Time, Place and Person" which requires one to check either "Oriented," "Disoriented, partially intermittently," or "Disoriented." Another four-page form, "Periodic Appraisal," has a tiny section called "Orientation to Person, Place and Time." It requires the physician or nurse to "Mark One Only" of six choices: (1) "Oriented," (2) "Disoriented—Some Spheres, Sometimes," (3) "Disoriented—Some Spheres, All Times," (4) "Disoriented—All Spheres, Sometimes," (5) "Disoriented—All Spheres, All Times," and (6) "Unconscious." Forms such as these are clearly poorly organized for the geriatrician who "does need sound information about intellectual impairment which has important implications for diagnosis and management."[36] Furthermore, by "intellectual impairment" it means not only the patient's memory but also his orientation, calculations, and knowledge of current information, and thus the term is used quite generally and does not in itself sort out the various processes and structures of mentation.

Assessment of both cognitive and conative mentation in the elderly is of critical importance if the geriatrician is to relieve distress and make sensible decisions. Since, for the physician, disorders primarily affecting mentation are integrated with disorders of the body, especially of the brain and central nervous system, assessment of mentation is itself assessment of the bodily component, so-called "organic brain damage." To accomplish adequate assessment of mentation, some geriatricians have used a particular mental status questionnaire (M.S.Q.), which runs as follows: (1) name of this town? (2) this place (e.g. address or hospital)? (3) today's date? (4) what month is this? (5) what year is this? (6) how old are you? (7) what year were you born in? (8) what month were you born in? (9) who is the prime minister [or president]? and (10) who was the prime minister [or president] before him? L.A. Wilson and W. Brass conclude that the M.S.Q. is "a powerful single measure for detecting and roughly quantifying intellectual impairment."[37] In addition, they claim that the M.S.Q. score reveals a high correlation with dementia ratings made independently by a physician. That is, in addition to completion of the M.S.Q. by some 207 patients, intellectual impairment was assessed on the basis of a physician's "own observations of the patient's conversation, behaviour and appearance, on information from the general practitioner, and, when available, on previous hospital records and history from supporters;"[38] this complex assessment was only based upon one highly competent physician's *"overall judgment"* and was labeled *"dementia rating."* With all due respect to Dr. Wilson, the hard work entailed in the analysis of the structure of mentation in the elderly can not be replaced by the ten-point instrument, M.S.Q. For the M.S.Q. is primarily focused on temporality; specifically it attends to memorial mentation. Temporal and memorial consciousness are, in fact, involved in grasping and responding to questions (3) through (10). Questions (1) and (2) involve naming: (1)name of this town? (2) this place (e.g., address or hospital)? Furthermore, as Dr. Wilson himself points out, question (1) might

well be excluded since it "adds little to discrimination."[39] Moreover, it is suggested that the patient be approached with the request: "How is your memory? I would like to test it."[40] Hence, it is not quite right to conclude that "all the M.S.Q. does is to help to disclose, and roughly measure, *intellectual impairment* at one point in time. . . . "[41] It is more precise to say, as does Dr. Wilson, that " . . . failing mental powers can be brought to the notice of an unsuspecting family."[42] The M.S.Q. cannot be credited with discriminating all forms of temporal mentation, spatial orientation, calculation, and current information or even "intellectual failure." What is surely correct is that it can identify if a rather significant alteration of mentation has occurred (for whatever reasons). For dementia includes such clinical features as irritability, procrastination, loss of initiative, and difficulty in adaptation to new situations and environments. All of this adds up to loss of mental capacity, and as time goes on, memory defects become more noticeable with deterioration most obvious in recent memory while remote memory may remain intact. But other cases of dementia reveal features like profound disorientation, social maladjustment, and incontinence. And it is often the case that dementia must be differentiated from psychotic depression which "may mimic senile dementia closely but, unlike dementia, sometimes responds well to therapy."[43] Moreover, senile dementia, which is usually associated with cerebral atrophy often of undetermined cause (certainly not caused by senility), must be distinguished from arteriosclerotic dementia.[44] Hence, the dementia we are discussing here is present in the absence of cerebral arteriosclerosis. In spite of distinctions based on specific clinico-pathological features, dementia is not itself a very clear concept. As one physician states, "the central loss in these disorders is the capacity to be responsible for directing one's daily life. If a person knows when to get out of bed, wash, dress, eat, and pay his bills, he is not a case. If someone has to do some or all these things for him or regularly remind him to do them, he is a case of dementia."[45] In this description no particular neurological or cortical lesion is brought forth as a warrant for the diagnosis "dementia." Such an account obviously fails to give due weight to all—if any—of the clinical phenomena.

But worse than this cavalier and unfortunately prevalent attitude toward assessing dementia, medicine has been complacent and remains unclear about the essential structural alterations in mentation in the very aged. It is little wonder that terms like 'senility,' 'dementia,' 'intellectual impairment,' and 'disorientation' proliferate madly. It should not go unnoticed that this dissatisfaction is shared by many geriatricians. In 1962, Drs. L. Wilson and I. Lawson pointed out that "dementia in the elderly requires as much care in its *interpretation* and investigation as dementia in younger people." They continued, "The use of 'senility' to explain general frailty is equally unsatisfactory and often covers a lack of diagnostic interest and effort."[46] The work to be done, then, is by no means complete today. The central question to ask is how does mentation differ structurally at different points in a person's age? To rectify this basic limitation in our knowledge and to avoid all twaddle (not on the part of old brains but rather among the younger analytic ones) like the

unsubstantiated generalizations of a physician from Liverpool, Dr. Robert Kemp, who claims that it is "normal" for persons over the age of 75 to be "frail and unsteady, dozing by day and wakeful at night, confused about people and places, forgetful and untidy, repetitive and boring, selfish and petty perhaps, and consumed by a fear of death,"[47] it may be of some value to turn our attention to a few physicians who offer clinical evidence which enables us to grasp the phenomena for ourselves.

IV. Alterations in the Structure of Mentation

Some years ago in response to a series of generalizations about aging profferred by Dr. Robert Kemp of Liverpool, a letter to the editor appeared in the September 29, 1962 issue to *The Lancet.* In his letter, Dr. J.N. Agate challenged Dr. Kemp on many points in his "Diagnosis of Old Age." Among them, Dr. Agate underscored the fact that illness in the old differs quite remarkably from illness in other age groups. He cited the frequent lack of exact symptoms (a "remarkable paucity of physical signs even in serious diseases"), and most important for our purposes, "a tendency for a mental disturbance to be the first evidence of physical disorder."[48] Failure to take these factors into account, he suggested, can only lead us to falsely attribute to "old age" what is in fact abnormality.

For trained geriatricians,[49] unsteadiness, disorientation, and the tendency to doze by day and be wakeful at night are indeed symptoms and signs to be carefully pursued. Furthermore, the biology of those who have entered not only senescence (which may be said to begin in the early forties) but senectitude (the post-climacteric or old age proper) reveals this uniqueness. Dr. Robert Butler points out:

> For example, an older woman, for some reason not an older man, receiving a certain anticoagulant, has a greater likelihood of untoward bleeding reactions. We are not sure why. Some of the tranquilizers which in a younger person may have a calming effect may create a dangerous drowsiness in an older person. The barbiturates which we think of as being sedatives or hypnotics to help people sleep at night may create the opposite reactions in older people.[50]

In addition, mental deterioration (confusion) is not a uniform process in the elderly, and it must be assessed for each patient with the physician taking into account the particular impairment-inducing conditions of that patient:

> Often it is not possible to point to a single cause of confusion in an ill old person. It may be due partly to the primary illness, partly to removal from familiar surroundings, partly to dehydration or electrolyte disturbance, partly to the complications of venous thrombosis or pressure sores, and partly to the drugs used. If there is any underlying

> dementia then the more severe the dementia the less specific and clear cut the cause of a confusional state is likely to be.[51]

This further underscores the heterogeneity within the aged group as well as the inadequacy of any view that seeks a singular cause to account for the relationship between being old and being 'confused.' In a report entitled "Similarities and Differences Between Psychological Deficit in Aging and Brain Damage," Gerald Goldstein and Carolyn Shelly conclude that in their study of four groups (young brain-damaged, young nonbrain-damaged, old brain-damaged, and old nonbrain-damaged), the effects of aging do not appear to run parallel with the effects of diffuse brain damage in a global way. They remark that "the discrepancy between the brain-damaged and nonbrain-damaged old subjects was not greater or smaller than what was found in the young groups."[52] They open their discussion by pointing out that "the major conclusion that can be reached appears to be that one cannot speak of mental decline with aging in a global way. First of all, there does not appear to be a decline in all intellectual functions. Indeed, tests of language abilities were performed better by the old nonbrain-damaged group than they were by the young nonbrain-damaged group."[53] Of even greater interest for us here is their conclusion that "there appears to be a decline in memory and problem-solving abilities with age, but the extent of the decline does not appear to be greater in brain-damaged individuals than it does in the nonbrain-damaged."[54] Most importantly, the researchers' report contains the admonition that "treating the decline in ability with aging as a monolithic entity would appear to be unwarranted, as would be the tendency to attribute this decline to either exclusively organic or sociocultural influences."[55] Thus the variables of nonverbal memory, language ability, motor ability, and psychomotor problem-solving need to be kept conceptually and operationally distinct. Empirical research suggests that the "pattern of intellectual decline with aging is not a simple one but requires consideration of specific kinds of abilities."[56] From the point of view of the interest of these researchers, then, for certain parameters of mentation there may well be resemblances between the normal and brain-damaged aged, but for other parameters there is clearly no good reason to assume that aged persons who reveal a particular *style* of mentation possess any kind of organic impairment like brain lesions.

In a most important paper, "Confusion in the House: Assessment of Disorientation for the Familiar in the Home," Ian Lawson reviews his critical appraisal of six of his female patients, all of whom experienced alterations in mentation, including what would appropriately be called 'dementia' in a few cases, and concludes that the *situation* of these brain damaged oldsters was a central component in understanding and managing their lives at home. Hence, in addition to the most accurate clinical assessment of organic, neurological syndromes and other forms of cerebral dysfunction as revealed through examination of perceptual distortions or illusions, he writes, the home situation may contain unique material that is not always available to later inspection when the patient is departed; and, indeed, when observed with patient *in situ*

naturale, may indicate quite alternative management to in-patient care. . . ."[57]

Observations of one of these patients in her natural surroundings revealed that disorientation in mentation is not comprehensible to the clinician without a full appreciation of the situation and milieu of the patient. A modification of wallpaper pattern, for example, served to alienate one patient from her surroundings. Although the presence and voice of her daughter, with whom she lived, was taken by her (through deductive inference) to mean that she was indeed at home, she in fact "did not *feel* herself to be there."[58] So when we say quite glibly, for example, that "old people tend to live in the past," we must ask ourselves if we have examined the situation in which the person's memorial consciousness is revealing itself. Have we explored the structure of mentation, in the best sense, which necessarily includes an examination of the *curriculum vitae,* life style, context, situation, and temporality of the aged? I believe we are compelled to respond in the negative. In short, if there is a correctly construed "loss" of mentation in some respects, it is probably not *mere loss* but a restructuring of the patient's entire mentation. The lady who was "disturbed" by the wallpaper had, we should note, no strict visual loss. Rather, she was impelled, writes Dr. Lawson, by what she saw into "a sense of bodily translation out of her familiar environment into the quite unfamiliar territory of 'the country.' "[59]

Carefully acquired clinical evidence, then, is the *sine qua non* for achieving an adequate assessment of mentation in the aged, and it is important to begin by assessing the mentation of the healthy, normal aged. Patient protocols like those of Dr. Lawson reveal even more: alterations in mentation are *not always permanent,* even in the aged infirm. Furthermore, 'confusion' and 'disorientation' in space and time are pejorative terms, since the norm is taken to be the mentation of those of us who have not yet reached senectitude or even senescence. Generally speaking, our psychology and philosophy are the products of the middle years and have normative implications for judging the penultimate years. Everything is directed to middle life or the "prime" when we are said to be at the "apex of our aggregate powers, ranging from twenty-five or thirty to forty or forty-five and comprising thus the fifteen or twenty years now commonly called our best."[60] But where alteration of mentation is not *reversible* (implying that we tend to prefer it to return to the mode of our middle years, if not our youth), it may well be restructured into a new totality, configuration, or Gestalt. One can now begin to put evidential teeth into the views of Robert Butler, who confesses that "I personally have always believed . . . that the study of aging is not just the study of decline—loss—and decrement which does indeed accompany aging and is found in later years."[61] 'To age' is not simply a replacement for the verb 'to decline.' Or as one researcher has put it more empirically, "old age is a poor prototype of deterioration associated with organic injury. . . ."[62] To avoid utilizing the model of organic impairment as the paradigm for alteration of mentation in the aged, we may well take a more serious look at what is *absent* amid the disciplines which proliferate Western culture.

We are now conscious of the fact that senescence and senectitude, which

occur in objective time, have a biological and mentational 'ontogenesis.' Since we are speaking of the penultimate phases of our existence, the term 'gerontogenetic' serves several purposes, containing as it does the Greek *Geron* and both (1) 'ontogeny' and (2) 'genetic,' which signal, respectively, (1) biologically rule-governed alteration occurring (2) in temporal phases. For 'ontogeny' refers to the development of the individual including the astonishing changes during its specific process of development and need not, of course, only apply to the embryo. In short, we are concerned with the cognitive *and* conative processes which undergo modification, configurational alteration, and even decline in the penultimate years. Hence, we call for a new area of inquiry: the study of *gerontogenetic mentation.*

V. *The Original Model: Piaget's "Epistémologie génétique"*

Almost as common as the notion that "old people live in the past" is the notion that very old people are living out their "second childhood." When Dr. Kemp identified the "normal" behavior of those persons over 75 as being frail and unsteady, forgetful and untidy, and consumed by a fear of death, he also remarked that it was "as normal as the comparable behavior of early childhood"[63]; discussing the behavioral changes in the elderly, he observed that these problems "are similar to those of childhood. . . ." And as if that were not enough, he concluded, "older people, like children, are unable to sort out their needs for themselves." Finally he confessed that "the elderly always seem to me to be on the reverse slope of childhood."[64] Fortunately, we can locate the opposite viewpoint among such eminently qualified researchers as J. de Ajuriaguerra and R. Tissot of the Psychiatric University Hospital of Geneve (Switzerland), who point out that "disintegration is not always a mere negative reflection of integration."[65] From their research setting where they investigate psychoneurologic disintegration in senile dementia, they quite carefully point out that "it is not our intention to derive from these studies a facile formulation of the elderly reverting to infancy. . . . Instead it is to demonstrate and attempt to understand, in the course of progressive deterioration, how functional dissolutions are produced which resemble the functional stages of infants—without neglecting the essential differences." The authors thus warn of too close a comparison between the senile disintegration process and infantile integration. Thus, they stress the fundamental differences between disintegration (retrogenesis) and integration (ontogenesis). As they put it, "the problem of steriotypias is a difficult one."[66]

In 1955 another Swiss intellectual—philosopher, biologist, psychologist, mathematician—Jean Piaget (at that time Professor at the Sorbonne and at the Faculté des Sciences à Genève) established a "Centre international d'Epistémologie génétique" and originated the first publication in the series "Etudes d'épistémologie génétique."[67] Notwithstanding current opinion, the Center was not concerned with what we Americans call "child psychology." It was not devoted to a study of behavioral parameters except in a very subtle

sense, a sense captured better by the French term *comportement* rather than the English word "behavior." The opening page of the first volume of the *Etudes* established the purpose of the *Centre* and the *Etudes:*

> The purpose of the Center at Geneva is thus to assure the possibility of teamwork between a few specialists who came from different directions during a specified time in order to share in the study of some well-defined questions of scientific epistemology from the point of view of development.[68]

The point is not so much the convening of multidisciplinary specialists representing logic, child psychology, mathematical physics, information theory, cognitive psychology, and epistemology. Rather, one should appreciate the purpose of the Center as directing its research to the understanding of those conditions, processes, and mechanisms which, if understood, would yield a systematic account of the origins of and developmental stages leading to scientific cognition. That is, Piaget was primarily concerned with determining the conditions for the possibility of the positive sciences. He was interested in the cognitive (rather than conative)[69] achievements of infants and children and the bearing of these accomplishments on what later is revealed as a cultural enterprise whose outcome is the generation of knowledge. Hence, the relevance of *'épistémologie,'* a term employed by philosophers to denote questions to be faced in the development of a theory of knowledge. Piaget's aims are thus quite unambiguously revealed when he discusses the *Programme et méthodes de l'épistémologie génétique:*

> . . . genetic epistemology is the study of successive states of a science *S* in terms of its development. Thus conceived, genetic epistemology is capable of being defined as 'the positive science, empirical as well as theoretical, of the becoming of the positive sciences in so far as they are sciences.'[70]

Thus conceived, Piaget's genetic epistemology is devoted to the study of those mechanisms which enable us to bring forth the positive sciences. His is a study of mental processes, having its roots in the earliest philosophical investigations into the structure of human cognition. Piaget's interests were, therefore, directed to psychology in a very carefully defined sense—the psychogenesis of those structures of cognition which give rise to the positive sciences (physics, biology, mathematics, and logic). Piaget's program is best summarized by a member of his original team, Wolfe Mays, professor of philosophy at the University of Manchester: "Piaget embarked on the study of cognitive development in children in the hope that it would help to elucidate the problem of knowledge in adults. Arguably this hope is misconceived in principle but it has issued in the most substantial body of related observation and theory so far to appear in developmental psychology."[71]

Piaget was interested in how "the logical and causal thinking of the child was

different from the adult,"[72] with adulthood not including senescence or senectitude but only the "prime" years in which scientific accomplishments come forth. In mathematics and the mathematical sciences the creative period tends to occur during the later 20's and early 30's. To understand the development of these processes, Piaget studied the overt activities which eventually take on a conceptual character. As Mays expresses it, Piaget's approach moves from the understanding of "knowing how" to "knowing that" in the child's thought.[73]

Appreciating the significant difference between perceptual and conceptual structures, Piaget attended to such domain-specific studies as time, space, speed, atomism, number, chance, causality, and 'conservation.' One important outcome of the work of the Center is the discovery that the principles of formal logic do not occur in the child's thought until adolescence, since classification and serialization, critical to logical thought, do not appear in the young child's cognition. A very high order achievement, cognitively speaking, is the notion of the number 12, for example, which is eventually "conceived as the class of all equivalent classes having twelve members," a formulation made salient by the logicians Frege and Russell. Most importantly (since we cannot explore Piaget's entire project at this time), Piaget always gave full regard to the child's action and behavioral activities; "the concept of length, for example, started off in the child as a group of behavioral activities such as comparing, ordering, etc. He [Piaget] would, however, hold that in the case of adult intelligence these activities have now obtained a symbolic expression in the form of mental operations, thus obviating the need for their overt performance."[74] Thus the child's operations, his or her actions as a system of *bodily* movements, eventually become interiorized, but earlier they were only exteriorizations of the child's lived body, the body as motile and acting on objects in the immediate, reachable sphere.

This approach to the development of cognitive achievements reveals the structure of *adult* thought, to be sure, but not the thought of persons who have entered senescence and senectitude, the penultimate phases of life. Perhaps it is true that the very aged, irrespective of infirmity, are no longer capable of scientific reasoning, analysis, and comprehension. That surely seems the case with respect to the demented aged, given a correct clinical assessment of that complex phenomenon. Still, are we to write off the mentation of the aged for this reason? Are scientific, mathematical, and logical reasoning, and the conditions of cognition which serve as their prerequisites, to be valued over all other forms of cognition? Is not scientific thought only one achievement and expression of the human condition? Is it any less an acknowledgement of the logicomathematical reasoning of scientists to point out that the magnificent operations of scientific thought are but one way to construe the world? Has the time come to describe the mentation of the senescent human actor?

To give due acknowledgement to the postscientific mentation of the aged, I have refrained from referring to the new discipline I mentioned earlier as "Gerontogenetic Epistemology." One must restrict the notion of epistemology to Piaget's very specified concerns (I leave aside the complaints voiced by the

philosophers who balk at Piaget's *genetic* epistemology).[75] Thus, I suggest that we study the gerontogenetic *mentation* of the aged and assess its phases with other than empirical, psychological models. That is, Piaget's successful approach can be taken as analogue for a study of the mentation of the aged. We may discover new phases, altering through time, thus enabling us to explicate the gerontogeny of the very aged geronto-genetically. We can stay with a model of the aged actor as a unified self which, as I have stressed, justifies the term 'mentation' and not 'mind' or 'psyche' or 'soul.' Moreover, since preliminary work has already been accomplished by psychologists interested in Piaget's earlier work, we have a place from which to start. But we must be careful to take Piaget's suggestions seriously: "Most tests of intelligence measure the latter behavior, but our real problem is to discover the actual operational mechanisms which govern such behavior, and not simply to measure it."[76]

Some guidelines for research are in order. First, we must be careful that we do not rush to develop instruments to measure aged mentation. It was this conservatism that elicited my earlier worry over the use of the M.S.Q. (mental status questionnaire) by geriatricians in the much needed assessment of their patients' mentation. Alterations in mentation, which we take for granted in children, are, we can hypothesize, not necessarily expressions of inevitable pathology or dysfunction but are integral to senescence and senectitude. The M.S.Q., however, tells us nothing of the mechanisms of temporal and memorial mentation, nor of the mechanisms of disintegration. Even more problematic is the danger of the overuse of such instruments as the M.S.Q. As Professors Ajuriaguerra and Tissot remark, "Despite the importance which may properly be assigned to disorders of memory . . . they must not be given too prominent a place in the field of demential disorganization, lest we risk explaining everything by a mechanism of amnesia."[77] Secondly, if our task is to understand the mentation of the very aged, not just the so-called "cognitive development," it is crucial that analyses not stop with the examination of the *content* of responses. It will be more important to uncover the structure of the *operations* which "lie below" the expressions of the aged. And thirdly, we must abandon the view that regression in elderly mentation is always a change to a lower order stage as it existed *previously*. That is, as J. Langer and W.R. Looft point out," the developmental direction in aging is backward, but it is backward to the forms of functional structures and actions that are present; the regression is never back to earlier, childhood forms of operation. An older person may give responses in a testing situation . . . that are very much like those of a child in the same situation, but these responses, though similar in content, may be the product of quite different cognitive operations."[78] We turn, finally, to the exploration of these insights.

VI. Genetic Epistemology in Transition to Gerontogenetic Mentation

Judith N. Hornblum and Willis F. Overton of Temple University and Kenneth F. Rubin of the University of Waterloo, Canada have published the

results of their research which examines Piaget's concept of 'conservation.'[79]

'Conservation' is perhaps best defined by describing the experimental procedure which attests to it: in full view of a subject, an experimenter begins with two identical medium-sized glasses containing *equal amounts* of water. The experimenter then pours the water from one of the two identical glasses into a tall, thin glass, removing the empty medium-sized glass. The subject is then asked to give the following three judgments and explanations: (1) do these glasses (one medium and one tall and thin) contain the same amount of water? how do you know? (2) does one of these two glasses have more water? how do you know? (3) does one of these two glasses have less water? how do you know? If the subject responds to the first question in the affirmative and the latter two in the negative, then one usually concludes that the subject *conserved* the amount of liquid. Affirmative responses to the latter two questions reveal that the subject has not related the size of the glasses to the height and volume of the liquid and has not, therefore, compensated for the fact that the tall, thin glass has a higher water mark than the medium-sized one. If this is the case, *conservation* has not been operative. Similarly, one can ask a child of ten, for example, whether he believes that sugar dissolved in water is *conserved,* even though the sugar particles become more and more invisible while the sum of particles remains constant.[80]

To investigate the operation of *conservation* in the elderly, a few research protocols were devised to make up for the "little information available concerning the effects of conservation training with elderly subjects." Hornblum and Overton began by distinguishing "performance" from "competence." That is, responses of elderly subjects to conservation tasks revealed either limitations in "performance" or, more significantly, *structural alterations in mentation* called "competence." If an elderly subject could be retrained to activate conservation (achieved by age 7, according to Piaget), then this suggests that the cognitive operation of conservation only required *reactivation.* In other words, the subject may not have undergone an alteration in the *structure* of mentation. On the other hand, and more importantly, these researchers suggest that there is often a structural alteration of cognition (mentation) in the elderly. Employing ingenious conservation tasks, Hornblum and Overton, did, in fact, and perhaps for the first time, train elderly subjects to perform tasks, thus revealing conservation performance. They believe that "it is most likely that [verbal] feedback activated existing operational structures."[81] Hence, they conclude that the elderly who were unable to distinguish between those concepts required for conservation probably reflected a "superficial problem" rather than an operational deficit or lack of competence. There is no need, however, to assume that operational modifications are always "deficits" which signal "loss" or "a *lack* of competence." That is precisely what one must discover. We should ask: do the elderly undergo an underlying structural alteration of mentation during senectitude? If so, is it always loss, deficit, and modification which can be reinstated by retraining? Although it may indeed be "more parsimonious to assume that training has influenced superficial performance factors (e.g., attention, motivation) than to assume that training has influenced underlying

structural competence,"[82] it is still necessary to investigate the question of the structural change of mentation in the elderly.

I strongly agree with William Looft that "further research should begin to provide answers regarding the structural properties of cognitive operations of this [old age] time of life."[83] The programmatic possibilities for the study of gerontogenetic mentation far exceed the exploration of temporality, memory, spatiality, orientation, and operations like conservation. One might consider, for instance, the concept of 'causality,' which (though necessary for scientific constructions and explanations and, therefore, of special interest to Piaget) has special import for the elderly, who may perhaps be incapable of scientific conceptualizations.

As a final illustration, then, let us consider causality which Piaget has shown appears on the sensory-motor level at the age of three or four months. Piaget writes:

> The infant discovers by chance that by pulling a cord which hangs from the roof of his cot he can shake, rock and rattle the celluloid toys (which contain small shot) attached to the roof. The proof that he sees causality in this is that later on, the roof being cleared of toys, a new object has merely to be hung up there when he immediately reaches for the cord and pulls on it looking expectantly at the object.[84]

This Piagetian analysis is illustrative of what Aristotle called "efficient cause." The child, through his activities—the cord-pulling with outstretched arm—eventually takes his egocentrism as the source of events in the world, a world which he can affect through his intentional activity. What might we postulate as the structural change in aged mentation? Does *prolonged* and *restricted activity* of the infirm aged produce a modification in the structure of their mentation? If so, does the aged and infirm patient, for example, adopt a mode of existence in which objects in the world overpower him? If so, does the category of causality, as Kant would have it, function differently in the total cognitive scheme (the human understanding)? These and similar questions are not only addressed to the psychologist but signal philosophical problems which should be taken up by philosophical psychology or philosophy of mind. In short, work for philosophers is not lacking in the domain of aging and the aged mind.

VII. Résumé and Proposal

In the early 1920's very little was known about children's strategies, intellective processes, and cognitive stages of development. The child was simply a "little adult" who, when he did his best, reasoned in the same way as the adult. Thanks to Piaget and his collaborators in Geneva and the proliferation of the published Piagetiana, the child has been emancipated. But thus far only sporadic efforts of scholars and researchers during the past fifteen or twenty

years have actually confronted problems ingredient in the processes of aging in that heterogeneous group we all too simply call "the aged."

Piaget for many years has been regarded as an anachronism and (with pun intended) viewed as the Swiss watchmaker pouring over the observations made by himself and others while gazing at the innocent activities of infancy and childhood. It is now apparent that we need another watchmaker to pour over the fully assembled instrument—the very aged human agent for whom time is "running out."

On August 9, 1976 Piaget celebrated his eightieth birthday. Today we need the "Piaget of the aged" whose efforts could serve to break the strangle hold of the predominating ethic of benign neglect of the aged. In the arena of health care and geriatric medicine, to the extent that it exists in the United States, Robert Kastenbaum is no doubt correct: "Convert this octogenarian into a child again, and we will innoculate him from life threatening disease, and stand ready to hurl every weapon in our medical arsenal against any prospect of untimely death. But careers are not made nor programs funded on the mission to convert an old man of eighty into an old man of eighty-one."[85]

A first step is to appreciate the point that the penultimate years of senescence and senectitude are truly different *in kind* from the extended middle years. A simple question which takes into account this qualitative alteration is asked by Robert Butler: "what happens to a person's memory as he grows older . . . ?"[86] This question straightforwardly calls for "the study of the normal processes of development—continuing growth and creativity, judgment and wisdom—which are fundamental to life and about which we know precious little."[87]

Thus far I have tacitly called for the establishment of a center for gerontogenetic mentation. Now I call for it openly. The ultimate purpose of such a research center would be, to use Robert Butler's words, "to improve the well-being of man. . . ."[88] Just as Piaget's genetic epistemology yielded knowledge with respect to the early years of the child's growth, this new discipline, gerontogenetic mentation, would eventually yield knowledge of mentation (including cognitive and conative functions) in the penultimate years. The study of gerontogenetic mentation would disclose growth and development as well as decline in senectitude, knowledge which might well assist us in understanding, preventing, and managing multiple conditions of infirmity and disability in the very aged. If indeed, as some claim, we are on the threshold of understanding the mysteries of the "cognitive style" and structure of persons in their penultimate years, can we be satisfied with less than revealing the many secrets of aging and perhaps even having the opportunity to apply them to making the later years more vigorous and dignified? As Dr. Agate asks, "It cannot, surely, be said that illness in the old 'differs little' from illness at any age? There are many differences including a tendency for a mental disturbance to be first evidence of physical disorder."[89] Furthermore, evaluation of elderly persons who present at hospital entails both a delicate professional relationship (often in emotionally charged situations) as well as an accurate assessment of mentation before admission.

Lest it be assumed that all problems associated with aging and the aged

reduce to medical problems, which are in truth a subset of the wider class of health problems within the even wider set of social problems, it is useful to return to the conclusion of Simone de Beauvoir's eight hundred page *The Coming of Age.* She argues that modern man is "rendered hopeless by the want of meaning in his present life."[90] The meaning of our existence, she says, has already been stolen from us "from the very beginning." Even if health can be given back, meaning cannot be restored in the final years. For a man to be and remain a man, she says, "he would always have to have been treated as a man."[91] Society's "humanism" is mere window dressing, therefore. "Old age exposes the failure of our entire civilization," she writes; "It is the whole man that must be remade. . . . "[92] She has not, however, drawn all the appropriate inferences from her own insight: If the whole man must be remade and if our entire civilization has failed, then our only hope may lie in our children, while *we* do our best not to make things any worse.

It is not by accident that Piaget's work led quite naturally to the emancipation of the child, who is no longer construed as a "little adult" doing his best to make it to adulthood while biomedical science and clinical medicine do their best to see him through to age 40 and beyond to 65. Emancipation is a natural outcome of the knowledge of human mentation, and the time has come to release the very aged as Piaget released the child (without becoming by the way, a "child psychologist") and as Pinel released the insane (is it a mere historical accident that Pinel first coined the term *dēmence*?). In any case, de Beauvoir's insights deserve to be pushed to the limit. We can begin by following the suggestion of Elizabeth E. Bohning who, in her "Suggestions for Research on the Literary Depiction of the Aging Process," points out that "Myths about the helplessness of the aged are difficult to dispel, for they have been ingrained in us during childhood, and indeed through children's literature." She continues to argue that a "study of the stereotypes of older people in children's literature is just as sorely needed as the many studies of the role of girls and women in children's books."[93]

In *Janet the Janitress,* a melodrama acted by and for young children, Craddock Crabtree McCrum,[94] archaeologist and curator of the Hillendale Museum and villain extraordinaire, seeks to gain the hand of Janet, janitress in Hillendale, by threatening Janet's mother, also a janitress. The script is revealing:

JANET: Before you hired me, I was out of work for two years. Mother and I were down to our last bean!
McCRUM: (Icily) Touching.
JANET: Speaking of mother, you don't mean to fire her, too, do you Mr. McCrum? You couldn't be so heartless!
McCRUM: (Aside) She doesn't know me very well!
JANET: If you throw her out, she has nowhere to go but the Old Janitors' Home.
McCRUM: I'll be glad to pay for her taxi.

Robert Kastenbaum has suggested that our society needs a new script and alternate scenario[95] for the penultimate years of its citizens—a script thus far unwritten. The cryptic image in *Janet the Janitress* is, of course, transparent. It signals that we are obliged to affect the imagination of our children, since the child is father to the man. *Janet the Janitress* is only a melodrama, however, and in that we can take solace. Were it not the script of a melodrama we might indeed give up all hope, for not only our responsible citizens but our children too would be cruel.

Notes

[1]During the preparation of this paper, Ian R. Lawson, M.D. (F.R.C.P. Edin., F.A.C.P.) gave unselfishly of his time, experience, and cogent criticism. His impeccable clinical discrimination served to stimulate my reflections on the mentation of the aged. The setting was the Hebrew Home for the Aged (Hartford) during the time of Dr. Lawson's appointment as medical director, a context in which he stood as exemplar of the physician, totally devoted to the care of his patients. I also wish to thank the residents and the staff of the Home for allowing me to participate, on occasion, in their activities during these past three years. Whatever I have learned is in great measure due to this fulfilling experience. The limitations of this paper are, however, entirely my own, and I apologize in advance to those for whom ignorance is always offensive.

[2]Excerpted from *La vieille en regrettant le temps de sa jeunesse* ("Les regrets de la belle hëaulmière") in *The Complete Works of François Villon,* trans. Anthony Bonner (New York: David McKay Co., 1960), pp. 48-49. Translation: "And now he's dead these thirty years, and I live on, gray-haired and old. Oh, when I think of those good old days, what I was then—what I've since become! When I look at my naked body and see myself so changed, poor, skinny, dried out and shrivelled, I almost lose my mind."

[3]"Humanism and the Humanities of Aging." *The Gerontologist,* 16, No. 2 (1976), p. 184.

[4]*The Coming of Age,* trans. Patrick O'Brian (New York: Warner Paperback, 1973), p. 134, p. 149.

[5]Ibid., p. 147.

[6]*Plea for an Age Movement* (New York: Vanguard Press, 1942), pp. 8, 14, 16.

[7]Perry, p. 15.

[8]*House of Representatives* (May 11, 1976), p. H-4266. In 1975 there were 42 million persons over 55 and about 32 million over 60. Today more than 22 million (or 10.5% of the population of the United States) are over 65; 8.5 million are over 75, and 1.9 million are over 85. For some like Anne R. Somers the fact that in 1974 only 10.3 percent of the United States' population was 65 years of age or older "probably accounts for the relative lack of attention to geriatrics in this country" (p. 475). A 10% figure seen as low, when in absolute numbers that is in excess of 22 million persons, seems odd indeed. See her "Geriatric Care in the United Kingdom: An American Perspective," *Annals of Internal Medicine,* 84, No. 4 (April 1976).

[9]This point, which I owe to Professor Edward J. Kollar, is of central importance in understanding the negative influence of Darwinism on current attitudes toward the elderly. See François Jacob's *The Logic of Life* (New York: Pantheon Books, Random House, 1973) and Gene Bylinsky, "Science is on the Trail of the Fountain of Youth," *Fortune,* 94, No. 1 (July 1976); reprinted at the request of Mr. Pepper in *The Congressional Record—House* (July 29, 1976), pp. H-8007-H-8010. Mr. Bylinsky

observes that "to put it bluntly, nature has little interest in the survival of individual members of a species once they have had time to give birth to and rear their young" (p. 8009).

[10]François Jacob, *The Logic of Life,* pp. 17, 20. Jacob notes that generation (the novel creation always requiring the intervention of some external force) has become reproduction—the intrinsic property of all living, organic systems, a notion which made its appearance only toward the end of the eighteenth century. Until the eighteenth century, living beings were thought of not as reproduced but as engendered, generation being the result of a creation, the intervention of a divine force, something like the production of a work of art by man.

[11]Quoted in de Beauvoir, *Coming of Age,* p. 218.

[12]"Exit and Existence: Society's Unwritten Script for Old Age and Death," unpublished paper prepared for the "Human Values and Aging" project, Case Western Reserve University (Nov. 1975), p. 27.

[13]Ibid., p. 14.

[14]In the January 3, 1976 issue of *The Lancet* (Vol. I, No. 7949, pp. 47-48), J. P. Crawford registered his complaint in a letter to the editor. He suggests that hospitals be "designated" in terms of the predominant kind of causes of death of patients in that hospital. Thus a psychogeriatric hospital like Stone House Hospital (Dartford, Kent) should be designated "geriatric" since the vast majority of patient deaths are due to disorders of a nonpsychiatric sort, including dementia and confusion which, he admits, are "cerebral organic states." Aye, there's the rub . . .

[15]"Aging in America," *The Congressional Record—Senate* (July 29, 1976), p. S-12750. See also L. A. Wilson, I. R. Lawson and W. Brass, "Multiple Disorders in the Elderly," *The Lancet* (October 27, 1962), p. 843. Here the Aberdeen geriatricians, Drs. Wilson and Lawson, caution us in the use of the expression "the frailty of old age." "Indeed," they point out, "we are less impressed by the frailty of old age than by the astonishing resistance and endurance it may show in the face of an overwhelming weight of illness."

[16]Somers, pp. 470-72.

[17]R. W. Canvin and N. G. Pearson, eds., *Proceedings of a Seminar Held at the University of Exeter, March 1-3, 1972* (Exeter: Univ. of Exeter, 1973), pp. 1-9.

[18]*De Anima,* trans. J. A. Smith (Oxford: Clarendon Press, 1931), Bk. I, Ch. 4, 408b18-19.

[19]Ibid., 408b20-30.

[20]"Ethics and Old Age," unpublished paper prepared for the "Human Values and Aging" project, Case Western Reserve University (Oct. 1975), p. 16.

[21]Statistical data reveal that, although it is true that the life expectancy of any *individual* in 1976 is not much greater than a citizen of Rome in the first century A.D. successfully living to age 40, we do, of course, respect the fact that many more persons constitute the total population over 65 than ever existed before at any one time in the historical past. This jibes with Dr. Robert R. Kohn's remark at the first meeting of the "Human Values and Aging" project (Cleveland, Ohio; October 11, 1975): "Even if the major killers are unefficacious, life expectancy will not change much, and so appreciably extending the quantity of life is no longer a major consideration." Cf. A. Comfort, "Study of Ageing Processes," in John N. Agate, ed., *Medicine in Old Age: Proceedings of a Conference Held at the Royal College of Physicians of London, 18th and 19th June, 1965* (London: Pitman Medical Publishing co., 1966). "He [the geriatric physician] is operating between the 60 and 80 mark. . . . If he were to abolish every disease of old age, cardiovascular, malignant, and all the others that we know of, the evidence suggests that

he . . . would cause ages of death to be distirbuted more normally about the specific age of 75 to 80. He would not, so far as we could now estimate, move the curve so far to the right that people would die at 90 and 100 instead of 70 and 80, because the number of diseases goes up exponentially as vitality declines exponentially" (p. 62).

[22]Fletcher cites Sir George Pickering, Regius Professor of Medicine at Oxford, in Joseph Fletcher, *The Ethics of Genetic Control* (New York: Anchor Doubleday, 1974), p. 112.

[23]These remarks are excerpted from an address presented by Dr. R. Butler to the National Council of Senior Citizens at their Convention in Chicago on June 4, 1976, and published as "Biomedical Research for the Elderly." *Congressional Record—House* (June 7, 1976), p. H-5398.

[24]"Aging in America," *The Congressional Record—Senate* (July 29, 1976), p. H-12750.

[25]Bylinsky, p. H-8008.

[26]Ibid.

[27]John G. Freymann, M.D., *The American Health Care System* (New York: Medcom, Inc., 1974), p. 26.

[28]*Senescence: The Last Half of Life* (New York: D. Appleton and Co., 1922), p. vii.

[29]Kastenbaum, p. 25.

[30]*The Phenomenology of Perception,* trans. Colin Smith (New York: Humanities Press, 1962), p. 412.

[31]See Stuart Spicker, "Inner Time and Lived-Through Time: Husserl and Merleau-Ponty," *Journal of the British Society for Phenomenology,* 4, No. 3 (October 1973), pp. 235-47.

[32]"Historical Development of the Multiplicity of Times and Implications for the Analysis of Aging," *The Human Context,* 7, No. 1 (Spring 1975), pp. 117-29. Also see Georges Gurvitch, *The Spectrum of Social Time* (Dordrecht, Holland: D. Reidel, 1964). In this work the author distinguishes between enduring, deceptive, erratic, cyclical, retarded, explosive, and alternating time as well as time in advance of itself. This is a most important book for those interested in a more accurate description of the temporality of aged mentation.

[33]John N. Agate, "The Geriatric Physician's Viewpoint," in Agate, ed., *Medicine in Old Age,* p. 127.

[34]A. M. Ostfeld, "The Aging Brain: Alzheimer's Disease and Senile Dementia—Discussant's Perspective," in *Epidemiology of Aging,* ed. A.M. Ostfeld and Don C. Gibson (Washington, D.C.: U.S. Department of Health, Education and Welfare, 1975), p. 130.

[35]Ibid.

[36]L. A. Wilson and W. Brass, "Brief Assessment of the Mental State in Geriatric Domiciliary Practice: The Usefulness of the Mental Status Questionnaire," *Age and Ageing,* 2 (1973), p. 92.

[37]Ibid., p. 98.

[38]Ibid., p. 93.

[39]Wilson and Brass, p. 100.

[40]Ibid.

[41]Ibid., p. 99. My italics.

[42]Ibid.

[43]Michael L. Shelanski, "The Aging Brain: Alzheimer's Disease and Senile Dementia," in *Epidemiology of Aging,* p. 114. I omit reference to Alzheimer's Disease since the clinical picture is similar to, though often more severe than, senile dementia in elderly patients. That is, Alzheimer's disease (presenile dementia) often arises at a younger age, i.e., prior to 65. The term 'senile dementia' is often employed as a synonym for 'chronic brain syndrome.'

[44]See Wilson, Lawson and Brass, p. 841.

[45]Ostfeld, p. 131.

[46]Wilson, Lawson and Brass, p. 841.

[47]"Diagnosis of Old Age," *The Lancet* (September 15, 1962), p. 515. The late Professor Dr. med. Herbert Plügge, an astute physician, was equally open to mistaken generalization: "Even a practiced and perceptive physician will in many cases be unable to decide at the time of the initial observation of his patient whether he is dealing with someone critically ill or sorely beset by old age." This is simply medico-mythical nonsense for which a lay person could be excused, but not a physician. If it is typical of currently held opinion among physicians, we had best look to improving clinical medical education. See Plügge's "Man and His Body," in S.F. Spicker, ed., *The Philosophy of the Body* (New York: Quadrangle Books, 1973), p. 310. The original text is *Der Mensch und sein Leib* (Tubingen: Max Niemeyer Verlag, 1967).

[48]Ibid., p. 657.

[49]Anne Somers reminds us that, according to the Royal College of Physicians, geriatrics is "the branch of general medicine concerned with the clinical, preventive, remedial, and social aspects of health and disease in the elderly" (p. 467). And recent evidence suggests that Professor Somers is no doubt right in her judgment that "Geriatric care is probably the most complex, neglected, and challenging aspect of health care facing the developed countries during the last quarter of the twentieth century" (p. 466). In this context it may well be useful to distinguish *elderly patients* from *geriatric patients,* the latter requiring long term care for ever shifting sets of multiple problems. For our purposes this distinction is not of critical importance, however.

[50]"Biomedical Research for the Elderly," *The Congressional Record—House* (June 7, 1976). p. H-5399.

[51]Tom Dunn and Tom Arie, "Mental Disturbance in the Ill Old Person," in *Medicine in Old Age,* ed. Martin Ware (Tavistock Square, London: British Medical Association, 1974), p. 83.

[52]*Journal of Gerontology,* 30, No. 4 (1975), p. 453.

[53]Ibid. Cf. Robert Butler, "Aging in America," *Congressional Record—Senate* (July 29, 1976), p. S-12750, "Scientific studies show, contrary to what many think, that learning capacities do not diminish with age. If you compare a group of 70-year olds with a group of 20-year-olds, it might appear that there's a loss in intellectual function among the older people. But longitudinal studies—those which follow the same people over a long period—clearly show that intellectual abilities of healthy people grow greater through the years, not less."

[54]Ibid.

[55]Ibid., p. 454.

[56]Ibid. Cf. "Aging Needn't Lower I.Q. Behavioral Study finds," *Times* (New York), 14 September 1976. A report of the work of Richard L. Sprott, a psychologist at the Jackson Laboratory, Bar Harbor, Maine. See Giuseppe Girotti and Angelo Beretta, "Apparent Verticality Following Short-Term Sensory Deprivation: Differential Performances in Young and Old," *Cortex,* V, No. 1 (March 1969), pp. 75-87. This

experimental study of the perception of verticality in young and old people suggests that old people "seem to revert to a more egocentric spatial organization" (p. 85), yet "No significant changes are induced in old men's performance by short-term sensory deprivation" (p. 86). The late psychologist Bernard Kutner, who dedicated his life to rehabilitation, frequently pointed out that "aging involves change rather than necessary decrement and decline." He thus proposed the notion that aging is a process of redifferentiation and reintegration, processes reminiscent of Jean Piaget's "assimilation" and "accommodation"; "Aging and Disability," *Duke University Council on Gerontology: Proceedings of Seminars 1961-1965* (January 9, 1962), pp. 41-42.

[57]*Psychiatric Quarterly,* 43 (1969), p. 238. See also Tom Arie ("Dementia in the Elderly," in *Medicine in Old Age*) who writes, "An organic psychiatric syndrome should always be assessed initially at home because it is an old person's capacity to function in his or her normal surroundings that needs to be assessed. Assessment at home also makes it possible to see the physical surroundings and often to make practical suggestions for domestic rearrangements" (p. 98).

[58]Ibid., p. 232, L. A. Cahn writes, " . . . even in very demented patients behavior is never a thing apart, but still remains the result of environmental factors especially those related to interhuman contact"; in *Senile Dementia: Clinical and Therapeutic Aspects,* ed. Ch. Muller and L. Ciompi (Switzerland: Hans Huber Pub., 1968), p. 82.

[59]Ibid., p. 237.

[60]Hull, p. vii.

[61]Butler, "Biomedical Research for the Elderly," p. H-5399.

[62]C. E. Hallenbeck ("Evidence for a Multiple Process View of Mental Deterioration," *Journal of Gerontology,* 19 [1964], pp. 357-63), cited by Goldstein and Shelly, p. 448.

[63]*Lancet* (Setpember 15, 1962), pp. 515-16.

[64]Ibid., p. 517.

[65]"Some Aspects of Psycho-Neurologic Disintegration in Senile Dementia," in *Senile Dementia,* p. 77.

[66]Ibid., pp. 78, 80.

[67]*Epistémologie génétique et recherche psychologique,* Vol. I, eds. W.E. Beth, W. Mays and J. Piaget (Paris: Presses Universitaires de France, 1957).

[68]Ibid., pp. 1-2, my translation. "Le but du Centre de Genève est donc d'assurer la possibilité d'un travail d'équipe entre quelques spécialistes venus d'horizons différents pour mettre en commun, durant un temps donné, l'étude de mêmes questions délimitées d'épistémologie scientifique sous l'angle du développement."

[69]This neglect of the child's conative development was recently criticized by Howard Gardner: "Piaget hias consistently neglected the realm of feeling. We learn much from his writings about children's conceptions of water, little about their fear of floods, their love of splashing, their desire to be minnows, mermaids or mariners. So, too, some aspects of consciousness may be captured in a child's verbal reflections upon his physical actions. But the subtle and perennial tensions among conscious, preconscious and unconscious processes are missed. Vast realms of awareness—occasions of existential anxiety, peak experiences, the often-overpowering imagery of daydreams and nightmares—are bypassed in this 'civilized,' streamlined and somewhat mechanistic view of human consciousness." Cf. "The Grasp of Consciousness." *The Times Book Review* (August 1, 1976), p. 2.

[70]Ibid., p. 13, my translation: ". . . l'épistémologie génétique est l'étude des états successifs d'une science *S* en fonction de son développement. Ainsi conçue l'épistémologie génétique pourrait se définir comme la science positive, aussi bien em-

pirique que théorique, du devenir des sciences positives en tant que sciences."

[71]"The Philosophy of Psychology: A Résumé," *Journal of the British Society for Phenomenology,* 6, No. 3 (October 1975), p. 210.

[72]"The Epistemology of Professor Piaget," *Proceedings of the Aristotelian Society,* n.s., 54 (1954), p. 49. See Jean Piaget, *Genetic Epistemology,* trans. Eleanor Duckworth (New York: Columbia Univ. Press, 1970), especially pp. 1-19.

[73]Ibid., p. 50.

[74]Ibid. p. 57.

[75]Professor Mays reminds us that "We are sometimes told [by philosophers] that epistemology merely concerns itself with the structural non-genetic elements of thought occurring in a quasi-logical setting, as opposed to their genetic treatment which falls within the province of psychology." The philosophers have branded Piaget's genetic studies "irrelevant" to the philosophical analysis of cognition, since they maintain that philosophical epistemology is "engaged in a rational reconstruction of thought or a normative study" and hence recourse to the empirical facts of a child's development is irrelevant. The most striking form of this objection to *genetic epistemology* is Reichenbach's: " . . . it will, therefore, never be a permissible objection to an epistemological construction that actual thinking does not conform to it" (Ibid., pp. 53-54).

[76]Piaget, *Logic and Psychology* (New York: Basic Books, 1957), p. xviii.

[77]*Senile Dementia,* p. 69.

[78]"Egocentrism and Social Interaction Across the Life Span," *Psychological Bulletin,* 78, No. 2 (August 1972), p. 87. Looft cites J. Langer's *Theories of Development* (New York: Holt, Rinehart and Winston, 1969). I am grateful to Professor Glenn Affleck for bringing this and other related psychological research papers, pertinent to aging and the concept of "conservation," to my attention.

[79]"Area and Volume Conservation Among the Elderly: Assessment and Training," *Developmental Psychology,* 12, No. 1 (1976), p. 69. W.R. Looft remarks: "Not surprisingly, there has been little research with adults and older persons using Piagetian tasks. Piagetian-adult research efforts are growing in number, and the findings to date have been intriguing." Looft also says that current findings "are highly suggestive of structural changes in cognitive abilities in old age" (p. 83). See K.H. Rubin, "Extinction of Conservation: A Life Span Investigation," *Developmental Psychology,* 12, No. 1 (1976), pp. 51-56. Rubin seems to opt for the view that alteration in elderly cognition is due to "decline in cognitive competence and is a function of growing neurological decreement with age" (p. 55).

[80]Piaget, *Insights and Illusions of Philosophy,* trans. Wolfe Mays (London: World Publishing Co., n.d.), p. 149.

[81]Ibid., p. 73.

[82]Ibid., p. 69.

[83]Looft, p. 89.

[84]*Insights and Illusions of Philosophy,* p. 147.

[85]"Exit and Existence," p. 15.

[86]"Aging in America," *The Congressional Record—Senate* (July 29, 1976), p. S-12751.

[87]"Biomedical Research for the Elderly," *House* (June 7, 1976), p. H-5399.

[88]Ibid., p. H-5398.

[89]*The Lancet,* p. 659.

[90]de Beauvoir, p. 804.

[91]Ibid., p. 805.

[92]Ibid., p. 806.

[93]A paper prepared for the "Human Values and Aging" project, Case Western Reserve University (Oct. 1976), p. 7.

[94]Superbly acted by Glenn D. Spicker (age 10), Webster Hill School, West Hartford, Connecticut (July 23, 1976).

[95]"Exit and Existence," p. 23.

Kathleen Woodward

MASTER SONGS OF MEDITATION: THE LATE POEMS OF ELIOT, POUND, STEVENS, AND WILLIAMS[1]

"It must be believed," wrote Emerson in an essay entitled "Old Age," "that there is a proportion between the designs of a man and the length of his life: there is a calendar of his years, so of his performances."[2] Behind Emerson's statement lies a theory of creation in which he would have us trust for reasons of both personal and cultural health. The extent to which old age creates its own culmination in poetry is too large a question to explore here. Whatever doubt we may have about Emerson's theory of a just proportion between performance and age we must limit to specific cases. In this essay the question becomes: considering four of our greatest Modern American poets—T. S. Eliot, Ezra Pound, Wallace Stevens, and William Carlos Williams—did aging and old age bring poetic fulfillment? I propose to show that in the form of superb meditative poems, these four poets offer us insights into the experience of successful aging and the sources of its wisdom. The four poems in particular which will be dealt with here are Eliot's *Four Quartets* (1943), Pound's *Pisan Cantos* (1948), "To an Old Philosopher in Rome" from Wallace Steven's *The Rock* (1954), and the fifth book of *Paterson* by William Carlos Williams.

The appropriate place to begin is with T. S. Eliot whose work, reviewed briefly, can provide us with the historical poetic context in which to understand these late Modern American poems. In 1915 Eliot introduced the world to "The Love Song of J. Alfred Prufrock," and in that portrait of a middle-aged man whose life is one of endless indecision, Eliot anticipated the uncertainty spawned by the World War One years. Prufrock was bored and exhausted, so worn out in fact that by 1920 he had aged to become Gerontion, a shrunken man living in a rented house with nothing but tired thoughts to keep him company. As Eliot, thirty-two years old at the time of the publication of "Gerontion," describes this figure, he is "a dull head among windy spaces" who, having lost his "sight, smell, hearing, taste, and touch," is capable only of "thoughts of a dry brain in a dry season."[3] Then, two years later, Eliot

inaugurated in "The Waste Land" a new genre which itself expressed the fragmentation and sterility of the modern secular world, a culture which had no informing symbols and was characterized by only a "heap of broken images." Together these three central poems—"Prufrock," "Gerontion," and "The Waste Land"—launched what has come to be known as the Age of Eliot.

But if the Age of Eliot began in exhaustion, it ultimately ended in affirmation. It is nonsense to conclude, as does a critic of Wallace Stevens, that "American poets have not, in general, aged well, because they have been unable to live their agedness with any fulness of being."[4] On the contrary, while the English Romantics, for example, burnt themselves out when they were young, these American poets reached old age with renewed intellectual vigor and poetic force. Pound was sixty-three when the *Pisan Cantos* were published in 1948, and both Stevens and Williams were seventy-five when their last books appeared, *The Rock* in 1954 and *Paterson V* four years later. Eliot is an exception. His seventies were not poetically fertile. The *Four Quartets* was published when he was only in his early fifties, but its voice and theme are definitely that of an older man. In these last poems one large theme dominates individual variations: we do not find odes of dejection or the dusty thoughts of a Gerontion but an energy and wisdom which are profound and sustaining. These poets are our ancestors, our fathers, our grandfathers. They are men who lived for a long time, and as poets they must be lived with for a long time. And we owe it to ourselves to listen openly for, as Eliot has said, "you don't really criticise any author to whom you have never surrendered yourself."[5]

These four books are bound together by more than an affirmative vision. Again Eliot takes the lead and provides a model. The *Four Quartets* differs radically from "The Waste Land" not only in its final tone of resolution, but also in its personalism, meditative mode, and lyric clarity. And in general these characteristics also appear in the late work of Pound, Stevens, and Williams.[6] We no longer encounter the careful impersonality of the poet which was the hallmark of much early American Modernism. Nor do we find the irony which only imposes distance. Instead there is a new closeness, a more open dialogue between the poet and himself and between the poet and the reader. The Modern poet is no longer invisible. He shows us himself. The *Four Quartets*, the *Pisan Cantos, The Rock, Paterson V*—all represent the culmination of long poetic careers and all strive for transcendence of historical time, seeing history, as Eliot does in "Little Gidding," as "a pattern/Of timeless moments."[7] In these poems the confusion of the urban collage of "The Waste Land" is untangled, if only tentatively. And in them we encounter the central image of the *sanctuary*, partly ironic, partly paradoxical, of the small closed room.

The condition of these poems could be said to be that of solitude. The first four books of Williams' long ambitious epic poem, *Paterson*, are dominated by the landscape of that industrial New Jersey city with its polluted rivers and crowded elevators. The last book, written after the incapacitating stroke which compelled him to abandon his medical practice, focuses on the quiet of the religious space of the New York Cloisters. Age for Williams forced upon him a kind of disengagement. This was a new situation for him, and the remedy he

Restoration by "fire" is a possibility not only for saints. The meaning of "refining fire" is open to many interpretations—the discipline of the Christian religion, the cultivation of art, the confession which accompanies the life review. It does not exclude pain and anger:

> Do not let me hear
> Of the wisdom of old men, but rather of their folly,
> Their fear of fear and frenzy, their fear of possession,
> Of belonging to another, or to others, or to God.
> "East Coker"

Surely in the last of the *Four Quartets* the well-known Eliot of skepticism and despair persists. But he yields to the Eliot of skepticism and faith. The wise man advises: from humility, consciousness, and confession will come transformation of the self and restoration of the self. Tortured Eliot, his doubt perhaps aggravated by age, nevertheless ends his poem in "another intensity." No longer the space of the everyday which offers "bitter tastelessness of shadow fruit" and "empty desolation," it is the inner space of enlightened age, the space of an inner exploration:

> Old men ought to be explorers
> Here and there does not matter
> We must be still and still moving
> Into another intensity
> For a further union, a deeper communion
> Through the dark cold and the empty desolation.

What is the union which Eliot speaks of? It could be communion with the literary tradition to which he belongs—the ghost he meets in London's chill streets.

II. The New Meditative Mode

It cannot be an accident that in the wake of the increasing fragmentation of industrial society, Late Modernism witnessed developments not only in poetry but also in the fields of anthropology and psychology which reveal an interest in wholeness and integration. As the intellectual historian Merle Curti observes, "in the later 1940's and throughout the 1950's the age-old quest for absolutes was pursued with fresh zest," and the answer given, he says, was essentially a religious or humanist one.[10] Thus on the one hand, Erich Neumann and Erik Erikson (the former a Jungian and the latter a neo-Freudian) have proposed theories of psychological development and maturation which offer hope for what Jung has called centroversion, the achievement of psychic wholeness in the last phases of life. And on the other hand, the anthropologists Gregory Bateson and Victor Turner have looked at the West from both within and without and concluded that we must adopt an ecological theory of mind, a systemic view of

social change. What this suggests is that the common concerns of these psychologists and social scientists over the last thirty years have been anticipated, or at least paralleled, by the poets.

Gregory Bateson conceives of a work of art as fundamentally a quest for grace.[11] Although he writes about "primitive" visual art, we can apply his observations to self-conscious poetry. The connotations of the word 'grace'—religious favor, prayer, compassion, good fortune, the unerring beauty of poise, the Greek goddesses, moral virtue—capture perfectly some of the concerns and qualities of these late poems of Eliot, Pound, Stevens, and Williams. But for Bateson grace is ultimately something more abstract. It is essentially a problem of integrating the diverse parts of the mind, and this integration exists on not just an individual level but a cultural level as well. Every culture, he concludes, has a characteristic species of grace toward which it is striving, and this can be read in its art. The terms that he uses to describe this integration are essentially Jungian: art delivers "a message about the interface between conscious and unconscious."[12] Rather than holding to the Freudian notion of art as symptom, Bateson believes that art *speaks* a *hidden* truth; it does not hide a truth.

Taken together, our American poems of old age reveal a conclusive distrust of the conscious, muscular, Promethean act of the mind. They signal a return to tradition, to metaphor, and to a reliance on the creative readiness which can yield the epiphanic moment. In this way the history of American Modernism fulfills Bateson's notion of the more specific role art has to play today if we are ever to extricate ourselves from the nightmare of our technological civilization. For art, he believes, calls attention to an ecological view of life which compensates for our *too-purposive* Western view of life. This is the wisdom which art can impart. "Wisdom," he writes, "I take to be the knowledge of the larger interactive system—that system which if disturbed, is likely to generate exponential curves of change."[13] Humility is a part of this wisdom, the knowledge that man is only part of a larger system and that the part can never ultimately control the whole. This is the humility that the American Moderns call for, either explicitly or implicitly. As Eliot writes in the *Quartets:*

> The only wisdom we can hope to acquire
> Is the wisdom of humility: humility is endless.

Pound echoes this in the *Pisan Cantos.* He confesses, "J'ai eu pitié des autres/probablement pas assez, and at moments that suited my own convenience" (LXXVI).[14]

Perhaps more importantly, this humility is also dramatized by the mode of these meditative poems. It is possible, Bateson believes, that the cure for the excesses of conscious purpose lies first with the individual rather than the wholesale reform of institutions. In art, dreams, and religion the whole person is involved and "must necessarily relax that arrogance [of the conscious mind] in favor of a creative experience in which his conscious mind plays only a small part," he writes, concluding that "in creative art man must experience himself—his total self—as a cybernetic model."[15] At its best, in other words, the

meditative mode of these late poems operates on a new principle of selecting "information." It provides us with a model of correct thought, just as the romantic landscape poem did in its time. The meditative mode is thus a way of uniting the self and the world through the agency of the mind, but we must not make the mistake of understanding mind as being limited to only conscious mind.

Here the model of mind described by Bateson converges with that of the psychologist Erik Erikson. The wisdom of the meditative mode parallels the wisdom and strength of what Erikson calls the eighth and final stage of psychosocial development. The decisive choice in this stage of old age, Erikson explains, is between the attitudes of integrity and despair:

> *Wisdom, then is detached concern with life itself, in the face of death itself.* It maintains and conveys the integrity of experience. . . . If vigor of mind combines with the gift of responsible renunciation, some old people can envisage human problems in their entirety (which is what "integrity" means) and can represent to the coming generation a living example of the "closure" of a style of life. Only such integrity can balance the despair of the knowledge that a limited life is coming to a conscious conclusion.[16]

Strength thus comes in being able to continue with dignity, *to be,* while facing the reality of *not being.* Erikson's phrase *"detached concern"* provides us with a key to understanding the process of achieving this state of mind, this state of grace: the meditative mode requires not so much an *act* of the mind as a *state of receptivity* to experience. In this final stage of life unity is discovered not by the disciplined, arduous jesuitical meditation Loyola recommended: composition, discourse, and colloquy.[17] The kind of thinking involved in other words, is not category-making and abstraction. The goal is to *discover* rather than to impose or to reason.

How is such thinking described? We find the "kind of pattern which we perceive in our own lives," Eliot wrote, "at rare moments of inattention and detachment, drowsing in sunlight. It is the pattern drawn by what the ancient world called Fate; subtilized by Christianity into mazes of delicate theology; and reduced again by the modern world into crudities of psychological or economic necessity."[18] As Eliot writes in "Little Gidding," we must look and not look, hear and not hear:

> At the source of the longest river
> The voice of the hidden waterfall
> And the children in the apple-tree
> Not known, because not looked for
> But heard, half-heard, in the stillness
> Between two waves of the sea.

The illumination of the "unexpected moment" appears when one is not con-

sciously, purposively, looking for it. The meditative mode of these poems of old age is, in other words, Heideggerian. It is characterized by a quiet openness to the primal realities of human experience which allows them simply *to be*, to disclose themselves before the gaze of the whole mind. What is revealed to Eliot, as we have already seen, is the possible meaning of his whole life as it extends beyond middle age into old age and forms a strong bond with a tradition which reaches back far beyond the twentieth century. But for Eliot such timeless moments have more than a personal meaning. They also are essential to the health of a culture. In the last of the *Quartets* we read, "A people without history/Is not redeemed from time, for history is a pattern of timeless moments." Pound would agree, and the *Pisan Cantos* are invested with just this spirit of disclosed romance—the goddesses of myth, for example, appear in his tent.

The meditative mode of these poems of old age is, however, perhaps best illustrated by Wallace Stevens' last book of poems, *The Rock*, certainly the most profoundly personal group of poems and to my mind the best collection he ever wrote. Of them, "To an Old Philosopher in Rome," portrays perfectly the quality of being—integrated, receptive, completed—possible in old age. In such earlier poems as "Sunday Morning" and "The Owl in the Sarcophagus," Stevens offers us only self-conscious *arguments* meant to counter death. In "Philosopher in Rome" he gives us a picture of an old man near death. It is a portrait of both himself and Santayana, the American philosopher who chose to live out the last eleven years of his life in a Roman Convent cell of the Blue Nuns with only a few books as company. In this poem we see that the last lesson of the philosopher is that the *whole of life* can be comprehended in its entirety, grasped as a gestalt in time. As Santayana himself put it in his preface to *Realms of Being*, "our distinction and glory, as well as our sorrow, will have lain in being something in particular, and in knowing what that is."[19]

This realm of being has its own mode of meditation. Stevens describes Santayana as "half-asleep," both "intent" and "dozing in the depths of wakefulness."[20] "Intent" here does not mean strenuous concentration but rather absorption, fascination, and interest. In "Old Philosopher in Rome," it is not intellectual speculation on a fiction which grants happiness and peace, but absorption in the particulars of this constricted environment—the smell of medicine, "the particles," as he puts it, "of nether-do." In the vocabulary of gestalt psychology, "*spontaneous* concentration, not deliberate concentration, brings *contact with the environment* resulting in a detailed, vivid, structured, and humanly meaningful organization of experience."[21] This mode of meditation is the poet's condition of "vague receptivity" which Stevens describes in his late essay "A Collect of Philosophy."[22] It is also the "vivid sleep" of "The Rock," and the "ease of mind that was like being alone in a boat at sea" in "Prologues to What Is Possible." What is possible are "not balances That we achieve but balances that happen," as he called such moments in "Notes Toward a Supreme Fiction."

Thus these poems of *The Rock* record Stevens' movement beyond the disciplined, deliberate act of the mind into a condition of receptivity to ex-

perience. As he wrote in a letter in 1950 about the privacy which Hartford, Connecticut offered him, "It seems easier to think here. Perhaps this is balanced by the possibility that one has less to think about or, rather, less occasion to think. Yet that does not seem possible. Then, too, it is not always easy to tell the difference between thinking and looking out of the window."[23] One could speculate here to what extent this kind of thinking characterizes partially or totally a last stage of life—senectitude. With the contraction of space, the imposition of physical immobility, and the condition of solitude, perhaps a new kind of thinking, satisfying and non-Promethean, originates.[24] Santayana is both alone and not alone:

> The life of the city never lets go, nor do you
> Ever want it to.

He is at one with the city. At the end of the poem a temporary stay against death has been erected:

> It is a kind of total grandeur at the end,
> With every visible thing enlarged and yet
> No more than a bed, a chair and moving nuns,
> The immensest theatre, the pillared porch,
> The book and candle in your ambered room,
>
> Total grandeur of a total edifice,
> Chosen by an inquisitor of structures
> For himself. He stops upon his threshold,
> As if the design of all his words takes form
> And frame from thinking and is realized.

The "total edifice" which stands as shelter is the self that he has composed through the act of writing. He is now able to stop the flow of time and to live completely within the present which extends before him infinitely.[25] The climax of the poem has the quality of apocalypse, of a monumental, visionary, and yet fully human poise.

Much of Stevens' poetry is a poetry of evanescence and epiphany. In such poems as "Examination of a Hero in a Time of War" or "The Owl in the Sarcophagus," moments of grace and vision disappear in the last stanza. But in "To an Old Philosopher in Rome" the still point is not a single heightened moment. It is a quiet state of being. It is a point of perspective in one's entire life. The mood is one of elegy and farewells in keeping with Stevens' "wintry temperament."[26] But it is predominantly that of quiet confidence, of Stevens' acceptance of what his life has been (the poems he has written—these, not memories—are the testaments to his existence) and what his life could be now.

In "To an Old Philosopher in Rome" we read Stevens' method for living out

the end of one's life with nobility, for transforming the extreme of the unknown into the extreme of the known:

> How easily the blown banners change to wings . . .
> Things dark on the horizons of perception,
> Become accompaniments of fortune, but
> Of the fortune of the spirit, beyond the eye,
> Not of its sphere, and yet not far beyond,
>
> The human end in the spirit's greatest reach
> The extreme of the known in the presence of the extreme
> Of the unknown.

First, the wise man must build his city in snow. By this Stevens means that man must clearly confront the death of the gods and his own death, not reason death away or lull himself to sleep with fairy tales of a life beyond. And by this Stevens also means that reality must be stripped to its simple essentials—"No more than a bed, a chair and moving nuns." Secondly there must be "a solitude of the self," a solitude which is necessary but not sufficient for the composition of the whole man, the integration of the self. This Stevens explicitly states in "Things of August":

> When was it that the particles became
> The whole man, that tempers and beliefs became
> Temper and belief and that differences lost
> Difference and were one? It had to be
> In the presence of a solitude of the self,
> An expanse and the abstraction of an expanse,
> A zone of time without the ticking of clocks,
> A color that moved us with forgetfulness.
> Where was it that we heard the voice of union?

Related to this "solitude of the self" is the equally necessary condition of "human dignity":

> The threshold, Rome, and that more merciful Rome
> Beyond, the two alike in the make of the mind.
> It is as if in a human dignity
> Two parallels become one, a perspective, of which
> Men are part both in the inch and in the mile.

And finally and perhaps most importantly, Stevens identifies a mode of meditation which is a mode of being characterized by receptivity to experience. Given these conditions the "extreme of the known"—understanding before death—becomes possible. The minor house of the convent becomes a great

structure. The two worlds, the real world and its heightened, imagined counterpart, become one—"a perspective" in which to live out old age.

III. The Wise Old Man as Hero

In these poems a new image of nobility and authority surfaces: the figure of the wise old man as hero. This is perhaps startling because so much has been said about the adolescent hero in our literature and the frenetic cult of youth in America. But it is the corrective we needed and still need. The Tradition of the New, still rampant, necessitates its opposite, the wisdom of the Tradition of the Old made New. If we can read the shape of history from literature, then in the forties and fifties we desired a new form of heroism, or at least, a new sense of tradition and continuity to counter a throw-away culture. For the abundance of America can no longer be thought of in terms of increasing consumer indexes. The people of a once-expanding land of plenty must reconceive space in interior terms. It is clearly no longer appropriate, nor correct, to apostrophize the United States, as Whitman did, as the greatest poem, for the country is no longer a new and virgin land.

But the compensation could be this: in these four great Moderns we see that the American Adam has grown up, and more importantly, he has grown old with grace and dignity. In these poems of old age the supreme humanist symbol is that of the wise old man in search of what will suffice. In fact, within the late poems of these elderly American poets, it is often the very presence of a teacher himself, the embodiment of tradition and continuity, which they themselves seek. Stevens' Santayana and Eliot's composite figure of his literary ancestors (the ghost), Pound's Confucius and Williams' Toulouse Lautrec, to whom he dedicates *Paterson V*—all represent not only tradition but are also doppelgängers, secret selves.

For a literary symbol, in addition to its historical context, has a personal dimension. It is a magical object which transforms the self. In the experience of the symbol we understand just how important these master figures are for these poets and, in turn, just how important for us are these aging poets: they have given us qualified images of wisdom arduously achieved only after a long life of reflection and creative work. As Theodore Roszak argues in *Where the Wasteland Ends,* "true symbols transcend intellectual deciphering, calling forth another level of consciousness which eludes words. They are, as it were, doors leading into dark chambers of reality, like the entranceways of the old mystery cults. We must take our whole life in with us and be prepared to be totally transformed. A true symbol must be *lived into,* that is how its meaning is found."[27] Our culture, in other words, must absorb these poems into the body politic and thereby take the words to heart.

Let us look briefly at the Williams of *Paterson V.* If the Williams of *Paterson I-IV,* a man in his mid-sixties, were to be described, we would characterize him as a lusty old man. One of the questions he asked himself was:

Doctor, do you believe in
"the people," the Democracy? Do
you still believe—in this
swill-hole of corrupt cities?
Do you, Doctor? Now?
(III, i)[28]

The answer he gave throughout those four books was, on balance, yes. But if we were to ask this same question of the Williams of *Paterson V* the answer would be "no," he does not still believe in that swill-hole. Now he wants to "avoid/the irreverent" (V, iii). At this point he is the wise old man reminiscent of the elder Eliot, Pound, and Stevens, a calmed figure who has won some measure of peace over much doubt and anguish and seeks to preserve tradition in the only form now available—art. Williams himself says as much in *I Wanted to Write a Poem,* which was published in the same year as the fifth book of *Paterson:*

> . . . *Paterson V* must be written, is being written. . . . Why must it be written? *Patterson IV* ends with the protagonist breaking through the bushes, identifying himself with the land, with America. He finally will die but it can't be categorically stated that death ends *anything.* When you're through with sex, with ambition, what can an old man create? Art, of course, a piece of art that will go beyond him into the lives of young people, the people who haven't had time to create. The old man meets the young people and lives on.[29]

Williams finds himself able to face the mortality of the "aging body" only through the medium of art, the continuity of tradition represented by the famous fifteenth-century Unicorn tapestries of the New York Cloisters:

—the aging body
with the deformed great-toe nail
makes itself known
coming
to search me out—with a
rare smile
among the thronging flowers of that field
where the Unicorn
is penned by a low
wooden fence
in April!
(V, iii)

Although "weakness dogs him," through art he escapes the pressure of time:

Through this hole
at the bottom of the cavern

of death, the imagination
escapes intact.
(V, i)

The wise old man personifies the strength of both tradition and creation. He is the "patron of origins," in Stevens' phrase. His is not, of course, an undisturbed serenity. On the contrary, such balance is not easily won or preserved. In the *Pisan Cantos* Pound is by turns cranky and exhausted, irreverent, irate, as well as benevolently wise. Williams exhorts Paterson (himself) to "keep your pecker up/whatever the detail!" (V, iii). And the tone of *The Rock,* although ever well-measured, is alternately one of a balanced tranquility, delight, and an almost weary sadness; in taking stock of his life and his work, Stevens acknowledges a sense of failure as well as new-found pleasures and ways of being. On the whole, then, for these four poets, the condition of integrity, to use Erikson's term, achieved in, or imagined for, old age is no simple state of being. Above all, perhaps, it is characterized by a humility which contradicts the Western way of thinking about man in the world—imperialism over nature and other peoples. Old age brings an end to domination. Man stripped of such physical, perhaps overbearing strength is what Stevens imagines in "Lebensweisheitspielerei," which I quote here in full:

Weaker and weaker, the sunlight falls
In the afternoon. The proud and the strong
Have departed.

Those that are left are the unaccomplished,
The finally human,
Natives of a dwindled sphere.

Their indigence is an indigence
That is an indigence of the light,
A stellar pallor that hangs on the threads.
Little by little, the poverty
Of autumnal space becomes
A look, a few words spoken.

Each person completely touches us
With what he is and as he is,
In the stale grandeur of annihilation.

It is "the finally human" which "touches us," a deepening of the human spirit made possible in old age.

IV. Tradition, Creation, and the Life Review

Of the four poets Pound was submitted to the most severe physical,

psychological, and social distress in his old age. The *Pisan Cantos* are nothing less than a survival piece. Pound, sixty years old and locked up in a hellhole of a wire cage, had only the notebooks to keep him alive in which he worked on translations of Confucius and his *Pisan Cantos.* His fervent dream for Italy and his frenzied belief in Mussolini ("Ben") had finally twisted into a personal nightmare. The sequence opens:

> THE enormous tragedy of the dream in the peasant's bent
> shoulders
> Manes! Manes was tanned and stuffed,
> Thus Ben and la Clara *a Milano*
> by the heels at Milano
> That maggots shd/ eat the dead bullock
> DIGENES, διγενές but the twice crucified
> where in history will you find it?
> (LXXIV)

Like Manes, the Persian sage who founded the sect of the Manicheans, Mussolini and his mistress Clara Petacci were crucified for their teachings. Thus Pound's Italy was gone. He had been stripped of his freedom, his wife, his books, and perhaps of his self confidence:

> we will see those old roads again, question,
> possibly
> but nothing appears much less likely.
> (LXXIV)

He had to start again, to find not only what could "suffice," in Wallace Stevens' cool term, but what he could live on. After all he was branded a traitor (understandably since he had spoken in favor of the enemy) and his betrayal was a result of believing in the wrong values at the wrong time in the wrong place. His solution would be a return to the past, not a projection into the future.

What he could live on is, in part, the memory of both people and places, art works and historical events and monuments. Robert Butler has suggested that the predominance of the shades of memory in the elderly is not necessarily a sign of senility or psychological imbalance, but may very well be a functional mechanism by which man comes to terms with his past life.[30] Certainly this is the case for Pound. He asserts "Senesco sed amo" (LXXX), which is both a personal revelation and a declaration as to how to live, and in these Cantos we see him honoring the dead in order to live by that rule. It is, in other words, not so much out of nostalgia as out of desire to pay homage to what he has loved in his life that Pound composes his hymn to the dead. He recites the litany of restaurants and cafes ("Dieudonne," "La Rupe," and "Dullier") and the litany of artists of his generation ("Jepson" and "Newbolt" and others: "Lordly men are to earth o'ergiven" [LXXIV]). And as a result of this, which is first and foremost an act of love, Pound plots the curve of his own past: "I am getting old

but I love." That past extends beyond his own life to the troubadours of the twelfth century, the literature of Greece and Rome, and African myth.

Perhaps just as significantly (and this is a kind of lesson in politics of the elderly), one of the primary catalysts in transforming his life in prison into at times magical moments of paradise, is his acknowledging brotherhood with other prisoners—criminals—of the camp. Paradoxically the forced space and forced time provided him, although against his will, the freedom for a life review. Thus in the *Pisan Cantos* Pound moves beyond the elite sphere of history, literature, and myth and into the world of outcast men. He magnificently unites the two, learning much, re-making himself, and creating one of his finest poems.

Earlier I referred to the anthropologist Victor Turner whose work I think can help us understand both how Pound was "made new" and how the elderly today form a key sector along the frontier of cultural adaptation.[31] In his recent study *Dramas, Fields, and Metaphors,*[32] Turner discusses our fundamental need for what he calls *communitas,* a condition of social unity (community) characterized by undifferentiated social status, by what Martin Buber has termed the "I-Thou" relationship of the self to the other, and by a time which is not socio-historical time but a sacred time. Above all communitas is not merely metaphorical; it is a relationship between concrete individuals (the pilgrimage is an excellent example of communitas). To communitas Turner opposes *structure* by which he means the hierarchal, stratified, bureaucratic structure we encounter everyday in the institutions of the family, the orthodox church, the corporation, and so on. The dialectic of the two poles of communitas and structure, Turner argues, is a useful conceptual tool for understanding the process of social change which includes the revitalization of institutions, the replacement of one institution by another, and so on. It is communitas which is the condition "for the production of root metaphors, conceptual archetypes, paradigms, models" and which thus provides the impetus for significant social change.[33] Of the four poets, it is only Pound who succeeds in clearly dramatizing this *need for community* and showing just what power the condition of communitas has. In the prison camp of Pisa he and the other prisoners are divested of all status, as are the elderly in our society, and from their mutual bondage, a close social bond is formed. This bond is paralleled by Pound's recognition that love and humility are basic personal and social virtues:

> filial, fraternal affection is the root of humaneness
> the root of the process.
>
> (LXXIV)

Significantly, communitas in the domain of the social world implies analogous communitas in the domain of the natural world. The principal actors of Pound's world are not just his fellow prisoners—Snag and the pistol-packing Burnes—but also the ant, the wasp, the lizard, the lynx, the eucalyptus. Hierarchy is dissolved. This is how Turner would explain this phenomenon:

> In a sense, when man ceases to be the master and becomes the equal or fellow of man, he also ceases to be the master and becomes the equal or fellow of non-human beings. It is culture that fabricates social distinctions in liminality, but in so doing culture is forced to use the idiom of nature, to replace its fictions by natural facts—even if these facts themselves only possess what reality they have in a framework of cultural concepts. Thus it is in liminality and also in those phases of ritual that abut on liminality that one finds profuse symbolic reference to beasts, birds, and vegetation.[34]

From the condition of communitas in the Pisan prison camp rises a conceptual archetype for a society different from that of our Western civilization—the African myth of Wagadu, an image of the Utopian city.[35] Pound's genius in the *Pisan Cantos* is thus to strike a balance between communitas (the prison camp, the green world, Wagadu) and structure (the China of Confucius), to write a lyric poem, an epic poem, about man and society in a time of severe personal distress and old age. This is something which neither Eliot, nor Stevens, nor Williams could do.

In his essay on "Art and Time," the depth psychologist Erich Neumann uses the word 'transcendent' to describe the quality which is found in the work of great artists in old age:

> In these works of man a numinous world is manifested in which the polarity of outward and inward—nature and art—seems to be resolved. Their secret alchemy achieves a synthesis of the numinosum at the heart of nature and psyche.
>
> These aged masters seem to have attained the image and likeness of a primal creative force, prior to the world and outside the world, which, though split from the very beginning into the polarity of nature and psyche, is in essence one divided whole.
>
> ....
>
> This art no longer relates either consciously or unconsciously to any historical time; the solitary monologue of these 'extreme' works is spoken, as it were, into the void.
>
> ....
>
> But in the rare instances when the phenomenon of transcendence occurs, the transpersonal seems, even though it has passed through the medium of the human, to have achieved its own objectivity—to speak, one might say, with itself. It is no longer oriented toward the world or man, the ego or the collective, security or insecurity; instead, the creative act which mysteriously creates form and life in nature as in the human psyche seems to have perceived itself and to shine forth with its own incandescence. The creative impulse seems to have liberated itself. United on the plane of artistic-creation, the self which man experiences within him and the world-creative self which is manifested outwardly achieve the transparency of symbolic reality.[36]

Although I am not sure in what way historical realities are ever transcended in a work of art, I do understand, and accept, what Neumann points to. The poems of Stevens, Eliot, Pound, and Williams do possess an orphic quality, a timeless dimension, which links them with what can only be called the age-old wisdom of humanity. For Neumann, man is not a one-dimensional political or economic animal. Rather Neumann calls for a "mystical anthropology"; he is concerned with *homo mysticus,* mystical man, with mysticism not limited to the experience of God but understood as a fundamental, broadly-based category of human experience. Following Jung's model of individuation (the striving of the individual toward psychic wholeness), Neumann argues that different forms of mysticism accompany the three major stages of psychological development: we find source mysticism in the uroboros stage where the unconscious is dominant, hero mysticism in the second phase where the ego is dominant, and mature mysticism in the final stage where the self emerges; opposites are reconciled, and harmony is achieved between the conscious and unconscious aspects of the mind. More specifically, the final stage of Old Age he identifies with the mysticism of the Egyptian God Osiris and the Tibetan Book of the Dead. In this stage the self becomes transparent, he says; the world becomes transparent, and the mystical experience is a conscious one. The possibility of the symbolic life is revealed, and life in the world becomes possible, even in the face of death. Thus Neumann explores the archetype of the Wise Old Man through its manifestations in texts drawn from both literature and the visual arts which are themselves the creations of men in old age. Literature is thus shown to reveal the achievement of wisdom in our time and to record the potentialities of human experience. Jung's description of the archetype of the Wise Old Man not only accords with Neumann's findings (this is not surprising) but also dovetails with Erikson's notion of the final stage of man's development in old age:

> In the encounter with life and the world there are experiences that are capable of moving us to long and thorough reflection, from which, in time, insights and convictions grow up—a process depicted by the alchemists as the philosophical tree. The unfolding of these experiences is regulated, as it were, by two archetypes: the anima, who expresses *life,* and the "Wise Old Man," who personifies *meaning.* . . . This aptly describes the character of that spirit or thinking which you do not, like an intellectual operation, perform yourself, as the "little god of this world," but which happens to you as though it came from another, and greater, perhaps the great spirit of the world. . . .[37]

The involuntary character of the archetype fits the description which the poets gave of the meditative mode and the symbols which emerge from this state of being. The long life of the imagination compensates almost automatically for the losses of the social world. A mystical experience is possible. It does not result from an "intellectual operation" which one performs like a "god." It simply happens, and happens as the result of a long life of writing, a long life of working with images. All of this is metaphor for the creative process. Neumann describes it this way:

> It is characteristic of the creative process that in it the ego cannot cling to its position of consciousness, but must expose itself to encounter with the nonego. In so doing, the ego renounces conscious reality, in which the world is experienced as contradiction, and an encounter occurs between ego and nonego in which the contradictions of the world, ego, and self are suspended. This encounter, wherever it may occur, we designate as mystical.[38]

This is the still point, with the reconciliation of opposites being described in psychoanalytical terms. The mature phase of old age, we see, is thus characterized by a new synthesis between the conscious ego and the non-ego; it is a final integration of the personality with the self, not the ego, at the center. What psychoanalysis describes as an archetype or abstract process, each of these poets had explored throughout their lives in poetry. The process was difficult, and the final achievement of the imagination secure.

Notes

[1]I would like to extend my warmest thanks to Professor Roy Harvey Pearce of the University of California at San Diego, and Professors Michel Benamou and Justin Replogle of the University of Wisconsin at Milwaukee, whose help in the formulation of this paper has been invaluable.

[2]Ralph Waldo Emerson, *Society and Solitude* (Boston: Fields, Osgood, & Co., 1870), p. 296.

[3]*The Waste Land and Other Poems* (New York: Harcourt, Brace, and World, 1962), pp. 19-22.

[4]Merle E. Brown, *Wallace Stevens: The Poem as Act* (Detroit: Wayne State Univ. Press, 1970), p. 175.

[5]Quoted in Stephen Spender, "Remembering Eliot," in *T. S. Eliot: The Man and His Work,* ed. Allen Tate (New York: Dell, 1966), p. 55.

[6]These Modern meditative poems resemble what M. H. Abrams has called the greater romantic lyric ("Structure and Style in the Greater Romantic Lyric," in *Romanticism and Consciousness,* ed. Harold Bloom (New York: Yale Univ. Press, 1970), p. 201.

[7]*Four Quartets* (New York: Harcourt, Brace, 1943). All references will be to this edition and will be identified by the name of the Quartet only.

[8]A. Alvarez, "A Meditative Poet," in *T. S. Eliot: Four Quartets: A Casebook,* ed. Bernard Bergonzi (London: Macmillan, 1969), p. 240.

[9]*The Coming of Age,* trans. Patrick O'Brian (New York: Warner Paperback Library, 1973), p. 14.

[10]*The Growth of American Thought,* 3rd ed. (New York: Harper and Row, 1964), p. 767.

[11]*Steps to an Ecology of Mind* (New York: Ballantine, 1972).

[12]Ibid., p. 138.

[13]Ibid., p. 433.

[14]*The Cantos of Ezra Pound* (New York: New Directions, 1970). All references will be to this edition and will be identified by the number of the Canto only.

[15]Bateson, p. 438.

[16]*Insight and Responsibility: Lectures on the Ethical Implications of Psychoanalytical Insight* (New York: W. W. Norton, 1964), pp. 133-34.

[17]See Louis Martz's *The Poem of the Mind: Essays on Poetry/English and American* (New York: Oxford Univ. Press, 1966) and *The Poetry of Meditation: A Study in English Religious Literature of the Seventeenth Century* (New Haven: Yale Univ. Press, 1954) for the opposite point of view. On the other hand, Roy Harvey Pearce (*The Continuity of American Poetry* [Princeton: Princeton Univ. Press, 1961], p. 43) has pointed out that for American poets the appropriate meditative model is Puritan, not jesuitical: "For the Puritan (particularly the New England Puritan, who was much more conservative than his English peer) meditation, then, was a matter not of disciplining one's self into knowledge of God (which was impossible) but of being lucky enough to catch a sudden glimpse of that knowledge as God might make manifest."

[18]"John Marston," *Elizabethan Essays* (New York: Haskell House, 1964), p. 194.

[19]Quoted in *The Development of American Philosophy,* eds. Walter G. Muedler, Laurence Sears, and Anne V. Schaback (Cambridge: Houghton Mifflin, 1960), p. 463.

[20]*The Collected Poems of Wallace Stevens* (New York: Alfred A. Knopf, 1968). All references will be to this edition and will be identified by title only.

[21]Frederick Perls, Ralph E. Hefferline, and Paul Goodman, *Gestalt Therapy: Excitement and Growth in the Human Personality* (New York: Delta Books, 1951), p. 63.

[22]*Opus Posthumous* (New York: Alfred A. Knopf, 1966), p. 197.

[23]Letter from Wallace Stevens to Barbara Church, February 1, 1950, in *Letters,* ed. Holly Stevens (New York: Alfred A. Knopf, 1966), p. 664.

[24]Stuart Spicker's "Gerontogenetic Mentation: Memory, Dementia and Medicine in the Penultimate Years" also raises this question (see this volume).

[25]For a discussion of aging and time from a philosophical point of view, see C. Davis Hendricks and Jon Hendricks, "Historical Development of the Multiplicity of Times and Implications for the Analysis of Aging," *The Human Context,* 7, No. 1 (1975), 117-29.

[26]Helen Vendler, *On Extended Wings: Wallace Stevens' Longer Poems* (Cambridge, Mass.: Harvard Univ. Press, 1969), p. 47.

[27]*Where the Wasteland Ends: Politics and Transcendence in Post-Industrial Society* (Garden City, New York: Doubleday, 1973), pp. 128-29.

[28]William Carlos Williams, *Paterson* (New York: New Directions, 1963). All references will be to this edition and will be identified only by the number of the book and the section within that book.

[29]*I Wanted to Write a Poem,* ed. Edith Heal (New York: Beacon Press, 1958), p. 26.

[30]"The Life Review: An Interpretation of Reminiscence in the Aged" [1963], in *Middle Age and Aging: A Reader in Social Psychology,* ed. Bernice L. Neugarten (Chicago: Univ. of Chicago Press, 1968), pp. 486-96.

[31]Gerald Gruman's "Cultural Origins of Present-day 'Age-ism': The Modernization of the Life Cycle," makes this point. See this volume.

[32]*Dramas, Fields, and Metaphors: Symbolic Action in Human Society* (Ithaca: Cornell Univ. Press, 1974).

[33]Ibid., p. 38. Turner associates communitas with "liminality," a term he borrows from Van Gennep; liminality, referring to a threshold situation, a gap between one ordered world and another, is an appropriate metaphor for these late poems.

[34]Ibid., pp. 252-53.

[35]For background about the myth of Wagadu see Leo Frobenius and Douglas C. Fox, *African Genesis* (London: Faber and Faber, 1938), pp. 109-10.

[36]Erich Newmann, *Art and the Creative Unconscious,* trans. Ralph Manheim (Princeton: Princeton Univ. Press, 1971), pp. 103-05.

[37]Carl Gustav Jung, *Mysterium Coniunctionis: An Inquiry into the Separation and Synthesis of Psychic Opposites in Alchemy,* trans. R. F. C. Hull, 2nd ed. (Princeton Univ. Press, 1970), p. 233.

[38]Erich Neumann, "Mystical Man" [1948], *The Mystic Vision,* Bollingen Series XXX: Papers from the Eranos Yearbooks, Vol. 6, ed. Joseph Campbell (Princeton: Princeton Univ. Press, 1969), pp. 375-415.

III. AGING, DEATH, AND DESTINY

Steven R. Smith

DEATH, DYING, AND THE ELDERLY IN SEVENTEENTH-CENTURY ENGLAND

Within the broad cultural tradition of western Christianity, attitudes towards death and dying have not remained constant, but have changed over the centuries. In the twentieth century, there is a tendency to fear death and to hide it. It is not something openly discussed and it often takes place in secret. Even mourning is minimized and elaborate funeral services and cemetery monuments are out of style today. By contrast, in seventeenth-century England the death of an individual was a highly significant event accompanied by elaborate and socially useful rituals. In this paper the attitudes of that society will be explored and the lives and deaths of some individuals will be described to illustrate the particular applications of society's attitudes as well as to show the rituals which accompanied death.[1]

For seventeenth-century England, some of the most significant work is that being done by the historical sociologists E.A. Wrigley, Peter Laslett, and the Cambridge Group for the History of Population and Social Structure.[2] What emerges from such studies is a picture of society as different from the twentieth century as are its attitudes towards death and dying. These attitudes were in part formed by the unique demographic structure of early modern England. This comes as no surprise; we could expect that a society in which most persons died young would have a very different view of death than one in which death normally came in old age. One of the most striking features of that demographic picture is the very short life expectancy at birth: it was somewhere in the late twenties. The main reason for this was the high infant mortality rate; by far the most dangerous were the first years of life. Though there were changes over the course of the century, overall age distribution was skewed towards youthfulness. Gregory King, one of England's earliest demographers, estimated in 1695 that some 45% of the population was children. Yet the overall youthfulness of the population and the short life expectancy at birth are a bit misleading: a person who survived childhood had a fairly good chance of living to an old age. King's figures show that about one

out of ten persons in 1695 was sixty years old or older.[3] The passage through the years between childhood and old age was not easy, of course. The relatively crude state of medical knowledge and the general lack of sanitation meant that many people died of illnesses and injuries which today are rarely the cause of death. Nor was there any defense against the plagues which swept the country several times during the century. Thus death was always close to the daily lives of these early modern people.[4]

In order to understand a society's attitude toward death, we must also investigate the history of the family. If there was a significant proportion of the population over the age of sixty, we might ask how those persons were cared for and where did they live. And for those who survived into old age, was there a period of retirement, or was work ended only by death? While life expectancy at birth was low, the average age at marriage was fairly high: twenty-four for women and nearly twenty-eight for men. Marriage almost always meant the creation of a new household since married sons did not, as a rule, remain in the homes of their parents and it was rare for two married couples, whether parents and children or brothers and sisters, to live in the same household. Thus, after the children had married, the parents were left alone as a separate household unit unless there were unmarried children. Since marriage was far less universal then now, the possibility of unmarried children was certainly not uncommon, but what needs to be emphasized is that in early modern England old persons did not usually move in with their married children. The statistical evidence being gathered by the Cambridge Group suggests that many aged persons lived alone, or, perhaps for financial or physical reasons, as lodgers in the homes of other families.

Demographic circumstances and household arrangements represent only two factors influencing attitudes towards death. Keith Thomas and Natalie Zemon Davis have pointed out in their studies of popular religion that the Protestant Reformation brought a major shift in thinking about the dead.[5] This will be dealt with at length later. Yet, although the Reformation brought with it modified attitudes towards the dead, society did of course remain deeply religious. For those who might have wished to avoid death or to postpone it, there remained the centuries old theological explanation of its necessity. The doctrine of original sin not only justified all human suffering, including that which accompanied illness and old age, but also revealed the cause of death. At the beginning of the world, death had been neither natural nor necessary, and God's original plan had been that man would live eternally. Adam's sin and the consequent fall of man, however, had altered that plan and the wages of sin had proved to be death.[6] Thus in a certain sense, it is impossible to separate the Christian attitude towards death from the Christian attitude towards life. All of earthly life was seen as preparation for the life-to-come. Death was the welcomed end of hardship, illness, sin, and suffering and the beginning, at least for some, of eternal bliss. On the other hand, death was also the time of judgement when a person would be held responsible for his manner of life on earth.

A typical expression of this Christian attitude can be found in Nicholas

Byfield's *Cure of the Fear of Death,* which was published in 1618.[7] After explaining that the Christian should welcome death, Byfield, a Puritan and the author of several other religious books, acknowledged that many people preferred to live long lives and to postpone death as long as possible. Yet, if death is the end of misery and suffering, he argued, there should be no reason to want to defer it. Indeed, human life, no matter how long it might last, is short when compared to eternity, and earthly pleasures, no matter how intense they may be, are insignificant when compared to heavenly bliss. Byfield urged his readers to be prepared for death, arguing that the nearness of death in old age should stimulate religious conversion, especially in those who had lived long sinful lives and thus had much to repent before death.

Another theological question raised in the religious literature of the century concerned the different life spans of individuals: if everyone shared the inheritance of original sin, why did some persons live longer than others? Could a person prolong his life by righteous living or shorten it by sinfulness? Could medicine and diet add years to one's life?[8] Francis Bacon was one of several writers who thought it possible to preserve youthfulness. His *History of Life and Death* is full of suggestions as to how one might postpone death. Most of its advice is based on the medical theories of the day which held that moisture and softness were characteristic of youth while dryness and hardness were characteristic of old age: death could thus be postponed if the body could be kept moist and soft.[9] But any medical attempt to prolong life could be viewed as interference with the will of God, just as the use of astrology to predict the time of death was considered to be unchristian because it acknowledged heavenly bodies as the determiners of man's destiny. William Lilly, one of the best known astrologers of the century, admitted that he was frequently asked to determine the date of someone's death, but responded that the most prudent course was to avoid such predictions.[10]

In addition to medical and astrological theories, there were many other folk beliefs in the seventeenth century concerning special circumstances which might influence the length of a person's life and signal the nearness of his death. It was widely believed that men who looked more like their mothers than their fathers generally lived longer, and that children born to young parents would have long lives. Bacon suggested that children conceived in the morning when parents were "not too lusty and wanton" lived longer than those conceived at other times. He also reported that hairy legs and black or red hair were considered to be signs of longevity.[11] Sir Thomas Browne, a physician and writer, in describing the death of a friend, recorded that "the moon was in motion from the meridian" at the time of death (it was commonly held that more deaths occurred at such a time than at any other time). He also thought it significant that this person had died at night, which was the time of the birth of Jesus. In his last days, this man had dreamed of his dead friends and had concluded that this was a sign of imminent death, but Browne thought this unlikely.[12] Taken together, these attempts to find some signs of long life or to use astrology to predict the length of life suggest that there was not some little anxiety about death. And, ironically, the inaccuracy of those

signs and predictions might well have reinforced the Christian notion that one must always be prepared for death.

Richard Allestree, a popular religious writer, dealt with the problem of the different life spans of individuals in *A Discourse Concerning the Period of Human Life* from a strictly theological point of view. After arguing that God has the power to set an arbitrary number of years for the life of any particular person, Allestree said that there is, nevertheless, a "common period of human life," which in seventeenth-century England was considered to be approximately the seventy or eighty years promised to each man in the Old Testament (the normal life span varied from place to place and from time to time, depending on such factors as the climate). As for the lengths of particular lives, there were two possible explanations: God immutably determined the length of each person's life, or, an individual's life span could be extended or shortened according to circumstances. Allestree was inclined to the second view since it introduced a degree of human responsibility: while God made the final decision, that decision would be influenced by what a person did with his life here on earth. Thus a person's life could be shortened or lengthened by his manner of living. Allestree based his opinion on Scriptural evidence and on human experience, which demonstrated that natural means for preserving life, such as medicine, were usually ineffective and that it was far safer to rely on good living and obedience to moral precepts to extend life expectancy.[13]

Despite the absolute necessity of death and the ultimate inability of man to postpone it, we are not surprised to find that in the seventeenth century many people were rather reluctant to welcome it. However, fear of dying, to some extent, was mitigated by the Christian doctrine that there were two kinds of death: carnal and spiritual. Carnal death, or death of the body, was the necessary death resulting from original sin. Spiritual death, on the other hand, occurred for those who remained cut off from God. Thus the Christian could hope for eternal spiritual life even though he could not prolong earthly life. John Moore's *Map of Man's Mortality,* published in 1617 only two years before his death, explained the standard Christian position on these two kinds of death and argued that death was not a curse as it had been for Adam and others who died before Christ, but rather was a blessing which initiated eternal happiness for the true Christian. Moore acknowledged that many people naturally fear death since it separates them from their families and friends and means that they will be judged by God for their sins. But these fears could be overcome by Christians who repented and reversed their values, placing eternal happiness before wordly pleasures. Carnal death itself was nothing to be afraid of: "Nothing better resembleth death than our sleep, and when do we ever better rest than at that time."[14]

John Dunton, author of an essay on death, also used the analogy of sleep in describing death. Death, he said, could be no more painful than birth, an event which no person remembers. Dunton described the experiences of two men who had been thought dead and who, upon reviving, explained what they had experienced. One was a man who had been hanged, the other had almost drowned. The hanged man reported that he had felt no pain, but had simply

The distraction fit, lost in a shaft of sunlight,
The wild thyme unseen, or the winter lightning
Or the waterfall, or music heard so deeply
That it is not heard at all, but you are the music
While the music lasts.

"The Dry Salvages"

Such timeless moments populate the *Four Quartets.* For our purposes in this paper, the most revealing of them occurs in a passage from "Little Gidding" which has been called one of Eliot's finest pieces of writing.[8] The other unattended moments of the *Quartets* exist in a timeless and spaceless dimension where Eliot is not present as a character, but Eliot does appear in "Little Gidding." It is the most personal and intimate passage of all the *Quartets.* It is his last poem. In this section he meets a ghost—a figure which represents his literary past, his creative tradition—in the wartorn streets of early morning London. He reveals himself, a man in his fifties, and he discloses what he fears his future as an old man might be. He projects himself into that foreign territory of old age, which is just what Simone de Beauvoir counsels us all to do: "If we do not know what we are going to be, we cannot know what we are: let us recognize ourselves in this old man or in that old woman. It must be done if we are to take upon ourselves the entirety of our human state."[9]

The message which Eliot sends himself, and us, is a message from the dead. First, it is purgatorial. The vision of old age is bleak and bitter:

Let me disclose the gifts reserved for age
  To set a crown upon your lifetime's effort.
  First, the cold friction of expiring sense
Without enchantment, offering no promise
  But bitter tastelessness of shadow fruit
  As body and soul begin to fall asunder.
Second, the conscious impotence of rage
  At human folly, and the laceration
  Of laughter at what ceases to amuse.
And last, the rending pain of re-enactment
  Of all that you have done, and been; the shame
  Of motives later revealed, and the awareness
Of things ill done and done to others' harm
  Which once you took for exercise of virtue.
  Then fools' approval stings, and honour stains.

"Little Gidding"

This could be Shakespeare's Jacques speaking. Old age, the ghost reveals, will be unendurable because:

From wrong to wrong the exasperated spirit
  Proceeds, unless restored by that refining fire
  Where you must move in measure, like a dancer.

For Eliot the still point is an ideal which has imaginative force as a symbol. But as we read in the third of the *Quartets,*

> But to apprehend
> The point of intersection of the timeless
> With time, is an occupation for the saint—
> No occupation either, but something given
> And taken, in a lifetime's death in love,
> Ardour and selflessness and self-surrender.
> "The Dry Salvages"

Grasping the still point—living in such a state of wholeness—is a possibility only for saints. One can aspire to it but never wholly achieve it. What is possible for an individual life? Eliot gives two answers: art and moments of mystical experience. In lines which recall Keats' famous "Ode on a Grecian Urn," Eliot acknowledges that although the body must die, pattern—the form of language and music—survives:

> Words move, music moves
> Only in time; but that which is only living
> Can only die. Words, after speech, reach
> Into the silence. Only by the form, the pattern,
> Can words or music reach
> The stillness, as a Chinese jar still
> Moves perpetually in its stillness.
> Not the stillness of the violin, while the note lasts,
> Not that only, but the co-existence,
> Or say that the end precedes the beginning,
> And that the end and the beginning were always there
> Before the beginning and after the end.
> "Burnt Norton"

It is pattern—continuity—which incarnates the still point, the locus of being and non-being, of beginning and end. Pattern is immortal ("Only by the form, the pattern,/Can words or music reach/The stillness") and thus gives sustenance to man. Art in the widest possible sense (including ritual and religion as well as literature) is the medium by which man, Eliot believes, can be in touch with the still point. Mediation is necessary. Eliot, of course, chose both poetry and Christian existentialism.

Although man cannot attain the still point as a continuous state of being, he can be graced with flashes of mystical experience. They are "unattended." They come when one is not looking. The mode of meditation is more Zen than strictly Christian:

> For most of us, there is only the unattended
> Moment, the moment in and out of time,

At the still point of the turning world. Neither flesh nor fleshness;
Neither from nor towards; at the still point, there the dance is,
But neither arrest nor movement. And do not call it fixity,
Where past and future are gathered. Neither movement from nor towards,
Neither ascent nor decline. Except for the point, the still point,
There would be no dance, and there is only the dance.
"Burnt Norton"

The desire is for wholeness, for a reconciliation of opposites ("Neither flesh nor fleshness;/Neither from nor towards"), for a state of being which is balanced at the source of change but not touched by it, for a moment of pure present-ness which can counteract the tyranny of biological and historical time without degenerating into stagnation ("do not call it fixity"). That point of stillness is the origin of meaningful creation, individual and cultural ("Except for the point, the still point,/There would be no dance"). It is a point of unity and deep peace, the point of eternal return, which is described elsewhere as:

The inner freedom from the practical desire,
The release from action and suffering, release from the inner
And the outer compulsion, yet surrounded
By a grace of sense, a white light still and moving,
Erhebung without motion, concentration
Without elimination, both a new world
And the old made explicit, understood
In the completion of its partial ecstasy,
The resolution of its partial horror.
"Burnt Norton"

The still point is an image of a state of "grace," "still and moving." Released from the demands of the world and inner pressures, one stands outside of time and gains the perspective of wisdom ("both a new world/And the old made explicit"). Thus it symbolizes the ultimate goal of a man's life: enhanced spirituality, increased consciousness, and the inner peace which comes from an acceptance of the "partial ecstasy" and "partial horror" of one's life and culture. The hope, as Eliot puts it in the concluding lines of "Little Gidding," the last of the *Four Quartets,* is that

We shall not cease from exploration
And the end of all our exploring
Will be to arrive where we started
And know the place for the first time.

One's life is a journey whose end will hopefully illuminate one's beginnings. One's end is a threshold where ideally "past and future are gathered."

sought was equally unparalleled in his past life: the acceptance of the European tradition, the shelter of the museum. For Pound, the humiliating and stifling U.S. prison camp in Pisa, Italy in which he was incarcerated in his sixties yielded, paradoxically, a kind of grace. And in Stevens' "To an Old Philosopher in Rome," written to his former mentor Santayana when Stevens was very old, the broad expanse of the West has contracted to the silence of a small convent room. With the lessening of mobility imposed by age, social pressures, and personal choice, in these poems space shrinks and disengagement from the social sphere takes place. But through the exercise of the imagination, memory, and the meditative mode this contraction is not lethal. On the contrary, it brings to the poets new insights and new possibilities for personal integrative experience. Accordingly their poetry provides us with symbols for psychic wholeness.

Thus for these writers the poetry of old age came as fulfillment. Although each poet moved *in his own way* toward a bearable closure to his life in poetry, their individual solutions offer one general answer to the problems of old age. And their poems speak to broad cultural as well as personal needs. They provide a counterstatement to the American frenzy for invention and the Tradition of the New. They share characteristics which together form a distinctive genre (understood as a literary form whose elements are stable and consistent) that is:

1. informed by a new symbol, "the still point," which defies the coercive power of clock time,
2. structured by a method of reflection, a new meditative mode, which denies the long-held Cartesian view of the act of the mind as conscious, voluntary, Promethean, and dominating, and stresses instead an easy penetration of mind and world, an ecology of mind,
3. populated by a new hero, the wise old man, in a society which worships youth, and
4. dedicated to tradition and the creative act as a stay against chaos, and characterized by the life review.

Since all of these qualities are tightly bound together, it is difficult to consider one in isolation from the others; given the broad scope of this topic, I will concentrate on only one poet in each of these areas, sketching the line of development and suggesting conclusions.

I. The Still Point

In these late poems the past and tradition are not repudiated but rather are re-created and from what Eliot had earlier called the West's waste land of broken images a new image emerges which is potent and integrative—the still point:

lost consciousness and seen a bright red light surrounded by darkness. Both of the men, it is significant, described the experience as similar to being asleep. In addition to attempting to dispell the fear of death as a painful experience, Dunton also recognized that people feared death because it meant the end of the love and comfort of earthly friends. Most of his essay argues that on the contrary, these ties would be renewed in heaven, for heavenly bliss would be incomplete without the acquaintance of old friends and relatives.[15] While Moore had urged people to change their values and to replace wordly love with love for eternity, Dunton suggested that perhaps the absence of companionship would not be altogether permanent.

Moore's view, however, was certainly the more common. It can be found, for example, in *A Fountain of Tears,* a book written especially for women by John Featley, onetime chaplain to Charles I. The book covers a wide variety of topics, and the twenty-sixth chapter deals with death. Featley thought that most people paid little attention to death until the prospect was near and that then the dying person was most troubled by the prospect of Hell and eternal suffering. Yet the basic problem was that people were too much in love with earthly things and did not care enough for heavenly things. Featley provided a list of questions for the dying woman to ask herself. The proper answers would give assurance of salvation, but if that assurance could not be had, the woman should pray for additional time in which to repent.[16] The wisest course of action, Featley counseled, was to live each day as if it were the last.

Here again we encounter the inseparability of the Christian attitude towards life and the Christian attitude towards death: all of life must be a preparation for death. William Perkins, a popular and prolific writer, articulated this belief in *A Salve for a Sick Man* which went through many printings during the century: "For the life of a Christian," he wrote, "is nothing else but a meditation of death." Perkins expressed the same idea in a shorter work, *Death's Knell,* which reminds its readers that death could come at any time, unexpectedly. Similarly, an anonymous seventeenth-century ballad entitled "Death's Dance" warns that most people, engaged in sinful activities or worldly and trivial affairs, never aware of the closeness of death, would be shocked to meet it. Richard Baxter even suggested that good health might be a dangerous thing as it could deceive one into thinking that death was far off, thus lulling the soul and conscience to sleep. James Cole, a merchant, not a theologian, wrote *Of Death, a True Description* to warn his fellow merchants of the necessity for constant preparation. In it he likened the man who is always prepared for death to the soldier who has his weapons ready before he actually sees the enemy. Cole also compared life to a candle; if the candle is not to be used up, it should never be lit. Death is a necessary consequence of being born and to speak against death is to speak against life itself. Concomitantly, people should not fear death since there is no way of escaping it. Yet some people do fear it, Cole said, because it means the loss of earthly pleasures and friends. Cole thus agreed with Moore, but provided his readers a different argument: this fear too was foolish since the dead, having no bodies, could not possibly miss earthly things and people. Only the fear of judgement

remained, but here again, Cole reasoned, there could be no legitimate fear on the part of the righteous.[17]

Although spiritual preparation for death was the primary obligation of the Christian, there was also an obligation to make proper disposition of any material goods. According to William Jones, a minister in the Isle of Wight who wrote two treatises on the subject of wills, the making of a will was a Christian duty, since failure to do so could cause strife among the heirs. The will should be drawn up well in advance of death and all of the children should be present so that they might know the disposition of property and use the occasion to strengthen their faith. The primary purpose of the will was to provide for the support of a surviving spouse or minor children, but after such provision was made, the remainder should be used, wrote Jones, for Christian charities.[18]

Providing for Christian charities in wills was one of the consequences of the sixteenth-century Reformation. In the Middle Ages, such funds would have been used for masses for the deceased or the endowment of religious houses. But the entire shift in attitudes towards the dead which accompanied the Reformation apparently raised questions in the minds of many as to the appropriateness of mourning and the proper funeral ceremonies and manner of burial. Medieval Christianity had required that the living provide certain services for the dead and imposed on survivors obligations—particularly for souls in Purgatory (traditionally, ghosts had been important in enforcing the fulfillment of those obligations). In England, after the Reformation, the building of elaborate monuments served as a sort of substitute for the earlier obligations, but even this practice had begun to wane in the seventeenth century.

Moreover, the traditional Christian doctrine of death as the release from suffering and earthly cares caused some problems with mourning. The acceptable attitude towards mourning for the deceased was summed up well by the author of *The Doctrine of Dying Well:* the death of a close friend or a loved one should not cause sorrow, but rejoicing. The merchant Cole accepted that theological position, but added that it was neither unseemly nor ungodly to mourn for the dead and cited Biblical examples to justify his position. Yet continual mourning was not good, and Cole suggested both "external" and "internal" remedies. The external remedy was to find some "new joy." The internal remedies were human reason and the word of God. Human reason taught that man should not be surprised at losses; death is both necessary and universal. From the Bible, man should learn to accept the will of God.[19]

While mourning continued to be accepted in seventeenth-century England, the Puritans did object to the practice of ritual mourning for the dead. Following the Reformation, there was a trend towards simpler funerals. This was in keeping with the Reformed doctrine of predestination and the belief that there was nothing that the living could do for the dead. It may also have reflected a desire to use whatever money was available for the benefit of the survivors and for charity rather than for elaborate funerals.[20]

The heart of the Protestant funeral service was the sermon which, like any

other sermon, was primarily exposition of a Scriptural text. A brief eulogy was usually added at the end, though many Protestants thought of any eulogy as a "popish" practice (Puritans objected to Anglican eulogies on the grounds that they were too generalized and failed to distinguish between good lives and bad lives). Yet after 1640 when the Puritans had become more powerful, elaborate eulogies for prominent Puritans were common and sometimes even preceded the exegesis. Certain themes appeared regularly. One was the idea of saintliness, a notion derived from the doctrine of Election which described a state of being to which all should aspire. Another common theme was worldliness and its evils. Listeners were warned of the dangers of sin and of loving this earthly life too much. A third theme was the transitory nature of life on earth and the over-riding importance of eternal life.[21] In different ways, all of these themes stressed the necessity of preparing for and facing the reality of death. The funeral sermon could either precede or follow the burial of the body. In the sixteenth century, as the elaborate rituals of the medieval church were discarded, the sermon generally was preached in the church after the burial. Usually the ceremonies began with a silent procession to the grave where a few psalms and other scripture verses were read.[22]

Just as these theological writings of the seventeenth century emphasized the close relationship between life and death, so did sermons and other literary descriptions of death: a good life meant a good death. Furthermore, in them the approach of death is also connected to the life cycle. While death frequently came at early ages, the old, who so often lived apart from their children, felt themselves close to death, and their immediate preparation for death was clearly a part of the preparation for the final years of life.

A few illustrations of actual individuals approaching old age and death will show, I hope, how the attitudes toward death and dying were reflected in the lives of these people. One source of such autobiographical material is the diary, which many kept for religious reasons as a record of God's blessings and trials and of the writer's conversion experience. Like all literary evidence, however, the diary reflects only one segment of the population. Those used in this paper are even narrower in scope in that they were written by clergymen. Nevertheless, they do offer glimpses of the life cycles and attitudes towards death of some seventeenth-century Englishmen.

Adam Martindale, a Presbyterian minister, teacher, and writer who was born in 1623 and died in 1686, completed his memoirs in the year before his death. The omnipresence of death is illustrated by Martindale's life. In 1632, when he was not yet five years old, his mother died. Today, her death might be described as unexpected for it came after an illness of only a few days, but such was not unusual in the seventeenth century. Shortly after his mother's death, Martindale's sister and her husband moved from London to Lancastershire "so that my father and she might be comforts and assistants one to another." But this arrangement lasted a very short time; the sister died later in the same year. Nine years afterwards, in 1641, Martindale's father, at the age of about sixty, decided to reduce his farming activity and entered into an agreement

with one of his sons, Thomas, who took half of his father's house and half of his land in exchange for an annual payment of ten pounds sterling. However, the civil wars caused such reverses for Thomas that he was forced to quit the annual payments and instead paid an undisclosed sum to his father. In 1658 the father, approximately eighty years old, died. In his final illness he sent for Adam and "seriously desired me to advise him to the best as to his eternal state." The three surviving children decided on a grand funeral and furnished "good meat and strong ale in plenty" for all who came to the house. Following the funeral sermon and the burial, the children provided another "rich dinner" at a tavern for relatives and friends. Martindale himself died at the age of sixty-three. At the age of sixty-one, he had been actively seeking appointment and noted in his memoirs that the death in 1684 of his patron, Lord Delamer (formerly Sir George Booth) deprived him not only of a good friend, but also of any hope for "employment at Dunham" which Delamer might have provided.[23]

Martindale's autobiography reveals something of the latter part of the life cycle of his father. His father was widowered when he was in his early fifties and left with a five year old son and several other children, some of whom were married. Unlike many of his contemporaries, he did not remarry. His daughter was willing to move from London in order to be near him, though there may well have been some less-than-altruistic motives involved. When he was about sixty, he began a sort of retirement process, turning over to his son part of the estate with the provision for what was to have been a steady lifetime income. Though he lived alone at the time of his death, he did summon at least one of his sons, who happened to be a clergyman, and sought assurance of salvation. His death was marked with two separate funeral meals as well as a sermon.

Another clergyman who recorded the details of his life was Ralph Josselin. Like Martindale, Josselin lost his mother while he was quite young; he was not yet eight years old when she died in 1624. Some years later, his father remarried when Ralph was fourteen or fifteen. His father died when Ralph was nineteen and was completing his education at Cambridge. The only young child left by his father's death was a five-year-old daughter born of the second marriage. Ralph's relationship with his stepmother was strained; after referring to a dispute with her over his father's estate in 1637, he did not mention her again in his diary until her death in 1668 at the age of eighty. Josselin married in 1640 at the age of twenty-three, and during the following twenty-three years, he and his wife had ten children, three of whom died in infancy. His oldest son, Thomas, died at home at the age of twenty-nine. Josselin's second surviving son, John, caused his father many problems and there were frequent references in the diary to John's unreligious lifestyle and irresponsibility. John did not finally leave his father's home until he had turned thirty and had married without his father's consent or knowledge. When he was fifty-five, Josselin began a sort of retirement or withdrawal process and began to break up the estate which he had acquired. Over the next eleven years, he turned over portions of his property to his children, but the bulk of it was not given to them until a few months before his death in 1683.

Josselin referred to himself as an "old man" in his sixtieth year, but he was still doing manual labor on his farm when he was sixty-five, one year before his death. He had several grandchildren, the oldest of whom was nearly ten at his death. His grandchildren, the children of two of his daughters, were frequent visitors in his home, sometimes spending weeks with their grandparents. His attitude towards them "appears to have been one of kindly concern, without any signs of meddling or moralizing." Josselin's attitude towards death as reflected in his diary, was ambivalent. Sometimes he showed Calvinist confidence; at other times he expressed fear. The entries near the end of his life were often pleas for God's assurance.[24]

Josselin's life reveals a life cycle pattern very different from Martindale's. Both of his parents died before he was an adult, and he was left with a stepmother with whom he was uncomfortable. He fathered a large family and lived long enough to enjoy his grandchildren. And although there was never a clear end to his career, he did begin a process of retirement along the lines of what sociologists might call "disengagement."

A third clergyman, Henry Newcome, kept a diary from which an *Autobiography* was abstracted. He was born in 1627 in Calcot, Huntingdonshire, the fourth son of Stephen and Rose Newcome, who produced a family of seven sons and one daughter. When Newcome was ten years old, both of his parents died within a few days of each other, his mother apparently from grief following her husband's death. They were buried in one coffin in February 1641, less than three months after the birth of their daughter. Since Stephen Newcome had owned the church living at Calcot, it was inherited by his oldest son, Robert, who, too young to perform the pastoral duties, received only a portion of the income. The older brothers were able to keep the family together and to raise the younger children, though it is not clear how they coped with their baby sister. This was done at some sacrifice since they had to remain single in order to discharge their obligations to the family.[25]

Henry Newcome, however, did not have to postpone marriage and married at a relatively young age. While the exact year of his marriage is not known, his first child, a daughter named Rose after her grandmother, was born in April of 1649 when Henry was not yet twenty-two. Henry and his wife had five children, three sons and two daughters, whose births were spread over an eight-year period. Like Josselin, Newcome had problems with his second son, Daniel, who got into trouble as an apprentice in London and was sent to Jamaica. A few years later he was back in England and married without the knowledge or consent of his parents. Daniel was often in need of money but Newcome was reluctant to provide it. As he approached fifty, he was concerned about the education and setting up of his youngest son, Peter, and he noted his wish that "it may please God to take Daniel off me." Daniel was first to provide a grandchild; his daughter, Jane, was born in April of 1678. Daniel's wife died the following month, he remarried seven months later, and in October of 1679, his second wife provided Newcome with a grandson, Pares. Daniel died in February of 1684 at the age of thirty-three. During his final illness, Newcome and another son, Harry, who was also a clergyman, sat with Daniel,

urging repentance. A posthumous son was born in April of 1684 to Daniel's widow. At the age of fifty-seven, Newcome assumed financial responsibility for this infant grandson.[26]

In the summer of 1695, Newcome made his will, providing that after his debts and funeral expenses were paid, the remainder of his property was to go to his wife, for herself and their unmarried daughter, Rose, "who I know will not leave her in her old age and great infirmities." At his wife's death, the estate was to be divided between his two daughters; Rose would get three-fifths and another daughter, Elizabeth, two-fifths. With the exception of two books—one designated for the man who would preach the funeral sermon, and the other a dictionary for his grandson (only if he should continue in school), Newcome left his entire library to be divided between his two surviving sons. Two months after making this will, Newcome died.[27]

The life of Henry Newcome illustrates a life cycle pattern different from those of Martindale and Josselin. When Newcome's parents died, they left a family with several infant children to be raised by their older brothers. Newcome's parents died before any of their children had married and thus they never knew any grandchildren. And Newcome's life is unusual in that all of his children survived into adulthood, and he not only knew several grandchildren, the oldest of whom would have been in teens at the time of his death, but had financial responsibility for one of them. His oldest daughter was unmarried at forty-six and apparently still at home when he died, leaving her the responsibility for caring for her aged and ill mother. Ultimately, however, she would inherit the bulk of his estate and her two brothers shared only their father's library.

Other, though less satisfactory, glimpses into the cycle of life and death can be obtained from biographical material, much of which was didactic in nature. The life of John Dunton was sketched by his son and included in a collection of Dunton's works. Dunton was born in 1628 in Little Misscenden, Buckinghamshire, the son of John Dunton, a minister. He had three sisters, all of whom lived into adulthood. Although Dunton's father died when John was about thirteen, he was able to complete his education, going up to Cambridge when he was sixteen. When he was in his early twenties, he became the minister in Graffham, Huntingdonshire, and it was there that he married. Several years later, their son, John, was born, but his wife died three months later "of that tormenting disease called the twisting of the guts." Dunton resolved not to marry again for at least seven years. After seven years, he moved to Aston Clinton, Buckinghamshire and married again. He and his second wife had four children.[28]

Dunton must have been about thirty-eight when he married the second time. He died at the age of forty-eight. His final illness, caused by "the stone," was very painful, but he was fully prepared for death and certain of his own salvation. His son reported several lengthy deathbed speeches about the glories of Christ and heaven. About twenty hours before Dunton's death, he

suffered "fainting fits," his face paled, and his feet grew cold. In his last minutes he said that he could see "Glorious Angels waiting at my bedside to convey my soul into Abraham's bosom." He gave practical advice to his wife and children, counselling his wife, if she should marry again, to be careful not to estrange her new husband from her children. He told his children that he thought that stone was hereditary, but might be avoided by moderate diet and sufficient exercise. And in addition to advice on vocations, marriage, and raising children, he urged his children to maintain the "bond of love" among themselves and to get together at least once a year. After final religious exhortation, he died on November 4, 1676.[29]

Samuel Clarke's *The Lives of Sundry Eminent Persons* provides accounts of the deaths of a number of persons, five of which we shall look at briefly. Clarke was a Puritan divine who was anxious to provide his readers with model lives and model deaths. In almost every account of death, whether it were the death of a younger person or of an older person, Clarke remarked on courage and faith at the time of death. The saints did not seem to fear death.

Sir Nathaniel Barnardiston, a prominent Puritan layman who died at the age of sixty-five in 1653, had begun preparing for his death by making his will some two years before his death. His final illness began with a swelling on his side which he interpreted as a "messenger" of death. Despite the pain of his illness, Barnardiston continued to participate in family prayers. On the day before he died he spoke to his children, warning them of the dangers of worldliness and urging them to be steadfast in faith. Another of Clarke's "eminent persons," Hugh Broughton, a London clergyman, became ill in November of 1611. He realized that he was dying, but from his bed continued to speak with his friends, "giving them many pious and godly exhortations." He died in August of 1612 at the age of sixty-three. Clarke noted that the sixty-third year was supposed to be particularly dangerous since it was a climatical year (a climatical is every seventh year of life and the forty-ninth year—seven times seven—and the sixty-third—nine times seven—were thought to be especially dangerous).[30]

One of the several women included in Clarke's collection, and one of the few whose age at death was mentioned, was his wife, Katherine Clarke. "In her old age, though she was crazy," Clarke writes of his wife, she continued to work and bore her infirmities with patience and good will. In her last years, she was often ill and seemed near death, but she always prepared for death. On May 25, 1675, in her seventy-third year, she had some friends in for dinner, and, while they were eating, she became ill "with a kind of shivering" which was later diagnosed as distemper. She survived for almost a month and during those final weeks, she blessed her children and grandchildren. Katherine and Samuel Clarke were unusual in that they had been married fifty years at the time of her death.[31]

Samuel Fairclough, another Puritan minister, survived not one wife, but three. When he was close to seventy years old, "this aged person was forced to marry (a third time) an aged gentlewoman to be his nurse. . . . " At the time of this marriage, Fairclough was living in a fairly crowded household. He lived

with one of his daughters and "some" of his sons who had lost their church livings after the Restoration. The sons and the daughter were married and had their children with them. In addition, there was a housekeeper who had her aged mother living there. Shortly after their marriage, Fairclough and his wife moved in with another son and his wife. After the death of his third wife, Fairclough went to live with one of his daughters, but his youngest daughter, "covetous also to have her child's part of his presence and company," persuaded him to come live with her. He lived with that daughter until his death which came after a one-day illness at the age of eighty-three. Clarke noted that "he died of no disease but that of old age."[32]

A detailed description of dying was included in the sketch of another minister, Dr. Samuel Winter. Winter became ill with distemper on Sunday, October 16, 1666, in the sixty-third year of his life, a climatical year. On the following Sunday, he told his wife that during the previous night, he had talked with "spirits" and that God had given him a "clearer sight" of the glory of heaven. Other members of Winter's family were summoned so that they could hear his final testimony. Yet, when they arrived, he "was so swallowed up in the contemplation thereof that he could not utter what he desired." On that evening, some friends visited him and they discussed various Bible verses for several hours. Then, after an hour's rest, Winter called his family and friends to his side and told them that he had but a short time left to live. He told them of his vision of the previous night and urged them to keep God's commandments. "And so with much weariness of spirit, looking up towards heaven, he begged of God that the words of a dying man might make a deep impression upon the hearts of his hearers." He lived through the night and spent the following day praying and praising God. From time to time, he called his wife and asked her "whether he were in the body or out of the body, for he could not tell." On Monday afternoon, the ninth day of his illness, he died with a smile on his face.[33]

These glimpses into the final days of some individuals from the seventeenth century indicate that the deathbed rituals were significant, and, that, whenever possible, the dying person was surrounded by family members. They also suggest that many people did prepare for death. The rituals of dying were partially for the benefit of the dying person, providing an opportunity for a review of life and preparation for the judgment of God. But, together with the funeral sermon, these rituals also served a social purpose, creating a special time for final instructions and exhortations. Surviving into old age might have had certain rewards. There was a commonly held belief and a Biblical teaching that old people deserved honor and respect. Old people could enjoy their grandchildren. For those with sufficient resources, there was the opportunity to withdraw from active life and even to divide one's property among one's children, but forced retirement was exceptional. On the other hand, old age brought some hardships. Old people did not always get the respect to which they thought they were entitled. Illness and infirmity could make life difficult. Old persons, particularly widows, might find themselves dependent on others. But in any case, the way one died was important. One not only had to live well,

which itself was a method of preparing for death, but one had to die well. It was not something done quietly, privately, or secretly. Death was neither hidden nor ignored. The obligations to family and society continued right up until the moment of death.

If we are to understand the problems and processes which confront us in this last quarter of the twentieth century, we must look to the past. Too often, in looking at the problems of the aged in our society, we lament the present and look longingly for a simple past when the problems were not so complicated. Such romanticizing cannot help but to distort our knowledge of the present. It may well be that because of the high proportion of older persons in western societies today, the past will offer no models for the solution of the problems of older persons in our societies; nor is it likely that understanding past attitudes towards death and dying will be of much comfort to the bereaved of the present. But to study the present situation and to consider only the present problems and attitudes will never lead to a complete understanding of old age and aging. We need to see which of our present problems are new and which are not, and we need to understand the evolution of attitudes and ideas. We must understand the different living arrangements of the past and how old age and death were handled then. Until we understand these things about the past, we cannot hope to understand the present. The historian, with his combination of the tools of the social scientist and the values of the humanist, is in a particularly useful position to help us understand these things. The work has begun, but there is much still to be done.

Notes

[1] In recent years, several historians have written about death and dying. One of the most significant works is Philippe Ariès, *Western Attitudes Toward Death From the Middle Ages to the Present,* trans. Patricia M. Ranum (Baltimore: Johns Hopkins Univ. Press, 1974). See also: David E. Stannard, "Death and Dying in Puritan New England," *American Historical Review,* 77 (1972), 419-44, and Stannard, ed., *Death in America* (Philadelphia: Univ. of Pennsylvania Press, 1974). A discussion of some of the early literature on death, with particular emphasis on Jeremy Taylor's *The Craft of Dying,* appears in Nancy Lee Beaty, *The Craft of Dying,* Yale Studies in English 175 (New Haven: Yale Univ. Press, 1970).

[2] Peter Laslett, *The World We Have Lost* (London: Methuen, 1965); Laslett, ed., *Household and Family in Past Times* (Cambridge: Cambridge Univ. Press, 1972); E.A. Wrigley, "Mortality in Pre-Industrial England: The Example of Colyton, Devon Over Three Centuries," *Daedalus,* 97 (1968), 546-80. See also J.D. Chambers, *Population, Economy, and Society in Pre-Industrial England* (London: Oxford Univ. Press, 1972).

[3] Laslett, *The World We Have Lost,* p. 103.

[4] Religious literature and sermons directed at young people also contained warnings about death and the importance of religious conversion. Young people often associated death with old age, and, therefore, tended to postpone consideration for religious salvation, but they were urged not to exchange the short-lived pleasures of sin for the eternal pleasures of heaven. Seventeenth-century mortality rates were such that by his mid-teens, a person probably would have experienced at least one death in his im-

mediate family and perhaps the death of a friend. See Steven R. Smith, "Religion and the Conception of Youth in Seventeenth-Century England," *History of Childhood Quarterly,* 2 (1975), 503-04.

[5] Keith Thomas, *Religion and the Decline of Magic* (New York: Scribners, 1971), pp. 602-04. Natalie Zemon Davis, "Some Tasks and Themes in the Study of Popular Religion," in *The Pursuit of Holiness in Late Medieval and Renaissance Religion,* ed. Charles Trinkaus and Heiko A. Oberman (Leiden: E.J. Brill, 1974), pp. 326-32.

[6] John Moore, *A Map of Man's Mortality* (London: 1617), pp. 7-21.

[7] *The Cure of the Fear of Death* (London: 1618), pp. 140-144.

[8] The entire question of prolongevity was not new in the seventeenth century, nor was it peculiar to Christianity. Ancient thinkers had raised this question, and, for the most part, had rejected the possibility as a violation of either natural or divine law, or both. In the Middle Ages, alchemists had developed theories of prolongation of life. For example, Roger Bacon, one of England's best known thinkers, had argued that pharmacology could help replenish the body's moisture and thus extend life. Somewhat later, an Italian, Luigi Cornaro, theorized that temperance was the key to long life; moderation in eating, drinking, and exercising could help preserve the moisture of the body. See Gerald J. Gruman, *A History of Ideas about the Prolongation of Life: The Evolution of Prolongevity Hypotheses to 1800,* Transactions of the American Philosophical Society, NS, vol. 56, pt. 9 (Philadelphia: American Philosophical Society, 1966). Interestingly, a twentieth-century English physician has quoted passages from Cornaro's work and found them good advice for the prevention of heart attacks. Malcolm Carruthers, *The Western Way of Death; Stress, Tension, and Heart Attacks* (New York: Pantheon Books, 1974).

[9] *The History of Life and Death* (London, 1638).

[10] Thomas, *Religion and the Decline of Magic,* pp. 315-16, 358, 90.

[11] Bacon, *Life and Death,* pp. 62, 113, 120, 121.

[12] *A Letter to a Friend Upon Occasion of the Death of His Intimate Friend* in *The Prose of Sir Thomas Browne,* ed. Norman J. Endicott (New York: W.W. Norton, 1967), pp. 352, 355.

[13] *A Discourse Concerning the Period of Human Life: Whether Mutable or Immutable* (London: 1677), pp. 55, 56, 63, 78, 82, 99, 116-17.

[14] Moore, *A Map of Man's Mortality,* pp. 123, 225-27, 230.

[15] *An Essay Proving That We Shall Know Our Friends in Heaven* (London: 1698), pp. 86, 88, 6-40. Dunton's descriptions of dying are not unlike those in Raymond A. Moody, Jr., *Life After Life; the Investigation of a Phenomena—Survival of Bodily Death* (Atlanta: Mockingbird, 1975).

[16] *A Fountain of Tears* (Amsterdam: 1646), pp. 639-44, 646-47.

[17] *A Salve for a Sick Man* in *The Works of William Perkins* (London: 1612), I, 496; Perkins, *Death's Knell: Of the Sick Man's Passing Bell,* 9th ed. (London: 1628); *Death's Dance* (London: 1631); Richard Baxter, *A Christian Directory* (London: 1673), p. 65; James Cole, *Of Death, a True Description* (London: 1629), pp. 3, 17, 18, 29, 50-4, 59-60.

[18] *A Pithy and Short Treatise Whereby a Godly Christian Is Directed How to Make His Last Will* (London: 1612), pp. 3-5.

[19] *The Doctrine of Dying Well* (London, 1628), p. 32; Cole, *Of Death,* pp. 165-69.

[20] Thomas, *Religion and the Decline of Magic,* pp. 604-05; Stannard, "The Puritan Way of Death: A Study in Religion, Culture, and Social Change," Diss. Yale University 1975, pp. 133-34.

[21] Selmar Neville Westby, "The Puritan Funeral Sermon in Seventeenth-Century

England," Diss. Univ. of Southern California 1970, pp. 18-31, 75, 101, 129-30.

[22] Alan Fager Herr, *The Elizabethan Sermon: A Survey and a Bibliography* (1940; rpt. New York: Octagon Books, 1969), p. 46.

[23] *The Life of Adam Martindale,* Chetham Society Remains, 4, ed. Richard Parkinson (Manchester: Chetham Society, 1845), pp. 17-8, 21-3, 119-20, 233.

[24] Alan Macfarlane, *The Family Life of Ralph Josselin, a Seventeenth-Century Clergyman: An Essay in Historical Anthropology* (Cambridge: Cambridge Univ. Press, 1970), pp. 15, 16, 126, 118-123, 98-99, 168-69.

[25] *The Autobiography of Henry Newcome,* Chetham Society Remains 26, 27 (Manchester: Chetham Society, 1852), pp. 3-4, 5-6.

[26] Ibid., pp. 181-84, 215, 217, 225, 228, 229.

[27] Ibid., pp. 284-86.

[28] *Dunton's Remains* (London: 1684), pp. 1-3, 12, 17, 19, 20-21.

[29] Ibid., pp. 45, 57.

[30] Samuel Clarke, *The Lives of Sundry Eminent Persons* (London, 1683), II, 114-16, I, 7.

[31] Ibid., II, 156-57.

[32] Ibid., I, 176, 185-86.

[33] Ibid., I, 98-100.

David Luke

"HOW IS IT THAT YOU LIVE, AND WHAT IS IT THAT YOU DO?": THE QUESTION OF OLD AGE IN ENGLISH ROMANTIC POETRY

The central concern of the Romantic poet was man's changing nature in a mysteriously changing universe. One critic has recently said that "Romanticism is the measuring of time by life."[1] Yet we might rephrase his statement to stress more specifically that Romanticism is the scrutiny and evaluation of *times of life*—that is, of being young and of becoming old. Many people think of the Romantic poet as wholly preoccupied with youth, but for nearly every image of youth in Romantic work there is a specter of old age nearby. Still, as the Romantic essayist William Hazlitt observes, people often play "hide-and-seek" with their consciousness of old age, and "we think ourselves too lusty and too nimble for that blear-eyed decrepit old gentleman to catch us."[2] Certainly, nimble modern critics have been adept at avoiding the emergence of that "decrepit old gentleman" in Romantic narratives. The Romantic fascination with mountains and ruins as enigmatic emblems of temporal processes of growth, endurance, and decay is of course well known, but the related Romantic interest in "the old man" has been curiously neglected.

Prior to the period, the old man generally entered English literature only as a comic and peripheral distortion of the norms and ideals of various social roles. Thus his development in much Romantic writing as a central, sympathetic, and symbolic character is indeed distinctive. Coleridge's "Ancient Mariner," Wordsworth's "Old Cumberland Beggar," Shelley's decrepit "Rousseau"—all are at the center of their respective works and promise provocative revelations of the possible consequences and values of prolonged metamorphosis. To digress from poetry for a moment, we might even consider the most famous horror story of the age as a disguised parable of the supposed horrors of old age, a parable of the old man as monster, insofar as the unnamed creature of Mary Shelley's *Frankenstein* (1816) emerges from his creator's desire to "examine the case and progress of decay" and to "renew life where death had apparently devoted the body to corruption."[3] Indeed, likened

to a "hideous mummy" with his "yellow skin" and "shrivelled complexion," the monster seems to have been born old. He seems to represent, as it were, the quintessential birth of the Romantic old man. And he also seems representative of his Romantic age in that his most remarkable narrative feature is the fact that, in the words of one commentator, he "is more human than his creator."[4]

I want to discuss the significance of some of these Romantic old men, and, more specifically, I want to examine some of the ideas and attitudes about old age in the poems of Wordsworth and Keats. In intriguing ways, Wordsworth and Keats convey quite different thoughts about old age, and their differing perspectives both reflect contrasting Romantic values and illuminate some of our current cultural controversies on the subject.

I

William Wordsworth (1770-1850) lived a long life, yet, like Victor Frankenstein, he exhibited a youthful interest in "the case and progress of decay" and created "the old man" in his poetry at an early age. "The Old Cumberland Beggar" (1797/1798) is one of the most significant of these early poems about old age, and it concerns an "aged Beggar" whom Wordsworth encounters during one of his walks among the mountains of Northern England.[5] But at the apparent center of the poem is a broad question which persists today as a vexing social issue—should the old, the infirm, and the impoverished be kept in institutions, or should they be free to roam about and seek the voluntary charity of their local communities? Adopting the "Old Cumberland Beggar" as a specific example, Wordsworth argues the latter alternative by suggesting that the old man serves as a spiritual benefit for his rural village in that even its "poorest poor" can gain "hope in heaven" by giving food to him. But if so, a curious question arises. Since the beggar himself is clearly *poorer* than the "poorest poor" of the village, what or to whom can he give? That is, within the context of the assumed relationship between material charity and spiritual value, what then are the beggar's resources for salvation? It is an intriguing question, and one which inevitably directs our attention toward the circumstances of the beggar beyond the village, among the "wild unpeopled hills" that surround it, for those circumstances both begin and end the poem, and in fact displace its social issues.

Wordsworth's intitial description of the old man alone with his "scraps and fragments" of food—"the dole of village dames" (9)—is hardly heartening:

> Surrounded by those wild unpeopled hills,
> He sat, and ate his food in solitude:
> And ever, scattered from his palsied hand,
> That, still attempting to prevent the waste,
> Was baffled still, the crumbs in little showers
> Fell on the ground; and the small mountain birds,

> Not venturing yet to peck their destined meal,
> Approached within the length of half his staff.
> (14-21)

Though the lines may suggest a vague sense of pastoral peacefulness, they are deceptive. The naked fact of the passage is that the old man is helplessly fighting for food with the "small mountain birds." He is "attempting to prevent the waste," and his apparent prodigality is but a grim aspect of his palsy. Moreover, his decrepitude is further suggested by the fearless approach of the birds "within the length of half his staff" in anticipation of their "destined meal." In short, the old beggar's situation is ominous. He is trapped in a minutely but exhaustively predatory environment.

Yet Wordsworth's sense of this situation in the final stanza of the poem is strange:

> Be his the natural silence of old age!
> Let him be free of mountain solitudes;
> And have around him, whether heard or not,
> The pleasant melody of woodland birds.
> . . . .
> And let him, *where* and *when* he will, sit down
> Beneath the trees, or on a grassy bank
> Of highway side, and with the little birds
> Share his chance-gathered meal; and, finally,
> As in the eye of Nature he has lived,
> So in the eye of Nature let him die!
> (182-185, 192-197; Wordsworth's emphasis)

For one thing, the irony of celebrating the "pleasant melody of woodland birds" whether or not the old beggar can hear it makes one aware of the gap between the speaker's feelings and whatever his subject's sensibilities may or may not be. And the gap increases when, with a single verb, Wordworth radically transforms his earlier record of the old man's state in nature by now presuming that he "shares" his food with the birds (and by thus implying that this is how the beggar gains his "hope in heaven" too). In the first stanza of the poem, Wordsworth's *actual* description of the beggar suggested a grim contrast between the beggar's sustenance and his decay, and an equally grim contrast between the charity of the village and the ruthlessness of nature. But in the final stanza, Wordsworth's *imagined* description mitigates awareness of the old man's decrepitude and conceals the predatoriness of the birds by, in effect, translating the qualities of the village into an implicit sense of nature itself as an inherently moral and benevolent community.

Wordsworth intends the allusive thrust of his final stanza as a subtle confirmation of his central argument in the poem. " 'Tis Nature's law," he asserts, that "a spirit and pulse of good,/ A life and soul" is "to every mode of being/ Inseparably linked" (73, 77-79). Such is the inevitable vision, he further

insists, of man's "heaven-regarding eye" (81). Thus as the poem develops, Wordsworth interprets his sense of the law of nature as a virtual revelation of the law of Heaven, and, in doing so, affirms the beggar's state in nature via the declaration, "Let him bear about/ The good which the benignant law of Heaven/ Has hung around him" (166-168). That is, Wordsworth ultimately evaluates the nature of old age in terms of his fundamental idealization of nature itself.

Even so, there are undeniable elements in the poem which evidence a "mismatching between illustration and argument" that many readers find recurrent in Wordsworth's works.[6] And at least one of Wordsworth's friends, Charles Lamb, also felt uncomfortable about some of the assumptions in the poem, and said so in a letter to him: "Here the mind knowingly passes a fiction on herself, first substituting her own feelings for the Beggar's, and, in the same breath detecting the fallacy, will not part with the wish."[7] Certainly, Wordsworth rather willfully idealizes the deprivation and decrepitude of the old man. On one hand, he acknowledges that the beggar himself is "Bow-bent, his eyes for ever on the ground" and that "one little span of earth/ Is all his prospect" (50-52). But on the other hand, his own "heaven-regarding eye" transcends whatever might be the old man's earthly concerns. It inspires Wordsworth to distance himself from thoughts of the old man's decay and to leave him to his own manifest lack of resources.

In a poem closely associated with "The Old Cumberland Beggar" and composed in the same year, Wordsworth similarly idealizes old age via his idealization of nature, but more specifically celebrates the emotional decay which he presumes accompanies the physical decay of old age. The old man of "Animal Tranquillity and Decay" (1797/1798)

> . . . is insensibly subdued
> To settled quiet: he is one by whom
> All effort seems forgotten; one to whom
> Long patience hath such mild composure given,
> That patience now doth seem a thing of which
> He hath no need. He is by nature led
> To peace so perfect that the young behold
> With envy, what the Old Man hardly feels.
> (7-14)

Here, Wordsworth describes the old man as so divested of animation that he seems to lack even that vestige of residual energy which we customarily associate with the emotional quality of "patience." Nevertheless, Wordsworth asserts that the old man is "by nature led" to this "perfect peace"—as if the essence of nature was not constant change but consummate quiescence. Wordsworth does not explicitly identify this sense of nature with any overtly spiritual idea here, yet, in the concise terms of the poem's title, he translates his presumption of the old man's "decay" into the thought of what is for him an implicitly blessed and transcendent "tranquillity." All in all, "Animal

Tranquillity and Decay" is a powerfully succinct little poem. In reading it, one does not sense any "mismatching between illustration and argument" because any potentially credible or detailed image of the old man is all but obliterated by the declarative force of Wordsworth's argument. Wordsworth does not dramatically distance himself from whatever might be the old man's concerns (as he did in "The Old Cumberland Beggar"), but simply *precludes* any thought of the old man's having any concerns. And yet, Wordsworth's very assertiveness is perhaps a hint of his hidden anxiety about old age.

This anxiety is apparent in "Resolution and Independence" (1802/1807). Here, however, the old man at first seems another picture of supposedly ideal passivity:

> Such seemed this Man, not all alive nor dead,
> Nor all asleep—in his extreme old age:
> His body was bent double, feet and head
> Coming together in life's pilgrimage.
> (64-67)

And Wordsworth's figurative thought of his collapsing body as the effect of a "pilgrimage" seems spiritually reassuring. Still, Wordsworth anxiously questions the old man about the circumstances of his life: " 'How is it that you live, and what is it you do?' " (119). The old man calmly replies that he gathers leeches for a living, from ponds scattered over the wilderness of the moors, and then adds:

> "Once I could meet with them on every side;
> But they have dwindled long by slow decay;
> Yet still I persevere, and find them where I may."
> (124-126)

In the symbolic context of the poem, the decline of the leeches is clearly more than a mere economic matter—it is symptomatic of the old man's own "slow decay," and indeed of the fact of dissolution as a universal principle. Nevertheless, the old man's stoic exertion in the midst of this decay seems praiseworthy. He seems to embody the august terms of the poem's title. But Wordsworth is at first strangely troubled by the old man's activity:

> While he was talking thus, the lonely place,
> The old Man's shape, and speech—all troubled me:
> In my mind's eye I seemed to see him pace
> About the weary moors continually,
> Wandering about alone and silently.
> (127-131)

Hearing "other matter" from the old man "cheerfully uttered" (134-135), however, Wordsworth concludes at the end of the poem:

I could have laughed myself to scorn to find
In that decrepit Man so firm a mind.
"God," said I, "be my help and stay secure;
I'll think of the Leech-gatherer on the lonely moor!"
(137-140)

Though we are not told the details of the old man's "other matter," it is implicit that it is "other" than his emphasis of decay, and, moreover, that it surely concerns in some way his simple belief in God. Speaking earlier in the manner of "Religious men, who give to God and man their dues" (98), the Leech-Gatherer had said to Wordsworth that "From pond to pond he roamed, from moor to moor;/ Housing, with God's good help, by choice or chance" (103-104). What accounts for Wordsworth's sudden depression at the thought of the Leech-Gatherer wandering about the "lonely" and "weary" moors, then, is his momentary severance in his "mind's eye" of the Leech-Gather's explicit association between earthly perseverance and divine providence. That is, Wordsworth momentarily envisions the old man's effort *only* as an exercise in exhaustion and futility, and as devoid of spiritual significance. But hearing again the "other matter," he is reassured, not by the example of the old man's energy in his waning world, but by the example of his spiritual belief which supersedes that energy and transcends the necessities of such a world. Thus, we glimpse any discrepancy between illustration and argument only for a moment via Wordsworth's dramatically divided response to the old man, and the discrepancy in fact disappears as the subject of the illustration, the Leech-Gatherer, himself assumes and articulates the argument. In short, as a dramatic symbol of Wordsworth's sense of old age, the Leech-Gatherer evolves beyond a representation of complex forces of life and death, and becomes a seemingly secure sign of simple salvation.

It is significant that the poem's notion of salvation involves an idealization of forces beyond rather than within nature. Whereas in "Animal Tranquillity and Decay" Wordsworth asserted that the old man was "by nature led" to "perfect peace," in "Resolution and Independence" he instinctively interprets the old man as evidence of "peculiar grace" and "a leading from above" (50-51). One critic has observed of certain central passages in an early version of Wordsworth's longest and greatest work, *The Prelude* (1805-1806/1850), "One can see . . . how Wordsworth will become fully Christian, how the resolution to descend into 'the Mind of Man' may result not in the psychological confrontation of his mortality and the understanding of it, but rather in the traditional Christian transmutation of it into continuing life."[8] We can see something of the same effect with regard to Wordsworth's resolution in "Resolution and Independence," and indeed can understand its relationship with another major poem which Wordsworth began in the same year, "Ode: Intimations of Immortality from Recollections of Early Childhood" (1802-06/1807). Though he was only in his thirties at the time, Wordsworth dramatizes himself as "the old man" in it, and expresses a "faith that looks

through death" (189) toward an assured sense of eternal life. Anticipating this explicit faith, the values of "Resolution and Independence" are not secular but spiritual. Wordsworth's implicit "resolution" in the poem emphasizes an "independence" not within the scope of earthly concerns, but apart from them.

Wordsworth's "old man" has his most sustained role in *The Excursion* (1795-1813/1814), and the poem in fact dramatically summarizes Wordsworth's sense of old age in that its intermittent composition spans nearly the whole of his productive poetic career. In it, Wordsworth describes his encounter with an old "wanderer" sitting beside a "ruined Cottage" on the moor. At first, Wordsworth is "stricken by the sight" of him, and indeed, when the old man finally speaks, his words are grim:

> "I see around me here
> Things which you cannot see: we die, my Friend,
> Nor we alone, but that which each man loved
> Dies with him, or is changed; and very soon
> Even of the good is no memorial left."
> (I, 469-474)

But there is a symbolic memorial left—the ruined cottage itself, with which the old man is so strongly associated. Sitting beside it, expressing its influence as it were, he tells the story of its former inhabitants. It is a story of a particular family's dissolution, decay, and death, yet its impact is general. It is a story which the ruined cottage tells by itself. And it is also a story that seems to define the old man's own destiny.

Yet Wordsworth prefers to think of the decayed cottage as a "tranquil Ruin," and the old man himself rhetorically asks at the end of his narrative, "Why should a tear be on an old Man's cheek?" (I, 598), and goes on to emphasize "the calm of nature" and the calming comforts of "natural wisdom" (I, 601, 604). We are given to understand that the old man's "natural wisdom" derives from his early communion with nature—specifically, from his mystical experiences as a youthful "herdsman" in the mountains:

> Early had he learned
> To reverence the volume that displays
> The mystery, the life which cannot die;
> But in the mountains did he *feel* his faith.
> All things, responsive to the writing, there
> Breathed immortality, revolving life,
> And greatness still revolving; infinite:
> There littleness was not; the least of things
> Seemed infinite; and there his spirit shaped
> Her prospects, nor did he believe,—he *saw*.
> (I, 223-232; Wordsworth's emphasis)

Such experiences had long inspired the old man to interpret the essence of nature not as a manifestation of dissolution or loss, but as a virtually visual revelation of the Bible's promise of immortality. Not all of the Romantic poets, of course, responded to mountains with such unqualified spiritual rapture.[9] But for Wordsworth, via his old wanderer, the mountain has become a living church.

In the final section of *The Excursion,* the wanderer implicitly draws upon his memory of the mystical mountains of his past, and comments at length on the landscape of old age:

"Do not think
That good and wise ever will be allowed,
Though strength decay, to breathe in such estate
As shall divide them wholly from the stir
Of hopeful nature. Rightly it is said
That Man descends into the VALE of years;
Yet have I thought that we might also speak,
And not presumptuously, I trust, of Age,
As of a final EMINENCE; though bare
In aspect and forbidding, yet a point
On which 'tis not impossible to sit
In awful sovereignty; a place of power.
. . . .
For on that superior height
Who sits, is disencumbered from the press
Of near obstructions, and is privileged
To breathe in solitude, above the host
Of ever-humming insects, 'mid thin air
That suits not them.
. . . .
And may it not be hoped, that, placed by age
In like removal, tranquil though severe,
We are not so removed for utter loss;
But for some favour, suited to our need?
What more than that the severing should confer
Fresh power to commune with the invisible world."
(IX, 44-55, 69-74, 81-86)

Wordsworth associates many of his old men with mountains, and indeed, as he does here, he often uses the image of a mountain as an explicit metaphor for conveying his sense of old age. With his "heaven-regarding eye," we remember, Wordsworth relegated the old Cumberland Beggar to "mountain solitudes." Likewise, he likened the old Leech-Gatherer to a "huge stone" that was "Couched on the bald top of an eminence;/ Wonder to all who do the same espy" (57-59). At the end of *The Excursion,* Wordsworth clarifies that "wonder."

Though at first glance Wordsworth seems partly to associate old age with "the stir/ Of hopeful nature," he in fact again more strongly defines it as beyond earthly concerns, as "above the host/ Of ever-humming insects." Indeed, Wordsworth instinctively describes the natural state of old age in negative terms and simultaneously interprets those terms as spiritual benefits. Thus, on one hand, he emphasizes old age as a state of "solitude" and "decay" and "loss," yet, on the other hand, he envisions old age as a "place of power" and a "privileged" state that is supposedly proximate to some transcendent "favour" from an "invisible world." Wordsworth had earlier referred to the "natural wisdom" of old age, but he now stresses its vision of the supernatural. In the capitalized terms of his underlying metaphor of the mountain, Wordsworth acknowledges old age as a descent into a "VALE" of decay, but he more forcefully idealizes it as an arrival at an "EMINENCE"—at a summit of spiritual promise and at the imminence of immortality. Yet the potential irony of Wordsworth's lofty presumption of the old man's communion with "the invisible world" is that one can lose sight of him. In the midst of such massive idealism, "the old man" can well become "the invisible man."

Certainly, if not invisible, Wordsworth's old men are unusually passive and remote, and Wordsworth places an unusual value on them as such. In poem after poem, he praises them for being "tranquil" and "serene," and interprets senescence as an esteemed quiescence.[10] We can better understand why this is so if we realize that, whatever the actual circumstances of his encounters with old men may or may not have been, Wordsworth's recurrent dialogue with them in his poems is essentially a dialogue with the "old man" within himself—that is, with his thoughts of becoming or being old. In his encounter with the old Leech-Gatherer, for example, Wordsworth reports:

> The old Man still stood talking by my side;
> But now his voice to me was like a stream
> Scarce heard; nor word from word could I divide;
> And the whole body of the Man did seem
> Like one whom I had met with in a dream.
> (106-110)

Before the old man of his dreams, however, Wordsworth is always "Perplexed, and longing to be comforted" (117) because the dream so often threatens to become a nightmare:

> My former thoughts returned: the fear that kills;
> And hope that is unwilling to be fed;
> Cold, pain, and labour, and all fleshly ills;
> And mighty Poets in their misery dead.
> (113-116)

The conjunction of Wordsworth's dream of the old man and his thought of "mighty Poets in their misery dead" is revealing. Quite simply, Wordsworth's

"old man" threatens him as a symbol of his own death.

If Wordsworth's dialogue with the old man within himself is as much a dialogue with his anxiety about decay and death as it is with his hope of immortality, then it becomes evident that his portrayal of the passive old man is as much a strategy for *suppressing* that anxiety as it is for expressing his spiritual assurance. Hence the ambivalence of his uneasy admission at the end of *The Excursion* that his sense of old age is "suited to our *need*" (my emphasis). Ultimately, Wordsworth is caught in a rigid dialectic whose terms have a common consequence with regard to old age. By viewing the old man as either a symbol of death or an image of divinity, Wordsworth effectively denies him an authentic earthly existence, and displaces a sense of value from the circumstances of his immediate life.

II

John Keats (1795-1821) had an absurdly short life, yet it symbolically approximated the experience of old age in some significant ways. For one thing, a sense of finitude was almost the daily consequence of his existence. When he was only twenty-three, he confessed in a letter to a friend, "I have never known any unalloy'd Happiness for many days together: the death or sickness of some one has always spoilt my hours."[11] Indeed, given the premature deaths of his parents and one of his two brothers, and given his awareness of the imminence of his own early death from tuberculosis, Keats could well say that "the World is full of Misery and Heartbreak, Pain, Sickness and oppression" (I, 281). He "saw too distinct into the core/Of an eternal fierce destruction" (I, 262).

One consequence of Keat's awareness of death was his emphasis that nature's inevitable lesson for all would-be hedonists and moralists alike was the loss of absolute or ideal value: "I do not at all believe in this sort of perfectibility—the nature of the world will not admit of it. . . . Look at the Poles and at the sands of Africa, Whirlpools and volcanoes—Let men exterminate them and I will say that they may arrive at earthly Happiness" (II, 101). Another consequence of Keats's awareness of death was his scorn of notions of spiritually transcending it. He entitled an early sonnet "Written in Disgust of Vulgar Superstition" (1816), and his skepticism did not disappear with the years. Referring specifically to Wordsworth's spiritual ideas, Keats wrote in 1818, "He makes a false coinage and deceives himself" (I, 223). He then added, "I will have no more of Wordsworth" (I, 224). At the beginning of one of Keat's most famous poems, "The Eve of St. Agnes" (1819/1820), two old spiritualists—the "ancient Beadsman" and the "palsy-stricken Angela"—had "Seem'd taking flight for heaven, without a death" (I, 8).[12] At the end, we are told only that:

> Angela the old
> Died palsy-twitch'd, with meagre face deform;
> The Beadsman, after thousand aves told,
> For aye unsought for slept among his ashes cold.
> (XLII, 6-9)

Here, Keats's ironic comment on the supposed spiritual benefits of old age is unmistakably grim. After a thousand prayers, there remains only the evidence of the "eternal fierce destruction."

But if Keats does not attempt to transform or transcend his awareness of aging as an advance toward death and nothingness, he does emphasize the value of continuing or renewed activity in the face of futility. In contrast to Wordsworth's celebration of the "settled quiet" of his old men, Keats exclaims, "God forbid we should what people call, *settle*—turn into a pond, a stagnant Lethe. . . . Better be imprudent moveables than prudent fixtures" (II, 138; Keat's emphasis). "Energy is of his essence," one critic has said of Keats.[13] And indeed, Keats's most important ideas about life characteristically allude far more to energy than to enervation.

For example, let us briefly look at a segment of Keats's description of a summer climb in 1818 up Scotland's highest mountain, Ben Nevis. Keats calls the mountain "old Ben" with obvious affection, and his account of it is in fact a symbolic comment of his sense of the circumstances surrounding old age.

> Talking of chasms they are the finest wonder
> of the whole—the[y] appear great rents in the
> very heart of the mountain . . . but other huge
> crags arising round it give the appearance to
> Nevis of a shattered heart or Core in itself. . . .
> Sometimes these chasms are tolerably clear,
> sometimes there is a misty cloud which seems
> to steam up and sometimes they are entirely
> smothered with clouds—After a little time the
> Mist cleared but still there were large Clouds
> about attracted by old Ben to a certain distance
> so as to form as it appeared large dome curtains
> which kept sailing about, opening and shutting
> at intervals here and there and everrywhere;
> so that although we did not see one vast wide
> extent of prospect all round we saw something
> perhaps finer—these cloud-veils opening with
> a dissolving motion and showing us the mountainous
> region beneath as through a loop hole—these
> Mouldy loop holes ever varrying and discovering
> fresh prospect east, west north and South (I, 353).

Note how different Keats's description of Ben Nevis is from Wordsworth's view of mountains. Whereas Wordsworth had idealized the mountain by stressing its summit as an emblem of immortality, Keats emphasizes its "chasms" as a symbol of "a shattered heart or Core"—as evidence, that is, of "the core/ Of an eternal fierce destruction." But in spite of his dark analogy, Keats still insists that these chasms "are the finest wonder of the whole" and in turn associates their "wonder" with the "ever-varrying" clouds of "old Ben" which

are paradoxically "opening with a dissolving motion" and "discovering fresh prospect." That is, we can see clearly here how for Keats metamorphosis is as much a matter of emergence and discovery as of dissolution. And insofar as his account of the geological and atmospheric processes of "old Ben" is partly a symbolic comment on the circumstances of old age, it suggests that if old age dramatizes the disappearance of things, it can still reveal an intermittently developing energy as well. And a "fresh prospect." In short, for Keats "old Ben" is as much a symbol of life as of death.

Keats dramatized these qualities and values in his great fragment of *Hyperion* (1818-1819/1820)—a poem, in Keats's words, about "Many a fallen old Divinity/Wandering in vain about bewildered shores" (III, 8-9). Partly modeled on Milton's epic, *Hyperion* is Keats's "Paradise Lost," and it concerns the Greek myth of the fall of one generation of gods, the Titans, and the rise of another, younger generation, the Olympians. The dialogue of the fallen gods thus constitutes, as it were, a symbolic compendium of the various "voices" of old age. At its beginning, the poem presents an immediate image of the giant decay of Saturn, the now only nominal ruler of the Titans:

> Deep in the shady sadness of a vale
> Far sunken from the healthy breath of morn,
> Far from the fiery noon, and eve's one star,
> Sat gray-hair'd Saturn, quiet as a stone,
> . . . .
> Upon the sodden ground
> His old right hand lay nerveless, listless, dead,
> Unsceptred; and his realmless eyes were closed;
> While his bow'd head seem'd list'ning to the Earth,
> His ancient mother, for some comfort yet.
> (I, 1-4, 17-21)

But the only earthly comfort which at first seems possible for Saturn derives from simply knowing the truth of his own new mortality. Oceanus, the submerged Titan of the sea, tells the fallen gods, " 'We fall by course of Nature's law' " (II, 181), and concludes, " 'Receive the truth, and let it be your balm' " (II, 243). Otherwise for the gods, there only remains "fear, anxiety, revenge,/ Remorse, spleen, hope, but most of all despair" (II, 94-95).

There is, however, Hyperion, the transitional god of the sun, who—destined to fall yet not fully fallen—embodies the residual magnificence of an almost endlessly extended sunset. Coelus, the sky-god, tells Hyperion:

> "This is the grief, O Son!
> Sad sign of ruin, sudden dismay, and fall!
> Yet do thou strive; as thou art capable,
> As thou canst move about, an evident God;
> And canst oppose to each malignant hour
> Ethereal presence."
> (I, 335-340)

In effect, Coelus redefines heroic value in terms of energy and effort rather than in terms of accomplishment, and does so with an open admission of Hyperion's ultimate fate before the force of the "malignant hours." In response, Hyperion "plung'd all noiseless into the deep night" (I, 357). He prolongs his light.

The poem's final image of Hyperion pictures him on a "granite peak" overlooking "the sad spaces of oblivion" (II, 359) and the mountainous mortality of the gods: "Regal his shape majestic, A vast shade/ In midst of his own brightness" (II, 372-373). Hyperion still shines in spite of the "vast shade," the shadow of death, within. And the narrative breaks off at a point which emphasizes the value of his indefinite energy. Hyperion is rallying the resources of the dejected gods (even Saturn is finally on the move again), and, by doing so, like Keats atop "old Ben," is "discovering fresh prospect" in the very midst of inevitable defeat.

Keats's great odes are condensed expressions of these dramatic conflicts, and I should like to comment on the perspectives of two of them. In the "Ode on a Grecian Urn" (1819/1820), Keats contemplates the possibility of an ideal conception of human life as an eternal work of art, yet covertly argues against the supposed virtues of remaining "for ever young." In the ode "To Autumn" (1819/1820), he insists on the changing environments of life, and suggests a sense of value in growing old.

The picture on the "Grecian Urn" that primarily attracts the poet is one of eternally young lovers happily settled in an Edenic setting. Here are Keats's first feelings about them:

> Fair youth, beneath the trees, thou canst not leave
> Thy song, nor ever can those trees be bare;
> Bold Lover, never, never canst thou kiss,
> Though winning near the goal—yet, do not grieve;
> She cannot fade, though thou hast not thy bliss,
> For ever wilt thou love, and she be fair!
>
> Ah, happy, happy boughs! that cannot shed
> Your leaves, nor ever bid the Spring adieu;
> And, happy melodist, unwearied,
> For ever piping songs for ever new;
> More happy love! more happy, happy love!
> For ever warm and still to be enjoy'd,
> For ever panting, and for ever young;
> All breathing human passion far above,
> That leaves a heart high-sorrowful and cloy'd,
> A burning forehead, and a parching tongue.
> (II, 5-10; III, 1-10)

But in spite of Keats's obvious idealization of eternal love and eternal spring, there is a latent negativism in his tribute. The thought of "never" subtly

counterpoints and even punctures the affirmation of "ever." "Bold Lover, never, never canst thou kiss,/ Though winning near the goal—yet, do not grieve." And this negativism results in a reversal of attitude in the final stanza of the poem:

> O Attic shape! Fair attitude! with brede
> Of marble men and maidens overwrought,
> With forest branches and the trodden weed;
> Thou, silent form, dost tease us out of thought
> As doth eternity: Cold Pastoral!
> When old age shall this generation waste,
> Thou shalt remain, in midst of other woe
> Than ours, a friend to man, to whom thou say'st,
> "Beauty is truth, truth beauty,"—that is all
> Ye know on earth, and all ye need to know.
>
> (V, 1-10)

Now Keats views the transfixed lovers as mere "marble men and maidens overwrought," and his earlier presumption of them as "for ever warm" has given way to a sense of them as impervious emblems of a "Cold Pastoral." Evidently, to be "for ever warm" can be quite chilling. At one point in *Hyperion,* Keats provocatively refers to "pale immortal death" (III, 128). Read one way, the phrase suggests the thought of immortality as a virtual state of death. In the "Ode on a Grecian Urn," Keats's final sense of the figures painted on the urn—figures caught in the immortal pretense of art—is similar. His initial empathy with their seemingly ideal space vanishes. For Keats, the "Grecian Urn" has become a funeral urn.

And yet this funeral urn does have a vital revelation for "old age" in the midst of "woe" and "waste." Ironically, however, that revelation is the *inverse* of the urn's presumption as a work of art. " 'Beauty is truth, truth beauty'." When Keats imagines the urn's message as this famous and seemingly enigmatic epigram, he alludes to the dual propositions which inform all of his greatest work: namely, that the central "truth" of life is of inevitable change ("that is all/ Ye know on earth"), and that this truth can be one of a sufficient "beauty" (that is "all ye need to know"). The beauty and truth of breath, of "breathing human passion." Perhaps the "passion" of Keats's own poem—of its passionately changing evaluation of the urn—is itself expressive of this beauty and truth. Perhaps, at its best, art can be a work of life. But ultimately, Keats's urn and Keats's poem suggest that life itself is preferable to art. The urn empties the poet of his own illusions of it as a work of art, but fills him with an aesthetic sense of life within his experience of loss. Correlatively, the urn dissolves the poet's illusions of eternal youth, but generates a sense of value in the midst of his imagined experience of old age. And this is why the urn will remain "a friend to man."

These revelations directly affect Keats's dramatic exploration of the illusory "art" of autumn in his ode "To Autumn" which remains as one of the finest

symbolic poems about old age ever written. The beginning of the poem pictures the art of autumn as a virtual cornucopia of seemingly endless abundance:

> Season of mists and mellow fruitfulness,
> Close bosom-friend of the maturing sun;
> Conspiring with him how to load and bless
> With fruit the vines that round the thatch-eves run;
> To bend with apples the moss'd cottage-trees,
> And fill all fruit with ripeness to the core;
> To swell the gourd, and plump the hazel shells
> With a sweet kernel; to set budding more,
> And still more, later flowers for the bees,
> Until they think warm days will never cease,
> For Summer has o'erbrimm'd their clammy cells.
> (I, 1-11)

At first glance, autumn's only purpose seems to be to "fill all fruit with ripeness to the core." Yet even the first line hints at the deceptive quality of autumn—it is a season of "mists" as well as of "fruitfulness." And the end of the stanza suggests a capacity for delusion in the bees who think of autumn as a season of eternal ripening, who "*think* warm days will never cease" (my emphasis).

In the second stanza, autumn's deception is strained further by the shifting implications of the poet's personification:

> Who hath not seen thee oft amid thy store?
> Sometimes whoever seeks abroad may find
> Thee sitting careless on a granary floor,
> Thy hair soft-lifted by the winnowing wind;
> Or on a half-reap'd furrow sound asleep,
> Drows'd with the fume of poppies, while thy hook
> Spares the next swath and all its twined flowers:
> And sometimes like a gleaner thou dost keep
> Steady thy laden head across a brook;
> Or by a cyder-press, with patient look,
> Thou watchest the last oozings hours by hours.
> (II, 1-11)

Keats's imagined figure of "Autumn" seems strangely and dramatically androgynous. Initially pictured as a sort of indolent "Mother Earth" lazily presiding over field and granary, the figure becomes more of an alert "Father Time" who, with lethal "hook," watches the "last oozings" of the cider "hours by hours." Within this dramatic shift, the earlier sense of ideal space gives way to revelations of time and process, and the feeling of infinite fertility yields to a realization of imminent death. The apple has become cider, and the cider is

almost at the end of its flow.

Yet something intriguing happens in the last line of this stanza: the "last oozings" are extended "hours by hours," and the momentary evocation of death is succeeded by the emphasis of indeterminate duration. It has often been said that one of the harshest aspects of old age is that it lacks that sense of an "infinite future" which the young supposedly enjoy. This may be so, but here Keats symbolically suggests the possible value for old age of an *indefinite* future—a future which can even dissipate the fact of death to the extent that death itself is an indefinite actuality (that is, it is certain that death will come, but uncertain when it will come).[14]

The developments of the third and final stanza of the poem derive from the context of this indefinite future:

> Where are the songs of Spring? Ay, where are they?
> Think not of them, thou hast thy music too,—
> While barred clouds bloom the soft-dying day.
> And touch the stubble-plains with rosy hue;
> Then in a wailful choir the small gnats mourn
> Among the river sallows, borne aloft
> Or sinking as the light wind lives or dies;
> And full-grown lambs loud bleat from hilly bourn;
> Hedge-crickets sing; and now with treble soft
> The red-breast whistles from a garden-croft;
> And gathering swallows twitter in the skies.
> (III, 1-11)

Here, Keats simply says that autumn has its "music" too. And within its medium of a simultaneously finite and indefinite future, that "music" is the music of motion and immediate energy. Yet this is not really just the music of old age. It is the magic of all ages. Thus all the sights and sounds of an autumn countryside at sunset blend together in the final stanza in a rich inconclusiveness which symbolically suggests the possibility of new beginnings and "fresh prospects" even within the abiding sense of an ending. Rhythms of ascent and descent, images of life and death, converge in confusing intensity. Puns (mourn/morn, bourn/born) implicitly compound the "bloom" and "rosy hue" of the now "stubble-plains." "And gathering swallows twitter in the skies." The poem's ending line may suggest a sense of final migration, but it more actively reveals the immediate presence of sustained song in the very heart of the wasteland.

Ultimately, "To Autumn" neither celebrates fulfillment nor laments an ending. Like *Hyperion,* it dramatizes the implicit value of a mode of energy that eludes limited categories of definition, and its extended revelation is simply that a great many things can and do happen throughout autumn. As a sustained symbolic comment on old age, then, the poem suggests values beyond the harvest of the past and experiences beyond an anxiety about the future. It suggests that old age is more than a time for memory and more than a time of death. It emphasizes the immediate and remarkable life of old age.

III

While Wordsworth and Keats both associate the "old man" with nature's ambivalent forces of growth and decay, then, their ultimate estimates of nature and the nature of old age strongly differ. Reflecting one impulse of the Romantic poets, Wordsworth records the bewildering effects of nature, yet simultaneously idealizes those effects in terms which eventually result in his affirmation of a spiritual value beyond nature. Likewise, he depicts the grim effects of old age, yet instinctively envisions the old man as the virtually disembodied premise of this spiritual value. In contrast, and reflecting a contrary impulse of the Romantic poets, Keats continues to confront the bewildering forces of nature without trying to spiritually transform them into something else. Doing so, he dramatizes the circumstances of old age as an intense convergence of desire and despair, and sustains his response to the old man as an emblem of enigmatic energy in the midst of his own decay. In short, for Wordsworth, the old man reveals a spiritual mystery. For Keats, he reveals the mystery of life.

If Wordsworth and Keats do not specifically address social issues in their poems about old age, their ideas and attitudes nevertheless have certain social implications which were as pertinent in their time as they are now. For example, while Wordsworth's spiritual ideals may reassure some of the elderly, they can also readily become the pretext for the massive neglect of the aged. Certainly there is no great cultural distance between the presumption of the spiritual tranquillity of old age and the forced tranquilization of the aged which commonly occurs today in supposedly ideal "homes."[15] The youthful scientist Victor Frankenstein wants to kill the "hideous mummy" that he has created. Wordsworth does not actually want to kill his old man, but he does want to tranquilize him. Perhaps this is to ascribe too harsh a motive to Wordsworth, but it is worth noting that at least one of his acquaintances, the eminent essayist and historian Thomas Carlyle, said of him in his later years, "Wordsworth maintained a stern composure, and went his way, content that the world should go quite another road," and added, "He was essentially a cold, hard, silent, practical man."[16] Be that as it may, when Wordsworth serenely refers to "the wholesome air of poverty" with which he envelops so many of his imagined old men (*The Excursion,* I, 306), one realizes the danger inherent in not making a distinction between the assertion of spiritual principle and the toleration of stark deprivation. And one further wonders what the relationship might be between Wordsworth's increasing Christianity in later life and his equally increasing political conservatism. At any event, in her impressively wide-ranging study of old age, *The Coming of Age* (1973), Simone de Beauvoir sharply rebukes such spiritual postures when they mask the severe realities of the elderly. "This mystical twaddle is indecent," she writes, "when we look at the real condition of the immense majority of old people: hunger, cold and disease certainly bring with them no kind of moral gain."[17]

Keats's stance on the subject is akin to that of Mary Shelley's shriveled

monster who defiantly tells his youthful creator and tormentor, "Life, although it may only be an accumulation of anguish, is dear to me, and I will defend it."[18] In contrast to Wordsworth, Keats strenuously admires "those to whom the miseries of the world/ Are misery, and will not let them rest" (*The Fall of Hyperion,* I, 148-149). Such declarations have a wide variety of modern implications. On one hand, Keats's continual authentication of death *as death* is clearly relevant to the values of our contemporary culture's increasingly open "dialogue" with death. But on the other hand, his emphasis on the value of immediate energy exerted in the face of death concurs with the many current efforts to embrace the obvious and rightful vitality of the aged in all areas of life.

These distinctions between Wordsworth and Keats with regard to old age are not unlike some of the issues raised by Robert Butler's recent criticism of Erik Erikson's view of elderly people. In such works as *Identity, Youth and Crisis* (1968) and *Life History and the Historical Moment* (1975), Erikson conceives of old age as a period for summarizing one's experiences, primarily one's past experiences, as evidence of one's ultimate "identity" and "integrity."[19] That is, with the evolution of cultural sensibilities, Wordsworth's old man as a reflection of an imagined future, of God, has become Erikson's old man as a symbol of an imagined past, of self. But in his massive text *Why Survive? Being Old in America* (1975), Butler argues that Erikson's concept is "potentially regressive" in that it unnecessarily constrains the elderly within passive roles derived from the past and minimizes the value of their encounter with new possibilities of identity and experience in the present. "I cannot accept Erikson's passive view of life," Butler concludes; "His claim that Integrity versus Despair is *the* psychosocial issue of old age does not fit my experience with older people, whose anger, despair and other evidence of not accepting one's fate are healthy."[20]

Certainly, despair is a significant element in modern narratives of old age. Divested of his mysticism, Wordsworth's old man reveals the voice of T. S. Eliot's "Gerontion" (1920):

> I am an old man,
> A dull head among windy spaces.
>
> . . . .
>
> I have no ghosts,
> An old man in a draughty house.
>
> . . . .
>
> And an old man driven by the Trades
> To a sleepy corner.

Even Eliot, however, can sometimes hear "Whispers of Immortality" from the wasteland of old age. But there are other voices. Dylan Thomas urges only that "Old age should burn and rave at close of day;/ Rage, rage against the dying of the light" ("Do Not Go Gentle into That Good Night" [1952]). As if in response, Bernard Berenson, in *Sunset and Twilight* (1963), emphasizes at

eighty-three, "I for one have never touched bottom in self, nor even struck against the surface, the outlines, the boundaries of this self. On the contrary, I feel the self as an energy only which expands and contracts."[21] No doubt the encounter with old age will always be as various as the lives which lead to it. Still, those of us who do become old will all experience something of the same vanishing landscape. And:

One must have a mind of winter
To regard the frost and the boughs
Of the pine-trees crusted with snow;

And have been cold a long time
To behold the junipers shagged with ice,
The spruces rough in the distant glitter

Of the January sun; and not to think
Of any misery in the sound of the wind,
In the sound of a few leaves,

Which is the sound of the land
Full of the same wind
That is blowing in the same bare place

For the listener, who listens in the snow,
And, nothing himself, beholds
Nothing that is not there and the nothing that is.

As Wallace Stevens knows in "The Snow Man" (1923), even in winter there is the promise of the "nothing that is." And as Keats said to a friend, "Nothings . . . are made Great and dignified by an ardent pursuit" (I, 243).

Notes

[1] Karl Kroeber, "The Relevance and Irrelevance of Romanticism," *Studies in Romanticism,* 9 (1970), 299.

[2] William Hazlitt, "On the Feeling of Immortality in Youth," *The Complete Works of William Hazlitt,* ed. P.P. Howe, Centenary Edition (London: J.M. Dent, 1933), XVII, 191.

[3] *Frankenstein* (New York: New American Library, 1965), pp. 50, 53.

[4] Harold Bloom, "Afterward," *Frankenstein,* p. 215.

[5] Quotations from Wordsworth's poems are from *Wordsworth: Poetical Works,* ed. Thomas Hutchinson, rev. Ernest de Selincourt (London: Oxford Univ. Press, 1969). The double dates in parentheses respectively represent the date of composition and the date of publication.

[6] Geoffrey H. Hartman, *Wordsworth's Poetry 1787-1814* (New Haven: Yale Univ. Press, 1964), p. 255.

[7] *The Letters of Charles Lamb,* ed. E.V. Lucas (London: J.M. Dent & Methuen, 1935), I, 239. The letter is dated January 30, 1801.

[8] Richard J. Onorato, *The Character of the Poet: Wordsworth in "The Prelude"* (Princeton: Princeton Univ. Press, 1971), pp. 138-39.

[9] In "Mont Blanc" (1817), for example, Shelley calls the highest mountain of the Alps "a flood of ruin" and "a city of death."

[10] Even seeming exceptions to this pattern still suggest the positive value of the "passive old man" for Wordsworth. In "Simon Lee: The Old Huntsman" (1798/1798), for example, Wordsworth dramatizes the helpless grief of an old man who tries to take active care of a plot of land but is unable to. The underlying implication of the poem is that he would have been better off being "tranquil" and "doing nothing."

[11] *The Letters of John Keats,* ed. Hyder E. Rollins, 2 vols. (Cambridge, Mass.: Harvard Univ. Press, 1958), II, 123. Hereafter, references to this edition are by volume and page number in parentheses within the text. I have retained Keats's original spelling and syntax.

[12] Quotations from Keats's poems are from *Keats: Poetical Works,* ed. H. W. Garrod (London: Oxford Univ. Press, 1970). The double dates in parentheses respectively represent the date of composition and the date of publication.

[13] Lionel Trilling, "Introduction," *The Selected Letters of John Keats,* ed. Lionel Trilling (New York: Farrar, 1951), p. 24.

[14] As Simone de Beauvoir says, "Over all living things, whatever their age, there hangs an inescapable exterior fate: [but] in no case is there a set moment at which this fate will strike. The old man knows that he will die 'soon': the fatality is as present at seventy as it is at eighty, and the word 'soon' remains as vague at eighty as it was at seventy." She even goes on to argue that, "It is not correct to speak of a relationship with death: the fact is that the old man, like all other men, has a relationship with life and with nothing else. What is in question is his will to survive." See *The Coming of Age,* trans. Patrick O'Brian (New York: Warner, 1973), p. 659.

[15] There is a potential correlation between Wordsworth's ideals of old age and Philip Slater's ideas in *The Pursuit of Loneliness: American Culture at the Breaking Point* (Boston: Beacon Press, 1970). Slater's general theme concerns the negative consequences of a "flush" culture which obsessively denies and displaces all revelations of waste and decay.

[16] Recorded by Sir Charles Gavan Duffy, *Conversations with Thomas Carlyle* (London: Sampson Low, Marston, 1892), pp. 54-55.

[17] de Beauvoir, p. 469.

[18] *Frankenstein,* p. 95.

[19] *Identity, Youth and Crisis* (New York: Norton, 1968); *Life History and the Historical Moment* (New York: Norton, 1975). Also see *Childhood and Society,* 2nd ed. (New York: Norton, 1963).

[20] *Why Survive? Being Old in America* (New York: Harper & Row, 1975), pp. 400-01.

[21] *Sunset and Twilight: From the Diaries of 1947-1958* (New York: Harcourt, Brace and World, 1963), p. 64.

Walter G. Moss

WHY THE ANXIOUS FEAR? AGING AND DEATH IN THE WORKS OF TURGENEV

For Ivan Turgenev (1818-1883), one of the world's great prose writers, aging, old age, and death were sources of fear and anxiety, although death at least might act to put an end to one's inner suffering. Youth, on the other hand, he saw as the "realm of light and colour," warmth and happiness. With few exceptions, these attitudes remained constant throughout Turgenev's career.

In "Steno," a long ambitious narrative poem written as he was approaching his sixteenth birthday, he laments the transient nature of life and the uncertainties of death. In this poem, Steno, the protagonist, has lost his religious faith, and substitutes for immortality do not appeal to him. He notes that we dream of glory, but asks what use is it if you are condemned to be food for worms. Despite these thoughts and his horror of what might occur after death, he commits suicide. The agonies which his life and mind cause him, it seems, are even harder to bear than the uncertainties of death.

Except for the absence of nostalgic words about youth, which will appear as early as 1844 in Turgenev's first published prose story, "Steno" accurately foreshadows Turgenev's later attitudes towards aging and death. Because of this consistency in his thinking throughout his life, the approach taken here will be to analyse Turgenev's thoughts on youth, aging, and death as they appear in his works[1] without emphasizing unduly his own age at the time a particular work was written. In the first section of this paper I will also make no attempt to indicate why I believe certain of his characters at times reflect the author's own thinking. Among those familiar with Turgenev, however, there would probably be little argument in regard to these assumptions. The second section of the paper will explore why he held the views he did and in the process of so doing, place them within the total context of his life and works.

I. Aging and Death in Turgenev's Works

Youth to Turgenev is not the same as childhood. In fact, for many of his characters that very early stage was a difficult period of life. A surprisingly significant number of his heroes and heroines were either orphaned by the death of one or both parents, or for various reasons were treated like orphans. And some would share the feeling of Lavretsky in *A Nest of the Gentry* (1859)[2] who says: "I was crippled in childhood."[3] As a result, many of these characters would later approach the period of their youth with a feeling of loneliness.

Although it is difficult to be precise, in general one could say that youth, as Turgenev uses the term, begins sometime after the age of puberty and extends into the mid-twenties. It is for him, however, more a state of mind than a chronologically determined stage, although the two most often coincide. A few of his characters, such as Natalya in *A Month in the Country* (completed in 1850), note that they were never young themselves. On the other hand, sometimes, but very seldom, older Turgenev characters act in a youthful manner. Lavretsky in *A Nest of the Gentry,* for instance, is in his mid-thirties when the young Liza briefly restores in him some of the sensations of youth. And Muza in "Punin and Baburin" (1874) can say, "some old men are younger than some young men," and Turgenev apparently agrees for he pictures Baburin as a hard-working idealist in Siberia up until his death at the age of sixty-seven.

To capture the tone of Turgenev's feelings about youth as well as to suggest some of its characteristics, a few excerpts representative of his thinking seem in order. In "The Region of Dead Calm" (1854), Veretev expresses the author's viewpoint when he says, "it was the time of youth, of mirth and happiness, the time of unlimited hopes, and invincible powers." Aleksei in "A Correspondence" (1856) speaks of the moments when he was youthful in this way:

> We entered, with sinking heart, into some sort of blissful waves . . . from the crimsoning sky, from the illuminated earth, from everywhere, it seemed as though the fresh and fiery breath of youth was wafted abroad, and the joyous triumph of some immortal happiness. . . . Do you remember that purity, that kindness and trustfulness of ideas, that emotion of noble hopes, that silence of plentitude?

Turgenev opens a piece from *Poems in Prose* written in 1878 with "O Realm of azure! O Realm of light and colour, of youth and happiness!" and proceeds to describe "a dream of sea, sky, and sun; of laughter and song; of enchanted islands with beautiful flowers and birds;" and the whole scene he says "spoke of love, of happy love!" In other passages, youth is spoken of as a time when our vital forces seeth, when we yearn for bliss and yet are carefree and self-confident. Turgenev does acknowledge from time to time that youth is not without some problems, but basically he sees it as a joyous stage of life. As he says in "First Love" (1860): "Oh, youth! Youth! You don't care for anything,

you seem to possess all the treasures of the universe; even sorrow comforts you, even grief becomes you."

In general it is Turgenev's male characters who are most nostalgic about their youth and the young, pure love which they experienced then. This love, of course, is usually awakened by a girl or woman, but occasionally strong attachments to male friends also provide great satisfaction. In "Yakov Pasynkov" (1855), for example, which is based to some extent on Turgenev's own youth, the narrator of the story recalls that as a young teen-ager he loved an older fellow student, Yakov Pasynkov, and describes a starlit night when they nestled together under a lilac bush and Yakov pressed his hand and recited a few lines of poetry. The narrator adds: "A devout tremor coursed through me; I turned cold all over, and sank down on his shoulder. My heart was filled to overflowing; where are those raptures now? Alas! in the place where youth is also."

For Turgenev a person was in general either youthful or old; he recognized no significant intermediate stages, such as middle age.[4] Our attention turns next, therefore, to his perceptions of the transition from being young to being old. The central factor which seems to cause such a change is the fading or disappearance of hope and idealism which most often occurs as a result of frustrated love. The case of Lavretsky in *A Nest of the Gentry* is a good example. Although he first falls in love at a considerably older age—twenty-five or twenty-six—than most Turgenev heroes, he remains young for several years until he discovers that his loved one, who has since become his wife, has been unfaithful to him. Then, Turgenev writes, skepticism "crept into his heart. . . . He became indifferent to everything around him." Four more years pass, and in his own mind he becomes old. He is ready to believe now, as Pavel more eloquently expresses it after his own loved one dies in "Faust" (1855), that "Life is a heavy toil," not "the fulfillment of cherished ideas and dreams, no matter how lofty they may be, but the fulfillment of duty, that is what man must take heed to." But then, although he is by this time in his mid thirties, he falls in love with the eighteen-year-old Liza. He becomes almost young again, but his happiness is soon ended when he discovers that his wife, whom he had thought dead, is very much alive. Liza soon afterwards enters a convent. The author gives us one final glimpse of Lavretsky: "During these eight years [since Liza had left him] he had at last turned the corner of life . . . he had really stopped thinking of his own happiness and self-interest. He had quieted down and, to be frank, had grown old not only in face and body, but in heart."

Another factor which Turgenev suggests contributes to the aging process is the Hamletlike mind which is troubled and indecisive. One of the characters in *A Month in the Country* hints at this: "If you know too much, you'll grow old before your time." And Rudin in the novel of the same name (1856) identifies staying young with following the inspirations of the heart. He writes to the young Natalya: "No matter how long you live, always follow the inspiration of your heart, never subject yourself either to your own or to another's mind." Rudin, as well as Turgenev, seems to feel that the mind can interfere with the spontaneity of the heart, and thereby subvert the hopes and optimism that are typical of youth.

Since Turgenev regrets the passing of youth, his most common attitude toward aging is one of dismay, at times almost of despair. His characters often comment on the quick passage of time ("Years of gladness,/Days of glee,/Like torrents of spring,/They flee, they flee!"). Although youth does not always bring great happiness, Turgenev believes that at least the hope and sometimes the reality of bliss are there, even if for a short period of time. His characters are therefore usually nostalgic about their youth. Accompanying this nostalgia is often a feeling that life has not lived up to its promise, that perhaps something has been missed, and that it is probably too late to do much about it. Most all of these feelings are well captured in a long monologue by the narrator of "An Excursion to the Forest Belt" (1857), a man who is probably no older than Turgenev himself at that time. After talking about his youth he says:

> Then the shadows began to grow and move forward; it became darker and darker around me; the monotonous years flew past more dully and quietly—and sadness descended like a stone upon my heart. . . . Oh, life, life, how art thou gone without a trace? . . . Has thou deceived me, or have I failed to make use of thy gifts? . . . My soul has thirsted for such full happiness. . . . Oh, golden chords that quivered so sensitively, so sweetly once upon a time, I hardly heard your song . . . when you broke. Or, perhaps, happiness, the direct happiness of my whole life has gone by close to me, has passed me, smiling with a radiant smile, and I have failed to recognize its divine countenance. . . . Oh, can it be that there is no hope, no return. . . . Strive to forget if thou desirest repose. . . . Do not look back, do not remember, do not aspire there where it is bright, where youth smiles, where joy profound flutters its azure pinions, where love, like the dew in the crimson dawn, beams with tears of rapture; look not there where bliss dwells and faith and power.

Although in this passage the narrator tells himself not to look back on his youth, he cannot resist. Nor can many of Turgenev's other characters. It might bring sadness, but for them, as for Turgenev, it is often a sweet sadness. And memories were better than a bleak, dark present. In one of his poems from *Poems in Prose* written in 1878 he advises an old man (perhaps himself?) to have recourse to his memories, but not to look forward.

Despite his nostalgia for lost youth, Turgenev's attitude toward attempting to remain young is somewhat ambivalent. He certainly seems to admire those who, like Baburin in "Punin and Baburin" and the grandfather in "The Two Friends" (1853), can somehow remain "young" in spirit. He also appears sympathetic with characters like Lavretsky in *A Nest of the Gentry* or Pavel in "Faust" who fall in love again and feel young again in their middle thirties. With older lovers or would be lovers, however, he is not especially tolerant (even though in his own life he was infatuated with a young actress when in his sixties). In Turgenev's works there is nothing like Galsworthy's touching picture in "The Indian Summer of a Forsyte" of an old man rejuvenated by infatuation.

In "A Hapless Girl" (1867), for example, the heroine tells of her uncle who tried to seduce her and who said: "An old man's heart is sometimes more ardent, and if the old man falls in love with anyone, his love is as firm as a stone wall! . . . Yes, yes; old men must not be despised!" But she relates that she found him revolting and disgusting, and Turgenev seems to agree.

While allowing Lavretsky and Pavel to fall in love again, and while certainly empathizing with them, Turgenev is ready when the romances collapse to admit, as he does at the end of *A Nest of the Gentry,* that "to keep one's heart young in old age, as some people say, is both difficult and almost absurd." And even though he finds it distressing to observe the traces of time on one's face or body, he is not very sympathetic with those who, like the count in the play *A Provincial Lady* (1851), dye their hair or use other artificial means to try to maintain the appearance of youth.

Such are Turgenev's feelings about aging. Now, what about his attitudes toward old age? It cannot be denied that on occasion Turgenev presents us with positive portraits of older characters—for example, the seventy-year-old Marya Dmitrievna in *A Nest of the Gentry,* the old couple in "Old Portraits" (1881), and Father Aleksei in "Father Aleksei's Story" (1877). A number of attractive older characters also appear in *A Sportsman's Sketches* (1852). But all of them are individuals who are appealing more in spite of their age than because of it. Whenever any of his characters or Turgenev himself speaks of old age, it is not to praise it but to curse it.

The "Region of Dead Calm" was written when Turgenev was thirty-five; he puts the following words into the mouth of the fortyish Veretev who is speaking to another character of about the same age: "And now you and I have grown old and stupid, we dye our moustaches, and saunter on the Nevsky, and we have become good for nothing; like broken-winded nags, we have become utterly vapid and worn out." Turgenev goes on to describe Veretev's acquaintances: "All of them were men no longer young, though unmarried; some of them had lost their hair, others were growing grey; their faces were covered with wrinkles, their chins had grown double, in a word, these gentlemen had all long since passed their prime." It is true that Veretev and probably his friends were aging playboys for whom Turgenev had little liking. But as we have seen, the prospects for happiness of much nobler souls of the same age, such as Lavretsky in *A Nest of the Gentry,* are not a great deal better. In "The Torrents of Spring," the portrait of old age is even more severe. The fifty-two-year-old narrator of this story—this was just about Turgenev's age when he wrote this work—observes that all of a sudden "old age comes upon you and with it the increasing, corroding, and undermining fear of death. . . . And, of course, you are lucky if that is the way you finish your life. For it is quite possible that before the end . . . there will be sickness and suffering." Finally, Turgenev himself speaks directly to us in his prose poem "The Old Man," written when he was approximately sixty:

> Days of darkness, of dreariness, have come. Thy own maladies, the sufferings of those dear to thee, the chill and gloom of old age. All that

> thou hast loved, to which thou hast given thyself irrevocably, is falling, going to pieces, the way is all downhill.

At least part of the explanation for Turgenev's fear of aging is that it involves the passage of time and therefore brings death that much closer. In his writing he bemoans the quick passing of time, frequently perceiving it as a destroyer of man's works, as well as of man himself. Steno, that creation of the young Turgenev, speaks of time the destroyer (the image of smoke in the novel *Smoke* also suggests the impermanence and mutability of humans and their works: "everything seemed to be smoke. . . . everything vanishes without a trace, without achieving anything"). In "It Is Enough" (1865) the narrator discusses the futility of life, but then asks himself whether art does not help to redeem it. His answer to himself is: "Its [Art's] perishableness, and again its perishableness, its decay and dust, that is what deprives me of courage and of faith." And a little later he says of nature that "she tolerates nothing immortal, nothing unchangeable. . . . She creates by destroying. . . . How are we to stand up against those heavy, coarse, interminably and incessantly oncoming waves." Yet it is ironic that in "The Diary of a Superfluous Man" (1850) the quick passage of time can provide consolation while at the same time depressing the narrator who has only a couple of weeks left to live. "To what extent," he proclaims, "are fourteen days less than fourteen years, or fourteen centuries? In the face of eternity, they say, everything is a mere nothing."

In Turgenev's works many of his characters confront death. Some die by their own hand, others as a result of violence perpetrated upon them, especially in duels, and still others as a result of sickness. In examining attitudes of these characters toward death, we find that their primary concern is not with the process of dying itself, but with the fact that life will come to an end and with what will or will not come after death.[5] Like many other themes, this is already evident in "Steno," Turgenev's first ambitious work. Along with the despair that life will cease to exist, a number of Turgenev's protagonists are saddened by the thought that their lives have not been lived well or that opportunities have been missed. We have already seen a similar regret expressed in regard to the irrevocability of youth. Some of the fears and anxieties triggered by approaching death are well articulated by the narrator of "A Diary of a Superfluous Man":

> I am afraid. Half bent over the silent, yawning abyss, I shudder, I turn away, I examine all around me with ardent attention. The least article is doubly dear to me. . . . It is hard for a living being to part from life! . . . And will it [his heart] really grow still forever, without once having experienced happiness.

The doctor in "A Country Doctor," one of Turgenev's *Sportsman's Sketches*, echoes one of those fears when he says: "It's dreadful to be dying at twenty-five, without having loved anyone." And the narrator in "Yakov Pasynkov" expresses a similar regret in regard to his beloved friend: "I feel pained, affronted,

that such a man, with so loving and devoted a heart should have died, without having even once experienced the bliss of mutual love."

Despite the apprehension which some of his characters experience in relation to thoughts of death, a few face it with equanimity (see, for example, the sketch entitled "Death" in *A Sportsman's Sketches*). And still others choose it rather than life. The doctor in "A Country Doctor" begs God to take his patient and he with her. And in that strange story "Klara Milich" (1883), Aratov contemplates the joining of Klara, whom he has come to love only after her death, and says: "Death no longer scares me now. It cannot destroy me, can it? On the contrary, only like *that* and *there* shall I be happy." And often the same character both fears and chooses death, as we have seen with Steno and as is the case with Nezhdanov in *Virgin Soil* (1877). Even the Superfluous Man writes, "Yes, it is good, it is good to be cut off at last from the exhausting consciousness of life, from the urgent and restless feeling of existence!" For the most part Turgenev's characters come to the tentative conclusion that nothing exists after death but the quiet of the grave. Turgenev, however, is never quite sure, and occasionally a character is allowed to hope, as does Aratov in "Klara Milich." Turgenev's many mysterious tales, such as "Phantoms" (1864) or "Knock . . . Knock . . . Knock" (1871), also hint at least of the possibility of life beyond the grave, whatever its nature might be.

II. Why the Anxious Fear?

The question that continued to beg for an answer as I proceeded to examine Turgenev's attitudes toward aging and death is: "Why?" Why did he seem to have such a negative view of aging and such strong anxieties about death? Although some might regard such feelings as natural, they did not seem so to me. Ernest Becker in *The Denial of Death*[6] and Norman O. Brown in *Life Against Death*[7] might both be correct in regarding the fear of death as the principle motivation for human activity. But let us suspend judgement for a while on both that and on Turgenev's feelings concerning death, and turn to his thoughts on aging.

Although a dislike of aging might be considered "normal" in our culture and in many others, certainly Turgenev's infatuation with the stage of youth and his failure to recognize redeeming qualities in later phases of life seem somewhat excessive. The methodological question which must be confronted here is just how to approach this excess. Is it largely influenced by historical, social, or psychological conditions? Now, one of the chief ways of understanding the attitudes of a writer toward any subject is by tracing the intellectual influences on him. The fact that Turgenev grew up in the period of the "Romantic Agony" and exhibits the strong influence of such individuals as Byron is certainly relevant to his attitudes toward aging and death. But while I do not wish to minimize this factor, it seems that in Turgenev's case there is a more basic source for these attitudes which demands investigation—his relationship to his parents. Although we do not know as much as we would like about this

relationship, Turgenev himself has left us one magnificent clue to help us understand it and thereby better understand his treatment of aging and death. This clue is his story "First Love."

The reader should be warned, however, that the path to an understanding of the attitudes we are interested in is not a straight one. As will be seen, they are intricately connected with other feelings and experiences, and only toward the end of this paper will I be able to attempt to pull all the loose ends together. If my interpretation is correct, however, it should lead not only to a better comprehension of Turgenev's attitudes about aging and death, but also provide additional insights into Turgenev's personality and works.

"First Love" was written in 1860, and Turgenev referred to it as the most autobiographical of all his stories. He assured a number of individuals that it was an account of events which, except for some minor changes, he actually experienced. In his biography of Turgenev, David Magarshack concludes that the events must have taken place in 1831 when the future writer was almost thirteen, his father thirty-eight, and his mother forty-four.[8] The most recent Russian edition of Turgenev's works suggests 1833 as the year. In any case, the story is presented as a recollection of a man named Vladimir. It revolves around the triangular relationship of Vladimir, sixteen, his father, and the twenty-one-year-old Princess Zinaida.

Vladimir is a romantic, idealistic youth, and his love for the princess resembles that of page for his queen—in fact, she actually pretends that he is her page. He is willing to do whatever she commands. He says at one point, "I would love and worship you to the end of my life, regardless of what you did and how much you tortured me." On another occasion he states, "I would gladly have caressed every fold of her dress and apron. The tips of her shoes peeped from under her skirt. I could have knelt in adoration to those shoes!" Also of interest is Vladimir's consciousness of the fact that he is still a boy and the sense of inferiority, especially in relationship to his father, that this produces in him. Yet at the same time the fact that he is a boy seems to enable him to receive an almost maternal affection from Zinaida, which she would not bestow upon a man and which brings him some special blissful moments.

The princess herself is a "fascinating mixture of cunning and carelessness, artificiality and simplicity, tranquility and playfulness." She can be passionate or cold, tender or harsh, and a certain capriciousness and willfulness seem to mark her character. She sometimes toys with Vladimir "like a cat with a mouse." He says, "Sometimes she would flirt with me, and I became all agitated and melted with emotion, at other times she would suddenly push me away."

The father "always dressed very exquisitely," was a magnificent horseman, and "despised timid people." His son recalls that he had "never seen a man more exquisitely calm, self-assured, and despotic." His character, however, can best be seen in the following description which the narrator gives of his boyhood relations with his father:

> My father had a strange influence on me, and our relations were strange. He took hardly any interest in my upbringing, but he never

> hurt my feelings; he respected my freedom, . . . he was even polite to me; but he never let me come close to him. I loved and admired him. He seemed to me to be a model of a man, and my God how passionately I would have become attached to him if I hadn't been continually aware of his rejecting hand.

Vladimir goes on to recall how once—but only once—his father had caressed him with such tenderness that he almost burst into tears, how at other times his father "would suddenly turn cold," as only he could, and seemed to care only for himself. Finally, he stresses his father's emphasis on the importance of a strong will.

Fundamental to the story is the strong jealousy which the young boy feels when he discovers that Zinaida is in love with someone. He takes a penknife and contemplates intercepting his rival, whoever it might be, on the way to a tryst—it would seem from many clues that the boy should have realized the rival was his own father, but he did not. When he discovers from a hiding place that his father is approaching, he becomes terrified. The narrator recalls the scene: "Jealous Othello, ready to murder, was suddenly transformed into a schoolboy. I was so frightened by my father's unexpected appearance. . . . I felt terribly ashamed." Still, however, he does not fully, consciously recognize that his father is the lover. A little later when he does finally accept the fact, he does not in his heart reproach his father, he is simply crushed.

A little later in the story, the narrator once again recalls that he not only bore no ill will against his father, but that his father seemed to have risen in his estimation as the result of his love affair. And toward the end of the story, after he had accidently seen his father with the princess, the narrator remembers that his "first impulse was to flee. Father will look around, I thought, and I shall be done for." That same night the young Vladimir dreams that his father is in a room with a whip with Zinaida who has a red mark on her forehead and that behind them both is still another rival for her affections who is covered with blood and who shakes his fist angerly at the father.

Six months later the father is dead—Turgenev's father died two days after Ivan's sixteenth birthday—and in the interval Vladimir has aged considerably. Four more years pass, and the princess dies. A few days later Vladimir goes out of his way to observe the death of an old woman and the terror of death that is in her eyes. The final words of the story are those of the narrator who says: "And I remember that there, beside the deathbed of that poor old woman, I felt afraid for Zinaida, and felt like praying for her, for my father—and for myself."

Although the role of the mother in "First Love" is not a central one, we should also note that she is ten years older than her husband—Turgenev's mother was six years older than her husband—and that on one occasion when she accuses him of being unfaithful, he reminds her of her age. This also apparently really took place between Turgenev's parents. But what characterizes the relationship of the boy to his mother in this story? Except for presenting her as fairly authoritarian in her relationship to her son and at one point having him kiss her hand and at another receive her blessing before going to bed, Turgenev

depicts little of their relationship. We cannot help but remark, however, that in a number of ways the princess resembles Turgenev's mother and that the relationship of the boy to Zinaida is similar to that of a small, adoring boy to his mother.

What I am suggesting here, of course, is that the princess is a surrogate mother figure and that basically the story turns on the traditional oedipal conflict—son loves mother and competes with father, in fact wishes the father dead, but then realizes that the father is stronger and that he disapproves of his son's behavior. Therefore, due to the fear of retribution for his incestuous desires and for his murderous impulses, the son represses them.

We know that Freud, among others, speaks of the Oedipus complex passing in early boyhood into a latency period, which in turn comes to an end at about the time of puberty. At that time the newly aroused sexual instincts once again reactivate oedipal feelings towards the parents until the son finds a replacement for the mother as a love-object. Whether Turgenev was actually twelve or fourteen at the time, he still would have been at about the right age for a resurgence of oedipal feelings. The selection, however, of a mother surrogate as a love-object and his father as a rival would doom him to repeat the oedipal cycle once more.

If my hypothesis—and I claim nothing more for it—is correct, then some of the mysterious elements of the story would be clarified. The failure to recognize the clues that his father was his rival could be attributed to repression. Did he not subconsciously know when he waited with his penknife that it was his father for whom he was waiting? And does he not protest too much when he says that after he was conscious that his rival was his father, he felt no ill will toward him? Are not the fear and trembling that he feels in front of his father due in part to the guilt he feels for subconsciously being antagonistic toward him? And in the dream that he has after seeing his father and Zinaida together, does the character who is covered with blood and shakes his fist at the father really represent Vladimir?

Finally, if the boy felt hostile to his father, and subconsciously wished for death or other harm to come to him, would he not feel guilty about the father's death? Psychologists tell us that this often occurs after someone's death even if the hostile feelings formerly directed at the dead person had no connection with his or her death. Would this explain why at the end of the story after watching the old woman die (who, by the way, kept saying "Lord, forgive me my sins" and had a look of the fear of death on her face), Vladimir has a strong desire to pray not only for Zinaida and his father, but also for himself?

We should not forget, however, that although Vladimir might have hated his father as a rival, he also "loved and admired him," and thought of him as "a model of a man." True, the case might be overstated here out of guilt. But such ambivalent feelings are quite common. Let us, however, leave for the time being this portrayal of a father-son relationship, remembering especially the admiration of the boy for his father, his feeling of inferiority as compared with him, the father's coldness toward the boy, and finally, the subconscious and

repressed resentment, envy, hatred, and consequent guilt that the boy probably felt toward his father.

Before outlining the many motifs of "First Love" which are repeated in subsequent Turgenev works and before dealing with the relationship of these motifs with Turgenev's anxieties regarding aging and death, let us briefly look at some facts about Turgenev's parents and his relationship to them.

Turgenev's mother was at times a notoriously cruel, sadistic woman. Ivan was her favorite child; there were two other sons in the family, Nicholas who was two years older than Ivan, and Sergei, an epileptic who died when he was eighteen and who was three years younger than Ivan. Their mother was throughout her life terribly possessive about her favorite son. Avrahm Yarmolinsky expresses a common opinion when he concludes that especially in regard to Ivan there was "something morbidly exaggerated about her maternal passion." She once wrote to her son, "I myself blush when I think of how very precious you are to me, maybe, it's a sin." Yarmolinsky also points out that she wrote Turgenev letters, in which she referred to herself as "most tender father and friend," and said "I alone conceived you," and "all that I am, you are."[9]

There is ample evidence to indicate that Turgenev had ambivalent feelings about his mother, loving her deeply but, especially as he got older, resenting her possessiveness and general cruelty. Nevertheless, he found it excruciatingly difficult to oppose her, and she seemed to be a master at inducing guilt in him whenever he dared to do so. In the reminiscences of a foster daughter of Turgenev's mother who came to the Turgenev household in 1833, we are provided with some scenes which were typical of the mother-son relationship. One such scene occurred in late 1846 or early 1847. Turgenev got up his nerve to mildly protest his mother's treatment of her serfs and of his older brother. She in turn became terribly upset with him, and as often happened when she became so upset, the estate doctor was sent for to give her laurel drops. Ivan grew alarmed, kissed his mother's hands, begged her to calm herself and forgive him. She asked, however, just how she could calm herself when he was intending once again to go abroad. The foster daughter notes then that Turgenev "bowed his head in his hands, and was silent, then with a griefstricken, almost despairing expression, he turned away."[10] Indeed, from 1838 when he went abroad for three years until his mother's death in 1850, he often turned away from her because she was an impossible woman to live with. But it was never easy and without reproaches. Some months before her death, they had another argument, and she refused to see him. He never saw her again.

In the meantime, however, in 1843 he had met another woman, Pauline Viardot, who in a number of ways resembled his mother but was not quite so possessive. She was an opera singer of Spanish descent and married to a Frenchman twice her age. Although she and Turgenev were perhaps once lovers, their relationship soon evolved into one in which Turgenev was thought of by all of the Viardots—Pauline, her husband, and the children—as an amiable and harmless member of the family who resided with them from time to time. Although Turgenev had brief liaisons with a number of other women,

both before and after meeting Pauline, he never married, and she was to remain his "woman on a pedestal" for most of his last four decades.

Of Turgenev's father we know much less than we do of his mother. A few of his letters have been preserved, and in some ways they substantiate Turgenev's portrait of him in "First Love," but in other ways they present him in a somewhat more favorable light, especially in regard to his concern for his children's education. These letters also indicate, however, that notwithstanding his connections with some liberals of his day, the elder Turgenev appreciated the necessity of military discipline and conventions. He enrolled his oldest boy in an artillery school in 1833, and apparently in 1832 had intended a military career for Ivan, but for some unknown reason soon changed his mind.[11] What would seem most important to us, however, is how Turgenev himself perceived his father. And most Turgenev experts agree that the portrayal in "First Love" is the most accurate perception that we have of Turgenev's image of him. It is also interesting to note that a few years before his own death, Turgenev was planning a novel in which one of the characters would be based upon a bastard of Turgenev's own father. Turgenev in the plan for the novel added that his father was "reputed to be a well known Don Juan." In addition to discovering his father's infidelity with the real life "princess," Turgenev undoubtedly had other opportunities for noticing that his father's feelings were much warmer toward other women than toward his own wife. The servant, for example, who traveled abroad with Ivan in 1838, and with whom he was on friendly terms, was reputed to be an illegitimate son of his father and was also said to resemble Ivan.

On the whole, the relationship of Turgenev's mother and father to each other does not seem to have been a happy one. She seems to have captured the handsome, young cavalry officer primarily because of her wealth. In "First Love," the grown son recalls the parents' situation: "My mother's life was miserable: she was always getting upset, always jealous and angry, though never in my father's presence. She was terrified of him and he treated her in a stern, cold, and distant manner." Madame Turgenev also seems to have resented the inconveniences necessitated by her husband's lingering health problems.[12] From patterns that can be discovered in many of his later works, it would seem that Turgenev sympathized with his mother as a result of the sufferings caused her by her husband.

At this point it would seem appropriate to put forth still another hypothesis—that Turgenev never overcame this triangular relationship and that his works in many ways reflect what psychologists would call a repetition-compulsion. In them, mother, father, and son appear time and again in different guises and forms, as if somehow Turgenev was subconsciously trying to work out through his art a problem that had earlier been repressed.

In his essay on "Turgenev and the Life-Giving Drop," Edmund Wilson repeats the story that Turgenev once told about a boy who had sick parents and was very unhappy because he could not cure them. One day he hears of a miraculous drop of water that, if drunk, could enable the drinker to cure diseases of the body and soul. The boy braves the competition of snakes and

reptiles and finally obtains the drop and cures his parents. In Wilson's interpretation of the story he does not stress, however, the most important point which is that Turgenev, at least subconsciously, wanted to help make his parents happy, desired perhaps to atone for guilt feelings toward them, and perhaps most of all wished to earn their love.[13]

Although the triangular relationship can be seen in numerous Turgenev stories, novels, and plays, perhaps the story of "A Hapless Girl" and the play *The Parasite* (completed in 1848) are most interesting from our point of view. In the first piece, Peter reminisces about his past when he was eighteen and had a close friend, Fustov, who was twenty-five. Fustov has a similar gracefulness, self-confidence, calmness, physical ability, and appeal to women ("a modest Don Juan") as does the father in "First Love." Fustov introduces Peter, who was called by his school comrades "the institute girl," to Susanna, the heroine of the story and Fustov's girl friend. In the ensuing pages we become familiar with the girl's background. It reminds us and must have reminded Turgenev of his mother's horrible youth.[14] In both cases there was a cruel step-father, an attempted seduction of the daughter (by the foster-father in life and by an uncle in the story), and an unpleasant uncle. Meanwhile, Fustov is told a malicious lie about Susanna, believes it, and no longer has anything to do with her. Peter, however, becomes very sympathetic to her. He finds out about the lie and tells Fustov about it. He asks his older friend if he loves Susanna, and Fustov becomes defensive and says he was ready to marry her, even though she is older than he. Peter, having a premonition of evil, asks his friend to go to her immediately, but Fustov says he will do so on the following day. It turns out, however, that the next day is too late. A short time after Peter's premonition, she committed suicide due to despair over Fustov's breaking off their relationship. All that remains of importance to us toward the end of the story is to note the sense of superiority that Peter comes to feel over Fustov, who seems to him now "almost a baby" and "a petty man." Peter thinks how completely differently he would have acted in his place.

In *The Parasite* we see an analogous pattern, although here it only figures as background material. An unfaithful husband drives his loving wife to seek consolation in the arms of a good, kind friend who lives with them. The very next day, however, after the wife has gone astray and in the process conceived a child, the husband falls off his horse and dies. Not long after giving birth to the child, the mother also dies.

My interpretation of these two situations is similar. Turgenev subconsciously presents to us here, in disguised forms, the basic oedipal conflict. Only in the first work, as opposed to "First Love," the son figure emerges the psychological winner, and the father figure appears as the loser. Does this reflect Turgenev's belief, although perhaps repressed, that if his father had been as loving, warm, and understanding of his mother as was Ivan himself as a boy, then perhaps his mother's life would have turned out better? After all, were not some of her faults due to the miserable experiences of her youth, and could not a loving husband have understood this and through his love made her a happier woman? In *The Parasite,* we again see a Don Juan type responsible for the unhappiness

of his wife. But the turning of the wife to another man in the household (a son figure?) is followed by the death of the husband (as sons in oedipal conflicts sometimes hope will occur), then of the wife (in retribution?), and the subsequent guilt and unhappiness of the third member of the triangle.

In other Turgenev works we find various combinations of the motifs in these two stories and in "First Love." We see the oedipal triangle in such works as "Andrei Kolosov," "The Bully" (1847), *A Nest of the Gentry* (Lavretsky, Liza, and Panshin), *Smoke* (Litvinov, Irena, and her husband), "Three Portraits" (completed in 1845?), "The Diary of a Superfluous Man," *On the Eve* (1860), "Faust" (Vera, her husband, and Pavel), *Rudin* (Rudin, Natalya, and Volintsiev), "The Torrents of Spring" (Sanin, Gemma, and Herr Klüber), "The Song of Triumphant Love" (1881), "The Watch" (1876), and *Virgin Soil* (Nezhdanov, Marianna, Solomin).

It is not always easy to recognize Turgenev's mother in these works, for at times her image seems to have been split in two—the predatory, possessive, sexual woman, such as Marya in "The Torrents of Spring" or Irena in *Smoke,* and the pure young virginal woman, such as Liza in *A Nest of the Gentry.* There are various explanations given as to why this psychological phenomenon occurs, including the repression of incestuous desires directed toward the mother. It does not, however, appear to be an uncommon experience, although psychologists seem to feel that its persistence reflects an arrested psychological development.[15]

The picture is further clouded by the belief of some psychologists that in the type of sadomasochistic relationship which we see between Marya and Sanin in "The Torrents of Spring," the sadistic woman represents for the masochistic sufferer his father, who is punishing him for his incestuous desires and for his hostile attitudes toward him as result of the oedipal conflict.[16] In fact, there can be little doubt that Turgenev himself had a strong streak of masochism and that his nature was somewhat of the passive kind that both Freud and Reik associate with masochism. One could also speak of certain homosexual tendencies which Turgenev seemed to display and which also are habitually revealed in the male masochistic personality.[17] These observations, however, do not lessen the importance of the basic oedipal conflict; rather, in the case of Turgenev, they seem to reinforce its significance.

With Turgenev's father we also are repeatedly faced with the splitting of the father image, which reflects the ambivalent love-hate relationship of the son to the father.[18] We know that Turgenev's father appeared calm and self-confident and placed a great deal of emphasis on the importance of a strong will. In such characters as Insarov in *On the Eve,* Bazarov in *Fathers and Sons* (1862), the older cousin in "The Watch," and Solomin in *Virgin Soil,* we see these characteristics manifested. These figures are to some extent like the Don Quixote type that the more Hamletlike Turgenev admired. In each of the above cases, the men of strong character are admired by weaker, more passive, boylike characters who are in love or infatuated with the same woman, but give way to the stronger man.[19] In the case of *Virgin Soil,* for example, Nezhdanov even goes so far as to make way for Solomin by committing suicide.

The reverse side of the image we have already seen in Fustov. This personality type reminds us of Turgenev's father because he is often self-assured, composed, and very determined. In addition, he is also frequently a Don Juan, like the Prince in "The Diary of a Superfluous Man," who trifles with a woman's affections or seduces her. Turgenev also often portrays him as a basically cold person who is all show with magnificent manners. Characters like these include the bully in the story of the same name, Panshin in *A Nest of the Gentry*, Irena's husband in *Smoke,* Veretev in "The Region of Dead Calm," the Baron in "A Dream" (1876), Herr Klüber in "The Torrents of Spring," Teglev in "Knock . . . Knock . . . Knock," Vasily Lutchinov in "Three Portraits," Muzzio in "The Song of Triumphant Love," and Platon in "The End" (completed in 1883).

As compared with the Turgenev-like character's willingness to give way before the *positive* type figure such as Insarov, the Turgenev personality type is not usually willing to renounce his affections in favor of the more *negative* type described above. Rather, jealousy and strong hostile feelings are often harbored against him, and violence sometimes results. In both "The Bully" and "Three Portraits," a duel occurs as a result of conflict over a woman, and the noble or innocent figure is killed by the willful one. In "The Diary of a Superfluous Man," there is also a duel between the two male rivals, but no one is seriously injured. In "The Song of Triumphant Love" the seducer is almost killed by his rival. And in *A Nest of the Gentry,* Lavretsky wins a psychological victory over his rival Panshin but, as we have seen, he loses Liza in the end to a convent.[20]

Thus, where the father and son figures come into conflict, violence and death often result. Even when the son gives way peacefully, such as in *On the Eve* and *Fathers and Sons,* the strong willed father figure dies at an early age, as did Turgenev's own father after Turgenev declined to openly compete with him over the prototype for the princess.

Given what we know of the oedipal conflict, however, these situations should not surprise us. Violent feelings on the part of the son are common, and because of these feelings, as well as because of incestuous feelings toward the mother, the son fears violence from the father in retribution. And for these same reasons it is not surprising that many of Turgenev's lovers are guilt-ridden and have premonitions of evil occurring to them as a result of their love.[21] For if as with the Turgenev-type lover in "Faust," he challenges, like the son in an oedipal conflict, the husband-wife relationship, it is no wonder that he feels "like a criminal," and tragedy results.

By this time, I hope that it has become at least a little clearer why Turgenev had the attitudes toward aging and death which he did. Let me, however, interpret as best I can the significance of his oedipal conflict for these attitudes.

In regard to his infatuation with youth, it would seem that several interpretations are possible. First, we might conclude that emotionally Turgenev never wished strongly enough to grow up, to leave the father-mother-son context. This could have been due in part to the fact that his father died before he was able to resolve his conflict with him. But although this might explain why he continued to experiment, probably subconsciously, with oedipal conflicts in

his writing, it does not really indicate why he felt youth was such a wonderful time of life. After all, if my interpretation is correct, he must have suffered guilt feelings, although perhaps repressed, after his father's death, as well as during earlier oedipal conflicts. And he allowed the protagonist "Steno," created before his sixteenth birthday, to commit suicide because he could not live with the demon (guilt?) inside himself.

A second interpretation is made possible by the insights of Ernest Jones in a paper on "Jealousy." Jones sees jealousy as often resulting from a need to be loved and a fear of losing it. The love is necessary to an individual because it helps to protect him psychologically from his own guilt and the fears of the father which have resulted from oedipal conflict.[22] We often find in Turgenev's characters and in his own relations with Pauline Viardot indications that love was valued for some such purpose. We perceive the desire to lose oneself (one's nagging guilt?) by becoming absorbed by the loved one. Youth, therefore, would be especially desirable because it was the stage of life when such dependent love was most possible and permissible.

Thirdly, we can infer that youth was more important to Turgenev as a kind of mythic Garden of Eden than as a real stage of life. It represented for him innocence, passivity, the promptings of the heart and the id, spontaneity, love and security, as opposed to guilt and a guilt-ridden mind, the super-ego, anxiety, uncertainty, insecurity and the fear of death. It certainly does not truly represent any stage past the first few years of life.

My preference for an explanation is a combination of all of the above interpretations. Turgenev's fear of aging could then be attributed to his fear of the opposite of youth with all its psychological implications. His feeling that life was passing him by and that it was not living up to its promise could have been due to the fact that in many ways both perceptions were true. He did not experience the joys and satisfactions that he had hoped he might, and that someone not stuck in an oedipal mire might have.[23] Aging also meant that death was coming closer, and we have referred numerous times to Turgenev's anxieties in that regard. They could be due to various causes. A certain amount of anxiety regarding death seems normal, whether repressed or not. One also must note that Turgenev did not have many "crutches" to lean on as a substitute for mortality. He was not able to have faith in traditional religious beliefs regarding life after death. Nor did he seem to be able to derive much satisfaction from the knowledge that his writings and his illegitimate daughter by a seamstress who worked for his mother would both continue to live on after his death.

Even granted these factors, however, one must conclude that with Turgenev these anxieties were greater than normal. One can perhaps attribute this in part to the feeling that he seemed to have that he had not lived a complete, fulfilling life, and therefore was not as ready for death as would be one who had. But excessive guilt would also seem to be part of the explanation. He portrays death in various male and female guises. And it is not too far fetched to understand these as mother and father images coming to claim a son who in reality was not able to satisfy his mother's possessive demands and who probably desired the death of his father.

Of the fact that Turgenev was guilt-ridden in regard to his parents there seems little doubt. I have attempted to indicate this in a number of ways, and further exploration into other avenues of Turgenev's personality—his fetish for kissing hands, his hypochondria, his indecisiveness, etc.—would, I think, establish this beyond a doubt. A number of writers have hinted at his guilt in regard to his relationship with his mother.[24] But I think not enough has been made of the oedipal conflict of the author of *Fathers and Sons* with his own father, and the resulting guilt.

In the short work "Three Meetings" (1852), the narrator, a Turgenev-like figure, has a dream about a beauty with whom he is infatuated. She flies away from him up to the sun. However it turns out not to be the sun, but an Italian spider (a spider in other passages of Turgenev appears as a death symbol). The narrator describes his dream, saying that in it he shouts, "I'll show him up for what he is: I saw him stealing oranges from other people's gardens." A few paragraphs later, the narrator recounts how in the dream he attempts to reach the beauty but is blocked by an old man who says: "Recognize in me Don Quixote de La Mancha. . . .All my life long I have been seeking my Dulcinea, and I have not been able to find her, and I will not tolerate it that you shall find yours." The narrator then asks him to stand aside, but instead the knight kills him with his spear.

Are not both the spider and Don Quixote in this dream disguised figures of Turgenev's father who "stole the fruit" (sexually pursued) from "other people's gardens" (women other than his wife), but yet never stopped seeking and was never satiated?

We have also seen, however, that Turgenev had ambivalent feelings toward death. This seems easy enough to understand. If indeed death leads to the end of all consciousness, then it also leads to the end of all anxiety and guilt. In one of Turgenev's final stories, "Klara Milich," Turgenev's longing for escape from these two demons through the loss of himself in love is merged with that other approach to the problem, death; and the hero falls in love with a dead woman and succeeds in joining her. Even though the story suggests some sort of blissful afterlife, the possibility of consciousness in such a state seems less important than the fact that these two approaches—love and death—to the ending of anxiety and guilt are merged.[25] And we are left with the irony that while love and death, as interrelated in the Oedipus complex, might have contributed in a major way to Turgenev's anxieties and guilt, they also ultimately presented themselves fused together as perhaps the only way to peace of mind.

III. Conclusion

In Simone de Beauvoir's *The Coming of Age* she quotes the following remark of Turgenev: "Do you know the worst of all vices? It is being over fifty-five."[26] She also gives many other examples of such attitudes from the lives of other significant persons. And it seems that she would have us believe that such attitudes represent a rather natural human response to aging.[27] In this essay, on

the other hand, I have attempted to demonstrate that Turgenev's works reflect an obsessive and irrational fear regarding aging and old age. And I have also attempted to indicate the probable main cause of this gerontophobia, as well as of his severe anxieties regarding death.

The question then is whether such beliefs as those of Turgenev are a natural, appropriate response to the phenomena of aging, old age, and death, or whether they are more likely to be manifestations of a neurosis. One does not have to accept every detâil of Erik Erikson's eight stage developmental theory in order to perceive that there is something healthier and more in keeping with the proper nature of man in such an approach than in the attitudes of Turgenev.[28] We tend to feel that a person who can look upon aging as an opportunity for inner growth, who can accept each stage of life as a new challenge, and who finally can meet death without cringing is somehow a fuller human being. Perhaps Nadezhda Mandelstam is a bit hard on those who fear old age when she writes: "I am now seventy years, and I know that only empty people fear old age and indulge in the absurd cult of youth. Each age of man has its own unique content."[29] Nevertheless, we are inclined to appreciate the essential "healthiness" of such a tough old woman who can embrace old age and regard death as a "triumph," who neither wishes at the end of her days "to be artificially kept alive," or to be destroyed, but who asks only "to remain human at the moment of final suffering."[30] For Turgenev, on the other hand, we feel more a sense of pity. Despite his great literary achievements, we feel that he failed to experience as much of the full richness of the life cycle as he might have.

Finally, the question as to whether attitudes like those we have examined of Turgenev are natural or neurotic is perhaps not without some significance for our own attitudes. For if we regard them as natural, it seems that we are in danger of perpetuating and strengthening such beliefs in ourselves and others. Whereas if we suspect that they are more likely to be reflections of a neurosis, then it would seem that we would increase our chances of approaching aging, old age, and death in a different and more positive manner.

Notes

[1]Although Turgenev's first published work was a long narrative poem, "Parasha" (1843), his reputation is based almost completely on his novels, short fiction, and plays. The first of his plays, as well as "Andrei Kolosov," his first published short story, both appeared within about a year of "Parasha," and he soon all but abandoned the writing of verse.

[2]Unless otherwise indicated the date in parenthesis indicates when the work was first printed.

[3]Many of the translations of quotations from Turgenev's shorter works are taken from *The Novels and Stories of Ivan Turgenieff,* trans. Isabel F. Hapgood, X-XIV (New York: Charles Scribner's Sons, 1904), although I have occasionally modified a translation. For the other translations, I have utilized as a guide a wide variety of English translations. I have, however, tried to insure that all quotations are faithful to the original Russian.

[4]This is especially true in regard to the author's male characters. With some of his female figures, such as Irena in *Smoke* (1867) who is in her late twenties, he seems to recognize that they are neither young nor old. And his male characters are strongly attracted to such mature women, as well as to more youthful, innocent ones.

[5]As compared with the subject of Turgenev's attitude toward aging, where I was able to discover only passing references to it in secondary sources, Eva Kagan-Kans devotes a significant section of her book *Hamlet and Don Quixote: Turgenev's Ambivalent Vision* (The Hague, Netherlands: Mouton & Co., 1975) to the subject of his treatment and feelings regarding death. While my analysis of his views on this latter topic are based primarily on a reading of his works, I am indebted to Kagan-Kans for reinforcing some of the tentative conclusions at which I had arrived, and for helping me to perceive the interrelationship of Turgenev's thoughts about death with some of his other ideas. My attempt to explain the psychological origins of Turgenev's feelings about aging and death—which will follow in the second section of this paper—is, however, except where indicated, based almost completely upon my own perceptions.

[6]*The Denial of Death* (New York: Free Press/Macmillan, and London: Collier Macmillan, 1975).

[7]*Life Against Death* (New York: Vintage/Random House, 1961).

[8]*Turgenev: A Life* (London: Faber and Faber, 1954), p. 30.

[9]*Turgenev: The Man, His Art and His Age* (New York: Collier Books, 1961), pp. 40, 45, 73.

[10]V. Zhitova, *The Turgenev Family,* trans. A.S. Mills (London: The Harvill Press, 1947), p. 112.

[11]See M.K. Kleman, "Otets Turgeneva v. pismakh k synovyam," *Turgenevskii Sbornik,* ed. A.F. Koni (Petrograd: Kooperativnoe izdatelstvo literatorov i uchenykh, 1924), pp. 131-43; V.V. Protasov, "K biografii I.S. Turgeneva," *Russkaya Literatura,* No. 2 (1971), pp. 123-24.

[12]Turgenev's father suffered off and on for many years as a result of a defective gall bladder. See T.P. Den, "S.N. Turgenev i ego synovya," *Russkaya Literatura,* No. 2 (1967), p. 131.

[13]Turgenev and the Life-Giving Drop," in *Turgenev's Literary Reminiscences,* trans. David Magarshack (New York: Minerva Press, 1968), pp. 13-15, et passim.

[14]I am aware that the story was based upon an actual occurrence of Turgenev's youth, but this in no way lessens the importance of the similarity of the girl's fate to that of Turgenev's mother.

[15]See Theodor Reik, *Psychology of Sex Relations* (New York: Grove, 1966), pp. 21-28, and Ernest Jones, *Hamlet and Oedipus* (Garden City, New York: Anchor-Doubleday, 1954), p. 97.

[16]Theodor Reik, *Masochism in Sex and Society* (New York: Grove, 1962), p. 205.

[17]Ibid., pp. 204-06.

[18]See F.L. Lucas, *Literature and Psychology,* 1st American ed., rev. (Ann Arbor: Univ. of Michigan Press, 1957), p. 53.

[19]It is sometimes overlooked that Arkady in *Fathers and Sons* considered himself in

love with Anna, before transferring his affections to her younger sister, Katya.

[20]In "The Dream" a special twist is given to the oedipal conflict. A seventeen-year-old boy, who says of his thirty-five-year old mother "I adored her, and she loved me," discovers that an evil man, the baron of the story, had years ago raped his mother and thereby become the boy's father. At the end of the story the baron is found dead on the beach. An equally sinister seducer, Platon, is pictured in the last story which Turgenev wrote, "The End." Although an oedipal conflict is not presented in it, it seems highly possible that Platon is a subconscious caricature of Turgenev's father. At the end of the story, Platon is brutally murdered.

[21]See Kagan-Kans, pp. 58-61, where she gives many examples of Turgenev's linking of passion with death, but does not mention that the linkage might be due to guilt which has arisen as a result of Turgenev's unresolved Oedipus complex.

[22]*Papers on Psychoanalysis,* 5th ed. (Boston: Beacon, 1961), pp. 358-59.

[23]The issue Turgenev's father made of the fact that his wife was older than he seems to have impressed Turgenev, but by itself it would not seem to have been enough of a factor to explain Turgenev's attitude toward aging.

[24]See, for example, Kagan-Kans, pp. 80-81, and Magarshack, *Turgenev: A Life,* pp. 125-27.

[25]One is reminded here of Leslie A. Fiedler's *Love and Death in the American Novel,* rev. ed. (New York: Dell, 1966). This work is rich with insights regarding the interconnections of attitudes toward love and death, as well as the relationship of both to the desire to remain a child. See, for example, pp. 50-51 regarding love and death.

[26]*The Coming of Age,* trans. Patrick O'Brien (New York: Putnam's, 1972), p. 284.

[27]I do not mean to imply, however, that de Beauvoir feels that such a response should be applauded. She obviously admires Victor Hugo's more positive approach to his own aging process. Nevertheless, she thinks that his attitude was exceptional and that for all but a privileged few, old age is a parody, and given the present social conditions that is about all we can expect. See de Beauvoir, pp. 505-11, 539-41.

[28]Erikson's theory is outlined in his *Childhood and Society,* 2nd ed., rev. (New York: Norton, 1963), pp. 247-74. Robert N. Butler in his *Why Survive? Being Old in America* (New York: Harper & Row, 1975), pp. 400-01, offers some criticism of Erikson's theory, especially in regard to his final stage of development where he feels Erikson's approach accentuates to too much of an extent a passive approach to life. Butler believes that anger and other evidence of an unwillingness to accept one's fate can be healthy. He does not mean by this, however, that we should not accept our own aging process and old age itself when it comes. Such a refusal he feels would be "self-sabotaging." See p. 14.

[29]*Hope Abandoned,* trans. Max Hayward (New York: Atheneum, 1974), p. 257.

[30]Ibid., pp. 106-08.

David Bronsen

CONSUMING STRUGGLE VS. KILLING TIME: PRELUDES TO DYING IN THE DRAMAS OF IBSEN AND BECKETT

"Les extrêmes se touchent." This venerable French saying states in effect that when attitudes and behavior are pushed to their uttermost limits, they take on the characteristics of their antitheses. The orientations to life I shall be dealing with that are mutually exclusive but converge at a certain point, are those expressed in the dramas by Henrik Ibsen and Samuel Beckett.

The differences between the works of the two dramatists are much more readily apparent than the elements that would seemingly justify their comparison, first of all because they derive from radically different traditions. Ibsen worked largely in the frame of realism, while Beckett belongs to that disparate medley of the tragic and comic which goes by the name of the "grotesque." Realism, by its natural impulse and vision, is intent on clarifying and bringing about resolution. While comedy normally gives rise to reconciliation and tragedy to resolution, the grotesque, on the other hand, offers no answers and its finale is not final, thus leaving the door open for a further round of the absurd it has already portrayed. From the medium in which he worked it follows that Ibsen saw himself as a pedagogue during the greater part of his dramatic career, one who offered examples, propounded self-realization and was eager to influence men's minds. Beckett, by contrast, not only offers no answers, his entire work from beginning to end keeps saying with unvarying insistence, "Nothing to be done" (the opening line of *Waiting for Godot*),[1] and that it is impossible to change man's lot.

While Ibsen attended to his tightly structured plots with the carefulness of a Flaubert, marshaling exposition, conflict, reversal, climax and denouement with practiced craftsmanship, it is questionable whether some of Beckett's more recent plays live up to Aristotle's minimum requirement for a drama as an action having a beginning, middle and an end. Ibsen is the past master of analytical plot, in which the present is determined by and derived from the past. In Beckett, the past is an archaeological deadweight alluded to but

seldom unearthed, so that it remains as meaningless and eventless as the present, and just as opaque. Contrary to Ibsen's pattern of the constantly forward-moving plot, Beckett's plays consist of endless diversions in which nothing of significance is happening and that lead nowhere. Since there is no will that can bring about change or external action, the "action" that does occur consists of waiting and the real antagonist becomes time, against which all else is powerless. When time alone is the prime mover, all that can ensue is suffering and boredom, both of which are essentially passive. Decisions are not thought out and acted upon; no real contest occurs and no visible counterforce appears. As a result, on two occasions Beckett has been able to convey his "message" in puppet-like mimes, in which the forces involved are reduced to abstractions. Since Beckett's dramas are mostly lacking in meaningful development and external action on the part of the characters consists of repetition while waiting for things to end, dramatic structure is predictably circular, so that plays end where they began.

The characters of Beckett and those of Ibsen in his final plays have in common that they are self-centered and introverted, with limited ability to relate to others and given to living in isolation. But whereas Ibsen's characters are highly individualized and, with few exceptions, eminently analyzable in psychological terms, Beckett's are largely impervious to such analysis. Instead, they lack in what normally passes for motivation and in virtually all instances are fragments of a composite and undifferentiated persona. In contrast to the characters in Ibsen's late plays, whose dedication to their professional commitments is identified with meaning and for whom the world has been a battleground of achievement, those of Beckett reject achievement and yearn, instead, for the process of life to come to an end. It is precisely these seemingly radical differences which, under certain circumstances, will be seen to touch and merge.

Ibsen offered testimony to his being an author of the nineteenth century by the broad compass of his themes, which range from the historical and the political to the mores of contemporary society, personal ethics, social problems and studies in psychological imbalance. Beckett marks himself an author of the twentieth century, and more specifically, a congener of Kafka, Genet, Ionesco and Arrabal, with his suggestion of obsession in forever mining the same vein. Beckett's universal theme is that of existential despair, and his undeviating loyalty to his narrow but intense vision through a lifetime of creativity has given his novels as well as his plays the imprint of an unmistakable style. The major development in his prose works is that they get more obscure and hermetic, and as a consequence, nearly unreadable. His plays become briefer and dialogue fades to monologue and near silence, while his characters grow more immobile and moribund. At the same time Beckett's plays, if that is the right term for them, evince an originality and genius in technical innovation and dramatic conception that are probably not equaled by any living playwright.

What Ibsen and Beckett do have in common is that for both of them writing is an existential act and their virtually exclusive activity, to the point where

they seem to exist only as an extension of their work. It is symptomatic that both writers are expatriates whose literary creations became their real home. In addition to their need to escape from what they left behind in their native countries, their expatriation also answered to an equally urgent need to dedicate themselves unstintingly to their writing. Ibsen lived abroad for twenty-seven years and of his fifteen mature works, all but the last four were written while living away from his native Norway. The Irishman Beckett has spent almost all of his creative years in Paris. Ibsen's professed desire was, as he put it, "to live in isolation, occupied exclusively with my work."[2] Beckett is also referring to his work when he says, "One creates one's own world, *un univers à part,* to which one retires . . . in order to flee chaos."[3]

The three late plays by Ibsen this essay will focus on—*The Master Builder* (1892), *John Gabriel Borkman* (1896) and *When We Dead Awaken* (1899)—have in common with *all* of Beckett's dramas that they deal with aged people. The characters in these works by Ibsen and those of Beckett are caught up in the absorbing preoccupation of how to cope with life while posing insistent questions that imply they have never found peace. None of the oldsters of Ibsen and Beckett live up to the ideal that Kant would attribute to the aged: "Age is not content with representing merely an accretion of years but wants to be looked upon as meritorious and to stand as an example."[4] Ibsen's characters are too troubled, their lives too "unfinished," to measure up to such a standard, and Beckett's are too deprived of human sustenance and self-esteem to serve as anything but bad examples.

Ibsen, who spent the middle portion of his productive years with the struggle for self-liberation in such plays as *A Doll's House, Ghosts,* and *An Enemy of the People* in which the enemy is always the other or is found in the dictates of society, progresses to psychologically oriented plays in which the struggle is directed simultaneously against oneself and the outer world, as in *The Wild Duck, Rosmersholm, The Lady from the Sea, Hedda Gabler.* Finally, in his depiction of old age in *The Master Builder, John Gabriel Borkman* and *When We Dead Awaken,* internal conflict takes over for which there is no resolution, much less liberation, because in each instance the protagonist is at once the captor and the prisoner, which leads to an indeterminate contest that can only be severed by death.[5] These plays of Ibsen's final years turn away in large part from the realism of his social plays and are informed by a poetic symbolism of the unconscious. All three are laments over misspent lives, and the main characters—Solness, the architect of *The Master Builder*—Borkman, the banker and financier—as well as Rubek, the sculptor of *When We Dead Awaken*—look backward, full of self-reproach and "post mortems," to use a term that figures prominently in Beckett's *Krapp's Last Tape,* a play which is similarly oriented.

These plays, which Ibsen wrote during the period of his sixty-fourth to his seventy-first years were, somewhat surprisingly, foreshadowed in *Brand* and *Peer Gynt,* the dramas that first served to make him famous nearly three decades earlier. Together these late plays represent parallel lines of inspiration which can be traced through many of the dramatist's other works. Brand is a

stern clergyman who, in Kierkegaardian fashion, lives with a total commitment to the absolute, sacrificing everything to his ideals and denouncing compromise as hypocrisy. His unyielding severity turns his parishioners against him, alienates his mother on her deathbed and indirectly brings about the death of his wife and child. In the end, having offered up everything to what he saw as his mission in life, Brand is left with rending doubt regarding the life he has led and whether, indeed, his actions might not have been inimical to his professed ideal.

Peer Gynt, the companion piece which followed two years later, has the hero living by the motto of the trolls, "to your self be enough,"[6] spending his life in compromise and self-gratification, devoid of ideals and without any clearcut pattern to his life. When, at the end of his life, the button-molder—an allegorical incarnation of death—appears to inquire what he has done with his life, Peer Gynt, lacking for an answer, is thrown into a panic.

Between the two of them, Brand and Peer Gynt serve to establish the canon of human variability in Ibsen's dramas.[7] Brand, who is characterized by austere idealism, is all superego, totally harnessed to obligation and undeviating in his direction, while Peer Gynt is all id, unbridled freedom and non-direction.

Peer Gynt, in fact, can be seen as an example of Sartre's *mauvaise foi.* He is the inauthentic man who flees from or denies his identity, rushing from one experience to another, never exhausting the potentialities of any and rarely involving himself in anything that goes beyond the transitory. Thus his aimless quest leads him all over the world in a flight from himself. The verdict of the button-molder is, "Yourself is just what you've never been." Gynt, whose life has consisted of temporary roles, is compared with an onion of many layers without a core.

> The Gyntian self—it's an army corps
> Of wishes, appetites, desires.
> The Gyntian self is a churning sea
> Of whims, demands, necessities—
> In short, whatever moves my soul. . . .

The Gyntian self, then, lives completely on a narcissistic level and is indifferent to responsibility or continuity. There is no prolonged striving; self-interest predominates at all times and hedonism is the strongest of enticements. Peer Gynt does, however, have some saving graces: he projects exuberance as well as a joy of life that are completely lacking in Brand. He is gifted with imagination and playfulness and makes of life an adventure, none of which enters into Brand's scheme of things. Despite all of his faults, Peer Gynt is saved in the end by the love of a woman, Solveig, in a variation of the Gretchen motif in Goethe's *Faust* and *The Flying Dutchman.* By contrast, Brand, the dour man of God, is buried in an avalanche moments after he cries out, "If not by Will, how can man be redeemed?" and is answered by a voice through the thunder, "He is the God of Love."[8] It would seem that the truth

Peer Gynt's Solveig is intended to symbolize corresponds to the principle of love and redemption from which Brand had cut himself off.

Brand is as far removed from the Sartrian *salaud* as one could imagine. That which is ethical is for him a categorical imperative, and far from living by a double standard, his demands on himself are always greater than those he asks of others. Unlike Peer Gynt who is a perpetual opportunist and a chronic liar, Brand is unflinching in standing up for what he sees as the truth and he has in great abundance the self-mastery so pitifully lacking in his counterpart. While Peer Gynt is forever squandering his energies, Brand never loses sight of his goal. The total mobilization of his powers makes Brand a nearly irresistible force, and indeed, he strives to realize his ideal "To be wholly oneself," which admits of no diffusion of identity. But the very knowledge of his sincerity and the self-assurance which derives from it become destructive, for sincerity grown fanatical is a virtue often shared by tyrants and monomaniacs. Brand is lacking in human sympathy and little moved by the suffering of those who do not share his views. His lofty mission in life serves to make him forbidding and unapproachable. As the totally inner-directed man, Brand's self is overdetermined, with no place for empathy. He is unable to relate to what he is not or, for that matter, to be anything other than the reformer with a mission. He has no alternative but to subject everyone he comes in contact with to his ascetic regime of total order and principle. The passion that rules Brand's life results inevitably in his having to assert control not only over himself but others as well. Thus, while Peer Gynt is constantly opening himself to new and unexpected possibilities at the expense of direction, Brand, through his constant control, is closing out prospects and thereby also the leavening of humor and irony. Brand's soul becomes an incarnation of the "Ice Church" referred to in the play.

Both plays, that of the reformer and the drifter, are statements of misspent lives and the failure of synthesis. Brand is locked into himself and the victim of his inner dictates, while Peer Gynt is the prey of constant dispersion. Brand and Peer Gynt, with their mutually exclusive life styles and diametrically opposed tensions, represent the seminal forces that inform the searching introspective plays of the dramatist's late years.

Solness, the architect, Borkman, the banker, and Rubek, the artist, have reached their sixties and are looking back on lives which were given over entirely to the ruthless exercise of ambition. Although all three remain seemingly vigorous and assertive, they are marked by the inroads of age and their period of meaningful achievement is clearly behind them. Solness no longer builds churches, but rather devotes himself to the lesser challenge of constructing houses. Rubek, a renowned sculptor, has long since completed the masterpiece that made him famous and taken to fashioning busts of people he despises. And Borkman, who years ago was engaged in a gigantic financial and industrial project that would have changed the face of Northern Europe, was convicted and imprisoned for embezzlement and has since spent many years sequestered in his home, waiting for the day when he will be called back, as he sees it, to run the financial affairs of his country.

The three men have in common their lowly beginnings and the fact that they see themselves as self-made men. Solness started out as a poor boy from the country and reached the top of his profession. Borkman is a miner's son who used to go down with his father to the pits. Rubek's background is not alluded to directly, but it is clear that, in contrast to his present opulence, his early years were spent in indigence. Over-compensation, then, appears to be one of the elements that would explain why these men are so driven.

There is also a barely suggested sense of self-doubt in Solness and Borkman, which, in the manner of intensely competitive men, they strive to extinguish through achievement. Otherwise, all three talk of the sense of power and overweening confidence that they felt in themselves in their youth, feelings that were fired by the heady sense of ambition. "I was so unshakably certain of victory," Borkman affirms.[9] He, like the others, lived with powerful images of himself: "I was about to sail across an uncharted and perilous ocean." The craving for success represents an immense longing for these men, a consuming desire that fills their beings. "My lust for power was overwhelming," Borkman says. For Solness the feeling was so urgent that he feels it was ordained: "Don't you think . . . there are people singled out by fate who . . . desire [something] so passionately that, ultimately, they must be granted it?"[10]

All three have lived by the motto that Brand gave voice to—"All or Nothing"—both in their commitment to and their desire for accomplishment, but with the difference that for Solness, Borkman and Rubek, it is the world that offers the rewards they seek. To insure the realization of their goals, each of these men has entered into an equivalent of the Faustian pact with the devil, selling their affective soul for the sake of the magic power of achievement. "I struck the bargain," Borkman says, meaning he renounced the woman he loved so that his would-be rival would back him in his endeavors and further his cause. Solness makes it clear that he has substituted his profession for his life: "The terrible price I had to pay . . . —to be able to build homes for others I had to renounce all hope of having a home of my own." And in a statement that seems to partake of wishful thinking, he remarks that the early death of his two infant children, which he sees as God's will, was a prerequisite of his success: "It was so that I should have nothing to bind me. No love or happiness or anything, you see. I was to be a master builder—nothing else. And all my life was to be spent building for Him." Rubek, too, makes clear that to succeed meant that he was never to involve himself in life: "I was convinced," he tells the girl he had loved and who served as his model in his distant youth, "if I desired you sensually, my vision would be profaned so that I would never be able to achieve what I was striving after."

In order to buttress themselves in an ethic which laid personal happiness on the altar of ambition and to sustain the relentless discipline, control and perpetual sublimation their way of life demanded, each character, either explicitly or implicitly, makes reference to the grandeur of his mission in life. In what amounts to a commentary on this kind of personality, Freud, who, incidentally, looked upon Ibsen as one of his favorite playwrights, describes the situation in which an individual seemingly transforms what would

otherwise be unbearable for him by engaging in a brand of wishful thinking which becomes central to his reality.[11] The hardships and resistance that Ibsen's achievers have to overcome are themselves signs of mastery and afford a sense of self. Similarly, the strenuousness of these men's endeavors and the harshness of their self-abnegation become measures of achievement. Sacrifice is turned into ennoblement and renunciation leads to self-aggrandizement and an apotheosis of the self. Living with their conviction of having been specially chosen has served to make these characters egocentric, domineering and arrogant. Brand is at one point forced to admit that he saw himself as the greatest of men and the same holds true for Solness, Borkman and Rubek.

For each, life has been not merely a matter of conquering but also destroying, as their egos became a devouring force that consumed those around them. Borkman says, " . . . I could spare neither family nor friend—I had to *take*. . . ." There is no place for equals in the lives of these men, with the result that others are used and depreciated. Nowhere is this clearer than in the relations these men have with their women. Borkman and Rubek have betrayed the women they loved and married others to whom they are indifferent. Solness married the woman whose estate he used to advance his career. These women whom Borkman and Rubek abandoned, as well as the one whom Solness made his wife, have withered and been sapped of life. One's profession, not one's woman, is the deeper bond; hence Borkman can maintain, " . . . if need be, one woman can be replaced by another. . . ." When Rubek had no further use for the model he was so attached to, he forgot her. Because women have demands of their own which can stand in the way of achievement, Borkman states angrily, "Women! They corrupt and pervert our lives. They deflect us from our destinies, rob us of our triumphs." Solness, in like manner, finds, "Everything I have created . . . I must [pay for] not only with my happiness, but with the happiness of others too. . . . [My wife] had to be destroyed and annihilated so that I could follow my calling and gain a—a kind of triumph." Thus success is a form of active aggression in which some must be humbled so that others can rise.

As long as there was forward movement in their careers and a feeling of climbing "toward the heights," a phrase that Borkman uses, their way of life brought its desired rewards and the rigidity and oppressiveness of their self-imposed *habitus* were tolerable. None of the three, however, can cope with the advent of age which brings with it a loss of former mastery and power. At this point each finds himself beset by fears that until then have been held successfully in check. Borkman clings to an illusion of new accomplishments, saying in the midst of his brooding, "Life still lies ahead of me," while holding on harder than ever to the memory of the man he once was. Solness, when confronted with the wish of his apprentice, whom he has so long held back, to strike out on his own, responds with near panic: "I shall never make way for anyone! Not of my own free will. Never, never!" In order to maintain power over his apprentice, whom he sees as indispensable, Solness has manipulated the man's father and fiancee, both of whom he keeps in his employ for this purpose.

But with advancing age the tightly held cohesion of the self starts to crumble and all three men, feeling that they are no longer fully in command, show signs of obvious stress. Solness, in a projection of his feelings about himself, thinks (falsely as it turns out) that others look upon him as deranged. Earlier forms of self-identification begin to break down and former goals lose their meaning. Rubek feels that the greatness of his past achievement no longer counts, having been blotted out by time, and voices his disillusionment by rejecting as empty and hollow the vocation of the artist which in the past had given direction to his life. Most damaging of all, he makes it clear that he has lost his passion for work.[12] All three also feel tormented by ill-defined guilt and are given to a self-torturing introspection, which makes a burden of memory and the past a source of self-reproach. The women of all three men feel that they have led wasted lives, and their behavior makes it clear that the affective sides of their personality have not been nurtured. At one point or another each man responds with the equivalent of Solness's anguished self-defense: "I can't do otherwise. . . . I am what I am. And I can't create myself anew." But he, like the others, ends up with a feeling of having lived in vain: " . . . when all the accounts are closed, I have been nothing really . . . It all adds up to nothing. Nothing. Nothing." Rubek, in similar fashion, speaks of "remorse for a forfeited life."

But when men who have defined themselves exclusively through achievement and recognition negate their reason for being with the cry of *vanitas,* the control that preserved them may be turning into self-destruction. The long submergence of the instinctual life and the revulsion over the substitute existence they had contented themselves with means that the total control of Brand gives way to the utter self-surrender of Peer Gynt. The first clear sign that this is happening occurs when these men start to yield to emotions they had previously repressed. The power and preeminence these men have achieved were attained at the cost of isolation, and isolation now becomes a source of anxiety. These men who identified their lives with the momentum of their activity now experience a sense of passivity and a starvation of emotions. Solness, who like Borkman has maintained distance from his wife, confides: "What I feel so keenly—almost painfully—is the need for someone who is close to me."

Each of the three men turns to the equivalent of Peer Gynt's Solveig in what Ibsen intends to be seen as a reaching out for an archetype of sustenance and replenishment of life. Rubek tells Irene, who reenters his life after decades of absence, "I have been waiting for you. For years. Without knowing it." "Help me to start living again!" Borkman tells the woman he had loved but deserted, "We two belong together, Ella: you and I." And Solness makes a similar declaration to Hilde, a young woman of twenty-two who unexpectedly enters his life. Each man attempts to enact what is expressed in *Little Eyolf,* the fourth play of Ibsen's old age, namely "to fill [the] emptiness with something. Something resembling love."[13]

How convincing is this late attempt at redress on the part of Solness, Borkman and Rubek? Are they perhaps filling the emptiness not with love but with

what might seem to resemble it, the self-love of the would-be survivor, and thereby only displaying a further example of their underlying egoism? The question arises because the endings of the three plays are the only elements in them that are not entirely convincing. Solness can at best be responding to an intoxication of the senses brought on by a young woman more than forty years his junior. Rubek's long-lost love is a desperately troubled woman who seems not likely at this late stage to be able to fulfill his expectations. Only Borkman's Ella would seem to be a fitting mate, but a degenerative illness, for which Borkman is at least in part responsible, leaves her only a short time to live.

In any case, the declaration of love is in each instance tantamount to extinction because death follows immediately afterwards. Hilde, by taking the place of Solness's obsession, becomes herself an obsession to the point where he tells her, "I begin to think there is no part of me that is safe from you." At her urging and against his better judgment, he climbs, in an act of self-abandonment, to the top of the tower he has built in order to hang a wreath, only to fall to his death. Borkman, in the company of Ella who admonishes him of his folly, rushes out of his home in a storm and dies of a stroke. Rubek and Irene, who find themselves on a mountainside in the midst of a mounting storm, ignore warnings to take cover and, like Brand, die in an avalanche.

All three men are involved in climbing as they meet their end. In symbolic terms they are engaged in an effort at self-transcendance and reaching out for a fatal attempt at freedom; but by breaking their old bonds, they also destroy themselves. In their final acts they do what they always did—they strive against the elements. Thus, in this final confrontation with life, they have still not made peace with themselves. The attempt to undo what they always stood for leads not to a new synthesis but rather to a specious *Liebestod.* Having ruled emotion out of their lives, they are destroyed by emotions they can no longer govern. What seems like atonement in these characters becomes self-rejection. The end of their lives is marked by the disgust which, as Erik Erikson has pointed out, mars a person's old age when he finds himself incapable of achieving a "wise integrity."

Thomas Mann's assessment of *When We Dead Awaken*—that it is a ghastly confession by a man who has lived entirely for his work and ends up too late in making his declaration of love to life—[14] applies equally to the other two plays under discussion. There is a deep-lying pessimism in these plays, an implication that genuine fulfillment is not really attainable. But even more disturbing is the suggestion that perhaps Solness, Borkman and Rubek never had any options from the beginning. Their Mephistophelian pact may not have been entered into as a matter of choice but of necessity. It is possible that for all three men a precariously held self and the fear of integration with others made it inevitable that they would attempt to buttress themselves by seeking out positions of dominance which would enable them to be the master of others and thereby keep them at a distance. All three at various times cry out, as Borkman did about the act which led to his imprisonment, " . . . I had to do it . . . because I was myself—because I was John Gabriel Borkman. . . . "

Or is it a rule of life that unparalleled performance in one area entails at least a partial failure in others, as suggested in two lines by William Butler Yeats:

> The intellect of man is forced to choose
> Perfection of the life or of the work.[15]

Aldous Huxley once remarked about a fellow Englishman that he was "one of those great men for whom one feels intensely sorry, because he was nothing but a great man."[16] One recalls Irene's reproach to Rubek, "...you were ... only an artist, not a man."

Ibsen's characters, while unbalanced in their orientation to life, require no special effort at comprehension on our part because they are not really alien to the world with which we are familiar. By contrast, the intensity of hopelessness to which Beckett's characters are subject is so extreme that we are likely to experience it personally only in occasional attacks of severe depression. Ibsen's characters are doers and they define themselves through that fact as well as through their professions, their status, and their achievement. Beckett's characters are loosely anchored in life; no profession, no occupation requires their daily application, thus leaving them infinitely free to engage in the contemplation of self which was foreign to Solness, Borkman and Rubek until they collided with the impasse of old age. For Ibsen's characters, life is legitimized by struggle and accomplishment, while those of Beckett do not struggle overtly with life but never really accept it either. Because Ibsen's characters live for a future of total attainment, the present for them is no more than a waystation, while Beckett's live in a deadening present that makes the prospect of the future seem still more oppressive and intolerable. His characters have been run over by life and their sense of self is badly eroded. If Ibsen's characters are poised for conquest, Beckett's, having abandoned hope, are predestined to defeat.

Whereas the lives of Ibsen's characters debouch into an old age in which work and illusion no longer serve to buoy them up, Beckett's cast of characters live their lives in a state of perpetual disaffection that makes striving and not striving equally irrelevant. No one in Ibsen's gallery of old men is portrayed as feeble or debilitated. By contrast, the dotards in Beckett's plays are moving constantly to a more advanced stage of decomposition and a deepening sense of unjoyous bafflement. These oldsters are out of sympathy with themselves, dealing with their meaninglessness and corporeal decay ironically and jeeringly. No author has dealt with old age more disturbingly than Samuel Beckett, for whom suffering takes on the expression of farce. And hardly anyone has proposed a more acerbic remedy for human needs: the height of wisdom "consists not in the satisfaction but in the ablation of desire."[17]

Life offers no prizes to Beckett's down-and-outers and his mime play *Act Without Words II* establishes that neither the go-getter nor the laggard is ever awarded anything for his struggle. Aside from this playlet, Beckett has seldom depicted anyone who is greedy for life's rewards and certainly no one who has

made heavy demands on himself in the process.

There is a mime play, however, that stands as a paradigm for Beckett's view of creation. *Act Without Words I* runs to eight and one-half pages in very large print and took about twenty-five minutes to perform when I saw it staged a number of years ago in Paris. The setting is: "Desert. Dazzling light."[18] The barrenness of the set stands for the starkness and essential nakedness of the human condition which is about to be symbolically enacted. Aloneness is represented as a world without shelter and the glaring light suggests the impossibility of refuge or escape.

The stage directions read: "The man is flung backwards on the stage from right wing. He falls, gets up immediately, dusts himself, turns aside, reflects." The fact that he is flung backwards onto the stage makes it apparent that the figure is not entering the world of his free will. Rather, this act of symbolic birth is an enactment of Heidegger's *Geworfensein*; one is thrown into a world of deprivation in which one immediately suffers a blow. Still, the figure rises immediately, pauses to assess the situation, and prepares himself for his next move:

> Whistle from right wing.
>
> He reflects, goes out right. Immediately flung back on stage he falls, gets up immediately, dusts himself, turns aside, reflects.

The whistle, which will issue forth its shrill command throughout the play, is a prod to action. One is prodded into activity by instinct, by training, by social pressure or by coercion from others. The figure's reflection marks him as attempting to draw inferences from his experience and relates him to the orderly Cartesian world of *cogito ergo sum.* The world, however, obviously does not function in the reasoned manner he would attribute to it and deals him a further blow for his pains.

Several repetitions of this action and repeated attempts at learning from his rude experiences soon have the figure growing doubtful about his ability to master a refractory and hostile world seemingly bent on frustrating him at every turn and making his struggle into a mockery.

In further bits of action a tree, with its promise of shade, descends from the flies, followed by other useful implements as well as a bottle of water. Each time the man attempts to avail himself of these objects they are withdrawn just beyond his grasp. He is then offered implements that might enable him to reach what is just beyond his finger tips, only to be foiled once again. It might appear as though the figure is reenacting the attempt at mastery of humankind's first tools, but in this rendition no mastery is possible. When everything fails he attempts suicide, but that possibility is also denied him. By the end of the mime the figure lies prostrate and unmoving. The bottle of water descends from the flies and dangles about his face, but he ignores it as well as the tree which is again offered. He has stopped responding to the whistle, and the water as well as the tree disappear. The figure lies supine, apparently impervious to any temptation that pretends to preserve life and

carry on the business of living. As the curtain drops, he contemplates his hands which, together with his mind, have proven powerless to assure survival. None of his responses proved effective, the will itself has been paralyzed, and the life cycle draws to an end, its sole lesson being that the resources of life are unobtainable. What remains is an image of T. S. Eliot's "Hollow Man": "Paralyzed force, gesture without motion. . . ."[19]

It is significant that Beckett's pantomime is enacted without emotion and with none of the frenzied activity which animates Kafka's tortured heroes. Kafka's characters are consumed with anxiety because they go on living to the end with the illusion that a final last effort might extricate them from their dilemma. The figure in *Act Without Words I* has, for his part, established by trial and error that there is no way to deal with life, just as there is no escape from it. Kafka's leading characters frequently end up in exhaustion and despair. The paradigm character in Beckett does not consume himself, rather his forces are slowly eaten away until, devoid of strength, he subsides into impotent resignation.

In the same way that Brand and Peer Gynt contain the psychic source material of a good deal that Ibsen wrote later on, the opening pages of Beckett's long essay on Proust, which he published eighteen years before he was to write his first play, offers a key to the understanding of the dramatic works which were to follow. Beckett exposes a claustrophobic vision under the guise of analyzing the author of *A la recherche du temps perdu*: "Proust's creatures . . . are victims of [their] predominating condition and circumstance—Time; . . . There is no escape from the hours and the days. Neither from tomorrow nor from yesterday . . . because yesterday has deformed us, or been deformed by us."[20] Beckett intones a dirge on the calamities perpetrated by time. The "Time cancer," as he calls it, has as its content "the boredom of living [which at times is replaced] by the suffering of being." Time, which is totally organized in the lives of Ibsen's achievers, becomes engulfment and demobilization in Beckett. In the later works of Ibsen as well as those of Beckett, however, time is equal to life and although the responses by the characters of each author are radically different, what is done with time represents in each case a basic adjustment that is intended to deal with the underlying intolerableness of life. The adjustment in each instance takes the form of a pact. The pact that Ibsen's characters have entered into in the name of attainment finds its explicit counterpart in Beckett: "Habit is a compromise effected between the individual and his environment. . . . Habit is the ballast that chains the dog to his vomit. . . . Life is habit [and] the pact must be continually renewed. . . ." Ibsen's characters have made their pact at great personal cost, but in anticipation of the reward of future attainment. Beckett's characters have no rewards in store for them, but the emptiness which is life is made bearable for them by the anodyne effect of habit. The endless reworking of the same routines in Beckett attests to the eternal repetition of habit which enables them to cope with boredom and suffering.

" . . . what is attainment?" Beckett asks in the same essay. "The iden-

tification of the subject with the object of his desire," we read; "The subject has died—and perhaps many times—on the way." Beckett grasps here what Ibsen's characters learn only when it is too late—the self that is to be crowned with success will, by the time it reaches its goal, no longer be the same person that started on the quest. But Beckett's insight into the problematic nature of attainment translates itself in his dramas into defeatism: the rejection by Beckett's characters of everything that could pass for illusion results in their making no investment of libido in the act of living. There is a suggestion of profound metaphysical gloom in Beckett, but one which excludes the supernatural and is devoid of faith. The only possible meaning in such a life might be found in intense religiosity, but this too is denied Beckett's characters, who instead give vent in *Waiting for Godot* and *Endgame* to explosive rage against God who has failed them because he does not exist.

Our "smug will to live," Beckett tells us, merely exemplifies our "pernicious and incurable optimism." The prime cause of all our sorrows is "that double-headed monster of damnation and salvation—Time." Although salvation here means life come to an end, no value is to be put on death, for "Whatever opinion we may be pleased to hold on the subject of death, we may be sure that it is meaningless and valueless."

In two successive pages of one of Beckett's prose works one reads, "life is a long . . . road, destination tomb,"[21] and "all dies so fast, no sooner born . . . ." The "long road" transcribes itself in Beckett's plays into the seemingly interminable process of waiting, yet there are statements in his dramas of an incredible compression of time in which the act of life and death are coextensive. In *Waiting for Godot* Pozzo, replying to a question regarding time, says, "Have you not done tormenting me with your accursed time! It's abominable! . . . one day [Lucky] went dumb, one day I went blind, one day we'll go deaf, one day we were born, one day we shall die, the same day, the same second. . . . They give birth astride of a grave, the light gleams an instant, then it's night once more." Vladimir responds in antiphonic fashion with language of Shakespearean power: "Astride of a grave and a difficult birth. Down in the hole, lingeringly, the grave-digger puts on the forceps. We have time to grow old. The air is full of our cries. . . . But habit is a great deadener." Beckett has continued to contract the metaphoric distance of birth and death to the point that in *Breath,* one of his later plays in which objects and sounds take the place of human beings, an inhalation and an exhalation following shortly on one another represent the interval between the womb and the tomb.

In Beckett's plays the time of one's waiting between birth and death is not assuaged in any meaningful fashion by human contact. The most that is offered is the physical presence of the other. The following exchange in *Endgame* is typical:

> Hamm: Why do you stay with me?
> Clov: Why do you keep me?
> Hamm: There's no one else.
> Clov: There's no one else.[22]

The relationship of Hamm and Clov is that of master and servant, which is also true of Pozzo and Lucky in *Waiting for Godot.* Husband and wife teams like Nell and Nagg in *Endgame* and Winnie and Willie in *Happy Days* as well as Mr. and Mrs. Rooney in *All that Fall* are crankily ill assorted, lacking in mutual comprehension, and bound to each other by inertia and a low level of symbiosis. Friendship also fails to be a source of meaning; Vladimir and Estragon in *Waiting for Godot,* for example, exasperatedly tell each other a number of times they are going to part, even though they never bring it off.

The play *Happy Days* exemplifies Beckett's basic situation of characters cast as clowns, playing out their miserable lot not with pathos but compulsive cheerfulness, as though in illustration of a point made in *Endgame:* "Nothing is funnier than unhappiness." While playing with the contents of her purse which serve as the symbols of life's daily trifles, Winnie is ensconced in a mound of earth up to her breasts in the first act. In the second act she is already buried up to her neck. Throughout it all she keeps up a steady patter of trivia while the decrepit Willy, who cannot stand upright, occasionally crawls about on his hands and knees behind the mound and at rare intervals delivers himself of a few words. The mechanical nature of Winnie's cheerfulness is pointed up by the repeated stage direction, "Happy expression off," as well as her constant rationalizing, "not a day goes by . . . without some blessing . . . ,"[23] at which point, in vaudeville fashion, Willie collapses.

The forced cheerfulness of the polyanna is never far from depression and hopelessness, as revealed in rare moments by such a statement as "the happy day to come when flesh melts at so many degrees . . . That's what I find so comforting when I lose heart and envy the brute beast." In referring to the mostly invisible presence of Willie and the fact that once in a while he even listens to her, she says, "That is what enables me to go on, go on talking, that is." Winnie, with her compulsive talk, is engaging in the sole activity that occupies Beckett's cast of characters: she is killing time. It is their way of defending themselves against boredom and the pain of existence, their clowning being a variation on precisely these themes.

The characters' intolerable existence in an uninhabitable world is further emphasized by their state of confinement. Here Beckett makes use of visual metaphors in contrast to Ibsen's use of symbols. Thus Hamm is tied to his wheelchair. His mother and father, Nagg and Nell, live in garbage cans. Winnie is embedded in a mound of earth. The characters in *Play* are implanted in urns. And with few exceptions, even those who do have use of their legs do not go anywhere. The immobility of all these characters is a statement of their paralysis of will and the impasse in which they find themselves.

In Beckett's world man's life is ruled by a fatalism which he cannot comprehend, from which no meaning is to be derived, and from which there is no escape. As Hamm puts it, " . . . you're on earth, there's no cure for that!"[24] Man is cast as victim pure and simple and the occasional victimizers, like Hamm and Pozzo, are themselves victimized by time and life. God Himself becomes a metaphor of hopelessness and the allusion to a life after death is turned into a sardonic joke. Clov asks Hamm, "Do you believe in the life to

come?" and gets a wisecrack for his pains: "Mine was always that." Having neither God nor will to turn to and no appetite for life, Beckett's characters move back and forth between the tight confines of inertia and paralysis, waiting for the freedom of extinction. The first line of *Endgame* has Clov saying, "Finished, it's finished, nearly finished, it must be nearly finished." The rest of the play consists of variations of the same theme: life is coming to an end and with it, the suffering of existence.

In *Oedipus at Colonus* Sophocles has the hero pronounce with solemn grandeur:

> Never to have been born is much the best;
> and the next best, by far,
> To return thence, by the way speediest,
> Where our beginnings are.[25]

Oedipus arrived at this point of view after a long life of titanic struggle with himself and the world and after having left his imprint on everyone he encountered. Beckett's characters, who capitulated before they even set out, have written life off without ever having gotten involved with it.

Of all his plays, *Krapp's Last Tape* is the closest that Beckett has allowed himself to come in portraying a dramatic character with a definable past. It also appears to be the only play by this author in which the central character has a personal history that serves to depict him in depth. Like all of Beckett's characters, Krapp is waiting for extinction while living out his life in hopelessness. But unlike the other plays, this one has scenes in which the main character dared for a time to hope, and he even continues to do so at intervals against his own wishes. It should also be pointed out that this play conveys one of the most powerful portraits of aging in world literature.

Krapp, on his sixty-ninth birthday, is engaged in doing what he does every year on that day—he listens to old tape recordings on which he has registered the events of the past and summarizes on a new tape what has occurred in the year gone by. The contrast in the voices of Krapp in the past to that of the man on the stage is a startling testimony to the ravages of age. Krapp has undergone a merciless series of reductions. His intellect has faded and his non-physical appetites have almost died. He has grown deaf and myopic, he talks with a broken voice and walks with difficulty. His memory has faded to the point that he no longer grasps the meaning of certain words he used previously.

Most of the time Krapp sits at his table which is illuminated by a strong white light, but periodically he moves out into the darkness which envelops the rest of the stage. Light and dark suggest life and extinction, while the tapes represent the attempt to find direction and the meaning of life. In addition, the recordings mark Krapp's effort to fix time and preserve the fleeting quality of existence.

It is appropriate that Krapp, who has placed such a high value on words and their preservation, is, like many of the characters in Beckett's novels, a writer,

although one who has lost his literary power and no longer sees any meaning in creativity. Since the present offers him so little, he subsists on the past, a proclivity that has been with him for the greater part of his life. As the play's title indicates, soon all of Krapp's life will belong to the past. As if in anticipation, Krapp sings to himself, "Now the day is over, night is drawing nigh. . . ."[26]

Krapp, like the hero in the old morality play *Everyman,* is in effect accounting for his life and taking stock of himself in the face of death. In both works there is the suggestion that something surpassingly significant has been left out of life and the protagonists are groping to find out what it was.

Three powerfully evocative scenes emerge from the past in *Krapp's Last Tape.* Encapsulated in a tape labeled "the black ball," which the old Krapp cannot even recall until he plays it, is the story of his mother's death. The Krapp of yesteryear sits on a bench near a stream in a biting wind and in sight of the window behind which his mother lies dying. He distracts himself with an unsuccessful attempt at flirtation and by tossing a ball to a little white dog. Finally, the blind goes down in his mother's window. The text of this part of the tape reads: "All over and done with, at last. I sat on for a few moments with the ball in my hand and the dog yelping and pawing at me. (*Pause.*) Moments. Her moments, my moments. (*Pause.*) The dog's moments. (*Pause*). In the end I held it out to him and he took it in his mouth, gently, gently. A small, old, black, hard, solid rubber ball. (*Pause.*) I shall feel it, in my hand, until my dying day. (*Pause.*) I might have kept it. (*Pause.*) But I gave it to the dog."

The black ball becomes an objective *non*-correlative, if I may alter T. S. Eliot's famous phrase. For Krapp, who apparently chose not to be present at his mother's death, fondling the black ball was the closest he could come to expressing mourning and giving the ball to the dog was his only way of opening himself up to loss. Since it was impossible for him to respond to his feelings directly, he took an emotional detour and moved back to his accustomed preoccupations with the self. In the play this is suggested by his concern with his bowel movements and by the fact that his conversation is mostly directed to himself.

The second tape, which is labeled "Memorable Equinox," has Krapp at thirty-nine years of age experiencing a revelation of existential force:

> Spiritually a year of profound gloom and indigence until that memorable night in March, at the end of the jetty, in the howling wind, never to be forgotten, when suddenly I saw the whole thing. The vision, at last. This I fancy is what I have chiefly to record this evening against the day when my work will be done and perhaps no place left in my memory, warm or cold, for the miracle that . . . (*hesitates*) . . . for the fire that set it alight. What I suddenly saw then was this, that the belief I had been going on all my life, namely—(*Krapp switches off impatiently, winds tape forward, switches on again*)—great granite rocks the foam flying in the light of the

> lighthouse and the wind-gauge spinning like a propeller, clear to me at last that the dark I have always struggled to keep under is in reality my most—(*Krapp curses, switches off, winds tape forward, switches on again*)—unshatterable association until my dissolution of storm and night with the light of the understanding and the fire. . . ."

Here Krapp curses and switches to a different tape.

The "profound gloom" that Krapp refers to is an expression of the feelings of imprisonment, human isolation, and meaninglessness which had been oppressing him. It is apparent that the intensity of his need for some kind of relief led to the experience of a breakthrough in which the barrier between self and object was overcome and a revelation of synthesis and meaning took place. But the elderly Krapp, as cramped and shut off as ever, has to protect himself from that seeming epiphany because he continues to be mired in the familiar gloom of the past.

The third tape, "Farewell to love," is one that Krapp has listened to and discussed on tape at various times over the years. It documents the love relationship in his younger years with Bianca whom he left, as the tape indicates, in order to devote himself entirely to the book he was writing. The break with a lover is a leitmotif that runs through many of Beckett's works, including *Murphy, More Pricks Than Kicks* and "First Love." In a delicate and moving passage which has no parallel in Beckett's other works, Krapp and Bianca drift in a boat on a lake past midnight. Krapp informs her that he thought "it was hopeless and no good going on," and then tenderly makes love to her: "I lay down across her with my face in her breasts and my hand on her. We lay there without moving. But under us all moved, and moved us, gently, up and down, and from side to side."

Like Ibsen's characters, Krapp has used his works as an excuse to forego meaningful human relationships. One learns that the "opus magnum" (Krapp's ironic phrase) was completed, and sold all of seventeen copies. Just as the frozen emotions of Krapp were incapable of expressing grief when his mother died, he was at a loss to hold on to a love relationship that represented a peak experience in his life. In both instances the retreat from closeness is a statement of human impoverishment. The younger Krapp and the older one insist that the relationship with Bianca was best put to an end, yet each continues to be haunted by her through the years, thus making it clear that no one ever really took her place. Self-discovery has not occurred, the lifelong colloquy with the self has led to nothing, and the collection of tapes with their compilation of fractured memories represents the only continuity this man has achieved.

Krapp is at various times peevish and ill-tempered, breaking out in anger at the supposed "fool" he used to be. The misdirected rage reveals the guilty obsession of not having fully lived, of having turned away from the vague, unaccepted awareness that he had always been an accomplice in the barrenness of his existence. The scene at the lighthouse suggests that the storm of his life was never allowed to surface, that always he was keeping something

from coming to light. The old Krapp, in making his last tape, mumbles, "Sometimes wondered in the night if a last effort mightn't—(*Pause.*) Ah finish your booze now and get to your bed." Krapp, forever dealing with unfinished business, ends up listening to a replay of the episode with Bianca until the tape runs out. The final line in the play before the curtain falls has *"Krapp motionless staring before him. The tape runs on in silence."* It is significant that Krapp stares into darkness and that the tape and not the actor ends the show.

The fatalism that Beckett's characters live by and which makes them non-functioning in life can be construed in a number of different ways that complement rather than exclude each other. There is the Pythagorean view, for which Plato is a source, that interrelates *soma*—body, and *sema*—the tomb. The body is a tomb, matter is evil, and the soul yearns to be set free. In Beckett's terms this would mean the world is uninhabitable because man's body is a charnel house.

The paralysis of Beckett's figures can also be seen as the despair that arises from acedia, the medieval concept of the spiritual apathy of those who, having taken holy orders, find themselves cut off from the source of their faith. In theological terms this is a form of sin that expresses itself in the refusal to love or be loved. Such people are fated to be consigned to the Christian hell of damnation.

A modern diagnosis, expressed in psychological terms, might explain the psychic affliction in question as an obsessive neurosis, and indeed, one of Beckett's French critics has characterized his point of view in this matter: *"la névrose est erigée en règle d'existence. . . .*"[27] Beckett's work is, indeed, neurosis raised to the level of universal existence. The infinitude of creation and possibility has been canceled out in Beckett's work in favor of a consuming nightmare of creeping extinction overtaking ill-defined characters largely lacking in human content. In *Endgame* Hamm refers to a friend as a convincing example of such an outlook, although he could just as well be talking about himself: "I once knew a madman who thought the end of the world had come. He was a painter and engraver. . . . I used to go and see him in the asylum. I'd take him by the hand and drag him to the window. Look! There! All that rising corn! And there! Look! The sails of the herring fleet! All that loveliness! . . . He'd snatch away his hand and go back into his corner. Appalled. All he had seen was ashes."

In contrast to such an orientation, Ibsen's characters, who climb steeples, brave snowstorms and look out on enormous vistas (as did Borkman just before he died), represent a fearful grandeur which is ennobling even when it is overwhelming. Unlike Beckett's characters who have never experienced the world as object and whose attitude is one of submission and surrender, those of Ibsen have known the self-confidence that comes from successfully pursuing the path they laid out for themselves. As the narrator of one of Beckett's prose works says, "I have never in my life been on my way anywhere, but simply on my way."[28] Beckett's characters, by reaching out for nothing, end up being lost to life and their non-involvement leaves them nothing to live for. Although

on the surface they seem to be making no claims on themselves or others, in reality they are asking for infinitely more than Ibsen's characters, namely that Godot should come and that the universe be put in order. In addition, the lifetime of misery and despair that Beckett's characters have suffered is every bit as strenuous and full of privation as that led by Ibsen's, while lacking in the rewards of the latter.

The work ethic of Solness, Borkman and Rubek recalls the piercing cry of Oswald in Ibsen's drama *Ghosts*: "Never to be able to work again! . . . To be dead while I'm still alive. . . . can you imagine anything so dreadful?"[29] This is a statement of terror which conveys the anguish of being deprived of one's mainstay in life. Ibsen's heroes, by equating work with life (Borkman says explicitly, "Life is work . . ."), have been marked by a *déformation professionelle,* a one-sided development in which part of their faculties and human qualities was left unnurtured and hence in a state of atrophy. One result of their one-sided accommodation to life is that they are left with hardly any resources for coping with old age and the prospect of death. Solness, Borkman and Rubek have lived with an illusion of immortality which turns into growing disquiet as the time approaches for them to give up their work. These men, who lived by the self-affirmation of their professional selves, suddenly find they no longer have anything to buoy themselves up. The anxiety that overtakes them in their late years when they are having to accept their comparative state of powerlessness for the first time stems from their clouded realization that life has not been lived.

At this point, when their energies are gradually being depleted and the commitment to work is not there to defend them against helplessness, Ibsen's characters subside into the forlorn state of Beckett's characters. In both cases they are paying the price of non-involvement and suffering from having missed out in life; both are left with emotional aridness and a state of non-contact.

Beckett quotes Proust as saying, "One lies all one's life long . . . notably to those that love one, and above all to that stranger whose contempt would cause one most pain—oneself." The characters of both authors have furnished themselves with an alibi for having deprived themselves of that which they most severely lacked. As a matter of fact, each has chosen unremittingly that which became the content of his life; ambition at the price of larger fulfillment on one hand and the uniqueness of metaphysical despair on the other. Krapp, no less than Solness, Borkman and Rubek, has taken lifelong flight into an evasion of self and into a brand of frozen consciousness whose never perceived motivation was to avoid awareness. Although their outward characteristics were different, each, driven by the fear of life, denied himself participation in the external world and thereby spared himself the unacceptable lesson that the answer to life is living it.

Although Ibsen's characters gave direction to their lives by setting goals that enabled them to make full use of their abilities and gave them the sense of purpose that comes from playing a role, no goals were conceived of that provided for fulfillment and meaning in their private lives. The result was that their professional commitment became an end in itself, ruling out other

considerations. In Beckett's characters the lack of an external commitment leaves them without the capacity to govern the direction of their lives and robs them of the ability to achieve discipline and involvement in the world's tasks. The lack of personal commitment has kept such a character as Krapp from growing into life and forced him to look backwards while trying to fend off despair.

Ibsen's characters, who are driven, and Beckett's, who are alienated, represent two widespread tendencies of modern society. Both types, because of their inability to live rich and rewarding lives, approach the end of life with a feeling of defeat and hopelessness. Dying is a part of life, and one usually dies as one has lived. After the death of Leonardo da Vinci a folio of his was found on which he had inscribed the sentence, "When I reach the point of having learned how to live, I shall have learned how to die."[30]

Notes

[1] Samuel Beckett, *Waiting for Godot* (New York: Evergreen Press, 1954). Note: references to editions of the plays by Ibsen and Beckett as well as Beckett's prose work *Proust* will be made only the first time they appear in the text except where possible ambiguity dictates otherwise. Page references will be given for quotations from works from all other authors.

[2] Henrik Ibsen, *Ghosts and Three Other Plays,* ed. Michael Meyer (Garden City, New York: Doubleday Anchor, 1966).

[3] Various Authors, *Materialien zu Becketts Endspiel* (Frankfurt am Main: Suhrkamp Verlag, 1968), p. 90. (My translation)

[4] Immanuel Kant, "Der Streit der Fakultäten," ed. Ernst Cassirer et al. (Berlin: Ernst Cassirer Verlag, 1922), VII, 413-14.

[5] Hedda Gabler arguably belongs in both categories, although she is still a young woman.

[6] Henrik Ibsen, *Peer Gynt,* trans. Rolf Fjelde (New York: The New American Library, 1964).

[7] Thus Gregers, the fanatic truthteller in *The Wild Duck,* is a further incarnation of the former, while Hjalmar, a self-indulgent character in the same play who manages to avoid decision-making at every turn, is one more instance of the latter.

[8] Henrik Ibsen, *Brand,* trans. Michael Meyer (New York: Doubleday Anchor, 1960).

[9] Henrik Ibsen, *When We Dead Awaken and Three Other Plays,* trans. Michael Meyer (Garden City, New York: Doubleday Anchor, 1960).

[10] Ibid.

[11] Sigmund Freud, *Civilization and Its Discontents* (Garden City, New York: Doubleday Anchor, 1958), p. 23.

[12] Cf. *When We Dead Awaken,* pp. 347 and 320.

[13] Henrik Ibsen, *Hedda Gabler and Three Other Plays,* trans. Michael Meyer, (Garden City, New York: Doubleday Anchor, 1961).

[14] *Kindlers Literatur Lexikon* (Zurich:Kindler Verlag, 1969), V, 263.

[15] Quoted by W. H. Auden in the Foreword to *Brand.*

[16] Quoted in the *Saturday Review,* February 21, 1976, p. 43.

[17] Samuel Beckett, *Proust* (New York, Grove Press, 1931).

[18] Samuel Beckett, *Krapp's Last Tape and Other Dramatic Pieces* (New York: Evergreen, 1960).

[19] T. S. Eliot, *The Complete Poems and Plays* (New York: Harcourt Brace, 1952), p. 56.

[20] *Proust.*

[21] Samuel Beckett, *Stories and Texts for Nothing* (New York: Evergreen, 1967).

[22] Samuel Beckett, *Endgame* (New York: Evergreen, 1958).

[23] Samuel Beckett, *Happy Days* (New York: Evergreen, 1961).

[24] *Endgame.*

[25] *Poetic Drama. An Anthology of Plays in Verse,* ed. Alfred Kreyborg (New York: Modern Age Books, 1941), p. 87.

[26] *Krapps's Last Tape.* This is a refrain that also occurs in *Waiting for Godot.*

[27] André Marissel, *Beckett* (Paris: Editions Universitaires, 1963), p. 106.

[28] Samuel Beckett, "From an Abandoned Work," in *First Love and Other Shorts* (New York: Evergreen, 1974).

[29] Henrik Ibsen, *Ghosts and Three Other Plays,* trans. Michael Meyer (Garden City, New York: Doubleday Anchor, 1966).

[30] Cf. Ludwig Marcuse, *Unverlorene Illusionen, Pessimismus—Ein Stadium der Reife* (Munich: Szcesny Verlag, 1966), p. 76. (My translation)

IV. THE POLITY AND THE ELDERLY: MODERNIZATION REVOLUTION AND EQUITY

Daniel Scott Smith

OLD AGE AND THE 'GREAT TRANSFORMATION': A NEW ENGLAND CASE STUDY

In the late spring of 1890 a fifty-one year old carpenter wrote a short, angry letter to the editor of a newspaper of Hingham, a town near Boston:

> Mr. Editor:—
>
> On the night of May 20th, the front gate was taken off and carried away from the premises of widow Xoa Dunbar at So. Hingham. If the very *cunning* perpetrators should sometime be thus unkindly used, they will then know how much they have annoyed one of the oldest residents now in her 86th year.
>
> Signed, *George Dunbar*

The fury of Mrs. Dunbar's son increased when, on the next Saturday night, the vandals hung the gate in a tree "at a considerable elevation, and in a battered, broken, and badly defaced condition." This *sixth* act of malicious mischief against his mother stirred George Dunbar to publish a four page pamphlet. In it he searched for the underlying sources of delinquency and presented reasons why the town should combat such misdemeanors.[1]

The destruction of the widow Dunbar's gate and her son's response are, of course, historically inconsequential. Yet such insignificant events and unimportant documents, when placed in broader context, do have potential for historians. In fact Dunbar himself also interpreted the incident in terms of history, both of the town and the nation. The mentality of the nineteenth century stamps his argument at nearly every point. But before we look at Dunbar's analysis, let us first take two other brief glimpses at points in the town's history and an inspection of the intervening trends which provide a context for assessing Dunbar's reaction to the incident of 1890.

The first of these historical moments gives Hingham its claim to distinction among New England towns today. In early 1680 the town "agreed to build a new meeting house with all convenient speed that may be for the good of the work." The Old Ship meetinghouse stands today as the oldest English church building

in North America. Instead of "convenient speed," however, controversy developed over its location, and as a result a remarkable set of documents delineating the social structure of the town has descended to the historian.[2]

Nearly bisecting the two centuries separating the social evidence relating to the construction of the Old Ship and the protest of George Dunbar is a quite different document, a perceptive and revealing sermon by the Reverend Ebenezer Gay. Climbing the pulpit on August 26, 1781, Gay marked his birthday and nearly sixty-four years as minister in the first parish of Hingham by preaching on Joshua XIV, 10, "And Now, Lo I am This Day Four Score and Five Years Old."[3] Although Gay was immediately remembered as a forerunner of Unitarianism and is now admired for his careful recording of vital events,[4] his sermon that summer Sabbath captured the ambiguous promise and inherent perils of being old in early New England.

Understanding these data extending over 200 years requires a theoretical perspective. Since the early nineteenth century, social theorists and others have attempted to comprehend the dimensions and significance of the problem of modernization, what Karl Polanyi has called the 'Great Transformation.'[5] Traditional and modern, feudalism and capitalism, *Gemeinschaft und Gesellschaft,* aristocratic and democratic, extended and nuclear—all these dichotomies cleave the seamless web perceived by historians, if not the historical record itself. One might add to the above list the chapter titles from David Hackett Fischer's recent work: "The Exaltation of Age in Early America, 1607-1780" versus the "Cult of Youth in Modern America, 1780-1970."[6] Believing that the great transformation is the crucial issue, I am attempting to discern what that means not with the conceptual sledge hammer of the classic sociological dichotomies but with the quantitative scapel of historical social indicators.

By 'modernization' I mean no more than the familiar facts of American social history—the shift from agriculture to commerce and industry as the principal means of livelihood, the transition from women bearing seven children or more to having only three, the change from most officeholders having fathers who occupied the same position a generation earlier to having an overwhelming majority of officials with no kin antecedents. As a result of one of these changes—declining fertility—the proportion of the population over sixty increased from about three percent in 1680 to fourteen percent in 1880. These great alterations in human behavior, and more as well, occurred during the quarter millenium between 1635 and 1880 I have been studying for the past eight years.[7] No historian can ignore these obvious and dramatic changes; but what is more important and interesting is the magnitude and interrelationships among the changes and the qualifications and limits on the 'Great Transformation.' By its very nature, old age cannot be "modernized" in the same sense that economic activity has been. Never forgetting the sledgehammer of modernization, the student of old age is much better served by the historical scapel.

Let us return, then, to how George Dunbar perceived the vandalism of his mother's property. Most of his pamphlet is concerned with justifying his protest

in the face of the absence of concern by the community and the town government. He emphatically rejected the fear that "the more notice you take of these things the more trouble you'll have." That point of view will lead, he argued, to "no security—for person or property." What had happened to the spirit of community and respect for law and order in the "Good Old Town of Hingham?" Not surprisingly, Dunbar responded with a litany of late nineteenth-century concerns and values. Because of the absence of a two-party system and the resultant complacency of the dominant GOP, he wrote, the town officials failed to react. Or perhaps, he argued, the three year terms of town officials made them unresponsive. But it was the community, he believed, more than the government that had failed to protect his mother. Most serious was the absence of civic concern. Progress itself was responsible for this attitude. The schools had failed; how else could one explain the "grin of satisfaction seen upon the faces of high school scholars and graduates at this particular outrage." Then, finally, he concluded,

> Isn't if *funny* to thus treat an aged person and have the approving smile of so many people of both sexes—teachers, female suffragists and all? Progressive Hingham with the light of the nineteenth century, incandescent electric lights at twenty-two dollars per light, and yet such indecency would seem to indicate in heathen darkness. Enterprise! Yes, enterprise! But the Enterprise that seeks to wipe out others to accomplish low and selfish ends is never found on the side of true progress.

Although we may smile at some of these items of progress that Dunbar felt were to blame, the values that he invoked to oppose the vandals are also integral to the nineteenth-century world view. Manliness, honor, citizen's rights, nobility, responsibility, patriotism—these individualistic values should stir the citizenry to action. Nowhere does Dunbar argue that the aged *per se* deserve respect or concern from the rest of the community. Unmentioned is any appeal to Christian obligations. Indeed, there is nothing distinctive about the old widow except her helplessness.

Dunbar's treatment of the "oldness" of the town reveals the flaw in his values and helps to explain the helplessness of his mother in this situation. Although the town was very old (it was founded in 1635) and the Dunbar family had been there since the seventeenth century, its great age was abstract and public. From George Dunbar's recall of the town grave of one of Washington's generals ("and one of his Army surgeons too") to Hingham's more recent heroic performance in the Civil War, only the public facts of Hingham's past were cited. It seemed important for Dunbar to mention that in 1861 his mother was willing "if need be, to lay her offering on the alter of liberty for the honor of the flag." But the son tells the community no more about his mother. In private matters, in the shared experience of generations, old and young, past and present, Hingham was perhaps as new as the rawest frontier county in the agricultural West or the dirtiest city in the industrial East.

Dunbar implicitly sensed that such indifference was a new phenomenon in Hingham's history. Yet historians must be skeptical in accepting such laments, common among nineteenth-century conservatives, for the passing of a more humane or better society. Had the status and image of the elderly actually declined with the development of an impersonal, modern, progressive society?

Over a century earlier the Reverend Gay had preached to a quite different community, no longer traditional but not yet modern. Most measures of behavior show the town's population then as being much closer to 1680 than 1890. But the superstructure of traditional values had badly deteriorated. Gay's perspective in this 1781 sermon nevertheless seems indistinguishable from the thoughts of other ministers of colonial New England.[8] Since the sermon was directed at the old, not the young, Gay omitted the positive attributes (greater wisdom, for example, and experience) often listed as reasons for venerating the old. The central theme was traditionally Christian—that this world was a prelude to the next, and that man was weak and passive, God mighty. Great longevity was due to the "goodness of God" who originally "took us out of the womb" and made us hope "when we hung on our mothers' breasts." Survival to old age was a gift from God, Gay reminded his congregation, and it "should be marvelous in our eyes, while we see so many dying around us ere they arrive of it."

Moreover, old age had definite advantages, especially for "the business of religion." The advantages related to decline and death; the old should not shrink from the inevitable. Gay scorned those who apparently believed "there is no man so old, but he thinks he may live a year longer." He insisted that "the young may, the old must die." By approaching death correctly the old could set an example for all Christians. Old age, Gay argued, exemplified Christian resignation for it "disableth us from following the world in eager and incessantly laborious pursuit—abateth the violence of sensual inclinations; and it exempteth from many temptations to sin, into which youth betrayeth men."

The personal experience of old age, Gay emphasized, was full of suffering and pain: "The bodily frame is so weakened, and such irreparable breaches are made in it, that its dissolution is daily to be expected. We may say as Job, Our breath is corrupt, our vital spirits wasted, our days are extinct, the graves are ready for us; we are tottering over them, and shall soon tumble into them." Such troubles were "a natural, unavoidable necessity." Although old age was a blessing of God, the loss of "most, or all, of our coeval friends, early acquaintance, and dear companions" was an additional "and not the least of the melancholy circumstances of old age." Disengagement and retreat were norms for all Christians, but these attitudes were especially fitting for the aged. "Remembering how old we are, our hearts should be loosened from this world; our affections to, our cares about, and pursuits after, the things of it, be moderated"; such worldly feelings were "inexcusable," "absurd," and "shocking" in the old.

We should not be misled by the negative features of Gay's sermon for the aged. In 1781 he was himself a very old man, a full quarter-century past his

sixtieth birthday. During the previous forty years he had ministered over a steadily declining religious impulse in the town; joining the church was becoming rarer, and men were abbreviating or omitting religious preambles in their wills. Nearly one-third of the brides he married and recorded in his register were already pregnant. Gay furthermore was not in sympathy with the Revolution, and one of his sons, Martin, had been banished as a Loyalist in 1778. No wonder Gay thought that "in respect of the public state of things the days are evil."

For all his catalogue of loneliness, affliction and impending death, Gay was, after all, still the active minister of the church. He would finally die, at the age of ninety, preparing his sermon one Sunday. He did not disengage or retire. Still he recognized withdrawal as an obligation, if weakness required it. "Should we have the trial of outliving our serviceableness in the world," he wrote, "and be laid by as vessels of no more use, the consideration of our being wasted and worn out with age, should make us contented, and others also, for whom we may seem burthensome; but still not long be so."

At the conclusion of his sermon he turned from generalities to his own case. As George Dunbar was to do eleven decades later, Gay pointed to the age of the town. In the 146 years since its founding, the first parish had had only three ministers. It was the *continuity of human interaction,* not the record of past heroes and public events of Dunbar's vision of Hingham's history, that Gay recognized. He specifically thanked the fathers, children, and children's children who had showed him affection. Recognizing and possibly apologizing for the tide of dechristianization, Gay admitted that his ministry had been more "acceptable" than "profitable." Nevertheless, Gay hoped to continue, to "finish the course of life, and the ministry I have received of him [God], together." Although Gay resisted retirement, he did endorse a central, and contradictory, principle upheld by both the older seventeenth-century community and the late nineteenth-century society in respect to the aged: respect and position in theory depended on *performance,* not on past service, ascribed power, or humane considerations. As he said, "As much as I dread and deprecate the being cut down as a cumberer of the ground in this part of the Lord's vineyard, I would not with my useless old age fill up the place, and deprive you of the help of a profitable labourer in it." Being "cut down" has, I sense, a double meaning—both a reaffirmation of man's general helplessness and Gay's personal fear of the desire of the congregation for a younger minister. His willingness to step down was more a principle affirmed than a promise given. Although retirement was not, to be sure, a matter of chronological age, his term ("useless old age") was vague and non-biological. Gay made no attempt to distinguish between infirm and healthy old age. Being old for Gay and for the traditional mentality was a religious and cultural condition, not a summary of empirical realities. High status and power might persist into old age, but Gay's sermon suggests such persistence had anti-social overtones.

More than a century of rapid economic and social development separates Gay's sermon and the protest of George Dunbar. Xoa Dunbar was an aged

widow of modest means, Gay an educated clergyman with a legacy of prestige and authority; the two cases are, of course, not directly comparable. We are concerned here not with experience but with the norms and values relating the elderly to the community. For Gay, the good of the community came before his own individual desires. In order to benefit the group, men, he argued, should yield scarce and valuable resources and positions to the next generation. Gay emphasized the uniqueness of the old and the value of that difference to the whole population, and he stressed the continuity on a personal level of the past and present. A little more than a century later, Dunbar was most appalled by the refusal of his Hingham neighbors to get involved over such a trivial matter. The failure of Dunbar's Hingham was inherent in its individualism; the town government itself had no larger function than to protect private rights from encroachment.

These two documents suggest a paradox—that the old who were economically and socially secure in the nineteenth century would not share Gay's ideal that they should yield to the next generation; at the same time those who were old and vulnerable could not look to the community for protection or assistance. A further distinction is latent in the two views. Gay's perspective was Christian and communal, Dunbar's secular and private. Although Dunbar's mother may have been isolated from communal support, her son vehemently protested in her behalf. If the experience of old age is indeed more a matter of private and familial sentiments and actions than generalized values and group decision, then the impersonality and individualism of the nineteenth century may have had very little impact on the old. Paradoxically the sense of community may have withered, but familial relationships between the old and the young may have become more cooperative and reciprocal. George Dunbar's individualism was a poor basis for community concern about the weak, but he obviously cared for more than himself.

To explore these paradoxical possibilities at the level of experience, we must move closer to the origins of this society now only glimpsed from the vantage points of 1781 and 1890 and turn from an analysis of values to one of social structure. The origins of Hingham lay, of course, in England and in the Puritan variant of English values and institutions.[9] In fact despite the importance of the Great Transformation, the Hingham of 1890 may be discerned in the character of the town two centuries earlier.

In the early 1680's we catch the community in the process of being taxed to build a new meeting house, fighting over its location, and being seated by a committee of the town in the new structure according to a complicated plan. On the surface and beneath, to a certain crucial point, we can find a gerontocratic society founded, as John Waters puts it, "by patriarchs, which gave office to its elders, not its youth, and believed in hierarchy."[10] Table 1 confirms that Hingham in the late seventeenth century was not a society of the young, but we find age-classes, not an age hierarchy. Before the age of forty, few men participated regularly in politics or held substantial amounts of property. Yet these indicators of status do not keep rising with age (see Table 1):

TABLE 1.–AGE AND SOCIAL STRUCTURE AMONG MALES IN HINGHAM, MASSACHUSETTS, 1680-1681

Age Group	Mean tax for building of the new meetinghouse (pounds)	Percent voting on location of new house	Percent serving as selectmen By 1680	Ever	No.
21-29	1.1	6%	0%	22%	(46)
30-39	2.1	20	4	32	(44)
40-49	4.1	43	29	52	(21)
50-59	4.9	48	38	48	(21)
60-69	4.4	60	67	67	(15)
Over 70	3.7	50	70	70	(10)

As we see, after the fifties mean wealth dropped, and after age forty the differential in voting is slight. The seating plan for the new meetinghouse best reveals the discontinuity after middle age. On the bench under the pulpit were the five "Elders" whose average age was nearly eighty but whose mean wealth was only forty-two percent of those on the seat of the current officeholders. Old age was honored and respected, but it did not command continued wealth or leadership position.

Why, then, was Hingham a society dominated not by the old but by the middle-aged? Values, institutions, and economic circumstances are all important elements in the explanation. Oversimplifying to some extent, we may define the conception of the family held by seventeenth-century Hinghamites as a future-oriented patriarchalism. Men had high obligations and responsibilities toward their families and descendants. Providing for one's own came well before charitable duties. In his sermon on wealth in 1682 Hingham's minister John Norton repeated the same point made by John Winthrop a half century earlier in the famous "Modell of Christian Charity": "He that provideth not for his owne . . . is worse than Infidel."[11]

Although it was believed that men were under a moral obligation to accumulate wealth for immediate and distant posterity, authority in the family extended over only one generation, not two. Grandparents did not exercise authority over the grandchildren. As John Robinson, the most important minister behind the migration to Plymouth, warned, grandparents were likely to overindulge their grandchildren, "seeing themselves further propagated in them, and by their means proceeding on to a further degree of eternity, which all desire naturally, if not in themselves, yet in their posterity.[12] The duty of parents toward their children, on the other hand, was to bring them to obedience. The suggested method was a traumatic crushing of the child's sinful will, a practice with ominous implications for the adult personality.[13] Such an obsession with genealogy, or what Edmund S. Morgan has called Puritan tribalism, implied parental obligations but not necessarily congenial

relationships with children. Through the Halfway Covenant of 1662 the children of unreborn church members could be baptised. The original conception of church membership was not discarded, and the beneficiaries of the compromise were the grandchildren, not the children, of the original Massachusetts Bay saints.

The family as a concept did not extend indefinitely into the past. This kinship principle is best illustrated by child-naming practices. If a man had a brother with the same first name as the father, he did not name a son for that father; his brother had first claim to transfer his own name. Men with first names different from their fathers were almost as likely to name their sons after themselves as men who were Jr.'s or III's[14] Both the tendency of grandparents to indulge their grandchildren and the childnaming customs can be traced to the English family system.

As a prerequisite to marriage in West-European societies men had to have access to economic resources to support an independent household. Although a young married man did not always have full title to these resources,[15] his status as a head-of-family gave him broad and exclusive powers over the members of his household. Thus the commitment to generational succession and the autonomy of family heads meant that the old could not have the same status and authority as the middle aged.

As the Reverend Gay's refusal to retire illustrates, norms are not identical to behavior. In all complicated human situations, there are in fact contradictory norms. Ideally, one infers, the younger generation would move into autonomous adulthood, and the older generation would continue more-or-less undiminished in status. The resolution of this contradiction was perhaps best expressed by the instructions to the seating committee of Windsor, Connecticut in the 1730's that each man was "to be seated according to his age and rates, but no man was to lose his rank."[16] But the ideal was not to be. In 1680-81 Hingham was just recovering from the fears of King Philip's War. In less than a decade the constriction of economic opportunities in Massachusetts would lead married couples to practice birth control.[17] Hingham was part of a world of uncertainty, scarcity, and constraint, not abundance and unlimited choice. Both individuals and the community had to make painful decisions.

How were these choices to be made? The existence of more important principles of stratification than age meant that the old were on the defensive. In the criteria used to seat New England meetinghouses, age typically was listed after wealth, and over time the age criterion and the use of seating committees disappeared. To pay for a new building, towns in the eighteenth century typically sold pew rights. Thus gradually these limited rights became indistinguishable from other forms of property. Wealth had always been the most important basis of inequality in New England towns, but over the course of the colonial period it became virtually the only principle. In this area, as in most matters, Hingham was conservative. Retaining the Old Ship structure, the town resisted demands for pews by individuals for nearly four decades before giving up in 1756. The Elder's Seat in the Hingham meetinghouse was not ripped out

until 1825. But the Elder's Seat was short, and its existence did not prevent the construction of family pews for the more prosperous.

High political office in the town was always a scarcer commodity than good seats in the meetinghouse. When the community was small and relatively undifferentiated in economic terms, a substantial majority of men eventually served as selectmen, and these men often served terms after their sixtieth birthday. The Founding Fathers of the town in particular often served into old age. The only eight men to be elected after age seventy in the whole era from 1650 to 1880 were concentrated exclusively in the four decades after 1670. As the population increased from about 800 in 1680 to nearly 2,500 in 1765, and as stratification widened, wealth and status (attending Harvard, for example, or having a father who previously held office) monopolized the positions of leadership. Between 1720 and 1840 few men over age sixty were elected to an additional term, and it was virtually unknown for a man to attain a position for the first time after age sixty (see Table 2):

TABLE 2.–AGE AT FIRST AND LAST ELECTION TO THE OFFICE OF SELECTMAN, HINGHAM, MASS., 1650-1880.

AGE AT FIRST ELECTION

Period	No.	-30	30-39	40-49	50-59	60-69	70+	Percentage over Age 50	Age 60
-1699	71	7	23	26	13	2	0	21%	3%
1700-1749	57	3	21	18	14	1	0	26	2
1750-1799	44	3	17	13	11	0	0	25	0
1800-1839	21	1	12	6	1	1	0	10	5
1840-1879	19	0	4	7	5	3	0	42	16

AGE AT LAST ELECTION

Period	No.	-30	30-39	40-49	50-59	60-69	70+	Percentage over Age 60	Age 70
-1699	64	0	10	14	22	11	7	28%	11%
1700-1749	65	1	2	21	38	12	1	20	2
1750-1799	37	1	7	13	12	4	0	11	0
1800-1839	21	1	8	5	4	3	0	14	0
1840-1879	20	0	1	5	6	8	0	40	0

Just as the town was not always to incorporate the symbolic meanings of community, the office of selectman after 1800 evolved into a specialized political function. Concomitant with the emergence of an institutionalized conception of town office, politicians (experts in a specialized business) could

continue to serve into very old age. Seth Sprague, for example, held office thirty-one years between 1857 and 1893, being seventy-six in his last year of service. DeWitt C. Bates died in office in 1905 at the age of seventy-eight. Of course, we must understand that holding office in the early twentieth century no longer was an emblem of social eminence.[18] Old leaders and specialized political elites were not unknown in the colonial period. Men served into old age and until death in colony-wide offices. In Connecticut, for example, the promotion of Assistants and designation of the Governor operated on a pure seniority system.[19] And during times of crisis, such as the Revolution, the old leaders were sometimes recalled to office, presumably because they were too old to be controversial.[20] But that is an exception which proves the rule: during ordinary times wealth and to a lesser extent family and education counted more than age and experience.

The defensive position and exclusion of old men from points of power quite often resulted from the previous history of conflict between young and middle-aged men. After a sorting-out process, New England towns emerged in the mid- and late seventeenth century with exceptionally homogeneous populations. Age was one of the few objective bases for conflict. Often these battles were over the location of a meetinghouse or over the formation of a new parish or town. Since the outlying areas around the town center were settled by the younger generation these fights could pit fathers against sons.[21] Although the struggle over the site of the Old Ship was not based on age, just two years later thirty-three year old James Hawke, "the candidate set up by the young men of the company," edged fifty-year old Thomas Andrews by a vote of fifty-five to forty-seven in the election for captain of the Hingham militia. The old faction in the militia band, an organization of males between sixteen and sixty, appealed to the General Court which reprimanded the Company for its irregular conduct.[22] Thus in public affairs we see that the middle-aged did not yield gracefully to the young, and this political struggle may exemplify an equally serious familial battle.

Most of the experiential history of old age is doubtless located within the family. Unlike governments or other social institutions, the family leaves little direct testimony about the nature of human relationships. We must rely on crude quantitative evidence and a degree of deductive reasoning. In a rapidly growing, high fertility population, the young could use their greater numbers against the middle-aged; they could temporarily win a militia election. Within the family the fathers held economic power, constrained only by the norms of generational succession or the fear of permanent outmigration by the sons. In a non-growing, purely agricultural economy the emergence of young men into economic adulthood necessarily involves the property of the older generation. A variety of strategies—primo- or ultimogeniture, joint residence or joint economic production, or even retirement for the older generation—exist for families to manage this crucial transition. It was clear that sons would eventually replace their fathers. But when?

Paternal death at a young age accelerated the attainment of desired adult statuses. In colonial Hingham and Concord, Massachusetts, and in Charles

Parish, Virginia, men whose fathers died young were able to marry at an earlier age than men whose fathers survived into old age.[23] If we control for other effects, such as age, through the statistical procedure of multiple regression, it becomes clear that the early death of the father significantly increased the value of real property a Hingham man held in 1749. In the agricultural economy of pre-industrial America, the economic interests of fathers and sons clashed. When the father did not die, the sons could not wait indefinitely.

Another quantitative indicator, the relationship of age to wealth, allows some insight into the outcome of generational friction and serves as a basis for comparison with other economic eras. In the United States in 1850 per capita wealth climbed continuously from the youngest to the oldest age group. Among Hingham males in 1680, farmers in the town in 1749, and in the entire country in 1850, a parabola illustrates the compromise between the retention of property and the obligation to help children get started in life (see Table 3):

TABLE 3.–THE RELATIONSHIP OF AGE TO WEALTH: HINGHAM, MASS., 1680 AND 1749; THE UNITED STATES IN 1850 AND 1963 (50-59=100).

Age-Group	Hingham 1680 Per holder	Hingham 1749 Artisans & Laborers Per holder	Hingham 1749 Farmers	United States 1850[1] Per Holder	United States 1850[1] Per Male	United States 1963[2]
21-29	22	23(13)	54(13)	38	13(20-29)	19(20-34)
30-39	44	46(29)	52(20)	57	43	50(35-44)
40-49	84	84(22)	56(30)	89	84	69(45-54)
50-59	100	100(23)	100(20)	100	100	100(55-64)
60-69	91	102(14)	72(18)	106	116	95(over 65)
Over 70	76	128(4)	70(11)	133	125	

[1]Lee Soltow, *Men and Wealth in the United States, 1859-1870* (New Haven: Yale Univ. Press, 1975), p. 70.

[2]Soltow, *Men and Wealth,* p. 85. Based on current dollars, families and unrelated individuals included; all other data relates to males only.

To be a farmer a man needed a substantial amount of property, regardless of whether he was twenty-five or fifty-five. Both because of lower capital requirements and because of the diversity of occupations, a man could get started in the non-farm sector much more easily. With the shift out of agriculture, property became more unequally distributed; fewer than ten percent of adult males held no property in 1680 compared to 47.2 percent of the total in 1880. Over the long-run, social stratification replaced intrafamilial age stratification as an important organizing principle of the town. Interestingly, the 1963 curve resembles the pre-industrial pattern, not that of the mid-nineteenth century.

Families may have tried to follow the Windsor rule "that no man was to lose his rank." Men passed over property to daughters at marriage and to sons at

several points, but they did not usually give away all of their holdings to their children. (Although I have not as yet studied the point systematically, end-of-life retirement contracts between fathers and sons appear to be rare.) Old men perhaps feared dependency on their sons. When a father made provision in his will for sons to care for their own mother, he left no detail untouched for filial concern or spontaneous affection. The number of cords of wood, the privilege of using a walk, garden, or well, which room or rooms in the house—all were precisely specified.

The Calvinistic childrearing experience and the recent memory of struggles over scarce familial resources may have led many sons "secretly to say within themselves," as John Locke bluntly put it, "When will you die, father?"[24] The underlying problem was the asymmetry of human relationships; after a transition in power, reciprocity was difficult to achieve. The Pilgrim minister John Robinson made the point abstractly, "Love rather descends, than ascends," and a New Hampshire minister in 1684 more graphically echoed the point: "Keepe the staffe in her owne Hand," he advised his second wife in his will, "that neither Forreigne nor domesticke claimmers may recover any thing of her, Her Bowells being more likely to yearne toward Her Children than theyrs towards theyre mother."[25] Although marriage was also a relationship between unequals, Puritan men often used terms of endearment to refer to their spouses in their wills; but very infrequent indeed was the designation of a son as "loveing" or "beloved." The difference here is instructive. The wife was always subordinate to her husband, and hence he could "love" her; the son would shift from powerless dependence to autonomy, and thus the father may have feared him.

My reading of the evidence for this Christian, communal, patriarchal, English, pre-industrial society certainly does not support any notion of a "Golden Age" for old people. Being a Christian culture, early New England held the signal attribute of old age to be nearness to death. Being communal, it granted able performance and the good of the group precedence over respect due age. Being partriarchical, it witnessed fathers both crushing and arousing hostility in their sons before being obliged to help them get started in life. Being English, it required autonomy to pass in considerable degree to newly married sons who headed their households. And being pre-industrial, it did not possess enough resources to satisfy all and thus economic conflict inhered in such an environment of scarcity. During most of the eighteenth century scarcity increased, and the older matrix of values sustaining respect for the aged withered.

A final bit of quantitative comparison helps to buttress the point that the material conditions for the old did not improve until the nineteenth century. There were, of course, always exceptions to general trends. The Reverend Gay could continue as minister because he remained capable, because few cared much for religious fervor, and because he decided to place his own interests first. In the whole period under consideration in this paper, the continued headship of a household by a male was a cultural norm and a defining characteristic of male adulthood. Single or married children might occasionally live with the father, but the key principle was the continuing headship of the

older male. Nearly eighty-five percent of all males over age sixty in Hingham in 1880 headed their own households; the figure was certainly no higher in 1790. Data on this point do not exist for the colonial period, but the figure reported by Peter Laslett for pre-industrial England points to continuity in practice (see Table 4):

TABLE 4.–HOUSEHOLD HEADSHIP RATIOS FOR MALES IN HINGHAM, MASS., 1790 and 1880, and in PRE-INDUSTRIAL ENGLAND.

	PERCENTAGE HEADING HOUSEHOLDS			
Age-Group	Hingham 1880	Hingham Maximum	in 1790[1] Minimum	Six places in England before 1800[2]
65-69	83%(92)	87%	82%(33)	
70-74	87 (56)	87	87 (15)	
75-79	84 (31)	78	64 (13)	
over 80	65 (26)	67	67 (6)	
over 65	82%(205)	84%	78%(65 or 61)	
over 60	84%(290)			81%

OCCUPATIONAL AND WEALTH DIFFERENTIALS IN HINGHAM, 1880

Occupation of males over 60	Pct. heading household	Town taxes assessed	Pct. heading household
Farmer	97%(34)	None	64%(72)
White collar	90 (48)	Less than $3.00	87 (86)
Skilled manual	92 (92)	$3.00 to $39.99	95 (64)
Laborer/unskilled manual	82 (61)	Over $40.00	93 (68)
Farm laborer	77 (13)		
No occupation	38 (24)	No real property Males over 60 in 1790	40-50%(16, 20)
Total	84%(290)	Holds property (1790)	96%(45)

[1]The 1790 figures were obtained by comparing the heads of families with the real property tax lists for 1790 and earlier years and the Hingham genealogy. Those not heading families were inferred, and some may have moved or died.

[2]Peter Laslett, "Societal Development and Aging," in *Handbook of Aging and the Social Sciences,* ed. Robert H. Binstock and Ethel Shanas (New York: Van Nostrand Reinhold, 1976), Tables 7a, 7b, pp. 108-09.

Between 1790 and 1880 there was no important change in the proportion of old men who were propertyless (26-30% versus 25%). Further, the proportion of propertyless males who headed their households is somewhat higher in 1880 than in 1790. The numbers involved are too small and the procedure used in 1790 too uncertain for firm conclusions. But it is striking that the general increase in propertylessness from fifteen to forty-seven percent for all males was not shared by those over age sixty-five.

With the transformation of the economy in the nineteenth century, fathers and sons did not have to struggle over scarce familial resources. Children were supposed to be autonomous and independent economically, and men much more frequently in their wills gave all the property to their wives.[26] Economic factors continued, of course, to structure the lives of the old; the occupational and wealth differentials in Table 4 confirm this obvious point. Poverty and dependency were still intertwined.

The weakening of the economic importance of the intergenerational connection does not mean that aging persons and their kin were separated. In 1880, for example, widow Xoa Dunbar headed her household with her son George being the only other member. Only 7.6% of males over sixty lived alone or with non-kin; the comparable figure for females is 13.4%. In the six pre-industrial communities studied by Laslett, nearly twenty percent of the males and twenty-five percent of the females lived apart from kin.[27] The figures for Hingham are quite low in view of the substantial outmigration of the young and the high proportion of those who never married (one-sixth of all females over age sixty). Nevertheless, two-thirds or more of all persons in each marital status group were living with kin.[28] Although there were very important changes in the family during the nineteenth century, the kin-composition of the household probably changed little. Not until after World War II can one find a substantial increase in the proportion of old persons living apart from kin.[29] When great abundance was finally achieved in American society, individualism would lead to the alteration of the conjugal household.[30]

In large part the attack on the widow Dunbar's gate was an isolated, atypical, and trivial exception to the increasingly secure position of the aged in the course of economic and social modernization. With politics a specialized business, old selectmen could serve, as can old Senators and Congressmen today, into old old age. With more economic opportunity, young men could get started without acquiring part of their father's property, and men could leave more resources to their widows. I have argued elsewhere that during the eighteenth century the middle-aged and young within the family were engaged in conflict, but that by the second quarter of the nineteenth century the crisis was resolved by the recognition of the substantive autonomy of young adults.[31] In a narrow sense the young triumphed. But it was a victory accepted by both sides. Parents, for example, less frequently named children for themselves and, if they did, added a distinctive middle name. Children symbolically were new individuals in the world, not the perpetuators of family lineages.[32]

We should be careful, however, not to go too far in this "whig" interpretation of the history of old age. Both Fischer and Achenbaum have demonstrated that

the positive element in the cultural evaluation of old age deteriorated after the colonial period. Fischer has stressed the emergence of a cult of youth.[33] The emphasis on youth expressed by literary figures and medical writers and their popular equivalents is important. In abstract and public contexts, men even act on such vague notions. In 1824 the newly established Jeffersonian Debating Society in Hingham could easily limit new members to those between twenty-one and thirty-five, and take away the voting and speaking privileges of members reaching their fortieth birthday.[34] Or in 1869 a first parish committee, with only one member over fifty, could recommend to the congregation that the century-old box pews be torn out and replaced with Victorian or open pews; a majority of the Society, "including the major part of its younger members, without whose active interest no society can live and prosper, believed the time to have fully arrived when the welfare of the parish demanded more comfortable pews on the lower floor." The work "was not one of destruction, but of preservation," argued the minister, and "great credit is certainly due to the more advanced in years for the cheerful spirit with which they have yielded their personal wishes in compliance with the wishes of the majority."[35] In the minds of Americans the earlier balance in preference between youth and maturity had shifted toward the former. Since the middle-aged had enjoyed the preponderant share of advantages stemming from the respect due age in pre-industrial New England, they, rather than the old, were the greater losers as a result of the emergence of a "cult of youth."

If such general considerations or prejudices had entered into decisions over public policy, the old could have been seriously affected. The massive, bureaucratic, routinized governmental agencies and private corporations of the twentieth century seem to require such prejudices. If jobs had been scarce, as in the Great Depression of the 1930's, or if average efficiency measurements had determined rigid hiring and firing rules, then the old definitely would have become victims of the ideological preference for the young. But during the nineteenth century the organizations which might have translated such abstract notions into action did not exist. The widow Dunbar was badly treated in May, 1890, and her injury was not felt by the community. It was the vandals who directly harmed her, not her sons as could have happened in the colonial era, nor the power of massive, organized institutions as would be possible in the twentieth century.

Finally, I must stress the continuity in the discrepancy between values and experience from the seventeenth century to the present. In the recent survey by the Harris organization, marked differences appear between the perception and reality of old age. Sixty-one percent of those under sixty-five, for example, believed that in general "loneliness is a very serious problem for old people," but only twelve percent of the old personally admitted that loneliness was "very serious" and only seven percent of those under sixty-five suffered from "very serious" loneliness.[36] The scattered historical evidence from Hingham suggests that this divergence is not at all new. Although respect and honor were due the aged in early New England, the striking attribute of the old was their nearness to death. With economic development in the nineteenth century, the material

circumstances and possibilities of autonomy increased for the old, yet the withering of the sense of community left them open for assault. While we should not underestimate the danger of the persistent negative image of the old, neither should we fail to understand the economic facts and human relationships that have sustained them.

Notes

[1]George Dunbar, *In the Good Old Town of Hingham* (Hingham: privately printed, 1890), p. 1. All the following references to Dunbar will be to this text and will not be identified by page number.

[2]John Coolidge, "Hingham Builds a Meetinghouse," *New England Quarterly,* 34 (December 1961), 435-61, 443. This article provides a good summary of the details of the construction of the meetinghouse.

[3]Ebenezer Gay, *The Old Man's Calendar. A Discourse on Joshua XIV. 10 Delivered in the First Parish of Hingham on the Lord's Day, August 26, 1781* (Boston, 1781; Hingham: rpt. Jedidiah Farmer, 1846). All the following references to Gay will be to this edition and will not be identified by page number.

[4]Daniel Scott Smith, "Underregistration and Bias in Probate Records: An Analysis of Data from Eighteenth-Century Hingham, Massachusetts," *William and Mary Quarterly,* 3rd. ser., 32 (January 1975), 100-10.

[5]*The Great Transformation: The Political and Economic Origins of Our Time* (New York: Farrar & Rinehart, 1944).

[6]David Hackett Fischer, *Growing Old in America: A Short History* (New York: Oxford Univ. Press, 1977).

[7]See my "The Demographic History of Colonial New England," *Journal of Economic History,* 32 (March 1972), 165-83; "Parental Power and Marriage Patterns: An Analysis of Historical Trends in Hingham, Massachusetts," *Journal of Marriage and the Family,* 35 (August 1973), 419-28; and with Michael S. Hindus, "Premarital Pregnancy in America, 1640-1971: An Overview and Interpretation," *Journal of Interdisciplinary History,* 5 (1975), 537-70.

[8]Fischer, *Growing Old,* Chapter 1; John Demos, "Aging in Pre-Modern Times: The Case of Early America," unpublished paper presented at the "Human Values and Aging" project, November 12, 1975.

[9]For the continuity of English habits between the mother country and Hingham, see David Grayson Allen, "In English Ways: The Movement of Societies and the Transferral of English Local Law and Custom to Massachusetts Bay, 1600-1690," Diss. Univ. of Wisconsin-Madison 1974. (A revised version of Allen's thesis is forthcoming from the University of North Carolina Press.) John J. Waters, "Hingham, Massachusetts, 1631-1661," *Journal of Social History,* 1 (1968), 351-70 (rpt. in *Colonial America: Essays in Politics and Social Development,* ed. Stanley N. Katz [Boston: Little, Brown, 1971], pp. 51-69), is an important treatment of the same theme.

[10]Waters, "Hingham, Massachusetts," in *Colonial America,* p. 69.

[11]Massachusetts Historical Society, Hingham, Mass., First Church Records, Box 7. Sermon number 7 of the Arthur Marble transcription of Matthew Hawke's shorthand

copy, p. 156; John Winthrop, "A Modell of Christian Charity," in *Puritan Political Ideas,* ed. Edmund S. Morgan (Indianapolis: Bobbs-Merrill, 1965), p. 79.

[12]John Robinson, "Of Children and Their Education (1628)," in *Child-Rearing Concepts, 1628-1861,* ed. Philip J. Greven, Jr. (Itasca, Illinois: F. E. Peacock, 1973), p. 13.

[13]John Demos, *A Little Commonwealth: Family Life in Plymouth Colony* (New York: Oxford Univ. Press, 1970), pp. 134-39; Lawrence Stone, "The Rise of the Nuclear Family in Early Modern England," in *The Family in History,* ed. Charles Rosenberg (Philadelphia: Univ. of Pennsylvania Press, 1975), pp. 36-49.

[14]Daniel Scott Smith, "Child Naming Patterns and Family Structure Change: Hingham, Mass., 1640-1880," *Newberry Papers in Family and Community History* (Chicago: Newberry Library, January 1977).

[15]Philip J. Greven, Jr., *Four Generations: Population, Land, and Family in Colonial Andover, Massachusetts* (Ithaca: Cornell Univ. Press, 1970).

[16]Henry R. Stiles, *The History and Genealogies of Ancient Windsor, Connecticut* (Hartford: Lockwood and Brainard, 1891), pp. 272-73.

[17]Smith, "The Demographic History of Colonial New England," pp. 165-83.

[18]Since the 1850's the age at terminating service in the U.S. House of Representatives has risen. For a discussion of institutionalization, see Allan G. Bogue, Jerome M. Clubb, Carroll R. McKibbin, and Santa A. Ataugott, "Members of the House of Representatives and the Processes of Modernization, 1789-1960," *Journal of American History,* 63 (September 1976), 275-302.

[19]I am indebted to Professor Edward M. Cook, Jr. of the University of Chicago for discussing the problem of age and office holding in colonial New England. See his *The Fathers of the Towns: Leadership and Community Structure in Eighteenth-Century New England* (Baltimore: Johns Hopkins Univ. Press, 1976).

[20]Robert A. Gross, *The Minutemen and Their World* (New York: Hill and Wang, 1976), p. 62; Fischer, *Growing Old,* pp. 45-48.

[21]For example, see Sumner Chilton Powell, *Puritan Village: The Formation of a New England Town* (Middletown, Conn.: Wesleyan Univ. Press, 1963), pp. 116-38.

[22]Massachusetts Historical Society. Hingham, Town Records, I (James Savage copy), p. 75.

[23]Smith, "Parental Power and Marriage Patterns," Table 1, p. 423; Gross, *Minutemen and Their World,* pp. 210-11; Daniel Blake Smith, "Mortality and Family in the Colonial Chesapeake: The Case of Charles Parish, Virginia," *Journal of Interdisciplinary History,* 8 (1977, forthcoming).

[24]John Locke, *Some Thoughts Concerning Education,* in Works, by John Locke (London, 1823; rpt. Darmstadt, Germany: Scientia Verlag Aalen, 1963), IX, p. 34.

[25]*New Hampshire Provincial and State Papers,* ed. A.S. Batchellor (Concord: Legislature of New Hampshire, 1911), XXXI, 275-79. John Robinson, "Of Children and their Education," in *Child-Rearing Concepts,* p. 13.

[26]Giving everything to the spouse is the standard practice in current American wills. See Marvin B. Sussman et al., *The Family and Inheritance* (New York: Russell Sage Foundation, 1970).

[27]Peter Laslett, "Societal Development and Aging," in *Handbook of Aging and the Social Sciences,* ed. Robert H. Binstock and Ethel Shanas (New York: Van Nostrand Reinhold, 1976), Table 7, pp. 108-09.

[28]These figures incorporate my finding that many of those recorded as "boarders" by the census were related according to the town genealogy. On the issue of boarding, see John Modell and Tamara K. Hareven, "Urbanization and the Malleable Household: An Examination of Boarding and Lodging in American Families," *Journal of Marriage and the Family,* 35 (August 1973), 467-79.

[29]I draw this inference from Albert Chevan and J. Henry Korson, "The Widowed Who Live Alone: An Examination of Social and Demographic Factors," *Social Forces,* 51 (September 1972), 45-53.

[30]For an elaboration of this argument, see my "The Periodization of American Family History" (unpublished paper presented at a seminar of the Davis Center for Historical Studies, Princeton University, November 1976).

[31]See especially Smith and Hindus, "Premarital Pregnancy in America," pp. 550-52.

[32]Smith, "Child-Naming Patterns," pp. 9-11.

[33]Fischer, *Growing Old*; W. Andrew Achenbaum, "The Obsolescence of Old Age in America, 1865-1914," *Journal of Social History*, 8 (Fall 1974), 48-62.

[34]*The Inaugural Address of President Jefferson, Constitution and Rules of the Jefferson Debating Society, and the Names of the Members* (Hingham: Farmer and Brown, 1828), p. 11.

[35]Calvin Lincoln, *A Discourse Delivered to the First Parish in Hingham, September 8, 1869, On Re-Opening their Meeting-House* (Hingham: First Parish of Hingham, 1873), pp. 8-9.

[36]Louis Harris and Associates, *The Myth and Reality of Aging in America* (Washington, D.C.: National Council on the Aging, 1975), pp. 29-33.

Thomas W. Ganschow

THE AGED IN A REVOLUTIONARY MILIEU: CHINA

During the three and one-half years (1964-1968) that I was teaching and studying in Taiwan, Hong Kong, and Japan, my Chinese and Japanese friends frequently asked me these questions: "Why do you Americans treat your old people as you do?" and "Why do you shut your parents off in old folks homes—what kind of civilization is that?" I found it impossible to give a civilized answer to them. For I believe the humaneness of a culture can be measured by the care and respect it devotes to the aged. During the time that I sought answers to these questions, I became more and more intrigued with the inquiries themselves: they reflected, it seemed to me, a leitmotif of East Asian civilization. The questions had roots in the earliest traditions of China, Japan, and Korea and were as culturally centered to the East Asian as were questions from me, an American, about China's political and economic institutions. At the same time I also began to wonder how the elderly have fared in the transition from a traditionally-centered to a revolutionary-motivated society. With this double perspective in mind, in this essay I will explore Chinese attitudes toward the aged throughout their history, focussing on (1) the philosophy of and treatment of the aged in pre-twentieth-century China, a traditionally-centered society, (2) the place of the aged in the People's Republic of China, a revolutionary society, from the point of view of Marxist-Maoist ideology, and (3) the treatment and circumstances of the aged in Mao's China, with special emphasis on travelers' accounts and literary sources.

I. The Aged in Confucian China

So many significant aspects of China's history revolve around her most important philosopher—Confucius. It may be an exaggeration to say that Confucianism and Chinese culture were once synonymous, but the hyperbole contains more truth than error. For over two millennia the Confucian philosophy "moulded the national character (of China); it touched every

corner of human activity; it permeated life in all its aspects, whether moral, political, or social."[1] When Confucius, therefore, expressed his concern and respect for the elders, especially for one's parents and the ancient sages, the Chinese people mirrored his words and actions in their everyday lives, up to the present century.

Not that Confucius originated the distinct motifs of the civilization, such as filial piety and ancestor worship, for these practices began in China long before the appearance of writing and philosophy.[2] We know that anthropologists such as Margaret Mead and Ralph Linton have recorded finding primitive societies in which the elders were not treated with any particular respect but rather found themselves in a precarious struggle with the young men who were trying to push them aside and establish new leadership. Linton writes that the "statuses ascribed to the old in various societies vary even more than those ascribed to children. In some cases they are relieved of all heavy labor and can settle back comfortably to live off their children. In others they perform most of the hard and monotonous tasks which do not require great physical strength, such as the gathering of firewood. . . . In most societies their advice is sought even when little attention is paid to their wishes."[3]

But in early China it would seem that the elders' advice was sought and listened to. Perhaps it was because the weak sedentary community was threatened with extinction by attacking nomadic tribes and as a result the young had to learn from the old the skills of building high and sturdy walls to keep out the invader. Perhaps it was because the northern area of China was subject to unpredictable droughts and floods, thus requiring the experienced builders of the society to teach the younger generation the vital knowledge of constructing and repairing the hydraulic projects. Or perhaps it was because, as Olga Lang has astutely noted, "China's intensive agriculture required not so much physical strength as a high degree of thoroughness, care, and experience—qualities which increase rather than decrease with age."[4] In any case, it would seem that as the Chinese took increasing pride in their traditions and showed greater consciousness of their history, they subsequently held the elders of the population in higher esteem, for they were the living source and memory of both history and tradition.

What Confucius and the *Ju* school (a more accurate term for Confucianism) did in China, then, was not invent a new morality of society's obligations to the aged—that was already present when Confucius came on the scene. Rather they embedded those extant obligations and traditions in a firm philosophical and ethical base. In modern terminology, we would say they institutionalized China's past and legitimized its guardians, the aged, for all future generations of China's dynastic history. Confucius himself confessed that he had grown up loving antiquity, respecting the lives of former kings, and idealizing a past golden age.[5] "For Confucius," writes Arthur Waley, "the *wen* (culture) *par excellence* was that established by the founders of the Chou dynasty [1122-256 B.C.]. To gather up the fragments of this culture and pass them on to posterity was the sacred mission entrusted to him [and his successors] by Heaven."[6]

Confucius imprinted upon Chinese civilization the requirement that the

younger generation show more than just respect for the elders; he insisted that their number of years of study and their accumulated experience made the aged the moral and ethical models of the society. Rather than just grow older and older, a man had the responsibility to be faithful to and love the ancients, never growing tired of learning and teaching others what he had learned, and slowly incorporating into his life the virtues of benevolence, wisdom, loyalty, righteousness, and others for correct living.[7] This was a gradual and necessary process that one went through to old age. Confucius, in fact, reflected on his own aging process in this way: "At fifteen I set my heart upon learning. At thirty, I had planted my feet firm upon the ground. At forty, I no longer suffered from perplexities. At fifty, I knew what were the biddings of Heaven. At sixty, I heard them with docile ear. At seventy, I could follow the dictates of my heart; for what I desired no longer overstepped the boundaries of right."[8] Even with respect to Taoism the countermelody in Chinese society, old age was important.[9] In Chinese tradition, then, wisdom might come with learning, but only wisdom *and* old age could produce a sage. As Arthur Wright has noted: "*Learning alone,* it was early recognized, *did not* make a sage—one whose wisdom and power over the minds of men could restore and maintain the desired harmony. A man became a sage only through *long* study and self-discipline which developed humaneness or love (*jen*) and gave him an almost mystical empathy for his fellow men and an acute sensitivity to all the delicate, balanced forces at work in the universe."[10] It is this which is so important about Confucius' belief: a man was made wise by reading history; a young man listened to the elders to enhance his chances of attaining wisdom; and ultimately wisdom in a person would be evidenced in his advanced age by the correctness of his life in the society.

Veneration of the past and the aged, then, became a fixed way of life for everyone in Chinese society, and, for better or for worse, it promoted and preserved those aspects of culture that the educated elite and the ruling bureaucracy found most desirable. Among others, these included the domination of male over female, of family life over the single state, gentry and peasant status over merchant and tradesman, and age over youth.

It was especially in the ritual of honoring their ancestors and the practice of filial piety that the Chinese most formalized the orthodoxy of age over youth. In these two ways, they paid respect to both the living and dead elders of society through rituals that insured and renewed the ruling position of the aged generation after generation, century after century.[11]

In order to maintain conformity and continuity in the practices of ancestor veneration and filial piety, thereby insuring the dominant position of age over youth, the Chinese codified these social values and practices. Codification took two forms: (1) written statutes that dealt primarily with more severe criminal behavior but also included some social duties and obligations,[12] and (2) what Ch'ü T'ung-tsu terms in *Law and Society in Traditional China* the "Confucianization of Law."[13] By this he means that order and regulation in traditional China were more dependent "on *li* [than written law] to maintain the social order and their implementation by moral education."[14]

The concept of *li* throughout Chinese history ran the spectrum of formal court ritual to the decorum of an individual in everyday behavior. As might be expected, *li* (the ritual of behavior, decorum, and propriety) developed out of respect for and in observance of hierarchical differences. As Derk Bodde has written, "*li* prescribed sharply differing patterns of behavior according to a person's age and rank both within his family and in society at large. . . ."[15] The point to be made here is that the rituals of conduct, for example, between grandfather and grandson, between father and son, between older and younger brothers, and other categories of age differences and rank differences were so important—the cement if not the heart of filial piety—that the rules of ritual and, to an extent, the principle behind them were recorded in the *Li Chi* (*The Record of Ritual*), a first century B.C. Confucian classic. And though *li* was important in all orthodox literature of Confucianism, the concept of the *li* stood pre-eminent in the *Li Chi. Li* is singled out for praise because of "all things by which men live, *li* [is] the greatest."[16] Looking back to antiquity for examples and quoting from Confucius for authority, this fascinating book defined for all Chinese, for all centuries, the ritual that children should use, for instance, for their parent's funeral. It also contained several sections that were especially concerned with the way young people should act in the presence of an elder. Here are some examples:

> 1. In going to take counsel with an elder, one must carry a stool and a staff with him (for the elder's use). When the elder asks a question, to reply without acknowledging one's incompetency and (trying to) decline answering, is contrary to propriety.
>
> 2. After sixty, (the coffin and other things for the mourning rites) were seen to be in readiness (once) in the year; after seventy, once in the season; after eighty, once in the month; and after ninety, every day they were kept in good repair.
>
> 3. The kings of the three dynasties, in nourishing the old, always caused the members of families who were advanced in years to be brought to their notice. Where an officer was eighty, one of his friends was free from all service of government; where he was ninety, all the members of his family were exempted from them. . . . Anciently the sovereigns of the line of Yü honoured virtue, and highly esteemed age; the sovereigns of Hsia honoured kinship, and highly esteemed age. Yü, Hsia, Yin, and Chou produced the greatest kings that have appeared under Heaven, and there was not one of them who neglected age. For long has honour been paid to years [age] under the sky; to pay it is next to the service of parent.[17]

The principles of the *Li Chi,* which to some degree both preserved and perverted the principles of Confucianism, guided Chinese society into the twentieth century. There seemed to be little question in the minds of the ruling

elite whether the young people really believed in the Confucian ideals or not. What was important was that they act as if they did and, then, in time they would come to believe in them. Like all such idealization there was a tendency toward an unwholesome parody of the beliefs and the believers; but at its best, they were sincere and poignant ideals that served as a foundation for other ideals of social behavior. And even when the Ch'ing dynasty was disintegrating and most of the traditional values were being questioned and examined, the principle of age before youth, the practice of filial piety, and the belief in the elderly as wise stood strong in China. But the ineptness of the Chinese government to face the challenges posed by the West and the glaring failures of the Confucian state, exposed through foreign wars and unequal treaties, caused the young radicals and reformers to realize these important, if exaggerated, points: China was failing under the leadership of the old; necessary reforms were often being hindered by the elders, and the response that China was going to have to make in order to survive the twentieth century seemed unlikely to come as long as the old system, under the old leadership and guided by the old philosophy, continued to dominate. Revolution was the order of the day.

II. The Aged in Communist Ideology

Communism calls one to revolution: revolution of the economic system, revolution of the mind, revolution of the whole society. "Communism," as I have written elsewhere, "is more than a temporary and fragmentary reform within an existing culture; rather, it should be considered a *weltanschauung,* or world view of life."[18] To create a new man so that he, in turn, can create a new society is its ultimate goal.

The history of past revolutions has demonstrated that it is the youth of a society which stands in the vanguard of both the revolt against the old order and the establishment of the new society. In a speech given to the Third All-Russia Congress of the Russian Komsomol in October, 1920, Lenin spoke of the importance of youth in the Communist revolution:

> . . . it may be said that it is the youth that will be faced with the actual task of creating a communist society. For it is clear that the generation of working people brought up in capitalist society can, at best, accomplish the task of destroying the foundations of the old, the capitalist way of life, which was built on exploitation. . . . I must say that the tasks of the youth in general, and of the young Communist Leagues . . . might be summed up in a single word: learn [communism]. . . . We can build communism only on the basis of the totality of knowledge, organizations and institutions, only by using the stock of human forces and means that have been left to us by the old society.[19]

Lenin calls, in other words, for the youth of the working men of all countries to unite in the proletarian revolution. To use a familiar analogy of Hegel's, the old things—can we also say the old people?—of society must become grist for the revolutionary grist mill. In fact, in the dialectic of historical movement, even the present is an anachronism.[20] Though Marxist theory requires that the future be built out of the past, even more important is the certainty of the destruction of the past. To the older generations, who may believe in enduring values and who may themselves have participated in establishing those values, Marxist declarations of the inevitability of revolution, the belief in the youthful vanguard of the revolution, and the call to destroy the old order must indeed be disturbing. In a certain sense, of course, all philosophical systems tend to indict the past for human failures and imperfections. Marx, however, indicts the past simply for existing. If each age must negate the past and, then, must in turn negate itself, what then must be the fate of the older generation in society? Let us see how Chairman Mao Tse-tung and the Chinese Communist leadership answered that question over the past quarter century.

During his remarkable revolutionary career, Mao Tse-tung added his views to the Marxist-Leninist declarations for revolution, for youthful leadership, and for the new Communist society. In a civilization that placed the aged of the society on a pedestal of respect and for millenia regarded the aged as guardians of China's traditions, Mao was indeed an iconoclast. Throughout his life Mao turned a jaundiced eye to China's traditional culture, rejecting the great sages as advocates of feudalism and slavery for the masses. In fact, Mao's suspicion and dislike for Confucius and the Classics intensified with his increased age and power.[21]

It was not Mao, of course, who was the first to criticize Chinese traditions and the elders who seemed to embody the traditional values. In particular, it had been the young Chinese intellectuals at the turn of the twentieth century who set fire to anti-tradition, anti-old, and anti-Confucian activities, which reached their intensity during the new culture movement of May 4th, 1919. Responding to a half-century of Chinese defeats and humiliations suffered at the hands of foreign powers, lashing out at incompetent republican governments and at warlord politics that proved unable to provide successful solutions to China's problems, these young radical intellectuals denounced what seemed to them to be the underlying causes of China's weakness, Confucianism and all those who supported it. The elders of the society were especially buffeted by the youthful attacks. One of the leaders of the May 4th Movement and the editor of the most important radical periodical of the time, *New Youth* (*Hsin Ch'ing-nien*), wrote in the first issue:

> The Chinese compliment others by saying, "He acts like an old man although still young." Englishmen and Americans encourage one another by saying "Keep young while growing old." Such is one respect in which the different ways of thought of the East and West are manifested. Youth is like early spring, like the rising sun . . . like a newly sharpened blade. It is the most valuable period of life. The

> function of youth in society is the same as that of a fresh and vital cell in a human body. In the processes of metabolism the old and rotten are incessantly eliminated to be replaced by the fresh and living. . . .
> What is the struggle [of youth]? It is to exert one's intellect, discard resolutely the old and the rotten. . . .[22]

Mao Tse-tung, in his mid-twenties at the time, took part in and sympathized with the struggle of youth in the May 4th Movement. He responded especially to the theme that a weak, old China had to be regenerated through the resurgence of youthful vigor and physical strength. Mao, for example, believed that the traditional disdain that the gentry class had toward vigorous exercise had to be replaced with a positive attitude toward physical education. "*Physical education,*" wrote Mao, "*really occupies the first place in our lives. When the body is strong then one can advance speedily in knowledge and morality, and reap far-reaching advantages. . . .*[23]

Years later Mao would couple his youthful nationalistic yearnings with more mature Communist thought, but throughout his life he continued to proclaim the need for a physically strong nation. Through peasant uprising and long difficult marches, swimming rivers and climbing mountains, and fighting external and internal enemies, Mao led the Chinese people to the Communist victory in 1949. And along the way Mao did not forget the role of youth in his victory: "What role have the Chinese youth played since the May 4th Movement? They have in a way played the role of the vanguard, and this is recognized by all the people of the country except the diehards."[24] And later Mao added these words:

> From ancient times the people who have created new schools of thought have always been young people without great learning. Confucius started at the age of twenty-three; and how much learning did Jesus have? Sakyamuni founded Buddhism at the age of nineteen; his learning was only acquired gradually later on. What learning did Sun Yat-sen have in his youth? He only went through higher middle school. Marx was also very young when he first created Dialectical Materialism. . . . When young people grasp a truth they are invincible and old people cannot compete with them.[25]

For Mao, revolution was a continuous process, especially against the "olds" of society. As new enemies and contradictions rose up to challenge the ongoing struggle to build communism, workers and peasants had to renew the revolution. In order to "bend the will of the people," especially the older, more conservative forces in the society, and in order to re-establish his will, especially with regard to his old comrades, Mao launched the momentous Great Proletarian Cultural Revolution in 1966.[26]

The Cultural Revolution, along with the anti-Confucius—Lin Piao campaign, was the final testimony to Mao's determination to have "unending revolution." Once again Mao called on the youth of Chinese society to stand at

the front of his efforts to root out conservatism, revisionism, feudalism, and traditionalism from the People's Republic. Launching out with an army known as the *Hung Wei Ping* (Red Guard), envisioning themselves as "revolutionary successors" and "revolutionary rebels," the youth were dedicated to the elimination of old thought, old culture, old customs, and old habits.[27] Many older Chinese felt the sting of Red Guard insults and many suffered public humiliation and physical abuse. Even old, formerly trusted comrades who had traversed the Long March with Mao on the way to the establishment of Communism in China, fell in shame by the onslaught of words and denunciations. Mao lamented the fact that too many of these people still clung to Confucian morality, feudalistic thought, and revisionistic feelings. "The dead still ruled," Mao believed, in too many areas of life and especially in the Communist Party itself.[28] Mao likened the Communist Party to a human body that had to have a vigorous circulation of blood and inhale fresh oxygen or else it became stale and lifeless. The waste matter of wrong thought, conservative ideas, and feudal ways had to be gotten rid of if communism was finally to be triumphant.[29] So as the "Children's Revolt" sought to root out the evil of the "olds" in Chinese society, no one was safe from their attacks. Everyone from Chou En-lai to Madame Sun Yat-sen (Soong Ch'ing-ling) were criticized to some degree. Mao's old comrade and chosen successor to his leadership role, Liu Shao-ch'i, was singled out for special condemnation and insults. He and "his gang of black guards" were accused of trying to restore capitalism in China and of promoting other bourgeois reactionary activities.

There are numerous stories about how the older people suffered during the years of the Cultural Revolution. Stanley Karnow recounts the story of old Madame Wong in Shanghai. Madame Wong was a sophisticated, brilliant, and somewhat arrogant woman who had been born into a northern family of great wealth, and had been educated at Oxford, where she met her future husband. Dedicated to his country, he offered his services to the Chiang Kai-shek regime during China's war against Japan. He was soon appalled by the corruption and ineptitude of the Nationalists and, consequently, he opted for the Communists rather than join Chiang in exile on Taiwan. During the early fifties the Communists tolerated and even encouraged the presence in China of selected foreign firms whose operations were useful. A few years after Ambassador Wong accepted the post of branch manager for a major British oil company in Shanghai, he died of cancer and his wife replaced him as manager of the British oil firm's Shanghai office. Karnow now relates the tragic conclusion:

> Despite her sensitivity to political developments, Madame Wong believed, like many other Chinese, that the Cultural Revolution was merely another "rectification" drive that would eventually dissipate. By the summer of 1966, however, she realized her error. . . .
>
> As friends who later fled Shanghai reconstructed the episode, Red Guards broke into Madame Wong's house. While some smashed her

> collection of antiques, others bound her hands behind her back, shaved her head, and, forcing her to kneel, ordered her to confess to her "sins." Declaring that she could redeem herself through menial labor, they assigned her to the task of charwoman in a government office.
>
> What followed has been described in two different versions, both tragic. According to one account, Mei [her daughter] learned of her mother's ordeal and, despite her purported indoctrination, killed herself. On hearing of her daughter's death, Madame Wong committed suicide by taking an overdose of drugs. According to the other account, Madame Wong made an abortive suicide attempt and Mei, believing her mother dead, killed herself—whereupon Madame Wong succeeded, this time, in committing suicide.[30]

If old people such as Madame Wong were surprised by the Red Guard eruptions, Mao himself seems to have been shocked by the violence and chaos they wrought. In July 1968, writes Immanuel Hsü, "Mao summoned the five student leaders representing major Red Guard groups in Peking to reprimand them for their 'ultraleftism, their sectarianism, and the mad fratricidal combat.' With tears in his eyes he said that they had let him down."[31] Whether it is true or not that Mao stated that he could no longer rely on "young intellectuals and students" to be the vanguard of the revolution, there is no doubt that Mao had never intended that the old people in the society would be so irrationally abused by the young nor that their practical and technical experiences be ignored. Mao had always stated, though not as emphatically as he had when speaking about the role of youth in the revolution, that the old had a role to play in the socialist society. The young people who had heard Mao's declarations about how youth had the ability to "grasp new things" faster than the "old fogeys," that they should "open fire on the old fogeys," and that it was "correct to crave greatness and success, to be impatient for quick results, to despise the past and put blind faith in the future,"[32] now found themselves chastised by the Chairman. Mao now called for a new alliance, a union of different elements that to the youthful radicals might even have seemed contradictory.

Admitting that he had renewed "faith in some of the old comrades who have made mistakes in the past" and arguing that "most of the old workers are skilled, even if their skill is not of a high order,"[33] Mao called for a "three-in-one combination" or "Three Way Alliance" between the old, middle-aged, and the young as well as the revolutionary masses, PLA representatives, and Party and state cadres. This "socialist new thing born in the great proletarian cultural revolution"[34] was not so much a condemnation of the young; in fact, youth's place in the revolutionary struggle was reasserted. But now it was tempered by the added experience and skills of the middle-aged and the old of the society. The old people, especially the peasants and workers, should not just be discarded as useless, Mao asserted, for they had valuable revolutionary experience as well as practical advice to pass on to the younger generation. But

the elders were not to regain the dominant position that they had once held in Chinese society. The youth, the new freshblood, had taken command in China and that is how it had to be Mao's conception of Communism. It was true that the youth had stumbled, but this did not at all mean that they had failed. As one editorial in China's major newspaper, *Jen-min Jih-pao* (People's Daily), explained it:

> People must learn to walk and also to stumble, and only by means of stumbling can one learn to walk. Having been tempered in the revolutionary war and in a long period of struggle, the old cadres should use their own glorious traditions and their own experiences and lessons to enlighten and help the younger generation. They must support and take care of the younger generation with wholehearted eagerness so that the latter can grow faster. The young cadres on their part should also humbly learn from the old cadres and draw on the latter's experiences to make up their own deficiencies. The old cadres and young cadres must acquire each others' strong points, unite as one and do their work still better together.[35]

All three age groups were required to return to the masses to learn correct revolutionary thinking and socialist construction from the workers and peasants.

III. The Aged in the People's Republic

Though over the past quarter of a century Mao had not been adverse to using force and to following the advice of his own axiom that "Political power grows out of the barrel of a gun," the counterpoise of that axiom had also been a part of Mao's strategy for change: "Our principle is that the Party commands the gun, and the gun will never be allowed to command the Party."[36] Revolutionary education, then, was Mao's key to change the old, the traditional, and even the complacent to active supporters of the revolution. Even Mao's old Party comrades had to go through periodic revivals to keep themselves from going astray from their Chairman's determined orthodoxy.

In the past couple of decades it is possible that every single older—and many a young—Chinese has had to criticize either himself or others in accordance with such criteria as class, background, revolutionary involvement, or political enthusiasm. Oldness particularly seemed to have a natural taint of Confucianism, feudalism, capitalism, or bureaucratism—concepts that obviously clashed with the model of the "New Chinese Man." Thoughts and memories locked in the hearts and minds of the aged linked the "new China" with a past history that Chairman Mao had condemned and villified. A modern Chinese poet has written that the scent of antiquity seeps from the very bones of China's aged,[37] and Mao, a poet himself, seemed quite aware of that irony within himself. Whenever Mao, or for that matter any

older, literate Chinese, penned a poem or essay and quoted the ancient philosophers—it is said that Mao quoted Confucius five times more than he did Marx in his speeches and writings[38]—the persistence of tradition was revealed in the use of historical allusions, the classical style of writing, and even in the very use of the Chinese Characters. Interestingly enough, it might be for this precise reason—the Chairman himself had not as yet rid himself of feudalistic ideas—that Mao so aggressively attacked Confucius and Confucianism in the last couple of years before his death. Mao was not without a solution to the problem of old ideas clinging to the minds of old people. For he had decided that the past was "past and gone!/For truly great men/Look to this age alone."[39]

Mao employed both traditional and, what we would call today, Maoist approaches to handle the aged in China's revolutionary milieu. On the one hand he ordered intense and continuous political education for all those judged heterodox in their thinking and actions. This revolution in education affected young and old alike in China. On the other hand, he attempted to draw the old people, along with the young, into actively uniting in constructing the socialist nation. Mao displayed his unique ability to couple theory and practice by using the old to teach the young Chinese farming skills, by drawing from the old their knowledge of traditional medicine, and by utilizing the old in such jobs as baby-sitting for the very young in state-run nurseries and in the home. As we have already seen in this paper, for centuries past the elders of Chinese society had taught the youth Confucian lessons for the future. And in the revolutionary milieu of today's China the elderly Chinese teach the youth about the horrors of pre-revolutionary days, especially about the misery and harshness of peasant life. Thus, along with the practical skills that the aged have been teaching, they have been giving the youth "political" lessons as well.

Mao, in fact, put himself forward as a model to his fellow older Chinese by reliving his past revolutionary struggles in his poetry. "Reascending Chingkangshan," written at the dawn of the Cultural Revolution, describes Mao's return to an old revolutionary haunt in May, 1965. Filled with nostalgia for bygone revolutionary days, Mao described his amazement at the changes that had taken place in that remote area of south China. New, fresh, and youthful scenes had replaced old, decrepit, and beleaguered ones. Because of the Communist Revolution, "Everywhere orioles sing, swallows dart/ Streams babble/And the road mounts skyward." Mixing genuine human emotion with a political call for continuous revolution, Mao wrote:

> Wind and thunder are stirring,
> Flags and banners are flying
> Wherever men live.
> Thirty-eight years are fled
> With a mere snap of the fingers.
>
> . . . .
>
> Nothing is hard in this world
> If you dare to scale the heights.[40]

With Chairman Mao as their example, scores of older Chinese stepped forward to recount to the young all over China stories about their pre-revolutionary days, their awakening to the Communist revolution, and the happiness they had attained since 1949. And, of course, in the process of recalling their past, the Chinese elders followed Mao's dictum to "criticize the old world, the old ideology and culture, and old customs and habits . . . which [are] antagonistic to Marxism-Leninism, to Mao Tse-tung's thought."[41] The following story is just one of many that were heard by foreign visitors to China. Its emphasis on past hardship, revolutionary struggles, and Communist success is typical:

> This old peasant woman begins to tell us her story of all the bitterness of the class struggle between poor peasants and landowners. Between 1966 and 1968, thousands of stories of this kind were presented as lessons to the "successors of the revolution" among the poorest peasants, helping the young realize just how deep is the abyss between them and the hated past. Having heard the horrors of the old society recounted, and the human sacrifices the old knew described, the young feel proud to be "successors to the revolutionary cause."
>
> "My name is Yang Man-kun," the peasant woman says. "Before the Liberation I lived under exploiting landlords who rented me three mou. The harvest from this land was not enough to pay the rent. One day when I was pregnant, during an icy winter, I had to go out to find grass to eat. I gave birth on the mountain, and the baby died of cold. Returning home, I left traces of blood along the trail."
>
> The old woman is crying quietly now, and the young peasant women watch her with tears in their eyes.
>
> "Our life was misery. We did not even have the right to medical treatment when we were sick. The village head said no, we were fine, and we had to work. One day my daughter was sick and I secretly took her to the doctor. Somebody told on us, told the village head we had gone to the doctor, and he was waiting for us when we got back to our shack. We were so frightened that we took the medicines and hid in another house; but he found us, pulled us out, and beat us with a rod. We were in perfectly good health, he said. My daughter and I fought back, and we were arrested. Since I had no money to pay the rent on the plot, the village head sent me to be a domestic in the landlord's luxurious house, and there I was assigned the worst tasks. I was illiterate, I couldn't go to school. For us, for peasants like us, it wasn't simply a matter of lacking education, we lacked even bread. When the Japanese invaders arrived, they burned my house. Nobody looked after me. . . ."
>
> The peasant goes on with the recital of her calvary. She has put the little red book on the table, and now and then she places her hand on it, like old women in Italy with their missals. She must have told this horrible story dozens of times, but everyone listens as if it was the first.

> "After the Liberation, Mao saved us from suffering. Our life changed. . . .[42]

Since most of these accounts are about China's poor peasants there is little deviation from one story to another. The result is that the old re-enforce in each other's mind the bleakness of life before the revolution and the improvements that have resulted in the aftermath. And one could hardly imagine any young person hearing such accounts and wishing for a "return to the good old days"; rather, we would expect the youth would be determined to continue with Mao's revolution.

In art and literature the pattern described above is reflected, but more dramatically. In the folk poem "An Old Eighth Route Armyman Comes to Yenan," the political lesson for China's aged is particularly clear. The poem tells of an old political commissar marching with younger members of the People's Liberation Army to Yenan again to seek the source of Revolutionary renewal. On the march the old man recalls the bitter times of his revolutionary days when he was a cowherd and the years of famine came and his parents died of hunger. The flashback continues:

> . . . and he just seven years old
> became an orphan, the savage
> landlord making a slave of him
> in exchange for back rent due.
>
> Each day he herded cattle
> by valley sides, each night
> lying by an old cow for warmth
> counting stars in the sky
> weeping at times, and then
> looking up at the Pagoda
> and calling it "Mother,"
> no family folk, no name even
> people just calling him
> "Little Cowherd."[43]

But then in 1935, "Chairman Mao came to north Shensi" and transformed the life of the poor cowherd. The Communist Party decided to put the boy's name in their "Family Records," and he learned "to write on birch bark, read the works of Chairman Mao in cliff-side caves," and "joined in a charge on the enemy," waving the red flag.

And now "thirty springs and autumns" later, the old Eighth Route Armyman returns again to Yenan to be refreshed by the revolutionary waters of the River Yen, where Chairman Mao himself once drank:

> Loving Yenan, thinking
> of his old mother, not willing

to go from the old pagoda!
But now mother Yenan has
changed again, its new beauty
ever unfolding;
. . . .
Old memories, new songs
intoxicate him, and staring
up at the Pagoda, hot tears come;
lightly willow twigs
caress his face, as a mother's
fingers would to her child,
and the old fighter's heart
is moved, as he once more
listens to his mother telling him
to again drink of the waters
of the Yen, prepare and return
to the struggle.[44]

What is especially interesting in this poem is the use of Yenan as the symbol of revolutionary renewal. In the history of the Chinese Communist Party it was at Yenan that Mao and the Communist Party regained their strength after the suffering and losses incurred during the famous Long March. Having fled the mountains of south China in October, 1934 with about 100,000 followers, Mao and the Communist army limped into Yenan about a year later with two thirds of the forces decimated. Yenan proved to be a boon to Mao. Thousands of students and other young people made the odyssey to the caves of Yenan to hear and read Mao's revolutionary speeches. They infused new blood into the membership of the party and strengthened the forces of the revolutionary army. Decades later thousands of old people made the trek to Yenan, either again, as did the old man in the poem, or for the first time, to retrace the steps of Chairman Mao, to reread the speeches he gave there, and to rediscover the source of the Chinese Revolution. It is in this way, then, that the old of China join in the three-in-one combination of the old, middle-aged, and young in order to bring up the new successors to Mao's revolution.[45]

IV. Some Concluding Remarks.

In the People's Republic of China there are approximately 120,000,000 people over 50 years of age, about 15% of the total population. About 50% is 20 years of age or under. Is there any wonder that Mao placed so much importance on youth, be they peasant or worker, during his years as leader of the People's Republic. James Reston has captured the youthful spirit of the Chinese scene in these apt words: "The extraordinary thing about this oldest civilization in the world is that it seems so young, you do not have the feeling here [in China]—so depressing and oppressive in some other parts of the Orient—of weariness, sickness and death, of old men and women spent before

their time, struggling against hopeless odds."[46]

As we have seen, the Confucian tradition and the people who supported it had largely been rejected by the young Chinese long before the Communists came to power in 1949, but it was Chairman Mao who, after that date, tried to bring about old China's total demise. His tenacious drives against the ghosts of China's past continued to his death, for as Richard Soloman has noted, "there is an important tension between Mao Tse-tung's personal conception of how China's political and social life should be organized in the country's search for new greatness, and the endurance of old social attitudes and political habits of millions of Chinese who embody the legacy of China's past."[47] What traumas such tensions caused for millions of China's aged have yet to be measured.

I have argued that Mao's opposition to traditional China made him, subsequently, uneasy with China's aged. There are historical, ideological, and personal reasons for this, and though I have tried to isolate them to some degree, they are intertwined in such a way as to make it difficult to make clear-cut distinctions. The passions of nationalism that Mao and many young Chinese fanned during the May 4 period, causing them to strike out at the old, especially those who supported the Confucian way, met in Mao's Marxist commitment and his revolutionary fervor. As a Marxist-Leninist, Mao found it impossible to live at peace with old China, for there were too many "antagonistic contradictions" between Marx and Confucius. John Fairbank is certainly right when he notes that "Confucius and Karl Marx had even less in common than the ideologies which bear their names, and the differences between Confucianism and Marx-Lenin-Maoism are as great as the similarities."[48] In any case, Mao found a way to turn the nationalistic but negative emotions of the Chinese youth toward the goal of destroying the old society and building the new Communist one. By unleashing the Red Guards in his determination to destroy the "olds of China" during the Cultural Revolution, Mao caused a crisis for the old people, especially for the old party members, that might have resulted in the young revolutionaries eating the old. And it was at this time that Mao—and other older revolutionary leaders—saw the irony of their own advanced age within the revolutionary milieu. And here again I think that Mao the Chinese, Mao the Marxist, and Mao the person sought a solution.

Mao may have observed how his own age, his educational training, his style of writing and speaking, and even his memories linked him to old China, to pre-revolutionary China. And he may have reflected, if the young are naturally curious about that past and the elderly are willing to tell them about it, then this could be either beneficial or harmful to the revolutionary cause. But Mao concluded that everything had to be subordinated to the Revolution, to his design for China—even the memory of an old man or woman. Another revolutionary leader, in another culture, might have tried to destroy the old in the society on any number of grounds. Perhaps because of his Chineseness, perhaps because he believed skills of the old were needed to help build the socialist society, perhaps because he did not want to set a dangerous precedent, or perhaps for all of these and even other reasons, Mao did not set

out to destroy the old people. In fact, he called for their inclusion in a "three-in-one combination" of old, middle-aged, and young Chinese that would unite to continue the revolution and build the socialist society. The way this was done and some of the results have been described in the last part of this paper. In particular, the old were called upon to describe their personal suffering in pre-Communist China, the struggle to transform the old to the new, and their happiness attained under Communism. They did indeed become links for the youth to the past but in a uniquely politically revolutionary way.

Notes

[1] Wu-chi Liu, *A Short History of Confucian Philosophy* (New York: Dell, 1955), p. 13. See also Yu-lan Fung, *A Short History of Chinese Philosophy* (New York: Macmillan, 1948).

[2] Herrlee G. Creel, *The Birth of China* (New York: Frederick Ungar, 1937), pp. 126-28. See also K. C. Chang, *Early Chinese Civilization: Anthropological Perspectives* (Cambridge, Mass.: Harvard Univ. Press, 1976), pp. 95-96, 168-71.

[3] Ralph Linton, *The Study of Man* (New York: D. Appleton-Century, 1936), p. 120. See also Margaret Mead, *Growing Up in New Guinea* (New York: William Marrow, 1930), pp. 212-13.

[4] *Chinese Family and Society* (New Haven, Conn.: Yale Univ. Press, 1946), p. 10.

[5] *The Analects of Confucius,* trans. Arthur Waley (London: George Allen & Unwin, 1938), Book 1, Verse 1.

[6] Ibid., Introduction by Waley, p. 40.

[7] *The Analects,* Bk. VII, 1, 2, 3. To acquire the Confucian virtues became a goal of the Chinese who wished to be truly educated and moral (*chün-tzu,* the gentleman).

[8] *The Analects,* Bk. II, 4.

[9] Legend had it that the sage of that philosophical school, Lao-tzu (which means "Old Master"), had been born a wise old man with a beard, having already spent decades in his mother's womb.

[10] Arthur F. Wright, "Values, Roles, and Personalities," in *Confucian Personalities,* ed. Arthur F. Wright and Denis Twitchett (Stanford: Stanford Univ. Press, 1962), pp. 5-6. My emphasis.

[11] Francis L. K. Hsu, *Americans and Chinese* (Garden City, New York: Doubleday, 1970), p. 236. See also his *Under the Ancestors' Shadow* (New York: Columbia Univ. Press, 1948), pp. 240-42.

[12] See Derk Bodde and Clarence Morris, *Law in Imperial China* (Cambridge, Mass.: Harvard Univ. Press, 1967), pp. 39-43. For examples, read cases 41-45, 88-89, 188-194.

[13] *Law and Society in Traditional China* (Paris: Mouton and Co., 1961), pp. 274-79.

[14] Ibid., p. 267.

[15] *Law in Imperial China,* p. 20.

[16] *Li Chi: The Book of Rites,* trans. James Legge, ed. Ch'u Chai and Winberg Chai (New Hyde Park, N.Y.: University Books, Inc., 1967), quoted from the *Li Chi* (Bk. XXIV, 1) in the introduction, p. xxxvi.

[17] Ibid. Quotations are from the *Li Chi* in the following order (1) Bk. I, pt. II, 1; (2) Bk. III, Sec. V, 4; (3) Bk. III, Sec. V, 12 and Bk XXI, Sec. II, 15. The three dynasties

that Confucius and his followers held up as models for later generations were the Hsia (legendary to this day), the Shang-Yin (c. 1766-1122B.C.), and the Chou (c. 1122-256 B.C.). The sovereign Yü is thought to be the founder of the Hsia dynasty.

[18] Thomas W. Ganschow, "Introduction" to "Strategies of Economic Development," in *Comparative Communism*, ed. Gary K. Bertsch and Thomas W. Ganschow (San Francisco: W.H. Freeman, 1976), p. 321.

[19] "The Tasks of the Youth Leagues, October 2, 1920," in *The Lenin Anthology*, ed. Robert C. Tucker (New York: W. W. Norton, 1975), pp. 661-62.

[20] Karl Marx, "Critique of Hegel's *Philosophy of Right:* Introduction," in *The Marx-Engels Reader*, ed. Robert C. Tucker (New York: W.W. Norton & Co., 1972), p. 12.

[21] Edgar Snow, *Red Star Over China*, rev. ed. (New York: Random House, 1968), pp. 131-37. In recounting his autobiography to Snow, Mao emphasized his dislike for his father, the Confucian Classics, and the old Chinese society. But his intense dislike for Confucius seems to have developed late in life, for Mao's early writings are sprinkled with quotes from the Classics. A recent and interesting, if highly speculative, study that explores Mao's attitudes toward Confucius and Confucianism, along with a host of other psychological questions, is Lucien Pye's, *Mao Tse-tung: The Man in the Leader* (New York: Basic Books, 1976).

[22] Tse-tsung Chow, *The May Fourth Movement* (Cambridge, Mass.: Harvard Univ. Press, 1960), pp. 45-46. For a more complete translation see Ssu-yü Teng and John K. Fairbank, eds., *China's Response to the West* (Cambridge, Mass.: Harvard Univ. Press, 1954), pp. 240-41. The conflict that raged between the old and the young during this period of China's history is especially heightened in Pa Chin's *Family*, the first part of a trilogy entitled *Turbulent Stream*, 1931.

[23] "A Study of Physical Education" (April 1917), in *The Political Thought of Mao Tse-tung*, ed. Stuart R. Schram, rev. ed. (New York: Praeger, 1969), p. 154.

[24] "The Orientation of the Youth Movement," May 4, 1939, in *Selected Works* (New York: International Publishers Co., Inc., 1954), III, 17.

[25] Mao Tse-tung, "Talks at the Chengtu Conference" (March 1958), *Chairman Mao Talks to the People: Talks and Letters 1956-1971*, ed. Stuart R. Schram (New York: Random House, 1974), pp. 118-19.

[26] For more detailed explanations of the causes and results of the Cultural Revolution, the reader might wish to see: Richard Baum and Louise B. Bennett, eds., *China in Ferment: Perspectives on the Cultural Revolution* (Englewood Cliffs, N.J.: Prentice-Hall, 1971) and Jean Esmein, *The Chinese Cultural Revolution* (New York: Doubleday, 1973).

[27] Immanuel C. Y. Hsü, *The Rise of Modern China* (New York: Oxford Univ. Press, 1975), p. 845. See also Mao Tse-tung, "On Contradiction" (August 1937), in *Selected Works* (New York: International Pub., 1954), II, 21, 38-40. Mao wrote, "It is always in such a manner that the new displaces the old in the world, that the old is superseded by the new, that the old is eliminated and the new is brought forth, or that the old is thrown off and the new ushered in."

[28] Mao Tse-tung, "The Dead Still Rule Today," in *The Political Thought of Mao Tse-tung*, p. 368. In this case Mao was referring to the arts.

[29] Mao Tse-tung, *Peking Review*, No. 43, October 25, 1968, p. 5.

[30] *Mao and China* (New York: The Viking Press, 1973), pp. 215-17. See also Ma Sitson, "The Red Guards: Escape from Terror," in *Life*, June 2, 1967, pp. 22-29, 63-66. Older writers, such as Hu Feng and Ting Ling, were also severely criticized during the Hundred Flowers campaign and later in the Cultural Revolution. See Merle Goldman, *Literary Dissent in Communist China* (Cambridge, Mass.: Harvard Univ. Press, 1967).

[31] *The Rise of Modern China,* pp. 847-48.

[32] "Talks at the Chengtu Conference" (March, 1958), in *Chairman Mao Talks to the People,* pp. 119-21.

[33] "Talk at the First Plenum of the Ninth Central Committee of the Chinese Communist Party" (April 28, 1969), in *Chairman Mao Talks to the People,* pp. 283-84, 287.

[34] The concept had its beginning in January 1967, in the Tenth National Congress of the Party and in the Fourth National People's Congress which "summed up this valuable experience created by the masses of the people, and included the 'three-in-one combination' of the old, the middle-aged and the young . . . " (Mao quoted in Chi Hsüan-yen, "Adhere to the Principle of 'Three-in-One Combination' of the Old, the Middle-aged and the Young," in *Jen-min Jih-pao,* January 7, 1976). The importance of the unity of these three elements in society is actually stated in the Constitution of Communist Party of China adopted on August 28, 1973 and in the Constitution of the People's Republic adopted on January 17, 1975.

[35] Kung Yeh-p'ing, "Young People Are Our Hope," in *Jen-min Jih-pao,* December 9, 1975.

[36] Mao Tse-tung, "Problems of War and Strategy" (November 6, 1938) in *Selected Works,* II, 272.

[37] This is a paraphrase of the poet Tai Wang-shu (1905-50) who wrote: "The scent of antiquity seeps from the graves," in "Sunset," *Twentieth Century Chinese Poetry: An Anthology,* trans. and ed. Kai-yu Hsu (Ithaca, N.Y.: Cornell Univ. Press, 1970), p. 183.

[38] Pye, *Mao Tse-tung: The Man in the Leader,* p. 240.

[39] "Snow," "Mao Tse-tung: Poems," *Chinese Literature,* No. 4 (1976), p. 26.

[40] "Mao Tse-tung: Poems," *Chinese Literature,* pp. 51-52. Chingkangshan, or the Chingkang Mountains, encompasses parts of Kiangsi and Hunan Provinces. Chairman Mao established China's first rural revolutionary base area there in October, 1927. A sketch of Mao's return to Chingkangshan can be seen in Hsu Kang, "The Creator of Spring," *Chinese Literature,* No. 3 (1976), pp. 77-83.

[41] "We Are Critics of the Old World," in *The Great Socialist Cultural Revolution* (Peking: Foreign Language Press, 1966), p. 18. This was translated from *Jen-min Jih-pao,* June 8, 1966.

[42] Maria Antonietta Macciocchi, *Daily Life in Revolutionary China,* trans. Kathy Brown et al. (New York: Monthly Review Press, 1972), pp. 225-26.

[43] Lu Yao and Tsao Ku-chi, "An Old Eighth Route Armyman Comes to Yenan," *Chinese Literature,* No. 11 (1972), pp. 55-56.

[44] Ibid., pp. 57-58.

[45] This was the call to the Chinese people after Mao's death in the "Message to the Whole Party, the Whole Army and the People of All Nationalities Throughout the Country," from the *Hsin-hua* News Agency, September 9, 1976.

[46] "The New York Times," *Report From Red China* (New York: Avon Books, 1972), p. 234.

[47] *Mao's Revolution and the Chinese Political Culture* (Berkeley, Calif.: Univ. of California Press, 1971), p. 1.

[48] *The United States and China,* 3rd rev. ed. (Cambridge, Mass.: Harvard Univ. Press, 1971), p. 49.

Thomas Halper

PATERNALISM AND THE ELDERLY

Rhetorically, this is an age of altruism. Governmental activities as diverse as the war in Vietnam and the war on poverty are justified in terms of helping the less fortunate; charitable contributions and expenditures routinely set records every year; corporations stress their social responsibilities and, aside from stockholders meetings, rarely speak of profits except in tones of apology; and writers claiming virtue in selfishness are dismissed as essentrics or moral retardates.

Yet in this age of altruism, no position is less fashionable than paternalism. The very word, in fact, is a term of abuse, and no one—conservative or liberal, businessman or laborer, Republican or Democrat, white or black—has talked kindly of it in recent memory. Men who can agree on little else, for example, the free market advocate, Milton Friedman, and the former radical activist, Tom Hayden, can agree that the "thorough-going paternalist . . . is our opponent."[1] At once quaintly Victorian and deeply repulsive, paternalism has achieved the status of epithet.

There is an obvious and disturbing irony which, like a vulture over carrion, seems suspended above discussions of paternalism and the aged. "Paternalism," derived from the Latin *pater,* suggests a relationship in which those in authority assume a posture toward the citizenry analogous to that a father would assume toward his young children. Yet when directed toward the aged, the paternalistic roles are reversed, so that the older party, instead of dominating the younger, is dominated by him. Perhaps it is the discomfort caused by such a role reversal that is responsible for the commonplace comparisons of old people with children.[2] In a literal sense, of course, "never on any plane does the aged person lapse into 'a second childhood,' since childhood is by definition a forward, upward movement."[3] Moreover, the "second childhood," unlike the first, seems to outsiders ridiculous, embarrassing, frequently even repulsive. In a youngster, slurred syllables may appear cute and

soiled diapers just a fact of life, but in an elderly person, these behaviors rarely provoke the same good-natured tolerance.[4]

In any case, the key to paternalism is what may be called the "paternalistic assertion" by officials of a right to interfere coercively in the life of the ordinary citizen *for his own good.* Its current unpopularity notwithstanding, this assertion has an ancient and not altogether dishonorable tradition in the theory and practice of Western law and politics. A recurring theme in the Platonic and Christian heritages is society's obligation to use its authority and resources to improve and uplift the flawed individual. Thus, Plato's ideal limit, the philosopher-king, unlike the "multitude [who do not] believe in the existence of any Real Essence,"[5] is sketched as capable of discerning justice and pursuing it, and this unique capacity gives him the right and responsibility to further the multitude's proper interests. A main task of the state, as a consequence, is teaching virtue and thereby shaping human nature. Similarly, in Augustine's temporal state, order is imposed upon and Christian beliefs inculcated in a populace whose natural tendencies are, self-destructively, in other directions. Nor need one return to Hellenic Athens or fifth-century North Africa for defenders of paternalism. Prior to the Depression of a generation ago, paternalistic assertions by American businessmen were commonplace,[6] and even today companies are occasionally described as "just like a big family"[7] and a recent President likened the "average American" to a "child in the family."[8]

It is difficult, in fairness, to ascribe paternalism either to the liberal or conservative persuasions, for in truth neither has maintained a consistent stance on the question. Liberalism has moved from a preoccupation with process to product, as the classical liberalism of Adam Smith, stressing the importance of freedom of choice, has been superseded by the contemporary liberalism of John Kenneth Galbraith, stressing the importance of making the proper (i.e., egalitarian) choice. Such a development is hardly surprising; it is surely not easy to retain a belief in the primacy of private decision-making when one is convinced that the outcomes of private decisions embody policies inferior to those of governmental decisions. Meanwhile, conservatism, for its part, has changed from the societal orientation of an Edmund Burke to the individualistic orientation of a Robert Nozick.[9] Nor is this development surprising, either; in the eighteenth century, threats to order and property were seen as coming largely from private citizens, but today they often appear to derive from official action itself. As a result of these historical crosscurrents, liberalism which had generally been hostile to paternalism is now frequently sympathetic towards it, while conservative opinion has altered in the opposite direction. The zigs and zags in each philosophical tradition, however, ensure that nearly all parties must feel some ambivalence on the issue.

I. Against Paternalism for the Aged

No adult portion of the population is the object of as much paternalistic attention as the elderly. The critical factual assumption is that of pervasive

incapacity. "Unintelligent, unemployable, crazy and asexual"—this, observes a prominent gerontologist, is how our society tends to view the elderly.[10] Thus, according to the unsubstantiated observations of one physician, the aged's "normal" condition is to be "frail and unsteady, dozing by day and wakeful at night, confused about people and places, forgetful and untidy, repetitive and boring, selfish and petty perhaps, and consumed by a fear of death."[11] The common short-hand term for these symptoms is senility, and it is likely to be viewed as a progressive and irremediable deterioration of the faculties, mental and physical. Thus unable to care for themselves, unable sometimes even to assure their own continued survival, the elderly are said to be in need of substantial outside help, whether they know it or not. Unless some outside institution, a private charity or a public agency, acts to impose its vision of their best interests upon the aged, they will surely be lost. In fact, probably, the more they oppose this aid, according to this view, the more they truly need it; for their opposition is taken as a denial of the incapacitation that is the central fact of their existence, and any person capable of such monumental self-delusion can hardly care for himself in a hostile or indifferent world.

To the anti-paternalist, this argument and the policies it supports are merely the latest incarnation of a long-standing revulsion toward and neglect of the aged that runs, like a thread of tears, through the fabric of Western civilization. Even the humanistic tradition, so widely venerated for its focus on the human spirit and its compassion for human problems, cannot escape blame, for it "long glorified youth and maturity and left old age out of its realm."[12] These flippancies of Shakespeare, therefore, are representative of an outlook that is itself venerable:

> Age I do abhor thee, youth I do adore thee.[13]
> [W]hen the age is in, the wit is out.[14]

Seen in this light, the current efforts of comedians like Johnny Carson and Jonathan Winters to get laughs by ridiculing stereotypical doddering old persons not only reflects and reinforces contemporary attitudes; they also are part of an odious and destructive tradition in which "old age is life's parody."[15]

Against paternalistic policies toward the elderly, four arguments may be made. The first three are essentially variations on the theme that when applied to the real world, these policies do not work well. The last seeks to demonstrate that paternalism is inherently offensive, and must therefore be rejected, irrespective of the development of problems in its actual operation.

First, though the aged citizen will not invariably perceive his own self-interest, he will do so more often than will public officials or even family members, for only he can appreciate his desires, fears, needs, and perspectives with the unalloyed purity of the insider. As John Stuart Mill put it, speaking in the broader context of an archetypical citizen:

> He is the person most interested in his well-being; the interest which any other person . . . can have in it, is trifling compared with that

> which he himself has; the interest which society has in him individually (except as to his own conduct to others) is fractional, and altogether indirect; while, with respect to his own feelings and circumstances, the most ordinary man or woman has means of knowledge immeasurably surpassing those that can be possessed by anyone else.[16]

The paternalistic analogy, therefore, is viewed as inadequate and misleading. Political and legal authorities, unlike idealized fathers, are not ordinarily all wise, loving, and knowledgeable in regard to the elderly, who, for their part, unlike small children, are not ordinarily immature, naive, and ignorant.[17]

The lesson here is one of humility: officials, no matter how noble their intentions, are necessarily ignorant about many critical factors. Decisions, as a result, invariably carry with them a certain number of unanticipated consequences, and these on occasion may seriously reduce the good designed to be accomplished. The adoption of Social Security, for instance, was greeted as a great boon to the elderly, and yet it is obvious by now that its blessings have been very mixed. For the assertion of a governmental responsibility to provide for the aged would seem to have permitted the loosening of the bonds of family responsibility and thereby made it easier for persons to neglect their debts to their elderly relatives. It is not quite so hard to shunt them aside, after all, when one believes that the government will take care of them. In addition to hastening the elderly's isolation from their family, Social Security also has encouraged their withdrawal from the economy, for the law severely limits the income that can be earned without incurring a reduction in benefits. This is not, of course, to argue that Social Security is a colossal blunder that has done more harm than good. And yet any system designed to aid the elderly that speeds their separation from their family and from productive work plainly has very serious flaws. As a very wise man observed a quarter century ago: "we must be aware of the dangers that lie in our most generous wishes. Some paradox of our nature leads us, when once we have made our fellow men the objects of our enlightened interests, to go on to make them the objects of our pity, then of our wisdom, ultimately of our coercion."[18] It is the old story of government beginning by doing things for the individual and ending by doing things to him.

Second, paternalism, by seeking to impose a risk-free, danger-free life on the aged, may deny them the opportunity to mold a challenging existence for themselves from their penultimate years. This aim, to be sure, may be neither realistically attainable nor safe. Yet its achievement—or even mere efforts at its achievement—may prove more rewarding than the frustrating environment in which a well-meaning government or family protects a person from himself. The popularity of this argument is indicated by the innumerable repetitions of a cliché like "nothing ventured, nothing gained" and the continued vitality in song and story of a tale like *Don Quixote.* Yet there is an unmistakable reluctance to apply this reasoning to the elderly who, (say) after weighing the comfort of old friends and familiar surroundings against the growing inconvenience of housekeeping and threat of criminal victimization, choose to remain in their old neighborhood. The family may fail to perceive physical

security as a normative value that is not desired by everyone to the same extent, and may attempt to impose its value schema on the elder. His choice, therefore, might be viewed not as one on which reasonable persons may differ, but rather as one so outrageously foolish that a nursing home seems the only recourse for the aged decision-maker.[19]

Talk of a challenging existence for the elderly, in any event, is apt to be greeted with incredulity. Do their challenges not better belong to a past when their capabilities were greater? This is a widely held view, and its social corollary, that the aged might as well be warehoused in custodial facilities since their potential is so meager, has had powerful practical consequences, indeed.[20] Much of our everyday experience seems to confirm this impression, and the media provide their own reinforcement. But there are reasons to believe that the existence of the incapacitated aged is not nearly so common as popular stereotypes would suggest, and that the process may not always be as natural and inevitable as it might appear.

For one thing, this view seriously overstates the real extent of true senile dementia. Often, gerontologists have pointed out, "senility" is a "hastily [applied] label"[21] that is "an utterly unjustifiable substitute for an accurate diagnosis"[22] that, in turn, is intended to "cover a lack of diagnostic interest and effort."[23] Even when the effort is made, the results may well be unsatisfactory. Standardized psychological tests, for example, may appear to place a scientific imprimateur on a diagnosis of mental deterioration, but in fact, by emphasizing factors like speed or adaptability, such tests are usually heavily biased against the aged. Memory, for instance, does not fail in old age so much as it simply takes longer to work. It was with good reason, therefore, that one physician complained, "There is almost a complete absence of good diagnostic psychological procedures for older people."[24] The much publicized "mental deterioration rarely occurs among normal older people before the eighties,"[25] and so-called senility may instead be caused by malnutrition, excessive medication, walking pneumonia, anemia, or literally dozens of other reversible factors.[26]

The stereotype of the incapacitated elderly may also be related to an unsatisfactory notion of aging itself. Aging, in the words of one student of community medicine, is commonly viewed as a biological process, "something that happens to us. Old age is a disease, biology robs us, and death is the ultimate mugger."[27] Viewed from this vantage, the individual emerges as a passive victim of impersonal forces. In truth, however, the individual is also the victim of our—and his—expectations. Over the course of a lifetime, the individual learns how an aged person "ought" to behave, and this, together with very widespread social reinforcement, contributes to his adopting that role, incapacities and all. And the rest of us, afflicted with the natural tendency to see what we expect to see and discard much of the remainder, usually have little difficulty in finding examples to confirm our pre-existing views. But even when the elder's incapacity is not, in this sense, "learned," it may have social and not biological causes. Depression, for instance, may result from the elderly person's sense of isolation and loss of social standing and purpose, and what seems to be

dullness may actually be a rusting away of personality brought on by simple disuse. Cut off from productive work, detached from families long dispersed and friends recently dead, many institutionalized elders have more contact with social workers, volunteer women, and practical nurses than with their own children or chosen companions. All of this suggests that the costs of seeking to impose a secure life on the elderly may be real and major, indeed, if not undertaken with extraordinary sensitivity, caution, and compassion, qualities hardly in abundant supply.

Third, as a practical matter, paternalism often serves as a convenient rationalization for self-interest. Authorities and families, that is, may "aid" the older person for their benefit. The story is all too familiar: an older person comes to be seen as a burden by his family and is put away in a nursing home, ostensibly for his own good. This rationalization provides a justification for the outside world and a salve for the family's conscience, but the true cause is simply that the older person has become a nuisance, an imposition, a pest.[28]

And fourth, paternalism necessarily implies an official intolerence for the citizen's foibles and a subordinate relationship with his government that are at war with the presumption of equality and thus "in plain conflict with democratic doctrine."[29] Moreover, the very attempt to treat citizens in this fashion denies them valuable opportunities to learn from their own mistakes and rejects the distinction between public and private spheres that is essential to the preservation of privacy.[30] A well-meaning attack on the rights of the aged, in this view, might promote habits of thought within the government and the populace that could be used to justify similar attacks against other groups in the future. For an official denial of the citizen's freedom to manage his purely personal affairs infringes upon his status as a rational, moral, autonomous being, and as Mill argued in his classic essay, "On Liberty," such a denial of the individual's intelligence, virtue, and ability to choose amounts to a denial of nothing less than his humanity.[31]

For all these reasons, paternalism—at least, in the abstract—seems to nearly everyone an odious doctrine, unworkable, tempting to abuse, and profoundly and fundamentally flawed. The vulnerability of the aged, further, renders the doctrine's application to them especially disturbing.

II. In Support of Paternalism for the Aged

The existence of paternalistic policies suggests that the paternalist—if, indeed, any spokesman could be found who would accept the label—is not without arguments of his own. Four basic contentions can be distinguished, of which the first three are largely refutations of opponents and the last a more positive claim for the doctrine itself.

First, anti-paternalists seek to maximize freedom, in the sense of a literal self-determination, because like Mill they believe that a free man is most fully a man.[32] For most people, however, freedom is not the highest value, but, despite the gushing press it has received in recent centuries, is merely an instrumental

value. We desire freedom, in other words, because we feel that its exercise will help us achieve that deeper goal which Mill dismissed as "much too complex or indefinite an end to be sought," namely, happiness. But paternalists contend that freedom is not the only path to happiness, and that sometimes, in fact, freedom may actually lead in the opposite direction. Thus, they conclude, when paternalism will maximize happiness, it ought to be pursued, even at the cost of some freedom. To do otherwise would be to confuse means with ends.

Yet, it might be replied, how can we be certain that a paternalistic policy will in fact maximize happiness? The answer is, of course, that we cannot be certain, for we cannot compare paternalistic and nonpaternalistic policies with the rigor of a laboratory experiment. But one sign that a paternalistic policy at least conduces to happiness would be its popularity, and it is obvious that many variants of paternalism affecting the elderly do not seem all that unpopular to those they serve. Social Security's Old Age and Survivors Insurance Program, for example, can be characterized fairly as "compelling individuals to use some of their current income to provide annuities for their old age;"[33] the main purpose is to help them and not to help society by preventing their becoming public charges. Yet such a program is so widely supported that virtually no politician dares utter a dissent.

Second, the anti-paternalists seem to postulate an unrealistically sharp distinction between the private sphere (from which government coercion would pretty much be excluded) and the public sphere (within which some coercion would be allowed). The public and private strands, however, are by now so entangled that the dichotomous approach amounts to no more than an Alexandrian solution to a most knotty problem. The entanglement, in fact, has proceeded so far that a pure case of paternalism toward the aged is exceptionally rare. Thus, the Medicare regulation requiring three days of hospitalization as a precondition for reimbursement of subsequent home health services is designed not merely to protect the aged against the consequences of an underestimation of the severity of their ailment. In addition, the regulation has the effect of protecting physicians who might too easily dismiss the complaint and be greatly disturbed by the awful result, the family and friends of the aged person who might view an obligation to provide attentive care at home as a real hardship, and hospital employees who might otherwise discover that their facilities are underutilized and that they are unemployed. Perhaps, one might reply, though the conventional self-interested motivation is present, the paternalistic motivation is dominant. This, however, is very difficult to establish, and, in any case, does not touch the contention that the conventional motivation was itself necessary or sufficient to justify government action.

Third, in today's extraordinarily complex world, there are countless opportunities for the aged citizen's ignorance or short-sightedness to assert itself with devastating consequences. Even Mill, in his exemplary argument against the doctrine that individuals should be protected from themselves, conceded that we may forcibly prevent a man from crossing a bridge if there is no time to warn him that it is about to collapse, for we are warranted in assuming that he is unaware of the danger and does not wish to fall into the river. The perils of

ignorance in a modern, technological society may be more subtle, but no less real for that. In fact, their nature may be such that we cannot assume that the aged citizen will "outgrow" his need for guidance, as a child outgrows his need for paternal authority. On the contrary, a citizen may actually need more guidance when he is elderly than he did when he was more youthful, for much of the information and skills that he possesses may be so obsolete as to be of little help or perhaps even dangerous. A deterioration of the mental faculties, of course, would serve only to underline this need. Social paternalism, therefore, need not be temporary, in the sense that literal familial paternalism is.

Fourth, despite paternalism's unsavory reputation, it is worth noting that at its core is the desire to help others, still possibly the most widely admired of virtues. It is true that paternalism links altruism to arrogance, for it involves not only doing something for someone but also determining that he needs this assistance occasionally in the face of his own entreaties to the contrary. Yet the Golden Rule also has its arrogant element: the assumption that others have the same desires as you, so that doing unto them as you would have them do unto you accords with their wishes.[34]

Furthermore, the attacks on paternalism, by focusing on the harm allegedly done to the citizen, quite ignores the authorities' moral obligations. Like all men, they are of course obligated to do good and reduce suffering when it is in their power to do so. Individuals, lacking the vast resources of the state usually cannot be expected to accomplish much, except on an *ad hoc,* case by case, basis; but public authorities, according to this argument, can and should do more, even if this might involve their saving someone from himself. Viewed from this perspective, the paternalistic assertion seems to stand the Golden Rule on its head. For the official believes not only that he would like to be protected by government if he were an ordinary citizen, but also that the citizen would see his obligation to protect if he were an official.

III. A Modern Problem

Thus far, the problem of paternalism and the aged has been discussed in rather abstract terms, with the main focus being directed toward protecting the elder against some external danger, like destitution. But what of internal dangers? Can we justify the relegation of aged persons deemed incompetent to mental institutions or nursing homes by the same rationale by which we might justify the compulsory taking of a portion of the paycheck for Social Security?

This is a very modern kind of problem, for it reflects twentieth-century concerns, twentieth-century ambitions, and twentieth-century capabilities. The urge to extend paternalism to the psyche, after all, is partly due to a contemporary compassionate revulsion against the harshness of the past in which the mad were either imprisoned in "Bedlams" like criminals or left free to suffer and be preyed upon by an indifferent or hostile society.[35] Partly, too, this paternalism has been a product of the scientific and technological character of the age. Vulgarized, distorted, and misconstrued, science paradoxically

suggests both the trap of determinism[36] and the possibility of manipulation.[37] Certain classes of deviants, therefore, may be seen as behaving as they do because of their socioeconomic environment, their early childhood experiences, a mental defect or disease, but in any event because of some factor or factors beyond the deviant's control. They are, as a result, neither responsible for their actions nor able to raise themselves to the level of social acceptability or individual fulfillment.[38] Therapists, however, benefitting from newly acquired knowledge and the impressive resources of the state, can treat these persons, hopefully rendering significant numbers of them fit to return to society, so that they can lead satisfying and productive lives. It is, thus, not only the individual's *acts* but also his very *self* which are to be altered.

Vastly increasing the impact of these attitudinal changes has been that peculiarly modern phenomenon, the bureaucracy. In times past, authorities on occasion assumed the right and obligation to try to reconstruct the selves of deviants, often under the press of ecclesiastical demands. But these periods, requiring as they did an enthusiasm indistinguishable from fanaticism, could not last long. Intensity would wane, routine would reassert its dominance, and the project would be put aside for a while. But with the onset of bureaucracy, personality alteration has become institutionalized. Agencies and their employees see it as their *raison d'être.* Thus routinized, it is no longer the product of a temporary fervor that is invariably subdued by the mundane; it *is* the mundane, the routine, and, therefore, the permanent.

The impact of these twin modern developments of scientism and bureaucracy upon the aged has been especially pronounced, for of the whole society it is their mental health that is most likely to come under question. It is generally assumed that the incidence of psychopathology rises considerably with age[39] to the extent that the prevalence of moderate to severe psychopathology in the elderly has been estimated at fully twelve to twenty-six percent of the entire elderly population.[40] Among nursing home residents, the percentages, of course, are apt to be even higher. Thus, one careful study of the behavior of 1144 residents in a variety of institutional facilities found that only forty-seven percent of the aged were mentally alert and at least half needed assistance with the simple activities of daily living.[41] The bureaucratic imperative of manageability is often sought through such products of science as the drug Thorazine, which facilitates custodial care by benumbing the elders, or behavioral techniques like Reality Orientation (RO) which has become a common type of therapy to reduce symptoms of senility. In its more structured format, RO features daily classroom sessions of fifteen to thirty minutes involving a therapist and four or five patients who are asked to read an RO board on which are attached cards with such basic information as day, date, and weather. Another version of RO involves the staff's continually reminding the patient who and where he is. Though such approaches have their defenders,[42] there is some evidence that RO may in practice not inhibit confusion but generate it, and that the technique is oppressively meddlesome in that "it morally and officially imposes one group's definition of living on another in the name of allegedly 'objective' rehabilitation."[43]

Many will recoil from such paternalistic practices and conclude that paternalism applied to the internal psychological realm is profoundly different from traditional paternalism applied to the external realm. In the latter case, we may speak of what the elder does will and ought to will; in the former case, we reject the claim that he has the capacity to reason which renders the self capable of meaningfully willing anything at all; in the latter case, we assert control over a small and probably inconsequential portion of the elder's life; in the former case, we assert virtual total authority over his whole being, including even the right to alter his basic personality. In both cases, the elder's desires may be frustrated by government action designed to save him from serious harm, but clearly the implications of officials using the power of the state to deny the very existence of a reasoning self—and assuming that function for themselves—are far more profound and frightening.

The question such a practice raises is not whether specific elders have occasionally been improperly committed due to bureaucratic malice or error; undoubtedly, in such a large enterprise mistakes have occurred and may be expected to occur again. The question, instead, is whether the compulsory commitment of anyone who has not broken the law or harmed another person can be justified. The practical magnitude of the problem is suggested by a pioneering study of the decision-making process involved in the admission of elderly persons to a psychiatric ward in which it was found that nearly all of the elders were admitted for their own good. Only about five percent had actually harmed others and a similar percentage were classed as "potentially harmful."[44]

Sting is added to the issue when we observe how certain psychiatrists distinguish the well from the sick. Fredrick Redlich, conceding that marginal deviation from the norm may permit various conclusions, adds in a tone of reassurance, "I think we psychiatrists know what the seriously ill person in a given culture is. That we do know. In this respect we agree, incidentally, with the clerk in the drug store. Our crude diagnostic criteria are reasonably similar."[45] Far from allaying our fears, such a statement instead reinforces our doubts regarding the scientific medical bases for incarceration. The psychiatrist, like the rest of us, Redlich seems to be saying, relies upon mere common sense, but this is plainly not how other medical specialists would determine that a patient had emphysema or meningitis. Moreover, there is an element of implicit circularity: mental illness, in practice, is defined as a set of behaviors, permitting us to infer from one's actions that he is mentally ill; the psychological dimension, which is ordinarily associated with mental illness, is irrelevant to its determination. At the other extreme, it is worth noting that an eminent English psychiatrist has opined that "normality may be a form of madness which goes unrecognized because it happens to be a good adaptation to reality."[46] Lest such a remark be dismissed as an ill-advised self-parody, consider the conclusion of two researchers that much of the no-talk, no-interaction behavior exhibited in institutions for the elderly reflects a desire for social distance and privacy on the part of elders who are denied ordinary privacy by an environment of constant enforced proximity to others.[47]

By this point, it becomes clear that the main threat of paternalism to the liberty of the aged results from good intentions and not ill, and, adding to the heavy irony, is the more potent and insidious for that. Acting from pure motives, paternalists are not restrained by conscience but propelled by it; and opponents are to some extent disarmed by the apparent nobility of their foes.

Yet, it may be replied, surely this argument against the paternalism of the internal is overdrawn. Of what value is liberty to an elder buffeted by the violent inner winds of the mind? Does not liberty presume a minimum level of rationality and maturity (which is why, for example, children are not free to bind themselves through contracts) that the seriously mentally ill simply do not possess? Is anything gained in clarity by terming the elderly schizophrenic and the senile "deviants," as if their departure from the norm were minor and theirs to initiate and to end? Can the deteriorations of aging be dismissed with the fatuity that growing old is a psychosomatic or sociosomatic illness? If it is true that with the best of intentions it may be difficult to determine who requires the help and protection of the state, does this amount to conceding that no one needs it unless he first asks for it? Or is this merely a rationalization for a callous evasion of responsibility? Granted that the current grasp of the causes and cures of mental illnesses may be unsure, does this constitute sufficient reason to abandon the entire enterprise until such time as we can be confident in our understanding and treatment? If so, how do we essay this quantum leap in learning if we cannot in the meanwhile proceed on the basis of our incomplete knowledge; and how confident ought we to be; and how do we determine that? The questions attack en masse, and, like piranhas, in small bites devour the flesh of our certitudes.

IV. Some Premature Conclusions

"Paternalism" typically is greeted with all the enthusiasm reserved for a dead mouse in a dustpan. So powerful, in fact, are the word's pejorative connotations that in common speech it performs double duty: it describes a phenomenon and signals our distaste for it, both at the same time. But this apparent economy is very costly, and the price is paid in terms of vagueness, ambiguity, unexamined assumptions, and confusion.

Muddying the waters still further is a fundamental dilemma posed by the political strategy adopted by the aged's advocates. Rhetorically, this strategy consists essentially of two assertions: first, the elderly are suffering grievously and will suffer even more in the future; second, their problems are unique to their age group and require programs uniquely targeted at them. Both of these assertions are open to some question. Thus, a careful study of the changing status of the aged reveals that, with respect to health, income, occupation, and education, there has been substantial improvement over the past decade and that this will probably continue to rise for the rest of the century. The gap between the elderly and the rest of society, moreover, is narrowing.[48] And the cry that "the problems of the American elderly have gone practically un-

noticed"[49] is heard so frequently that one is reminded of Kerensky's sobriquet as "history's most famous forgotten man." Nor is it clear that the elderly's problems—health, mobility, employment, low income, loneliness—differ so much from the rest of society in kind rather than in degree.[50]

Nonetheless, in accordance with these by now familiar assertions, a whole range of programs and services are directed exclusively, or nearly so, at the elderly: Medicare, reduced property taxes, discounts on mass transit—the list could be extended indefinitely. The problem is that the aged cannot be singled out for special advantages without also being stigmatized as being incompetent or needy. And this stigma can operate as a self-fulfilling prophecy, for both society and the aged themselves may well view these policies as an official societal judgment as to the aged's inferiority. This judgment, in turn, may support not only programs that aid the elderly but also paternalistic programs that strike at "the linchpin of the quality of life for the aged," their sense of self-esteem.[51] Thus the dilemma: in order to receive aid, the elderly must be portrayed as living so wretchedly that the remedial programs will likely threaten such basic assets as their independence, social status, and sense of worth, as well. On the other hand, if the elderly are not so portrayed, they will probably be beaten out by other interests making claims on the public purse. Either way, the aged's gains seem certain to be accompanied by major losses.

All of this suggests that the larger question of paternalism and the aged is also one of very mixed consequences. Viewed from one perspective, paternalism is by no means the unmitigated evil that it is generally taken for granted to be. Instead, it is often a realistic response to the elder's preference for happiness over freedom in a world dominated by forces too enormous and complicated for him to manage himself. Founded on altruism and propelled by real public needs, paternalism *per se* is neither morally repugnant nor politically unpopular. This, of course, is not to argue for a thorough-going paternalism, for such a system presumes a ruling elite divinely endowed with virtue and knowledge, a kind of contemporary reincarnation of Plato's philosopher-kings. But, by the same token, it seems clear that paternalism properly has an important if limited role to play in modern democracies and, indeed, although it is rarely defended with candor, that it actually plays such a role. Naturally, reasonable men of good will may differ on the advisability of specific paternalistic policies, but opposition to paternalism as such appears unjustified.

Yet, granting the utility of a limited paternalism for the aged, the problem remains of how to confine it within its proper bounds. Such bounds, of course, are entirely abstract and represent a human effort to impose order upon a disorderly nature. As such, bounds are to some significant and irreduceable degree arbitrary judgments. Participants and observers, therefore, will surely differ as to where the lines should fall, and, lacking an impersonal mechanism or objective arbiter to whom such disputes might be brought, will have recourse only to the legislative or bureaucractic political process, a process in which rationality is merely one of many (and by no means always the most important) inputs.[52]

The bounds, in any case, would be drawn not with stakes but with words, and

terminological agreement may not end the conflict but merely provide it with another arena. Broad phrases tend to be vague, ambiguous, and confusing; narrow phrases can rarely anticipate an uncertain future or permit sufficient administrative flexibility. Exacerbating the problem further is the ongoing disintegration of what once seemed to be sturdy pillars of moral authority; plainly, the family, the church, the school, and the state have lost much of their power to define the limits of right and wrong. In a society as heterogeneous as the United States, furthermore, consensus except in particular locales would seem practically impossible. Cultural, economic, religious, racial, and ethnic differences obviously constitute enormous obstacles in the way of creating useful nationwide standards.[53] Moreover, even if these difficulties could somehow be handled, the prosaic but immense problem of enforcement would remain: how could one insure that the agreed upon criteria were in fact being followed? Many of the aged subjected to government paternalism would be perceived as nuisances or superfluous deviants for whose welfare the rest of the society is little concerned. Self-interested politicians and pressure groups, therefore, would have small incentive to perform a watchdog role, which, presumably, would devolve upon altruists who are commonly lacking in stamina, skills, and funds. Adding special poignancy to the situation is the likelihood that many elders might be so vulnerable and weak as to be quite ineffectual when confronted by the power and inertia of a modern bureaucracy. Thus incapable of protecting themselves, they would seem to require paternalists to protect them from abuse from the hands of other paternalists. Since the second set of paternalists is not infallible, either, a third would be required to safeguard against abuse from them. At this point, one realizes that the logic of the solution has directed him into an infinite regress, which itself must constitute something of a refutation. The specter of innumerable competing paternalists, resembling a Pirandellian parody of Madisonian checks and balances, is as unworkable as it is absurd.

In specific contexts, of course, the problem of setting limits to paternalism is fundamentally ethical, which is to say that it depends upon values that can be defended but never indisputably confirmed like a fact or refuted like a hypothesis. As a realistic matter, it is probable that paternalistic decision-makers would speak of the necessity of balancing the elder's rights with his limitations: his interest in his own autonomy with society's interest in protecting him. Such rhetoric, invariably the logic of the self-anointed "practical man," however, is little more than a linguistic deceit, for it begs the basic problem of identifying the values and quantifying them. In other words, balancing suggests a visual metaphor of scales, in which the uniform and impersonal force of gravity "decides" which of two weights is heavier; but in "balancing" arguments, there may be no consensus even on what the "weights" are. (For example, in addition to the elder's interest in his own autonomy and society's interest in protecting him, does he have an independent interest in a society with strong protective impulses and does society have an independent interest in maximizing autonomy among its aged?). And even if the weights could be agreed upon by the competing parties, there is no uniform and impersonal force

analogous to gravity that can "balance" the claims with incontrovertible objectivity. Instead, the decision-maker must inescapably fall back upon precedent, personal values, current social thought, and so on, none of which affords a precisely demarcated and insurmountable barrier against cynical or well-intentioned governmental abuse. By refusing to require subject consent—normally the first line of defense against abuse in phenomena as disparate as political democracies and medical experiments on humans—we undermine our own authority to protect ourselves. If we grant officials the right to interfere in our lives for our own good in some instances, how can we stop them from interfering in others? After all, the assumption is that *they* know best, and not we.

Again, it may be retorted that the anti-paternalist exaggerates the nature of the problem which may simply be a variation on the classic political dilemma of how one constructs a government strong enough to do what is asked of it, without becoming so strong as to tyrannize those whom it would serve. Such a problem can yield no answer in the mode of a problem in geometry—clear, final, and unassailable. And yet we do not on that account renounce all government. The drawing of such a conclusion Bentham labelled the "fallacy of distrust, or what's at the bottom?"

> The measure G, which is good, is to be thrown out because, for aught we can be sure of, some day or other it may happen to be followed by some other measure B, which may be a bad one. . . .If on this ground it is right that the measure would be rejected, so ought every other measure that ever has been or can be proposed. For of no measure can anybody be sure that it may not be followed by some other measure or measures of which, when they make their appearance, it may be said that they are bad. If, then, the argument proves anything, it proves that no measure ever ought to be carried, or ever ought to have been carried, and that therefore that all things that can be done by law and government, and hence law and government themselves, are nuisances.[54]

Plainly, the recognition of the possibility of abuse—whether intended or not—makes us not blindly hostile to power and government *per se,* but instead sensitive to noting and endeavoring to correct what we take to be official failures. The price of liberty, in other words, does in the last analysis turn out to be eternal vigilance, and this general recognition might serve us well in warding off the development of an all-powerful paternalistic state, too.

Paternalistic arguments, as a consequence, can hardly be offered in the spirit of the evangelist. Viewing them as weapons, the reader is likely to look beyond them to what a British political theorist called "the inner fortress itself—the vision of life for the sake of which the war is being waged."[55] Meanwhile, dogmatic anti-paternalism, though marbeled with the fat of fictions and unpalatable when served raw, superficially seems to be a defense of the Free Society and the Human Spirit, each pronounced with capital letters. Thus, while many of its arguments may appear naive or sophistic, anti-paternalism (at least in the abstract) will doubtless ward off all attacks with the self-righteous

assurance of one who has been dominant a long time. The anti-paternalist, as Berlin said of Mill, "perceived something profound and essential about the destructive effect of man's most successful efforts at self-improvement in modern society; about the unintended consequences of modern democracy, and the fallaciousness and practical dangers of the theories by which some of the worst of these consequences were (and still are) defended.[56]"

All of that is true and needs to be said. The fallibility of those in authority, no matter how well intentioned, should never be forgotten, nor should the fact that they are not always well intentioned to begin with. And yet this is, after all, only a partial truth, for the aged are fallible, too, and vulnerable often even beyond their own fears. A humane society requires that this truth be served also.

Notes

[1]Milton Friedman, *Capitalism and Freedom* (Chicago: Univ. of Chicago Press, 1962), p. 187; Tom Hayden, "Welfare Liberalism and Social Change," in *The Great Society Reader: The Failure of American Liberalism,* ed. Marvin E. Gettleman and David Mermelstein (New York: Random House, 1967), pp. 480-81.

[2]See Robert Kemp, "Diagnosis of Old Age," *Lancet,* 15 Sept. 1962, pp. 515-17.

[3]Simone de Beauvoir, *The Coming of Age,* trans. Patrick O'Brian (New York: Putnam's, 1972), p. 472.

[4]As René Dubos, *Mirage of Health* (New York: Doubleday, 1961) suggests, "the semi-senile oldster[s] who [were] expected to spend [their] last years rocking on the porch of the family homestead . . . are likely now to become inmates of mental institutions because they cannot find a safe place in the crowded high-pressure environment of modern life. . . . The problem of our time may be less an actual increase in the numbers of mental defectives than a decrease in the tolerance of society for them."

[5]Plato, *The Republic,* trans. Francis M. Cornford (New York: Oxford Univ. Press, 1945), p. 201.

[6]See, for example, the famous anti-union remarks of George F. Baer, president of the Philadelphia and Reading Railford Co., *New York Times,* 21 Aug. 1902, p. 2, col. 6.

[7]*New York Times,* 22 Nov. 1974, p. 19, col. 1. The article focuses on the paternalistic reign of Charles A. Cannon, head of Cannon Mills for over half a century. Of course, in nineteenth-century France, this attitude had been taken far more seriously by the Saint-Simonians, who sought to combine business enterprise and religious idealism in a kind of feudal industrialism that would benefit the working classes.

[8]Richard Nixon, quoted in Garnett D. Horner, "Interview With the President," *Washington Star,* 9 Nov. 1972, p. A1, col. 8.

[9]Adam Smith, *An Inquiry into the Nature and Causes of the Wealth of Nations* (New York: Modern Library, 1937 [1776]); John Kenneth Galbraith, *The Affluent Society* (Boston: Houghton Mifflin, 1958); Edmund Burke, *Reflection on the Revolution in France* (London: Dent, 1910 [1790]); Robert Nozick, *Anarchy, State and Utopia* (New York: Basic Books, 1974).

[10]Alex Comfort, *A Good Age* (New York: Crown, 1976).

[11]Kemp, "Diagnosis of Old Age," p. 515.

[12] Joseph Freeman, "Humanism and the Humanities of Aging," *Gerontologist,* 16 (1976), 184.

[13] William Shakespeare, "The Passionate Pilgrim," x, 15, in *The Complete Works of William Shakespeare* (New York: Books, Inc., 1947), p. 1222.

[14] William Shakespeare, *Much Ado about Nothing,"* III, v, 36, in ibid., p. 142.

[15] Anatole Broyard, *Aroused by Books* (New York: Random House, 1974), p. 235.

[16] John Stuart Mill, "On Liberty," *On Liberty and Other Essays* (New York: Macmillan, 1926 [1859], p. 90.

[17] Debate on the validity of the analogy between father and governor, family and polity, has been a recurring theme in the Western intellectual tradition. Plato in the *Statesman* argued for the comparability of state and household; Aristotle in the *Politics* declared this a "mistake"; Filmer in his *Patriarcho* followed Plato's path; Locke in his *First Treatise* followed Aristotle's.

[18] Lionel Trilling, *The Liberal Imagination* (New York: Viking, 1950).

[19] Dorothy Rabinowitz and Yedida Nielsen, in their moving *Home Life: A Story of Old Age* (New York: Macmillan, 1971), tell of a son who is tormented by the idea that his mother, who lived alone, might fall and break her hip. Though he telephones her daily and she walks without difficulty, he believes that eventually she will fall with disastrous results. Viewing her contented situation as unreasonably risky, he finally succeeds in having her sent to a nursing home, where her refusal to deteriorate is undermined and destroyed.

[20] Thus, approximately one million elderly are currently institutionalized. Due to the expected rapid growth of the upper age population, a one percent increase in the proportion of the institutionalized elderly by the year 2000 will probably double their number to approximately two million.

[21] Robert N. Butler, Director of the National Institute on Aging, "Biological Research for the Elderly," *Congressional Record,* 7 June 1976, p. H 5398 (daily ed.); Boris Kobrynski, "The Mentally Impaired Elderly—Whose Responsibility," *Gerontologist,* 15 (1975), 408.

[22] John N. Agate, "The Geriatric Physician's Viewpoint," in *Medicine in Old Age,* ed. John N. Agate (London: Pitman Medical Publishing Co., 1966), p. 127.

[23] L. A. Wilson and W. Brais, "Brief Assessment of the Mental State in Geriatric Domiciliary Practice: The Usefulness of the Mental Status Questionnaire," *Age and Aging,* 2 (1973), 92.

[24] A. M. Ostfeld, "The Aging Brain: Alzheimer's Disease and Senile Dementia—Discussant's Perspective," in *Epidemiology of Aging,* ed. A. M. Ostfeld and Don C. Gibson (Washing: HEW, 1975), p. 130.

[25] Dr. Robert E. Rothenberg, quoted in Senator Charles Percy, "Opening Statement—Medicine and Aging: An Assessment of Opportunities and Neglect," U.S. Senate, Special Committee on Aging (Washington, D.C.: GPO, October 13, 1976), p. 3.

[26] Butler, "Biological Research for the Elderly, p. H5398.

[27] Jack Geiger, Book Review of *A Good Age* by Alex Comfort, *New York Times Book Review,* 28 Nov. 1976, p. 5, col. 1.

[28] For a moving fictional portrayal of such an event, see May Sarton, *As We Are Now* (New York: Norton, 1973). In line with this, the Department of Health, Education and Welfare estimates that up to a quarter of the institutionalized elderly are being "un-

necessarily maintained in an institutional environment" (*Congressional Record*, 2 Feb. 1977), p. E544 ed. On the question of family abandonment, however, Ethel Shanas, a University of Illinois (Chicago) medical sociologist, reports that fully eighty percent of older men and sixty percent of older women live with their spouse or children. A disproportionate number of institutionalized elderly, on the other hand, had previously lived alone. If "a person has no family," she concludes, "that nonexistent family cannot neglect him" (*Des Moines Register*, 4 April 1974, p. 12).

[29] Yves Simon, *Philosophy of Democratic Government* (Chicago: Univ. of Chicago Press, 1951), pp. 8-9.

[30] Privacy seems of particular value to the aged. See Phyllis Baldock, "Geriatric Services—The Patients' Views," *Gerontologia Clinica*, 13 (1975), 19.

[31] Mill, "On Liberty," pp. 69-70.

[32] Thus, Locke, for example, maintains that the individual does not have the right to renounce his freedom by such irreversible acts as committing suicide or becoming a slave. Mill agrees that one ought not be permitted to sell oneself into slavery. "The principle of freedom," he contends, "cannot require that the individual should be free not to be free. It is not freedom to be allowed to alienate his freedom." Of course, this comes perilously close to forcing one to be free.

[33] Friedman, *Capitalism and Freedom*, p. 187.

[34] Arquably, activistic altruism is inherently tainted by the ego, like chicken salad made with spoiled mayonnaise. It is not to be wondered therefore, that revisionists, discovering that even saints are human, have begun to tear at the reputations of such figures as Schweitzer and Gandhi.

[35] In still earlier times, of course, the mentally ill were often regarded as possessed by devils.

[36] See, for example, Sigmund Freud, *Introductory Lectures on Psychoanalysis* (New York: Horace Liveright, 1920), pp. 37-38; B.F. Belby, "Psychoanalysis and Crime," *Journal of Criminal Psychopathology*, 4 (1943), 647.

[37] See B. F. Skinner, *Beyond Freedom and Dignity* (New York: Knopf, 1971) and *About Behaviorism* (New York: Knopf, 1974). To the extent that paternalism rests upon coercion, Skinner may not be a true paternalist, for operant conditioning stresses not coercion (which depends upon the subject's perceiving a thread of punishment) but inducement (which depends instead upon the subject's perceiving an offer of reward).

[38] On environmental determinism in the context of anti-poverty policy, see Thomas Halper, "The Poor as Pawns: The New 'Deserving Poor' and the Old," *Polity*, 6 (1973), 71.

[39] Group for the Advancement of Psychiatry, "Toward a Public Policy of Mental Health Care of the Elderly," vol. 7, Report 79 (1970).

[40] Edith Buss and E. Pfeiffer, "Functional Psychiatric Disorders," in *Behavior and Adaptation in Later Life*, ed. Buss and Pfeiffer (Boston: Little, Brown, 1969).

[41] Leonard E. Gottesman and Norman C. Bourestom, "Why Nursing Homes Do What They Do," *Gerontologist*, 14 (1974), 507, 503.

[42] See, for example, J. Folsom, "Reality Orientation for the Elderly Mental Patient," *Journal of Geriatric Psychiatry*, 1 (1968), 291; L. P. Stephens, ed., *Reality Orientation* (Washington: APA Hospital and Community Psychiatry Service, 1965); L. R. Taulbee, "Nursing Intervention for Confusion of the Elderly," *Alabama Nurse*, 22 (1968), 1.

[43] Jaber F. Gubrium and Margret Ksander, "On Multiple Realities and Reality Orientation," *Gerontologist,* 15 (1975), 145. Nursing home abuses, of course, have been so widely reported in the media as to have become a kind of cliché. For a popular muckraking treatment, see Mary Adelaide Mendelson, *Tender Loving Greed* (New York: Knopf, 1974). Thus, the public is accustomed to reading such items as the revelation that fifty-nine percent of all certified skilled nursing homes failed to meet federal fire safety requirements two full years after they were handed down; the more numerous intermediate care facilities presumably have a still worse record (*Des Moines Register,* 16 Jan. 1974, p. 2). Perhaps equally telling is the conclusion of two meticulous observers that only a tiny portion of the activities in skilled nursing homes consists of skilled nursing. Gottesman and Bourestom, "Why Nursing Homes Do What They Do," p. 504. But it is a widespread "lack of human dignity in patient care"—a lack justified by paternalistic sentiments—that most impressed the Senate Aging Committee's subcommittee on long-term care in its report, *Nursing Home Care in the United States: Failure in Public Policy* (Washington, D.C.: GPO, 1976). Moved by these changes, Representative William S. Cohen (R., Me.) proposed a nursing home patients' bill of rights that was profoundly antipaternalistic, *Congressional Record,* 11Jan. 1977, p. E116 (daily ed.).

[44] Marjorie F. Lowenthal, *Lives in Distress* (New York: Basic Books, 1964), pp. 204-05.

[45] Frederick C. Redlich, *Interrelations between the Social Environment and Psychiatric Disorders* (New York: Milbank Memorial Fund, 1953), p. 120.

[46] F. Glover, "Medico-Psychological Aspects of Normality," *British Journal of Psychiatry,* 23 (1932), 1965. Of course, this is a contradiction in terms. If normality is madness, then there can be no normality and no madness, either; for the existence of each concept depends upon the other.

[47] Arthur N. Schwartz and Hans G. Proppe, "Perceptions of Privacy among Institutionalized Aged," *Proceedings of the 77th Annual Convention, American Psychological Association,* 4 (Pt. 2) (1969), 727-28.

[48] Erdman Palmore, "The Future Status of the Aged," *Gerontologist,* 16 (August 1976), 297.

[49] Note "Discrimination against the Elderly: A Prospective of the Problem," *Suffolk Law Review,* 7 (1973), 918. Thus, in a day picked at random, the *Congressional Record* 31 Jan. 1977 (daily ed.), contained no less than twenty-one items on the elderly, all of them sympathetic; this was not an election year or a time of especially heightened interest in the plight of the aged.

[50] Undeniably, however, certain medical problems frequently have different causes and treatments in the elderly, such as headaches, weight loss, altered cholesterol levels, mental changes, fevers, arthritis, and diabetes. This recognition—in addition to an urge to spur gerontological research and humanize care of the elderly—lies behind the current effort to induce or coerce medical schools into creating a specialty in geriatrics.

[51] Arthur N. Schwartz, "An Observer: On Self-Esteem as the Linchpin of Quality of Life for the Aged," *Gerontologist,* 15 (1975), 470.

[52] See Paul Diesing, *Reason in Society* (Urbana: Univ. of Illinois Press, 1962), pp. 171-234.

[53] Those downplaying this problem might do well to review the Supreme Court's apparently foredoomed efforts to create workable national standards in that policy area

of comparatively modest importance, obscenity.

[54]Jeremy Bentham, *The Handbook of Political Fallacies,* ed. Harold A. Larrabee (New York: Harper and Brothers, 1962 [1824]), p. 101.

[55]Isaiah Berlin, *Four Essays on Liberty* (London: Oxford Univ. Press, 1969), p. 201.

[56]Ibid.

Donald Marquis

ETHICS AND THE ELDERLY: SOME PROBLEMS

There is growing interest in the problems of the elderly. There should be. In the first place, the number of those over sixty-five in this country is rapidly increasing, both in absolute terms and as a proportion of the total American population. Because of medical advances, many diseases can be either cured, prevented, or controlled. The most noteworthy exceptions to medical progress are those diseases whose occurrence is correlated with age: cardiovascular diseases and cancer. Consequently, an increasing percentage of the population is living beyond the age of sixty-five. Now almost ten percent of the American population is sixty-five years of age or older; by the year 2000 this percentage may nearly double. In the second place, there is growing awareness that the elderly are not as well off as other age groups in the population. As a group they require much more medical care than do others. Few of them are in the work force. Their incomes from private pensions and social security are lower than the incomes of those of working age. They are discriminated against in various ways. They are often retired or fired from their jobs solely on account of their age. We suspect that a "You can keep your job only if you are under 65" policy is no better than a "Whites only" hiring policy. Many of the elderly are excluded in one way or another from the normal affairs of society. Whether they are isolated from the community in retirement homes or whether they lack adequate transportation to get to places where they wish to travel, the effect is the same: many of them are isolated and lonely. Furthermore, our culture is youth-oriented. Young people and middle-aged people do not like to grow old; the old are often perceived as living through a stage of life which is disvalued. Being old is perceived as waiting around to die. If the fountain of youth were discovered, its owner would make a fortune selling bottled water. People grow old, not because they want to, not because they value age, but because the only alternative to growing old is dying.[1]

We are, and should be, bothered by this family of moral concerns. We feel it is wrong that so many of the elderly live so close to, or below, the poverty level.

We feel it is wrong that the elderly are discriminated against. We feel it is wrong that being old is disvalued. We feel ashamed that the quality of the lives of many of the elderly is so poor. And we feel that something ought to be done about these matters.

Many people have these moral sentiments; I have these moral sentiments. But in moral philosophy moral sentiments are not enough. For one thing we may have conflicting moral sentiments in certain situations, as when a lie may further benevolent ends. Merely having moral sentiments does not tell us the right thing to do in such a situation. In the second place, moral sentiment does not establish for us the *extent* of our duties. Surely some persons' moral sentiments toward the elderly are stronger than others. But this does not seem to be sufficient to show that the duty of some toward the elderly is greater than the duty of others.

What we would like to have, then, is not merely a set of moral sentiments toward the elderly, but an *ethics* which relates to the elderly. By an ethics I mean a set of moral claims about our obligations toward the elderly which form a coherent whole and which are justified by an appeal to basic moral principles. We would like to have some account of the obligations of the non-elderly to the elderly such that those obligations would be not merely moral sentiment, not merely moral opinion, but would be *reasonable* moral claims.

There is no such account. So far as I know there is no literature whatsoever that consists of sustained ethical reflection on the nature, extent, and justification of our obligations toward the elderly. Furthermore, I think it can be shown that several ethical theories which are or have been popular and which are regularly studied in courses in ethics do not (at least do not obviously) imply that we have obligations toward the elderly such that if we acted as we ought to act, the condition of the elderly would be measurably improved.

I am not making the trivial point that one cannot deduce substantial obligations toward the elderly from ethical egoism or from the moral principles found in the ethical treatises of Attila the Hun. There are difficulties with the deduction of substantial duties toward the elderly even from those ethical theories which contain the basis for the derivation of significant obligations to others.

The ethical theories I shall discuss are not theories which belong merely to the ethics class or the scholar's bookshelf. These theories are taken seriously by the philosophical community because they are theories which do seem to make explicit some of the basic moral intuitions of our culture and perhaps of mankind. That we may not be ready to accept all of the implications of these theories shows only that often we do not work out carefully the consequences of our beliefs. Furthermore, it is clear that sometimes, when we do work out the consequences of even our basic convictions, we then decide to revise those convictions. The purpose of the following pages is to examine some ethical principles which, when first considered, seem very plausible and to show that they do lead, upon analysis, to moral stances toward the elderly which seem quite unacceptable. Only by this sort of process of reflection can we make progress both in ethical theory and in a search for reasonable and justified policies toward the elderly.

I

When I began reflecting upon the ethics of the treatment of the elderly, I asked many of my colleagues in philosophy for their thoughts concerning the conjunction of ethics and the problems of the elderly. One replied that there are *no* special ethical problems concerning the elderly. The correct moral stance toward the elderly, he said is simple: Elderly human beings are human beings. Therefore, one has the same obligations toward them that one has toward other human beings.

This particular philosopher does ethics in the tradition of Immanuel Kant. As I reflected on my friend's remark I began to see that if one has only those obligations that are generated by reflection within at least one version of the ethical tradition of Kant or within similar traditions, what might be described as a rather hard-hearted policy toward the elderly would emerge. In particular, positive obligations toward the elderly, obligations that require some positive action on our part, emerge with difficulty, if at all.

This point requires a bit of explanation and analysis. Put briefly, and perhaps oversimply, the key test of a moral standard for Kant, what Kant calls "the categorical imperative," involves asking whether one could rationally will that one's own rule of conduct become a universal law; that is, one asks whether one could rationally will that one's rule of conduct become everyone's rule of conduct.[2] A rule of conduct is morally permissible if and only if one could rationally will that such a rule of conduct be adopted by everyone. For example, the rule of conduct "Whenever it is to my advantage, I shall not tell the truth" is morally impermissible because if that were everyone's rule of conduct, no one would believe what a person said when it was known not to be in his interests to tell the truth.

It is worth noting here that Kant's categorical imperative does capture and attempt to make explicit what many people intuitively regard as basic to morality. Furthermore, this imperative, if not pressed too hard, does generate interesting and exceptionless duties relating both to non-interference in the lives of others and to keeping contracts. One cannot rationally will "Whenever it is to one's advantage, one shall not keep a contract" since if that were everyone's rule of conduct, others would not make contracts unenforceable by law; hence, one could not use contracts unenforceable by law for one's own purposes.

The obligations whose generation via the categorical imperative are most obvious seem to be *negative* duties, duties *not* to interfere with persons or arrangements. Furthermore, such Kantian negative duties are "perfect" duties; that is, such duties are exceptionless. Kantian morality is very rigorous and does not appear to provide for exceptions to these duties even in unusual circumstances. In spite of the rigor of Kantian negative duties, such duties are not difficult to fulfill, for they do not require us to *do* any particular thing. They only require us to refrain from certain actions. Kantian morality does not generate for us an abundance of obligations or relatively onerous ones.

Positive duties, duties which require some action, have a different, and more

disputable, status in Kantian ethics. The duty of benevolence is such a duty for Kant. Kant calls this duty an imperfect duty. Its imperfection manifests itself in at least two ways: First, one cannot be benevolent to everyone (though one can refrain from lying to everyone). So the duty of benevolence *cannot* be "perfectly" fulfilled in the way the duty not to lie or the duty not to kill can be. Secondly, the categorical imperative does not tell us how benevolent we ought to be even toward a particular person.

Although Kant did not think so, it seems to me that reflection upon the "imperfection" of the duty of benevolence yields the conclusion that the duty of benevolence may not exist for me at all. Suppose one is well situated financially. Is it immoral to adopt the rule of conduct "Under no circumstances help those in need"? I don't see why not. One may prefer to will that rule of conduct as a universal law rather than some universal rule of conduct involving benevolence. For if the probabilities of being in need are slight, a universal rule involving any degree of benevolence is more likely to deplete one's resources than succor one's needs. The duty of benevolence turns out on Kant's *principles* (on this interpretation) to be a *very* imperfect duty; indeed, it is so imperfect that there are persons for whom it does not exist at all! Duty, on this account of things, does not consist primarily in helping others, but in leaving a man alone to see what he can make of himself.

One can arrive at this conclusion by a different route. Kant regarded another formulation of the categorical imperative to be equivalent to the version we have been discussing. In this formulation one ought to treat humanity "never simply as a means, but always at the same time as an end." Kant's moral principle is an explicit statement of a moral conviction of many: persons are never to be used merely for our own purposes, but are also to be treated as having intrinsic value. So, for example, an employer is not prevented from using an employee for his own interests by this dictum. But such a use must be compatible with the employer regarding the employee as a person, not merely as an instrument of his will.

Although Kant would not agree, it is most unclear how we can deduce much of a duty of benevolence from this first principle. It is one thing always to regard others in our dealings with them as persons, never just as means for our own satisfaction. If so, certain behavior is *forbidden.* It is quite another thing to reach out actively to others with whom we would not otherwise interact.

What account of our obligations toward the elderly is given by such ethical principles? Surely we are left with an ethics of benign neglect. Of course, the elderly are not to be killed or harmed. Of course, they should not be discriminated against solely on grounds of age. But it follows from none of this that we should be particularly morally concerned if they are isolated from society or if many of them live at or near the level of poverty or if they do not have adequate medical care. To provide them with medical care or to provide them with transportation or to provide them with the material comforts or even necessities of life are all positive acts. If these acts are obligatory, they are positive obligations. On my reading of Kant's *principles,* "positive obligations" are not particularly obligatory, if obligatory at all.

The distinction between negative duties and positive obligations that is invidious to positive obligations is often made on other grounds.[3] Sometimes it is merely regarded as intuitively evident. One plausible basis for the distinction is that while fulfilling negative duties does not "cost" us anything, that is, an expenditure of time, effort, or money to fulfill them is not typically required, positive obligations require us to give up something on which we (apparently) have a claim. Thus, determining the extent of our positive obligations involves balancing those claims against the claims of others. However the distinction is justified and explained, many who accept this distinction will not feel any very urgent obligations toward the elderly or any obligations which cause them a great deal of inconvenience.

The problem is that obligations toward the elderly, if they are to remedy those matters that are described as the plight of the elderly, will cause other age groups a lot of inconvenience. Consider the current flap over Social Security. It is estimated that in ten years there will be only 2.3 persons in the work force for every person receiving Social Security benefits. Providing an adequate level of benefits will require quite large deductions from the salaries of the work force. This burden is rightly perceived as onerous; it does require sacrifice. Paradoxically, the very qualitative and quantitative dimensions of the problems of the elderly, those features of the problem that increase the magnitude of our concern, also make it much less than obvious how that problem should be dealt with—at least within the ethical traditions we are considering.

One important reason for this problem is that the situation of the elderly is in important respects unprecedented. The existence of a large number, of a very substantial proportion, of elderly people in our society who do not live with their children creates a problem for ethics that did not exist earlier. As long as one thinks of relations of obligation as existing only between relatively autonomous agents who can function capably as long as their actions are not interfered with, then an ethics of negative duties is fairly plausible. Positive obligations impose constraints upon our actions that negative obligations do not. Negative obligations only require us to *avoid* doing certain things; as long as those things are avoided, doing what we want is possible. Positive obligations extract from us either time or money. They curtail the freedom of an autonomous individual to do what he wants. In a complementary manner, if those negative obligations are observed, then *others* can do what they want. A system of negative obligations, if adhered to, sets the moral stage, so to speak, for the free action of autonomous individuals without interfering with the freedom of action of others. Duty consists of staying out of everyone else's way.

This picture of society will not quite do, of course. Special provisions must be made for non-working women and children. But such women and children are seen, on this account, as supported by a male wage-earner. The act of marriage is seen as a contract. Marital and parental obligations are assumed by entering into that contract and on a Kantian view of things, a violation of that contract is as serious as the violation of a negative duty. Still, familial and

parental responsibilities are not *required* of us on this view. We are free not to enter into the contract at all.

Many of the elderly simply do not fit into the picture I have sketched. A vast number of the elderly just are not autonomous agents who can fulfill their lives as they wish merely by being left alone. In addition, a high percentage are not in good health by the standards of health that apply to a forty-year old. Many are not able to get employment because they are not physically capable of holding down an ordinary job; or are not able to get employment because of mandatory retirement policies; or are not able to engage in what those in other age groups would consider to be ordinary human activities. In short, they do not fit into the autonomous agent role in the traditional picture. But the elderly do not fit into the family role either, for many well-known reasons. Hence, the elderly are excluded from the picture or model of society that the ethical principles I am considering presuppose.

I have been arguing that there is a certain theory of morality—an ethics—which does not justify the claim that we have substantial obligations to the elderly. The view that we do not have such obligations flies in the face of my moral sentiments and, I am sure, the sentiments of many others. Accordingly, I am inclined to think that the notion of morality embodied in the interpretation of Kant considered here and in other similar theories must be given up. But this must be done in the recognition that the ethical theory we have been discussing is intuitively plausible and persuasive if not pressed too hard. Furthermore, this ethical theory does undoubtedly make explicit the basic, if unspoken, moral intuitions of many people. What is interesting here is that the sorts of obligations we have to the elderly apparently cannot be based upon some randomly selected ethical theory; even a theory which is as scrupulous about respecting the rights of others as is Kant's moral philosophy.

II

If we find that one kind of ethical theory will not justify and explain the obligations toward the elderly we surely have, it seems reasonable to examine a different sort of theory. There are other ethical theories that do generate positive obligations toward others. The best known is utilitarianism. Utilitarianism comes in a variety of forms. It may be a criterion of rightness for individual acts, rules, attitudes, social policies, or acts of legislatures. A utilitarian claims that whatever is being evaluated morally is right if and only if the consequences of that act, rule, attitude, policy, or law are more valuable than alternative acts, rules, and so forth. For the purposes of this discussion we need be concerned only with social policies. What we want to know is whether obligations to the elderly that entail a greater allocation of resources to them can be justified on utilitarian grounds.

Utilitarianism clearly entails some positive obligations—indeed, it entails significant positive obligations. To over-simplify matters a bit, if one is contemplating a choice between performing some action A and not performing it,

and doing A produces more of value than not doing A, then one has an obligation to do A even if all the value produced by A accrues to others. The ethics of utilitarianism is clearly not an ethics of benign neglect. It commands that value be maximized. To whom these values accrue is not an object of utilitarian assessment.

Accordingly, there will be a utilitarian justification of a social policy of beneficence toward the elderly only if the value gained by allocating resources so as to benefit the elderly is greater than the value lost to other age groups because of the allocation. Clearly utilitarianism, in order to be operative, requires a theory of value. The classical utilitarians regarded pleasure as the sole ultimate value, but we need not make this assumption. For the purposes of our limited analysis here, we might regard as valuable whatever people in our culture at this time do regard as valuable.

This quite clearly sets a problem for us. For it is a truism that the prevailing cultural attitude in late twentieth-century America is not to perceive value in the lives and the activities of the elderly as compared to other age groups. Of course, many "humanistically" oriented studies of the aged in contemporary America attempt to contest this attitude; they do attempt to find value in the activities and lives of the aged.

What are we to make of this? Surely exceptionless generalizations about the capacity of the aged to realize value in their lives or to perform those activities that are generally regarded as worthwhile are one and all false. Assertions about the declining achievements of persons over 65 will be inevitably met by counterexamples. Nevertheless, if we are concerned about *social* issues, if we are concerned about the plight of the elderly as a *group* in contemporary America, then *tendencies* are significant, even if there are not infrequent exceptions to those tendencies. It is surely incontrovertible that there is a decline in the physical and intellectual powers of the elderly. Whatever the achievements of some of the elderly, *in general* they are not capable of creating value to the extent that those in younger age groups are. If this is the case, surely there will be difficulties with any utilitarian argument in which it is maintained that there should be a reallocation of social resources so that the elderly have more and other age groups less.

The difficulty here can be made more perspicuous if we compare the situation of the elderly with the situation of children. There are good utilitarian arguments for education, indeed, for public education, because education provides human beings with the opportunity and the encouragement to create things of value. Education is value creating, and the children who benefit from education use that education to produce and achieve those things that are regarded as socially valuable. Subsidization of the aged, in general, does not have at all the same effect. Their careers are over; their productive and intellectual powers are declining; their creative capacities are dimmed. Their futures are, by comparison to children, quantitatively slight; their capacity for creation is qualitatively diminished. By comparison, then, the argument for investment in them *if it is a utilitarian argument,* is much weaker.

Discussions of geriatric medicine refer to a similar problem. It is often said that many physicians do not spend enough time with their older patients, that they neglect their older patients in favor of their younger patients. The reason that is given for this practice is that whereas there is the possibility of producing genuine improvement or even cure in the case of middle-aged or younger patients, the degenerative diseases of the aged are not cured. Indeed, improvement in the condition of the elderly is often impossible. Medical care in these elderly often amounts to battling degeneration on even terms and ultimately merely to slowing the rate of degeneration. It is often alleged that many physicians do not find sufficient positive reinforcement to continue those efforts. What this comes to is that some physicians do not see medical care of the elderly as productive of sufficient value to merit their efforts. It is better in their eyes that they treat patients who can really profit from medical care. Notice that this seemingly callous approach is not egoistic; it seems certainly utilitarian.

Perhaps the problem here can be made even more salient by means of an analogy. Suppose that the voters in some community are being asked to vote approval for bonds to finance the construction of a new bridge across a river that runs through the middle of town. Shortly before the bond election they are told that the bridge will probably last only eight years before it must be torn down and that even during its life span, it will not be able to support heavy truck traffic. Voters will be unlikely to approve the bonds. For there are severe limitations on the *time* of value production for this investment and also limitations on the value produced by that investment during the time that investment is productive. The analogy with a utilitarian justification of policies of beneficence toward the elderly is plain to see.

But there is even a further problem. Education is justified on utilitarian grounds, not only because of its benefits for each and every student, but because those benefits have a "multiplier effect." Education benefits not only those who receive it, but also those who interact in various ways with those who receive it. A person who is educated benefits others by being a good citizen, by producing goods and services that others use, and by raising the cultural climate of the community for the benefit of others. Beneficent policies toward the elderly will lack many of these secondary beneficial effects. The elderly are not, in general, members of the work force. Policies that benefit them do not, therefore, have the effect of returning more goods and services to the economy. The benefits, by and large, *stop* with the elderly.

One might object here that the problem I am raising presupposes a biased theory of value, that I am assuming that the values to be promoted by social policy are to be the values of those who are younger than the elderly. But why should this be? Perhaps we should count as valuable what the *elderly* count as valuable. Perhaps what the elderly count as valuable should be judged to be as valuable as that which younger members of society count as valuable. If so, it might be alleged, the problems with a utilitarian justification of a policy of beneficence to the aged do not arise.

I do not think that this line of objection succeeds. Interpersonal com-

parisons of relative value among age groups *are* possible. Let us consider a thought experiment. Suppose that every eighty-year-old person were given the opportunity of becoming forty years old and that every forty-year-old were given the opportunity of becoming eighty years old. I submit that there would be considerably fewer people who would take the opportunity of becoming older than people who would take the opportunity of becoming younger. *One* reason for such a decision, of course, would be that an eighty-year-old would have less of a future; to decide to be eighty is to decide to shorten one's future. But surely *another* reason for such a decision would be that one would judge the quality of one's life to be better at forty than at eighty. Presumably, if we were given just ten years to live and we had the choice of the age at which to live them, then one would prefer to live them at middle age rather than old age. But if this is so, then our problem with the utilitarian justification of a policy of beneficence toward the elderly remains.

The problems here run very deep. Utilitarianism is a *future* oriented ethics; present actions are justified in terms of future pay-offs. The elderly, almost by definition, have less future than those in younger age groups. Less future, less pay-off. The problem here is also related to our attitudes toward death. When a man dies in the prime of life, we pity him. We feel it was a bad thing for him to die because of the future that he lost.[4] When a man dies at age ninety, we often feel that such a death is more acceptable because little is lost. This fits well with the view that the latter life is less valuable than the former.

III

There are other difficulties which concern utilitarian ethics and the elderly. I have so far assumed that the ethical issue concerning treatment of the elderly should be analyzed with respect to a fixed population and that the fundamental issue we need to consider is how resources should be distributed within this population. But there is no reason to consider this assumption sacred. It may well be possible to maximize value by altering the population—say, by killing off its less valuable members. Indeed, there is an argument—a pretty good argument I think—for the view that a utilitarian ethics would justify genocide of the elderly. And if such an argument succeeds, then we have even better reasons than previously offered not to attempt to wrap ourselves in the mantle of utilitarian standards in order to attempt to justify a policy of beneficence to the elderly.

Perhaps this problem can be developed by considering the ethics of killing at the beginning of life. The moral permissibility of abortion is often defended on utilitarian grounds. Those who defend the moral permissibility of abortion often cite in their favor the population explosion, the significant disruption of life plans if a woman continues with an unwanted pregnancy and the diminished value of a child's life if the fetus is discovered to have some dreadful defect. These considerations are in fact taken (by many) to be sufficient to justify killing very young members of the species *Homo sapiens* on a

very large scale. As far as I can tell these considerations are utilitarian in character. It is worth noting—and worrisomely so—that similar considerations apply also to the elderly. Killing them off would diminish the surplus population; killing them off would relieve the work force of the burden of supporting them; the value of the lives of many of the elderly *are* diminished.

It will be objected that there are differences between killing fetuses and killing old people: fetuses do not suffer anguish and apprehension over being killed; fetuses do not suffer while they are being killed. However, such objections do not establish a moral asymmetry from a utilitarian point of view. If we were to adopt a policy of genocide of the elderly, we would not wish, of course, for killings to be *painful.* Painful killings should be (and can be) avoided. Nor need there be anguish involved. If we are to take utilitarianism seriously, the elderly, since they are of good character, will be able to perceive the rightness of their deaths. Much of the anguish and apprehension associated with death (perhaps all) is associated with dying, not the state of death.

Although I am not defending these conclusions, I am concerned with what may be the consequences of utilitarian ethics for treatment of the aged. Of course these consequences are morally outrageous. They are suggested, however, not only by an analogy with utilitarian arguments defending abortion, but also by an analysis of the principle of utility.

Utilitarianism commands us to maximize value. Suppose that life on the whole is valuable. (If it is not, then some killing would seem to be permissible.) According to a view which has been called "total utilitarianism," one might conclude that one has a moral obligation to bring children into the world. The injunction "Go forth and multiply" would have significant moral force. If another one hundred million people, if born in this country, would be happy and would not decrease everyone else's happiness too much, then the mothers of America with a bit of noble assistance from the fathers of America would have an obligation to create those people. Now this consequence of utilitarianism is counterintuitive. It can be avoided if we renounce "total utilitarianism" and if we take the principle as a directive to maximize the *average* amount of value in a society. What the utilitarian attempts to increase, then, is the figure arrived at by totalling the value of the lives of each and every member of the population divided by the number of members of the population. This version of utilitarianism, which might be called "average utilitarianism," does not have procreative consequences. Unfortunately, it has worse consequences. For we can increase the average value of the lives of the population merely by ending the less valuable lives. Surely the elderly would be the group most abused by such a policy.[5]

I think there are a great many reasons, then, for *not* attempting to justify our moral sentiments toward the elderly by appealing to utilitarian moral theory. Any utilitarian justification of a policy of beneficence toward the elderly is obviously subject to enormous difficulties. This does *not* show, of course, that we cannot retain our moral sentiments toward them. What this

does show is that *another* attempt to place those moral sentiments in the context of a general ethical theory where those moral sentiments can be justified and explained, is subject to enormous difficulties. What this shows is that we do not yet have a genuine *ethics* for the elderly.

IV

The difficulties with a utilitarian justification of policies of beneficence toward the elderly will come as no surprise to those familiar with the literature of moral philosophy. Although on the face of it the utilitarian principle seems to be a plausible first principle of ethics and although it promises relief from an ethics of overly rigid rules, it appears to generate moral claims that are quite literally incredible. In particular, utilitarianism appears to generate "obligations" that violate human rights.

This not unusual view in philosophical ethics suggests that beneficent policies toward the elderly are to be justified, not by an appeal to a theory of obligation as conceived either in the tradition of Kant or Mill, but rather by a theory of rights. On this view of things the obligations that those who are not elderly have toward the elderly are justified in terms of the *rights* that the elderly have. These rights are justified because the elderly are persons, and all persons have such rights.

Obviously this approach requires careful elaboration. Nevertheless, it is possible to explain why the task of justification of our moral sentiments by this approach is far from easy. Let us suppose, for the sake of argument, that the elderly do have a right to have their essential needs met. Let us suppose that it can be established that they have the right to medical care, to minimally decent housing, to adequate food, to some minimally decent standard of living. Who is to provide all this? It will have to be provided by members of the workforce. But at this point problems emerge.

It is facile to argue here that if the elderly have a right to X and cannot provide X for themselves, then others have an obligation to provide X for them. On the contrary, Judith Thomson has argued that from the claim that a fetus has a right to life and from the claim that it cannot live independently, it does *not* follow that its mother has a strict obligation not to have an abortion. The reason for this is (roughly) that the fetus is making a claim on the mother's body, and that body if *hers*. What happens to it is something she has a right to decide.[6]

I am not endorsing Thomson's argument. Yet it is clear that she has made a point whose analogue in the case of the elderly merits examination. Satisfaction of the needs of the elderly involves taking from the non-elderly what they *earn,* something that, in the view of the non-elderly, they have a right to as just recompense for their labors.

This is no mere intellectual issue. Keeping the Social Security system solvent, funding pension plans for government employees, and funding medicare *do* take from the work force what they earn. These facts have been

widely noted in the press. To be sure, governments have traditionally used tax monies for similar purposes, for example, funding facilities for the mentally retarded. But the resources used for such purposes are relatively small and easily go unnoticed. The amount of the reallocation of resources through government to benefit the aged is enormous. We notice it. And when we do, it is reasonable to ask for an ethical justification. Presumably such an account would be given in terms of some adequate theory of justice.

The philosophical issue of justice, an old, honorable one, remains in dispute today. There are various and disparate accounts of the nature of justice discussed within the philosophical community at the present time. From these, widely divergent views of what counts for a just allocation of resources to the elderly can be inferred.[7] Hence, there is no standard, accepted account of the nature of justice which justifies our moral sentiment that resources should be re-allocated for use by the elderly. Actually, American philosophers have done very little work on the theory of justice until recent years. Presumably the newly awakened interest in those theories within the philosophical community will produce results that will go further to justify certain policies toward the elderly than anything which is available now.

V

The argument of this essay has been developed on the basis of an assumption which many will regard as dubious—at least from an ethical point of view—and which should, as a consequence, receive some discussion. I have assumed that the population of this country over the age of sixty-five is an overwhelmingly dependent population.

The problems that arise in working out an ethics for the treatment of the elderly are all based upon this fact. Yet one might argue that it *need not* be the case that the elderly population be almost entirely a dependent population. The dependency of the elderly is based, it is argued, not on their inability to work, but on mandatory retirement policies. The elderly are *forced* to retire; hence, they are forced to become dependent. Since we feel that their essential needs should be provided for in some way, and since they cannot provide for their own essential needs through their labor due to retirement policies, then it becomes the task of the non-elderly to provide for those needs.

What we have here is not just the ferreting out of an assumption upon which some of the issues concerning the elderly are based, but also the basis for an argument against mandatory retirement policies. If employers did not have mandatory retirement policies, then more persons over sixty-five would remain in the work force. If so, the necessary income transfers from those who are employed to those who are not would not need to be as great. That would be a good thing.

The argument here is not as simple as it might at first appear. It is not at all clear that the disappearance of mandatory retirement policies would cause very many of the elderly to remain in the work force under all assumptions. One wants to distinguish what would happen if mandatory retirement policies

were abolished and retirement plans are such that voluntary retirement is possible *and* what would happen if mandatory retirement were abolished in a context where retirement plans are *not* adequate. There is evidence that where pension plans are generous and retirement is voluntary, only a small percentage of workers prefer to continue to work.[8] But if only a small percentage of employees prefer to remain at their jobs after a time when they are eligible to draw an *adequate* pension, then the *social* advantages of voluntary retirement policies seem to be slender. It seems quite reasonable to argue that if the price of gaining significant social benefits from voluntary retirement policies is less than adequate pension benefits, then that price is too high.

Of course one might argue against mandatory retirement on other grounds. One might argue that it is *unjust* that one be required to retire on the grounds that one has reached a certain age, that mandatory retirement unfairly discriminates against older persons in our society on the very simple ground that they are denied the right to retain a job although that right is accorded those who belong to other age groups.

Whether or not this argument succeeds depends upon whether or not one has a right to a job. It is not at all clear that there is such a right. It is much more likely that one has a right to have one's essential needs met, and if these can only be met by holding a job, then one has a right to a job. But this right is quite different from our former right. This right is quite compatible with mandatory retirement policies so long as adequate pension benefits are available to the retiree. It may well be that the case against mandatory retirement rests primarily not on some general right which human beings have, but rather upon a specific set of social conditions which happen now to exist in our society. In fact pensions are often inadequate.

Much could be added in support of mandatory retirement policies from the point of view of employers. Consider the case of an employer without a legally enforceable mandatory retirement policy. How does he dismiss employees who, although they have served him faithfully for many years, are no longer capable of performing their work? I suspect that this task becomes easier, the better the employer-employee relations to begin with and the more the work of the employee involves physical labor. When the task involves considerable physical labor, the employee is able to recognize when he is unable to complete it. Furthermore, the informal and sometimes paternalistic relationships in small business may ease the burden of dismissal considerably. Surely this matter is much more difficult in an organization where mental labors rather than physical labors are required and where work rules and dismissals are a matter of informal agreement and not contract. "Senility hearings" for older employees in such situations are too horrible to contemplate. Indeed, one begins to realize that mandatory retirement policies have an important advantage: an employee is laid off, not because *as an individual* he is no longer capable of doing the work his job requires, but because of a competence-independent standard (in the individual case). This is, in important respects, a much more dignified way to leave the work force.

Mandatory retirement policies seem to be as much a product of the size and

impersonality of many businesses as they are a product of age discrimination. An independent craftsman does not have to worry about mandatory retirement policies. He can make his work day shorter or longer as he chooses without anyone else being affected. If he is no longer able to supply a good product, then his customers may leave him. Then he will leave the work force. Business enterprises cannot employ this method of retirement. Additional problems are created by the size of the enterprise and by standardized work rules beyond the caprice of employers and foremen. Workers, for good reasons, desire such standards. But one man's caprice is another man's sound judgment. To abandon arbitrary practices is also to give up the right of employers or foremen to make individual and delicate judgments concerning the ability of each older employee to continue on the job. Since senility hearings are out of the question, the only alternative seems to be for firms to adopt the rule that an employee is guaranteed continued employment as long as he or she *believes* (or at least, *affirms*) that he or she is capable of continuing in his or her job. I take it that no one is seriously proposing such a policy.

It seems fair to conclude that if a case can be made against mandatory retirement policies, that case will have to overcome serious obstacles. In the first place, there is good reason for thinking that in the presence of adequate pension benefits the elderly would not benefit substantially from voluntary retirement policies. In the second place, it is not at all clear that mandatory retirement is always unjust. In the third place, mandatory retirement policies may well have certain advantages over alternative policies, especially in large impersonal enterprises. Here is another instance in which the justification of a "pro-elderly" policy is much less obvious than it initially appears.

VI

I have not been attempting to argue against beneficent policies toward the elderly. Indeed, I believe that beneficence with respect to the elderly by those of us who are not yet elderly is appropriate. What concerns me is that the justification of these pro-elderly policies does not always leap into view; indeed, there are accepted standards for ethical conduct in terms of which such justifications do not seem to be forthcoming. This should bother anyone with appropriate moral sensibilities toward the elderly and with a capacity and concern for critical systematic reflection on his duties toward others. What is needed in this area is not just additional policies, projects, or programs, but a moral point of view regarding the elderly which is grounded in basic moral precepts; in short, an ethics for the elderly.

Notes

[1] For a good survey of the plight of the elderly see Robert N. Butler, *Why Survive? Being Old in America* (New York: Harper and Row, 1975).

[2]Immanuel Kant, "Groundwork of the Metaphysic of Morals," trans. H.J. Paton, *The Moral Law* (London: Hutchinson, 1948).

[3]On this topic see Gilbert Harman, "Moral Relativism Defended," *Philosophical Review*, 841 (1975), 3-22; Robert Coburn, "Relativism and the Basis of Morality," *Philosophical Review*, 851 (1976), 87-93; and Richard Trammell, "Saving Life and Taking Life," *The Journal of Philosophy*, 721 (1975), 131-37.

[4]On this point see Thomas Nagel, "Death," *Nous*, 4(1970), 73-80.

[5]This argument is developed in a convincing and more precise way by Richard G. Henson in "Utilitarianism and the Wrongness of Killing," *Philosophical Review*, 80 (1971), 320-37. For an objection see L.S. Sumner, "A Matter of Life and Death," *Nous*, 10 (1976), 145-72.

[6]Judith Thomson, "A Defense of Abortion," *Philosophy and Public Affairs*, 1 (1971), 47-66.

[7]See John Rawls, *A Theory of Justice* (Cambridge: Harvard Univ. Press, 1971) and Robert Nozick, *Anarchy, State, and Utopia* (New York: Basic Books, 1974).

[8]Experience at General Motors is instructive. See "Inflation Hits Private and Public Pension Plans Equally," *The Kansas City Times*, 8 March 1977, p. 9A.

V. THEORETICAL CONSIDERATIONS

Gerald J. Gruman

CULTURAL ORIGINS OF PRESENT-DAY "AGE-ISM": THE MODERNIZATION OF THE LIFE CYCLE[1]

My purposes in this paper are:

1. to analyze historically the cultural factors which underlie contemporary forms of prejudice against the elderly;
2. to inquire into the ideological presuppositions that bring about restrictive definitions of age-and-generation categories; and
3. to challenge disengagement theory and to seek an intellectual basis for the re-engagement of older people into the mainstream of modern life.

In thinking about ageism and the declining status and narrowing role options of the elderly, we require a large frame of reference. Therefore, in addition to gerontology *per se,* we shall turn to the concepts of human development, the multidisciplinary field that studies the entire range of the life span. Also, we shall refer to theories of modernization, in which history blends with the social and behavioral sciences in attempting to clarify fundamental changes in life style and world view that cross the usual historical and geographical boundaries.

In this paper I shall trace contemporary forms of the disparagement of the old to the acceleration of modernization which began about the turn of the twentieth century. Thus, special attention will be given to the period 1890-1930, the crucial years of modernistic transition and the heroic, formative era of gerontology and geriatrics.[2] In addition, the analysis of the modernist ethos and its concomitant ageism must include the major ideological upheaval of the last two decades of the nineteenth century and the early years of the twentieth—the revolt against positivism. Out of the struggle to contain that rebellion, there arose a new version of positivism—*neo*-positivism—that has furthered the typology of age stages and acts to sever the elderly from common humanity.[3] "Neo-positivism" here refers to an ideology of social import; it is not meant to signify a philosophy of science—logical positivism—nor does it relate directly to the practices called positive thinking.

On the basis of this investigation, I shall propose an interpretation of modernization which differs from the currently prevalent ones.[4] And as a corollary of that explication, we shall deduce a hypothesis of re-engagement to serve as an alternative to the theory now dominant in psycho-social gerontology—disengagement.[5] Such a re-engagement theory will include the depth psychologists' insights into and respect for the individual, aside from normative strictures of age and sex. Re-engagement theory also requires the perceptions from world history and anthropology that our culture is built on conditional and partial values rather than completed and universal ones; therefore, it is subject to change and improvement,[6] and the aging population, whose very presence is a remarkable modern innovation, can be seen as embodying a key sector of cultural adaptation. It is just such civilizing inventiveness, or modernization, that at present constitutes, according to the philosophy of historicism, the open, on-going dimension of human nature.

I. The Contemporary Aging Crisis

Negative views of senescence have hindered the efforts of gerontology and geriatrics from their very beginnings as specialized fields of endeavor, but it was not until 1968 that Robert N. Butler identified such prejudices as 'age-ism': a form of discriminatory thinking comparable to racism, sexism and the biased stereotyping of ethnic groups and socio-economic classes.[7] The study of ageism is all the more compelling at this time because of what I have referred to as an "aging crisis."[8] Older persons are so markedly uncertain of their status, and society itself so profoundly insecure about later life's meaning and goals, that questions of senescence cut directly to the core values of contemporary culture,[9] just as sexual problems did in Freud's time.

The situation is strikingly ironic. A considerable part of the nation—10.5 percent or 22.4 million in 1976 America—has surpassed sixty-five years and been classified, uniformly and arbitrarily, as "old."[10] These senior persons can expect an average of twelve to fifteen years of continuing life. However, the mood generally is not one of satisfaction. There is an existential tone of a sentence or condemnation to this period of being. Although engendered by officially approved activities of modern public health, organized science, and expansionary economics, an aging population was not desired or even responsibly foreseen. Moreover, it has appeared when central beliefs about modernity have been questioned sharply and sent into retreat. Thus, the elderly and their allies find themselves culturally under siege. The paradoxical interchange between traditional and modern means that the aged have come to be viewed as something new and strange. Instead of symbolizing the reassuringly familiar, they seem threateningly alien.

The old strangers of today are too aware of their vulnerability to seek heroic roles as exemplars of family or folk. Their behavior, even more than that of adolescents, has been veering to the defensively mercurial, "protean" pattern posited by R.J. Lifton. Kenneth Keniston's notion of "non-commitment as a

way of life" and Paul Goodman's definition of the "early resigned"—both descriptions previously associated with alienated adolescence—now are applicable to elders.[11]

To a historian, the aged waver precariously between two worlds. The very term 'modern' connotes mode or fashion, the 'now.' Since the Renaissance and Reformation, preference has gone to *first* principles, *young* geniuses, *primal* nations, *rising* classes, the *New* World. A sense of ever-continuing motion and a system of updates on stylistic trends have been provided by novels, newspapers, periodicals, journals, and the cinema. On the other hand, the quandaries and catastrophes of this century strongly suggest that the West itself has reached old age. Security and survival have become the preeminent goals. And enigmatic meditation, akin to anticipatory grief, replaces ameliorative action. The wish to be safely out of it prepares the way for announcements of the end of ideology and the onset of the post-modern or even post-historic epoch. At its bicentenary, the American Republic, like some latter-day Venetian patriciate, seemed to dwell obsessively on past gains. Apprehensions of a downward curve of Western culture and the parallel failure of nerve in individuals past middle life measure the depth of the aging crisis.

Our society's tendency to opt out of its responsibilities for supposed reasons of age has ominous implications for the genuinely senescent. An older population cannot be helped significantly without *further* advances in modernization. When a nation sets its sights on a stationary model, institutions resort to attritional weeding of borderline categories—women, black people, those in mid or late life, and youth too. Following the teachings of scarcity economics, allocations of sacrifice in such a situation are meted out according to the outcome of the stark clashes of organized interests. Modernization in reverse gear is a decidedly unpleasant phenomenon.

II. The Discovery of Age-ism

The term "age-ism" was formulated by Robert N. Butler,[12] then practicing psychiatry in Washington, D.C., in 1968, a year of nation-wide racial violence that reached a crescendo when troops in battle gear patrolled the Capitol building itself. At almost the same time, student revolts in France, the United States, and other countries forced an awareness of a portentous gap between generations. Another unsettling influence was the bio-medical revolution, a time bomb which appeared destined to call into question generally-accepted notions about sex and marriage, illness, aging, and death itself. Earlier, Butler had conceived of antagonism toward the elderly as a possible result of medical advances that could extend life expectancy and swell the numbers of the aged; there might, he argued, develop a basis for a *future* conflict of generational interest groups. But instead, the pressure of actual events caused the concept to be applied to the kind of hostility that justifies an already established pattern of deprivation and neglect. A year later, Butler presented his rationale for identifying age-ism as another form of bigotry.

In addition to Butler, several others also had argued that negative, stereotyped categorization of the elderly going quite beyond biomedicine permeates the general culture.[13] As early as 1953, Milton L. Barron had argued in a pioneering paper that the elderly were taking on the behavioral features of a new minority group. Michael Harrington warned in 1962 that the problems of age were not simply results of increased life expectancy. Harrington, however, spoke of the cultural devaluation of the aged only in such general terms as social "rejection." In 1963, Jules Henry analyzed the dehumanizing effect of social "obsolescence," and in 1966 he demonstrated that neo-positivist social thought, typified by Durkheim, tended to exacerbate institutional depersonalization of the aged. In the meantime, Lifton was working out an interpretation of the breakdown of continuity in life-span development and the increasing proclivity of youth to victimize the old as people no longer "really alive." Butler's identification of age-ism brought these several insights to a conceptual focus. This was of great consequence for gerontological theory: attention was shifted from a phenomenon which might appear sometime in the future, as Butler had earlier suggested, to one that exists in the here and now. Age-ism, in other words, *was given* a history.

The essentials of age-ism were presented to Butler in a Chevy Chase, Maryland housing conflict. And the word 'age-ism' first appeared in March 1969 in a *Washington Post* article, headed "Age and Race Fears Seen in Housing Opposition," by Carl Bernstein who described the controversy in which Butler was involved.[14] Public housing authorities, looking for apartments for older citizens, had requested the use of a local building; two open hearings in the largely white, middle class suburb exploded into middle-aged riot. The angry faces reminded Butler of the scenes of furious, generational confrontation between students and police which he had witnessed in Chicago in August of 1968. Just as in Chicago, in Chevy Chase there were not only economic and racial concerns but also tensions about age itself (ranging from overly-defensive denials to outspoken avowals of hostility to having "all those old people" in the area).

It is noteworthy that the contending forces were deployed along the boundary between token existence and comfortable living. The aged were on the defensive in the face of assumptions that retirement is respectable only if made possible by ostensibly independent, hard-earned economic arrangements. Value judgments about work and security surfaced in the charge that the building was too luxurious and the neighborhood too affluent. The battle swirled about such features as a swimming pool, air-conditioning, and parking facilities—i.e., consumer goods that symbolically separate the people of the 1930's and 1940's, who had struggled through depression and war and were now senescent, from those who had enjoyed the fruits of victory and the affluence of the 1950's and 1960's. This generational division is highlighted by the historical turning-point recently chronicled by John Morton Blum: on the one hand, the Economic Bill of Rights, promised in 1944 but never implemented, that sketched a picture of post-war freedom from want even in old age, and on the other hand, the actual policies that emerged from the war years directed towards "eternal consumer

spending" and "*more* for everybody" of the "things that consumers want" and culminating in a "spending spree."[15]

In the distinction between maintenance and living well, so fiercely guarded against the dependent elderly, there is such lack of generosity that the term 'thrift euthanasia' comes to mind. As we see in this conflict, the elders come to be viewed as people who ought not to be alive in the sense of *really living.* This has deep historical roots. Ever since the quantification of life-and-death matters initiated by the Calvinist work ethic, there has been a growing concern about those who live "too long." According to the similar presuppositions of mercantilism, what one person gains *must* be the loss of someone else. Thus, in regard to the public supplementation of the economic well-being of elders, a distinction is made between "just enough" and "too much": although a modest maintenance ought to be provided, society should avoid, it would seem, going to unusual lengths and need not strive to keep the old living freely and enjoyably.

The Chevy Chase episodes recounted by Butler illustrate the paradoxical fact, central to the aging crisis today, that the old now are seen as new and unsettling, an alien force threatening to the community. And although conceding that a campaign of community education might have prevented some of the alarm, Butler concluded that the rush to judgment indicated the presence of prejudiced stereotypes and myths—bigotry. In a later work, he summarized: "Age-ism can be seen as a process of systematic stereotyping of and discrimination against people because they are old, just as racism and sexism accomplish this with skin color and gender."[16] Like racism and sexism, age-ism insists that *inherent biological factors determine traits of personality and character.* As Butler has observed, one of the greatest handicaps of aging is the decrease in the range of choice, a loss which results not only from physiological and economic limitations but also from the restrictive norms of a biased culture.

Our culture seems to institute such restrictive norms of behavior almost more rapidly than critics can question them. In 1956, J.C. Furnas bade goodbye to Uncle Tom, and in 1963 Betty Friedan discredited the components of the feminine mystique.[17] But racial and sexual role stereotypes persist, and age-graded categories have increased, with old age set in an especially derogatory mold. We discover, in fact, similarities in the roles and characteristics attributed to the three groups. Stereotyped "good" attributes ascribed to black people have included: skill in handling children and animals, musical and dancing ability, loyalty as servants and as menial employees, and a feeling for religion. These same traits are linked to women and (except for the song-and-dance) the elderly. Such "favorable" characterizations can be especially deceptive. As Friedan warned, the glamorization of women can mask a surrender of the search for one's own identity. Similarly, Simone de Beauvoir launched in *The Coming of Age* (which, it is noteworthy, followed her analysis of sexism in *The Second Sex*) a campaign against the pretended idealization of aging because it emphasizes alleged differences of the elderly from the rest of humanity and thus enables an exploitative society to get rid of older working people. One might speak of an "aging mystique": as Robert Kastenbaum

satirically observes, "The gracefully aging person has the knack of making us [professionals] feel better. This type of elder is . . . content with his or her lot . . . is non-competitive, noncomplaining . . . knows his place . . . also eats watermelon and fried chicken and has a natural sense of rhythm."[18] Thus the "good" old person merges with Jump Jim Crow. In contrast, the "bad" elder, like Friedan's liberated woman, risks abrasiveness in affirming a complex, ambiguous individuality.

More ominous than the categorizing of "good" and "bad" roles is the trend in the twentieth century toward an *absence* of role. Ernest Burgess called it a "role-less role," and it has a biological counterpart which has been termed a "running out of programme."[19] Bio-gerontologists confront generally the evident lack of purpose for senescence in the scheme of natural evolution. And, in particular, they must face the theory of the great geneticist August Weismann that the individual, after the years of reproduction, is no longer of use to the evolution of the species and somehow is programmed for death. On this question, British scientists (P.B. Medawar, for example, and Alex Comfort) have argued that nature does not kill older organisms but rather is *indifferent* to their fate: when the inherited, genetic blueprint runs out of instructions, the aging animal is rendered more and more disorganized and vulnerable. This British rejection of natural teleological purpose was intended to keep the way clear for culturally-defined purposive values regarding the aged (historically, the Beveridge Plan of 1942 and proposals for large-scale research were at stake).[20] The American sociologist Burgess also pressed for remedial measures. The undecided situation of the elders can become a plus to the extent that it provides an opportunity for meliorist action; neglected, it falls to an appalling minus. Thus age-ism, as Butler noted, is a prejudice that is both insidious and deeply destructive.

III. The Modernist Transformation

In the 1890's a crucial turning point took place in American attitudes toward growth and development, initiated by the perception that rapid, relatively easy expansion (especially the Westward movement of the frontier) was coming abruptly to an end. As Frederick Jackson Turner stated in 1893, "to the frontier the American intellect owes its striking characteristics."[21] Most of the traits he listed now seem to be almost synonymous with present-day notions of youthfulness—restless, nervous energy, buoyancy and exuberance, and quick inventiveness. The frontier experience had kept America vital by forcing a continual rebirth of culture in a milieu of barbarous challenges at the advancing border of settlement. The biological metaphors of birth and development were in keeping with Turner's epigenetic theory of history that considered a nation to be like a living, growing organism.[22]

It is significant that while Turner's frontier imagery today connotes youth, what he had in mind was vigorous, mature manhood continuing into later life. Studies of the history of age groupings[23] indicate that the concept of adolescence

was not yet known in the 1890's, and that "youth," from about fifteen to twenty-five, still was viewed as a clumsy, undesirable time. Therefore, the termination of the frontier signified a most disturbing sort of coming of age. "And now," Turner wrote, "four centuries from the discovery of America . . . the frontier has gone, and with its going has closed the first period of American history."[24] This closing, a sign of the imminent diminishing of a healthy maturity, brought about the great transformation in age values. Adulthood began to appear a problematic phase, the elders to seem definitely inadequate, and the young loomed as a raw but promising national resource.

The new awareness of limitations influenced every realm of life and thought. The United States was no longer the fortunate land with no history. A worried search was begun for sources of renewed national momentum. Such concerns had decisive implications not only at the governmental level but also for the individual, since the American idea of progress had been interrelated to a remarkable degree with upward mobility and personal success.

In America after 1890, there was an urgent attempt to *form a generation* with the characteristics considered requisite for keeping the country moving ahead. And this massive re-evaluation of work drives and fighting qualities fostered what has come to be known as ageism. The "strenuous life," a neo-romantic cluster of virtues, in line with the values of the work ethic and business enterprise, became preeminent as Theodore Roosevelt moved towards the Presidency.[25] Borrowed from France, *morale* was to be the increasing preoccupation in industrial, military and governmental circles. And Roosevelt's secular sermons set the pace:

> I wish to preach . . . the doctrine of the strenuous life, the life of toil and effort, of labor and strife. . . . We of this generation . . . have our tasks, and woe to us if we fail to perform them. . . . When men fear work or fear righteous war, when women fear motherhood . . . well it is that they should vanish from the earth. . . .[26]

The either/or tone in these precepts, a hallmark of modernism, intimated severe threats to those who failed to measure up. It was indeed to be a century marked by massive purges in many lands of supposedly parasitic, inferior, deviationist, and alien elements. Roosevelt's doctrine was an omen of things to come.

From the first, the outlook for the elderly in an era of strenuous life had been far from reassuring. Theodore Roosevelt, himself a bespectacled, wealthy Easterner, was enthralled by young men who could "hit the line hard."[27] The few aged persons he mentioned favorably were highly unusual paragons of vitality and ceaseless work. He invoked mythic memories of frontier days "when the weakling died as the penalty of inability to hold his own." His insistent alarm about the "least touch of flabbiness" expressed a profound intolerance for anyone who becomes dependent or has to be carried. The Rough Rider used stereotypes of an incipient ageism to lash out at "elderly men, of fine records in the past, who are no longer fit to break through routine and to show . . . ex-

traordinary energy . . . initiative . . . and willingness to accept responsibility." In particular, his do-or-die distinction between "real" men and women and the "hideous" category of the "mere cumberer of the earth" represents the most destructive component of contemporary ageism.

This attitude caused a decisive shift in immigration policy. First the frontier had ended, and now the Golden Door began to close against categories of people considered of only marginal use in the planned resurgence of national strength and productivity. Americans had become less willing to gamble that the "refuse" of the Old World would be revitalized by opportunity. State encouragement of immigration was slowed and then reversed; Ellis Island became an Isle of Tears as newcomers were turned back. Exactly how many were rejected is difficult to estimate since most decisions to bar entry were made by steamship companies before departure from Europe. In the 1920's, screening processes were transferred even further away, from shipping lines to overseas consulates. As policy had become more and more discriminatory, a *show* of objectivity, typical of neo-positivist management, surfaced in "tests" of literacy, work skills, health, and employability. Even the blatantly racist system of the 1920's was disguised by a flurry of "scientific," statistical activity which supposedly determined the quotas.

The age bias within the quota system is an important field for further research. It is clear that the older person was looked upon by shipping companies and consulates as much more of a risk in regard to illness, unemployment, and the public welfare rolls. Generational prejudice is revealed in the fact that children of citizens were non-quota, thus bypassing the apparatus of exclusion, but parents of citizens were controlled by quota allotments. In 1927, twenty-one per cent of the population but only about nine per cent of the immigrants were above forty-five.[28]

Among the hardest hit by generational discontinuity and incipient ageism were immigrants who did succeed in reaching America between 1880 and 1924. Mostly young, they nevertheless rapidly became a lost generation viewed, with remarkable unanimity, as expendable in the securing of a beach-head for the next, Americanized generation. With the arrival of the first child in school, the family order was dramatically reversed as the young took the key role of mediator between home and society. Adolescence brought crisis and a predictable dénouement: the elders were discarded just as others previously had been left in the Old World. The melancholy equation of youth's success as a distancing from home had not been unfamiliar to American parents, long used to migrations to the frontier. But the East and South European immigrants had an unusually shattering fate. The feverish quest to make good, as the door was closing forever, had a destructive effect on both young and old. The contemporary, modernist life cycle, with alienated youth and rejected aged, first was enacted by those in the final wave of mass immigration. Their plight foretold that of the nation and the nation's elderly. They had poured into "a society moving toward fixity," and they mirrored the country's dilemma: "The old people, growing older, could see the day ahead when there would be none of their kind left, . . . the decline of their group was associated with their own aging

. . . a young America had welcomed them in the power of their youth when their energies were serviceable, but now was discarding them to escape the pressing issues of its [America's] own maturity."[29]

In the 1890's a hierarchy of ages, races, and stages of development was invoked to justify domestic and foreign policy. If the American mainland frontier had closed, it was felt that new territories abroad had to be conquered and domestic "weaknesses" curbed. This can be seen during the Spanish American War when an overseas empire was won, while at home racist Jim Crow laws came into wide use. The cluster of value-laden images which underlay these policies reveals much about the development of ageism. On the one hand, blacks were stereotyped as too child-like and primitive to qualify as citizen-soldiers and skilled workers. On the other hand, enemy Spain was pictured in terms of international legal incompetence because of senility. And in contrast to the seemingly undisciplined blacks and decrepit Spaniards, America symbolized a masterful maturity, taking up the White Man's Burden and guiding "little brown brothers" (Filipinos) and "sister republics" (Latin Americans). Theodore Roosevelt sounded the metaphors of a "young" America pushing aside the "medieval" Spanish, just as the "iron" Roman once had prevailed over "corroded" Greeks; his similes of social mortalism—"rust," "dry-rot," "corruption," "feebleness," "flabbiness," and "decadence"—pointed always to the menace of age and decline.[30]

To summarize: the status of the elderly cannot help but be affected in an innovative, highly competitive society by an *age symbolism* pervasively applied to ethnic, national and racial groups. Particularly relevant to gerontology is the fact that the developmental hierarchy of peoples and races, although replete with biomedical analogies, essentially reflected cultural values of a particular society with an ideology of generational displacement. Adult maturity and healthful vigor were conceived in terms of skills and attitudes assumed indispensable in the global rivalry of business, industry, and war. Thus, metaphors of the social contract and the work ethic were dominant in Senator Beveridge's statement in 1900 which urged Americans to accept their mission of being God's "master organizers" of peoples either too juvenile ("savage") or too old ("senile").[31] For a time, the elderly in America could take pride in being members of an elect nation, and in the next decades they were granted measures of social insurance within a welfare-warfare state. But their position was destined to be endangered in a climate of opinion which focused on intensive contests that push aside the weaker group.

That the phrase "welfare-warfare" is not mere irony can be seen in the manner in which the great steel battleship, the symbol of the mature nation, acted as a cutting edge of social exclusiveness and the mandatory retirement of the elderly. Along with blacks and the "worn-out" peoples (the South and East Europeans, and the Chinese), elderly Anglo-Saxons too came to be separated out from the elite new navy. The great bulk of recruits were mere boys. Theodore Roosevelt, president at only forty-two, loved to dwell on the slowness and over-caution of the Spanish fleet. During the 1907 world tour of the American battle fleet, younger officers were put on display and the decision was

made to set chronological barriers that would get rid of senior officers "too old for the responsibilities and arduous duty."[32]

This new retirement policy presaged the tone of Social Security legislation to follow. In fact, some of the mysteries of Franklin D. Roosevelt's attitudes about social insurance and age-categories might be revealed by inquiries into the long years (1913-1920) in which, like T.R. before him, he served as Assistant Secretary of the Navy. Such studies might help explain why the elderly were excluded from the New Deal's pension plan while much larger resources were directed into aid for the young. The puzzling and disastrous fight against the "nine old men" of the Supreme Court in 1937 called forth statements by F.D.R. reminiscent of the strenuous life doctrine: "A lowered mental or physical vigor leads men to avoid an examination of complicated and changed conditions. . . . [N]ew facts become blurred through old glasses fitted . . . for the needs of another generation; older men . . . cease to explore or inquire. . . . [S]ystematic addition of younger blood will vitalize the courts. . . .[33]

In America after 1890, the sciences, especially biomedicine and psychology, were caught up in measuring and shaping the population for the tasks of mass production and marketing and military preparedness. The call to heroic virtues was supplemented by a vast elaboration of neo-positivist methods for standardizing human aptitudes and traits: the I.Q. gradient, time-motion studies, life expectancy tables, tax brackets, and clothing sizes. From these were to come such stigmatizing categorizations as the moron, the 4-F, the odd size and, of course, the "old fogeys" of sixty-five. Insistence on highly-motivated energy and the elaborate network of quantitative typologies acted to set apart presumably deficient strata, groupings, and peoples.

In the 1890's and early 1900's, it became standard practice for industry to shut out workers over the age of forty. The song "Everybody Works but Father" (1905) depicted the general downfall of the head of the house. In philosophy, the cultural displacement of parental values had been summed up for shock effect in Nietzsche's statement of the 1880's that God, the Father figure, is *dead.* In psychology, the death in 1896 of Sigmund Freud's own father had provoked an emotional breakdown leading to the formulation of the famous Oedipus complex which uses archetypal myth to justify, as universal, the rivalry of son with father and the displacement of the elder—actually relatively new features of a particular social order. This situation did not improve: in 1935, as in 1905, the social and cultural onset of old age continued to move in on the "middle-aged" man of forty.

In 1905 the American physician William Osler had touched this raw nerve in a much controverted lecture:

> I have two fixed ideas well known to my friends. . . . The first is the comparative uselessness of men above forty. . . . Take the sum of human achievement . . . subtract the work of the men above forty, and . . . we would practically be where we are today. It is difficult to name a great and far-reaching conquest of the mind which has not been . . . done between the ages of twenty-five and forty—these fifteen golden years. . . . [34]

Osler's second belief was the absolute uselessness of men over sixty; he felt it would be an incalculable benefit if all men stopped work at that age.

Presented in wintry February of 1905, Osler's ideas about later life stimulated a rebuttal in mild July in an address by Sir James Crichton-Browne to the Royal Institute of Public Health.[35] We already have noted, in the opposition to Weismann's mortalism, an English propensity towards fondness for the elderly. It is fascinating to compare the New World physician Osler, with his nervous theory of human development as a series of discontinuous stages, leaping upward and then tumbling, with the placid English physician Crichton-Browne who viewed development as a steady, cumulative process in which gains outnumber losses, at least in realms most worthwhile. Both are eloquent and both are modern. But where Osler's modernism was that of an evolutionist positivism, close to neo-positivism, which saw the golden years as twenty-five to forty, Sir James was the spokesman for a more relaxed, long-range modernism which stemmed from the Italian Renaissance humanism of Luigi Cornaro. Old age, according to Cornaro, is a great blessing, for only long years permit the forming of true wisdom, virtue, the gathering of full honors and, for that matter, considerable wealth.[36] This easy humanism of Southern Europe still was free from the Reformation rejection of pleasure and "good works." Indeed, Crichton-Browne enjoyed poking fun at the kind of puritanical, Low Church reductionism which would rid life of its "superfluous" fullness and richness. In this humanist, meliorist, and hedonistic tradition of modernization, Sir James listed, in answer to Osler, many examples of valuable work done after the age of forty, and sixty also, and concluded:

> We should, I think, take a frankly optimistic . . . view of old age. We should not gauge it simply by its capacity for toil. . . . The world is not a sweating-den nor a big round factory in which piece-work is strictly enforced. No; it is, or ought to be a home . . . in which each man should be allowed to live . . . his whole life. . . . But his whole life is not finished at sixty and . . . it should not be assumed that he is henceforth useless and a cumberer of the ground.[37]

What Osler had been expounding was a version of the generational sequence[38] rationalized by positivist kinds of social thought prevalent in Victorian Britain, Bismarckian Germany and in America after about 1876. In this model of society, the young, due to the march of progress, are considered innately superior because they come on the scene at a later, more advanced time. Thus, the sons displace the fathers; as Osler put it, they are "born of us, fated to excel us." Although Freud felt it a duty to defend this onward-upward seriation, he could not help laughing at times at a culture ruled so absolutely by "His Majesty the Baby." To Osler, raised on the frontier (in Upper Canada), succession and displacement seemed almost self-evident. The idea was reinforced in his student days when he read Herbert Spencer, who taught the sort of positivism most acceptable in England and America. At the turn of the century, generationism and mortalism were toughened by the pessimistic social Darwinism identified with Weismann's theories of aging and death. Thus

Osler, who had retained much of the evangelical Anglicanism of his upbringing, came to approach the neo-romantic elements of tragic striving and sacrifice that were incorporated into the new positivism of this century. It was this shift to neo-positivism that underlay the modernist transformation and the rise of contemporary age-ism.

IV. The Positivist Ideology of Age and the Revolt that Failed

In order to understand the increased age-ism and generational displacement that accompanied the modernist transformation after 1890, we must review the ideas about age and senescence generally held during the nineteenth century, their systematization by positivist ideology, and their transition, despite challenges, to the new positivism of this century. Although the revolt against positivism failed, it constituted the major cultural movement of the turn of the century and was characterized by creative brilliance. Thus, to comprehend present-day age-ism and to picture a conception of life-span development which differs from contemporary notions, we shall turn briefly to a pre-positivist view of the norms of human development, as exemplified in the thought of Crichton-Browne. Then we shall note how that classical model of aging, as a cumulative process which gives preference to elders, has been challenged by patterns which emphasize discontinuity and give preference to earlier years.

a. Pre-positivist Views on Age and Aging

Crichton-Browne's rebuttal against age-ism was based on assumptions inherited from Renaissance humanism and the Enlightenment. The former, typified by Cornaro, was mentioned in the previous section. The latter, the eighteenth-century norm of development, focused on adult maturity as a long, relatively homogeneous and unbroken phase of life, adapting the classical model of the four ages of man from Hippocrates, Aristotle, and Galen.[39] Childhood and youth were considered to be preparatory stages; it is only in the proto-adult phase that a person becomes interesting (we may think here of the famous fictional characters Tom Jones and Candide). Through formative experiences and the inculcation of prudential virtues, a person firms into a definite adult personality and then hopefully will continue on the long plateau of adulthood, gradually using up inner reserves but gathering knowledge and wisdom, status and wealth. Thus, life was seen as a history of the molding of character, and the elders held the high ground: "older is better."

Analogously, the eighteenth century tended to view social progress in continuous terms of material improvements and the rise of class (bourgeois) and nation. Crichton-Browne's especially amiable outlook stems in great part from the developmental regularity and continuity of the English Reformation (which came from above) and the Revolution of 1688, which was "gloriously peaceful." We should note that his engaging humanistic meliorism is shared by both Ilya

Mechnikov and Ignatz Nascher,[40] founders of gerontology and geriatrics respectively; it appears also in Butler's belief that a civilization is no better than its treatment of average, ordinary members.

On the basis of the classical hypothesis of aging as a predominance in the body of "cold" and "dry" qualities, one could predicate either a limited or an extended span of years. To bourgeois prudence it seemed sensible to "burn" the God-given, vital fuel (hot and moist, like oil) evenly in a thrifty way, so that one lived as long as possible and then was benefited by a "natural" death—a flickering out as painless as sleep. The sons would gather at the paternal home to hear the last words and blessing as the accumulated property was handed on. But thinkers who grasped the prospects of the new sciences went beyond that circumspect, bourgeois plan of life and predicted means for replenishing vital forces. In the context of bourgeois, natural death, aging was accepted as a normal process; Benjamin Franklin, however, listed senescence as a "disease" to be conquered like other ills. Thus, it was logically possible for Condorcet to postulate, in a vista of historical progress, a practically illimitable increase in longevity. Crichton-Browne's compromise between guarded bourgeois and visionary *philosophe* allotted to everyone a hundred years of "useful and honored" life; Mechnikov projected the doubling of the Biblical three score and ten.[41]

Challenges to the continuous, cumulative pattern of human development came from diverse sources and as early as the ancient Greeks. Let us briefly review that history. Platonism's speculative aspect opened the way for the Roman defense of age by Cicero, but the defense was a disruptive one in that he lauded age as a *special* phase above normative adulthood. Furthermore, in Neo-Platonism, the very naturalness of the life cycle was doubted, and re-imaginings of it were stimulated, such as those of the alchemists, Paracelsus, and the pietist Lutheranism which inspired German romantic (and later, Eriksonian) ideas of an upward, metamorphic struggle proceeding level by level.

In the second century, a number mysticism of the Pythagorean and Neo-Platonic sort influenced the scientist Ptolemy to transform *four ages to seven,* a figure in keeping with the sway of the seven planets, and coincidentally attractive to the symbolism of Judeo-Christian tradition. This was quite different from classical representations of the course of life which were, for the most part, not highly conscious of time stages. Aristotelean thought, for example, lacks feeling for historical development, and in ethics, the golden mean was calculated in a largely horizontal time milieu. But to Neo-Platonism, every individual phenomenon has its unique properties, or soul, and the searching hierarchical classification of diseases, drugs, organs, and the *stages of life* had a tremendous effect on biomedicine. That this kind of discontinuity could be pessimistic is revealed in Marcus Aurelius' idea that at age forty an individual passes the "fullness" of life and enters a period of grim, dutiful endurance in the service of the state.

Medieval Christianity took up the seven-ages model, infused it with a stations-of-the-cross pathos, and institutionalized it by sacramental steps.

However, the traditional age of Christ at death—a few months past thirty-three—placed the latter part of life under a shadow. Since Christ's sacrificial death took place in the midst of life, and since forty was the customary turning point, the golden years would be from about twenty-six to forty—from seven years before to seven years after the Crucifixion (such an interpretation, pervading Christian thought and supported by the Stoic "fullness" of life, was reflected in the evangelical and classical upbringing of Osler). We should not be surprised then to find that in Medieval Europe, the elderly were regarded with an unfriendly eye.[42] The seven ages model was later given definitive expression by Shakespeare's Jacques in *As You Like It.*

The transition from gerontophobia to age-ism can be seen in Jonathan Swift's well-known account of the Struldbrugs in *Gulliver's Travels* (1726), a reworking of the legend of Tithonus who requested immortality but forgot to stipulate everlasting youthfulness. Swift could count on his public being familiar with an entire range of gerontophobic traits through reading Juvenal, Ecclesiastes, Erasmus, and Shakespeare. Thus, the Struldbrugs are described as vain, opinionated, covetous and garrulous; but Swift pressed beyond classical restraints and dwelled on the overriding passion of these unfortunate creatures eaten up by burning envy and impotent desire. These are the ingredients underlying the "old witch" and "dirty old man" stereotypes of today's age-ism. Gulliver's revulsion and his salute to death extended into a general call to arms lest such long-lived beings, driven by greed, the "necessary consequent of old age," might completely absorb control of the nation.[43]

Finally, let us turn to the influential belief conveyed by the romantic aphorism, voiced by Wordsworth, that "the child is father of the man." The concept, noted earlier, that older is better seems to be the opinion of a new class already comfortably in power. When the fight has yet to be won, a right of revolution is asserted in which newer (and younger) is better. Thus the stalwart old Roman Cato, so glorified by Addison, is replaced by youthful heroes: Nathan Hale in America, the legendary young Bonaparte in France. The quick-step of the "*Marseillaise*"—*allons, enfants!*—outpaces the elders. Modern revolution, in other words, may break away from cumulative development and become a total war with unlimited goals. Malthus had warned of the ethical problem in such images of progress in which the present generation suffers and is then discarded for the benefit of an elite, future generation. With modern class revolution, counter-revolution, and world war, that dilemma came to a startling reality as entire generations have been consigned to the "dustbin" of history. Indeed, the young *per se* can be viewed as a kind of class.

b. Age Stages in Positivism

In nineteenth-century positivism, an attempt was made to bring together Enlightenment and romanticist ideas of human development. The result was a sequence of ages and generations systematically organized so that experts could intervene to guide the individual through crucial transitions. Also each age

category was given a functional meaning that was meant to contribute to social harmony.

The fundamental concepts of positivist philosophy were set forth as early as 1800, in Paris, by a circle of intellectuals known as the Ideologues. These thinkers had been shocked by the violence of the Revolution (1789-1799); they wished to prevent another destructive crisis by taking control of the domain of thought and opinion. Their aim was to adjust continuously the prevailing pattern of ideas, or "ideology," in order to keep the public in step with the flow of changes that are inevitable in an industrializing society. They would channel human drives away from divisive "metaphysical" questions of value and focus them on practical "positive" problems of technique and management.

The important scientist, Bichat, sought to apply the "ideological" approach to biomedicine. At a time when clashes between secularism and orthodoxy were disrupting orderly research, Bichat evaded the debate about ultimate purposes and emphasized the generally-accepted medical function of staving off "premature" death. The tactic of utilizing death as the *defining* limit of the physician's activity has been denoted "medical mortalism."[44] The effect, in the absence of a strong commitment to life affirmation, was that mortality was removed as a catastrophic ending to life and instead was disseminated as a series of little deaths throughout the life span, from birth on. Consequently, the transitions of life and the functions of age groupings came to be viewed in terms of a succession of *engagements* against the forces of mortality, in which resistance becomes less and less effective and acceptance is increasingly appropriate. Thus, the *intellectual foundation for disengagement theory* was presented more than a century ago.

Auguste Comte, lauding Bichat, adopted a related stance for sociology which was to be based only on "positive" observable facts and was to avoid all speculative "metaphysical" issues.[45] The scheme, of course, carried implicit values of its own, and, in fact, tended to bypass both history and psychology. Nevertheless, Comtean doctrines were adopted wherever a regime wanted an ideology to concentrate energies on material expansion while skirting controversial questions of value and purpose.

In a move towards generationism, Comte divided life into a series of functional age groupings. In 1852, he outlined a succession of nine social "sacraments."[46] The first, *presentation,* at birth, begins fourteen years of childhood. The second, *initiation,* launches seven years of schooling. *Admission,* at age twenty-one, marks a seven-year apprenticeship, and *destination,* at age twenty-eight, the start of a definite career. *Marriage,* the fifth sacrament, varies from twenty-one to twenty-eight for women and twenty-eight to thirty-five for men. *Maturity,* for men only, initiates, at age forty-two, a golden twenty-one years of truly productive work, after which the person moves into *retirement* and becomes an advisor. Death is euphemistically called *transformation,* and the ninth sacrament, *incorporation,* is a judgment seven years later, after which the sanctified remains of the meritorious are transferred to a monumental cemetery.

Nearly every feature of the Comtean life plan did come to be put into effect in

the modern West. Chronologically determined retirement, embalming of the deceased, elaborate cemeteries, memorial days, and so on, actually were established. Most significant for our purposes is the functionally-organized generational sequence. The young are carriers of innovation; the elders are intrinsically conservative; and "natural" attrition is counted on to weed out the unproductive old. Thus, positivism not only was mortalist in the defensiveness of its resistance to inevitable decline, but also in its built-in *need* for death as the guarantor of its version of progress.[47] And the pattern of sons displacing fathers was set, to the discomfiture of many a bourgeois family. With the advent of the Darwinist struggle for existence, the golden years no longer would begin at age forty-two but, as Osler stated, would end there.

c. *Rebellion*

The revolt against positivism was so broad and various that it almost defies analysis. One aspect of it is suggested by the term 'expressionism,' connoting the direct artistic and literary communication of primal emotion. Another element of the rebellion was 'neo-romanticism,' meaning the reassertion of the subjective and the irrational and a concern with redemptive suffering. The greatest German anti-positivist, Nietzsche, transcends classification, and the French philosopher, Henri Bergson, also is part of the revolt but rises above it.

The most cogent attack on positivism was that of the Russian thinker Nicholas Fyodorov (1828-1903). In a synthesis of scientific and Christian humanism, Fyodorov sketched a "Common Task" that could unify humanity in a struggle against earthly evils. He attacked three major tenets of positivism: its mortalism, its idea of progress, and its generationism. First, in the West, Comte's Religion of Humanity was received, despite its mortalist bent, as a kind of secular Catholicism. Therefore, the power of Fyodorov's thought resides in his affirmation that Christianity is centered on a radical rejection of death, and that consequently the mortalism of Comte is a terrible betrayal. While Fyodorov declared that true piety requires an awareness of one's mortality, his concern about death was not acceptance but an ethical imperative to "begin to do" something about actually overcoming death: "science must not be the knowledge of causes only without the knowledge of . . . what *ought to be.*"[48]

Secondly, the positivist version of progress was criticized sharply by Fyodorov as a flow of curious consumer items and dreadful armaments rather than a program of human betterment. He urged the learned professions to look beyond their elite position and to recognize that they too are vulnerable to the "common misfortunes"—aging, despair and death.

And finally, in regard to the generation gap, Fyodorov asserted that son-father displacement is a poor guideline for social advance since it is based merely on "the sons' sense of superiority over their fathers, and in the sense of superiority of the living over the dead." Satirizing the age-ism implicit in positivism, he wrote: "Of course, the learned are able to say that in former times the aged were killed while now they are only despised; isn't it progress to replace physical murder by spiritual murder?!"[49]

d. From Neo-Positivism to Disengagement Theory

The greater part of the revolt against positivism was not intransigent or profound. Rather it was largely a heretical rebellion from within which sought limited goals and changes of emphasis. Such hesitant insurrection was defeated by the rise of a new positivism that took on characteristics of romantic heroism and Darwinist conflict as the great powers entered, in the 1890's, an era of intensified rivalry. Neo-positivism especially adopted neo-romantic themes.

The best example of a neo-positivist thinker is Emile Durkheim who adapted the fashionable revival of interest in the subjective and primitive to give greater appeal to Comtean social solidarity. Durkheim particularly worried about individual assertiveness and disturbed social morale which, in terms of mortalism, he saw as an opening wedge of dire decline.

Durkheim and his students produced a social science infused with moral fervor and an emphasis on individual sacrifice for the collectivity. They selected evidence from primitive cultures that reinforced the belief that contemporary political and economic situations express universal human values. Their famed studies of the division of labor, "egoistic" suicide, the basic forms of religious life, and "obligatory" gift-exchange were geared to the "moral consolidation" of the Third French Republic and its empire. The main themes of Durkheim's thought were taken up by Talcott Parsons in America, who has applied them to urge society's sub-groups to fulfill their functional obligations—to "stabilize their contracts."[50] And these sub-groups now include age and generation categories. Thus, despite the revolt at the turn of the century, today "modern Western civilization is positivistic. . . . That is the kind of culture most people live in."[51]

It is important to recognize that the immense reordering of activities, persons, and ideals at the dawn of the twentieth century scarcely can be summed up as a cult of youth. This was a process which required youth also to sacrifice genuine choice and identity. Indeed, there were marked similarities between the creation of groupings of the young and the old. The psychologist G. Stanley Hall, who discovered both adolescence and senescence,[52] followed an epigenetic theory like that in Turner's philosophy of history and, recently, in Erikson's outline of psychological development. In 1904, Hall defined the adolescent and within two decades youth were being excluded from the work force and directed into prolonged education as junior citizens. In 1922, Hall's book *Senescence* defined the elders, and, by 1935, social security began their official exclusion from the work force and their prolonged retirement as senior citizens. In both cases, cultural conjectures and biomedical hypotheses justified the classification of millions of persons in sub-systems of society with specialized tasks, functions, and ethical codes—as if human development could be parcelled out by the method of the division of labor.

These were large steps towards a normative model of sequential age-generation stages, from cradle to grave, each phase guided by experts in the displacement and attrition of the elders. In 1957, the separation of the aged was given concise intellectual formulation in the theory of disengagement, which

argues that society in general and the elderly themselves, *aware of the inevitability of on-coming death and the absence of a future,* mutually, inescapably, and beneficially take measures of detachment, so that final termination occurs with minimal disturbance.[53]

V. Modernization Theory and the Re-Engagement of the Elderly

The disengagement formula has a number of crucial shortcomings. For one thing, it contradicts the melioristic drive which is a central component of modern biomedicine. The theory also is faulty in its reliance on the relatively static, positivist notion of social harmony which neglects the powerful forces for change revealed in both history and depth psychology. And its segregating implications are disclosed in the statement that, as people grow older, they come to be "equilibrated" at a greater and greater distance from others.[54] This latter feature stimulated the sociologist Arnold M. Rose to make an incisive reply. Rose, known for his collaboration with Gunnar Myrdal's great inquiry into racism in America, reasoned that the kind of social thought that underlies disengagement theory ignores history and does not take into account cross-cultural variations. Rose advocated studies in cultural history and the dynamics of social transformation as better guides for theories of age than positivist concepts of balancing within a particular system.[55]

The re-engagement theory offered in this paper is meant to challenge the basic assumptions of neo-positivist ideology. And, in the light of the philosophy of historicism, a redefinition of modernization will be presented in which the aged do have a future ("historicism" here means the belief that history provides unique insight into the nature of cultural values by considering them in the context of temporal, developmental processes). It is essential to note too that, in the perspective of world history, many manifestations of modernism—abstract art, quantum physics, the sexual revolution—represent only the comparatively recent working out of processes of modernization that have been under way for centuries, since the Renaissance or earlier yet. This distinction between the "modernist" movement, from the Victorian to the contemporary, and the much more comprehensive, long-range trends systematized by modernization theory is a salient point in this study.[56] Such a differentiation is of decided consequence in dealing with the problems of an aging population, a phenomenon seemingly at cross purposes with most modernist tendencies after 1890.

Our analysis of the ideological framework of the modernist ethos, and its concomitant ageism, concluded that the revolt against positivism, in its effect on establishment opinion, was not victorious but led to a new form of positivism. That neo-positivist ideology has determined the attributes and direction of modernism down to the present time. Specifically, neo-positivism has promoted the categorization of age and generation in a sequence programmed to displace the elderly. This has meant severe valuational difficulties for gerontology and geriatrics.

Today, we have the task of recognizing that no nineteenth-or twentieth-century society ever aimed to create an aging population. Contemporary gerontology, therefore, must relate itself to a theory of modernization that, unlike the neo-positivist one, is committed to humanist, meliorist, and liberating goals, and on a scale comprehensive enough to apply to an entire population stratum of elders. It is important that gerontologists perceive disengagement not so much as a component of modernity but rather as part of a school of sociology geared to the managing of a highly particular social system. In considering the basis for an alternative plan of life-span development, it is helpful to utilize the insight from comparative history and ethnology that the culture of our time, dominated by imperatives of productivity and short-run profit, is contingent and amendable.

In attempting to establish a view of modernization different from the neo-positivist one, we shall outline contrasting interpretations of a number of central issues.

1. Sacrifice. Despite the supposed hedonism of our time, this key element in neo-positivism continues to have great appeal. The theme of sacrifice already was prominent in Comte's dictum that education must prepare people to live for others, an anti-individualist and anti-liberal interpretation patterned on the hierarchical society of the Middle Ages. More directly relevant to America, Durkheim's work evaluated suffering and sacrifice as indispensable in giving meaning to personal life and cementing the unity of the overall community. As a government spokesman during World War I, he infused Comtean social solidarity with the rationalized asceticism of total mobilization. The military aura of such sociological terms as 'morale' and 'disengagement' stems in part from Durkheim's influence.

The tenet of sacrifice is continued in Talcott Parsons' theories which have had a profound influence on American social and behavioral sciences. The obligatory altruism in contemporary culture is analyzed in Parsons' studies of American attitudes about death and dying.[57] Applied to aging, his viewpoint strongly endorses disengagement.

The significant, epigenetic developmental scheme of Erik Erikson[58] is not positivist, but the flow of his eight stages of life and their neo-romantic content blend with some of the aims of neo-positivism. His stage sequence, in particular, is applicable to neo-positivist generationism: youth is given the creative role of identity delineation, while the elders are left with a sacrificial part to play. The eighth, or final, age does not challenge disengagement directly but centers on "responsible renunciation" and "closure." Butler has criticized his placing of the elderly in a position of heroically defending an identity and style formed long years before: "people are locked in by such a theory."[59] Indeed, the eighth age is reminiscent of positivist mortalism's "show of resistance" to an inherently overwhelming fate.

In an alternative view of modernization, a hedonist ethic of pleasure over pain would have to be prominent. The elders thus would strive for satisfying and continuing creativity and self-assertion. Anger and despair, as Butler suggests,

can serve to motivate the quest for happiness in old age. It is necessary, especially, to fight against taboos which block sexuality in the aging, including the absolute proscription of inter-generational relationships.

2. Mortalism. Disengagement, like positivism, sees death as the *defining* absolute and accordingly elaborates functional groupings to adapt life, the variable, to the escalating probability of dying—and with the least possible amount of "neurotic" disturbance or social disruption.[60] The elderly are pressed to conform to a policy in which morality is a simplified ethic of professional skills, progress is smooth-running administration, and order is an unquestioned good—the kind of system satirized in *Catch-22.*

An alternative modernization theory would reject mortalist insistence on the omnipresence of death and the inevitability of increasing vulnerableness at higher stages of development. Instead, it would assume life to be the defining absolute and ethical goal in terms of biomedical strategy through time, and society would seek to diminish death, the variable, moving target. This connotes efforts to extend the length of *healthful* life.[61] Progress in that area would contradict the supposition of a static, universal human condition which underlies disengagement theory.

3. Social particularism and/the division of labor. The lack of historical and ethnological perspective in neo-positivism means that a particular, work-ethic, social-contract kind of society is held to be the final culmination of the universal needs of human nature. Therefore, the division of labor allocates specialized functions to supposedly natural categories (based on biological analogy): age, sex, generation and, to some extent, race and class.

An alternative plan of modernization would bring the individual, on one hand, and overall humanity, on the other, back into the picture and thereby give the elders and the gerontologists a much deeper and broader range of comprehension and choice. Moreover, society would be treated not so much in line with fixed equations of social harmony but more in terms of dynamic processes of transforming development.

4. Discontinuity. Neo-positivist ideology postulates an *interruption* in creative development in the aging and elderly which brings about the generation gap and gives rise to disengagement theory.

An alternative would be similar to Goethe's paradigm of personality formation in which *all* the stages of life are considered to be equally inventive and meaningful. It is noteworthy that Goethe was able to go beyond the romantic developmental formula, with its fixation on heroic self-sacrifice, because of the strong influence on him of Italian Renaissance hedonism and self-assertion. This portion of his thought resulted from his fascination with the prolongevity ideas of Luigi Cornaro and also from his joyous trip to Italy in middle age. A similar concept of "open," ever-renewed creativity, including a sensual component, appears too in Nietzsche's thought in relation to transcendent endeavors to realize the full potentialities of human nature. In this perspective,

the discontinuity of mandatory retirement at sixty-five especially should be repealed.

5. *Attenuation of values.* In neo-positivism, essential questions of human values are excluded from consideration because they are felt to lead to the unknowable realm of metaphysics or the danger of disrupting personal or social calm.

An alternative modernization hypothesis would embody the deep valuational commitments of Enlightenment and romanticist humanism and would follow these beliefs into the realm of abstract thought as well as that of practice. The controversial and "disruptive" issues often are the very ones that serve to reconnect the aging to the social and cultural mainstream.[62]

6. *The individual and psychology.* Durkheim's concept of the person as a "collective representation" of social reality, a living fetish, must be challenged by the assertion of individual worth.[63] The elderly especially must be liberated from restrictive behavior norms, such as those of disengagement, which are meant to carry out the supposed functions of socio-biological groupings. Genuine modernization cannot by-pass, as neo-positivism tends to do, the methods and findings of depth psychology. Contrary to mortalist ideology, the formulation by Freud in *Civilization and its Discontents* (1930) of the struggle between the forces of Eros and those of Thanatos is a compelling statement of on-going creativity as a saving factor in preventing another holocaust of nuclear war and genocide.

7. *Progress and history.* A hallmark of alternative modernization is melioristic progress, the striving to implement the Enlightenment program of not only comforting the aged but also *freeing* them. The word 'meliorism' was introduced by the great English novelist George Eliot, a would-be convert to Comtean doctrine who could not bring herself to accept the positivist theme of resignation or the dictum that "pain is not an evil." Her own outlook, the meliorist ethic of human betterment, included deep respect for history, regard for the worth of ordinary individuals, and Christian humanist caring that sought the alleviation of life's anguish. Her empathy with the masses of humanity helped to carry the Enlightenment impulse of philanthropy into the Victorian epoch and down to the present century. Crichton-Browne and the great nineteenth-century physicians—Lister, Pasteur, Simpson and others—played a similar role. Indeed, the principal source of the prestige that modern biomedicine enjoys is the fact that it was the one professional group that seriously took up the imperative of melioristic progress from the Enlightenment. That is why Albert Camus, in his novel *The Plague,* turned to the physician to exemplify the kind of heroism that has not been reduced to "absurdity" even in the mass society of the twentieth century—for biomedicine carries forward the transcendent Judeo-Christian quest for salvation from evil and death.

Along with meliorist progress, an *open historicism* seems to me the key to a modernization different from the neo-positivist one. In his profound analysis of

the crisis of twentieth-century culture, Ernst Nolte has reasoned that human nature, to a historian, seems to be something still not finished but rather pressing towards its potential wholeness and superseding the past in an unfolding realization through historical time. Nolte considers this adaptational dimension to be intrinsic to human nature. Thus, he states that man is "not a complete unit" but rather a "transcendental creature," developing towards a wholeness that is "from one aspect, more than himself."[64]

In this perspective, central questions of meaning and value that are baffling today ought not to be pushed to premature closure but should be kept open for future resolution. This is the historicist answer to the positivist dilemma about the "unknowable"; instead of banning metaphysics, ultimate problems are to be put into the context of the evolving progress of human thought. Unfortunately, particularistic cultures tend to fix their gaze regressively on a traditional past. Nolte, therefore, insists on the importance of humanity's being allowed to work freely through the anxious, but fulfilling and liberating, process he terms 'modernist transcendence.'[65] The historicist view he outlines provides a significant alternative to the static structure and attenuated aims of neo-positivism with its reiterative "whatever is, *is.*" To Nolte, philosophy necessarily involves a phase of alienation from the world of "existing and familiar things" in which one reaches beyond current conditions to sense possibilities of betterment and thus is enabled to "exert a critique on that which is."

A life span that is truly modern in attaining humanist, meliorist, and individualist values still is ahead. At present, the worth of the individual is not so much a fact as a goal. This interpretation requires the confronting of the truism in contemporary culture that resources should be invested preferentially in the young, because they have a future and the elderly do not. However, in the furthering of a genuinely modern culture, it is the aging who actually have pride of place; they are where the action is, for they are something historically *new* as a large population sector. The solving of their problems is a make-or-break task for the modern forces that brought them into being. Moreover, the elderly, as individuals, face challenges *new* to themselves which call for successive, creative renewals of identity. And as part of humanity, they live in a historically early, or *new*, phase of accelerated modernization. *Thus, the aging population does have a future, as it becomes re-engaged at the frontier of modern cultural adaptation and realization through historical time.*

Notes

[1]This paper is dedicated to the memory of Prof. Ernest S. Falbo (1923-1975), a soldier against bigotry; Distinguished Flying Cross, 1945, and founding editor of *Italian Americana*, 1974. Parts of the study were reported to the Washington (D.C.) Society for the History of Medicine and to the 29th Annual Meeting of the Gerontological Society. I wish to acknowledge earlier support by a John Simon Guggenheim Memorial Fellowship and a National Institute of Mental Health Research Fellowship directed by Robert Kastenbaum and H. L. P. Resnik.

[2]About 1903, the term 'gerontology' was originated by Ilya Mechnikov and, in 1909, 'geriatrics' was put into use by Ignatz Nascher. See Mirko D. Grmek, *On Ageing and Old Age: Basic Problems and Historic Aspects of Gerontology and Geriatrics* (The Hague, Netherlands: W. Junk, 1958) and my articles: "An Introduction to Literature on the History of Gerontology," *Bulletin of the History of Medicine,* 31 (1957), 78-83, and "Longevity," *Dictionary of the History of Ideas: Studies of Selected Pivotal Ideas,* ed. Philip P. Wiener, 5 vols. (New York: Charles Scribner's Sons, 1973-1974), III, 89-93.

[3]To refer to the prevalent nineteenth-century ideology, I introduced the phrase 'establishment positivism' in my "Remembrance: The Media as Historians of the Book of Life," in *Communicating Issues in Thanatology,* ed. Thomas J. Fleming et al. (New York: MSS Information Corp., 1976), pp. 11-28. To indicate the twentieth-century form of establishment positivism, I used the term 'neo-positivism' in "An Historical Introduction to Ideas about Voluntary Euthanasia: With a Bibliographic Guide," *Omega: The Journal of Death and Dying, 4* (1973), 87-138. The concept was developed further in "The Aging Crisis in Modern Thought: Romanticism, Positivism, Counter-Culture," presented 29 Dec. 1973 to a session on "The Aged in History: Cross-national Perspectives," at the 88th Annual Meeting, American Historical Association, San Francisco (to be published in *International Journal of Aging and Human Development*); "The Modern Intellectual Crisis about an Aging Population and Cultural Decline," presented 2 May 1975 to a Colloquium on "Aging: Myths, Rituals, and Values," University of Southern California (Humanities Division and Andrus Gerontology Center), Los Angeles; and "Ethics of Death and Dying: Historical Perspective," *Encyclopedia of Bioethics,* ed. Warren T. Reich (New York: Macmillan-Free Press, in preparation).

[4]The need in gerontology for long-range historical perspective in understanding modernity is evident in the important work edited by Donald O. Cowgill and Lowell D. Holmes, *Aging and Modernization* (New York: Appleton-Century-Crofts, 1972), in which efforts to formulate a set of cross-cultural hypotheses are weakened by insufficient measures to distinguish primary modernization steps in "developing" nations from secondary, modernist changes in "advanced" countries.

[5]The prototype statement of disengagement theory is in Elaine Cumming and William E. Henry, *Growing Old: The Process of Disengagement* (New York: Basic Books, 1961). Generally, the intellectual foundations of the theory have not received adequate attention; an exception is Arnold M. Rose, "A Current Theoretical Issue in Social Gerontology," *The Gerontologist,* 4 (1964), 46-50.

[6]A major difficulty for re-engagement is society's reluctance to invest in projects lacking short-run profitability or established kinds of esteem; this has been identified as the chief cultural cause of the aging crisis by Margaret Clark and Barbara Gallatin Anderson, *Culture and Aging: An Anthropological Study of Older Americans* (Springfield, Ill.: Charles C. Thomas, 1967), pp. 421-33.

[7]Robert N. Butler, *Why Survive? Being Old in America* (New York: Harper and Row, 1975), p. 11.

[8]I initially summarized this interpretation as a confrontation between death and progress; see my monograph, *A History of Ideas About the Prolongation of Life: The Evolution of Prolongevity Hypotheses to 1800* (1966; rpt. New York: Arno-N.Y. Times, 1977), pp. 5-9, 74-77, 83-91. The present study has benefited from Gerhard Masur's "Crisis in History," *Dictionary of the History of Ideas,* ed. Philip P. Wiener (New York: Charles Scribner's Sons, 1973-74), I, 589-96.

[9]The contemporary, cultural, and ideological crisis that besets the aging is brought out with urgent clarity by Margaret Clark, "Cultural Values and Dependency in Later Life," in *The Dependencies of Old People*, ed. Richard A. Kalish, Occasional Papers in Gerontology, No. 6 (Ann Arbor: Inst. of Gerontology, Univ. of Michigan-Wayne State U., 1969), pp. 59-72; and Robert Kastenbaum, "Exit and Existence: Society's Unwritten Script for Old Age and Death," presented 13 Nov. 1975 at a Conference on "Human Values and Aging" at Case Western Reserve University, Cleveland.

[10]The sixty-fifth birthday is a disturbingly arbitrary social criterion of aging, as Paul Woodring states in "Why Retire at 65?" *Washington Post*, 5 Sept. 1976, p. B4. The question needs more investigation, if age-ism is to be combatted in an informed way. Some of the social and political factors are indicated by Leonard D. Cain, "The Growing Importance of Legal Age in Determining the Status of the Elderly," *The Gerontologist*, 14 (1974), 167-74 and J. Douglas Brown, *An American Philosophy of Social Security: Evolution and Issues* (Princeton: Princeton Univ. Press, 1972), pp. 5-10, 116-25. A medical tradition, setting sixty-five as the onset of old age, originated from a work (1857-1860) by the German physician Lorenz Geist: see Grmek, *On Ageing and Old Age*, pp. 24, 71.

[11]The relevant references to adolescent psychology are Robert Jay Lifton, *History and Human Survival* (New York: Random House, 1970), pp. 311-73; Kenneth Keniston, *The Uncommitted: Alienated Youth in American Society* (1965; rpt. New York: Dell, 1970), pp. 73-89; Paul Goodman, *Growing Up Absurd: Problems of Youth in the Organized Society* (New York: Vintage, 1960), pp. 170-90.

[12]See his articles "The Effect of Medical and Health Progress on the Social and Economic Aspects of the Life Cycle," *Industrial Gerontology*, 1, No. 2 (June 1969), 1-9, and "Age-Ism: Another Form of Bigotry," *The Gerontologist*, 9 (1969), 243-46.

[13]Milton L. Barron, "Minority Group Characteristics of the Aged in American Society," *Journal of Gerontology*, 8 (1953), 477-82; Michael Harrington, *The Other America: Poverty in the United States* (1962; rpt. Baltimore: Penguin, 1963), pp. 111-30; Jules Henry, "Human Obsolescence," *Culture Against Man* (New York: Random House, 1963), pp. 389-474; Robert Jay Lifton, *History and Human Survival*, pp. 332-73; and Jules Henry, "Personality and Ageing" (1966), in *On Sham, Vulnerability and Other Forms of Self-Destruction* (New York: Vintage Books, 1973), pp. 16-39.

[14]Bernstein, *Washington Post*, 7 March 1969, p. A6.

[15]John Morton Blum, *V Was for Victory: Politics and American Culture During World War II* (New York: Harcourt Brace Jovanovich, 1976), pp. 245-54, 323-32.

[16]Butler, *Why Survive*, p. 12.

[17]Furnas, *Goodbye to Uncle Tom* (New York: Apollo-Sloane, 1956); Friedan, *The Feminine Mystique* (1963; rpt. New York: Dell, 1964).

[18]Kastenbaum, "Should We Have Mixed Feelings About Our Ambivalence Toward the Aged?" *Journal of Geriatric Psychiatry*, 7 (1974), 97.

[19]Ernest W. Burgess, ed., *Aging in Western Societies* (Chicago: Univ. of Chicago Press, 1960), pp. 20-21. On "exhaustion of programme," see Alex Comfort, *The Biology of Senescence* (New York: Rinehart, 1956), pp. 37-41, 138-39.

[20]A key statement of meliorist gerontology, opposing Weismann's mortalism and related to World War II ideology is P. B. Medawar's "Old Age and Natural Death" (1945), *The Uniqueness of the Individual* (New York: Basic Books, 1957), pp. 17-43.

[21]Turner, "The Significance of the Frontier in American History" (1893), in *The Turner Thesis,* ed. George Rogers Taylor, 3rd ed. (Lexington, MA: D. C. Heath, 1972), pp. 4, 27.

[22]'Epigenesis,' a term from embryology, denotes a concept of development in which the organism does not grow simply in a quantitative sense but goes through a series of *stages* of metamorphic change. Such a view was taken up also in biological evolution, biomedicine, the psychology of human development, and the philosophy of history. Turner spoke of it as the "germ theory." See the superb essay by Owsei Tempkin, "German Concepts of Ontogeny and History around 1800," *Bulletin of the History of Medicine,* 24 (1950), 227-47.

[23]Joseph F. Kett, "History of Age Grouping in America," in *Youth: Transition to Adulthood,* Report of the Panel on Youth (Washington: Government Printing Office, 1973), pp. 9-29.

[24]Turner, "Frontier," pp. 4, 28.

[25]Theodore Roosevelt, *The Strenuous Life: Essays and Addresses* (New York: Century, 1903), pp. 1-21.

[26]Ibid., pp. 1, 4.

[27]For references in this paragraph, Ibid., pp. 3, 92-93; 108-09, 164, 182, 255-57, 281, 313.

[28]See the Immigration Law and statistical tables in the *World Almanac for 1929,* ed. Robert H. Lyman (New York: New York World, 1929), pp. 256 ff. Percentages were calculated from the tables.

[29]This paragraph is based largely on Oscar Handlin's *The Uprooted* (New York: Grosset and Dunlap, 1951); the quotations are from pp. 293 and 300.

[30]Roosevelt, *The Strenuous Life,* pp. 6, 9, 38, 183, 221-23, 257, 281.

[31]Quoted in Louis L. Snyder, *The Idea of Racialism: Its Meaning and History* (Princeton: Anvil-Van Nostrand, 1962), pp. 167-68.

[32]Roosevelt, *The Strenuous Life,* pp. 6, 37-38, 196, 203; and Robert A. Hart, *The Great White Fleet* (Boston: Little, Brown 1965), pp. 30, 48.

[33]Quoted in Basil Rauch, *The History of the New Deal: 1933-1938* (New York: Creative Age Press, 1944), pp. 270-71. On the limitations of the Social Security Act, see Paul K. Conkin, *F.D.R. and the Origins of the Welfare State* (New York: Thomas Y. Crowell, 1967), pp. 60-62.

[34]Osler, "The Fixed Period," *Aequanimitas: With Other Addresses,* 3rd ed. (Philadelphia: Blakiston, 1932), pp. 373-93, 381-82.

[35]Crichton-Browne, *The Prevention of Senility* (London: Macmillan, 1905), pp. 3-68; on the "superfluities" of life, see pp. 9-13.

[36]On Luigi Cornaro and his influence, see my *History of Ideas about Prolongation of Life,* pp. 68-74.

[37]Crichton-Browne, *The Prevention of Senility,* p. 66.

[38]For an introduction to generationism, see Julían Marías, "Generations: The Concept," *Encyclopedia of the Social Sciences,* ed. David L. Sills (New York: Macmillan-Free Press, 1968), VI, 88-92 and Alan B. Spitzer, "The Historical Problem of Generations," *American Historical Review,* 78 (1973), 1353-85. For Osler's ideas and

up-bringing, see the great biography by Harvey Cushing, *The Life of Sir William Osler* (New York: Oxford Univ. Press, 1940).

[39]The classical four ages are discussed by Mirko Grmek in *On Ageing and Old Age.* Also see Drmek (p. 24) on the seven ages concept.

[40]On Nascher's ideas, see Joseph T. Freeman, "Nascher," *The Gerontologist,* 1 (1961), 17-26.

[41]On the longevity ideas of Franklin and Concorcet, see my *History of Ideas about Prolongation of Life,* pp. 83-84, 87 ff.; on Crichton-Browne's, see his *Prevention of Senility,* pp. 67-68; on Mechnikov's, see his *The Nature of Man,* trans. P. Chalmers Mitchell (1903; rpt. New York: Arno-N.Y. Times, 1977), pp. 281-84.

[42]On the harshness of the medieval attitude to the old and moribund, see T. S. R. Boase, *Death in the Middle Ages* (New York: McGraw-Hill, 1972) and William Munk, *Euthanasia* (1887; rpt. New York: Arno-N.Y. Times, 1977), pp. 93-96.

[43]Jonathan Swift, *Gulliver's Travels* (New York: Modern Library, 1950), p. 244.

[44]Michel Foucault, *The Birth of the Clinic: An Archaeology of Medical Perception,* trans. A. M. Sheridan Smith (New York: Vintage, 1975), pp. 124-48, 195-99.

[45]Frank E. Manuel, *The Prophets of Paris* (Cambridge: Harvard Univ. Press, 1962), pp. 249-96; and John Stuart Mill, *Auguste Comte and Positivism* (1865; rpt. Ann Arbor: Univ. of Michigan Press, 1961).

[46]Auguste Comte, *The Catechism of Positive Religion* (1852), trans. Richard Congreve, 3rd ed. (1891; rpt. Clifton, N.J.: Augustus M. Kelley, 1973), pp. 90-97.

[47]Karl Löwith, *Meaning in History* (Chicago: Univ. of Chicago Press, 1949), pp. 87-88.

[48]Nicholas F. Fyodorov, "The Question of Brotherhood, or Relatedness" (1906), trans. Arleigh E. Moorhouse and George L. Kline, *Russian Philosophy,* ed. James M. Edie, James P. Scanlan and Mary-Barbara Zeldin (Chicago: Quadrangle, 1969), III, 11-54; reprinted in *Death as a Speculative Theme* (New York: Arno-N.Y. Times, 1977).

[49]Ibid., p. 38.

[50]Parsons, *The Structure of Social Action,* 2nd ed. (1949; rpt. New York: Free Press, 1968) and *The Social System* (New York: Free Press, 1951).

[51]Roland N. Stromberg, *An Intellectual History of Modern Europe,* 2nd ed. (Englewood Cliffs, N.J.: Prentice-Hall, 1975), p. 302.

[52]G. Stanley Hall, *Adolescence,* 2 vols. (New York: D. Appleton, 1904) and *Senescence: The Last Half of Life* (New York: D. Appleton, 1922).

[53]Cumming and Henry, *Growing Old;* M. Elaine Cumming, "New Thoughts on the Theory of Disengagement," *New Thoughts on Old Age,* ed. Kastenbaum (New York: Springer, 1964), pp. 3-18; William E. Henry, "Engagement and Disengagement," *Psychobiology of Aging,* ed. Robert Kastenbaum (New York: Springer, 1965), pp. 19-35.

[54]Henry, "Engagement and Disengagement," p. 32.

[55]Rose, "A Current Theoretical Issue," *Gerontologist* (1964).

[56]For historical differentiation between the "modernist" era and long-range modernization, see Richard D. Brown, *Modernization: The Transformation of American Life: 1600-1865* (New York: Hill and Wang, 1976), pp. 3-22, 187-201.

[57]Talcott Parsons and Victor Lidz, "Death in American Society," *Essays in Self-Destruction,* ed. Edwin S. Shneidman (New York: Science House, 1967), pp. 133-70; and Talcott Parsons, Renée C. Fox and Victor M. Lidz, "The 'Gift of Life' and its Reciprocation," *Death in American Experience,* ed. Arien Mack (New York: Schocken, 1973), pp. 1-49; Talcott Parsons, "Old Age as Consummatory Phase," *The Gerontologist,* 3 (1963), 53-54.

[58]Erik H. Erikson, *Childhood and Society,* 2nd ed. (New York: W. W. Norton, 1963), pp. 247-74; *Insight and Responsibility* (New York: W.W. Norton, 1964), pp. 111-57.

[59]Butler, *Why Survive,* pp. 400-01.

[60]Neo-positivist concern to prevent disruption of prevalent values can be seen in Parsons' antagonism to any direct challenge to racial segregation and his equating of the sick role with a deviant one (Parsons, *The Social System,* pp. 281-83, 478).

[61]See my *Prolongation of Life,* "Longevity," "Aging Crisis," "Aging and Decline," and "Ethics." See also Alan Harrington, *The Immortalist* (New York: Random House, 969), and Albert Rosenfeld, *Prolongevity* (New York: Alfred A. Knopf, 1976).

[62]Re-engagement is directly in contradiction to the opinion of Parsons (*The Social System,* p. 315) that to "sellout" is actually a process of "getting well."

[63]On positivist fetishism, see Henri de Lubac, *The Drama of Atheist Humanism,* trans. Edith M. Riley (1950; rpt. Cleveland: World, 1963), pp. 89, 114, 117. On Durkheim's concepts of the individual and "collective representation," see Parsons, *The Structure of Social Action,* pp. 344-68.

[64]Nolte, *Three Faces of Fascism,* trans. Leila Vennewitz (New York: Holt, Rinehart and Winston, 1966), pp. 429-34.

[65]Ibid., pp. 450-54.

Additional References

The following references, not cited in the notes, were crucial during the research phase of this paper—G.J.G.

Boorstin, Daniel J. *The Lost World of Thomas Jefferson.* 1948; rpt. Boston: Beacon, 1960.

Boorstin, Daniel J. *The Americans: The Democratic Experience.* 1973; rpt. New York: Vintage, 1974.

Briggs, Asa. "Welfare State." *Dictionary of the History of Ideas.* Ed. Philip P. Wiener. New York: Charles Scribner's Sons, 1973-74. IV, 509-15.

Buckley, Jerome H. *The Triumph of Time: A Study of the Victorian Concepts.* Cambridge: Harvard Univ. Press, 1966.

Butler, Robert N. "The Life Review: An Interpretation of Reminiscence in the Aged" (1963). *New Thoughts on Old Age.* Ed. Robert Kastenbaum. New York: Springer, 1964, pp. 265-80.

Butler, Robert N. "The Destiny of Creativity in Later Life" (1964). *Psychodynamic Studies on Aging.* Ed. Sidney Levin and Ralph J. Kahana. New York: International Universities Press, 1967, pp. 20-63.

Butler, Robert N. and Myrna I. Lewis. *Aging and Mental Health: Positive*

Psychosocial Approaches. St. Louis: Mosby, 1973.
de Beauvoir, Simone. *A Very Easy Death.* Trans. Patrick O'Brian. 1965; rpt. New York: Warner, 1973.
de Beauvoir, Simone. *The Coming of Age.* Trans. Patrick O'Brian. New York: G. P. Putnam's Sons, 1972.
Fox, Daniel M. *The Discovery of Abundance.* Ithaca: Cornell Univ. Press, 1967.
Gibson, Charles, ed. *The Black Legend: Anti-Spanish Attitudes in the Old World and the New.* New York: Alfred A. Knopf, 1971.
Gossett, Thomas F. *Race: The History of an Idea in America.* New York: Schocken, 1965.
Handlin, Oscar, ed. *Immigration as a Factor in American History.* Englewood Cliffs, N.J.: Prentice-Hall, 1959.
Heilbroner, Robert L. *An Inquiry into the Human Prospect.* New York: Norton, 1974.
Hughes, H. Stuart. *Consciousness and Society: The Reorientation of European Social Thought: 1890-1930.* New York: Vintage, 1958.
Iggers, Georg G. "Historicism." *Dictionary of the History of Ideas.* Ed. Philip P. Wiener. New York: Charles Scribner's Sons, 1973-74. II, 456-64.
Jaspers, Karl. *Nietzsche: An Introduction to the Understanding of His Philosophical Activity.* Trans. Charles F. Wallraff and Frederick J. Schmitz. 1965; rpt. Chicago: Regnery, 1969.
Kardiner, Abram and Edward Preble. *They Studied Man.* New York: Mentor, 1963.
Kümmel, Friedrich. "Time as Succession and the Problem of Duration." *The Voices of Time.* Ed. J. T. Fraser. New York: George Braziller, 1966, pp. 31-55.
Lerner, Max. "Life Cycle of the American." *America as a Civilization.* New York: Simon and Schuster, 1957, pp. 543-620.
Lichtheim, George. *The Concept of Ideology.* New York: Vintage, 1967.
Mandelbaum, Maurice. "Historicism." *Encyclopedia of Philosophy.* Ed. Paul Edwards. New York: Macmillan-Free Press, 1967. IV, 22-25.
Marcuse, Herbert. "The Ideology of Death." *The Meaning of Death.* Ed. Herman Feifel. 1959; rpt. New York: McGraw-Hill, 1965, pp. 64-76.
Marcuse, Herbert. *One Dimensional Man: Studies in the Ideology of Advanced Industrial Society.* Boston: Beacon, 1964.
Meinecke, Friedrich. "Historicism and Its Problems," trans. Julian H. Franklin. *Varieties of History.* Ed. Fritz Stern. New York: Meridian, 1956, pp. 267-88.
Mosse, George L. *The Culture of Western Europe: The Nineteenth and Twentieth Centuries.* Chicago: Rand McNally, 1961.
Myrdal, Gunnar. *An American Dilemma.* 2 vols. 1944; rpt. New York: Pantheon, 1962.
Neugarten, Bernice L., ed. *Middle Age and Aging.* Chicago: Univ. of Chicago Press, 1968.
Neugarten, Bernice L. "The Old and the Young in Advanced Industrial

Societies." Lecture presented 29 Aug. 1969 to 8th International Congress of Gerontology, Washington, DC.

Neugarten, Bernice L. "Social Implications of a Prolonged Life-Span." *The Gerontologist,* 12 (1972), 323, 438-40.

Neugarten, Bernice L. and Nancy Datan. "Sociological Perspectives on the Life Cycle." *Life-Span Developmental Psychology.* Ed. Paul B. Baltes and K. Werner Schaie. New York: Academic Press, 1973, pp. 53-69.

Paris, Bernard J. *Experiments in Life: George Eliot's Quest for Values.* Detroit: Wayne State Univ. Press, 1965.

Rejai, Mostafa. "Ideology." *Dictionary of the History of Ideas.* Ed. Philip P. Wiener. New York: Charles Scribner's Sons, 1973-74. II, 552-59.

Roazen, Paul. *Erik H. Erikson: The Power and Limits of a Vision.* New York: Free Press, 1976.

Rokeach, Milton. *The Open and Closed Mind.* New York: Basic Books, 1960.

Semmel, Bernard. *Imperialism and Social Reform.* 1960; rpt. Garden City, N.Y.: Anchor, 1968.

Stern, Fritz. *The Politics of Cultural Despair.* 1961; rpt. Garden City, N.Y.: Anchor, 1965.

Weg, Ruth B. "Physiology and Sexuality in Aging." *Sexuality and Aging.* Ed. I. M. Burnside. Los Angeles: Andrus Gerontology Center, 1975, pp. 7-17.

Wyllie, Irvin G. *The Self-Made Man in America: The Myth of Rags to Riches.* 1954; rpt. New York: Free Press, 1966.

Robert N. Butler

AFTERWORD: HUMANISTIC PERSPECTIVES IN GERONTOLOGY

Perhaps it should not surprise us that a range of feelings about the elderly, from ignorance and ambivalence at best, to hatred and distaste at worst, are found in the works of artists, writers and humanists, as in the culture at large. The cultural arts reflect our strongest fears and desires to avoid that period of human life which constitutes old age. A negative, stereotypic theme which enables us to close our eyes to the realities of old age—including the joys as well as the pains—permeates much of our literature.

Simone de Beauvoir's book *The Coming of Age* was motivated by her desire to improve the treatment of the elderly in Western civilization. Ironically, her book's purpose was offset by her reinforcement of a multitude of stereotypes about aging. A limited view of the old and a resistant attitude toward aging become especially apparent in de Beauvoir's cliches. To quote her:

> Old people find it very hard to adapt themselves to new situations . . . they resist change.
>
> For every individual, age brings with it a dreaded decline.
>
> Old age . . . reduces emotion.

And she says of the old man, "He takes pleasure in erotic literature, licentious works of art, dirty stories, the company of young women and furtive contacts; he indulges in fetishism, sado-masochism, various forms of perversion, and after the age of eighty, in voyeurism." Her work suffers from incomplete scholarship, ideology, élitism, and obvious subjectivity as regards aging. It is probable that de Beauvoir worked from the armchair in Parisian libraries and made few forays among the elderly. She detests aging and the older person in herself.

Some of the most perceptive works on old age have been composed by those who have lived through this special period of life. The older Wallace Stevens comprehended old age. He displayed it in his statement about Santayana in "To an Old Philosopher in Rome":

> The sounds drift in. The buildings are remembered.
> The life of the city never lets go, nor do you
> Ever want it to. It is part of the life in your room.
> Its domes are the architecture of your bed.
> The bell's keep on repeating solemn names.
> It is a kind of total grandeur at the end
> With every visible thing enlarged and yet
> No more than a bed, a chair and moving nuns,
> The immensest theater, the pillared porch,
> The book and candle in your ambered room.

And the younger John Updike could also appreciate old age. As he wrote in *The Poorhouse Fair,* there is "death at their sides, the third guest at every meal."

The message is simple. The student, the artist, the scientist, the humanist—regardless of age, they must all form their own attitudes through the depth of individual past and present relationships with older people. One must become absorbed and immersed in any subject worthy of study, such as old age. Artists must become enveloped in it in order to experience it and communicate it. Scientists, too, must involve themselves in depth in order to understand it. Humanists, in order to appreciate and comment upon old age, must have been openly and directly touched by it (not alone through books). The message is simple, but made difficult when the great and worthy object of study creates in us fear and uneasiness, dread and confusion. Thus, it is all the more necessary to spend time, a great amount of time, with older people to even begin to sense the mysteries and realities, the possibilities and the limits. Sit then and listen, walk with, talk with, and relive the past with the elderly as they review their lives.

It was refreshing to read Kenneth Koch's *I Never Told Anybody: Teaching Poetry Writing in a Nursing Home.* Koch went into the nursing home. There he could listen to and read what the ninety-four year old Nadya Catalfano could write about autumn:

> Your leaves sound different.
> I couldn't understand why
> The leaves at that time of year
> Had a rustle about them
> And they would drop
> At the least little thing
> And I would listen
> And pick up some of them.

Both older people and those interacting with them may be swept up in the special time perspective that can make old age a period of enjoyable, emotional and sensory awareness. The elemental things of life—children, plants, nature, human touching (physical and emotional), color, shape—may assume greater significance as people sort out the more important from the less important.

Tolstoy wrote in his marvelously outrageous, controversial "What is Art?":

> We are accustomed to understand art to be only what we hear and see in theatres, concerts and exhibitions; together with buildings, statues, poems and novels. But all this is but the smallest part of the art by which we communicate with one another in life. All human life is filled with works of art of every kind—in cradle-song, jest, mimicry, the ornamentation of houses, dress, and utensils, to church services, buildings, monuments and triumphal processions. It is all artistic activity.

The songs of the nursing home, those sung in Koch's nursing home, are by people in their seventies, eighties, and nineties, most with limited education and from the working class—messengers, short-order cooks, domestic servants. For those who might take the elitist view of art that such songs do not justify the term 'art,' Tolstoy had harsh words: "The highest art has always been comprehensible to normal people. What fails to infect normal people is not art." To Tolstoy, "Art in a human activity consist[s] in this, that one man consciously by means of certain external signs, hands on to others feelings he has lived through, and that others are infected by these feelings and also experience them."

This, the twentieth century, has witnessed the emergence of old age. Our social perceptions and social institutions were not prepared for the increase in the number and relative proportion of older people. What should be a triumph of human progress is viewed instead as an enormous "problem," a macabre joke. Just as televised war and violence weaken our sensibility, the great numbers of older people overwhelm and numb us. Rather than fall prey to the further pitting of generations each against the other and rather than responding to these growing numbers with mandatory retirement, social resistance and prejudice, we can hope that all ages might meet together, exchange views, deal with common enemies of injustice, inequity, poverty, racism, and ignorance.

I should like to see more attention given to humanizing old age. Thoughtful persons of all walks of life, particularly our writers, artists and humanists, should consider old age not only as it is now, but as becoming a new, fresh old age—with a new identity and novel indications. As we cure diseases, end obligatory retirement, offset programmed obsolescence, and foster mental and physical vigor through effective prevention and new knowledge, the artist's profile of aging should change.

The vision of humanists, like the vision of gerontologists, should include the future of aging and not be restricted only to dealing with contemporary myths and realities. This volume marks an important beginning for understanding the changing and diverse patterns of old age.

NOTES ON CONTRIBUTORS

Geri Berg, M.A., is Assistant Professor of Art History, School of Health Services, The Johns Hopkins University, Baltimore, Maryland.

David Bronsen, Ph.D., is Professor of German and Comparative Literature, Department of Germanic Languages and Literature, Washington University, St. Louis, Missouri.

Robert N. Butler, M.D., is Director, National Institute on Aging, National Institutes of Health, Public Health Service, Department of Health, Education, and Welfare, Bethesda, Maryland.

Erik H. Erikson, LL.D., Sc.D., Soc. Sci.D. (h.c.), is Professor of Human Development, Emeritus, Harvard University, Cambridge, Massachusetts.

Joan M. Erikson, LL.D., is Senior Consultant in Psychiatry, Mt. Zion Hospital, San Francisco, California.

Richard Freedman, Ph.D., is Professor of English, Department of English, Simmons College, Boston, Massachusetts.

Sally Gadow, R.N., Ph.D., is Assistant Professor of Philosophy, School of Health Services, The Johns Hopkins University, Baltimore, Maryland.

Thomas W. Ganschow, Ph.D., is Assistant Professor of History, Department of History, The University of Georgia, Athens, Georgia.

Gerald J. Gruman, M.D., Ph.D., is currently pursuing independent research; 3508 Napier Street, Silver Spring, Maryland.

Thomas Halper, Ph.D., is Associate Professor of Political Science, Department of Political Science, Baruch College of the City University of New York, New York City.

David Luke, Ph.D., is Assistant Professor of English, Department of English, The University of Minnesota, Minneapolis, Minnesota.

Donald Marquis, Ph.D., is Assistant Professor of Philosophy, Department of Philosophy, The University of Kansas, Lawrence, Kansas.

Walter G. Moss, Ph.D., is Associate Professor of History, Department of History and Philosophy, Eastern Michigan University, Ypsilanti, Michigan.

Barbara G. Rosenkrantz, Ph.D., is Professor of the History of Medicine, Department of the History of Science, The Harvard School of Public Health, Boston, Massachusetts.

Daniel Scott Smith, Ph.D., is Assistant Professor of History, Department of History, University of Illinois at Chicago Circle, Chicago, Illinois.

Steven R. Smith, Ph.D., is Associate Professor of History, Department of History, Savannah State College, Savannah, Georgia.

Stuart F. Spicker, Ph.D., is Associate Professor of Community Medicine and Health Care (Philosophy), Department of Community Medicine and Health Care, School of Medicine, The University of Connecticut Health Center, Farmington, Connecticut.

Harold M. Stahmer, Ph.D., is Professor of Religion and Philosophy, Associate Director, Center for Gerontological Studies and Programs, The University of Florida, Gainesville, Florida.

David E. Stannard, Ph.D., is Assistant Professor of American Studies and History, American Studies Program, Yale University, New Haven, Connecticut.

Susan S. Tamke, Ph.D., is Assistant Professor of Popular Culture, Department of Popular Culture, Bowling Green State University, Bowling Green, Ohio.

Lance Tibbles, LL.B., is Associate Professor of Law, Capital University Law School, Columbus, Ohio.

David D. Van Tassel, Ph.D., is Professor of History, Department of History, Director, "Human Values and Aging" project, Case Western Reserve University, Cleveland, Ohio.

Maris A. Vinovskis, Ph.D., is Associate Professor of History, Department of History and Center for Political Studies of the Institute for Social Research, University of Michigan, Ann Arbor, Michigan.

Evelyn Eaton Whitehead, Ph.D., is Assistant Professor of Theology, Department of Theology, The University of Notre Dame, Notre Dame, Indiana.

Kathleen M. Woodward, Ph.D., is Assistant Professor of English, Department of English, The University of Wisconsin—Milwaukee, Milwaukee, Wisconsin.

INDEX